DECISION MAKING IN SYSTEMS ENGINEERING AND MANAGEMENT

DECISION MAKING IN SYSTEMS ENGINEERING AND MANAGEMENT

Third Edition

PATRICK J. DRISCOLL, Ph.D., Editor
GREGORY S. PARNELL, Ph.D., Editor
DALE L. HENDERSON, Ph.D., Design Editor

WILEY

This edition first published 2023

© 2023 John Wiley & Sons, Inc. All rights reserved.

Edition History

1st edition (9780470165706) 2008, by Gregory S. Parnell, Patrick J. Driscoll, and Dale L. Henderson

2nd edition (9780470900420) 2010, by Gregory S. Parnell, Patrick J. Driscoll, and Dale L. Henderson

Registered Office

John Wiley & Sons, Inc., 111 River Street, Hoboken, NJ 07030, USA

Editorial Office

111 River Street, Hoboken, NJ 07030, USA

For details of our global editorial offices, customer services, and more information about Wiley products visit us at www.wiley.com.

Wiley also publishes its books in a variety of electronic formats and by print-on-demand. Some content that appears in standard print versions of this book may not be available in other formats.

Library of Congress Cataloging-in-Publication Data:

Names: Driscoll, Patrick J., editor. | Parnell, Gregory S., editor. |
    Henderson, Dale L., editor.
Title: Decision making in systems engineering and management / edited by
    Patrick J. Driscoll, Gregory S. Parnell, Dale L. Henderson.
Description: Third edition. | Hoboken, NJ : Wiley, 2023. | Includes
    bibliographical references and index.
Identifiers: LCCN 2022036178 (print) | LCCN 2022036179 (ebook) | ISBN
    9781119901402 (hardback) | ISBN 9781119901419 (adobe pdf) | ISBN
    9781119901426 (epub)
Subjects: LCSH: Systems engineering–Management. | Systems
    engineering–Decision making.
Classification: LCC TA168 .D43 2023 (print) | LCC TA168 (ebook) | DDC
    621.382/16–dc23/eng/20221003
LC record available at https://lccn.loc.gov/2022036178
LC ebook record available at https://lccn.loc.gov/2022036179

Cover Design: Wiley
Cover Image: © Titima Ongkantong/Shutterstock

Set in 10/12pt TimesLTStd by Straive, Chennai, India

Contents

List of Figures

List of Tables

Co-authors

It is difficult to imagine how our systems engineering, engineering management, and systems design curriculum at West Point would have advanced to the quality level it is currently operating at without the many contributions from our entire department staff and faculty. The first edition was the epitome of a team effort involving many of the folks listed in the following, several of whom are currently making outstanding contributions at other academic institutions and industry. As editions progressed to this 3rd edition, many of their contributions to this text live on, perhaps reshaped into a different format with a different emphasis, but with the same core intent maintained: to help develop the next generation of systems thinkers. The primary chapters to which they deserve co-authorship are noted next to their names below. And for that, we thank them profusely.

Roger C. Burk, Ph.D. Associate Professor of Systems Engineering, Department of Systems Engineering, U.S. Military Academy, West Point. [13]

John D. Caddell, M.S. Instructor, Department of Systems Engineering, U.S. Military Academy, West Point, NY. [10]

Matthew Dabkowski, Ph.D. Academy Professor and Systems Engineering Program Director, U.S. Military Academy, West Point, NY. [10]

Robert A. Dees, Ph.D. Former Assistant Professor, Department of Systems Engineering, U.S. Military Academy, West Point, NY. [9]

Patrick J. Driscoll, Ph.D. Professor Emeritus, Department of Systems Engineering, U.S. Military Academy, West Point, NY. [1, 2, 3, 5, 6, 9, 10]

Patrick J. DuBois, M.S. Instructor, Department of Systems Engineering, U.S. Military Academy, West Point, NY. [10]

Simon R. Goerger, Ph.D. Director of the Institute for Systems Engineering Research (ISER), Information Technology Laboratory, U.S. Army Engineering Research and Development Center (ERDC), Vicksburg, MS. [3]

Dale L. Henderson, Ph.D. Principal Research Scientist, Amazon Global Inventory Platform Team, Seattle, WA. [Illustrations]

Robert Kewley, Ph.D. Former Professor and Head of the Department of Systems Engineering, U.S. Military Academy, West Point, NY. [9]

John E. Kobza, Ph.D. Professor and Head of Industrial and Systems Engineering at Texas Tech University in Lubbock, TX. [3]

Paul D. Kucik, III, Ph.D. Senior Quantitative Manager, Amazon, Seattle, WA. [1]

Michael J. Kwinn Jr., Ph.D. Senior Principal Systems Engineer, Raytheon Corporation, Austin, Texas. [9]

Kenneth W. McDonald, Ph.D. Professor of Engineering Management, Department of Systems Engineering, U.S. Military Academy, West Point, NY. [12]

Heather Nachtmann, Ph.D. Professor of Industrial Engineering and Senior Associate Vice Chancellor for Research and Innovation, the University of Arkansas, Fayetteville, AR. [8]

Gregory S. Parnell, Ph.D. Professor of Practice, Department of Industrial Engineering, the University of Arkansas, Fayetteville, AR. [1, 4, 5, 6, 9, 10]

Edward Pohl, Ph.D. Professor and Head of the Department of Industrial Engineering, the University of Arkansas, Fayetteville, AR. [5, 11]

James Schreiner, Ph.D. Academy Professor and Systems Management Program Director, U.S. Military Academy, West Point, NY. [12]

Timothy Trainor, Ph.D. President, Mount St. Mary's University, and former Professor and Head of the Department of Systems Engineering, U.S. Military Academy, West Point, NY. [5, 6, 9]

Paul D. West, Ph.D. Former Assistant Professor in the Department of Systems Engineering at the U.S. Military Academy, West Point, NY. [3, 4, 7]

Preface

This third edition represents significant changes from the previous two. While the core material has been preserved, evolutionary changes in teaching and professional practice related to decision making in systems engineering and management had transformed both environments substantially, an effect only made more pronounced by the COVID-19 outbreak in 2020 and subsequent social interaction restrictions.

Ten years of teaching, applied systems decision support, and systems assessments have yielded valuable opportunities and insights. Project sponsors and clients expressed interest in understanding system modularity and integration levels as new and more network capable technologies were becoming part of Army operations, and recognizing advances that industry had already embraced. Deterministic modeling, while still useful, was universally recognized as needing extensions capable of addressing decision makers' personal risk, principally because of the high costs associated with system development and acquisition. In response, we developed a new technique called *realization analysis* that directly leverages Monte Carlo simulation to address this concern, providing decision support in a manner previously overlooked.

We continued our support for deployed or isolated analysts possessing limited access to specialty software, yet still needing to accomplish many of the tasks associated with systems discussed in previous editions. Open source and freely accessible software took on new importance in this light, motivating us to place a heavier emphasis on spreadsheets, programs like *SIPmath*, *Gephi*, *Vensim PLE*, and others both in practice and in our curriculum. Several examples in the third edition now illustrate their use.

The third edition material has been shaped with two reader groups in mind: students and faculty exploring effective decision support approaches and professional analysts engaged in systems projects and programs. Both groups require a book that enables them to quickly adopt new techniques and that will add value. Key chapter references have also been updated, but we also preserved those identifying earlier work that still shape current thinking.

Ideation techniques that leverage design concepts have taken on newfound importance in professional practice, echoed in part by efforts of the Stanford d.School which did not exist when the previous editions were being crafted. Several core elements associated with design thinking are now included in this edition.

This third edition makes several important refinements to our approach for supporting decisions since the second edition was published in 2010. Most notably, the book now includes techniques for including uncertainty modeling and analysis to augment the systems decision process (SDP), in particular to the major topics of value modeling, cost estimating, reliability, and risk analysis. No decision support is complete without such a treatment, especially when faced with the occasionally interesting and oftentimes frustrating challenges and complications that go hand-in-hand with systems design, acquisition, development, operation, and replacement. Regardless of whether these systems involve policy, organizations, technology, national security, law, politics, or the myriad of other interdependent entities that are now commonplace in our lives, it seemed a bit of injustice to leave the reader armed with only deterministic approaches when we were routinely applying a more expansive toolkit in practice and within our curriculum.

The book unabashedly advocates a philosophical systems thinking worldview that encourages "embrace and understand" approaches that recognize something important is lost when decomposition, component optimization, and reassembly activities are imposed on a system. One sees these holistic behaviors and characteristics when a system is assembled and operating, and observes them disappearing when attention shifts to individual system elements. Internet congestion, traffic jams, the "accordion effect" in traffic, queues at service windows, climate change, species adaptation, mechanical instabilities, market effects, restaurant failures, and so on are some of the plethora of system-level behaviors diagnosable from a holistic systems thinking viewpoint. Tools that support this engagement philosophy such as systemigrams, dependency structure matrices, system dynamics, and directional dependency diagrams are now included. And, when they are, they are connected to mathematics that reveal insights into system structure that supports actions within the SDP. Fourteen years of advising student team consulting efforts with outside organizations—called capstone design projects at West Point and other universities—have also informed changes to this edition.

Changes in the way that our faculty use textbook materials also affected the structure of the third edition. Whereas in the past, faculty would rely on book exercises for student assignments, that practice has largely disappeared. Custom assignments developed anew every semester by faculty has become the norm. So, chapter-end exercises have been removed, replaced in select locations with short checks on learning. Faculty textbook reliance persists, but only when methods and ideas are presented in a student-accessible manner they can build upon. Students continue to be encouraged to rely upon professional journal publications throughout our courses, motivating us to include an example addressing how to pursue these resources online.

We tried to make chapters more self-containing instead of asking readers to negotiate several chapters to piece together critical techniques associated with multi-criteria value models (MCVM) that we advocate. This also better positions the book for a digital edition should the publisher choose to do so.

While there are a handful of definitions endorsed by professional organizations mentioned in the book, it is difficult to pigeonhole systems engineering as an activity. In some cases, it is about tangible design and manufacturing. In others, it's focused on the activities that a disciplinary engineer is required to do once they have progressed beyond benchwork. In yet others, systems engineering leans toward product, systems, and services acquisition and, of course, decision support. This third edition recognizes this and provides methods that cross-cut all these interests.

It is customary to specify who this edition is intended to serve. For practicing professional, it is relatively easy to do: systems analysts of all types, acquisition professionals, systems engineers, and anyone engaged with systems decision support. For education, it fits well as a text for courses supporting systems engineering, operations research, decision analysis, and systems design and development, and especially well for courses intended to bridge these topics. The book's focus is on fundamental philosophies and techniques for supporting critical decisions throughout the life cycle of all system projects and programs from conceptual design to retirement. When these decisions involve truly competitive alternatives, stakeholders with vested interests, values, priorities, and a level of uncertainty that can be only be ignored at peril to the project or program, this book is uniquely positioned to help.

A word of apology is warranted as well. In the process of editing and creating material that gave birth to this third edition, we may have deleted one or more of your favorite sections that complemented a nice tea and biscuits during the long winter months. For that, we do apologize. But white space being scarce for book publishing, something must go to provide real estate for new topics. We do sincerely hope that you will find the same utility and comfort in those that now appear.

SLAINTÈ,
PATRICK J. DRISCOLL
West Point, NY

GREGORY S. PARNELL
Fayetteville, AR
May 2022

Chapter 1

Working with Systems

If your system doesn't work and you don't know why, it's quite hard to improve it.

—Jason Yosinski, Uber AI Labs

1.1 INTRODUCTION

So, let's begin with an idea that tacitly supports all of systems decision making and systems engineering (SE) in general. In 1928, Sir Arthur Eddington—a colleague and contemporary of Albert Einstein—published a small manuscript entitled "The Nature of the Physical World" [1] in which he attempted to explain in a relatively non-technical way some of the most challenging ideas from physics. And while most of what he addresses are topics not necessarily aligned with this book's purpose, a few are worth noting because of their direct relevance to the principles and practices of systems work.

In the context of describing the running down of the universe, he said that "[a]ny change occurring to a body which can be treated as a single unit can be undone. The laws of Nature admit of the undoing as easily as of the doing ... The common property possessed by laws governing the individual can be stated more clearly by a reference to time. A certain sequence of event running from past to future is the *doing* of an event; the same sequence running from future to past is the *undoing* of it ... Now the primary laws of physics taken one by one all declare that they are entirely indifferent as to which way you consider time to be progressing, just as they are indifferent as to whether you view the world from the right or the left. This is true of the classical laws, the relativity laws, and even of the quantum laws ... The reversibility is inherent in the whole conceptual

Decision Making in Systems Engineering and Management, Third Edition.
Patrick J. Driscoll, Gregory S. Parnell, and Dale L. Henderson
© 2023 John Wiley & Sons, Inc. Published 2023 by John Wiley & Sons, Inc.

scheme in which the laws find a place. Thus the question whether the world does or does not 'make sense' is outside the range of these laws. We have to appeal to the one outstanding law—the second law of thermodynamics—to put some sense into the world. It opens up a new province of knowledge, namely, the study of *organization*; and it is in connection with organization that a direction of time-flow and a distinction between doing and undoing appears for the first time."

Any loss of organization is equitably measured by the chance against its recovery by accidental coincidence. The practical measure of the random element which can increase in the universe but can never decrease is called *entropy*. Entropy continually increases. Its special feature is that the conclusions yielded by entropy are independent of the nature of the microscopical processes that are going on. It is not concerned with the nature of the individual; it is interested in the individual as a component of a crowd.

System level organization and behavior cannot be distributed to individual elements; it would be meaningless to say that an individual system component contains a fraction of the overall organization or behavior. In Sir Arthur Eddington's words, "[t]here is one [idea] which would look into each minute compartment of space to see what it may contain and so make a complete inventory of the world. But this misses any world-features where are not located in the minute compartments. We often think that when we have completed our study of *one* we know all about *two*, because 'two' is 'one and one'. We forget that we still have to make a study of 'and'." Here is the point: the study of 'and' is the study of systems. Without identifying, examining, and understanding what this one simple word 'and' means, system level characteristics and behavior are lost.

How and why individual system elements (components) interact and depend on each other together with identifying what moves between these elements define a system and its behavior. Avoiding the temptation to decompose a system into individual components retains a world view of the system, the only one capable of examining its organization and system level behavior resulting from its organization. The organization of a system is known as its *structure*. It is how individual system elements are organized so as to accomplish its purpose for being.

Left alone, the laws of entropy state that the world's organizations—the structure of individual elements—tend to disorder and decay. Bridges, governments, the human body, corporations, nature, automobiles, buildings, aircraft, societies, legal systems, religions, supply chains, cellular communications systems, species, and every other collection of individual elements in which a discernable level of organization is present, tends to disorganization and in some cases, decay. The process of adding organization or improving existing organization is called *engineering*. The branches of study that this process is applied to define primary engineering branches, all of their sub-disciplines, and interdisciplinary fields including systems engineering.

Systems engineers attempt to delay disorganization in systems by focusing on the system itself, making sure that all aspects of the system are considered as an integrated and interconnected entity, and then considering all the individual subsystems and components that support the system structure. Inevitably, these subsystems and components are designed and developed by specialty scientists, technologists, and engineering teams. Consequently, systems engineering is known as a truly interdisciplinary profession that, while led by systems engineers, have teams consisting of a wide range of professionals.

Decisions associated with modern systems are complicated and challenging. This book focuses on aiding those attempting to support these decisions, and to educate those who will assume their responsibilities in the future.

Systems either occur naturally or they are engineered by humans to accomplish very specific purposes. As a species, humans have little tolerance for disorder and confusion being part of everyday life. When present, these characteristics frustrate understanding of observed phenomena, motivating a natural tendency to bypass the whole and scrutinize individual objects to gain at least a partial understanding of what is transpiring. Partial understanding is better than no understanding, but disregarding interactions between objects that define the phenomena as a system is tenuous. When individual phenomenon can be contextualized as part of a larger identifiable entity, the actions and effects of observed phenomena make sense because relationships and interactions between and among individual entities and groups (components, subsystems) define the basis for their association. They interact because they need to in some sense, be it survival, profitability, security, pleasure, or other reasons.

Intentionally engineered systems are designed to do something for humans to make our lives a little (or a lot) better. Separating consideration of what a system *does* from what a system *is* defines one of the most fundamental and necessary ideas for all that follows in this book.

As an example, consider a legal system that is in-place for a small town. When laws are crafted in a complementary and coordinated way with other laws at town, state, and national level these connections define relationships that enables a legal *system* to exist. The legal system involves many elements than just the laws—courts, judges, forensic laboratories, police, vehicles, communication systems, municipal budgets, politicians, and many others, some of which contain key stakeholders to the legal system. While legislators work very hard at getting the wording of a new law correct, making sure that it does not conflict with other laws drives them to consider how this new law *integrates* within the larger system. Regardless of the system being considered, achieving successful integration in this manner is the most challenging task of systems engineers. For system decision support teams, it complicates the factors contributing to modeling and adds to the cost and value dimensions needed as described in this book.

However, if the legal system is engineered properly, it can achieve its fundamental objective (purpose) without conflict: to discourage or prevent chaotic and disruptive behavior among a population. It does so by having each system subgroup and component successfully performing *functions* at many levels. These functions describe what the system has *to do* to be considered successful. How well it performs these functions are determined by *measures*. The degree to which humans prioritize on each measure is set by their *values*.

Sewer systems and septic systems solve the problem of how to safely handle human waste, a great improvement over pit toilets and open air facilities. Cellular and internet networks reduce delays in communication and have enabled rapid business transactions and information exchange among people separated by thousands of miles and language differences. Aircraft, automobiles, boats, and trains have made the world a smaller place because of these transportation systems. In NYC, for example, Metro North, Path, New Jersey Transit, and the Long Island Rail Road provide rapid transit that enables commuters to live hours away from their place of work. And all these system are intentionally designed to operate, maintain, and retire the vehicles that are a part of a much larger system of interconnected elements.

Given the extent to which all the topics in this book rely on a solid understanding of what a system is, it is helpful to define it here. The *INCOSE Systems Engineering Handbook* [2] offers a two-part definition aligning with that of ISO/IEC/IEEE:

> … an integrated set of elements, subsystems, or assemblies that accomplish a defined objective. These elements include products (hardware, software, firmware), processes, people, information, techniques, facilities, services, and other support elements (*INCOSE*).
> … combination of interacting elements organized to achieve one or more stated purposes (ISO/IEC/IEEE 15288).

Another helpful definition was offered by Hitchins [3]:

> A system is an open set of complementary, interacting parts with properties, capabilities, and behaviors emerging both from the parts and their interactions.

Although slightly different, these definitions place a strong emphasis on the connected characteristic discussed earlier: "interacting elements," "interacting parts," and the "properties, capabilities, and behaviors" emerging from the parts as interconnected elements and the total organized collection of these into a system. These clearly convey that "the fundamental idea of a system is a purposeful whole that consists of interacting parts."

For conceptualizing and recognizing systems, it is useful to blend these into a single definition as proposed by Dickerson and Marvis [4] which aligns with the idea that an engineered system is designed and created with intent:

> A system is a combination of interacting elements integrated to realize properties, behaviors, and capabilities that achieve one or more stated purpose(s).

The objects supporting the structure of a system (its organization) are called "components" or "elements," terms that are used interchangeably throughout this book. The word "parts" is generally not used when referring to system objects because a part is the lowest level of item involved in a component and are generally below the concern of the main task of systems engineers: integrating components into a whole system.

The terms "process" and "analysis" are used throughout the book so it is helpful to define these as well before moving on.

Definition: The word *process* refers to a repeatable, logically organized, step-by-step sequence of actions or activities intended to achieve a specific outcome. The word "process" in this setting is a noun.

Definition: The term *analysis* is used to describe all the cognitive activities that attempt to gain insights into system behavior based on modeling results. When analysis succeeds, output is translated and interpreted in a manner that makes sense in the current context.

A shortened version of the aforementioned definition that is popular with students is: "analysis is the set of activities that take place after the correct answers are identified." Defining the term "analysis" is important because it means different things to different disciplines, and since most systems decision support teams have a blend of disciplinary expertise, a common understanding prevents misunderstandings. Analytical chemistry, for example, focuses on learning techniques that produce precise measurements such as the amount of nickel in a metallic substance. Identifying the correct amount of nickel to the level of precision needed ends analytical chemistry's definition for analysis. Not so for systems work. Output from design, modeling, engineering, computational calculations, mathematics, statistics, and other specialty techniques must be analyzed to illuminate insights, implications, ramifications, and potential opportunities that should be communicated to stakeholders.

The definition for systems engineering used by *INCOSE*, the world's leading systems engineering professional society, aligns with the philosophy of this book:

Definition: Systems Engineering is a *transdisciplinary* and *integrative* approach to enable the successful realization, use, and retirement of *engineered systems*, using *systems principles and concepts*, and scientific, technological, and management methods [2].

In this definition, the terms *engineering* and *engineered* are used in their widest sense as "the action of working artfully to bring something about," explicitly recognizing the creativity, thoughtfulness, and design-enabled characteristics associated with systems engineering and systems decision support projects. Engineered systems may be composed of any blend of people, products, services, information, processes, and natural systems.

The *INCOSE* definition highlights several key functions of systems engineering as a professional practice:

- Understanding stakeholders (including clients, users, consumers) to identify system functions and objectives to meet their needs.
- Measuring how well system elements will perform functions to meet stakeholder needs.
- Integrating multiple disciplines into the systems engineering team and in consideration of systems alternatives: engineering (aerospace, bioengineering, chemical, civil, electrical, environmental, industrial, mechanical, and others), management, finance, manufacturing, services, logistics, marketing, sales, and so on.
- Remaining involved in many tasks throughout the system life cycle (defining client and user needs and required functionality; documenting requirements; design; integration; identifying, assessing, and managing risks; and system validation).
- Participating in system cost analysis and resource management to ensure cost estimate credibility and an affordable system results.
- Performing system modeling and analysis to insure that a sufficient and comprehensive system representation is being considered at each decision gate of the system life cycle.
- Supporting engineering managers' decision making as they manage the system throughout the system life cycle.

These functions, among others, serve to clarify an important point: systems engineering and engineering management are inextricably linked. They work in a complementary fashion to design, develop, deploy, operate, maintain, and eventually retire successful systems that deliver value to stakeholders. So, what is expected of a systems engineer or a systems professional in general?

Systems engineers are leaders of multidisciplinary technical teams. Azad Madni, an *INCOSE* Fellow, describes the expectations of systems engineers in the following way [5]: "Systems engineers are required to be broad thinkers, capable of generating creative options and synthesizing solutions. They are lateral thinkers at heart, which underscores the natural multidisciplinary structure of systems engineering teams. They must be capable of formulating the right problem to solve and to challenge *every* assumption prior to accepting any. Systems engineers must have the necessary skills and knowledge to imbed esthetics into systems (solutions), to create required abstractions and associations, to synthesize solutions using metaphors, analogies, and heuristics, and to know where and where not to infuse cognitive engineering in the system life cycle."

There are a good many professional systems engineers who will contend that it is not possible for undergraduate students to learn the myriad of technical skills needed to properly function as a systems engineer in today's rapidly evolving world. One must first master the skills required by primary engineering disciplines: electrical, mechanical, chemical, nuclear, or environmental. Afterwards, one can move on to becoming a systems engineer when job requirements shift from benchwork to managing efforts to integrate components and subsystems into systems. This book's approach both agrees and disagrees with this position.

On one hand, being grounded in any technical, scientific, organizational, or engineering field affords substantial advantages when dealing with the intricacies of modern systems. On the other, in today's age all modern systems of reasonable complexity and technological sophistication are not the product of a single engineering field. And, those that are (or were) constructed in such a fashion frequently encounter issues once the system is deployed because 'things got missed' during design, build, testing, and deployment of the system. Gaining a foundation of understanding regarding processes and techniques that can help to avoid such costly mistakes while supporting important system decisions that must be made is well within the grasp of undergraduates.

Most often, the source of these issues is a narrow scope of perspective during system development. Some set of external systems involving stakeholders with vested interests have requirements or desires that were not taken into consideration when critical development decisions were made. This is especially evident for decisions that potentially are "latched," meaning that once they have been made, their ramifications cannot be undone without excessive rework, extraordinary cost increases, and unacceptable schedule delays. Again, it is helpful to remember that a decision is an irrevocable allocation of resources.

It would have been far better for such a team to have participating members whose cognitive processes focus on identifying multi-organizational interests that enrich design alternatives, integrating these interests into intentional design decisions, and developing models that provide insights into 'what if?' long before production begins. Doing so goes a long way toward preventing dysfunctional over-investment in any one stakeholder interest at the sacrifice of systems performance. Such an over-investment is call *sub-optimizing*.

It would be great if such an approach were applicable throughout the complete system life cycle, supporting the plethora of system decisions that must be made to ensure completeness is attained that benefits most, if not all, stakeholders. In this, it is important to recognize that following a well-defined decision process does not guarantee that a system will be produced with functionality that satisfies every stakeholder. Compromises must be made throughout the development stage that will dilute the expectations of some stakeholders in order to maximize the system's overall performance. However, using a well-defined process does dramatically increase the likelihood that good decisions will be made based a comprehensive consideration of multiple dimensions affecting the end result. Recognize also that once systems are put into operation, shortcomings will emerge if for no other reason than the fact that the environment within which the system must function has continued to evolve while the system was undergoing design, development, and deployment.

It is this dimension of systems engineering – decision making in systems engineering and management – that this book focuses on. The technical skills, philosophical perspectives, and encompassing processes associated with this activity can be successfully mastered by undergraduates, graduates, and professional practitioners alike, albeit to different levels of expertise. Inherent in this is a need for one to first understand the system of interest (what currently exists) and what stakeholders envision the system being and doing to be considered successful. Successfully connecting these bookends of a systems project with organized comprehensive activities is what the systems decision process (SDP) introduced in this book does.

This third edition recognizes several evolutions that have occurred since the second edition was published in 2010. First, the course that motivated the book in the first place has evolved and refined its content to capitalize on new developments and demonstrated success elements while letting go of others. While deterministic models continue to demonstrate value in supporting critical systems decisions, they more frequently deliver substantially more value when uncertainties affecting costs, risks, value, schedule, and so on are integrated into them. Models that embrace uncertainty repeatedly not only provide additional insights into what's best now, but also illuminate insights into potential opportunities or disasters that are lurking among important choices being made. The third edition expands it coverage to support this.

Second, teaching practices continue to adapt and evolve, and many instructors adopt custom materials from diverse professional sources that more appropriately meet their needs and the needs of their students. For published material, extracting segments from their sources requires that sections and chapters exist mostly as stand-alone entities largely decoupled from their collective whole. The third edition has been crafted to support this feature. Additionally, occasional checks on learning are used to better facilitate 'smaller bites' to aid digestion of the material.

Lastly, the software development community has largely moved away from selling or licensing individual proprietary products for educational purposes. Recognizing that students represent future adopters, many are allowing free or very low cost access to their applications for education and research purposes. The number of high-quality, open-source, community developed, free software applications available to support the techniques and ideas in this book has expanded quite a bit since the second edition. Several of these are used to illustrate technical approaches in the third edition, with appendices providing information on how to obtain these and basic getting started guidelines.

In all, this third edition is intended to assist students and practitioners to understand best practices for supporting systems decisions. The sections that follow recap briefly many of the essential ideas needed to do this.

1.1.1 Check on Learning

Concepts:

(a) The human body is considered a complex bio/neuro/chemical system. What does "being healthy" mean in this context? What does "being ill" mean?

(b) Under entropy, systems tend toward disorder. Is this the same thing as "aging" for humans?

(c) Is the education system actually a system? If so, then what is its purpose? What are its components? Are they integrated?

Comprehension:

(a) What does it mean to "integrate" components into a system?

(b) Is there a difference between "transdisciplinary" and "interdisciplinary" professions?

Application:

(a) Give an example of a "process" that you do every day.

(b) Systems have behavior that disappears when they are broken up into parts. Traffic jams, soccer plays, and the phrase "There's no 'I' in teams" are examples of this. Can you think of any more?

(c) Education often assumes that "in order for you to do C you must do A and B first." Can you provide examples where this is not true?

1.2 THE SYSTEMS ENGINEERING PERSPECTIVE

Humans form teams in an effort to overcome obstacles when faced with challenging tasks. Developing a new system or service, or improving an existing system is a challenging task complicated by having to deal directly with people and organizations each of whom have their own public, private, personal, and group motivations, biases, goals, values, and other distinguishing characteristics that establish differences between each entity. These distinctions are important when forming teams because multi-skilled teams tend to perform better in the face of complication and complexity than single dimensional teams. Consequently, a systems development project whose team members include various types of engineers, physical scientists, computer scientists, mathematicians, financial experts, lawyers, social scientists, manufacturers, logisticians, and others experiences a better chance that what may appear difficult for some will be easy(ier) for others. In this mix, it is the systems professional that supports critical system decisions, sewing together (integrating) each team member's effort, keeping them on track to meet requirements without over optimizing their contribution, and insuring that the resulting system meets or exceeds stakeholder expectations. This has become the world of systems engineers almost by default.

Systems engineering is a relatively new discipline that is, at times, difficult to pigeon hole because of its pervasive presence due to the demands of modern life. Of course, people have engineered large, complex systems since the Egyptians built the pyramids, Romans built their aqueducts, and fifteenth century sea captains prepared their sailing ships to go around the world. Until about a 100 years ago, system integration was generally in the hands of a craft specialist with a lifetime of experience in his or her craft, working mainly from a huge store of painfully learned rules of thumb.

The need for multidisciplinary engineering at the systems level was first widely recognized in the telephone industry in the 1920s and 1930s, where the approach became fairly common. Systems thinking and mathematical modeling got a further boost during World War II with the success of operations research, which used the scientific method and mathematical modeling to improve military operations. After the war, the military services discovered that systems engineering was essential to developing complex weapon systems in the computer and missile age. The private sector followed this lead, using systems engineering for such projects as commercial aircraft, nuclear power plants, and petroleum refineries.

The first book on systems engineering was published in 1957 [6], and by the 1960s degree programs in the discipline became widely available. The professional organization for systems engineers, known as the International Council on Systems Engineering (*INCOSE*) [7], was founded in 1990 with the mission to "enhance the state-of-the-art and practice of systems engineering in industry, academia, and government by promoting interdisciplinary, scalable approaches to produce technologically appropriate solutions to meet societal needs."[7]

1.2.1 Systems Trends That Challenge System Engineers

There are several important trends that have imposed significant systems engineering challenges, including the actions necessary to support key decisions that stakeholders must make. Systems have become increasingly more complex, more dynamic, and more interconnected, and involve more internal and external stakeholders than in the past. They also face increasing security challenges as less and less systems are designed and deployed as stand-alone entities.

Increasing complexity. Systems are more complex today in terms of function, form, integration, and technology. This not only concerns technical components and their assembly and integration into comprehensive, stable systems, but also on the processes and organizations associated with them. Creating and maintaining systems involve many disciplines from across the landscape of professional practice. And, while new technologies create new opportunities, they increase system complexity through their numbers, design variation, inherent adaptability, and extensive integration requirements.

More dynamic. Modern systems interact with their environment in real time, and the needs of stakeholders evolve in concert with these interactions. Rapid changes in the environment motivate new requirements that must be accommodated for the system to continue to provide value to consumers of products and services.

Increasing interconnectedness. Network advances in information technology have led to multi-layered direct collaboration that fuels a global economy with pervasive interconnectedness. International supply chains are common and frequent, intertwining concerns for regional stability into technical design for system elements. Artifacts of these concerns affect production, services, and personnel in new ways.

Many and varied stakeholders. Increasing system complexity and interconnectedness leads to an increase in the number and variety of stakeholders involved in the system life cycle.

In addition to considering the perspectives of scientists, engineers, and engineering managers, system engineers must consider the perspectives of functional managers (production, sales, marketing, finance, etc.), regulators, professional organizations, legislative bodies and regulation, cultural advocates, environmentalists, government lobbies, community groups, and international financial entities, just to name just a few who commonly have vested interests in existing and new systems.

Increasing security concerns. Many systems face increasing security challenges due to threats from malicious adversaries ranging from hackers to terrorists. Information assurance, which is the activity of protecting data and its flow across communication networks, is a major concern of system developers and users. In a similar fashion, physical security is an important design criteria for many systems as well. Protecting personal information in systems is now a major system challenge.

Complexity is a challenging concept when it comes to systems engineering and systems decision problems. Table 1.1 illustrates a modified and expanded spectrum of complexity across

TABLE 1.1 Dimensions of Problem Complexity [8].

Problem Dimension:	Low (Technical Problem)	Medium (Complex Problem)	High (Wicked Problem)
Boundary	Isolated, defined	Interconnected, defined	No defined boundary
Type	Similar to solved problems	Several unique features and new constraints will occur over time	Unique or unprecedented
Stakeholders	Few homogenous stakeholders	Multiple with different or conflicting views and interests	Hostile or alienated stakeholders with mutually exclusive interests
Challenges	Technology application and natural environment requirements	New technology development, natural environment, intelligent adversaries	No known technology, hostile natural environment, constant threats
Parameters	Stable and predictable	Parameter prediction difficult or unknown	Unstable or unpredictable
Use of Experiments	Multiple low-risk experiments possible	Modeling and simulation can be used to perform experiments	Multiple experiments not possible
Alternative Solutions	Limited set	Large number are possible	No bounded set
Solutions	Single optimal and testable solution	Good solutions can be identified and evaluated objectively and subjectively	No optimal or objectively testable solution
Resources	Reasonable and predictable	Large and dynamic	Not sustainable within existing constraints
End State	Optimal solution clearly defined	Good solutions can be implemented but additional needs arise from dynamic needs	No clear stopping point

Source: Parnell [52]/Springer Nature.

10 problem dimensions held in-common with systems decision problems based on the visual modeling approach of Clemens [9]. The third category called "Wicked Problems" is a recently characterized phenomenon typifying a growing number of systems in existence today. A recent outstanding publication by the *INCOSE* Complex Systems Working group lists and describes fifteen (15) characteristics of complexity [10] that are useful to bear in-mind early in the SDP's Problem Definition phase when a systems team is engaged with understanding a systems project's potential challenges. Table 1.2 is an extract from their efforts.

These descriptions are particularly helpful during the Problem Definition phase of the SDP when the systems team is dedicated to identifying the structure and characteristics of the system of interest.

1.2.2 Check on Learning

Concepts:

(a) Is there a difference between "system behavior" and "emerging system behavior"? If so, what is the difference based on?

(b) Is there a difference between a "stakeholder" and a "shareholder"?

Comprehension:

(a) If complexity is a system characteristic that does not go away, then what is a "complicated system"? How do complications go away?

(b) Is the daily process you identified in the previous learning check a dynamic process? How so?

(c) Laughter is considered an emergent behavior. Why would this be so?

Application:

(a) Can you give examples of a system boundary you encounter in daily life? Is the system associated with this boundary an engineered system?

(b) Cybersecurity is an example of a network system security concern. What other types of security are a system concern and can you provide specific examples?

(c) Can you identify an example where technology is changing rapidly? Perhaps one that changes a device that you were completely satisfied with into one that is frustrating? What aspect of technology changed rapidly to make this happen?

1.2.3 Fundamental Tasks of Systems Engineers

All participants in a system life cycle should use systems thinking. Although the trend is changing, systems engineers are the primary system thinkers on a systems team. There are three fundamental tasks for systems engineers and several key questions that systems engineers must answer for each task:

Task 1: Use an interdisciplinary approach to consider the complete problem in every system decision during every stage of the system life cycle.

TABLE 1.2   Characteristics of Complexity [10].

Characteristic	Definition
Diversity	The structural, behavior, and system state varieties that characterize a system and/or its environments. Complex systems tend to exhibit significant diversity.
Connectivity	The connection of the system between its functions and the environment. This connectivity is characterized by the number of nodes, diversity of node types, number of links, and diversity in link characteristics. Complex systems have multiple layers of connections within their system structure. Discontinuities (breaks in a pattern of connectivity at one or more layers) are often indications of complex system connectivity. Simple and some complicated systems may be characterized by simpler structures such as hierarchies.
Interactivity	The behavior stimulus and response between different components and functions of a system and the system with its environment. Complex systems have many diverse sources of stimulus and diverse types of responses. The correlation between stimulus and response can be both direct and indirect (perhaps separated by many layers of system connectivity). The types of stimuli and responses vary greatly. The levels of stimuli and responses can range from very subtle to very pronounced. The timeframe for system responses can vary greatly.
Adaptability	Complex systems proactively or reactively change functions, relationships, and behaviors to balance changes in environment and apply these to achieve system goals.
Multiscale	In complex systems, behaviors, relationships, and structures exist on many scales, are ambiguously coupled across multiple scales, and are not reducible to a single level.
Multi-perspective	Multiple perspectives, some of which are orthogonal, are required to comprehend a complex system.
Behavior	Complex system behavior cannot be described fully as a response system. Complex system behavior includes nonlinearities. Optimizing system behavior cannot often be done focusing on properties solely within the system.
Dynamics	Complex systems may have equilibrium states or may have no equilibrium state. Complex system dynamics have multiple scales or loops. Complex systems can stay within the dynamical system or generate new system states or state transitions due to internal system changes, external environment changes, or both. Correlation of changes in complex systems to events or conditions in the system dynamics may be ambiguous.
Representation	Representations of complex systems can be difficult to properly construct with any depth. It is often impossible to predict future configurations, structures, or behaviors of a complex system, given finite resources. Causal influence networks create a challenge in developing "requisite" conceptual models within these time and information resource constraints.
Evolution	Changes over time in complex system states and structures (physical and behavioral) can result from various causes. Complex system states and structures are likely to change as a result of interactions within the complex system, with the environment, or in application. A complex system can have disequilibrium (for example, non-steady) states and continue to function. Complex system states and structures can change in an unplanned manner that can be difficult to discern as they occur. Changes in the states and structure of a complex system are a natural function of (is often present in) the complex system dynamics. Changes can occur without centralized control, due to localized responses to external and/or internal influences.

TABLE 1.2 (*continued*)

Characteristic	Definition
System emergence (general)	Features/behavior associated with the holistic system that are more than aggregations of individual component properties.
Unexpected emergence (complex)	Emergent properties of the holistic system that are unexpected (whether predictable or unpredictable) in the system functionality/response. Unpredictable given finite resources. Behavior not describable as a response system.
Disproportionate effects	Details seen at fine scales can influence large scale behavior. Small scale modifications can result in radical changes of behavior. Scale can be in terms of magnitude of effect or aggregate amount of change. Weak ties can have disproportionate effects.
Intermediate boundaries	Complex system boundaries are intricately woven with their environment and other interacting systems. Their boundaries can be non-deterministic. The boundary cannot be distinguished based solely on processes inside the system.
Contextual influences	All systems reside in natural and social environments and relate to these. In the relationship between the system and the natural and social environments there can be complexity. This complex interaction depends on the social application of the system. Social systems often strive to achieve multiple, sometimes incompatible, objectives with the application of the same system.

Source: Adapted from [5].

Each stage of a system's life cycle generates its own unique challenges. An initial problem statement from one decision maker or stakeholder rarely encompasses all significant perspectives needed to define a complete systems problem. Several key questions associated with this first task are [11]:

- What is the system of interest?
- What is the actual problem needing to be solved?
- Who are the decision makers and stakeholders?
- What are the influencing factors and constraints imposed by the system environment?
- How will we know when we have adequately defined the problem?
- What value can the system provide to decision makers and stakeholders, including clients, system owners, system users, collaborators, and consumers of products and services?
- How much time is available to solve the problem?

Chapter 4 describes the first phase in the SDP, including some useful techniques for problem definition based on research and stakeholder analysis.

Task 2: Convert stakeholder needs into system functions, requirements, and performance measures.

Systems engineers work with stakeholders to determine what is and what should be. One of the most surprising facts of systems engineering is that it is not always easy to identify the future users or consumers of a system or its output. Many times, the organization funding the system is not the user or the consumer of the product or service. This is especially true when users do not directly pay for a service or product that the system provides, which is typical of many government systems decision support efforts. Working with stakeholders to determine the functions that the system must perform is a daunting task when dealing with complex, dynamic, interdependent systems involving many stakeholders and facing significant security challenges. Once these system functions are determined, system requirements must be specified and assigned to system elements (components) so that component engineers can begin design.

The following are some of the key questions for this task:

- Who are the stakeholders (clients, system owners, system users, collaborators, and consumers of product and services) holding a vested interest in the system?
- What methodology should be used to implement the systems engineering process to define system functions and requirements?
- To what extent should decision makers and stakeholders be involved in the process?
- What are the functions the system needs to perform to create value for stakeholders?
- What are the design objectives for each function?
- How should the ability of a designed solution to meet the design objectives be measured?
- What are the requirements for each function?
- How should system functions be allocated to system elements?
- How, when, and why do internal and external system elements interact?
- What are the design, operational, and maintenance constraints?
- How will we verify that elements meet their requirements and interfaces?

Chapter 6 describes the tasks and some useful techniques for functional analysis and value modeling. The screening criteria (the requirements that any acceptable solution must be able to meet) and the value model (which defines the minimum acceptable levels on each value measures) directly assess each candidate solution's ability to satisfy major system requirements.

Task 3: Lead requirements analysis, design synthesis, and system validation to achieve successful system realization.

After identifying system functions, requirements, and performance measures, a systems engineer must lead the requirements analysis, design synthesis and validate that the design solution solves the defined problem. The basis for system design and validation is usually an iterative sequence of functional analysis, modeling, simulation, development, test, production, and evaluation. For complex systems, a spiral development approach may be used to develop system prototypes with increasing capabilities until the system requirements and feasibility are established. Once the system design is validated, the systems engineer must continue to work on the successful system realization.

One of the most essential systems engineering tasks is to lead the resolution of requirements, configuration control, design integration, interface management, and test issues that will occur during the life cycle stages. The chief (or lead) systems engineer creates a professional and respectful environment that encourages early identification, multidisciplinary assessment, creative solution development, timely decision making, and integrated resolution of engineering issues. To achieve the value the system was designed to obtain, the following are some of the key questions involved in this task:

- How will we know when we have adequately solved the problem?
- How do we ensure that the design will meet the requirements?
- How do we resolve conflicting requirements, interfaces, or design issues?
- How can we allocate system performance to system elements?

- How can we identify and validate component and system interfaces?
- Can we trade off one performance measure against other measures?
- How will we verify that system performance has been achieved?
- How do we identify, assess, and manage risk during the system life cycle?
- How do we trade off system performance with life cycle costs to ensure affordability?

Several chapters of this book provide information on performance measurement:

- Chapter 3 provides techniques for modeling system performance and system suitability.
- Cost is almost always a critical systems performance measure. Chapter 8 provides techniques for life cycle costing.
- Chapter 6 describes the multiple criteria value model (MCVM) that identifies the value measures (often system performance measures) for the objectives of each system function. The value model captures the value added for each incremental increase in the range of each value measure. It also captures the relative importance of the value measure ranges to the system design.
- Chapters 3 and 3 describe modeling and simulation techniques for assessing system performance, screening alternatives and enhancing candidate solutions.
- Chapter 9 describes how to perform trade-off analysis among value measures and between system value and system cost.

Systems thinking is critical to each of the three fundamental systems engineering tasks. Systems engineers must help teams think about the problem and the solution that is being designed for the problem. Systems engineers must continue to be the consumer and user advocates as they help convert owner, user, collaborator, and consumer needs into systems functions, requirements, and value measures. In addition, they must define, validate, and test the element interfaces. These three fundamental tasks are made more challenging by increasing system complexity, dynamic changes, interconnectedness, number of stakeholders, and increasing security concerns.

1.2.4 Relationship of Systems Engineers to Other Engineering Disciplines

As noted in the opening quote of this chapter, systems engineering is only one of the engineering disciplines involved in a system's life cycle. Table 1.3 briefly compares systems engineering with other engineering disciplines' views on several dimensions. Scientists play a critical role by developing the fundamental theory that supports each of the engineering disciplines. Component (or discipline) engineers develop the technology that determines what can be. By performing the tasks described earlier, systems engineers work with stakeholders to determine what should be. Finally, engineering managers orchestrate the activities that produce what will be. A lead systems engineer or engineering manager approves all the products developed by the systems team and obtains client organizational approvals and the resources to design, produce, and operate the system of interest.

Systems engineers help provide design synthesis. To do this job they need to understand the system component engineering disciplines, work effectively with their engineering colleagues, and know when to bring interdisciplinary teams together to solve requirement, design, test, or operational problems.

TABLE 1.3   Comparison of Engineering Disciplines.

Comparison criteria	Systems engineering	Traditional engineering discipline
Problem characteristics	Complex, multidisciplinary, incrementally defined	Primarily requiring expertise in no more than a couple of disciplines; problem relatively well defined at the onset
Emphasis	Leadership in formulating and framing the right problem to solve; focus on methodology and process; finding parsimonious solutions that are often a balance between tradeoffs; associative thinking	Finding the right technique to solve; focus on outcome or result; finding parsimonious explanations; vertical thinking
Basis	Esthetics, envisioning, systems science, systems theory	Physical sciences and attendant laws
Key challenges	Integration: achieving multi-level inter-operability between new and legacy software-intensive systems; Architecting unprecedented systems; legacy migration; new/legacy system evolution;	Finding the most elegant or optimal solution; formulating hypothesis and using deductive reasoning methods to confirm or refute them; finding effective approximations to simplify problem solution or computational load
Complicating factors	Design, modeling, analysis, and decisions involve a wide span of organizations and environmental factors (see SDP)	Nonlinear phenomena in various physical sciences; advanced materials and new technology
Key metric examples	Technology and system readiness; system modularity; cost and ease of legacy migration; system complexity; ability to accommodate evolving requirements; ability to meet stakeholder expectations of value	Solution accuracy, product quality, and reliability; solution robustness

1.2.5   Education, Training, and Knowledge of Systems Engineers

Educating and training systems engineers occurs across the spectrum of undergraduate, graduate, continuing education, and professional certification programs. Most of these programs introduce and reinforce systems thinking and the tools needed to for projects throughout the entire system life cycle. Training programs are sometimes tailored to a stage in the system life cycle.

As a relatively new discipline, systems engineering programs are still being developed at colleges and universities. All engineering programs, including systems engineering, are accredited by ABET Inc. [12]. INCOSE is currently working with ABET to become the professional society to establish systems engineering centric accrediting standards for systems engineering programs [12]. In addition to undergraduate systems engineering degree programs, several universities offer masters and Ph.D. programs in systems engineering. These programs have different names such as systems engineering, industrial and systems engineering, and information and systems engineering. Many engineers have undergraduate degrees in another engineering discipline before obtaining a graduate degree in systems engineering. There are also several systems engineering continuing education programs offered. INCOSE established a systems engineering certification program in 2004 which has continued to expand.

As an evolving and growing field, systems engineering knowledge is available from many sources including online, textbooks, and technical books. Specific series have been established by various publishers to highlight a select offering of references considered foundational to understanding the principles and practices of systems engineering. Two examples are the Wiley Series in Systems Engineering and Management [13], and the CRC Press Complex and Enterprise Systems Engineering series [14]. For a broader list of systems engineering books, readers can refer to Wikipedia. A second source of useful reference material is contained in primers, handbooks, and bodies of knowledge. INCOSE versions of these type of reference materials are available on their website. Two other comprehensive references are available free from MITRE [15] and NASA [16]. The Systems Engineering Body of Knowledge (SEBoK) project (https://sebokwiki.org/), a collaboration between several organizations, is another excellent source for information regarding the principles and practices of systems engineering.

As is described in Section 1.3, the philosophy of systems thinking is what differentiates modern systems engineering from other specialty engineering disciplines such as civil, mechanical, electrical, aerospace, and environmental. Table 1.3 presents some of the more significant differences [5]. While not exhaustive, the comparison clearly illustrates that there is something different about systems engineering that is fundamental to the discipline.

The engineering thought process underpinning these other engineering fields assumes that decomposing a structure into its smallest constituent parts, understanding these parts, and reassembling these parts will enable one to understand the structure. Not so with a systems engineering thought process. Many of these engineering fields are facing problems that are increasingly more interconnected and globally oriented. Consequently, interdisciplinary teams are being formed using professionals from a host of disciplines so that the team represents as many perspectives as possible. **Definition**: The *systems engineering thought process* is a holistic, logically structured sequence of cognitive activities that support system design, systems analysis, and systems decision making to maximize the value delivered by a system to its stakeholders for the resources.

Systems decision problems occur in the context of their environment. The diversity of environmental factors shown in the SDP of Figure 1.8 clearly illustrates the need for systems engineering teams to be multidisciplinary. Each of these factors represent potential systems, stakeholders, and vested interests that will affect any systems decision and must be considered in the design and implementation of any feasible system solutions.

1.3 SYSTEMS THINKING

The Irish poet John Donne was very much a systems thinker. He envisioned the human race as being strongly interconnected to the point that "any man's death diminishes [him], because [he is] involved with mankind." Had he been living today, he no doubt would have been a strong advocate of social network theory [17].

As one of the current champions for using a holistic approach when developing models of real-world phenomena, Michael Pidd [18] poses two interesting questions earlier that go right to the heart of the discipline of systems engineering (SE). In a sense, whether systems are actual entities or simply one by-product of human perception and reasoning is irrelevant. If systems are the natural means by which we cope with and understand the highly connected, information intensive world we live in, it would seem illogical to not incorporate a strong consideration of the impact of this connectedness when making decisions about this same world. This is what systems thinking is all about.

 Why system thinking matters: how you think is how you act is how you are. The way you think creates the results you get. The most powerful way to improve the quality of your results is to improve the way you think [19].

This philosophy underscores a systems engineering thought process predicated on the belief that the study of the whole should come before that of the parts, recognizing that there are system level behaviors, interactions, and structural characteristics that are not present when the system is decomposed into its elements. This belief sets apart systems engineering from other engineering fields whose thought processes are founded on principles of decomposition as the basis of understanding. While decomposition certainly has its role in all analytical processes, focusing on the entire system has become an indispensable approach when addressing modern systems whose size and complexity are significant. Systems-of-systems engineering [20], model-oriented systems engineering [21], and techniques for designing complex systems [22] have emerged from the systems engineering community in response to this growing challenge. None of these approaches and their associated methods would exist in the absence of systems thinking.

The reason for departing from a pure decomposition principle at the onset of a systems decision problem is that decomposition is an activity that focuses on individual system element characteristics. It uses these individual characteristics to logically group or arrange elements so that the extent of shared characteristics becomes evident, thereby providing insights into how a more efficient or effective systems structure might be realized (by combining elements) or how a systems analysis might be more simply performed (because the analytical results associated with one element might apply to other elements possessing a high degree of shared characteristics with it).

Focusing on individual system elements tends to miss crucial interactions between the elements of a system or between composite groups of systems interacting as a whole. When these interactions or interdependencies are overlooked or insufficiently emphasized, the resulting modeling and analysis can suggest potential solutions that exhibit sub-optimal characteristics. Such solution alternatives, while attractive to the performance of individual elements, can actually hinder or degrade some performance measure of the overall system.

The risk (return volatility) for a portfolio of investments can easily increase because of an inappropriate over-investment in one particular asset, resulting in a loss of optimality for the portfolio [23]. In a similar fashion, installing high-intensity discharge (HID) headlamps into an older model vehicle may increase the lumens output (maximization effect for the headlamp element), but because the older model car is designed to accommodate filament bulbs, doing so results in improperly focused beam patterns and excessive glare to other road users. A safety measure associated with the older vehicle as a transportation system would degrade as a result.

Systems have emergent properties that are not possessed by any of its individual elements. Bottlenecks and the "accordion effect" observed in dense highway traffic flows are examples of emergent properties not possessed by individual automobiles; they become evident only when the transportation elements are viewed as a whole system. These properties result from the relationships between system elements, commonly described as the system *structure*. In many cases, this structure can be described mathematically. The functions and expressions resulting from these *mathematical* descriptions directly support modeling the system as described in Chapter 2.

Systems thinking enables one to progress beyond simply seeing isolated events to recognizing patterns of interactions and the underlying structures that are responsible for them [24]. It reveals structure in a way that enables teams to specify the boundary of the system, which sets apart the system and its internal functions from the environment external to it. Knowing this boundary enables teams to identify key system inputs and outputs and to visualize the *spatial arrangement* of the system within its environment. Critical systems thinking of the type required for systems engineering encourages creativity simply because of the strong interplay between conceptual visualization, detailed analysis, and unique measures of effectiveness (MOE) produced by synthesizing ideas.

The combination of systems thinking with engineering best practices has produced a variation of systems engineering second to none. The particular application of systems thinking advocated in this book is an adaption of general systems theory [25] with an emphasis on systems decision problems.

Systems have become increasingly more complex, dynamic, interconnected, and automated. Both the number and diversity of stakeholders have increased, as global systems have become more prevalent. Complexity presents itself as any combination of numerical, relational, or variational system characteristics that are persistent under any design alternative. In this way, interactions and dependencies between system elements are at least as important as the system elements themselves. Recognizing and leveraging this is the very foundation of systems thinking.

Systems thinking is a way of engaging with problem structuring, decision making, and design in which the interconnections and dependencies between system elements are at least as important as the elements themselves. In this manner, an understanding of the behavior exhibited by an entire system under study is needed before any decomposition of the system occurs. It is a holistic philosophy capable of uncovering critical system structure such as boundaries, inputs, outputs, spatial orientation, process structure, and complex interactions of systems with their environment [26].

For example, software companies take advantage of time zone differences to apply continuous effort to new software systems by positioning development teams in the United States, Europe, India, and Japan. Financial systems previously operating as independent ventures now involve banks, businesses, customers, markets, financial institutions, exchange services, and national and international auditing agencies. Changes occurring in one system impact in a very short time those they are connected to. A change in the Tokyo market, for example, propagates quickly to the US market because of strong relationships existing between not only these markets but the monetary exchange rates, trade balance levels, manufacturing production levels and inventory levels as well. In order to respond quickly to these market changes, buy and sell rules are automated so as to keep disrupting events from escalating out of control over time.

Military systems have dramatically increased in complexity as well. Currently, complex, interconnected systems use real-time satellite data to geo-locate themselves and to find, identify, and classify potential targets using a worldwide network of sensor systems. These, in turn, are connected to a host of weapons platforms having the capability to place precision guided munitions on targets. With systems such as these, a host of systems decisions arise. Is there a lower limit to human participation in a targeting process such as these? Are these limits defined by technological, cultural, moral, legal, or financial factors? Likewise, should there be an upper limit on the percentage of automated decision making? What measures of effectiveness (MOE) are appropriate for the integrated system behavior present only when all systems are operational?

In general then, for complex systems, how many system interactions do we need to consider when we are faced with analyzing a single system? Answers to this question shape both the system boundaries and scope of our decision support effort. How can we insure that critical interactions and relationships are represented in any model we build, and those that play only a minor role are discounted but not forgotten? For this and other important considerations to not be overlooked, a systems team needs a robust and consistent SDP driven by systems thinking that can repeatedly be applied during any system life cycle stage.

This way of thinking considers the system as a whole first, examining the behavior arising from a complete system without decomposing it into its elements. What the system does as a whole can be compared with what it was intended to do, creating information that can be used to modify the system's structure in a way that improves its performance. A system's structure can be apparent or underlying. Apparent structure can be observed; underlying structure requires modeling and mathematics to uncover and describe. Generally, a systems structure exists within boundaries, but not always. Strong dependency relationships with external elements outside of a system's boundaries can cause a boundary to flex, making what was once external to the system boundary now a part of the internal system elements for decision support purposes.

Understanding system structure enables system engineers to design, produce, deploy, and operate systems focused on delivering high value capabilities to customers. The focus on delivering value is what underscores every activity of modern systems engineering [27].

Systems thinking combined with creating value for stakeholders is a modern world view embedded in systems engineering as an effective way of addressing many of the challenges posed by the growing complexity of systems. Systems engineers necessarily must consider both hard and soft systems analysis techniques [28].

In applying the SDP that we introduce in Section 1.6 and use throughout this book, a significant amount of time is consumed in the early steps of the process, carefully identifying the core issues from stakeholders' perspectives, determining critical functions that the system must perform as a whole in order to be considered successful, and clearly identifying and quantifying how these functions will deliver value to stakeholders. Many of the techniques used to accomplish these tasks are considered "soft" in the sense that they are largely subjective and qualitative, as opposed to "hard" techniques that are objective and quantitative. Techniques used in later steps of the SDP involving system modeling and analysis, which are introduced in Chapter 3, lean more toward the quantitative type. Together, they form an effective combination of approaches that make systems engineering indispensable.

1.3.1 Check on Learning

Concepts:

(a) Is online shopping a system? If so, what components can you identify? Does it have a boundary?

(b) Can you give an example of a system whose performance suffers if one or more of its components are over-optimized (allowed to perform as much or as little as possible)?

(c) System thinking depends on perspectives. Can you give an example of an "outside looking in" and an "inside looking out" perspective that matters?

Comprehension:

(a) What is the difference between "thinking" and "system thinking"? How does this affect the actions taken?

(b) A common approach to fixing a complicated problem is to break it into parts, fix the parts, and put it back together. System thinking suggests not doing this at the start. Which category does medical surgery fall into?

Application:

(a) Is there something that you do that ignores the affect that it has on others? If so, is this an indication that you are actually part of system? What is the system?

(b) The expressions "I'm too close to the problem" and "I can't see the forest from the trees" are commonly used examples of needing to change perspective to gain a better understanding of a situation. Can you think of any other example phrases that indicate this as well?

1.4   SYSTEM LIFE CYCLES

Systems are dynamic in the sense that the passage of time affects their elements, functions, interactions, and value delivered to stakeholders. These observable effects are commonly referred to as system maturation effects. A system life cycle is a conceptual model that is used by system engineers and managers to describe how a system matures over time. It includes each of the stages in the conceptualization, design, development, production, deployment, operation, and retirement of the system. For most systems decision challenges and all system design problems, when coupled with the uncertainties associated with cost, performance, and schedule, life cycle models become important tools to help engineers and managers understand, predict, and plan for how a system will evolve into the future.

All systems have a useful lifetime during which they serve the purpose for which they were created. Just like a human lifetime, the degree to which a system achieves its purpose typically varies with age. New systems start out by hopefully meeting their performance targets. After entry in service, system elements and processes may begin to degrade. Degradation that occurs during a system's useful years motivates a host of specialized maintenance activities, some planned and some unplanned, intended to restore the system to as close to its original state as possible.

Eventually, most systems degrade to a point at which they no longer effectively meet stakeholder needs and are retired. At the retirement decision, the cost of further maintaining a system can easily exceed the cost of replacing the system. Mexico decided more than 20 years ago to not invest in any more old-style telephone infrastructure but rather go directly to the latest and greatest cellular systems for just this reason. Human-manned highway toll booths have likewise been replaced all along the New Jersey turnpike for similar reasons. Or, perhaps the system is operating as intended but it can no longer provide value to its stakeholders due to changes in the environment within which it exists or changes in stakeholder values and priorities. Media for musical sound recordings has changed many times since the first acoustic recordings in 1877 due to increased fidelity and performance offered by new technologies that better replicate a live performance. Eight-track technology for audio recording and playback is an example of a system that was retired because it lost its ability to compete in a consumer environment where "smaller is better" drove demand and new digital media offered a solution to the frustrating problem of tape contamination and damage. Network music streaming is now the dominant means for listening to music, but it also was a disruptive technology for the traditional record company model for how musicians were compensated. Interestingly, vinyl records—a product of the early twentieth century—are still being made in relatively small numbers compared with digital media, principally because audiophile stakeholder value for this media has held steady, and they are willing to pay the additional costs associated with this format.

In a similar fashion to human physiology, it is useful to think of a system as progressing through a succession of stages known as a life cycle. For living systems, this cycle consists of four stages simply described: birth, evolution, deterioration, and death [25]. A life cycle structure is an effective metaphor because it enables systems teams to:

1. Organize system development activities in a logical fashion that recognizes some activities must be accomplished prior to others.
2. Identify the specific activities needed to be accomplished in each stage to successfully move to the next stage.
3. Effectively consider the impact that early decisions have on later stages of the system life cycle, especially with regards to cost and risk (the likelihood and consequences of system problems).

As illustrated in Figure 1.1, system life cycle activities have a logical sequencing. They align with the transition of a system from its conceptual birth to eventual retirement. Notice that these activities are not the same as those described in the SDP. The SDP is a cycle of phases to support major systems decisions repeated at critical decision points (sometimes called gates) typically encountered once or more during each stage of the life cycle. The four phases of the SDP are described in Chapter 4 of this book.

As members of multidisciplinary teams, systems engineers maintain an appropriate focus on what needs to be done and when it needs to be done. The specifics of what, when, how, and why associated with these needs is dictated by the life cycle stage of the system. For example, the list of alternative solutions concerning a recently deployed system would consist of process and/or product modifications and enhancements designed to aid the system to better achieve the purpose

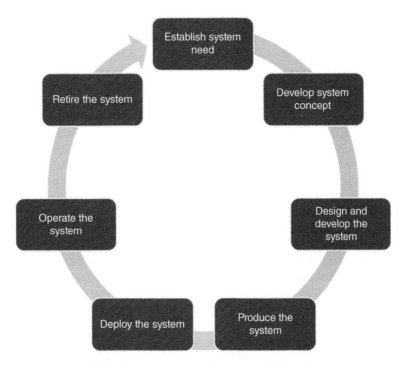

Figure 1.1 The stages of a system's life cycle.

for which it was created. In later life cycle stages, the list of alternative solutions might focus on new systems to replace the current system.

Some decisions made during early stages of system development are irreversible; once committed to a particular system concept (e.g. airplane) and a detailed design, consumer needs and resource limitations including time usually prevent the design team from switching to alternative design solutions. Other minor design decisions (e.g. paint color) can be altered readily without significant impact on project planning and execution.

However, all decisions have immediate and delayed costs associated with them. These costs can consist of a blend of financial, risk, environmental, technological, legal, and moral factors of direct concern to stakeholders, many of which may not be realized until later stages in the life cycle.

Not considering life cycle costs when making decisions early in the system life cycle could prove disastrous to long term system viability and survivability. The principle underlying this idea goes back to the Scottish enlightenment known as the Law of Unintended Consequences, more recently stated [29] succinctly as "[w]hether or not what you do has the effect you want, it will have three at least that you never expected, and one of those usually unpleasant." The least expensive and most effective hot water pipe insulating material to use in the northeast United States might be asbestos, but deciding to use asbestos without seriously considering the cost factors associated with the operational and retirement stages would not be wise.

This principle reminds us to be careful not to commit to a "whatever is best for right now" solution without examining the degree to which such a solution remains satisfactory during later life cycle stages as well. Hidden system costs emerge because someone failed to employ systems thinking over a complete system life cycle.

In practice, life cycles are driven by the system of interest. They serve to describe a system as it matures over time with regard to its functioning. A life cycle also guides professionals involved with sustaining the value delivered by the system to stakeholders thoughout this maturation. The life cycle stages need to contain sufficient detail to enable systems engineers, systems managers, operations researchers, production engineers, and so on to identify where their skill sets fit into the overall effort. At the same time, the stages need to be described broadly enough to accommodate related activities in a natural way.

System life cycles are planned and documented for success. Among the myriad of life cycle models in existence, two fundamental classifications arise: predictive and adaptive [30]. Predictive life cycle models favor optimization over adaptability. Adaptive life cycle models accept and embrace change during the development process and resist detailed planning. Once a life cycle for a particular systems decision problem is defined and documented, it is possible to structure the management system that will be used to support and perform each stage of the life cycle. This provides the data that are necessary to support major SDP decision gates to move to the next stage. Planning an effective management system prevents system development from occurring in a piecemeal or disjoint basis that has a tendency to increase risk.

The life cycle model in this text has the advantage of being able to simply represent stages in a system's lifetime along with the activities within each stage. The structured SDP process used to define and support systems engineering activities within these stages is naturally cyclic, providing a constant feedback mechanism that encourages revision, capturing ongoing changes in the system environment while taking full advantage of opportunities to capture and deliver value to the stakeholders. The SDP typically is used once in each stage to determine if the system should advance to the next stage.

As a consequence of defining the system life cycle separate from the SDP, the SDP provides the essential information for systems decision makers independent of the life cycle stage the system is in. Admittedly, each application of the SDP is tailored to the system and the life cycle stage. Some elements of the SDP may be truncated while others may be amplified for some systems in some stages. This adaptability feature is perhaps one of the SDPs greatest attributes.

1.4.1   System Life Cycle Model

The life cycle stages listed in Table 1.4 are broadly defined so as to apply to as many systems as possible. As can be seen in the sections that follow, various other life cycle models exist that

TABLE 1.4   System life cycle model for systems engineering and management.

System life cycle stage	Typical stage activities
Establish system need	Define the problem
	Identify stakeholder needs
	Identify preliminary requirements
	Identify risk factors and initial risk management plan
Develop system concept	Refine system requirements
	Explore system concepts
	Propose feasible system concepts
	Refine risk factors
	Assess initial performance, schedule, and technology risks
Design and develop system	Develop preliminary design
	Develop final design
	Assess initial development cost, market, and business risks
	Perform development tests to reduce risk
	Refine performance, schedule, and technology risk assessments; include mitigation steps in risk management plan
	Build development system(s) for test and evaluation
	Verify and validate design
	Test for integration, robustness, effectiveness
	Includes production scheduling, economic analysis, reliability assessments, maintainability, and spiral design implementation considerations, among others
Produce system	Produce system according to design specifications and production schedule
	Apply Lean Six Sigma as appropriate
	Refine development cost, market, and business risks; include mitigation steps in risk management plan
	Monitor, measure and mitigate performance, schedule, and technology risk
	Assess initial operational risk to the system
Deploy system	Refine operational risk to the system
	Develop a deployment plan
	Complete training of users and consumers
Operate system	Operate system to satisfy consumer and user needs
	Monitor, measure and mitigate operational risks
	Identify opportunities for enhanced system performance
	Provide sustained system capability through maintenance, updates, or planned spiral developed enhancements
Retire system	Develop retirement plan
	Store, archive, or dispose of the system

have specific types of system development models or systems engineering applications in mind. For example, the spiral design model illustrated in Figure 1.3 is frequently used in software system development with an eye toward highlighting risk management throughout the various life cycle stages.

Establish System Need. Establishing a clear system need is a critical first step in system management. Successfully addressing the purposes associated with this stage of the life cycle increases the likelihood of a match between the system that is truly needed and the one that is developed. The client faced with the problem that generates a system need is typically dealing with the problem's symptoms and resulting effects on a day-to-day basis. It is not unusual for someone in this situation to communicate an initial system need that is focused on treating these symptoms.

In the short term, treating the symptoms might improve the working conditions associated with the problem but it does not help to resolve the underlying cause(s) of these symptoms, which is much more difficult to uncover. The true cause(s) of observed symptoms typically evolves from a process of intensive interaction with stakeholders using techniques introduced in Chapter 5.

The first stage of the life cycle is about exploration, discovery and refining key ingredients necessary for the program to get off to a good start. This consumes a large proportion of time and effort. Once the actual problem, stakeholder needs, and preliminary requirements are successfully defined, the beginning steps are taken toward effective risk management and the system transitions into the next life cycle stage.

Develop System Concept. The life cycle stage of developing a system concept is centered on applying techniques designed to inspire creative thought contributing to effective, efficient systems designed to deliver maximum value to the stakeholders. These techniques generate novel system possibilities that meet stakeholder needs and eliminate any system concepts that are infeasible to further consider. Conceptual system models involving graphical illustrations, tables, and charts comparing and contrasting system characteristics, and a multitude of linked hierarchical diagrams are used to identify possible system concepts designed to address stakeholder needs.

In light of this initial set of feasible system concepts, various dimensions of system risk are identified and refined, such as performance (will the technology work?), schedule (can it be provided when needed?), and cost (is the system affordable?). The life cycle transitions to the next stage only when a sufficient number of feasible system concepts are identified that possess acceptable levels of risk.

Design and Develop System. The design and development stage involves designing, developing, testing, and documenting the performance of the chosen system concept. Quite often the models produced during this stage take the form of simulations, prototype code modules, mathematical programs, reduced and full-scale physical prototypes, among others. One must be careful to adhere to professional best practices when testing and analyzing the performance of competitive designs using these models and simulations (see Chapter 3), especially when it comes to verifying and validating model results.

A feasible concept along with a system model enables the system team to develop estimates of program costs along with market and business risks. Of course, the accuracy of these risk estimates depends strongly upon the assumptions made concerning the system deployment environment that will occur in the future. It is wise under these conditions to carefully develop a set of use case scenarios for testing the performance of the system design using models and simulations developed for this purpose. These use cases should reasonably reflect the full span of "What if?" possibilities. This is one way of identifying system design problems and limitations short of building, deploying, and operating a full-scale system. Engineering managers are fully engaged in the system at this point in the life cycle as well, developing plans to address all the dimensions of implementation noted. When satisfactorily completed, the decision gate naturally supports the system going forward into a production stage.

Produce System. Realizing success in the system production life cycle stage is as far from a foregone conclusion as one might imagine. This is a period in the system life cycle that stresses the management team charged with producing a system that serves its intended purpose, meets, or exceeds design requirements reflecting an acceptable risk across all risk dimensions, and does all this in an effective and efficient manner to achieve competitive advantage for the consumer of system products and services.

Ultimately, a system must deliver value to its key stakeholders or it will ultimately fail. However, systems can fail through no fault of their own simply because of changing environmental conditions. Remember that throughout the life cycle and all the efforts that have gone into making a concept a reality, time continues to evolve, raising the very real possibility that substantial threats to system success might become evident that were not present earlier in the life cycle. Thus, during this stage the systems team tries to identify and assess the types and levels of operational risks the deployed system will face.

Depending on the type of system to be delivered—product-focused or service-focused—Lean Six Sigma principles [31] are applied so that the production processes used to make the designed system a reality are as effective and efficient as possible.

A portion of the ongoing risk analysis engages in monitoring, measuring, and mitigating risks identified in the previous life cycle stages. Moreover, a good deal of effort goes into maintaining vigilance for any new risks that might emerge as a result of changes in the environment outside of the control of the team. This sensitivity naturally leads to a consideration of those external factors that could present risk to the system once it is placed into operation.

Operational risk [32] is emerging to be one of the least quantified, less understood, yet potentially largest impact areas of risk for systems engineering. While no single definition is dominant currently, operational risk is generally understood to mean the loss resulting from inadequate or failed internal processes, people, and support systems, or from environmental events. During this stage of the life cycle, brainstorming and other ideation techniques are again used to identify an initial list of operational risks that might threaten program success once the system is fielded and in the hands of users and consumers.

Deploy System. Successfully deploying a new or re-engineered system is the direct result of executing a well thought-out deployment plan that provides details concerning the activities necessary to place the system into an operational environment. The plan includes as a minimum a description of the assumptions supporting the current capabilities and intended use of the system, the dependencies that can affect the deployment of the system, and any factors that limit the ability to deploy the system.

In close coordination with the system users, consumers, and owners, many other deployment details are specified in the deployment plan as well. These include information concerning deployment locations, site preparation, database conversions or creation, and phased rollout sequencing (if appropriate). Training programs and system documentation are created during this life cycle stage. Specific training plans for system users and maintainers play a critical role in achieving a successful system deployment.

The systems team itself transitions into a support role during this life cycle stage as they begin to disengage from primary contact with the system and transfer system functionality to the client. Additional resource requirements for the design team are identified, support procedures designed, and a host of transition activities along with management roles and responsibilities become part of the deployment plan. Operations and maintenance plans are created and specified as well in order to provide explicit guidance to the system consumers and users as to how they might capture the greatest value return consistent with the intended design goals.

Finally, contingency plans are developed during this stage as well, some of which are included in the deployment plan and others are maintained internally by the systems engineering and deployment teams in case some of the risks identified and planned for in previous stages become reality. The operational risks identified previously are refined and updated as forecasted information concerning the system environment used to develop an initial list of potential threats to program success becomes reality.

Operate System. The most visible life cycle stage is that of operating the system in the mode it was intended. System users operate systems to provide products and services to system consumers. When we recognize the existence of systems in our environment, we are observing them in this stage of their life cycle. Some everyday systems that fall into this characterization include transportation networks, communications networks, electricity grid supply networks, emergency services, public and private education, tourism, law enforcement, national border security, politics, organized crime, and others.

Condition monitoring of a system while it is in operation is an activity that has traditionally consisted of use-based measures such as the number of hours of operation, number of spot welds performed, number of patients treated, and so on. Measures such as these have dominated reliability analysis for systems whose wear and tear during periods of nonuse is so small as to render its impact insignificant.

A good example of this can be seen in aircraft systems scheduled maintenance planning, which is based on flight hours of the aircraft in operation and not on the amount of time that has passed since the aircraft was placed into operation. Recently [33], many aircraft systems have switched to condition-based maintenance recognizing that not all pilots fly aircraft in the same manner. For military aircraft, condition-based maintenance recognizes that an hour flying routine missions imposes a significantly different level of system stress than does an hour flying in combat missions at night, in bad weather, or amidst hostile fire. Thus, system maintenance planning, which used to consist of executing routine tasks on a preset schedule, is evolving to the point where real time monitoring of system condition indicators is becoming more commonplace.

Any externally generated operational risks due to external influences on system elements, services, and performance to meet goals identified in previous life cycle stages are closely monitored during system operation. However, management focus during this life cycle stage is not exclusively centered on potential bad things that might occur. They also maintain a heightened awareness for possible opportunities to enhance system performance that could add value to the stakeholders or increase the competitive advantage of consumers and users.

In fact, when systems engineers are called upon to engage a system during one of its operational life cycle stages, the underlying motivation of the user organization is centered on this very principle of exacting increased performance value out of the existing system. This could mean re-engineering the system or its processes, applying optimization techniques to increase the efficiency of some dimensions of the system operation, using reliability methods to better understand and reduce the overall maintenance costs, or perhaps generating new ideas for system replacement that leverage recent developments in technology, knowledge, or the competitive landscape. Some of these advancements or changes in the operating environment may have been predicted and planned for during earlier life cycle stages, in which case system enhancements would be applied using principles of spiral development [34] as well.

Retire System. Finally, when users determine that it is no longer in their best interest to continue operating the system, it is retired from service. While the activities during this stage might be as simple as donating the existing system to a nonprofit organization or placing the system in storage, this life cycle stage can actually be quite complicated. One needs only consider the intricate requirements associated with taking a nuclear power plant offline in order to gain an appreciation for how complex this system retirement stage could be [35].

1.5 OTHER MAJOR SYSTEM LIFE CYCLE MODELS

As mentioned previously, there are several life cycle models in common use today. All of these life cycle models, including the one we use, are based on sets of professionally agreed standards, the primary ones being listed in Table 1.5 [36]. Despite their obvious differences, these life cycle models do have common characteristics. In the United States, the INCOSE has taken the lead on setting a common standard for professional practice and education against which programs and businesses can compare their quality levels.

TABLE 1.5   A Comparison of Standards-Driven Life Cycle Models.

Standard	Description	System life cycle stages
MIL/-STD/-499B	Focuses on the development of defense systems	• Pre-concept • Concept exploration and definition • Demonstration and validation • Engineering and manufacturing development • Production and deployment • Operations and support
EIA.IS 632	A demilitarized version of MILSTD499B	• Market requirements • Concept definition and feasibility • Concept validation • Engineering and manufacturing development • Production and deployment • Operations and support
IEEE 1220	Introduces the interdisciplinary nature of the tasks involved in transforming client needs, requirements, and constraints into a system solution	• System definition • Subsystem definition • Preliminary design • Detailed design • Fabrication, assembly, integration, and test • Production • Customer support
EIA 632	Focus is on defining processes that can be applied in any enterprise-based life cycle phase to engineer or re-engineer a system	• Assessment of opportunities • Solicitation and contract award • System concept development • Subsystem design and pre-deployment • Deployment, installation, operations, and support
ISO/IEC 15288	Includes both systems engineering and management processes at a high level of abstraction	• Concept process • Development process • Production process • Utilization process • Support process • Retirement or disposal process

TABLE 1.6   The ISO/IEC 15288 Systems Engineering Life Cycle Model.

Life cycle stage	Purpose	Decision gates
Concept	• Identify stakeholder needs	Execute next stage
	• Explore concepts	
	• Propose feasible solutions	
Development	• Refine system requirements	Continue current stage
	• Create solution description	
	• Build system	
	• Verify and validate	
Production	• Mass produce system	Go to previous stage
	• Inspect and test	
Utilization	• Operate system to satisfy user needs	Hold project activity
Support	• Provide sustained systemcapability	Terminate project
Retirement	• Store, archive, or dispose of system	

The last standard listed, ISO/IEC 15288, represents a modern interpretation of a system life cycle relative to the complex and heavily stakeholder dependent nature of the typical systems addressed in professional practice today. It represents the evolving standard of systems engineering practice in the United Kingdom. In this vein, the ISO/IEC 15288 system life cycle model is serving a purpose closely aligned with the life cycle model adopted in this book, except that, as can be seen in Table 1.6, they combine a life cycle model with various steps in an SDP. In this text, we separate the two processes into the system life cycle model discussed earlier and the SDP that supports decision making during all the stages of the system life cycle model.

Given the sequential representation shown in Table 1.6 [37], the ISO/IEC 15288 system life cycle implies one stage is completed before transitioning into the next. As a result, this life cycle model has been criticized for its lack of robustness in dealing with a wide variety of system problems. The waterfall model (Figure 1.2) is more robust because system problems arising in any stage can lead the systems team to recycle back through earlier stages in order to resolve them.

In contrast to the waterfall, the spiral life cycle model shown in Figure 1.3 formalizes the notion of repeated cycling through a development process. Each spiral produces increasingly more complex prototypes leading to a full-scale system deployment. In essence, the spiral model executes a series of waterfall models for each prototype development.

One attractive feature of the spiral model is the explicit recognition of the important role that risk plays in system development. This same consideration is intentionally incorporated in the system life cycle model used herein. In both life cycle models, various types of risks are identified during each prototype development cycle; for example, investment risk, performance risk, schedule risk, and so on. If these risks are successfully mitigated, the systems team evaluates the results of the current cycle, presents the results and conclusions in support of the decision gate, and, if approved, proceeds to enhance the prototype in the spiral model or moves to another stage in our life cycle model. Failing to resolve important risks can cause the program to terminate during any stage.

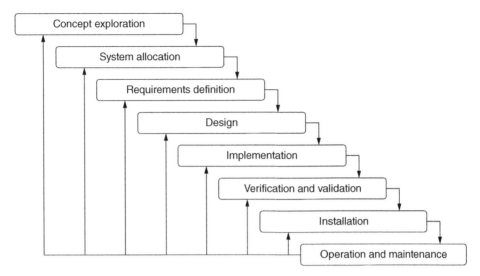

Figure 1.2 Waterfall system life cycle model.

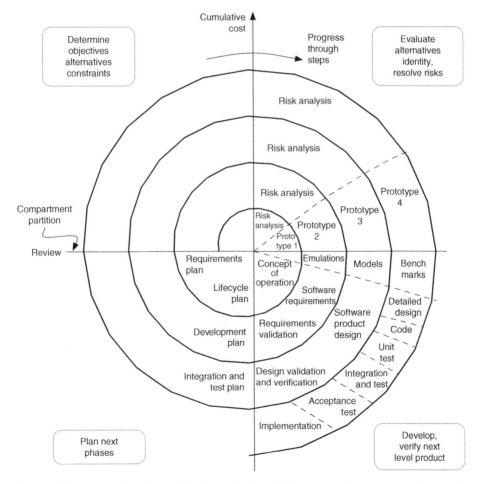

Figure 1.3 Spiral life cycle model with embedded risk assessment. Source: Boehm [38].

Several other specialized models are used for system development, although none as prevalent as the two already mentioned. Rapid applications development, a methodology created to respond to the need to develop software systems very fast, strives to deploy an 80% system solution in 20% of the time that would be required to produce a total solution [39], and agile life cycle models [40] are among these specialized models.

A system's performance level, its supportability, and all associated costs are important considerations in any SDP. The process introduced in Section 1.6 is fundamentally life cycle centered. In each stage of a system's useful life, systems owners make decisions that influence the well-being of their system and determine whether the system will continue to the next stage of its life cycle. The decision of whether or not to advance the system to the next stage is called a *decision gate*.

The performance of a system will degrade if it is not maintained properly and maintaining a system consumes valuable resources. At some point, system owners are faced with critical decisions of whether to continue to maintain the current system, modify the system to create new functionality with new objectives in mind, or to retire the current system and replace it with a new system design. These decisions should be made taking into consideration the entire system life cycle and its associated costs, such as development, production, support, and "end of life" disposal costs, because it is in this context that some surprising costs, such as energy and environmental costs, become clearly visible.

Consider, for example, the life cycle costs associated with a washing machine [41] in terms of percentage of its overall contributions to energy and water consumption, air and water pollution, and solid waste. One might suspect that the largest solid waste costs to the environment would be in the two life cycle stages at the beginning of its life cycle (packaging material is removed and discarded) and at the end (the machine is disposed of). However, as can be seen in Figure 1.4, the operational stage dominates these two stages as a result of the many packets of washing detergent and other consumables that are discarded during the machine's life. It is just the opposite case with the environmental costs associated with nuclear power facilities. The disposal (long-term storage) costs of spent nuclear fuel have grown over time to equal the development and production costs of the facility [42].

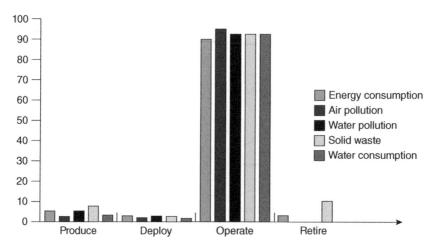

Figure 1.4   Life cycle assessment of environmental costs of a washing machine [41].

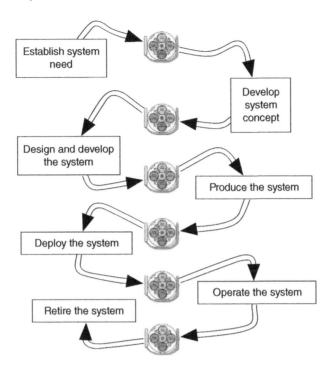

Figure 1.5 Systems decision process used throughout a system life cycle. Source: D/SE, 2010.

The system life cycle shown in Figure 1.5 is identical to that introduced earlier except for the SDP illustrations added between each stage. The stages of this life cycle are aligned with how a system matures during its lifetime. The SDP illustrations are positioned in this manner to communicate that there also exist decision gates through which the system can only pass by satisfying some explicit requirements. These requirements are usually set by system owners. For example, a system typically will not be allowed to proceed from the design and development stage to the production stage without clearly demonstrating that the system design has a high likelihood of efficiently delivering the value to stakeholders that the design promises. Decision gates are used by engineering managers to assess system risk, both in terms of what it promises to deliver in future stages and threats to system survivability once deployed.

Uncertainties are present to varying degrees throughout all of these considerations. While some cost components can be fixed using contractual agreements, others are dependent upon environmental factors well beyond the control of and well outside of the knowledge base of systems engineering teams. Illness, labor strikes, late detected code errors, raw material shortages, weather related losses, legal challenges, and the like are all phenomena of the type that impose cost increases despite the best intentions and planning of the systems team. Important modeling parameters such as cost coefficients used in cost estimating relationships and component performance estimates are based on past data which, as all investment professionals will proclaim, are no guarantee of future performance. Performing the proper due diligence to identify, assess, and manage the potential downside impact of events driven by uncertainty such as these is the role of risk analysts on the systems team.

Risk management involves a constant cycle of activities whose purpose is to leverage the most accurate information concerning uncertain events that could threaten system success to construct

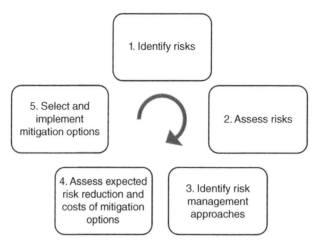

Figure 1.6   Simplified risk management cycle affecting systems decisions.

effective plans that eliminate, mitigate, relocate, or (accept and adapt to) the occurrence of these events. Figure 1.6 shows a simplified risk management cycle whose elements are in common to all risk planning efforts.

Risk is a fundamental concept in systems decision making. Various forms of risk present themselves throughout the life cycle of a system: business risk (does it make sense for the project team to undertake the effort?), market risk (is there a viable and profitable market for the products and/or services the system is designed to deliver?), cost/budget risk (how do potential future scenarios affect the planned for budget and what contingency funds need to be set aside to cover potential cost overruns due to risk events occurring?), system program risk (can technical, schedule, cost, and program risks be identified, mitigated, or resolved in a manner that satisfies system owners?), decision risk (how much exposure does the decision maker have to the possibility of bad outcomes?), and implementation risk (can the system be put into action to deliver value?). Risk management, including risk forecasting and mitigation planning, starts early and continues throughout a system's life cycle.

1.5.1   Check on Learning

Concepts:

   (a) Which life cycle stage has more risk associated with it? Is this dependent on the type of system? Can you give an example?

   (b) In what life cycle stage are costs most clearly understood and evident? Does this depend on the system, or in general?

   (c) Is the education system you are/were best described as a waterfall or spiral life cycle model? Or, do the life cycle stages described better fit?

Comprehension:

   (a) Does the "retire the system" life cycle stage really matter? Can you give an example of a system where supporting the answer "yes" and one supporting the answer "no"? Is this answer a function of perspective?

(b) In what system life cycle stages does professional architecture play a prominent role?

(c) Is a cellphone engineered to have a long "operate the system" life cycle stage? Why? Is this intentional by design or a function of a changing environment surrounding it?

Application:

(a) Are end of life costs a concern for electric vehicles? If so, what are these costs?

(b) Can you give a different example of a system that is in each of the life cycle stages? How near are they to the next life cycle stage? What are the indicators you would look for to confirm that they have indeed moved into the next life cycle stage?

1.6 SYSTEMS DECISION PROCESS

From conceptual design to retirement, a system competes for resources necessary to maintain its ability to deliver value to stakeholders by functioning as intended. Systems decisions involving the allocation of these resources are made during all system life cycle stages. As long as a system is operating successfully, other external system owners will look to leverage its capabilities to increase the performance of their own systems as well. These intentional collaborations forming what now are called "systems of systems" take a good deal of thought, again involving non-trivial decisions with substantial outcomes. There are many examples of this leveraging taking place, particularly in transportation, defense, health care, software, infrastructure, and telecommunications.

In all cases, having a structured approach—a repeatable process—to follow when making these decisions goes a long way towards ensuring that as many relevant considerations as possible have been integrated into the possible alternatives and the conditions for selecting among alternatives is grounded in best practices. Having a process to support systems engineers, project and program managers, and system designers is especially important given the job turnover that occurs in positions of responsibility throughout all levels of business and government.

What makes a quality decision? Matheson and Matheson used a chain illustration to identify the six elements of a quality decision for an R&D organization [43]. Each link in the decision quality chain is important. Our SDP includes each of the six elements as shown in Figure 1.7. The following is a brief description of each link in the chain.

- *Appropriate frame*. Our cognitive view of the problem must be appropriate to consider the full scope of the problem and all the needs of the stakeholders.
- *Creative, doable alternatives*. We want creative, feasible solutions that create value for the stakeholders and decision makers.
- *Meaningful, realistic data*. The data we use to generate and score candidate solutions must be understandable and credible.
- *Clear values and trade-offs*. The values we use to generate and evaluate solutions must be defined and trade-off analysis must be performed between system requirements, value measures, and resources.
- *Logically correct reasoning*. The mathematical techniques we use to evaluate alternatives must use a sound operations research technique. The SDP leverages multiple criteria decision making (MCDM), multiple objective decision analysis (MODA), and multiple criteria value modeling (MCVM) as its foundation.
- *Commitment to action*. Finally, the decision maker(s) and stakeholders must be committed to solution implementation. Implementation barriers and risks must be identified and resolved.

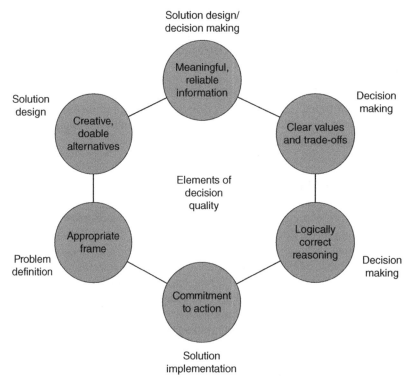

Figure 1.7   Elements of decision quality (the corresponding SDP phases are annotated in the diagram).

As a consequence, systems decisions have become more and more complicated as the number of dependencies on a system's elements or functions grows. Systems engineers need a logically consistent and proven process for helping a system owner (including all stakeholders) make major systems decisions, usually to continue to the next life cycle stage. The systems decision process (SDP) that is introduced in this book is shown in Figure 1.8. This SDP is a collaborative, iterative, and value-based decision process that can be applied during any system life cycle stage.

The SDP's focus on supporting system-specific decisions is a customization of a broader decision analysis context that integrates tenets of systems engineering, design, MCVM, and several other quantitative and qualitative disciplines into a cohesive methodology. Among the SDP's many advantages, six inherent characteristics are worth highlighting at this point:

- The SDP encapsulates the dynamic flow of system engineering activities and the evolution of the system state, starting with the current status (what is) and ending with a system that successfully delivers value to system stakeholders (what should be).
- It is a collaborative process that focuses on the needs and objectives of stakeholders and decision makers concerned with the value being delivered by the system.
- It has four major phases organized into a logical progression (problem definition, solution design, decision making, and solution implementation) that embrace systems thinking and apply proven systems engineering approaches, yet are highly iterative.
- It explicitly considers the environment (its factors and interacting systems) that systems operate in as critical to systems decision making, and thus highlights a requirement for multidisciplinary systems engineering teams.

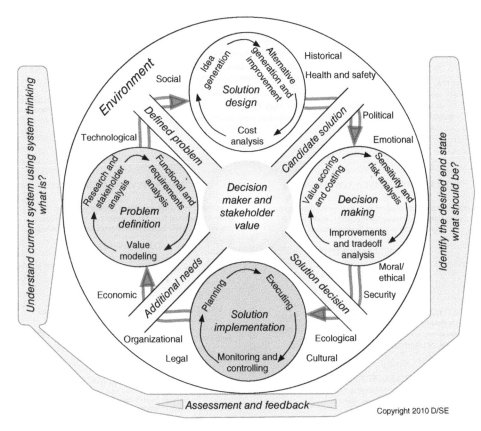

Figure 1.8 Systems decision process.

- It emphasizes value creation (value modeling, solution enhancements, and value focused thinking) in addition to evaluation (scoring and sensitivity analysis) of alternatives.
- It is acutely turned to focusing on entities that interact, and in this way maintains a holistic perspective throughout the process, even when decomposition is applied.

A mathematical foundation of the SDP is found in multi-objective decision analysis [44]. This approach affords an ability to qualitatively and quantitatively define value by identifying requirements (solution screening criteria) and evaluation criteria that are essential for guiding the development and evaluation of system solutions in all life cycle stages.

The definition of a "systems decision" is very encompassing because a system can be defined in many ways. The SDP is a broadly applicable process that can be used to support a variety of engineering, enterprise, and organizational decisions involving technical design, organizational strategy, policy analysis, resource allocation, facility design and location, personnel hiring, event planning, college selection, and many others. The concepts and techniques arising from systems thinking define a system, and the SDP provides the collaborative, dynamic, value-focused decision process that subsequently informs decision makers.

In practice and in educational settings, highlighting the modeling and analysis flow that typically accompanies the activities prescribed by the SDP greatly facilitates work breakdown and task assignments for team members. Coupled with anticipated work products, this information directly supports project budget estimates. Figure 1.9 illustrates a product perspective of a typical systems

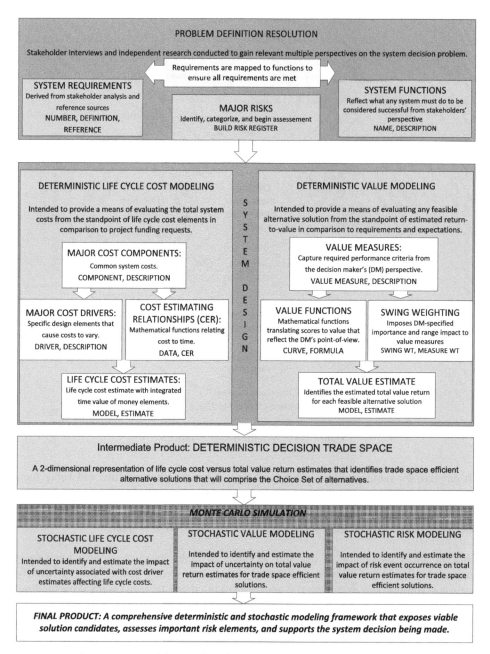

Figure 1.9   Modeling and analysis flow for typical SDP application.

decision support effort. While all of the elements shown are addressed in the chapters that follow, a few comments at this point will be helpful.

The diagram flows from top to bottom, aligning with the first three phases of the SDP: Problem definition, Solution design, and Decision making. It culminates with a comprehensive tradeoff space ("tradespace") that supports the system solution decision gate immediately preceding the

Solution implementation phase. All of the analysis products developed in this flow carry over to the Solution implementation phase once a solution decision has been made.

The top block contains the three primary products of the Problem definition phase that must be developed before proceeding on: proper identification and listing of systems functions, identifying and cataloging requirements, and identifying, categorizing, and assessing major risks. These represent what the system is, what it is expected to do, what every alternative must contain to be considered a feasible candidate as a solution, and a due diligence with respect to risk that every systems decision project should conduct.

The second block shows a parallel, yet separate effort to model and analyze life cycle costs and to estimate value returns for alternative solutions under an assumption that uncertainties associated with any parameters or information input will be addressed after these efforts have been successfully concluded. Both of these deterministic analyses require alternative solutions against which they will be used. Hence, they are shown as intrinsic to solution design. Cost is separated from the value model construction because cost defines the tradeoff dimension against which total value return is compared in the deterministic tradespace shown.

Finally, any uncertainty or probabilistic considerations associated with the models, their input, output, or modeling parameters are directly addressed. For most SDP applications, this is accomplished using Monte Carlo simulation, a technique discussed in detail in Chapter 10. Risk modeling, whether subjective or objective in nature, is purely a probabilistic venture wrapped with considerable uncertainty. To be logically consistent in modeling, risks factors, their distributions, and impacts are integrated as modeling adaptations once the deterministic modeling effort is complete. Chapter 10 addresses this in detail for both value and cost risk analysis. For completeness however, we note that once the overall risk management process has begun during a systems decision project's early phases, it is sustained and updated throughout the SDP.

The modeling and analysis flow ingrained in the SDP results in powerful decision support models. Teams developing these models need to keep in-mind both who the models are being developed for and what type of purpose they are intended to serve. The latter consideration prevents models from becoming unwieldy by containing unneeded levels of sophistication and detail, or by exceeding the project's scope. Adhering to the modeling purpose focuses team effort and prevents function creep from occurring as a result of late requirements imposed by stakeholders once the model is operating satisfactorily. The diagram in Figure 1.10 shows one such approach to identifying the modeling purpose [18].

The partitioned rectangle on top illustrates a spectrum of model use being distributed between 100% frequent and routine use on the left and 100% human interaction on the right. Arrayed along the axis below it are four modeling archetypes whose positioning approximates their characterization in the spectrum. Thus, a model whose purpose is purely exploratory in nature and whose results are intended to promote discussion among stakeholders would a position to the right extreme.

An example of an exploratory modeling purpose within the SDP framework would be a model constructed to examine the feasibility of futuristic, fully-automated ground force engagement

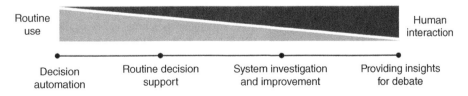

Figure 1.10 Spectrum of modeling purposes. Source: Pidd [18]/with permission of Springer Nature.

systems for the military. The interest in such a hypothetical case would not be in designing a system to accommodate stakeholder requirements, but rather to expose and discuss the implications with respect to the various environmental factors shown in Figure 1.8. Conversely, a decision support model built to aid a one-time systems decision might fall somewhere between the decision automation and routine decision support archetypes shown. While the cost, value, and risk models developed for a one-time decision require stakeholder interaction during their construction, they typically would not require intensive human interaction after their purpose has been served. Building sophisticated user interfaces to these models would not be a wise investment of the team's effort.

1.7 STAKEHOLDERS AND VESTED INTERESTS

The SDP focuses to a great extent on system stakeholders, the definitions of which have a long chronology in the management sciences literature [45]. A stakeholder, in the context of systems engineering, is a person or organization that has a vested interest in any system or its outputs. When such a system is an organization, this definition aligns with Freeman's—"any group of individual who can affect or is affected by the achievement of the organization's objectives" [46]. It is this vested interest that establishes their importance within any system-focused effort. Sooner or later, for any systems decision problem, stakeholders will care about the decision reached because it will in one way or another affect them, their systems, or their success. Consequently, it is prudent and wise to identify and prioritize stakeholders in some organized fashion, and to integrate their needs, wants, and desires in any possible candidate solution.

In the SDP, this is accomplished by constructing value models based on stakeholder input, insuring that the output of these models reflects their input, priorities, beliefs, and intentions. Their input as a group impacts system functions and establishes screening criteria which become requirements that any potential solution must meet. Alternatives failing to meet requirements are eliminated from further consideration.

Understanding stakeholder requirements, leveraging their values, and supporting the major decisions they must make are primary tasks for systems teams. This is important because the models created during the process must *not* reflect the modelers' values, but rather they must codify and express those of the stakeholders who have a vested interest in the system, its behavior, and its output. Accomplishing this requires a systems decision support team to initiate and maintain open channels of communication with key stakeholders right from the start, especially the decision maker(s). This is primarily accomplished during each phase using periodic interim progress reviews (IPR) to update stakeholders on project status, resource consumption and anticipated expenses going forward, anticipated products, scheduling and milestone updates, and any barriers anticipated that might disrupt the project plan.

For technology-based systems, decision makers may be the project/program manager or the chief engineering manager of the organization. For complex systems decisions the decision maker may be an operational manager, a military commander, a program manager, a functional manager, the chief technology officer (CTO), the chief information officer (CIO), or even the chief executive officer (CEO), among others. In government, equivalent positions are typically occupied by people serving at the senior executive service (SES) level. In the military, commanders at all levels are decision makers, having both responsibility and accountability for the decisions they make. Decision makers approve the resources to perform the SDP. Decision makers should "inspect what they expect" [47].

The team must involve decision maker(s) and key stakeholders in a systems project from the earliest possible time. Failing to do this will increase the possibility of stakeholders having unrealistic or incorrect project expectations. If the project becomes a "hands off" one from the stakeholders' perspectives, there is a very high likelihood that the team's recommendations will have to be "sold" to stakeholders in a less-than-receptive context.

Stakeholder involvement is critical to the success of the SDP. Stakeholder input and feedback ensure the appropriate frame for systems decisions; they help the systems decision support team acquire reliable and credible information. Their early involvement is essential to gaining their commitment to action necessary to implement any recommended decisions at the end of the project. Without stakeholder involvement, system decisions will not be sustainable and stakeholders may force costly changes in design and development later on.

A popular saying in economics and sociology is "where someone stands on an issue depends on where they sit." In other words, a person's perspective is relative to what they do and where they do it. The type of information that a stakeholder can be expected to provide, their interest in the system of interest, and their level of decision making is directly determined by their positions in their organization, as shown in Table 1.7. In general, there are three levels of decision making that involve systems: strategic, operational, and tactical. Systems exist in support of all three levels, so the decision maker for a specific system effort could be from any one of these levels.

Stakeholders at a strategic level have extensive knowledge regarding "the big picture" of how their organization is currently positioned to succeed in its purpose within its environment. They focus on the whole entity rather than an isolated unit. A majority of their time is spent looking outward from the organization at the longest horizon of interest. They typically control and allocate major resources in the present and set priorities for those planned for the future. As the outward face(s) of the organization, they interact on a regular basis with external entities, watchful for indications of internal and external changes that might offer opportunities or pose threats to the organization and its mission(s).

Stakeholders at a tactical level focus on the short term horizon, typically from the present extending a year or two into the future. Their concerns are inward looking on their processes and products, overseeing and conducting modeling and analysis that translates data from a host of sources into information that can inform ongoing activities and provide valuable insights that inform short and long term planning. The tactical level is where spreadsheet models are most likely to exist.

Finally, stakeholders at the operational level link strategic goals and objectives to tactical goals and objectives. They are the executors of established processes (e.g. production, purchasing,

TABLE 1.7 Stakeholder Levels and Focus.

Level	Focus	Data types	Accessibility
Strategic (executive and senior mgmt)	Achieving long term objectives	Knowledge (internal and external)	Very limited
Tactical (group supervisor and line mgmt)	Fiscal year objectives (budget, salaries, inventory, customers)	Information (internal and technical)	Limited
Operational (team supervisor)	Day-to-day activities	Data	Easy

accounting, payroll, safety) whose activities generate data. Each of these three levels has different stakeholder accessibility, and as one progresses upwards toward strategic stakeholders and decision makers, barriers to access are encountered by way of personnel (admin assistants) and policy. These will need to be accommodated by the systems decision support team.

Problem definition. Conducting research is a key activity for identifying potential system stakeholders. Stakeholders provide information about the environment that helps frame the problem and accurately specify the problem statement. They help identify the system objectives and the requirements. They provide insights to help identify the constraints and functions. Finally, they validate the value model and the final problem statement.

Solution design. Stakeholders participate in the solution design, assessment, and testing. They attend design reviews and provide comments on design solutions. They continue to identify constraints and requirements. They participate in spiral development processes by evaluating each prototype solution. Finally, they participate in test and evaluation programs. Stakeholders help identify the cost elements used in system cost analysis to ensure that the alternatives will be affordable.

Decision making. Stakeholders are involved in the value scoring and costing of candidate solutions. They provide the operational data, test data, models, simulation, and experts to obtain the scoring data. They participate in interim reviews and final decision presentations.

Solution implementation. Stakeholders are critical to solution implementation. They help identify the solution implementation plan, tasks, and controls. All tasks in this phase require stakeholder commitment to action.

It is important to recognize that all stakeholder input is conditionally valid based upon their individual perspectives and vested interests. In other words, from their experience with and relationship to the problem or opportunity being addressed, and within the environment of openness they have chosen, the information they provide is accurate and is used with this assumption in mind. In practice, this may not be the case, and is why a good percentage of time is consumed defining the actual problem rather than simply proceeding with an initial problem statement provided by a client representative, or one or two stakeholders. What if the client *is* the problem?

What acts to mitigate concerns regarding information accuracy and to fill any gaps in this information is independent research on the part of the team. Research starts as early as possible in a systems decision support project, and once begun it never stops; it may change focus, but it never stops. A substantial amount of research takes place prior to the first meeting with any client because communicating a high level of understanding and knowledge regarding the system under focus goes a long way toward motivating trust and confidence with the client, especially if the systems decision support team is not part of the client organization. This triumvirate of input, so critical to accurately defining a problem, is illustrated in Figure 1.11.

Managing stakeholder expectations has become so intrinsic to project success that a number of other formalizations have been developed to understand the interrelationship between key individuals and organizations and the challenges that could arise as a project unfolds. Mitchell, Agle, and Wood [45] posits that stakeholders can be identified by their possessing or being attributed to possess one, two, or all three of the following attributes, which we generalize here to systems.

1. The stakeholder's *power* to influence the system.
2. The *legitimacy* of the stakeholder's relationship to the system.
3. The *urgency* of the stakeholder's claim on the system.

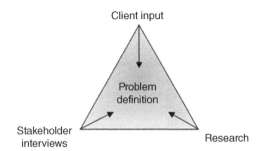

Figure 1.11 Three required ingredients for proper problem definition.

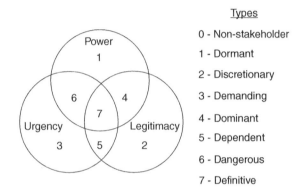

Figure 1.12 Stakeholder salience types. Source: Matty [48].

These attributes interact in a manner that defines *stakeholder salience*, the degree to which managers give priority to competing stakeholder claims. Salience then results in a classification of stakeholders by eight types shown in Figure 1.12.

Throughout the SDP, there is a strong emphasis on identifying, engaging with, cultivating a trust relationship with, and crafting high value system solutions for a stakeholder called the *decision authority*. Mitchell's characterization clearly illustrates why this is so. The *decision maker* is a salience Type 7 in Figure 1.12. The decision maker possesses an *urgency* to find a solution to the dilemma facing the system, the *power* to select and implement a value-based solution, and the recognized *legitimacy* by all stakeholders to make this selection.

Beyond understanding how stakeholders relate to one another and the system, these attributes are relevant to systems decision problems because Matty [48] has connected them to elements of value, which comprises one-half of the tradeoff space advocated by the approach presented in this book (see Chapter 5). Stakeholder legitimacy strongly influences value identification; power strongly influences value proposition; and urgency strongly influences value execution. Two other approaches have garnered broad interest in professional practice: the Stakeholder Circle™, and the Organizational Zoo [49].

The Stakeholder Circle™ is a commercially available software tool which originated in a doctoral thesis [50]. This was motivated by several decades of project management experience in which "poor stakeholder engagement due to not seeing where some stakeholders were coming from led to project delivery failure." The software provides a visualization tool that measures and illustrates various stakeholders' power, influence, and positioning. It leverages a useful metaphor of stakeholders in a concentric circle surrounding the project itself. A five step methodology is used to manage the stakeholder pool over the complete life cycle of a project: identify the stakeholders and their needs, prioritize the stakeholders, visualize their relationship to the project, develop an engagement strategy, and monitor changes over time.

The "Organizational Zoo" concept uses the metaphor of an animal kingdom and its familiar inhabitants to persuade stakeholders to see "how various situations and environments can facilitate or inhibit a knowledge-sharing culture." By associating key individuals with stereotypical behaviors expressed by lions, eagles, ants, mice, rattlesnakes, hyenas, unicorns, and other creatures, stakeholders gain an understanding of how and why they are likely to react to project-related situations. This approach is more stakeholder-centric in its application than the Stakeholder Circle™, though both methods possess similarities to the use of rich pictures in soft system methodology [28].

Notice that this notion of a stakeholder makes no distinction based on the motivation of stakeholder vested interest. System teams should allow for the possibility that for any system of reasonable presence in its surrounding environment, there exists a subset of adversarial stakeholders who are not interested in the success and well-being of the system of interest. On the contrary, they might have a vested interest in its demise, or at the very least the stagnation or reduction in the growth of the system, its outputs, and linkages. Market competitors, advocates of opposing political ideologies, members of hostile biological systems, and the like are obvious examples of adversarial groups that might typify this malevolent category of stakeholders. Cleland [51] and Winch [52] introduce and elaborate upon several useful techniques for mitigating the risk to project success posed by hostile stakeholders.

More complex and challenging to identify are the less obvious stakeholders; those persons and organizations that are once, twice, and further removed from direct interaction with the system under study but nonetheless have a vested interest that needs to be considered in a systems decision problem. A once removed stakeholder could be described as one whose direct vested interest lies in the output of a system that is dependent on output of the system under study. A similar relationship exists for further removed stakeholders. The environmental factors shown in the SDP of Figure 1.8 are very helpful in this regard. They are frequently used as memory cues during stakeholder identification.

For our purposes, the simplest complete taxonomy for stakeholders contains six types. In some systems decisions it may be useful to include additional types of stakeholders. For example, it may be helpful to divide the User group into two subgroups: operators and maintainers, in order more clearly identify their role in interacting with the system and to better classify their individual perspectives.

Decision authority. The stakeholder(s) with ultimate decision gate authority to approve and implement a system solution.

Client. The person(s) or organization(s) that solicit systems decision support for a project or program. The client pays for any needed system decision support. The client is some subset of the organization that owns the system, but can also be a separate organization charged with maintenance, upkeep, cybersecurity, and so on. They are the source of project compensation; and/or the stakeholder(s) that principally define system requirements. There is frequently only one.

Owner. The person(s) or organization(s) responsible for proper and purposeful system operation. There is frequently only one owner and they bear all the costs of ownership that are associated with the system. Owners are the stakeholders that are seeing a strategic need to develop a new system or improve and existing one.

User. The person(s) or organization accountable for proper and purposeful system operation. Often referred to as the *end user*, this group of people generate system interface requirements that must be met for the system to be used as intended. They are also the ones who have the most practical, hands-on experience with the situation that motivates a new system's purpose or an existing system's improvement and can describe the shortcomings and operational benefits that an existing system has. The user group is the sole focus of usability studies and assessments that generate and refine many functional requirements [53].

Consumer. The person(s) or organization(s) that realizes direct or indirect benefits from the products or services provided by the system or its behavior. They "consume" the system output. These stakeholders are sometimes referred to as the *customer*.

Collaborator. The person(s) or organization(s) that are virtually or physically connected to the system, its behaviors, its input, or output. Collaborators realize benefits, costs, and/or risks resulting from the connection. Although external to a system boundary, collaborators can provide a system with needed support such as information, materiel, energy, and so on.

For any given systems decision problem, it is perhaps easiest to identify the Client first, then the Decision authority, followed by the others in any convenient order. For example, on a recent rental car system re-design, the Client solicited assistance in identifying creative alternatives for marketing non-recreational vehicle rental in his region. When asked, the Client stated that although he would be making the intermediate gate decisions to move the project forward, any solutions would have to be approved by his regional manager prior to implementation. His regional manager is therefore the Decision authority.

An example will help to distinguish between a User and an Owner. A technology company purchases computer systems for its engineers to use for computer aided design. The company owns the computers and is held responsible for maintaining proper accountability against loss. The engineers use the computers and typically sign hand receipts acknowledging that they have taken possession of the computers. If, on a particularly bad Friday, one of the engineers (User) tosses her computer out the window and destroys it, she will be held accountable and have to pay for the damages or replacement. As the company's representative (Owner), the managing supervisor of the engineer is held responsible that all proper steps were taken to protect and safeguard the system against its loss or damage.

A Collaborator is one who coordinates and synchronizes their own separate set of activities, goals, capabilities, and behaviors to one or more of those output by the system under consideration. A passive collaborator establishes dependencies on a system, its behavior, its input, or its output without necessarily coordinating with other system stakeholders. An active collaborator creates a deliberate arrangement with system stakeholders.

This taxonomy can then be further divided into an *active* set and a *passive* set of stakeholders. The active set contains those stakeholders who currently place a high enough priority on the systems decision problem to return your call or participate in an interview, focus group, or survey in order to provide the design team with relevant information. The passive set contains those who do not. Membership in these two sets will most likely change throughout the duration of a systems decision project as awareness of the project and relevance of the impact of the decisions made increases in the pool of passive stakeholders.

A checklist of questions is often helpful when identifying system stakeholders. The following are a subset of the many types of questions one could pose, but are helpful nonetheless.

- Who or what (by role) are the system's primary users?
- Who installs, starts up, maintains, or shuts down the system?
- Who or what requires system support for ongoing tasks?
- Who or what are the system's secondary users?
- What hardware or software does the system handle?
- What other systems interact with the system? Who owns these systems?
- Do any elements interacting with the system perform multiple roles?
- Who or what relies on system output?
- Who or what is notified when something occurs within the system?
- Who or what provides information, materiel, energy, finances, or services to the system?
- Who or what helps the system respond to and complete a task?
- Who or what governs, audits, oversees, or controls the system's behavior?

1.7.1 Check on Learning

Concepts:

(a) Why does it matter which category a stakeholder falls into? Can you give an example supporting your answer?

(b) Could one person fit into all stakeholder categories at once, or are some of them mutually exclusive?

(c) Are computer hackers stakeholders to systems that they digitally break into? If so, what stakeholder category(ies) best fit them?

Comprehension:

(a) When designing a new computer, which stakeholder category is the most important to focus on? Why?

(b) Can you give an example where it would be a bad idea to let a User make key decisions regarding a system and its behavior?

(c) What stakeholder category is the US President with regards to the political system? Who fits into the other categories?

Application:

(a) Can you give examples of "collaborator" stakeholders for systems that you encounter in everyday life?

(b) What type of stakeholder is an apartment renter? Why?

(c) The chef/owner trend continues in the restaurant business today. What other stakeholders are involved with a restaurant?

REFERENCES

1. Eddington, A. (1928) *The Nature of the Physical World*. London: J.M. Dent & Sons.
2. Walden, D.D., Roedler, G.J., Forsberg, K.J., Hamelin, R.D., Shortell, T.M. (2015) *Systems Engineering Handbook*, 4th ed. New York: John Wiley & Sons.

3. Hitchins, D. (2003) *Advanced Systems Thinking, Engineering, and Management*. Boston, MA: Artech House.

4. Dickerson, C.E., Marvis, D.N. (2010) *Architecture and Principles of Systems Engineering*. Boca Raton, FL: Taylor and Francis Group.

5. Madni, A.M. (2006) 'The intellectual content of systems engineering: a definitional hurdle or something more?,' *INCOSE Insight*, 9(1), pp. 21–23.

6. Goode, H., Machol, R. (1957) *Systems Engineering: An Introduction to the Design of Large-scale Systems*. New York: McGraw-Hill.

7. Incose (2006) International Committee for Systems Engineering (INCOSE). Available at: http://www.incose.org. (Accessed 24 Feb 2002).

8. Parnell, G. (2009) 'Evaluation of risks in complex problems,' in *Making Essential Choices with Scant Information: Front-end Decision-making in Major Projects*, T.M. Williams, K. Samset, and K.J. Sunnevåg Eds. Basingstoke: Palgrave MacMillan, pp. 230–256.

9. Clemens, M. (2008) *The Art of Complex Problem Solving*. Available at: http://www.idiagram.com. (Accessed Nov 2021).

10. International Council on Systems Engineering (2021) '*A Complexity Primer for Systems Engineers*,' Revision 1, White Paper, INCOSE-TP-2021-007-01, San Diego, CA.

11. International Council on Systems Engineering (1997) *Systems Engineering Primer*. Reston, VA: American Institute of Aeronautics and Astronautics. Available at: https://www.aiaa.org/. (Accessed 24 Feb 2022).

12. ABET (2022) *Engineering Accreditation*. Baltimore, MD: ABET. Available at: www.abet.org. (Accessed 24 Feb 2022).

13. Sage, A.P. (ed.) (2014) *Wiley Series in Systems Engineering and Management*. New York: John Wiley & Sons.

14. Garvey, P.R., White, B.E. (2009) *Complex and Enterprise Systems Engineering*. CRC Press Series. Boca Raton, FL: Taylor & Francis Publishing.

15. The MITRE Corporation (2014) *The MITRE Systems Engineering Guide*. McLean, VA: MITRE Corporation. Available at: www.mitre.org/publications/technical-papers/the-mitre-systems-engineering-guide. (Accessed 24 Feb 2022).

16. NASA (2016) *NASA Systems Engineering Handbook*. Washington, DC: National Aeronautics and Space Administration. Available at: www.nasa.gov/sites/default/files/atoms/files/nasasystemshandbook0.pdf. (Accessed Jan 2022).

17. Wasserman, S., Faust, K., Iacobucci, D., Granovetter, M. (1994) *Social Network Analysis: Methods and Applications*. Cambridge: Cambridge University Press.

18. Pidd, M. (2010) 'Why modeling and model use matter,' *Journal of Operational Research Society*, 61(1), pp. 14–24.

19. Haines, S.G. (1998) *The Manager's Pocket Guide to Systems Thinking and Learning*. Amherst, MA: Centre for Strategic Management, HRD Press.

20. Jamshidi, M. (2009) *System of Systems Engineering*. New York: John Wiley & Sons.

21. Hybertson, D.W. (2009) *Model-Oriented Systems Engineering Science*. Boca Raton, FL: CRC Press.

22. Aslaksen, E.W. (2009) *Designing Complex Systems*. Boca Raton, FL: CRC Press.

23. Markowitz, H.M. (1952) 'Portfolio selection,' *Journal of Finance*, 7(1), pp. 77–91.

24. McDermott, I. (1997) *The Art of Systems Thinking*. London: Thorsons Publishing.

25. Skyttner, L. (2001) *General Systems Theory: Ideas and Applications*. Singapore: World Scientific Publishing Co.

26. *Systems Thinking Definition*. Available at: https://en.wikipedia.org/wiki/Systemsthinking. (Accessed 24 Feb 2022).

27. Keeney, R.L. (1992) *Value-Focused Thinking: A Path to Creative Decisionmaking*. Boston, MA: Harvard University Press.

28. Checkland, P. (1999) *Systems Thinking, Systems Practice*. New York: John Wiley & Sons.

29. Merton, R.K. (1936) 'The unanticipated consequences of purposive social action,' *American Sociological Review*, 1(6), pp. 894–904.

30. Archibald, R.D. (2000) *Max Wideman's PM Wisdom*. Available at: http://www.maxwideman.com/. Accessed 24 Feb 2022.

31. George, M.L. (2002) *Lean Six Sigma*. New York: McGraw-Hill Publishing.

32. Hoffman, D.G. (2002) *Managing Operational Risk: 20 Firmwide Best Practice Strategies*. New York: John Wiley & Sons.

33. Amari, S.V., McLaughlin, L. (2004) 'Optimal design of a condition-based maintenance model,' *Proceedings of the Reliability and Maintainability Society*, 2004 Annual Symposium (RAMS), pp. 528–533.

34. (1998) 'A Survey of System Development Process Models,' CTG.MFA-003. Albany, NY: University of Albany Center for Technology in Government.

35. (2002) 'Nuclear Regulatory Legislation,' NUREG-0980, 1(6), 107th Congress, 1st Session, Office of the General Council. Washington, DC: U.S. Nuclear Regulatory Commission.

36. Sheard, S.A., Jerome, D., Lake, J.G. (1998) 'Systems engineering standards and models compared,' *INCOSE International Symposium*, 8(1), pp. 589–605.

37. Price, S., John, P. (2004) 'The status of models in defense systems engineering,' in *Systems Modeling: Theory and Practice*, M. Pidd (ed) West Sussex, England: John Wiley & Sons.

38. Boehm, B. (2000) '*Spiral Development: Experience, Principles, and Refinements*,' CMU/SEI-2000-SR-008. Pittsburg, PA: Carnegie Mellon Software Engineering Institute.

39. Dogiparthi, H. (2019) 'Rapid application development,' University of the Cumberlands. DOI: 10.13140/RG.2.2.29407.41126. (Accessed 24 Feb 2022).

40. Agile Alliance (2010) *The Agile Manifesto*. Available at https://www.agilealliance.org/. (Accessed 24 Feb 2022).

41. AMI (2006) The University of Bolton postgraduate course offerings. Available at http://www.ami.ac.uk/. (Accessed 24 Feb 2022).

42. World Nuclear Association (2016) *The New Economics of Nuclear Power*. Available at: www.world-nuclear.org. (Accessed 24 Feb 2022).

43. Matheson, D., Matheson, J. (1998) *The Smart Organization: Creating Value Through Strategic R&D*. Cambridge: Harvard University Press.

44. Keeney, R.L., Raiffa, H. (1976) *Decision Making with Multiple Objectives: Preferences and Tradeoffs*. New York: John Wiley & Sons.

45. Mitchell, R.K., Agle, B.R., Wood, D.J. (1997) 'Toward a theory of stakeholder identification and salience: defining the principle of who or what really counts,' *Academy of Management Review*, 22(4), pp. 853–886.

46. Freeman, R.E. (1984) *Strategic Management: A Stakeholder Approach*. Boston, MA: Pitman.

47. Gude, C. (2000) 'Personal conversation with former vice president of technology for IBM,' Phrase was coined by Ginni Rometty, one of IBM's chief executives in Global Services.

48. Matty, D. (2010) *Stakeholder Salience Influence on Value Creation*, Doctoral Research. Cambridge, MA: Engineering Systems Division, Massachusetts Institute of Technology.

49. Shelley, A. (2007) *The Organizational Zoo: A Survival Guide to Workplace Behavior*. Connecticut: Aslan Publishing.

50. Bourne, L. (2005) *Project Relationship Management and the Stakeholder Circle*, Doctoral Dissertation. Melbourne, Australia: Graduate School of Business, RMIT University. Available at: http://www.stakeholder-management.com. (Accessed 24 Feb 2022).

51. Cleland, D.I. (1999) *Project Management Strategic Design and Implementation*. Singapore: McGraw-Hill Publishing.

52. Winch, G.M. (2004) 'Managing project stakeholders,' in *The Wiley Guide to Managing Projects*, Peter W.G. Morris, Jeffrey K. Pinto, Eds. New York: John Wiley & Sons, pp. 321–339.

53. Stanton, S., Hedge, A., Brookhuis, K., Salas, E., Hendrick, H. (2005) *Handbook of Human Factors and Ergonomics Methods*. Boca Raton, FL: CRC Press.

Chapter **2**

Applied Systems Thinking

It's about constellations, not stars.

—Ryan Quinn, Shakespeare Director

2.1 HOLISM—FRAMING SYSTEMS

Simply stated, most successful organizations have learned that attempting to solve modern system problems or pursue innovation and creativity in system design and development by focusing on individual system elements while disregarding the myriad of connections that exist between and among these elements and the world surrounding them is a wasted effort doomed to fall short of expectations. It's impossible to optimize system performance without understanding how it fits into its environment. Putting a phenomenal scope on a poorly functioning rifle will only do a better job of showing clearly the target missed. As a result, systems engineers working on systems decision support teams embrace systems thinking as a best practice. Among other benefits, doing this consistently helps illuminate dependency relationships occurring in space and time that must be addressed if a system solution is to be successful.

To recap from previous: systems thinking is a cognitive perspective that recognizes interrelationships and dependencies between real world elements in a way that allows the entirety of what is being looked at to be interpreted as a system. Interpretation defines perspective and uniquely determines possible actions and alternatives. At the heart of any decision process lies this framed understanding that is the result of conditioning through experience (good and bad), education, and explicit choice.

Decision Making in Systems Engineering and Management, Third Edition.
Patrick J. Driscoll, Gregory S. Parnell, and Dale L. Henderson
© 2023 John Wiley & Sons, Inc. Published 2023 by John Wiley & Sons, Inc.

The human body is a complex system with a host of internal biochemical and neurological controls that respond to ongoing continuous feedback signals. When a specific element of this system malfunctions or fails altogether, the body will adapt and adjust itself to compensate. There is a noticeable difference between the actions taken by a physician trained in Eastern medicine and one trained in Western medicine when this occurs [1]. Western medicine by and large frames treatment based on isolating the failed part or malfunctioning process and attempts to either adjust or replace it. This is known as *atomistical* philosophy. In other words, if pain is experienced in the lower back, the operating assumption is something in the lower back is amiss. This constrains treatments to physical therapy, pharmacology, and surgical alternatives. In many cases, this atomistical perspective works wonders to meet patients' hopes and expectations. In some cases however, it falls woefully short.

In comparison, Eastern medicine recognizes that while pain might be experienced in the lower back, the human body is a complex physical, biochemical, and neurological system that has a vast number and type of dependencies between system elements, including its external environment. The lower back pain could very well be the result of a cascade of responses to a stimulus or cause somewhere else in the body or external to the observable boundary defined by surface anatomy that is connected directly (first order) or indirectly (second and higher order) to the neural receptors in the lower back that are signaling pain to the brain. With this *holistic* philosophy, Eastern medicine focuses on restoring environmental, biochemical, or neurological balance to the overall system, giving it a chance to respond using its own alternatives available internally as a complex system. Once balance is disturbed, illness and injury sets in. Thus, holistic treatments such as herbal medicine, acupuncture, and moxibustion originating in Chinese medicine, and osteopathic medicine and chiropractic approaches originating in the United States are commonplace.

For systems engineering, holistic and atomistic thinking go hand-in-hand coincident with expansive and contractive thinking. Exclude one or the other and problems result. When observing a system in its environment, it becomes apparent that some subsets of system elements were not designed as systems or subsystems. Yet, they have observable interdependencies that have evolved over time and possibly are delivering a higher order purpose than any one subset was intended to do.

Some things existing in the real world are difficult to envision as a system or part of a system. But upon careful modeling, they reveal themselves to be functioning as a system or part of a system. Once a system is identified, the tools, techniques, and methods available for increasing its performance or augmenting its functionality increase. This is the magic of systems thinking. One who understands and engages in systems thinking cares at least as much (and most likely more) about the relationships between elements as the elements themselves.

This chapter presents a collection of tools and techniques that have been very successful to date, and are not going away any time soon. They are used on projects and system designs in professional practice and academic curriculum. By no means are these all there is. Table 2.1 provides an expanded listing of systems thinking methods that were available online in late

TABLE 2.1   A Selection of Systems Thinking Tools [2].

18 Words	Affinity Diagram	Conceptual Model	Context Diagram
Decision Matrix	Functional FMEA	Functional Means Analysis	Functional Modeling
Graphical Analysis	Influence Diagram	Input–Output Diagram	Matrix Diagram
Morphological Box	Multiple Cause Diagram	N2 Analysis	Quad of Arms
Rich Picture	Root Definition	Sequence Diagram	Spray Diagram
Systems Map	Tree Diagram		

Source: Adapted from [13].

2021 [2]. The handful or more of the ones addressed in this chapter are comprehensive enough to empower and enrich analytical support for systems decisions.

MITRE, a US government federally funded research and development center (FFRDC), refers to atomistic and holistic thinking as a two-step process involving analysis and synthesis in their Systems Engineering Guide [3]:

- *Analysis.* The ability to decompose an entity into deterministic components, explain each component separately, and aggregate the component behaviors to explain the whole. If the entity is a system, then analysis answers the question, "How does the system work?" Analysis results in knowledge of an entity; it reveals internal structure. For example, to know how an automobile works, you analyze it, that is, you take it apart and determine what each part does. This is essential to important activities like repairing automobiles or diagnosing and repairing problems of other, more complicated systems.

- *Synthesis.* The ability to identify the whole of which a system is a part, explain the behavior or properties of the whole, and disaggregate the whole to identify the role or function of the system in the whole. Synthesis answers the "Why is it what it is?" question. Synthesis is the mode of thought that results in the understanding of an entity (i.e., an appreciation of the role or function an entity plays in the larger system of which it is a part). As an example, the answer to the question of why the American automobile was originally designed for six passengers is because the average family size at the time was 5.6 people. Every MITRE systems engineer who has defined a system performance specification against mission or operational requirements has used synthetic thinking.

Notice that the term "analysis" is defined differently by MITRE than the way we define "analysis" in this book. So if you were working with systems engineers from MITRE or some other organization that adopted MITRE's Systems Engineering Guide, it would be beneficial to agree on common definitions for critical terms like "analysis" before proceeding on the project.

Based on the way that MITRE defines these terms, it is clear that systems thinking involves synthesis (holistic thinking) and then analysis (atomistic thinking) occurring in fast repeat cycles considering the system as a whole and its relationships to its environment before attempting decomposition to address the system's internal workings and relationships. Then the effort returns to system level to make adjustments. The research that happens right at the start of the systems decision process (SDP) is tightly linked to the framing of the system. Delving too deeply into a system's substructures before clearly understanding system interrelationships and behavior as a whole can waste a good deal of time and cause costly project restarts.

System representations of the type introduced in Chapter 3 start as a high level conceptual model of a system and its relationships with elements external to its initial boundary. This is an important feature of systems thinking because there are behaviors present at the system level that will disappear when decomposition takes place. Any subsequent decomposition then adds detail and clarity to the system, its configuration, its stakeholders, and the entities exchanged via interactions and dependencies, allowing for specific modeling and analysis to occur. These activities are intended to expose and examine the system's underlying structure.

For the SDP, creating high-level system representations is a great start to a systems decision support or systems engineering effort simply because these representations help to shape a common understanding among the team and the system stakeholders as to the characteristics of the system of interest. They also help to establish a base level of understanding among project participants, which can include individuals unfamiliar with the system of interest, particularly those from outside the client and owner groups.

As decomposition proceeds (what the MITRE SE Guide refers to as analysis), the representation elements—such as circles (nodes) as system objects and lines with arrows (arcs) as dependencies—then become clusters of lower-level sub-elements, which in turn have relationships with other elements. In reverse, clusters can be thought of as containers that decomposition opens to reveal system sub-elements. This also begins to expose indicators of system complexity as a result of increases in the number and type of relationships imbedded within the system, its output, and behavior, giving the system decision support team a sense of how difficult a project engagement is going to be.

Definition: Holism is a cognitive viewpoint that recognizes behavior resulting from element interactions. When taken as completely as possible, holism and systems thinking go hand-in-hand.

A point that can be overlooked is that as a system is being decomposed into subsystem structures and below, a number of relationships identified at the system level are actually connected to specific subsystems as opposed to the entire system. Identifying and re-representing these as necessary further refines the system representation, which can aid system development in a number of ways including identifying requirements and external collaborations that may have been missed had it not been done.

2.1.1 Systems Versus Analytic Thinking

Systems thinking in support of decision making consistently leads to deep understanding of most, if not all, of the various factors affecting possible alternatives. This success is largely due to two distinguishing characteristics: the manner in which it departs from analytic thinking, and its natural ability to reveal subtle but important relationships overlooked when pure decomposition approaches fail to consider "the big picture." [4, 5]

Applied to a system decision problem, analytic thinking is a more traditional approach to problem solving. Starting with the current system, analytical thinking identifies problems and issues, applies focused modeling techniques based on the mathematical characteristics of the identified problem, identifies possible solutions, and concludes with recommending solutions for changing some controllable dimensions of system activities that improve the system's operational state. Although the specific steps used in various disciplines may differ, this is the prevalent style of thinking imbedded in modern education. This type of thinking is most successful in situations where fine tuning of some system performance measures is called for but the system structure itself is assumed to be acceptable and no design changes (e.g., subsystem upgrade, added functionality, etc.) are needed. These decision problems are often referred to as "well structured." Improving the efficiency of established logistic supply networks, increasing the system reliability of telecommunication networks, and reducing transportation costs in package pickup and delivery systems are good examples of where analytic thinking has successfully supported decision making. In all these cases (and many others), the *operation* of the system lies at the heart of the decision to be made and not necessarily the system itself.

In contrast, systems thinking first and foremost centers *on the system itself* in relation to its environment. For the SDP, operational improvements such as the ones noted earlier, representing only one dimension of the overall system structure, are identified as part of alternative system solutions crafted with stakeholder goals, values, and ideals clearly in mind. Keeping the system's environment constantly in consideration goes a long way toward avoiding unintended consequences that ripple beyond a system boundary as the result of changes made to a system.

How you think is how you act is how you are. The way you think creates the results you experience. The most powerful way to improve the quality of your results is to improve the way you think. This is why systems thinking matters [6].

Adopting and maintaining a value focus in this setting is essential because as a system evolves through its life cycle and changes in size and complexity, the perceived value being delivered by the system likewise evolves. Sometimes this occurs in an undesirable way that drives system redesign efforts. Other times a more subtle adaptation occurs in which the system shifts its value focus, obscuring from system owners and stakeholders exactly how and where it is delivering value.

As is the case with most engineered systems, there will come a time at which a system continues to function exactly as intended but stakeholders' perceived value for it doing so either decreases or increases. The former case motivates system retirement and replacement. The latter case motivates support system augmentations or replacements. There is also an interesting situation in which an operating system has so many dependencies of all orders connected to it that it is considered 'too big to fail.' Systems thinking provides a frame through which to identify these subtle, but important considerations.

For any system decision problem, system thinking starts with the system output ("What should the system do? What is desired by the stakeholders?") and proceeds to work backward to identify system functions, processes, objectives, structure, and elements necessary to achieve this desired output. It then assesses the current state of the system ("Where is the system currently?") and asks, "What actions need to be taken to move the system from where it is to where it needs to be in order to maximize the value it delivers to stakeholders?" This natural focus on output (i.e., results, effects) provided by systems thinking creates a goal-oriented frame of reference that produces long term *system-level solutions* focused on the structure of the system rather than short term *symptom-level solutions* solutions that address subsets of the overall system. This point bears emphasis.

A systems thinking frame-of-reference helps one to distinguish between symptom-level and system-level phenomena. Symptom-level phenomena are typically of short duration and easily observable. When they incite stakeholder dissatisfaction, they can often be mistaken as a system problem rather than a symptom of a system problem. This is especially true for complex systems having a large number and type of dependencies between system elements that change and adapt over time, making it difficult to isolate phenomena resulting from structural system shortcomings.

For example, a recent debate centers on whether or not offering advanced course curricula to higher performing students in secondary education is disadvantaging other students. An observable phenomenon that sparked stakeholder dissatisfaction is the numerical imbalance that can often be seen in these courses by counting students according to racial identification. Symptom-level solutions are rather straightforward in this instance, but eliminating symptom-level phenomena provides short term relief but will not prevent their recurrence or others emerging in the future because the underlying system structure from which these symptoms arise is unchanged. Secondary education could easily be considered complex by our definition here. What shortcomings in the system structure are causing this symptom? What does the system structure look like? What are the potential system level solutions, and what system elements would they involve? Laws? Teachers? School districts? Funding? Parental influence? Educational assumptions? Students? What effect would they have on system element relationships and what are the second and higher order effects over time? These are difficult questions to address, but if long term system performance improvements are being sought, systems thinking offers a viable means of pursuing them.

While symptom-level solutions can provide an immediate value return (e.g., stop crime in a neighborhood), they are not going to alter structural elements of the system that give rise to the observed symptom (e.g., economic conditions, income disparity, educational shortcomings, cultural differences). Another way of saying this is that system-level solutions alter the fundamental system dynamics and relationships between system components; symptom-level solutions provide spot-fixes where these dynamics and relationships are failing. Risk-to-return on a specific investment instrument is a symptom-level phenomenon; elevated systemic risk shared across the entire derivatives market because of widespread use of credit default swaps is a system-level phenomenon. A single company deciding to no longer participate in these financial products would provide localized risk-relief but the underlying system-wide risk exposure still untreated will cause (possibly new) risk events to appear elsewhere.

System-level phenomena are persistent, presenting themselves in varying degrees across most if not all system components. These phenomena endure because they are an element or aspect of the underlying structure and organization of the system components that are connected by dependency relationships. System-level issues can be identified using techniques that focus on identifying failure modes, such as root cause analysis [7] that attempt to trace collections of symptom-level effects back to shared sources of generation.

It is possible in this framework that what is currently perceived as issues might not need fixing; they may actually be opportunities needing reinforcement. The perceived issues may very well be evidence of system functionality that is being imposed on the system by its users and is pushing against the constraints of the formally established structure and practices. In large organizations, "work-arounds" created by employees in order to properly accomplish tasks and the emergence of informal leaders assuming ad hoc roles and responsibilities outside of the established hierarchy are often indicators of just such a situation. The stakeholder analysis so critical to the successful application of the SDP properly frames these issues within a broader system perspective as they arise without assuming they must be eliminated.

2.1.2 Check on Learning

Concepts:
  (a) Can a system-level solution be a solution that simultaneously addresses subsystems and components needs as well? Can you give an example of this?
  (b) Is comedy a system level phenomena?

Comprehension:
  (a) Are their situations that applying a holistic perspective to would not be beneficial? What would these be? Is there a common characteristic between them?
  (b) Is getting the right answer to an engineering design question considered analysis? Why?

Application:
  (a) When you do online shopping at your favorite webstore, are you engaged in value focused thinking, alternative focused thinking, or both?
  (b) Teachers and bosses are always suggesting the best way to go about doing things. Can you give an example of a work-around that you developed to adapt to a particular occupational environment? Is the work-around successful?
  (c) Can you give an example of a system where ignoring element interactions caused problems? Would you say that it was intentional or accidental?

2.2 ELEMENT DEPENDENCIES

Identifying dependency relationships between system elements is critical to systems engineering and system design. When system element **A** is dependent upon system element **B**, it means that **A** cannot function completely until something arrives from **B**. Sometimes these dependencies are easy to recognize:

- **B** supplies electrical power to **A**, so **A** cannot operate until electrical power arrives from **B**. **A** depends on **B**; electrical power flows from **B** to **A**.
- A local regulation states that the town building inspector (**B**) has to provide a building permit before construction on house renovation (**A**) can begin. **A** depends on **B**; a building permit flows from **B** to **A**.
- An online investment account cannot execute user transactions (**B**) until login information (**A**) is supplied by the account holder and verified by the investment company's system. **B** depends on **A**; permissions information flows from **A** to **B**.

Sometimes they are more difficult to uncover because they are not immediately evident:

- A member of state congress (**A**) will not provide her endorsement to the local candidate (**B**) running for an open county supervisor position in an upcoming election until the candidate agrees to participate on her rural health services task force if elected. The endorsement flows in one direction: (**A**) to (**B**), and the agreement flows in the reverse: (**B**) to (**A**). As stated, it appears that the endorsement flow is waiting on the agreement, but in fact the agreement won't be provided unless the endorsement comes along with it. Diagrammatically, this would be represented by a two-headed arrow indicating bi-directional flow, or an edge with no arrow-heads on either end, indicating the same thing.
- In several military operations over the years, balloon-based airborne sensors and communications devices have been used to enhance line-of-sight communications. Units used to bring the balloons down if the devices were not working, until someone observed that adversaries changed their behavior (**B**) when the balloon was up (**A**) regardless of whether or not the devices were working. This was a unintentional system dependency that was not identified until someone happened to notice the change in behavior.

Sometimes the dependencies are of higher order and have to be traced to be identified. In this case, tracing is done by following connections between system elements along path segments over which the connecting substance (e.g., energy, information, influence, physical matter) flows, thereby creating a dependency relationship. Figure 2.1 illustrates this concept.

In Figure 2.1, the arrow at the end of each line segment indicates the direction of substance flow. Here, element **C** is directly dependent on something being provided by element **A**. There is only a single connector, so this is a *first order* dependency. Element **E** has a first order dependency on what **C** is providing, and a *second order* dependency on element **A**. That is, element **E** cannot properly function until element **C** supplies what it does, and element **C** cannot properly function until element **A** supplies it with what it needs to work properly. Elements **D** and **B** have *third order* dependencies on element **A**, and so on. Some software products, such as the Cambridge Advanced Modeler (CAM), accept a diagram of elements and directional connections in some form (called a *directional dependency* diagram or *digraph* in general), asks the user to identify the starting element for tracing (in this case element **A**), and then re-organizes and separates the circles

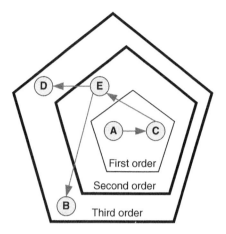

Figure 2.1   Ordered dependency tracing example.

(system elements) using geometric figures similar to Figure 2.1 to show the order of dependencies that exists.

All system representations attempt to make both system elements and dependency relationships clear. Intentional dependencies result from system decisions and design choices. Non-intentional dependencies (e.g., threat behavior change) are those created by stakeholders, system elements, and external systems that exist in the environment and interact with the system of interest. Non-intentional dependencies emerge post-design and deployment when they are needed by an external system, provide a competitive advantage to an external entity, or facilitate some element's adaptation to a changing environment. One example that combines all three of these reasons is the countless financial organizations that rely on up-to-date and accurate information flow from news and market service organizations (external systems). If the dependencies are strong enough and critical to the financial organization, they can be made part of the actual system through contractual agreements. This is a good example of how a system boundary can flex over time, as needed.

2.2.1   Check on Learning

Concepts:

    (a) What could possibly go wrong by ignoring higher order dependencies when making system decisions? Can you give an example?

Comprehension:

    (a) What dependency order describes the relationship between the university you choose to attend and your happiness?

    (b) Is the relationship between households and recycling operations an first order dependency or higher? Why?

Application:

    (a) What dependency order are microplastics in seafood? Is there an initial cause that initiated the chain of events? Can you identify the relationship links between the various dependency orders that have led to this phenomenon?

(b) Can you identify a non-intentional dependency on your university/job performance? Who or what is dependent upon this?

(c) Draw a diagram similar to Figure 2.1 that shows as many intentional and non-intentional dependency relationships propagating outward a local grocery store.

2.3 EXPANSIVE AND CONTRACTIVE THINKING

There are times during the SDP and other systems-related processes at which a systems engineer or systems decision support team broadens the project scope to conceptualize a widened space of possibilities regarding system performance and its effects on the environment, its design and development factors, the stakeholders influenced by varied performance, higher order relationships other than immediate elements, and possible system design alternatives, among other considerations. This is done in an attempt to avoid being trapped within an unintentionally limited set of design options, cost alternatives, system solutions, affected stakeholders with subtle but important vested interests, and system relationships and dependencies. The concern here is that important and consequential opportunities to innovate might be missed, causing value return to be overlooked or diminished.

Broadening project scope is one example of *expansive thinking*. In expansive thinking, one attempts to extend physical, functional, and behavioral boundaries upward, downward, and laterally, challenging assumptions that might appear to be constraints. Among the places where expansive thinking is beneficial, it is very useful early in the SDP Problem Definition phase when identifying "What is?" and "What should be?" with regard to the system of interest because the team's holistic perspective considers a wide variety of environmental elements and relationships prior to setting an initial system boundary. Setting a boundary is an example of *contractive thinking*.

Contractive thinking reduces scope by zooming in on select subsets of detail, thereby establishing boundaries that limit what is being considered and what is not. Contractive thinking occurs throughout the SDP as well, but is especially evident just prior to decision gates when a limited set of information is being presented to a decision maker for approval.

In a broad sense, there is a cycle of thinking between expansive and contractive thinking that takes place when engaging in a system design and development activity. For successful systems work, this cycle is intentional, identifiable, and manageable, taking place within the systems engineering team. Conceptual considerations of systems with boundaries naturally accommodates this cycle. So do projects.

Expansive thinking is a process of "zooming out" while contractive thinking equates to "zooming in" in some manner. For system representations, expansive thinking temporarily brings consideration of lateral and metasystems into the scope of a systems project to help decide what is "in" and what is not. Contractive thinking follows, narrowing this scope and establishing a revised system boundary. Expansive thinking reaches out to include less immediate stakeholders; contractive thinking narrows this set. Expansive thinking extends the possible ways a system may be designed to accomplish a needed purpose or objective; contractive thinking shrinks these possibilities. Contractive thinking can get "lost in the weeds," while expansive thinking can be held up by "dreamers." Expansive thinkers are more likely to see opportunity by conceptualizing a broader picture looking across lateral system interrelationships; contractive thinkers are more likely to understand internal workings of systems by digging deep into subsystems and lower level interactions.

In all this, the system of interest has not changed; but the perspectives taken by the systems team do and will change. There is no prescribed process for engaging in these two types of thinking while working a systems project except to point out that where brainstorming and other idea generating techniques are called for, they implicitly require imposed boundaries to blur and expansive thinking to engage. In contrast, points in any systems design and development process or the SDP at which a best set of alternatives is being pursued, contractive thinking is used in concert with modeling and analysis.

One warning comes with this and it pertains to working with stakeholders. There are system stakeholders who will be assertive and less flexible thinkers during meetings, group solicitations, or interviews. From experience, it appears that this is mostly due to either their dominant personalities or because of how they think they need to act given the organizational position they are in. They are not wrong in behaving like this, but in discussions they tend to seek confirmation of an idea or strategy they already favor and do not necessarily welcome novel input or alternatives that represent "thinking outside of the box," which is analogous to blurring boundaries and engaging in expansive thinking. Engaging them in a private discussion explaining the differences between expansive and contractive thinking and the advantages of both does help, especially if their idea is used to nucleate new ones.

2.3.1 Check on Learning

Concepts:

 (a) Is an innovative product the result of expansive thinking, contractive thinking, or both? Can you give an example?

 (b) How many expansive thinking—contractive thinking cycles were involved with your decision to attend university? Can these be arranged on a timeline? Which came first?

Comprehension:

 (a) Is improving the design of an Android cellphone while maintaining the product form factor an example of expansive or contractive thinking?

Application:

 (a) Have you encountered person who predominantly engages in contractive thinking? For what situations would this be a good thing or a bad thing to do?

 (b) Similarly, have you encountered a person who predominantly engages in expansive thinking? Again, for what situations would this be a good thing or a bad thing to do?

2.4 STRUCTURE

Understanding the workings of a system requires some conceptual thinking about its underlying *structure*. A system's structure is its organization. Structure depends on the number and type of relationships that connect system elements. Structure is described by identifying a system's elements (components), understanding which elements are connected and how they interact with each other to achieve the system's purpose, and understanding where this system lies relative to other systems that can impact its behavior or vice-versa. System structure has important characteristics that are useful to know when supporting systems decisions, such as the modularity of its design, its level of integration, the measured importance of components, elements that are single points-of-failure, and so on.

This organization may be *evident*, meaning that it is identifiable through direct observation. Evident structure motivates most system representations such as those discussed in Chapter 3. Structure may also be hidden from direct observation, requiring modeling and mathematics to reveal its *underlying* structure. A good example of underlying structure is an estimate of systems *modularity* as a function of component dependencies. Modularity is a general systems concept expressing the degree to which a system can be separated and recombined, important features for design and maintenance purposes. This is also referred to as the tightness of coupling between system elements along with the technical or procedural rules of the system that allow for mixing and matching of element capabilities [8].

Highly modular system designs consist of loosely connected (coupled) blocks (modules) that have significant intra-module (within the boundary of each module) dependencies and few inter-module (connections with entities external to each module) dependencies. When a system is highly modular, individual modules are designed to be replaced, repaired, upgraded, or retired as subunits to a system with relative ease, thereby reducing some of the costs associated with these activities.

The opposite of a modular system is one that is *integral*. A highly integral system consists of a very low number of modules with tight (strongly) coupling between modules. Systems that are highly integral involve costly, technically complicated, and time consuming maintenance activities rarely intended for a user to perform without significant training. For this reason, highly integral systems are typically intended for in-use replacement ("swapout") rather than repair.

Broadly speaking, modularity can be a desirable design characteristic of a system in some settings, and yet be undesirable in others. For example, a highly modular ground radar system with numerous individual system elements easily transported in a single Pelican case assumes a risk during use that components will be lost.

Modularity, and hence the exact definition of a module in a given system, depends on the type and strength of connections being considered. A system could be highly modular with respect to physical connections, and yet be highly integral with respect to another dimension of connectivity such as electrical power. Highly integral systems, such as modern smart phones, are designed to be totally replaced rather than repaired as components are damaged or fail. For example, Apple only recently began providing support for replacing damaged touchscreens on the iPhone series, previously leaving this type of activity to third party vendors. Prior to this, a user's only option was to replace the phone.

Processes also have structure because there is an organization to them that extends over time. Typically, processes are described and illustrated using a step-by-step listing similar to a cooking recipe or a flowchart. Processes can be quite complicated, such as the one shown in Figure 2.2 which shows the acquisition process for major capabilities used by the US Department of Defense. If this were a cooking recipe, it would be challenging for even the best of chefs!

Some processes appear to have a simple structure until they are closely examined and then begin to reveal their complications. Consider for a moment the process associated with purchasing an automobile. On one hand, this might appear to be a simply structured one: go to a local dealership, examine their inventory, compare prices to budget, and purchase the vehicle that comes closest to satisfying desire without violating your working budget limits. No doubt many people exercise this strategy on a routine basis. Knowing this propensity of potential buyers enables automobile manufacturers to craft enticing advertisements and marketing campaigns that can effectively reshape what a potential buyer thinks they want into what the manufacturer wants to sell. This is the heart of effective marketing [10].

On the other hand, applying a small amount of systems thinking to the car buying process reveals the purchase decision as highly connected in its structure. The car being purchased will become part of a system in which the automobile is a new element that interacts in various ways with other major systems: the transportation highway system (health & safety), banking (financial) systems, fuel logistic (technical and electric grid) systems, personal prestige and entertainment

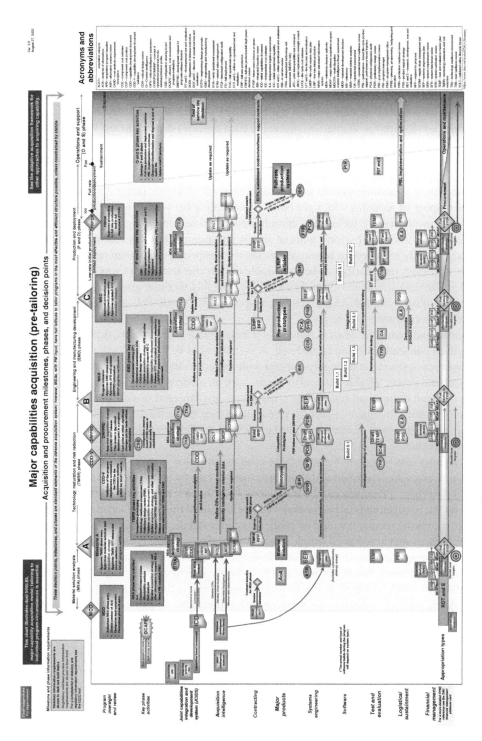

Figure 2.2 Major capability acquisition chart [9].

(social) systems, insurance (financial) systems, motor vehicle regulation (legal) systems, communication (technical) systems, ecological systems, law enforcement systems, and so on. From this systems thinking perspective, the purchase decision takes on a much greater level of importance than it may have otherwise. A diesel fueled monster truck may give way to an electric vehicle. The system solution clearly has an impact on each of these other systems in some manner that should be either taken into consideration or intentionally disregarded, but certainly not ignored.

In fact, one of the most significant failings of the current U.S. transportation system is that the automobile was never thought of as being part of a system until it had already reached a level of popularity in the United States that it became a household necessity and problems associated with the large number of automobiles arose. The automobile was developed and introduced during a period that saw the automobile as a stand-alone technology largely replacing the horse and carriage. So long as it outperformed the previous equine technology, it was considered a success. This success is not nearly so apparent if the automobile is examined from a systems thinking perspective. In that guise, the automobile has managed to fail miserably across a host of dimensions. Many of these can be observed in any major city today: oversized cars and trucks negotiating tight roads and streets, bridges and tunnels incapable of handling daily traffic density, insufficient parking, poor air quality induced in areas where regional geography restricts free flow of wind, and a distribution of the working population to suburban locations necessitating automobile use just to get to places of employment. Had the automobile been developed as a multilateral system interconnected with urban (and rural) transportation networks and environmental systems, cities would be in a much different situation than they find themselves in today.

What is important here is not that the automobile could have been developed differently, but that in choosing to design, develop, and deploy the automobile as a standalone system (actually, it is highly unlikely that anyone back then was engaged in the type of systems thinking we now do), a host of complementary transportation solutions that could replace the horse and buggy were not considered. Systems thinking would have helped to identify these potential feasible solutions. If they were subsequently rejected, it would have been for logically defendable reasons. In the business of supporting decision making, limiting the span of potential solutions tends to degrade the quality of the chosen solution, certainly when measured against criteria of robustness.

An example in a social setting can further illustrate this point. In the United States during the late 1960s, it was not uncommon to hear people taking positions on issues of behavior choices by saying: "Why should it matter to anyone else what I do? If I decide to do this, I am the only one affected. It's my life." While behavior is certainly within an individual's control, this statement ignores any and all connections, dependencies, and interactions between the individual and the environment.

 The poet John Donne recognized the importance of connections nearly four centuries ago in his poem *No Man is An Island*: "No man is an island entire of itself; every man is a piece of the continent, a part of the main." —John Donne (1572–1631)

The underlying (hidden) structure of a system is typically exposed and described by transforming a symbolic representation of the system into mathematical forms such as adjacency matrices which are discussed in Chapter 3. For example, it is straightforward and natural to represent a logistic system using a digraph because items (physical or digital) flow between locations (physical or virtual). By associating variables such as x_{ij} with the directional arrows, some quantity flows from element i to element j, establishing a dependency. Such a diagram can be transformed into a mathematical program whose solution(s) optimizes the operation of the system. These mathematical programs reach a solution much quicker when a special *network structure* is present, which a diagram helps to reveal.

Exposing underlying system structure requires a focus not simply on the elements of a system but also on the relationships existing between elements. These relationships are the binding material that defines a system's structure, and mathematics provides a means by which these relationships can be captured and analyzed. What is the nature of these relationships? What do they imply about the system itself? How do the relationships or the elements themselves change over time? If allowed to continue in its current operational configuration, what might the state of the system be sometime in the future? How long will it take for a system to stabilize after changes have been made? Are there single points-of-failure or over-dependencies? What are the long term effects on specific system elements? Many of the modeling methods discussed in later chapters are based on relationship characteristics.

An assumption at the heart of most mathematical system models is that the observable output of a system is a direct result of the input provided, internal processes, and the controls acting on the system. This relates input to output in a cause-effect manner that helps to reveal a system's behavior within its boundary along with the functions and sub-functions enabling this behavior.

Structure Example.
Consider the simple model for a system labeled as "collect intelligence" in Figure 2.3. It shows a box containing a system function that accepts input and transforms this input into output via some known or unknown transformation function that can potentially be expressed as a cause–effect relationship.

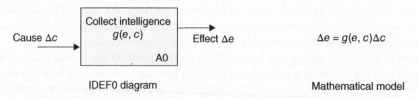

Figure 2.3   Two abstract system models: graphical and mathematical.

Let (c) represent the input (cause) information to the system and (e) the output (effect) intelligence report. Suppose that we impose a change in the input information (c), denoted by Δc. This change causes a change in the output e of the system represented as Δe. The exact translation or transformation of this change (*perturbation*), is accomplished by some transformation function denoted as $g(e, c)$. The nature of $g(e, c)$ defines the mathematical structure of the system. Its action moves the system used to produce intelligence reports from one state $S(e, c)$ to another $S(e + \Delta e, c + \Delta c)$. This idea of a *system state* is a general concept that can be used to describe a system's condition, location, inherent health, financial position, and political position, among other characteristics.

Is $g(e, c)$ linear or nonlinear? This can be determined by examining the proportionality of the effect response for various changes in input. If Δe is proportional to Δc, then $g(e, c)$

---

is linear. If not, then $g(e, c)$ is either discontinuous or nonlinear. Determining the best mathematical form of $g(e, c)$ is left to experimentation and data analysis using methods such as linear regression, spline fitting, response surface modeling, and others. Once $g(e, c)$ is identified, is there a best level of output for given ranges of input that the system can be tuned to produce? Optimization techniques such as linear and nonlinear programming, equilibrium models, and related techniques could be used to answer this question.

Does the transformation performed by the system function stay consistent over time? If so, then $g(e, c)$ is likely *time invariant* and time is not explicitly modeled in the mathematical system representation. Otherwise, time should be included in the system function representation: in some manner: $g(e, c, t)$. If $g(e, c, t)$ is nonlinear, is the system *stable*, or do the effects increase without bound?

Is the relationship between Δc and Δe known with certainty? If not, then $g(e, c)$ should include probability or uncertainty elements where they occur. This is typically the case for systems that are best represented by simulations, queuing networks, decision analysis structures, risk models, forecasting methods, reliability models, and Markov processes, among others.

The role played by the function $g(e, c)$ in this abstract system representation is crucial. In mathematical terms, the function $g(e, c)$ is referred to as a *system kernel* [11]. It fundamentally describes the incremental change occurring between input and output to the system, which can occur in discrete steps:

$$g(e, c) \equiv \frac{\Delta e}{\Delta c} \tag{2.1}$$

or continuously:

$$g(e, c) \equiv \frac{de}{dc} \tag{2.2}$$

The two expressions (2.1) and (2.2) are related by a limit expression as the incremental interval is made infinitesimally small:

$$\lim_{\Delta c \to 0} \frac{\Delta e}{\Delta c} = \frac{de}{dc} = g(e, c) \tag{2.3}$$

Figure 2.4 illustrates a slightly more complicated system structure to represent mathematically. The external feedback loop complicates the input to the system by adding a new input component that represents a manipulated portion of the system output. A common example of a structure of this kind can be envisioned by thinking about the creation of a political speech as an IDEF0 model's function, one element of a much larger political system. In this manner, we can construct a system boundary around the speech writing process from the perspective of a particular speech writer.

Constantly changing information flows into this system from the environment, acting as input dc to the speech writing kernel, $g(e, c)$, which processes this input to create the output political message for a speech, de. However, the speech writer also wisely takes into account the public reaction to previous speeches when crafting a new message to be delivered. This consideration of public processing of previous output de, creates a new system function called a *feedback kernel* which is part of an external system which we associate with the public. The output of this feedback kernel is *public* opinion relevant to the speech writer.

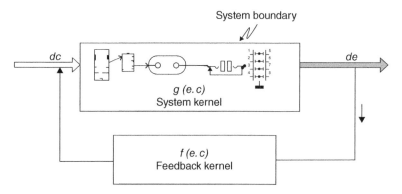

Figure 2.4 A system representation with external feedback.

The public takes the previous output *de* and uses *de* as input to the feedback kernel $f(e, c)$. The output of the feedback kernel, $f(e, c)de$, is added to the normal environmental input *dc* so that the total (new) input to the system becomes $dc + f(e, c)de$. Thus we have,

$$de = g(e, c)[dc + f(e, c)de] \tag{2.4}$$

Finally, by gathering common terms in Equation (2.4) and assuming that $dc \neq 0$, we see that the system kernel alters its form to a new form $g(e, c)_f$, where the subscript f simply designates that the feedback effects have been included in the system kernel:

$$\frac{de}{dc} = g(e, c)_f = \frac{g(e, c)}{1 - g(e, c)f(e, c)} \tag{2.5}$$

By thinking of the action $f(e, c)$ has on the previous system output *de*, and noting that the next output from the system kernel $g(e, c)_f$ is again acted on by the feedback kernel, we can easily get a sense that the feedback input is either being left alone ($f(e, c)de = 0$), amplified ($|f(e, c)de| > 1$), or dampened ($|f(e, c)de| < 1$) with each loop negotiation. This example begins to hint at some of the underlying system structure that can introduce system *complexity* arising from nonlinear dynamic changes, similar to those exhibited by this example when $g(e, c)$ is nonlinear. Complexity also arises when the system kernel $g(e, c)$ alters its structure in response to changes in input *c*. This ability of the system to adapt is again a characteristic of complex systems.

In a model representing sequenced functions, activities, or processes, feedback can also be represented in one of the two forms: control feedback and/or input feedback. Control feedback takes the output of a lower bounding box in the sequence order and connects it via an arrow to the control of an earlier bounding box in the sequence. A practical example of this can be seen in the organizational use of after-action reviews and similar activities that use system output to guide the system function. Similarly, input feedback takes the output of a lower bounding box in the sequence order and connects it via an arrow to the input of an earlier bounding box in the sequence. This situation is commonly encountered in rework situations, for example, in manufacturing or report writing.

Large systems are not necessarily complex systems. The presence of complicated and strong element interactions, nonlinear dynamic changes induced by system function kernels, and possibly self-organization behavior can impose complexity on a system; being large in size complicates an already challenging situation. Systems decision problems possessing some or all of these characteristics are recently being referred to as *wicked* problems [12]. Most often, the tool of choice to model and analyze a complex system is simulation.

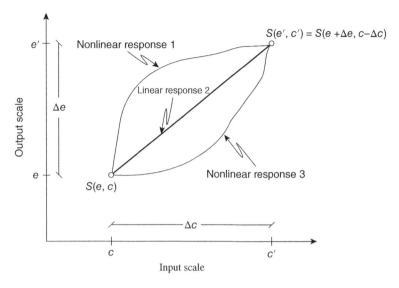

Figure 2.5   Three possible qualitative structures of a system kernel function.

Early in a system life cycle when input and output data for a system are likely unavailable, it is still possible to gain a qualitative sense of the mathematical structure of a system using this same mathematical structure approach without knowing the exact notational form of either the system kernel $g(e, c)$ or existing feedback functions. Optionally, it may be possible to use a graphical approach in collaboration with the system owner or user(s) to extract a more general, but still useful, approximation of $g(e, c)$ by simply focusing on input and output to the system. Figure 2.5 illustrates three possible resulting function forms for $g(e, c)$ for the case when the system kernel is assumed to be continuous.

The topmost concave nonlinear response curve 1 in Figure 2.5 describes a system kernel $g(e, c)$ that quickly drives the system state $S(e, c)$ to react to small increases in system input c. As the size of the imposed change on input Δc increases, the output response decreases. The bottommost convex nonlinear response curve 3 has just the opposite affect: the system kernel $g(e, c)$ translates large changes on the system input into large output responses but small changes have small response. The middle linear response curve 2 illustrates a proportional response that remains constant throughout the range of possible input changes Δc. Without knowing the exact details of how the kernel operates, varying inputs and observing outputs provides important clues as to what the mathematical model of this system function should be.

2.5   CLASSIFYING SYSTEMS

Challenging system decisions require a top-down classification scheme that starts with the "big picture" of the system and its observable behavior. Systems occur in many different forms but generally can be described using three classes for system types: physical, abstract, and unperceivable. A *physical* system, also referred to as a concrete system [13], exists in the reality of space–time and consists of at least two elements that interact in a meaningful manner. This is a system that is clearly evident in the real world and directly observable to the trained and perhaps untrained eye. An automobile is a good example of a physical system.

Physical systems further subdivide into four subclasses that can overlap in some cases:

- *Nonliving* has no genetic connections in the system and no processes that qualitatively transform the elements together with the whole and continuously renew these same elements.
- *Living* typically referred to as an organic system, is a system subject to the principles of natural selection such as an ant colony, a predator–prey relationship between species, and human biophysiology.
- *Manmade* physical systems intentionally created to augment human life such as transportation road networks, logistic resupply systems, and communication systems.
- *Natural* are those systems coming into being by natural processes, such as waterway networks created by natural processes associated with glaciers, tectonic plate shifts, and weather.

An *abstract* system is a system of concepts that are linked together in some manner, generally in an attempt to convey an initial design, a strategic policy, or some other idea that has not been implemented in some other form. Abstract systems are organizations of ideas expressed in symbolic form that can take the form of words, numbers, images, figures, or other symbols. In a sense, this type of system is an intermediate system pinched between reality and the completely intangible as its elements may or may not be empirically observable, because they are relationships abstracted from a particular interest or theoretical point-of-view.

Figure 2.6 is an example of the field of engineering management (EM) expressed as an abstract system. In its organization, the diagram conveys the order and purpose of the professional field of EM as emerging from the unique interaction of four separate disciplines: leadership, management, economics, and engineering. Each of these four disciplines could in turn be represented as systems. Permeating all of these systems are the environmental resource considerations of people, technology, time, and finances. A similar illustration could be used to show how the car buying decision (substituted in place of "EM" in the picture) impacts the other systems mentioned earlier.

An interesting point to note with regard to this figure is that the EM system as illustrated does not exist apart from the four discipline systems shown. It exists solely because of the interaction of these four systems. It is, in fact, a professional field delivered only at a holistic level of systems; it is not possible to decompose the abstract EM system representation into its multilateral system elements and still retain the complete character of EM. Bear this observation in mind when the concept of designing "system-level measures of performance" arises later in this book.

An *unperceivable* system is a classification that is largely based on the limitations of our ability to observe the system rather than some innate characteristics it may possess. These systems exist when an extreme number of elements and the complexity of their relationships mask the underlying system structure or organization. A system representation used to describe an unperceivable system is an approximation of the system at best, typically containing only as much detail so as to enable its inputs and outputs to be identified.

An example of an unperceivable system is the U.S. economy. A complete description that includes all of its elements and interrelationships defies our comprehension. At best, we resort to surrogate measures such as gross domestic product (GDP), the Dow Jones composite index, unemployment estimates, inflation rate estimates, foreign trade balance, monetary exchange rates, and new housing starts as indicators of how well (or poorly) the U.S. economy is performing. The complex nature of this system due to the number of elements, number of interactions, and evolving states of both these make it unperceivable as a system. This goes a long way toward explaining why, despite technology advances and Nobel laureate awardees in economics, error-free future state forecasts of this system remain impossible to attain.

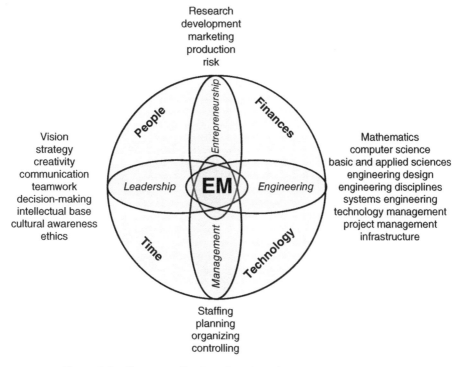

Figure 2.6 Conceptualization of engineering management system.

2.6 BOUNDARIES

The concept of establishing a *system boundary* is fundamental to working with systems. From a practical standpoint, a system boundary serves to delineate those elements, interactions, and subsystems that should be part of a system definition from those that should not. Generally, elements and systems that are strongly dependent on the system of interest should be considered inside the system boundary. This doesn't mean that they are technically part of what is being developed, but it does mean they are integrated into the system development project to a large extent and that they (and their stakeholders) can and will cause requirements that otherwise would not be present.

 If someone throws a fit because you set boundaries, it's just more evidence that the boundary is needed. —Unknown author

For example, by itself a 44-bottle wine refrigerator (a temperature and humidity controlling system) can be any size and shape that a manufacturer desires. However, the sizes actually set for these appliances are driven by cabinet manufacturers and kitchen design professionals who need versions of these appliances to fit into their cabinets (see Figure 2.7). Consequently, technical requirements for under-counter wine refrigerator sizes and the location and type of their electrical

Figure 2.7   Landmark® under-counter wine refrigerators. Source: Landmark.

connections are driven by requirements set by external cabinet systems and their stakeholders (who include consumers). Figure 2.7 shows how two separate 15-in. refrigerators were combined to meet one customer's storage requirements.

To a good extent, what is included within a system boundary is influenced by the systems decision because of the scope of the decision making—what the decision will affect and who is involved. If the design change or system improvement only affects some limited aspect of a system function, then the boundary for a project like this is quite tight, and may only be limited to a small engineering or technical team within design and manufacturing. For example, the boundary would be tight if Landmark® decided to change all their interior appliance lighting to LED. However, if they were deciding to completely replace the type of refrigeration compressor, enable WiFi connections to mobile phone apps, and use a newly designed storage shelving for the unit shown in Figure 2.7, these decisions will affect overall electrical and installation requirements. Cabinet and home electrical systems (and the building codes associated with each) will be considered inside of the wine refrigerator system boundary, as might the replacement part supply chain systems and WiFi networking standards.

Unfortunately, this means that there is no easy answer to setting a system boundary; every systems decision problem motivates its own appropriate system boundary and system definition. Systems engineers accomplish this using the information resulting from research and extensive interaction with stakeholders during the problem definition phase of the SDP. In this regard, the system boundary is one tool available to a systems engineer to help define the scope of a particular project.

Definition: A *system boundary* is a physical or conceptual boundary that contains all the essential elements, subsystems, and interactions necessary to address a systems decision problem.

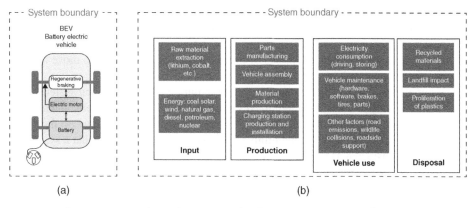

Figure 2.8 Two boundary options for the same BEV system of interest.

The system boundary effectively and completely isolates the system under study from its external environment except for inputs and outputs that are allowed to move across the system boundary.

A system's boundary distinguishes the system of interest from its environment. At the onset of a systems decision support project, the systems team identifies an initial system boundary to delineate the elements that will be considered within the system and those that will be considered external. For example, a project focused on electric vehicles as a replacement for conventional carbon fuel vehicles could establish an initial system boundary around a single electric vehicle and its components (a), or it could establish a system boundary around a wider group of elements encompassing more of the systems actual life cycle activities (b) as illustrated in Figure 2.8. With a system boundary such as (a), it seems clear that electric vehicles are good for the natural environment. However, the more expansive and inclusive boundary shown as (b) introduces elements that question this conclusion, especially when raw material mining (e.g., groundwater extraction of lithium) and vehicle production are considered internal to the system of interest. Depending on the nature of the questions being asked, and the fundamental objective of the systems project, one of these is more appropriate than the other.

Open systems interact with their environment in a specific way in which they accept inputs from the environment in order to produce outputs that return to the environment. *Closed* systems are isolated and hermetic, accepting no inputs beyond those used to initialize the system and providing no outputs to its environment. Closed systems do not need to interact with their environment to maintain their existence. The clearest form of a closed system is one proposed in physics and mechanical engineering: a perpetual motion device. Once the initial energy is provided to put the device in motion, it stays in motion forever with absolutely no inputs from outside of its boundary.

Closed systems generally do not occur in nature. More often, human intervention in the form of controlled scientific experiments create closed systems. Some systems are considered closed systems because some particular exchange across its boundary is discounted or ignored. Atoms and molecules can be considered closed systems if their quantum effects are ignored. Greenhouses could be considered closed systems if energy (heat) exchange is ignored. In mathematics, an abstract system on its own vector spaces represents closed systems: valid operations performed on the elements of a vector space remain in the vector space forever. Edwin A. Abbott (1838–1926), an English schoolmaster and theologian, wrote an interesting book titled *Flatland: A Romance of Many Dimensions* [14] about what life would be like in a two-dimensional world. The world he created was like a 2D photograph: people, places, and things were flat. A line would act as an impenetrable boundary for all the beings that existed in this world. This 2D Flatland was a closed system much like a vector space in linear algebra; all interactions between objects in Flatland resulted in an object or effect that existed in the same 2D world. No new elements entered from outside. It became an open system when one of the residents discovered how to move into a third dimension.

Most, if not all, systems we encounter and operate in our daily lives are open systems. Consequently, if an initial inspection of a system makes it appear to be a closed system, chances are we are overlooking some multi-lateral or hierarchical systems that are affecting input to the system.

The boundary of a system is the actual limits of the major system elements that a systems team decides should be considered as part of the system of interest. Inputs and outputs cross boundaries of systems. The boundary of a system must be selected to include all of the important interacting elements of the system of interest and exclude all those that do not impact the system behavior that makes it a system. Isolating the core system is an important part of a systems engineering project because doing so allows lateral systems, subsystems, and metasystems to be identified as well.

Figure 2.12 illustrates a hypothetical open system with each of the major system structural elements shown. The system accepts input from its environment, acts on that input via its internal functions, and again interacts with its environment by producing output. Input can take the form of physical material, as in sand being used as a source of silicon dioxide for making silicon wafers for computer microchips. Input can also possess a less tangible form, as in the case of information. For decision support systems used to predict stock performance or assign airline ticket prices, information is one input flowing across the boundary of these open systems.

While it may be natural to think of these inputs and outputs in terms of matter, energy, and materials such as raw materials used in a manufacturing or production facility, they can just as well be services, or induced effects such as influences and other psychological entities. These can all be appropriately defined as crossing a particular system boundary. The strength of this conceptualization predominately lies in its broad application across a very wide spectrum of disciplines and applications.

2.7   VISIBILITY AND SPATIAL ARRANGEMENT

In most broad terms, system structure can be described first in terms of its relationship with the environment and secondly in terms of what it represents and how it is organized to interact. We have seen one form of structure already open or closed systems that captures how the system interacts with its environment. Here we want to examine two other dimensions of system structure: visibility and spatial arrangement.

2.7.1   Visibility

From the systems perspective of input, transform, and output, we can describe system structure in terms of the degree of visibility that we have on the internal workings of the system. Are the elements and their interactions readily identifiable, or are some or all of these hidden from view? The answer to this question enables us to specify the system as one of the three basic structural models: a black box, a gray box, or a white box [13]. These three gradations of visibility into the inner workings of a system are illustrated in Figure 2.9.

A *black box* is a structure that behaves in a certain way without providing any visibility into exactly what internal elements are, how they are specifically linked, how they functionally transform inputs to the system to produce observable system output. Uncovering such information for

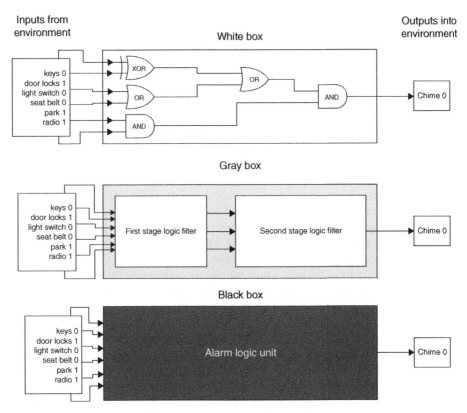

Figure 2.9 Degrees of internal understanding of a system.

the purposes of gaining deeper understanding of a black box system consists primarily of repeatedly manipulating the input to get to a point of producing reasonably predictable output(s). Extracting the functional linkage between input and output then becomes the task of design of experiments, regression, response surface methodology, and other data-dependent modeling techniques.

A good example of a black box system is human body temperature regulation. If a person's body temperature is too high, placing that person in a bath of cold water lowers it, as does administering loading doses of aspirin. If the person's body temperature is too low, slow heating in a hot tub or with human skin contact will gradually raise the temperature. How exactly the body is reacting to these external stimuli at a subsystem interaction level to make this happen is known, but generally not accessible to discovery without extremely sophisticated instrumentation.

A *gray box* offers partial knowledge of selected internal component interactions and processes (activities). This middle ground perspective is one that is often encountered in practice as even very complex systems have partially accessible and understandable internal processes. For example, in the United States economic system which is unperceivable, we could create groups of elements at various levels that would allow a partial view into the inner workings of this system, such as country elements engaged in foreign trade, all legal non-profit organizations engaged in charity work in the state of New York, and so on. In the gray box illustration of Figure 2.9, while a select number of system elements are visible, their interactions are not. Complete information concerning the system this represents cannot be acquired.

A *white box* perspective recognizes complete transparency on a systems internal elements and processes. This ability is rarely achievable when working with existing systems that are complex but very common in newly designed systems such as telecom networks, mechanical devices, business partnerships, athletic teams, and farming operations. It is possible to reasonably fill in gaps in understanding of internal elements and processes of white box systems by making assumptions and then validating these assumptions by measuring output variation in comparison to input changes, as would be done with a black or gray box system.

2.7.2   Spatial Arrangement

The natural state of affairs for systems is that they exist within and among other systems so that for any particular systems decision problem, a systems engineer is inevitably faced with a composite system environment. Determining where and how the specific system of interest is located relative to the other systems it interacts with is a necessary task for setting the scope of the program. Some systems will have extensive interaction with the system of interest, which means that changes occurring in one of these interrelated systems have an impact on the behavior of the system of interest. Systems of this kind have a high priority for being included within the scope of the project. As the degree of interaction between systems diminishes, systems falling into this category are more likely to be simply noted for the record and set aside.

One important note to consider is that systems often interact on an abstract level in addition to or in lieu of having linked system elements. Market effects, a consideration related to the financial environmental factor, are a good example of this. Competition for market share between, for example, Linux and Microsoft® Windows operating systems creates a strong interaction that must be considered when version updates and functionality revisions are being designed and developed. Likewise, two separate countries can be strongly linked politically because of shared vested interests even though no elements of their infrastructure are interconnected. Being sensitive to subtle interactions such as these and others helps identify and characterize lateral systems described in what follows. This is one of the uses of the environmental factors surrounding the four steps of the SDP shown in Figure 1.8.

A good visualization of the typical arrangement of systems interrelationships is useful for detecting the connections between various systems. Generally, systems either start out as, or evolve into being, part of other systems in one of three structural relationships: multilateral, lateral, and multilevel hierarchies. A multilevel hierarchical arrangement is one that is very familiar to large organizations because this is typically the manner in which they are structured to accomplish defined objectives. These arrangements are also referred to as *nested* systems. A more commonly encountered term is a "system-of-systems."

For a systems decision problem, recognizing and understanding the relationships between interacting systems, especially in a system-of-systems situation, is significant because these systems are likely to be at different stages in their individual life cycles. Mature systems tend to have a strong degree of presence in the composite system environment, an extensive network of connections, significant resource requirements, and are able to sustain a competitive situation for a long duration of time. In comparison, younger systems tend to have newer technologies, less presence in the composite system environment, less extensive interdependencies with existing systems, may have significant resource requirements, and their ability to sustain competition is less robust. Not recognizing this additional characteristic can result in unsatisfactory systems solutions being constructed. Moreover, notice that these observations, important as they are, say little about system

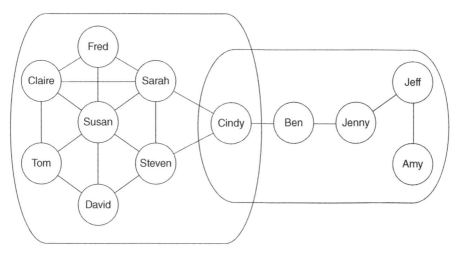

Figure 2.10 Multilateral friendship systems in a social network. Source: Pidd [17]/ John Wiley & Sons.

efficiency, effectiveness, ability to leverage resources or arrange cooperative strategic alliances, and a host of other concerns that address the long term survivability of systems. Each systems decision problem should be approached as being unique and it is up to the systems team to discern the relevant issues of concern from stakeholder and decision maker input to the SDP.

In a hierarchy, the system under study resides within a broader contextual arrangement called a *metasystem*. It in turn can have groupings of connected elements interacting to accomplish defined objectives. These are called *subsystems*. Within a hierarchical arrangement, like entities exist on the same level. Subsystems particular to these entities exist below them, and systems that they are a part of exist above them. Systems operating on the same level that share common elements are called *multilateral* systems. Systems on the same hierarchical level that are linked only by abstract or indirect effects (e.g., political influence, competition, targeted recruiting at the same population) are referred to as *lateral* systems.

An example of a multilateral arrangement from social network analysis [15, 16] is shown in Figure 2.10. Cindy is a person who exists as a friend to two separate groups of people that do not interact. The bridge relationship connecting the two social groups (systems) through the single individual (shared component) is multilateral systems structure. Changes that occur in one group have the potential for inducing changes in behavior in the other group through this shared component. The two multilateral friendship networks shown in Figure 2.10 would be considered to be in a lateral system arrangement if they did not share the element "Cindy" in common.

The positioning of a system within a hierarchy is relative to the system being examined, being determined in large part by the system purpose or how it functions in its relationship to other systems. It is this idea that motivates the construction of a functional hierarchy for systems decision problems.

Figure 2.11 presents two perspectives of the exact same group of hierarchical objects concerning the suspension system for an automobile. If the system of interest is the vehicle's complete suspension system, we would conceptualize the system hierarchy consistent with Perspective 1: the system would reside within the metasystem of the entire automobile and have as one of its subsystems the left rear brake drum and shock absorbing subsystem. If we were instead focusing on the

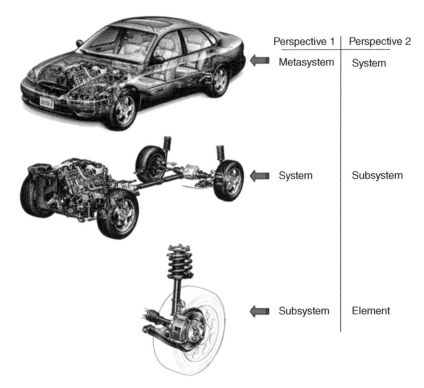

	Perspective 1	Perspective 2
	Metasystem	System
	System	Subsystem
	Subsystem	Element

Figure 2.11 Three hierarchy levels of system spatial placement. (Courtesy of Kevin Hulsey Illustration Inc.).

entire automobile as the system of interest, then Perspective 2 would be appropriate. The complete suspension system would be a subsystem and the left rear brake drum and shock absorbing object would be an element of this subsystem. One possible metasystem for Perspective 2 could be the rental car system that uses this automobile as part of its available fleet.

In hierarchical systems, the observable system behavior can easily change depending on the system being examined. At higher levels in a hierarchy a more abstract, encompassing view of the whole system emerges without attention to the details of the elements or parts. At lower levels, where subsystems and individual elements are evident, a multitude of interacting parts can typically be observed but without understanding how they are organized to form a whole [18].

In a pure multilateral arrangement in which the only connections between systems are shared elements, the relationship between these systems is essentially non-hierarchical. For situations such as this, it is then valuable to conceptualize the arrangement of systems as a *composite multilateral* arrangement [19]. Subsystems and elements can then have the same meaning as in a typical hierarchical structure. The environment shaped by the interactions emanating from the composite multilateral systems takes the place of a metasystem. This is a particularly useful construct for systems decision problems involving strategy and policy, where the dynamics of influence, power, or counteraction are key to shaping the decisions being made. Recent examples of such an arrangement arose when applying systems thinking to US border security policy [20], metropolitan disaster planning [19], and counter-insurgency strategy [21].

2.7.3 Check on Learning

Concepts:

(a) What level of visibility do you have with regards to your online music streaming service's system?

(b) Can you give an example of a "flat" organization that prefers to not operate as a hierarchy? Is it working for them?

Comprehension:

(a) Think of a local outdoor pond as a system. What dictates its structure? How easily is this structure disrupted? What would describe its evident structure and underlying structure?

Application:

(a) Can you identify a spatial arrangement for your local health clinic? What is its meta-system? What lateral systems either provide support to it or have dependencies on its output?

(b) How would you characterize the spatial arrangement your living space (dorm, apartment, house, tent, trailer, etc.) has with its neighborhood? What would be the metasystem to the neighborhood?

2.8 EVOLUTION AND DYNAMICS

As time progresses, a system of interest will evolve and many systems decision support elements change in concert. Perhaps not in a one-to-one fashion, but they most certainly will change. Some changes can be represented and analyzed in well-defined ways; others retain their challenge and are open areas for research and development. Let's first consider the system itself.

Different systems afford different levels of visibility into their inner workings. The relationships between elements can change dynamically over time, causing system evolution to become a concern. A portion of the output of a system can undergo *feedback* in which the environment uses the system output to create conditioned input that is fed back into the system. Interaction with the environment requires that a system be open, as a closed system has no interaction across its boundaries.

Figure 2.12 also illustrates the two major versions of system *feedback*: internal and external [11]. **Definition**: *Internal* feedback is the feedback of a system that is modified and recycled with the system boundary to alter inputs delivered to a system.

Internal feedback is entirely controlled by the system and is typically not visible from outside the system boundary. A common example of internal feedback is a manufacturing quality control process that sends work-in-progress back through manufacturing stages for rework prior to releasing the product for distribution. A consumer only sees the end product, not being privy to the internal workings of the manufacturing company. In education, intra-departmental reviews of courses, syllabi, programs, and teaching philosophies are other examples of internal feedback if a system boundary for an academic major were drawn around a department's operations.

Identifying internal feedback depends on having access to the inner workings of a system. If the owner of a system allows access to its internal processes and structure, then it is possible to identify internal feedback. Otherwise, internal feedback is invisible to external observation. When a Securities and Exchange Commission (SEC) accountant performs an in-depth financial audit of a publicly traded company in the United States, full access is required so that the inner workings of the company (aka: systems internal processes) can be identified and examined for adherence

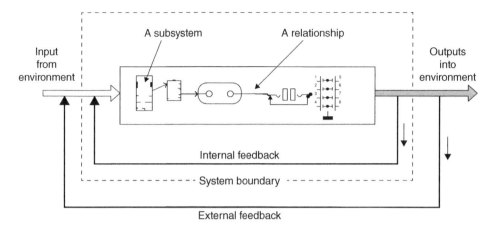

Figure 2.12   Structural organization of a system with boundaries.

to SEC regulations. In a similar fashion, ABET, Inc. requires such access to university academic programs in order to accredit systems engineering major programs.

Definition: *External* feedback is the feedback of a system that occurs in the environment outside of the system boundary, acting to alter inputs before they are delivered to a system. *Internal* occurs within a system boundary typically between system components.

A system "sees" external feedback in the form of its normal input. Without some means of external observation, a system is unaware of the external systems processes and interactions that are using or responding to some portion of its own output, integrating this output into their systems functions, and releasing modified outputs into the environment that becomes part of the system inputs. This underscores a very important point as to why systems engineers add value to customer programs even when the customer is extremely talented and knowledgeable at what they do: it always helps to have a fresh set of eyes on a problem if for no other reason than to provide objective clarity on systems operations.

Feedback complicates systems modeling and analysis. Modern systems, which are highly connected to other systems both to survive competition and to leverage cooperation, have designed processes enabling them to adapt to their surroundings as a means of attaining competitive advantage and improving performance. Systems that modify their output in a manner that actively responds to changes in their environment due to injection of other systems output are called *adaptive* systems. Adaptive systems tend to pose more of a modeling and analysis challenge principally, because the external (and possibly internal) feedback pathways need to be identified in the course of understanding how the system is operating.

It is also possible that while some open systems produce outputs that are simply transformed input as shown in Figure 2.12, this is not always the case. It is possible that the outputs of the system are simply there to allow the system to secure, through a cycle of events, more of the useful inputs it needs to survive.

In the conceptual system of Figure 2.6, the apparent boundary of the EM discipline would be the perimeter of the central, dark circle in the figure which sets it apart from the other overlapping systems.

While we may observe systems within a limited period of time, and subsequently gather data that we use to design, improve, or change systems, we must always bear in mind the fact that the system does not sit still and wait for us to finish what we are doing. A system is somewhat like an object in a pond. An extremely hard object like a glass ball would change little over time in this environment, yet the environment may radically change around it. Conversely, while the environment in a pond surrounding a saltine cracker may not change much, the internal structure of the cracker would indeed change over time. And so it is with systems.

Systems engineers concern themselves with how system elements interact both within and external to system boundaries at the time they are observing the system. They must also be aware of how these interactions and conditions affecting them might evolve in the time that passes between different team actions. For example, performance data for individual securities on the New York Stock Exchange would have to be continually updated in a systems decision problem concerning portfolio structuring. If this is not done, a potential investment strategy that would work at the time of data collection might not a week, month, or six months later. The sensitivity of these solutions to time is very large. The system dynamics are rapid, they have the potential for wide variation in performance, and they are filled with uncertainty. Any system representation and subsequent program planning should take these characteristics into consideration.

Chapter 3 introduces several techniques for modeling and analyzing systems and their effects when evolution is a consideration, whether the changes of interest are considered continuous or discrete. A continuous system is one whose inputs can be continuously varied by arbitrarily small changes, and the system responds to these continuous inputs with an output that is continuously variable. A discrete system is one whose inputs change in discrete amounts (e.g., steps in time, fixed increases in volume, number of people) that generally have a minimum size below which it does not make sense to reduce. Thus, the output tends to respond in a stepwise fashion as well [11].

There is an effect of time that is common to all modeling and analysis efforts but yet can easily be overlooked amidst all of the ongoing activities. The system environment, including stakeholders, evolves as a decision support project progresses. All elements of engagement will evolve as well including stakeholder priorities, value measures, stakeholder value return estimates, costs, available technologies, available alternatives, available information, project team members, competitors, threats, opportunities, risks, world state, and a litany of other first order changes that will have some level of effect on the end project results.

The key challenge with time effects is in determining the changes that are relevant, important, and will have a significant impact on the project effort and which ones can the team safely set aside. Let's discuss two here and leave the others for consideration as checks on learning.

Change elements associated with key stakeholders are generally handled by a consistent and frequent engagement strategy like that which we advocate for all systems projects. If a project engagement is handled in a removed fashion from key stakeholders—those with power, urgency, and legitimacy—some unpredictable amount of what the project team does will be overcome by events and will either be inaccurate or dismissed as irrelevant. The longer the execution time for a project, the greater the likelihood that this could occur. Consistent and frequent engagements with key stakeholders, especially those directly associated with the decision maker, will enable to project team to identify early indicators of potential changes and to be proactive in accommodating them.

Consistent and frequent engagement, often accomplished by including key stakeholders or their representatives on the project team, also nearly eliminates a need to "sell the solution" at the end of the project. By including these people on the project team, the ideas generated by team members and key stakeholders blend together extending a sense of ownership in results beyond the original project team. Selling isn't necessary because results are being developed by the very people would have had to sell the solution to.

The second change that is relevant and usually kept under close watch of a project team once modeling has commenced is the evolution of available alternatives and how they compete with each other as time progresses. As is discussed in Chapter 9, the truly competitive system alternatives

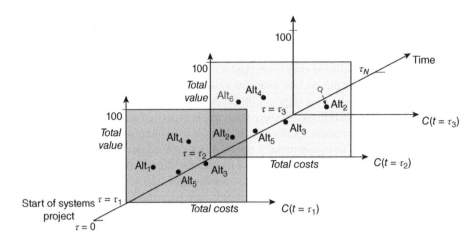

Figure 2.13   Alternative choice set evolution during a systems project.

comprise what is called a *choice set* of alternatives. These have made it through a screening process and have attained a level of value-cost efficiency that mandates they be considered as possible system solutions at any point in a system life cycle that the systems project applies. Figure 2.13 shows a conceptual illustration of this change effect as it relates to the deterministic tradespace created by applying the SDP when uncertainty is not explicitly modeled. A similar, but more complicated illustration applies in that situation as well.

Figure 2.13 shows a hypothetical deterministic tradespace result in which at time $t = \tau_1$ alternatives 1 through 5 ($Alt_1 \ldots Alt_5$) comprise the choice set C from among which a decision maker would be asked to select a system solution if this were being done at that time. The project started at time $t = 0$ and is currently at time $t = \tau_1$. Between times $t = 0$ and $t = \tau_1$, all the activities defined by the SDP stages leading up to Decision Making have taken place which involve, as a minimum, a subset of the change effects noted earlier.

The tradespace illustrated at the second time epoch $t = \tau_2$ shows that in the intervening time between τ_1 and τ_2, alternative 1 (Alt_1) has dropped from the choice set C and is no longer part of those being considered for selection, alternative 6 (Alt_6) has become part of the choice set C having gone through screening and evaluation against key stakeholder values and costs, and alternative 2 (Alt_2) has decreased in value and increased in cost. Among other possible considerations, what is immediately evident in this illustration is that had the choice set at τ_1 been retained for consideration at τ_2, Alt_1 might have been selected by the decision maker despite its unavailability, Alt_6 (a much better value for cost alternative) would have been missed, and the possible value-for-cost return shown for Alt_2 would have been incorrect. All of these potential outcomes specifically attributed to evolutionary time effects missed by the project team could be disastrous to the system project. An awareness of such possibilities by the project team develops a sensitivity to change effects and has the potential for the team to adopt and apply proactive best practices that contribute to success.

REFERENCES

1. Tsuei, J.J. (1978) 'Eastern and Western approaches to medicine,' *Western Journal of Medicine*, 128, pp. 551–557.
2. Burge Hughes Walsh Ltd. (2021). *Systems Thinking Tools*. Available at: http://www.burgehugheswalsh .co.uk. (Accessed 25 Feb 2022).
3. Rebovich, G. (2014) *Systems Engineering Guide*. Bedford, MA: The MITRE Corporation.
4. Jackson, M.C. (2003) *Systems Thinking: Creative Holism for Managers*. West Sussex, England: John Wiley & Sons, Ltd.
5. Pidd, M. (2004) *Systems Modelling: Theory and Practice*. Chicester, England: John Wiley & Sons, Ltd; 2004.
6. Haines, S.G. (1998) *The Manager's Pocket Guide to Systems Thinking and Learning*. Amherst, MA: Centre for Strategic Management, HRD Press.
7. Okes, D. (2009) *Root Cause Analysis*. Milwaukee, WI: ASQ Quality Press.
8. Shilling, M., Paparone, C. (2005) 'Modularity: an application of general systems theory to military force development,' *Defense Acquisition Review Journal*, 11 (3), pp. 279–293.
9. Pilling, T. (2020) *Major Capabilities Acquisition (Pre-Tailoring) Chart*. Fort Belvoir, VA: U.S. Defense Acquisition University.
10. Bullock, A. (2004) *The Secret Sales Pitch*. San Jose, CA: Norwich Publishers.
11. Sandquist, G.M. (1995) *Introduction to System Science*. Englewood Cliffs, NJ: Prentice-Hall.
12. Yeh, R.T. (1991) 'System development as a wicked problem,' *International Journal of Software Engineering and Knowledge Engineering*, 1(2), pp. 17–130.
13. Skyttner, L. (2001) *General Systems Theory: Ideas and Applications*. Singapore: World Scientific Publishing Co.
14. Abbott, E.A. (1952) *Flatland: A Romance in Many Dimensions*. New York: Dover Publications Inc.
15. Wasserman, S., Faust, K., Iacobucci, D., Granovetter, M. (1994) *Social Network Analysis: Methods and Applications*. Cambridge, England: Cambridge University Press.
16. Krackhardt, D., Krebs, V. (2002) *Social Network Analysis*. Scottsville, VA: Semantic Studios. Available at: http://semanticstudios.com. (Accessed 25 Feb 2022).
17. Pidd, M. (2003) *Tools for Thinking*. Chichester, West Sussex, England: John Wiley & Sons, Ltd.
18. Heylighen, F. (1998) *Basic concepts of the systems approach*. Principia Cybernetica Web. Available at: http://pespmc1.vub.ac.be/. (Accessed 25 Feb 2022).
19. Driscoll, P.J., Goerger, N. (2006) 'Stochastic system modeling of infrastructure resiliency,' ORCEN Research Report DSE-R-0628, New York: Department of Systems Engineering, U.S. Military Academy West Point.
20. Driscoll, P.J. (2006) 'Modeling system interaction via linear influence dynamics,' ORCEN Research Report DSE-R-0629, West Point, NY: Department of Systems Engineering, U.S. Military Academy.
21. Driscoll, P.J., Goerger, N. (2007) 'Shaping counter-insurgency strategy via dynamic modeling,' ORCEN Research Report DSE-R-0720, West Point, NY: Department of Systems Engineering, U.S. Military Academy.

Chapter **3**

System Representations

There seems to be a kind of order in the universe, in the movement of the stars and the turning of the earth and the changing of the seasons, and even in the cycle of human life. But human life itself is almost pure chaos.

—Katherine Anne Porter (1890–1980)

3.1 INTRODUCTION

Adopting a holistic perspective that embraces systems thinking sets the right mental framework to answer the first question asked in any systems engineering or systems decision support project: "What is the system that we are dealing with here?" The answer to this question is descriptive, portraying the current state of the system of interest as it is understood. Supporting this answer is the role of research and stakeholder interviews, which inevitably produce lists of internal and external system elements along with the relationships between system elements that define the system of interest.

Mapping these lists to a mental image is the very next thing that the human mind will do in an attempt to effectively summarize the current level of understanding in a neat and tidy picture or diagram. The form that this image takes depends on one's education and experience, but it is critical to every systems engineering or systems decision support effort. To make sure the project starts off in the right direction, all team members and key stakeholders need to have congruous mental models of the system of interest as the physical representation of this system will become the reference point for many activities that follow.

Decision Making in Systems Engineering and Management, Third Edition.
Patrick J. Driscoll, Gregory S. Parnell, and Dale L. Henderson
© 2023 John Wiley & Sons, Inc. Published 2023 by John Wiley & Sons, Inc.

A representation can become more than just a reference picture. It can be a base for modeling, leading to quantitative and qualitative insights into evident and underlying (hidden) characteristics of the system. Accomplishing this in a straightforward manner, generally requires representations that have a near one-to-one mapping between system elements and their interactions and the mathematical terms and expressions that translate this organization into a model. The ones discussed in this chapter have this property.

3.2 SYSTEM MODELING CONCEPTS

It is often said that *modeling*, the act of creating purposeful and accurate representations of some aspect of the real world, is more of an art than a science. While modeling certainly requires a healthy amount of creativity and cleverness at times, the fundamental process as it is represented in every discipline is described by a set of steps that have been refined over time by experience. These steps represent a repeatable pattern that can be tailored to some extent given the particulars of the situation you face.

Adhering to these steps and the principles guiding them gets you to a working model most every time. When applying these, it's helpful to think of cooking recipes rather than paintings and sculpture as an analogy to what you are doing. Following a recipe for sourdough bread will successfully yield sourdough bread, but it won't necessary taste like the sourdough bread you may have had in San Francisco. It takes customization and a holistic understanding of baking in the context of a particular environment (e.g. humidity, oven temperature stability, type of Dutch oven, yeast type and freshness, flour type and composition, steaming or not, timing, and so on) because that is what bakers do. They are system thinkers in this regard.

A model, like the recipe, produces correct results for the choices made: the steps followed (starter feeding, levain making, dough making), the parameters chosen (baking and proving temperatures, baking and proving times, equipment used), and the input provided (flour type, water, ingredients). When a recipe produces what was expected given all these, it passes *verification*. When the bread is served to friends or sold to customers and they enjoy it, the recipe passes *validation*. In other words, your approach to baking could be producing exactly the bread you expect, but the output needs to be compared or applied to the real world to determine its success. *Accreditation* takes place when an external reviewer tests your recipe at their location, determines it works, and formally states this fact. Complete success is achieved when your baking passes verification, validation, and accreditation (if available). The exact same thing applies to modeling.

Adjusting the model to more closely represent the real world behavior, phenomena, or system intended is a task called improving the *fidelity* of the model. Beyond beautification, improving model fidelity typically helps stakeholders understand its behavior and output because it more closely resembles the system and its setting that they are familiar with.

Modeling can get complicated. While it's easy to say "now you must validate your model," knowing which assumptions to relax and test (this can completely change the model type—changing the yeast or flour type can give you a completely different bread), what order to do this in (some model types are sensitive to this—vary the oven temp first? baking time? switch flour ratios?), and which parameters should be changed and whether simultaneous or sequential change combinations are appropriate are settled only with careful discussion. This is also true regarding improvements to input data by either gathering more or using a different source. Experience and best practices are the best teachers for knowing when to stop making changes because the model cannot get any better than it is.

Just as with playing a musical instrument or painting a picture, some people have more natural talent for modeling than others. However, everyone can improve their modeling skills with practice.

A note on data: All models need data. Data inform all the choices made when building a model, such as the type and value of parameters, whether a spreadsheet model possible or appropriate, the amount of data cleaning that will be needed (the data science side of modeling), whether censored or missing data needs to be accommodated, and so on. If questionable data is fed into a great model, the results are questionable. This doesn't mean that the modeling effort was wasted time, but it may mean that the team should pause the development effort to wait for better data.

A best practice when data are questionable is to use them everywhere you need it to build your model, but identify these locations to the client as placeholders for better data once it is available. This enables the systems team to discuss possible output displays with the client, explore effective information dashboard designs, examine information and insights the model is currently able to provide, plan follow-on changes to the model based on what the client or decision maker sees, and so on. In this sense, the model acts as a prototype for a number of modeling choices that must eventually be made.

This approach also commonplace when dealing with sensitive, proprietary, or classified data and the team wants to work on the model without the constraints that come along with securing the data. In such situations, the team should consider the option of never dealing with the actual data until very late in the systems decision support effort, and instead asking for representative sanitized data to use that is similar in characteristics and scale but not necessarily informative or compromising. For more involved modeling efforts than stand-alone models, such as intending to have a cloud-based analytical backend to a web-based client interface, making continual progress will be important to staying on schedule. As discussed in Chapter 10 when addressing uncertainty, be very careful when using time-lagged data or average data to create model parameters, coefficients, components, and such as it can easily become a source of problems.

3.2.1 What Models Are

In a systems decision support setting, a *model* is an abstract representation of the system of interest, or some aspect of its behavior. For example, a model of a supply chain system, also known as a logistic system, commonly takes the form of graphical information service (GIS) mapping software map overlays, directional dependency graphs, mathematical programs, and spreadsheets, all of which are abstractions of what the system is actually comprised of: people systems (unions, organizations, mechanics), machines (trucks, lifts, robotics, etc.), financial systems (billing, receiving, tolls, insurance), support systems (fuel, roads, maintenance, health care, waste management, legal), security systems (GPS tracking, event logging, surveillance, protection), and others. The abstract models created to represent these real objects and their interactive relationships and dependencies effectively inform business strategies that help supply chain companies to compete, survive, and prosper (or not) in the competitive environment they operate in.

A warning heard commonly in practice is that models are not the real world. While true, it is impossible to build a model without simplifying assumptions that leave some aspect of a system, its behavior, or its interaction with its environment out while focusing on that which is thought to be important. Be careful to not fall too much in love with your model no matter how complicated and elegant it may be.

Consider a model airplane. It could be a 1/72 scale plastic model that comes in a kit. The assembled model has some of the features of the real aircraft, such as the shape of the fuselage and the angle of the wings. However, it does not have a working engine or controllable flight surfaces.

Another airplane model is the ready-built radio controlled (R/C) airplane. It flies with the user controlling the elevator, ailerons, and speed. Electric ducted fans even replace jet engines! However, this model is also not the real aircraft. The weight and balance are different, the rudder is fixed, and the flight dynamics are different than the real aircraft.

Both of these are useful representations of the real aircraft system, but each has a different purpose. The model kit illustrates the shape of the fuselage in relation to wing angle. The R/C model demonstrates how the aircraft might perform while flying. Neither model is useful for predicting the maximum altitude or flying range of the actual aircraft. Their usefulness, as in all models, depends on what aspect of the actual system is being studied.

The *modeler* must choose what to put in and what to leave out of a model, as well as how to represent what is included. This is the essence of modeling. It can be very difficult to choose which key aspects of a system should be modeled and how to incorporate them into a workable model. A set of differential equations may accurately represent relationships among system elements, but this representation may not be useful if the equations cannot be solved in a practical amount of time.

3.2.2   Role of Models in Solution Design

The primary purpose of a model is to provide insights and understanding as to how an actual system design will or does perform. This information can then be used to design/re-design/replace the system in a way that meets its design purpose. It does this by delivering new functionality to stakeholders, or by offering improved and possibly optimized performance. The Wright brothers used a wind tunnel to gain understanding as to how a wing behaves; certainly a much better modeling choice than creating prototypes that some enthusiastic "volunteer" would attempt to fly. They used the information from wind tunnel experiments to design wings for their aircraft that successfully created lift.

There are three different types of solution design goals that modeling is used to inform: *satisficing*, *adaptivising*, and *optimizing* (Figure 3.1). A good question to ask is: "From whose perspective would one of these characterizations apply?" The answer, as is the case with almost all of the goals presented in this book, is the system stakeholders. The systems decision support team does not decide this for stakeholders because the choice has ramifications that stakeholders are both responsible and accountable for.

Satisficing is a term that comes from a concatenation of *satisfying* with *sacrificing*. Satisficing, as a solution design goal for an existing system, translates into seeking satisfactory system performance while sacrificing budget goals, advanced technology upgrade choices, performance possibilities, and so on. Satisficing is an overt and intentional tradeoff. For a new system, satisficing means that a good feasible design solution with acceptable intrinsic tradeoffs will be satisfactory to the stakeholders. Chances are that in such a design there are elements of the system that were

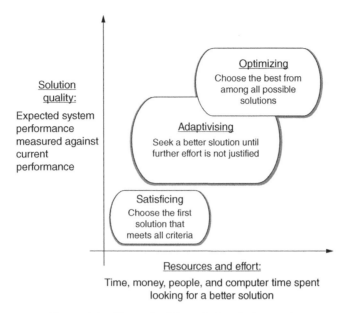

Figure 3.1 The tradeoff for solution design goals.

able to be optimized in some sense while others needed to deliver capabilities short of what was possible so that the system's purpose is achieved by intentional balance across all system elements. Making such a balance happen is the responsibility of system engineers.

The primary criterion for adaptivising design solutions is cost effectiveness although other criteria are possible as well. For existing systems, improving system performance is a commonly desired goal of stakeholders, but this goal is only pursued when it can be obtained at a reasonable cost. A small auto repair facility might be able to reduce the time it takes to diagnose automobile issues by purchasing the most recent specialty software, but may not be able to afford the training costs, repair delays, time consuming phone calls and emails to the software developer because of application errors, and increased salary burden associated with new personnel hires needed to operate the software on a daily basis.

It is important to keep cost separate from other tradeoff dimensions such as value return, not only for trade space purposes, but also because it is typically a factor that something creative can be done to relieve cost restrictions. What appears to be firm budget limit is often not so.

Satisficing accepts any solution that works reasonably well given the current situation. Adaptivising looks for "good" solutions among those that could work. In picking a walking route to the top of a hill such as Arthur's Seat in Edinburgh, Scotland, a satisficing solution could be to walk straight up. An adaptivising solution could be to walk a path others have made that leads up the hill. The tradeoff in this situation could be time or desired physical condition upon arriving at the top.

Optimizing solutions are at least as good and often better than all other solutions. They are the best according to a subset of targeted performance measures. However, they may require much effort or expense. If the goal is to get to the top of the hill in the quickest manner while being well-rested, the optimizing solution may be to land on top of the hill in a helicopter.

In recent years, stakeholders of all systems recognize that optimal solutions identified by modeling are informative but will rarely be implemented or worth the costs associated with trying to do so. This is because a single model cannot include all possible decision criteria, and some of the criteria intentionally left out are introduced after an optimal system solution is identified. When this happens, the overall goal retreats to adaptivising but with a better set of competing alternatives now that characteristics of a best solution are known.

The tradespace created by way of the systems decision process (SDP) accommodates all three of these goals using Pareto efficiency principles. Based on the information presented, decision makers or stakeholders select the alternative that meets their preference goal. Satisficing occurs by selecting system solutions that are feasible but not optimal in every category of value return. Adaptivising recognizes budget limitations and inviolate cost constraints when selecting a solution within the final choice set. And finally, optimizing takes place by choosing a Pareto efficient solution that represents the best (defined by the decision maker or stakeholders) among those included in the final choice set.

3.2.3   Qualities of Useful Models

Just as an artist must make choices when representing ideas or emotions in a tangible form, so a systems engineer must make choices when representing key elements of a system in a model. These choices are guided by seven qualifiers for good models that have emerged over time and are considered to be a comprehensive set of intentional choices that should be addressed while planning to build a model.

Parsimony. One of the primary characteristics of a model is the level of complexity intended to be represented. The principle of *parsimony* (also known as Occam's Razor) states that when choosing among scientific theories that make exactly the same predictions, the best one is the simplest [1]. Given several models of a system with comparable output in terms of the information provided, the best model is the simplest one. It is typically easier to understand in terms of its structure and interactions. It also may require fewer and more reasonable assumptions. For these reasons, parsimonious models are usually easier to explain to stakeholders.

Simplicity. Another characteristic is expressed by the relationship between the complexity of the model and that of the system it represents. The model's level of complexity typically increases in response to the system's level of complexity. This is not always the case, but a complex model for a simple system usually represents a lack of effort on the part of the modeler. It takes time, effort, and creativity to achieve simplicity in a model. A simple model of a complex system is truly a thing of rarest beauty. Moreover, a simple model inspires innovation better than a complex one because the human mind tends to drift towards thinking about design variations and possible alternatives after a person is convinced that they understand what they are looking at.

Accuracy. Accuracy is "the degree to which a parameter or variable, or a set of parameters or variables, within a model or simulation conforms exactly to reality or to some chosen standard or referent." [2] Here again as in the case of many disciplines, accuracy is not analogous to precision. An accurate but low precision model is useful. A precise but inaccurate model is folly. However, low accuracy models, often referred to as "quick and dirty" or "back of the envelope" representations can often be just enough to gain sufficient initial insight into a system's behavior.

Robustness. Robustness characterizes the ability of a model to represent the system over a wide range of input and parameter values. A model that is not robust only represents the system for a narrow range of inputs and parameter selections. For example, a weather model that represented local climate conditions only for a 30 minute time horizon under fair weather conditions would not be considered robust. Beyond this range, other models must be used or the structural parameters of the existing model must substantially change. This is not necessarily a problem. For example, if the narrow range of input values covers all of the alternatives from the Solution Design phase of the SDP, then it will serve its purpose. However, if the narrow range only covers a portion of the design space, other models will be needed, or a more robust model must be developed.

Scale. The scale of the model is an important characteristic that refers to the depth of detail incorporated into the model. Suppose an international policy model was created to represent how nation states interact. If all the complicated activities defining a nation state were represented by a single country element in a model, it would not have nearly the depth of detail as a model that decomposed nations into six major entities representing their health, financial, political, military, educational, and international trade systems. The scale selected for a model will follow naturally from the questions being asked about a system.

Fidelity. Fidelity is an overall characterization of how well a model represents the actual system of interest when observing the behavior and output of both. The more similar a model's behavior and output is to that of the system of interest, the higher fidelity it is. Higher fidelity generally corresponds to more complicated models, just as high-fidelity vinyl recordings are claimed to be truer to the actual sound produced by performer or group. Fidelity is an aggregate characteristic that brings together complexity (parsimony and simplicity), accuracy, robustness, and scale. A 100% replication of an actual system represents a duplicate or copy of the actual system.

Balance. Just as an artist must choose which aspects of an idea to convey and how to represent it in an art form, one must choose which aspects of a system are essential and how to represent them in the model. The modeler must balance and blend complexity (parsimony and simplicity), accuracy, scale, and robustness. (One definition of an expert is knowing what to ignore.) Among the choices the modeler must make is the type of model (or models) to use.

3.2.4 Building System Models

Just as there is no "correct" way to create art, there is no single "correct" way to create a model. However, much like learning the fundamentals of mixing oil paint colors, there are steps or processes that have been used in the past to successfully develop models and these are based on sound principles that help avoid missteps while ensuring that the modeling goal is achieved. This section presents one possible modeling process. Think of it is a list of things to consider while developing a model rather than a rigid step-by-step procedure. In fact, some of the steps listed in Figure 3.2 may need to be repeated several times in different orders as the model is developed.

Create a Conceptual Model Typically, a system model originates in a person's mind based on what is known about the system of interest. A *conceptual model* conceptual model of a system ties together important system elements and their interactive behavior among themselves and with major environmental elements. A conceptual model of a rocket launch is shown in Figure 3.3. A conceptual model tends to take form by way of diagrams and illustrations that logically represent the system of interest and a subset of its behaviors associated with the overall project goals. Once crafted, the project team discusses and critiques this model to determine if translating this

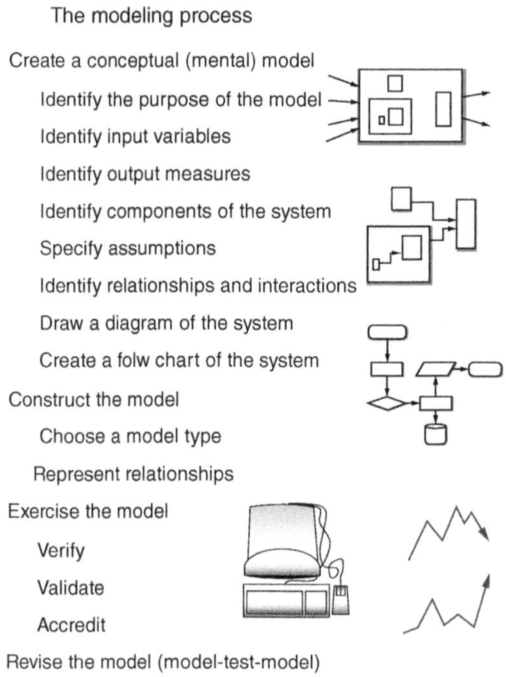

The modeling process
Create a conceptual (mental) model
Identify the purpose of the model
Identify input variables
Identify output measures
Identify components of the system
Specify assumptions
Identify relationships and interactions
Draw a diagram of the system
Create a folw chart of the system
Construct the model
Choose a model type
Represent relationships
Exercise the model
Verify
Validate
Accredit
Revise the model (model-test-model)

Figure 3.2 The modeling process.

Countdown procedures
Launch
First stage burn
Countdown failure
Staging and ignition
Second stage burn
Mission success
Burn failure
Staging and ignition
Third stage burn
Deploy payload
Staging failure
Mission failure
Deployment failure

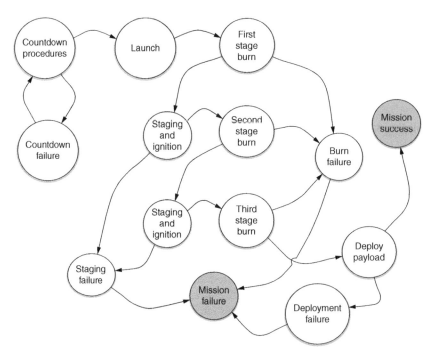

Figure 3.3 Rocket launch discrete event model.

concept organization into an actual model will meet the team's needs. Most conceptual models undergo many revisions before reaching a satisfactory form that enables a digital, mathematical, or physical model to be constructed.

Many of the items or steps in Figure 3.2 related to a conceptual model are discussed as part of the SDP (see Chapter 4). These include identifying system elements or components, specifying assumptions, analyzing data to identify relationships and interactions, and drawing diagrams and flowcharts for the system. Other items need to be considered as well. There are seven steps to address when building a conceptual model. These are:

1. **Identify the Purpose of the Model.** The first and most important consideration is the purpose of the model. Why is one needed? To predict how a specific system design will perform under various conditions? To replicate the current system behavior so proposed changes can be assessed in terms of cost and performance? To generate data that can be used to identify parameters for another model? To identify potential weaknesses in the current system design by approximating extreme stresses? Example settings that motivate purposes such as these are: How high should the flood walls be to protect the City of New Orleans from hurricane storm surges? How many satellites can be placed into space if two space shuttles or payload rockets are purchased? What is the worst-case response time to a distress call from manned lunar station?

2. **Identify Initial Assumptions**. There will never be a situation in which all the information, talent, budget, equipment, cooperation, and support needed to build an ideal system model will be on-hand at the start of a project. With modeling, information is typically the limiting factor at the start. Consequently, a starting set of assumptions must be made to avoid creating project delays. These are commonly referred to as *simplifying assumptions*. As a modeling effort and project moves along, new or more accurate information and resources become available, enabling some or all of the initial assumptions to be relaxed or eliminated, thereby improving the fidelity and applicability of the model.

3. **Identify Input Variables.** The purpose of the model affects the choice of model *input variables*. These could represent aspects of the design that a systems engineer can choose–sometimes called controllable or independent variables. Some of these directly follow from inputs to the system from outside its boundary or entities that flow from one system element to another. They can also represent choices made regarding parameters that can vary across a range of values, such as number of available flatbed trailers, water temperature, river depth, and so on. Input levels and parameter values are varied to create scenarios to explore "what if?" situations.

4. **Identify Output Variables.** Output variables represent what the modeler wants to learn from the model. In most models, outputs directly respond to changes in inputs and model parameter settings. Model outputs can also be more complicated, such as evolving graphical patterns created by sets of specific outputs.

5. **Identify Controls.** Identifying inputs, outputs, controls, and components (mechanisms) of a system provide the elements necessary to build in IDEF0 model. Of those, controls are often the most difficult to understand. The IEEE Standard for IDEF0 (IEEE Std 1320.1-1998) defines a control as "a condition or set of conditions required for a function to produce correct output." This may include a wide variety of conditions, including regulations, instruction manuals, or "trigger" events. IDEF0 models must have at least one control and at least one output, although typically a function will also include at least one input, which is transformed into an output by the function.

6. **Choose a Model Type.** Sometimes assumptions about the system lead naturally to a choice of model. If it is assumed that there is no randomness or uncertainty associated with system performance or behavior, then deterministic models are appropriate. The availability of data can also drive the choice of a model type. For example, lack of data for a certain input variable may lead to another model type that does not need that input. The type of data is also an influencing factor when choosing a model type. For example, if quarterly data are available, then a discrete-time model that moves in three-month steps would most likely be used. In addition, the goal of the model can be the primary factor in choosing a model type. For example, optimization models are likely to be used if the purpose is to find a best design solution among competing alternatives.

7. **Represent Relationships.** After the model type is chosen, the system relationships relevant to the goal must be represented in the model. Each type of model has specific ways of representing relationships. For example, system dynamics digital models use stocks, flows, and differential equations to link element interactivity. A linear model such as $y = mx + b$ relates m, x, and b using algebra. A Markov chain describing how a system moves from one state to another uses a state transition matrix to describe the movement of a system between various states. A graphical model uses directional arrows (arcs) to represent relationships that link system elements.

Interestingly, the same variable could be an input variable for one model and an output variable for another. For example, suppose a model is created to predict the probability of detecting an explosive device in a bag that is screened by Machine A and Machine B. An input value could be the detection rate for Machine B at an airport terminal. However, if the purpose of the model is to determine the detection rate for Machine B that maximizes the probability of detecting the device, then the detection rate for Machine B is an output variable. After the modeler understands the system and has created a conceptual model, the actual model can be built.

Construct the Model   One of the key decisions in constructing a model is choosing a type of model to use. There are several types of models including digital, physical, graphical, and mathematical. Even though these are distinct types of models, they are often used together.

Digital. Digital models are those created by and within specific software applications. These are arguably the most common models used to understand system behavior today, mostly because of their low resource costs (time, personnel, materials) and ability to rapidly assess complicated changes and alternative system designs. More and more of these are finding residence in network clouds which tend to have significantly higher digital storage, parallel and serial computing options, nearly unlimited computing memory, and advanced CPU and GPU capabilities not possible with all but the most expensive computers.

 When building analytical models in spreadsheets, a best practice is to not enter important coefficients and parameter values directly into the formulas used in cells (called *hard-wiring*), especially those that might change during sensitivity analysis and scenario explorations. Instead, where a coefficient or parameter is needed in a formula, create a separate section to hold these values and link each formula to the values it needs. In this way, adjustments can be made quickly when assumptions change, new information is obtained, or "What if?" explorations are performed.

Physical. Physical models involve a physical representation of the system, such as architectural prototypes for building designs, improved distributed armor for military personnel carriers, alternative crew capsule emergency evacuation systems for commercial rockets, and impact diffusion systems for electronic vehicle passenger compartments. Physical models are sometimes the only alternative when other options may not be practical. This was the case for many aerospace models until high-speed computers allowed real-time solution of mathematical formulas for fluid flow dynamics to replace, or reduce the number of physical wind tunnel tests.

Physical models need not always be miniature versions of the real system. Sometimes a physical representation is used to take advantage of a physical property. For example, soap film takes a shape that minimizes surface area. Before the age of computers, some optimization problems were solved using soap films and wire frames or glass plates with wooden pegs. Surprisingly, this technique is currently a topic of discussion concerning a fundamental research question related to computational complexity theory [3].

Sometimes physical models are based on analogies; something in the physical model represents a quantity of interest in the system. An interesting example of this is the analog computer. An analog computer uses electrical circuits to represent differential equations. Combinations of operational amplifiers, resistors, and capacitors are used to construct circuits that perform such mathematical operations as integration, differentiation, summation, and inversion.

Physical models have always had limited areas of application and digital models have further limited their use. However, they can still effectively demonstrate system performance. Seeing a truss design made out of small wooden toothpicks support a large weight can be pretty dramatic!

Graphical. Graphical or schematic models use diagrams to represent relationships among system components to represent feedback relationships or evolving conditions over time. These are used to uncover observable system structure, to illustrate potential system configurations, to highlight major dependencies between internal and external system elements, and other valuable system information. Sometimes these diagrams are the end product of the SDP and can provide an understanding of some aspect of the system of interest. Sometimes they are graphical precursors for computer packages that generate and execute code.

System dynamics software such as *Vensim PLE*® has this functionality. The relationships expressed in its stock-and-flow graphical diagrams are translated as differential equations inside the software application apart from user view. In other packages, such as the discrete-event simulation languages Simul8® and ProModel®, a graphical model represents the logical structure of system interactions between system elements over time (see Section 3.8). While a user concentrates on the details of the graphical layout, the underlying kernel runs extensive computations resulting in both numerical and graphical output.

Mathematical. Mathematical models use quantitative relationships to represent systems. Part of the challenge of constructing a mathematical model is translating from a spoken language or graphical diagram into an appropriate mathematical form. Sometimes this is straightforward, such as when using a directional dependency diagram to build a mathematical linear program as described in Section 3.4.1. And sometimes it takes very specialized talent to accomplish this translation.

Mathematical models can provide exact or approximate results as output. Approximations are models that provide results close to an exact solution. Although not as accurate as exact solutions, approximations are usually much easier to solve because the degree of approximation is chosen by the modeler. As an example, suppose we wish to determine the area under the function $f(x) = x^2$ between points a and b. The exact solution is:

$$\int_a^b x^2 dx = \frac{1}{3}x^3\big|_a^b = \frac{b^3 - a^3}{3}. \tag{3.1}$$

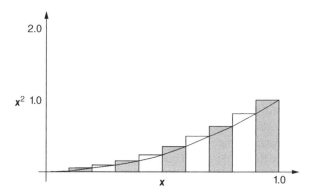

Figure 3.4   Area under the function $f(x) = x^2$.

An alternative is to use an approximate model to represent the area with a polygon. If this polygon was a trapezoid, the approximate solution would be

$$\left(\frac{a^2 + b^2}{2} \right)(b - a) = \frac{b^3 - ab^2 + a^2b + a^3}{2}. \tag{3.2}$$

If $a = 1$ and $b = 2$, the exact solution is 7/3 and the approximate solution is 5/2. The approximation error is 1/6. Using a different polygon would produce different approximations. For example, the area under the curve could be approximated as a rectangle (see Figure 3.4). Adding the area of each rectangle provides a different approximation than that obtained using trapezoids. In both cases, an advantage of using an approximation is that it did not require integration.

Mathematical models can be solved analytically or numerically. An analytical solution is a mathematical expression called a *closed-form* result. Exact numerical results are then obtained by substituting specific values into the expression. Numerical solutions are approximations that can be as close to exact as needed, depending on the time and resources available. Numerical approaches are useful when closed-form expressions for an exact solution are not available or are not practical.

Numerical solutions often use approximations, which can introduce approximation error. They may also have errors due to computation, such as when rounding or truncation occurs because of numerical precision settings in software. For example, consider the expression 3(4/3). Evaluated analytically, the result is 4. If it is evaluated numerically on a computer, the result is 3.9999999, because the computer cannot represent the exact value of 1/3.

Computers can be used to obtain either analytical or numerical solutions. Mathematical analysis software such as Mathematica® and Matlab® can solve many problems analytically. They also provide a variety of numerical tools for use in approximations.

3.2.5   Characteristics of Models

Models have*characteristics* that help systems engineers choose an appropriate model to use as it aligns to the characteristics of the actual system. Some of these characteristics are shown in Figure 3.5 and are discussed in the following text. These are discussed as exclusive choices simply for convenience. In practice, many models end up being a blend of types.

Descriptive versus Prescriptive. Descriptive models produce information regarding system behavior or observable traits. The results generated by *prescriptive models* are intended to inform stakeholders which course of action to adopt. A descriptive model of a Blue Origin payload rocket

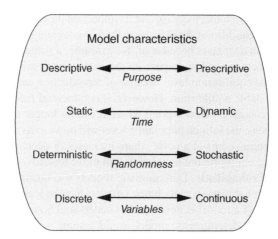

Figure 3.5 Model characteristics.

launch could represent the pre-launch, launch, and post-launch activities at a launch pad to compare the different possible locations for launch observers, security forces, emergency response teams, and launch monitoring cameras given the launch conditions created by the rocket (system). A prescriptive model of a rocket launch could be used to determine the proper mixture of rocket fuel and payload.

A descriptive model of automotive traffic on the Tokyo roadways during the Olympics could be used to unveil emerging congestion patters that occur over time. A prescriptive model of the same could be used to determine the timing for closing and opening on-ramp gates. Both models would pass verification if their output produced results as intended. Both models would have to be compared with real Tokyo traffic to pass validation.

Static versus Dynamic. Static models are intended to produce output that mimics a fixed value for a variable that changes in real life. Time, for example, is fixed rather than being represented as a changing variable. A static model of a marathon runner as a system might ask: "If a marathon runner's blood conditions are at these levels, what happens to muscle response?" Neither time nor distance is a variable in the model. In comparison, dynamic models are intended to represent a system's behavior over changing variables such as time, distance, gravitational attraction, or so on. A dynamic model of a marathon runner might ask: "As the race proceeds, what happens to the runner's glucose levels?"

Dynamic models can exhibit transient or equilibrium system behavior depending on the stability of a system over time. If a system is asymptotically stable, transient system behavior appears and then disappears at various times, settling down into one of a number of observable conditions (states) that no longer change as time goes on unless the model's initial settings are altered. These states are equilibria. It usually takes longer time settings in a model to observe equilibrium system behavior.

For example, when modeling salmon population in the Pacific ocean off the coast of Washington state in the United States, a dynamic model is used to understand how the population levels will change over time with fishing and other environment changes taking place at preset levels (model parameters). If the initial population is larger than the available food sources, then the carrying capacity of that location in the ocean is exceeded. The salmon population declines to a level at which it will stay over a long time horizon all other conditions being supportive of this. As the population increases because of reproduction, this increase and its impact on the environment are transient; the population will return to the equilibrium level because there is not enough food to sustain the higher population. If the population decreases because of, for example, a surge in commercial fishing or a one-time oil spill, this decrease and its impact on the environment are is transient; the salmon population will return to the equilibrium level because of reproduction and adequate food sources. This population level is a stable equilibrium. However, if commercial fishing is too extensive and sustained, the population can drop below a point where it can no longer climb to the equilibrium described. When this happens, the salmon population level will move to its other stable equilibrium: zero. An unstable equilibrium occurs at a point where increases or decreases in population levels determine which of the two equilibria the population will move towards.

Deterministic versus Probabilistic. Deterministic models use quantities that are assumed to be known with certainty. Probabilistic (or stochastic) models have at least one quantity with either uncertain or random values. If a model is developed to understand how beer sales will be affected over time by inflation rates, a deterministic model would assume inflation is set and known at a particular level (e.g. 6%). The output of such a model will be single point estimates for beer sales.

A probabilistic model would assume that inflation will change according to a pattern of increase and decrease likelihoods. This pattern is called an inflation distribution. The output of a probabilistic model are patterns of sales possibilities that have percent likelihoods associated with them, and these patterns are based on the patterns used to describe inflation variation.

Discrete versus Continuous. Whether a model is called discrete or continuous depends on the type of variables that are involved in the model. The variables in a model can be discrete, continuous, or a mixed combination of these two. Variables are *discrete* when the values they can assume are countable, and usually finite. In most cases, this means positive and negative integers, but discrete variables also can take on values from a finite set such as $\{red, blue, orange, green\}$ or $\{13.5, 21.908, 33, 11/4\}$. This becomes important when working with constructed scales.

Continuous variables can assume any values on an uninterrupted scale, which no matter how this scale is bounded or unbounded, means an infinite number of possibilities. Most commonly in systems modeling, continuous variables are used to represent practical quantities of interest such as costs, technical measurements, and reliability estimates.

 In modeling, information is always at a premium. Assumptions must be made when information is lacking. Maintain a list of these assumptions as the modeling process progresses. These assumptions form the basis for performing sensitivity analysis on modeling results later on.

3.2.6   Exercise the Model

Once a model is constructed, the modeler assesses how good the model is and how and when it is appropriate to use. This is referred to as exercising or testing the model. The major concepts related to this testing have already been introduced by way of the recipe example earlier: verification, validation, and accreditation. Here, the comparison is between the constructed model and the conceptual model.

Verification. Verification determines whether the constructed model matches the conceptual model [4]. That is, was the conceptual model correctly implemented in the constructed model? Verification is an inward focus on the model. Accomplishing this involves a small number of tests beginning with simple ones often referred to as 'sanity checks', and these are usually based on special cases where the behavior or condition of the system is known. For example, in a conceptual model of a rocket, if there is a limited payload and no rocket launch, there should be no satisfied demand for resupplies needed at a manned lunar base because the demand is dependent upon payload and successful launch. Does this happen in the constructed model?

Model verification checks typically involve testing known conditions with known results and testing extreme conditions for known results. If the model passes the simple tests, more complicated ones are tried until the model developer and accreditation agent are confident that the constructed model performs as the conceptual model states it should. Input variables and parameters may be varied over a range of values to determine the model's accuracy and robustness. If a conceptual model predicts that inventory will rise as demand decreases, does this occur in the constructed model? Actual data from the system of interest or a similar system may be used as input to the model and the output can then be compared with the actual behavior of the system of interest.

During this process, failure can be more enlightening than success. Parameters may need to be adjusted, external system elements may need to be added or deleted, or extra terms or components may need to be added to the model that were initially overlooked because of tacit assumptions being made that were not intended or specifically recorded. Sometimes the model does not represent the system well and a new type of model must be developed.

Validation. Validation determines whether the conceptual model (and constructed model if it is verified) appropriately represents the actual system [4]. Validation is an outward focus from the model to its environment. For example, a conceptual model may assume a linear relationship between thrust and speed; that is, speed increases proportionately as thrust increases. If the actual system includes both drag and thrust, then there may be times when speed declines because drag from the payload and atmospheric conditions are greater than the force generated by thrust. In this case, the underlying relationship might not be correct and the conceptual model is not valid.

Accreditation. Accreditation is an official seal of approval granted by a designated authority [4]. For systems decision support models, this authority is frequently the decision-maker or delegated technical representatives. Model accreditation signifies that the model has been verified and validated for an intended purpose, application, or scenario. Accreditation is more than just an administrative action. In a majority of instances, it is intended to represent the model user's interests or those who will depend on the model's output. All models and simulations used by the Department of Defense must be verified, validated, and accredited [4].

The process used to create a model and the testing involved in its development are both very important when judging a model. What characteristics were considered for inclusion in the model? What assumptions were made while developing the model? What value ranges or conditions were tested? The answers to such questions build confidence in the model's capabilities.

3.2.7 Revise the Model

As has already been discussed, test results may cause changes to a developing model. This linkage is sometimes called the *model-test-model* concept. The idea is to use knowledge gained about the system or the model to continually revise and improve the conceptual or constructed model. This is also the idea behind rapid model development techniques used in design thinking [5]. Revising the model is always an option and typically happens quite frequently during model development.

The Wright brothers' experience flying gliders and using data from others helped them to know what they wanted to measure and what they wanted to vary. Lift and drift were their output variables. The different types of wing shape and aspect ratios were their input variables. The wind tunnel gave them the means to do it. They spent over a month experimenting with the wind tunnel. This corresponds to verification and validation. They wanted to be confident that their model would yield useful results and they understood the conditions under which it would. At some point they had a discussion and agreed they were ready to collect data. This corresponds to accreditation. Once they were confident of how to use their model, they systematically explored the system by trying different wing shapes and aspect ratios.

3.3   SYSTEMIGRAMS

A systemigram is a graph diagram used by systems engineers to communicate to stakeholders the level of understanding held by a systems decision support team regarding major connections between the system of interest and its environment. Similar to a context diagram [6], it is a powerful and useful tool that can make complex or complicated systems understandable. The word systemigram is a combination of the words ***systemi***c and dia***gram***.

Two popular software applications for creating systemigrams are SystemiTool, a free web-based or standalone application distributed and maintained by the Systems Engineering Research Center (SERC) at Stevens Institute of Technology (https://sercuarc.org/serc-tools), and Plectica (www.plectica.com), a commercial tool developed by Plectica and offered with graduated pricing. The systemigrams shown in this chapter were created with SystemiTool.

A systemigram starts as an initial diagram created shortly after completing a significant amount of research and investigation into the system of interest's current state. This becomes a key diagram discussed during early meetings with decision makers and other stakeholders to communicate the team's understanding of the system and its relationship to its environment. Revisions occur as more complete information is provided by stakeholders and ongoing background research.

A benefit provided by systemigrams in comparison to other representations is that a single 2D diagram can capture and illustrate multiple types of interconnections and dependencies internally between system elements and with external environmental elements as well. This is done by way of the connection labels assigned to the directional arrows that show an action statement (or verb) that functionally connects two objects (nouns). In several other system representations, a single type of relationship defines connections (e.g. information flow), and the system structure associated with this one relationship is represented (e.g. physical connections). If a second type of connection is desired, then a second representation would be needed. Not so with a systemigram, partly because a systemigram attempts to tell a reasonably complete story regarding the system of interest.

Several support projects that the authors have undertaken ended early with success when a high quality systemigram was created and the client (and decision maker) realized that the system visualization effectively reframed their understanding of the organization's operation and purpose. Their previous "big picture" framing which had been effective for many years was showing indications that it was no longer sufficient to support day-to-day decisions relying on business sense and intuition because the organization's operations had become more complex—a greater number of elements and a greater number and type of interconnecting relationships.

3.3.1   Systemigram Rules

While creating an effective and aesthetically pleasing systemigram certainly involves creativity and a sense for organization, there are a small number of rules that should be followed for every systemigram.

The starting point is establishing a purpose statement for the system of interest along with any environmental elements that have important interactions and dependencies with the system. The system decision process (SDP)'s environmental factors that surround the four phase circles act as a checklist to cue one's thinking about system interconnections and dependencies that originate from outside the system boundary or are dependent on some direct or indirect system output.

There are six basic steps for creating a systemigram:

1. Create a *mainstay* connection of nodes starting with the system represented as a node in the upper left and ending with a node in the lower right of the diagram that represents the goal, purpose, or objective for the system. The initial system node should consist of only its major components. Additional system elements can be added as needed after the mainstay is created. The mainstay conveys the system purpose, acting as a backbone for the diagram around which additional elements are connected as they are identified.

2. Nodes must contain noun phrases because these represent system elements or objects. Ideally there should be 15–25 nodes used in a single systemigram, mostly because the diagram is created in landscape on 8.5 × 11 inch paper. However, as the number of nodes and connecting links increases beyond this, the diagram becomes more and more difficult to comprehend as a whole.

3. Links should contain verb phrases or verbs that describe how two nodes are related. Unlike other representations, systemigram links are typically one-directional between two nodes.

4. Nodes should not be repeated, although an initial diagram resulting from brainstorming or other ideation techniques might repeat nodes temporarily. These repetitions are eliminated by refining the systemigram before moving on.

5. Links should not cross-over one another. As noted by Rechtin [7], the ratio of actual links to the total number possible should be about 15%, which is held to be the optimal ratio of interfaces in a system relative to how many there could be.

6. Optionally use colors to distinguish classes of objects (nodes) to improve the systemigram's readability. This is useful when using the SDP environmental factors to trigger ideas (e.g. legal, safety, political, and so on).

As an example, consider the ongoing transition from internal combustion automobiles to one of the four types of electric vehicles: battery electric vehicle (BEV), plug-in hybrid electric vehicle (PHEV), hybrid electric vehicle (HEV), and a fuel cell electric vehicle (FCEV) [8] (see Figure 3.6). The majority opinion currently held by consumers is that for non-commercial transportation a BEV offers the best alternative to reduce carbon emissions and help mitigate or reverse global climate change. Almost without exception, BEVs have a reputation for having no detrimental impact on the environment based on their operational characteristics without a combustion engine. The primary purpose for a BEV system follows from this belief and is shown as the mainstay of the systemigram in Figure 3.7. This is the popular story associated with a BEV. Once the mainstay is created, engaging in some expansive systems thinking suggests that this reputation is based on a system boundary that ends with the vehicle itself, rather than including other system interconnections across the BEV boundary into its environment. Adding these interconnections begins to unveil a system that is more complicated than just a BEV itself.

Building on the BEV mainstay systemigram, considerations external to the BEV are used to create an initial systemigram shown in Figure 3.8. Notice that the expanded systemigram's BEV system node still only shows three of its major components, limiting consideration of BEV system elements that could be connected to other external systems. If the BEV system node was made larger to include its drive train, suspension system, passenger compartment, and other elements, categorically more connections would be identified and illustrated on the systemigram.

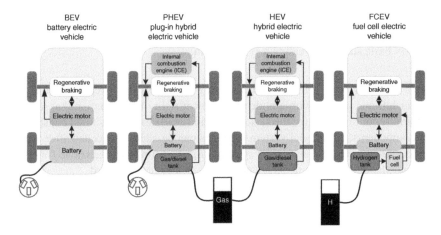

Figure 3.6   Types of electric vehicles and their major components [8].

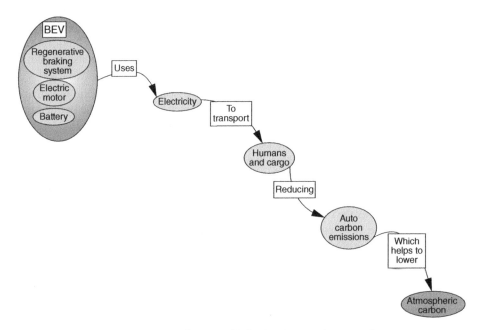

Figure 3.7   Battery electric vehicle (BEV) systemigram mainstay.

There is a practical limit to a systemigram's size, which seems to vary depending on the system of interest. Since a systemigram represents a "big picture" of a system's interconnections along with the system purpose on a mainstay, it would be better to limit the depth rather than the breadth of interconnections when expanding the mainstay. In this way, the resulting systemigram captures a shallow, yet comprehensive view of just how widespread of an influence that a system has on its environment (and vice-versa), better facilitating stakeholder identification and other follow-on activities.

Notice that the node "Electrical Grid" appears three times in the initial diagram shown in Figure 3.8, violating the "no duplicate nodes" rule. Also, the nodes "Roadside Service (AAA)" and

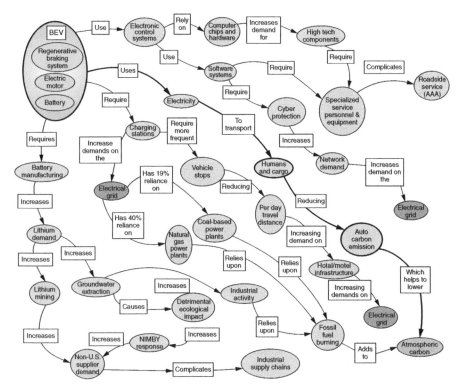

Figure 3.8   Battery electric vehicle (BEV) initial systemigram.

"Industrial Supply Chains" do not currently have connecting paths to the end node "Atmospheric Carbon." Revising this initial systemigram would include rearranging and redefining nodes and connections so that the systemigram would contain no rule violations.

3.4   DIRECTIONAL DEPENDENCY (D²) DIAGRAMS

A directional dependency diagram for a system, or (D²) diagram for short, is a 2D graphical representation of a system used as a stepping stone to further modeling. Follow-on modeling could be mathematical—as in logistic optimization models, structural—as in dependency structure matrices (DSM) as described in Section 3.5, or simulation—such as system dynamics simulations. In all cases, a D² diagram contains system elements as nodes that are determined by the systems decision support team to be within the current system boundary. If the system boundary contracts or expands, the system's D² diagram will lose or gain nodes and connections, respectively. The reason this is so is because the D² diagram and subsequent modeling are typically intended to expose some underlying system structure information that is not identifiable by observation.

A characteristic that sets D² diagrams apart from systemigrams is that D² diagram links describe a single connection type, whereas systemigrams can have multiple types of interdependencies relating nodes via links. Because of this characteristic, D² diagrams are analogous to influence diagrams, information flow diagrams, logistic network diagrams, network flow diagrams, and architectural diagrams, to name a few. Information, influence, energy, and matter are good examples to think of

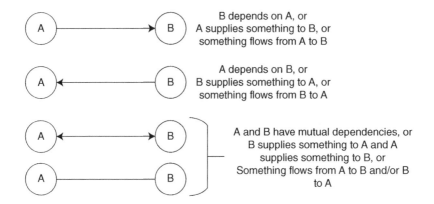

Figure 3.9 Directional dependency diagram relationships.

when working with D^2 diagrams, although this list is certainly not all-inclusive. Moreover, a D^2 diagram can be further enhanced by adding weights, costs, and other numerical quantities to each connecting arc.

Since D^2 diagrams are a jump off point for further modeling, it is important that the directed graph (*digraph*) property is maintained, so that a link with a single arrow head (arc) drawn to connect node **A** to node **B** means that some substance is identifiable as passing from node **A** to node **B**, and vice-versa. For some connections, such physical connections, the dependency relationship frequently is bi-directional. If node **A** is physically welded to node **B**, the arc between node **A** to node **B** would have an arrowhead on both ends, or no arrowhead on either end signifying bi-directional dependency. In mathematical terms, such a link is called an *edge*. Figure 3.9 shows each of these cases.

Creating a D^2 diagram is straightforward and most of the information needed to get started can be identified by answering very fundamental questions concerning the system of interest. All that is necessary is to adopt a systems thinking perspective. With this, some questions answerable by research and stakeholder interviews could be:

1. What does this system do? What output does it produce? What material, energy, information, or influences flow into and/or out of the system? Where do these come from?
2. Does the system, its behavior, and its output align with the human culture and/or politics existing in the system's environment?
3. What impact does this output have in its environment?
4. Is the output intended to generate profit? Provide security for someone or something? Enable human activities to occur (e.g. transportation, communication, medical services, etc.)?
5. Who outside of the system is depending on this system's output for what they do? What do they use it for?
6. Are there any safety considerations associated with the system, its behavior, or its output? What regulations or laws oversee or regulate the system's behavior?
7. Who or what outside of the organization that owns the system loses when the system succeeds in its designed purpose? Does the system openly compete with these entities? Does it threaten the status quo in the environment within which it operates?
8. What critical technologies or supplies does the system depend on to function properly? Where do these come from now and in the foreseeable future?

Then, objects identified by these questions become potential nodes; any two nodes that are related by the single connection type are connected by an arc or edge that defines the dependency direction(s) that exist between them, and keeping notes as to how/why these two are connected for discussion and revision purposes.

3.4.1 D² Diagrams into Math Representations

Once constructed, a D^2 diagram becomes a directed graph. This type of graph enables mathematical techniques from graph theory and social network analysis to be applied to expose a system's underlying structure. Optionally, the graph can be further transformed into a matrix structure for analysis. One such matrix structure is an *adjacency matrix*.

An adjacency matrix is a way of representing the relationships between system elements (nodes) in a 2D array. It is a square matrix in which the number of rows and columns are equal. For an unweighted D^2 diagram (one with no numerical labels placed on the links), if there is a first order connection between system elements i and j, then the numerical value placed at location a_{ij} in the matrix: row i, column j will equal 1. If there is no connection, it will equal zero. Two-way connections between system elements (nodes) indicated by an edge with no arrows or a two-headed arrow create matrix entries equal to 1 that are a reflection across the main diagonal extending from upper left to lower right position in the matrix. Which representation is used in the D^2 diagram – two-headed arrow or no arrows – is simply a modeling choice made for neatness and clarity. The numerical entries placed entries along this main diagonal are equal to zero. Figure 3.10 shows the correspondence between a small, unweighted D^2 diagram and its corresponding adjacency matrix. The same placement rules apply when other numerical values are being used (a weighted D^2 diagram, or weighted digraph).

This matrix form can be recreated and analyzed in spreadsheets as a matrix or a dependency structure matrix (DSM), exported as comma delimited files (*.csv) for import into other software tools, and/or directly entered and analyzed into specialty software such as *Mathematica* and *Gephi* to bring an expanded number of analytical options to examine the underlying system structure.

A second translation from a system representation into mathematics that is widely used occurs in the context of optimizing logistic systems. These diagrams are converted into continuous linear programs whose objective is to minimize shipping and handling costs while meeting demands. In operations research, this type of problem is known as a *minimum cost network flow problem* [9]. The mathematical formulation for this type of problem has been around since roughly 1968, with many revisions and techniques for addressing unusual and special cases developed since then. Logistic systems such as supply chains, package delivery, container shipping, and others which have physical presence are evident and plentiful. However, modern computer networks function as logistic systems as well. The "locations" in these systems can be physical, such as storage arrays,

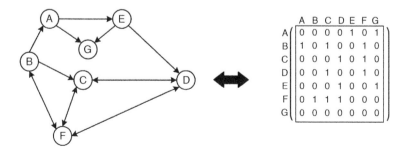

Figure 3.10   D² diagram and its adjacency matrix.

network servers, and routers locations. Or they can be virtual locations such as those defined in virtual networks and subnets.

From a systems perspective, each system element within a logistic system has a dependency with another system element. For both physical and virtual logistic system, these dependencies are directional, again conforming to a D^2 diagram. Some sort of resource is provided by the overall system, and this resource is typically controlled by a supplier who faces defined costs associated with delivering product or services to meet demands. This is an example of a flow dependency. The items flowing from one location to others could be material items, energy, information, data, services, and other objects created by a subset(s) of elements and distributed across its system pathways to internal and external elements typically owned and operated by someone else, although this does not have to be the case.

A *linear program* is a mathematical model that has two specific mathematical elements: an *objective function* expression that is the target expression being minimized or maximized, and a collection of inequality or equality expressions called *constraints* that, if properly defined, will allow solutions to be found that don't violate any of system's flow limitations or its operating conditions and will keep the software algorithms designed to solve these models from running off to infinity in either direction, positive or negative. When solutions are found that satisfy the entire collection of constraints, they are referred to as *feasible solutions*. The best feasible solution(s) are called *optimal solutions*. A linear program is an example of an optimizing, deterministic, mathematical model.

Searching on the web for the terms "linear program" will produce a wonderful amount of very informative explanations and examples. It is no exaggeration to say that this type of model is by far the most well-known and widely used of the various types of mathematical programs. For logistic systems projects, familiarity with this type of mathematical model is an absolute must. The following example illustrates the idea of translating (mapping) diagrams into mathematical expressions, assuming that a single type of material flow (i.e. packaged food boxes) is defining dependencies between locations. When the situation is more complicated and several types of resources are flowing between locations, the problem is known as a multi-commodity network flow problem [10].

As an illustration of how a D^2 diagram maps directly to mathematics, suppose that a single nonprofit food supplier has three locations at which it creates and packages high-quality meal boxes for charitable distribution to needy families: locations A, B, and C. The system boundary for this food operation includes the facilities and people at these three sites. Again, this could change, but initially let's use it as such. Each food location has a limit on how many meal boxes they can make and supply to distribution points during one time period, for example a week. These are shown to the left of each food packaging location.

The five locations that distribute these meal boxes to families (locations 1, 2, 3, 4, and 5) depend directly on the output of the food packaging company. These locations depend on the flow of packaged meals from the supply locations to satisfy their needs. The specific number of weekly meal boxes they need (demands) are shown to the right of each distribution location. When there is a distribution location that does not depend on a specific food packaging location for its meal boxes, no connecting arrow appears between sites. Figure 3.11 shows a D^2 diagram for the connections between system elements.

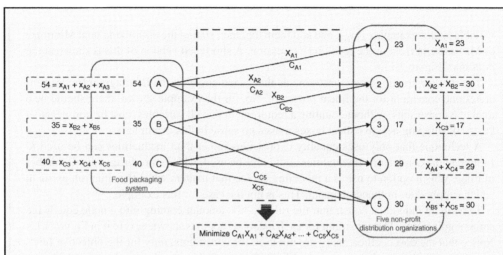

Figure 3.11 Example D² diagram for logistic system with associated mathematics.

Since the meal boxes are given away and not sold, the food supplier currently pays all shipping costs. The problem that the nonprofit food supplier has is to determine how many meal boxes it should ship from each supply location A, B, and C to each distribution site (1, 2, 3, 4, and 5) in a way that minimizes the overall total cost while satisfying each site's demands.

Suppose total supply available (adding up the three food packaging locations' capacities equals 129) equals the total demand (adding all five distribution locations' demands equals 129), and that there are enough connections between supply and demand locations so that the resulting mathematical model is guaranteed to have at least one feasible solution. This second point is a bit subtle: demand cannot be met if supplies cannot get to the locations that need them. So, there must be enough possible connections coming out of A, B, and C to enable this to happen. In some properly built logistic models, it can be frustrating to correctly translate the system diagraph representation into a linear program's expressions and then into a spreadsheet or other application only to get a response that says the problem is not feasible, meaning that some limitation represented by a constraint is being violated. There are methods for adding dummy variables to each of the constraint expressions that essentially absorb constraint violations like this while identifying which supplies cannot get from supply to demand locations [11].

On diagram in Figure 3.11, there is a variable x_{ij} associated with each connection signifying the unknown amount of meal boxes that should ship along each connection (arc) starting at location i and ending at location j (the flow direction indicated by each connecting arrow). Similarly, there is a numerical parameter c_{ij} labelled on each connection signifying the cost per meal box for shipping from location i and to location j, making this an example of a weighted D² diagram. Not all of the cost labels are shown to keep the illustration easily understandable. At this point, all D² elements are labeled and the digraph can now be translated into a linear program. This means that an objective function expression and the supply and demand constraints corresponding to this diagram need to be created.

To form the objective function, remember the rule: "arcs generate the objective function expression." Multiply each connection's cost label c_{ij} with its unknown shipping amount variable x_{ij}, for example $c_{A1}x_{A1}$, and add them together, stating the optimizing goal Minimize or Maximize in front of the resulting expression. A shortened version of this is shown at the bottom of Figure 3.11.

The rule for creating flow constraints is that "each circle on the D^2 diagram (node) generates one constraint for the linear program." So, for the example shown, there should be a total of 8 constraints, without counting a requirement that all variables must be non-negative ($x_{ij} \geq 0$); shipping negative meal boxes makes no sense in this example.

A technique that only uses equality expressions rather than inequalities can be used to formulate the constraints. Inequalities could also be used, which introduces a small number of rules. Which option to use is a modeling choice that matters when the situation exists in which supply does not meet demand. This is not the case for this example.

To form an individual constraint, the rule is: "the amount coming into a node equals the amount going out." The constraint for each location (node) is shown next to it in Figure 3.11. Notice that the cost coefficients c_{ij} are not used for constraints, only for the objective function. Constraints are only concerned with placing restrictions on the number of meal boxes shipped along each connection (arc): x_{ij}. The objective function has to have associated cost coefficients with shipping amounts x_{ij} because it will be the expression that will be minimized using some software application.

The full linear program model for this example is then:

$$\text{Minimize} \quad \sum_{i=A}^{C} \sum_{j=1}^{5} c_{ij}x_{ij}$$

$$
\begin{aligned}
\text{Subject to:} \quad & x_{A1} + x_{A2} + x_{A3} = 54, \\
& x_{B2} + x_{B5} = 35 \\
& x_{C3} + x_{C4} + x_{C5} = 40 \\
& x_{A1} = 23 \\
& x_{A2} + x_{B2} = 30 \\
& x_{C3} = 17 \\
& x_{A4} + x_{C4} = 29 \\
& x_{B5} + x_{C5} = 30 \\
& x_{ij} \geq 0 \quad i = A, B, C \quad j = 1, 2, \ldots, 5
\end{aligned}
$$

Depending on the software used, this linear program is entered into the application and solved using some efficient algorithm, producing an optimal plan for shipping meal boxes to each distribution location at minimum cost.

The link between two elements on a D^2 diagram defines an *interface* of some kind, one of the most important system features throughout its life cycle. System interfaces take many forms depending on type of elements being connected and what relates them in this way. Nowadays, human–computer interfaces are the ones that easily come to mind since computing devices of all kinds populate day-to-day life, and humans are readily identifiable users of these devices. By engaging in systems thinking, more varied system interfaces become apparent, revealing system elements and elements in the environment outside of a system boundary that interact with a system of interest, and not necessarily by technical means. Laws and regulations, other biological species, oceans and air, ambient noise levels, atmospheric temperature, human cultures and religions, and many others could contain elements whose system interactions are relevant to an ongoing project and will therefore have directional interactions with the system of interest.

Interface design is an important topic in systems engineering, one that is beyond the scope of this book to address in a comprehensive manner. An entire field called *Human Systems Integration* exists just to develop, aggregate, apply, and share best practices. Getting interfaces correctly designed, developed, and coordinated is a task that lies at the heart of systems integration. Done properly, system elements interact to produce system behavior that matches what is intended. Shortcomings in interfaces create dissatisfaction among stakeholders by imposing limitations on system performance or system sustainment activities. Human system interfaces have been shown to be a major factor influencing whether or not an end user is going to accept the system as-is [12].

3.5 DSM AND DMM MODELS

To understand the role of DSM and domain mapping matrices (DMM) in systems work, it is necessary to address some design basics. There are two fundamental approaches to design: algorithmic and axiomatic [13]. Both are deliberate, engaging processes with specific purposes in-mind. Algorithmic design is used when repeatability is desired. Given the exact same input, a successful algorithm produces the exact same output over and over to the degree of accuracy required. Creating a manufacturing line comprised of a system of intricate machines, computers, and personnel would require algorithmic design because once started on a particular product identical output is desired.

Axiomatic design is at the heart of the architecture of homes, buildings, bridges, landscape, and other physical objects. Axiomatic design engages activities in a structured fashion, but does so with innovation and creativity in-mind, hoping that for a specific design project if multiple organizations are given the exact same inputs, very different outputs will result. It is no surprise then that axiomatic design is at the heart of system architecture as well. Given the exact same stakeholder needs, wants, and desires that creat the same functional and nonfunctional requirements, two companies will develop very different systems that meet stakeholder expectations.

Figure 3.12 shows the four domains of axiomatic design aligned in chronological order from left to right. Comparing these to the SDP phases explicitly reveals why system decision making supported by the SDP and axiomatic design are compatible. The Customer domain is focused on understanding and capturing stakeholder needs, wants, and desires. The Functional domain translates requirements created during activities in the Customer domain into statements regarding what any successful system design must do to meet Customer requirements. These are called a system's *major functions*. A system that successfully performs its major functions is said to deliver its functionality to the end user. The Physical domain involves activities such as value modeling, cost analysis, design selection, subsystem integration, prototyping, test and evaluation, and final design. This stage readies the design for manufacturing and assembly. The Process domain defines how the system will be created, which could be a manufacturing or some other process depending on the type of system of interest. For the SDP, this equates to the Solution Implementation phase and the activities it involves.

3.5.1 Dependency Structure Matrix (DSM)

During problem definition and conceptual design, a *dependency structure matrix* (DSM), or equivalently a *design structure matrix*, is a useful representation for investigating the structure of a

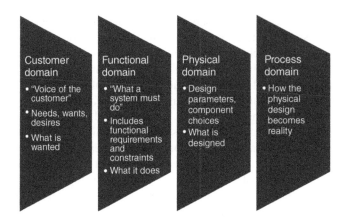

Figure 3.12 The four domains of axiomatic design.

system, for understanding layered interconnections that exist or are planned to exist between system elements, and for accomplishing tasks that involve interface management. DSMs have seen considerable use for software and hardware engineering design processes as well as applications associated with parametric analysis and modular design [14]. Originally developed for applications in process modeling [15], DSMs have since been used for modeling and management of products [16], supply chain improvements [17], stakeholder value networks [18], and knowledge management [19], among others.

A DSM is a square matrix in which the diagonal cells typically represent system elements (components, people, process activities) and the off-diagonal cells represent dependencies, interfaces, and interactions between these elements. The matrix's row and column labels are identical and in identical order starting at the upper left position. DSMs are a single domain matrix model, meaning that it represents activities or component/subsystem architecture within one of the axiomatic design domains. Most applications involve binary DSMs in which a dependency between two system elements is indicated by a 1 or zero (no dependency). Numerical DSMs have off-diagonal entries containing a number, which are used to indicate the strength or intensity of the connection. The main diagonal is typically not used because these represent dependencies of a system element on itself. Table 3.1 lists several types of interactions that create connections between system elements.

In their early years, DSMs were primarily a tool for engineering management focused on identifying and tracking interactions between low-level hardware and software modules, components and devices [20]. In more recent years, DSMs have been used by systems engineers

TABLE 3.1 Typical Interactions Used in DSMs.

Component Type	Interaction Type	Description
Hardware	Spatial	Identifies needs for adjacency between two elements; associations of physical space and alignment
	Energy	Identifies needs for energy exchange between two elements
	Information	Needs for data or signal exchange between two elements
	Material	Needs for material exchange between two elements
People	Level of Detail	Sparse (documents, email) to rich (face-to-face, models)
	Frequency	Low (batch, just-in-time) to high (on-line, real time)
	Direction	One-way or two-way
	Timing	Early (preliminary, incomplete, partial) to late (final)

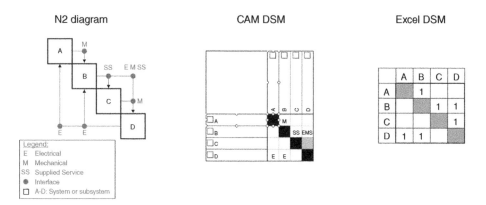

Figure 3.13 N2 and DSM representations for a four-element interaction.

and designers to represent a system's architecture and to unveil system structure characteristics not readily observable, such as modularity clusters and opportunities to restructure processes and teaming arrangements. The National Aeronautics and Space Administration (NASA) uses a DSM approach to identify interactions or interfaces between major system elements from a systems perspective, calling them by a different name: an N2 diagram (or equivalently, an (N × N) interaction matrix) [21]. The label 'N2' highlights the square configuration intended by the diagram. This is similar to a DSM whose row and column elements are identical and identically arranged.

Figure 3.13 shows a comparison between an N2 diagram and two DSM diagrams, all representing the same four-element system and its connecting relationships. There are differences between an N2 diagram and a DSM that can be observed in this figure: the N2 diagram is shown in a floating image format that isolates interactions, types, and elements; a DSM is portrayed in matrix form, either as a stand-alone matrix or more typically in spreadsheet form and its interactions can be indicated as binary (present or not) without calling out the type of interaction visually, or by cell-coding dependencies with various labels as done with the Cambridge Advanced Modeller (CAM) DSM shown [22]. Appendix B contains information regarding how to obtain CAM and getting started with CAM once downloaded. For Excel, multiple interaction types such as those shown in the N2 diagram could be indicated by color coding each non-zero/non-empty cell on a DSM and inserting a reference legend as required.

An input assumption – row or column – determines where connections are designated in a matrix representation, how dependencies are interpreted in a DSM, and whether a correct matrix multiplication results when manipulating a binary DSM. With row input, column elements depend on output or interaction coming from row elements. In the CAM DSM shown in Figure 3.13, the non-zero entry in row A, column B means that system element B depends on system element A via a Mechanical (M) type connection (interface). Similarly, element B depends on element D through an Electrical (E) type connection (interface).

An important representation capability that DSMs provide is highlighted in an N2 diagram by the use of a legend: multiple interaction types through interfaces can be represented on a single DSM. In Figure 3.13, the N2 legend highlights this fact as does the CAM DSM when the field editing option is chosen. A binary DSM in matrix form is assumed to represent a single type of dependency unless specified in a legend.

Another DSM feature to note is that the main diagonal entries from upper left to lower right are not used. Dependencies are not indicated in these cells based on an assumption that it is not necessary to show that a system element is dependent upon itself to properly function. If further detail is required regarding the internal dependencies of a single system element, a subsystem DSM is created and the appropriate internal connections are identified.

DSMs can also be created directly in software applications designed with systems engineering and design purposes in-mind. These often have a selection of DSM and graph algorithms imbedded in them, recognizing that encoding a DSM is the start point for system analysis purposes. For this book, an application called *Cambridge Advanced Modeller* (CAM) is used to highlight this feature. CAM is a powerful software application developed by the Engineering Design Centre (EDC) at the University of Cambridge, England.

It is also possible to craft custom Visual Basic (VBA) code as executable modules in Excel to accomplish DSM analysis, since VBA is integrated into all of the Microsoft O365 applications. Mirshekarian created an Excel macro-enabled file called *DSM Program* Version 2.1 for this purpose [23].

Row input is usually assumed when representing dependencies between system elements or process tasks in a DSM. Row input maintains consistency with D^2 diagrams in which the i, j subscripts on arc variables x_{ij} mean that something is being provided *from* row element i *to* to column element j, and that column element j is dependent upon row element i for this. In DSMs, a non-zero connection shown in a matrix cell corresponding to location row i, column j: $a_{ij} = 1$, indicates the same directional dependency relationship.

Activity DSMs are used to represent time-based ordering of tasks that occur with system processes, such as those associated with projects, project management, acquisition programs, manufacturing and assembly, case file review, and others. The connections between tasks illustrate movement or feed forward in a process (iteration) and movement backwards or feedback (rework). These DSMs are usually created starting with a reference D^2 diagram or any diagram whose circle elements (nodes) are tasks and arcs connecting them show directional dependency.

Figure 3.14 shows a D^2 diagram for a 7-task process designed to progress from task A to task G in alphabetical order and its equivalent DSM. This D^2 diagram contains feed forward and feedback

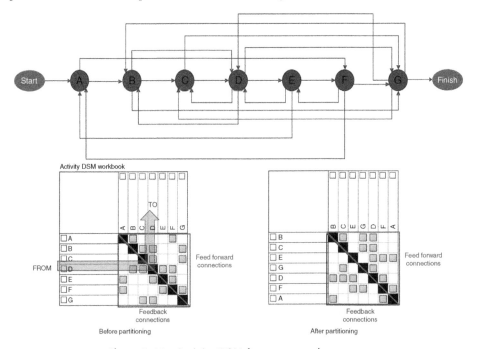

Figure 3.14 Activity DSM for a seven-task process.

connections that represent task skipping and rework to previous tasks. The same type connections are shown in the upper and lower triangular regions of the activity DSM, respectively. The superimposed arrow shows the "row to column" or "right and up" dependency direction, illustrating the row input assumption.

The analytical goal for activity DSMs is to rearrange and reorder tasks to eliminate process feedback, yielding a pure upper triangular DSM with feedback loops made as small (tight to connecting elements) as possible. The algorithm for doing this is called *sequencing* (www.dsmweb.org/sequencing-a-dsm) in some DSM applications and *partitioning* (www-edc.eng.cam.ac.uk/cam/documentation) in others. For complex systems and systems with substantial feedback, sequencing and partitioning are likely to only partially achieve this goal without eliminating or splitting process tasks. A good example is the righthand DSM in Figure 3.14 which has had partitioning applied to it. The task list shown in row entries has been reordered and feedback loops have been pulled inwards towards the main diagonal and linked elements as a result of a partitioning algorithm being applied to the matrix.

Component DSMs are commonly used to represent interfaces between system components and communication or information flow between people and devices in an organization. They are constructed in the same manner as activity DSMs except that system elements are listed as row and column labels arranged in the same order instead of tasks. Component DSMs are static representations of system elements and their interactions. Multiple types of interactions can be represented in a single DSM if some type labeling is used. Table 3.1 shows several different types of interactions for hardware and people products.

An analytical goal with component DSMs is to group the system elements into potential *modules* with relatively high internal interaction and relatively low external interaction. The algorithm for doing this is called *clustering*. For hardware systems, modules represent components and subsystems that are more compact and more easily replaceable because components outside of the module have fewer connections to the components within a module. For process DSMs, clustering into modules suggests potential team restructuring to co-locate individuals who have intensive information interaction with teammates.

The example that follows is a DSM created to show the physical dependencies between major aircraft system elements for the AgustaWestland AW101 helicopter.

Binary DSM Example: AW101 Helicopter. A simplified binary DSM system representation for the 19 major subsystems involved with the AW101 Helicopter is shown in Figure 3.15. Using row input in this case, each of the light grey colored locations represents a physical dependency between the row and column system elements shown (a one). For example, the highlighted row element called "Flight control systems" is providing some physical entity to the column element called "Avionics." This means that the Avionic subsystem is dependent upon the Flight Control Systems. Consequently, a light grey box was placed in the DSM location corresponding to this connection. Since no other information appears, it is clearly a binary DSM. Where no light grey square appears, no physical dependency exists between the row and column elements corresponding to this empty location (a zero).

A number of insights are immediately evident. There are three system elements upon which nearly every subsystem depends: Avionics, Bare fuselage, and Cables and piping. In the event of a failure in one of these subsystems, an immediate direct impact will be felt by a majority of the AW101's subsystems where a connection is indicated in the DSM.

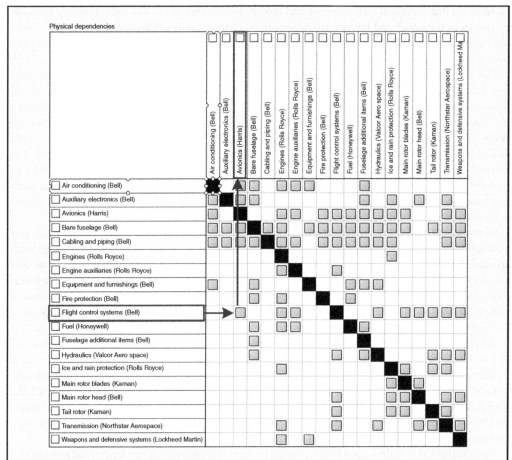

Figure 3.15 A binary component DSM showing physical dependencies for the AW101 Helicopter.

Some subsystems, such as the Transmission, has fewer dependencies on it (6). Here, however is an illustration of a binary DSM limitation: the intensity of the connection or its criticality is not shown. With no other system knowledge, all the physical dependencies are equivalent, which is generally not the case. A revision of this initial DSM could use a different CAM workbook option better suited to convey both the presence of a dependency and a level of importance to system performance, such as a DSM with dependency strength (Integer) and direction (Positive, Negative). See Appendix B for details.

In component DSMs, clustering can help provide insights into opportunities to create modules of system elements combined in such a way to make their connections less vulnerable to disruption. In activity DSM's, the results produced by clustering can inform options such as co-locating teams, or combining process steps to reduce the total number of individual tasks.

Example: Clustered AW101 DSM. In Figure 3.15, hypothetical aerospace companies have been added to the element labels to show that they are responsible for the subsystem design and manufacturing. With this information appended to the system element labels, the results of clustering shown in Figure 3.16 can provide additional management insights. The clustering algorithm attempts to identify sets of connections that can be pulled closely to the main diagonal, ideally forming a completely filled-in square, such as the one shown for the Main rotor blades and the Main rotor head.

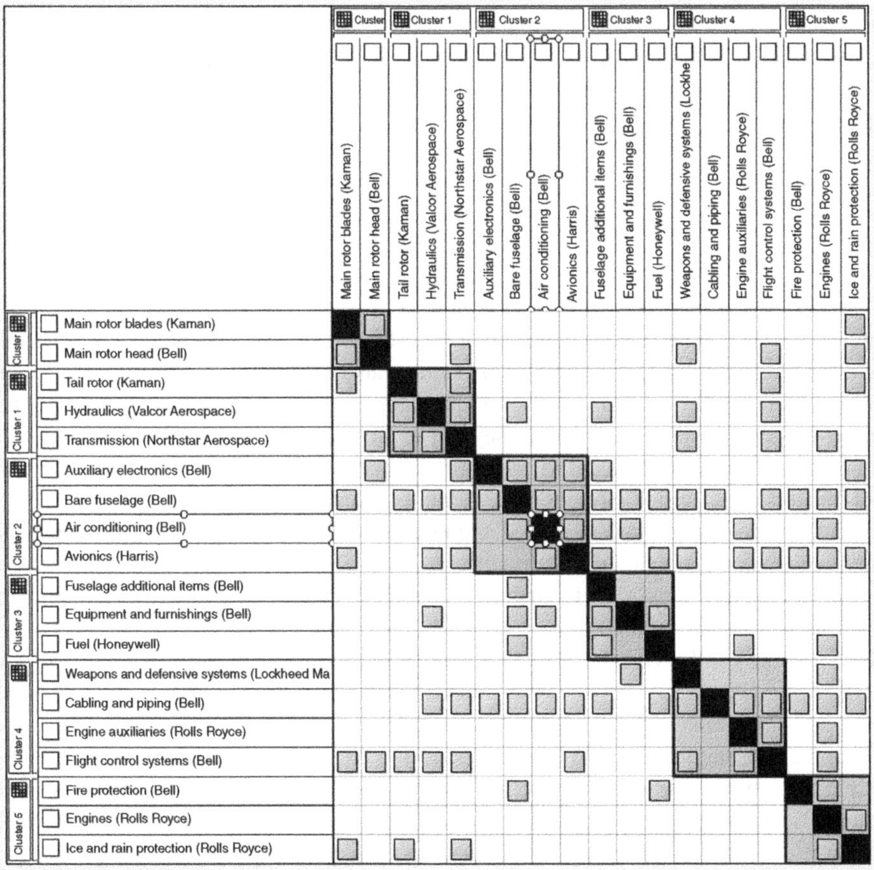

Figure 3.16 Clustered AW101 DSM showing potential component modules.

In this example, six (6) clusters have been identified as indicated by the shaded squares running down the main DSM diagonal from the upper left to the lower right of the DSM. By adding the company names to the subsystems, possible options can be considered for teaming or contracting, co-locating in some sense the different subsystem development teams base on the level of dependencies noted. By itself, this DSM is merely suggesting this as a possibility. In reality, far more factors are taken into consideration before such a venture is undertaken.

For the purposes of uncovering a systems underlying structure, DSMs are a better choice than N2 diagrams mainly because once created in software, they can be manipulated, analyzed, or exported as column separated values (CSV) files for import into other software applications whose mathematical and graphics tools greatly enhance analytical opportunities. Three such applications illustrated here are the commercially available Wolfram *Mathematica*, the open source and freely available software called *R*, and *Gephi*. Casting a binary DSM into an adjacency matrix in a common first step to doing this.

3.5.2 System Adjacency Matrices

A DSM's shape naturally leads to mathematical matrices and the many tools associated with linear algebra and network analysis. Since the main diagonal of a DSM is typically not used, zeroes are placed along the main diagonal to complete the matrix. For example, consider the binary matrix for the Excel DSM in Figure 3.13. In matrix form, this DSM becomes:

$$DSM_{4 \times 4} = \begin{bmatrix} a_{11} & a_{12} & a_{13} & a_{14} \\ a_{21} & a_{22} & a_{23} & a_{24} \\ a_{31} & a_{32} & a_{33} & a_{34} \\ a_{41} & a_{42} & a_{43} & a_{44} \end{bmatrix} = \begin{bmatrix} 0 & 1 & 0 & 0 \\ 0 & 0 & 1 & 1 \\ 0 & 0 & 0 & 1 \\ 1 & 1 & 0 & 0 \end{bmatrix}$$

A single DSM is a static system representation. This implies that each dependency indicated by a non-zero entry in a DSM is a direct dependency, also known as a *first order* dependency. A matrix like the one earlier is analogous to an *adjacency matrix* because a first order connection between two system elements means that they are as close as possible to each other with regards to the dependency; they are adjacent to each other. Once in adjacency matrix form, a number of structural insights into a system are possible, including estimating system modularity.

Figure 3.17 shows both the AW101 DSM and its equivalent adjacency matrix. In both instances, row input is maintained so that a non-zero entry in cell (i, j) indicates a directional dependency of column j on row i; equivalently, that something is being provided from the row i system element to the column j system element.

System structure can be visualized in a number of helpful ways in *Mathematica*. Appendix D contains the commands used to produce the graphs in Figure 3.18. *Mathematica* identifies potential system modules as *communities* using the same clustering characteristics as described earlier for DSMs. Graph clustering in *Mathematica* is a specialized form of clustering that uses graph structure to identify communities of nodes that are closely linked. In graph terminology, a *community* is a cluster of nodes (system elements) with a relatively high density of internal connections. In technical terms, it is a set of nodes with high modularity. Communities may overlap and they may also be nested, such that higher-level communities are formed from more localized communities. This highlights the importance of perspective: the spatial arrangement level chosen as the basis for representing a system graphically will influence the underlying structure revealed by graphical and numerical analysis.

What appears to be a somewhat balanced dependency structure in Figure 3.18(a) has three identifiable communities (modules) appearing in Figure 3.18(b). *Mathematica* has graphics options for displaying node labels for improved clarity, if desired. Both of these graphs are static; they do not have an automatic means for dynamically exploring the system structure through rapid re-visualization. The open source software *Gephi* was designed to do provide this functionality, and to easily interrogate the system structure using network measures that have meaningful interpretations when applied to systems.

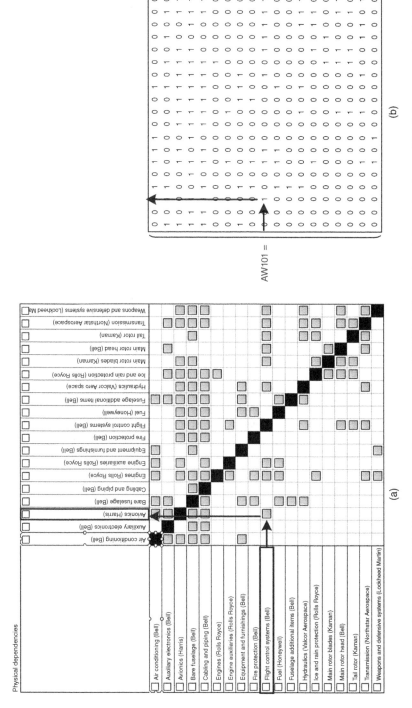

Figure 3.17 Translating the AW101 DSM into an adjacency matrix. (a) DSM with row input dependencies and (b) Adjacency matrix for DSM with row input.

113

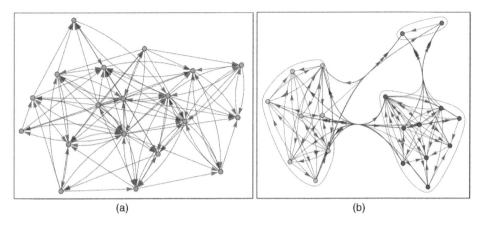

(a)   (b)

Figure 3.18 AW101 digraph and module clustering. (a) AW101 DSM as an AdjacentGraph and (b) Potential modules via CommunityGraph.

Network Structures The open source and free software called *Gephi* provides a unique capability for examining system structure based on very powerful visualization and network analysis methods. Not all network measures logically apply to system structures, but several do, including modularity, bridge nodes, shortest (directed paths) between system elements, average graph diameter, and others. The shortest directed path between two system elements (nodes) can be used to estimate change propagation to other system elements, especially when connections have associated time characteristics. Bridge nodes can indicate high dependency system elements that may present single points-of-failure.

For systems projects, *Gephi* offers an enhanced functionality beyond static plotting. It allows a user to dynamically interact with the layout in a host of ways not easily done with other applications, which is especially useful when seeking to understand a system's structural features. Here, a brief discussion is presented to illustrate several basic features. Appendix D contains information on how to obtain and install the software as well as useful "Getting Started" guidance and recommendations for helpful reference material freely available on the web.

Once a DSM is created in either CAM or Excel, the DSM can be exported and saved as a comma separated values (*.CSV) file that can be imported directly into *Gephi* software programs for exploration. Figure 3.19 shows the AW101 DSM as a CSV file on the left, and the initial *Gephi* workspace after importing the CSV file. The node labels have been toggled on to show the system element agreement between the two representations. In addition to visualization tools, *Gephi* has a large suite of powerful network science routines that can expose important system structure such as modularity, diameter, degree, minimum spanning tree, and others.

The AW101 DSM was imported as a mixed type of directed and undirected connections so that symmetric connections between two system elements would be represented as two arrows instead of an edge with no arrows. The upper right window indicates that the DSM has 19 system elements and 109 connections. A number of editing tools that affect the visualization appear on the left and bottom of the workspace.

System Modularity: SMI Once a system is represented as a DSM and translated into its adjacency matrix equivalent for export into other software programs, the system's level of modularity can be estimated, a helpful feature supporting system design and component/subsystem

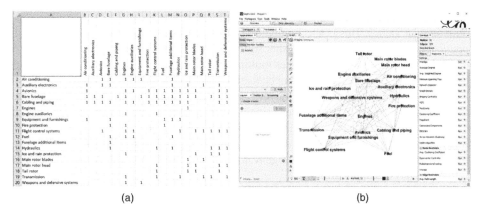

(a)   (b)

Figure 3.19 Microsoft Excel CSV file and network layout after importing into *Gephi*. (a) CSV file with labels and (b) *Gephi* layout with CSV imported.

replacement planning. Modularity is of interest in systems decision making because it can be a stakeholder requirement that translates into a value measure needing a numerical estimate. *Mathematica* and *Gephi* accomplish this based on algorithms for identifying graph communities.

A different approach was developed by Hóltta-Otto et al. [24] based on mathematical computations that leverage a numerically decreasing pattern present in an adjacency matrix's non-zero *singular values*. In linear algebra, singular values are the square roots of the eigenvalues of a matrix. These values represent structural elements associated with a matrix, so finding an association between these and system structure was a clever insight.

 The geometric interpretation of an $n \times m$ matrix A's singular values $\sigma_1, \sigma_2, \ldots, \sigma_n$ is that they represent the length of the n major axes of an n-dimensional ellipsoid created by multiplying AB, where the matrix B represents an n-dimensional unit circle (its axes of symmetry have length equal to 1) whose axes of symmetry are expanded and compressed by being multiplied by the singular values.

In terms of information, if a 9×9 matrix A has 5 non-zero singular values, it has 5 independent dimensions of information describing its structure (5 independent rows or columns in the matrix); it's missing 4 dimensions. This condition is known as being *rank deficient*, where rank is defined as the number of non-zero orthogonal (independent) dimensions. A matrix's rank equals the number of non-zero singular values it possesses. Image compression leverages this very interpretation to reduce an image's resolution to send over small bandwidth mediums.

The SMI approach is based on the idea that a matrix's singular values represent information related to its structure. Integral systems have very tightly coupled system elements. This characteristic corresponds to a matrix representing the system that has a small number of large, non-zero singular values. This means that the information content required to describe a tightly coupled integral system's connectivity is concentrated in fewer singular values than modular systems. A modular design requires more information to describe its connectivity completely, which translates into its matrix representation having more non-zero singular values, generally smaller in magnitude than that of an integral system.

A technique from linear algebra called *singular value decomposition* (SVD) is used to identify a matrix's singular values. This is a technique best left to a software application to perform, which *Mathematica*, routines in *R*, *Matlab*, and other software application accomplish well. SVD factors a real or complex matrix A into three matrices multiplied together: $A = UDV^T$, somewhat analogous to the way that a single number, say 24, can be factored into the product of one-dimensional terms: $24 = 2 \cdot 3 \cdot 4$. The middle matrix in this factorization, D, is a square matrix (i.e. same number of rows and columns) containing the non-zero singular values of A ordered by magnitude from high to low along its main diagonal starting in the upper left corner. This matrix is called a *diagonal matrix*. All other entries of D off of the main diagonal are equal to zero. Singular values also are the positive square root of the matrix A's eigenvalues, another mathematical element used in other engineering and physics applications.

This singular value modularity index (SMI) is calculated as:

$$SMI = 1 - \frac{1}{N \cdot \sigma_1} \sum_{i=1}^{N-1} \sigma_i(\sigma_i - \sigma_{i+1}) \tag{3.3}$$

where σ_i represents the ith singular value for the adjacency matrix associated with a system's DSM and N represents the number of system elements represented in the DSM. The first singular value, σ_1, has the highest magnitude. The SMI expression changed slightly in a later paper. This second version included a continuous exponential term that approximated the discrete singular value decreasing pattern modeled previously in Equation (3.3) [25]:

$$SMI_{new} = 1 - \frac{1}{N} \left(\arg\min_\alpha \sum_{i=1}^{N} \left| \frac{\sigma_i}{\sigma_1} - \exp^{-[i-1]/\alpha} \right| \right)$$

The SMI in this new expression is equal to the quantity σ^*/N that minimizes the error between an exponential decay and the actual decay structure across all singular values observed and modeled earlier. For use with DSM's, the earlier non-exponential SMI provides a more direct approach and will be used here.

The dependency (i.e. coupling) structure of a system (i.e. the number and pattern of non-zero entries) will determine how many singular values will be non-zero. The SMI value is theoretically bounded between 0 (highly integral) and 1 (highly modular). However, the actual SMI maximum and minimum values depend on the size of the DSM.

The SMI calculation is most useful when its results are expressed as a relative percentage on a spectrum between the SMI of a fully integral DSM and the SMI of a fully modular DSM all having the same size (*NxN*) as the DSM for the system of interest. A fully integral DSM is created by filling all entries of an *NxN* matrix with 1's except for 0's on the main diagonal. A fully modular DSM is created by having only entries immediately reflected on both sides of the main diagonal of the same size matrix with 1's and all other places including the main diagonal with 0's. Figure 3.20

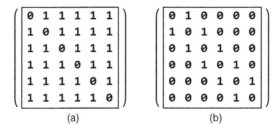

(a)   (b)

Figure 3.20 SMI bounding matrices for 6 × 6 DSM. (a) Fully integral and (b) fully modular.

illustrates these two SMI bounding matrices using 6×6 adjacency matrices. The next example illustrates this process with the AW101 system.

SMI Calculation Example: AW101 The AW101 system has 19 system elements. The singular values for the AW101's adjacency matrix shown in Figure 3.17 were identified by entering the adjacency matrix into *Mathematica*, applying the command `SingularValueDecomposition[N[AW101],19]` or `SingularValueList[N[AW101],19]` to the matrix. There were 19 non-zero singular values produced the set: 7.5253, 3.50937, 2.98288, 2.54021, 2.21623, 2.18772, 1.95859, 1.8162, 1.66825, 1.26593, 1.04766, 0.958673, 0.766056, 0.579295, 0.475827, 0.425994, 0.338195, 0.153658, 0.0292232, indicating that a large number of singular values having sets of similar magnitude are needed to describe the structure of the DSM, providing a rough indication that the system design as represented in the DSM is more modular than integral. Substituting these singular values into Equation (3.3), yielded an SMI(AW101) = 0.741957.

Applying the same procedures to the 19×19 fully modular SMI bounding matrix produced 18 non-zero singular values: 1.97538, 1.97538, 1.90211, 1.90211, 1.78201, 1.78201, 1.61803, 1.61803, 1.41421, 1.41421, 1.17557, 1.17557, 0.907981, 0.907981, 0.618034, 0.618034, 0.312869, 0.312869, 0. These values correspond to: SMI(Mod) = 0.941464.

Similarly, the fully integral SMI bounding matrix produced 19 non-zero singular values with most of the information concentrated into σ_1: 18.0, 1.0, 1.0, 1.0, 1.0, 1.0, 1.0, 1.0, 1.0, 1.0, 1.0, 1.0, 1.0, 1.0, 1.0, 1.0, 1.0, 1.0, and SMI(Int) = 0.105263.

To estimate the percent modularity of the AW101 DSM:

- Calculate the length of the interval between the bounding matrices' SMI:

$$0.941464 - 0.105263 = 0.836201$$

- Calculate the percent modularity as the proportion of the overall interval consumed by the modularity index of the AW101 DSM:

$$\frac{0.741957}{0.836201} \cdot 100 = 88.7295$$

This SMI result suggests that the current AW101 DSM element dependencies represent a system with 88.7% modularity, which is consist with earlier analyses based on the AW101 DSM.

Several other mathematical options are available for computing a modularity index based on system element coupling characteristics [26].

Estimating Change Propagation While easiest to think of adjacency as physical proximity, it can also be extended to cases where material, energy, information, or data is flowing between elements inside and/or outside of a system boundary. The effect of changing one element then propagates via these connections to other elements in the system of interest.

To identify how soon a subsystem failure or change might affect other system elements, one could start at a row location originating this effect, follow to the column element directly connected to it, re-enter the DSM at the row element identical to this column element, and repeat until a blank entry is encountered in the DSM. However, potential effect chains and loops within system representations can be identified, thanks to the use of the powers of the binary interactions matrix such as the DSM above [27]. Raising this matrix to the nth power yields a numerical matrix (with integer values) in which a non-zero element a_{ij} corresponds to the number of possible change propagation paths (chains) from element i to j, the length of which being exactly n.

For example, raising the previous matrix to the 3rd power, thereby seeking to identify any possible change propagation paths of length 3 in the system yields:

$$DSM_3 = \begin{bmatrix} 0 & 1 & 0 & 0 \\ 0 & 0 & 1 & 1 \\ 0 & 0 & 0 & 1 \\ 1 & 1 & 0 & 0 \end{bmatrix}^3 = \begin{bmatrix} 1 & 1 & 0 & 1 \\ 1 & 2 & 1 & 1 \\ 0 & 1 & 1 & 1 \\ 1 & 1 & 1 & 2 \end{bmatrix}$$

Potential loops can be identified by examining the diagonal elements of the resulting matrix, and potential chains can be identified using the non-diagonal elements. From these results, $a_{44} = 2$ indicates that there are 2 paths of length 3 starting at row element D and ending at column element D (indicating 2 loops since for a DSM the row elements are identical to the column elements): $D \rightarrow A \rightarrow B \rightarrow D$ and $D \rightarrow A \rightarrow B \rightarrow D$; 1 path of length 3 starting at row element C and ending at column element B: $C \rightarrow D \rightarrow A \rightarrow B$, and so on.

When project risks are used as system elements in this representation, a DSM becomes a Risk Structure Matrix (RSM) whose binary connections indicate causal interactions between risk elements [18]. The fact that a possible dependency has been identified between $Risk_i$ to $Risk_j$ means that when $Risk_i$ occurs, there is a chance of $Risk_j$ occurring as well as the consequence (impact) of $Risk_i$. Modeling risk stochastically, this chance is a conditional probability $0 \leq P(R_j|R_i) \leq 1$. Deterministically representing risk dependencies in this manner assumes that $P(R_j|R_i) = 1$ if a cause–effect relationship such as this exists.

Similar to fishbone diagrams in root cause analysis [28], which are used to show cause–effect pathways to a system failure, a risk structure matrix (RSM) representing cause–effect relationships between risks enables these chains to indicate how cause–effect events propagate to other risks, introducing a cascading of risk events. Identified chains and loops in DSMs and RSMs are then prioritized by decision makers, according to likelihood and severity.

3.5.3 Domain Mapping Matrix (DMM)

Systems development involves groups of different teams, in different locations, that can easily be performing work in different phases of development. There is always a risk that products and information created by one team will be lost or not considered when work is being carried out by another team. Even when only a single team is involved, project complexity can cause the same effect. A domain mapping matrix (DMM) facilitates synchronization of domain/phase products and activities to reduce the risk of this loss occurring [29].

In comparison to a DSM, a DMM is typically a multiple domain representation used primarily as a systems engineering management tool to illustrate or track connections or dependencies between different objects from distinct axiomatic design domains. When DMMs are used within a single design domain, they are used in the same fashion: to map between different development items. DMMs have been used for mapping personnel to tasks, tasks to resources, activities to design parameters [30], individuals to skills, activities to deliverables [22], or more commonly in a hardware or software development mode to bridge between design domains [29]. Since the column and row elements are different in a DMM, all the cells (matrix positions) are used including those on a diagonal.

For example, a DMM would be used to ensure that system requirements identified during Customer domain activities (stakeholder analysis in the SDP) are completely addressed by system functions identified in Functional domain activities (functional flowcharts, functional hierarchies in SDP). Similarly, DMMs are used to make sure that all system functions from the Functional domain are being performed by hardware and software components developed in Physical domain (parameters and specifications), and that these hardware and software components are being manufactured by processes in the Process domain.

The lower triangular illustration in Figure 3.21, adapted from [29], summarizes the primary DSM and DMM uses for system development. Along the main diagonal, square DSM's are shown. The off-diagonal locations show many of the cross item comparisons that generate rectangular DMM matrices, including those that might be used within a particular design domain. Stakeholder analysis, Requirements, and Specifications align with activities in the Customer domain and the Problem definition phase of the SDP. Functionality is identified and tracked in the Functional design domain and during the Problem definition phase of the SDP. The Product domain is concerned with Parameters and Products, as is the SDP Solution Design phase. Processes are the focus of the Process domain and the Solution Implementation phase of the SDP.

The cell entries in a DMM show connections between a previous domain's row entries (output from the domain activities, e.g. requirements) to the next domain's column entries (e.g. system

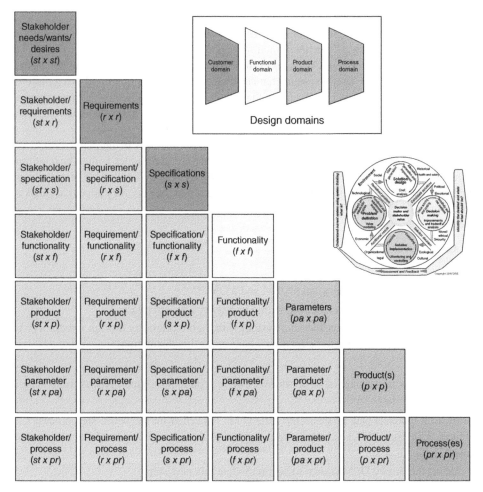

Figure 3.21 DSMs and DMMs commonly supporting system development.

	DMM	Functional domain			
		Function 1	**Function 2**	**Function 3**	**Function 4**
Customer domain	Requirement 1		■		■
	Requirement 2				
	Requirement 3	■	■		■
	Requirement 4	■	■		■
	Requirement 5	■			■
	Requirement 6	■	■		
	Requirement 7		■		

Figure 3.22   Example DMM with design defects.

functions). Since a DMM's row and column entries are not identical as in a DSM or RSM, the resulting matrix model is typically rectangular (m rows by n columns, $m \neq n$), not square (n by n). Quality function deployment (QFD) is a type of diagram that contains multiple DMMs in a single overall diagram.

Figure 3.22 shows an example of a hypothetical system development DMM that maps system requirements to system functions. Several things are worth noting here. While most system functions appear to align with requirements, Function 3 appears to not correspond to any of the seven stakeholder requirements. This could be an example of *function creep* that can happen with best intentions, yet could involve costly system elements that no stakeholder identified as a requirement. It could also be a low-cost functional add-on that the design team saw as a one-time opportunity to add significant value to the system. In either case, this defect must gain stakeholder agreement and approval or it must be removed.

The DMM also shows that Requirement 2 has no system functions being planned to meet the requirement. This also must be corrected before moving forward in a project. Either the requirement is a mistake, or the design team overlooked it when identifying system functions. These deficiencies can appear in any of the DMMs shown in Figure 3.21 and when they do, they appear as blank rows or blank columns.

3.5.4   Check on Learning

Concepts:

   (a) What is the difference between a DSM and a DMM?

   (b) Does a DSM represent a mapping within or between design phases?

   (c) Would a cellphone be considered a system with high modularity or high integrality? Does an indicator like "ability to be repaired" help make this distinction?

Comprehension:

   (a) Are systems best designed to be throw-away or repairable? Which type is more beneficial to society at-large? Why?

Application: Suppose a new process step called "M" is needed for the seven-step process shown in Figure 3.14. Step "M" needs the output from steps A, C, and F and sends its output to steps E and G.

   (a) Adjust the binary DSM shown to accommodate this new step.

(b) Calculate the singular value modularity index (SMI) for the original 7-step DSM and the new 8-step DSM. Has modularity increased or decreased with the addition of this new step?

(c) Apply partitioning or clustering to the 7-step and 8-step DSMs. Do teams established for the 7-step process need to change to accommodate the 8-step process?

(d) Convert the new 8-step DSM into an adjacency matrix. Has the third power loop structure changed from what existed before? What does this mean for the system elements if a change is made to step "M" after it is in-place? Which elements would feel the change immediately and which will have a time delay?

3.6 SYSTEM DYNAMICS

System dynamics is a modeling approach that is used to represent the behavior of a full range of systems—simple to complex—based on cause–effect relationships, feedback loops between system elements, and time delays that affect interactions between system elements. System dynamics models are intended to capture all applicable elements affecting the system of interest's behavior, including those outside of the system's boundary. Multiple types of relationships can be represented in system dynamics models.

System dynamics representations generally assume two forms: causal loop diagrams, and stock and flow diagrams intended to support system dynamics simulations. Causal loop diagrams are qualitative system representations containing words as objects and arrows (arcs) as directional interactions between these word objects. In this sense they are similar to systemigrams.

Causal loop diagrams do not require software to create, and can easily be created using pencil and paper. However, applications like *Vensim PLE* which is used here, are more tidy, motivate deliberate placing of elements and relationships, and have features such as color-coding, font styles and sizes, and so on that enhance readability.

These diagrams are static qualitative system representations intended to capture and convey system complexity introduced because of various interactions and feedback over time that influence how and to what extent specific system elements interact to produce system behavior. It is the "over time" aspect of causal loop diagrams and stock and flow diagrams that model a system of interest's dynamics.

Causal loop diagrams are one start point for creating dynamic system software simulations. For applications like *Vensim PLE*, the simulation is performing a numerical integration of a dynamical system. When the causal loop diagram is translated into a *stock and flow diagram* for simulation purposes, each cause–effect connection must be specified mathematically using functions. These functions can be anything from simple algebraic expressions to more complicated ones. Stock and flow diagrams are the extension of causal loop diagrams needed when quantitative insights into system behavior due to interactions and feedback are needed. Controlling parameters are also assigned to the objects they influence.

Stock and flow diagrams are a representation of the same system of interest captured in its associated causal loop diagram(s), but now targeted variables (stocks) are isolated and tracked. A desire to know how these stocks change over time is the start point for building a stock and flow diagram.

These stocks represent counts of interest whose levels change because of the mathematical functions and model parameters that describe the connections existing between system elements. There are a number of stock variables targeted for tracking in a typical system dynamics model. The graphical patterns showing how these stock levels change over time are a primary output of system dynamics models, providing insights into system behavior but also *when* decisions and subsequent actions should be taken.

In causal loop diagrams, all arcs represent cause–effect relationships. By definition, causal loop diagrams must contain at least one closed loop that represents feedback among system elements. A closed loop is defined as a path of connections starting at, say, element A, and continuing through one or more additional elements in the same direction and ending back at element A. Feedback loops are either reinforcing—meaning that the effects on each of the system elements are either all positive (growth) or all negative (decay); or they are balancing—meaning that positive and negative cause–effects exist in the same loop, one countering the behavioral influence of the other to some degree and causing stocks to approach limiting levels. The following example illustrates the key features of a causal loop diagram. Appendix A contains more extensive information for software implementation using *Vensim PLE*. Examples of stock and flow simulation models for COVID system dynamics models are available free of charge from Ventana Systems, Inc. for use with *Vensim PLE* (https://vensim.com/coronavirus/).

System Dynamics Example. Early in the outbreak of the COVID-19 pandemic, governments around the globe were scrambling to understand the dynamics associated with the spread of COVID-19 from a systems perspective, taking into account the interactions of all relevant entities affecting the disease. Researchers at the Indian Institute of Management Lucknow in Uttar Pradesh, India, adopted a systems dynamics approach this challenge to examine how lockdown and social distancing measures influence the behavior of people over time [31]. In this setting, system decisions regarding formal interventions are policy decisions, one of the application environments within which system dynamics models excel. Using *Vensim Pro*, they created an effective causal loop diagram which is shown in Figure 3.23. Several key elements of a causal loop diagram are illustrated in this figure.

- All the word objects are noun objects but they can be different objects. For example, **Birth** is a count, **Natural rate of transmission** is a rate, **Delay in behavior change** is a time measure, **Panic among people** is an observational characteristic, and so on.

- The word objects are connected to other word objects using arcs (arrows) that indicate the direction of the cause–effect relationship. For example, **Infected people from foreign countries** (cause) entering India has an effect on the India's **Infected population**.

- Each arc (arrow) connecting word objects has a positive "+" or negative "−" sign near the arrowhead, indicating the response direction of the affected system element by changes in the causing element. For example, if the number of **People died** increases (cause) then the **Panic among people** increases (effect) in response, which is indicated by a "+" sign next to the arrowhead going into the system element it affects. Similarly, if the **COVID fatality rate** increases (cause), the **People recovered** decreases (effect), as indicated by a "−" sign next to the arrowhead.

- Three feedback loops exist within the dynamics shown. The direction of their loops (clockwise or counterclockwise) are indicated by the surrounding arrows. Two are *balancing loops* (B_1 and B_2) and one is a *reinforcing loop* (R_1). All three loop influences proceed along their paths with connections indicated in the same direction(s). The circular shape involving **Infected population (symptomatic)**, **People died**, **Panic among people**, **COVID fatality rate**, and **People recovered** is not a loop because the arrows switch direction several times along this closed circle.

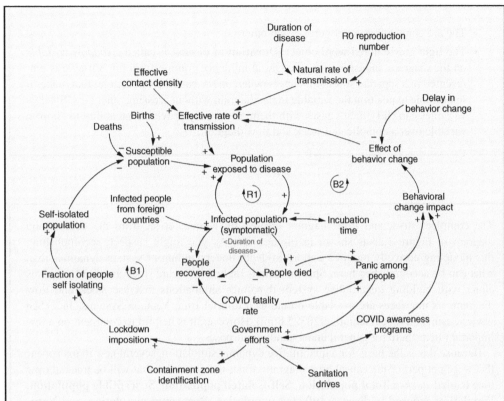

Figure 3.23 COVID causal loop diagram for major factors. Source: Kumar et al. [31]/with permission of Elsevier.

- The loop involving **Population exposed to disease** and **Infected population (symptomatic** is a positive reinforcing loop because increasing **Population exposed to disease** causes an increase in **Infected population (symptomatic)**, which then feeds back causing an increase in **Population exposed to disease**, again causing an increase in **Infected population (symptomatic)**, and so on.

- The two loops designated as B_1 and B_2 are balancing loops because within the loops formed they have both positive (growth) and negative (decay) cause–effects, indicating that the system dynamics imposes offsetting limitations on growth and decay. The extent to which this offset occurs - does it delay, stop, or reverse growth or decay over time - could be determined by converting this causal loop diagram to a stock and flow diagram and simulating the system behavior over time. Other phenomena that exhibit this kind balancing behavior are the clinical pharmacokinetics of ethanol in the human body [32] and the dynamics of fish populations in response to an area's carrying capacity [33] without emigration or immigration, among others.

- Since cause–effect relationships are assumed for all connections between system elements, there's no need to label arcs like what is done in systemigrams. Additionally, the mechanism conveying the cause–effect (e.g. physical contact, observation, data collection) is not explicitly conveyed in causal loop diagrams.

- The arc connections do not cross each other.
- The light grey colored word object: **Duration of disease** is called a *shadow variable* on the diagram, indicating that the causal influence coming from this variable is represented in a separate sub-model or elsewhere in the causal loop diagram that makes it impossible to position the variable in the diagram without crossing other arcs. Shadow variables can carry their causes with them, essentially providing an ability to "hop" a variable over a complicated stock and flow diagram.

The complete stock and flow diagram created by Kumar, et al. from the causal loop diagram in Figure 3.23 is shown in Figure 3.24. As you might suspect, accomplishing this modeling correctly requires a more in-depth understanding of system dynamics than what can be accomplished here. Specific details on how to create stock and flow diagrams along with building quantitative system dynamics simulations that use stock and flow diagrams as interfaces are available online as a tutorial from Ventana Systems, Inc. (See www.vensim.com/documentation/20325.html). However, it is helpful to comment on a few important items here for general understanding purposes.

Because this is the basis for a quantitative dynamic simulation, several new items appear that were not part of the causal loop diagram. First, the quantities that will be tracked over time (called *stocks*): **Total population**, **Self-isolated population**, **Susceptible population**, **Population exposed to disease**, **Infected population**, **Recovered population**, and **Number of people died** appear as rectangles connected by double-lined *flow* arrows. Stock levels are also known as accumulations or state variables, highlighting the underlying differential equations describing the mathematics supporting system dynamics models. Stocks and flow arrows use different menu items in *Vensim PLE* than those used to create causal loop diagrams. These flow arrows *do not* represent cause–effect relationships; they define the flow of stocks through the system of interest, terminating at collection points that end the flow (**Self-isolated population**, **Number of people died**, and **Recovered population**). The levels of these stocks change based on the user-specified mathematical expressions containing rates and other parameters.

For the **Total population** stock, there are flow arrows coming from and going to cloud-like objects. These clouds highlight and define the limits of the model, essentially saying that new population births come from somewhere outside of the COVID model, and deaths go outside of the model as well. This is also what is being represented by the flow rate injecting **Cases from foreign lands** into the model.

There are also arrows similar to those appearing in the causal loop diagram. When these are used to connect objects in the causal loop diagram, they represent cause–effect. In a stock and flow diagram in *Vensim PLE* these are called *information arrows*. It's not necessary to distinguish positive or negative influences on these arrows unless desired to enhance clarity. The light grey variables again represent shadow variables as in causal loop diagrams.

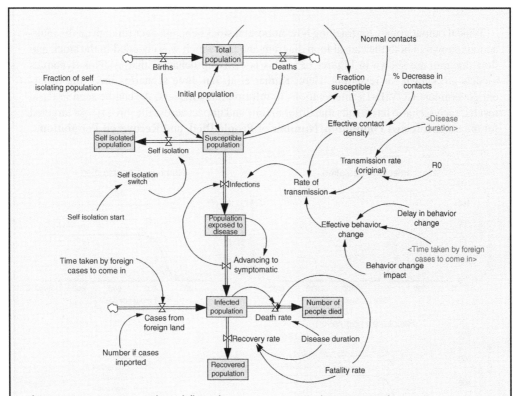

Figure 3.24 COVID stock and flow diagram supporting dynamic simulation. Source: Kumar et al. [31]/with permission of Elsevier.

When arrows are connecting model parameters to stocks (e.g. **Initial population** is connected to **Total population**), they are part of the mathematical expression defining the stock level they are connected to. Lastly, there are rates of change that control the flow of stocks through the model. These appear as hourglass looking shapes on flow arrows in *Vensim PLE*. Arrows connect objects to these hourglass shapes that are mathematically defining these rates (e.g. **Rate of transmission** appears in the expression for **Infections**). Similarly, arrows show these rates as being connected to other rates and stocks. Again, this means they appear in the expressions used by the object at the arrowhead. For example, the **Self isolation** start time appears in the expression for **Self isolation** switch, and it appears in the **Self isolation** rate that controls the flow between the **Susceptible population** stock and the **Self isolated population** stock.

The researchers chose 5 scenarios to examine for effectiveness based on the level of government intervention: no intervention (1), light (2), moderate (3), strict (4), and the actual government response regarding lockdown and social distancing (5). By then varying the parameter settings for percent decrease in contacts, behavioral delay, and percent of the population in self-isolation after an initial number of days, among others, each scenario could be represented in the same stock and flow model and run for a specific time horizon. The system dynamics (how system elements are connected) are assumed to not change between scenarios.

Typical output graphs for tracking how important stocks change over time given the inter-actions shown in both the causal loop diagram and that which was encoded in the stock and flow diagram are shown in Figure 3.25. This is evolving behavior that systems dynamics models are known for revealing. Here, Kumar et al. ran three scenarios involving differ-ent government COVID-19 interventions to inform policy makers. As can be seen in these results, each scenario has results that differ in time and impact across the three stocks targeted for tracking: **Infected Population, Number of People Died**, and **Recovered Population**.

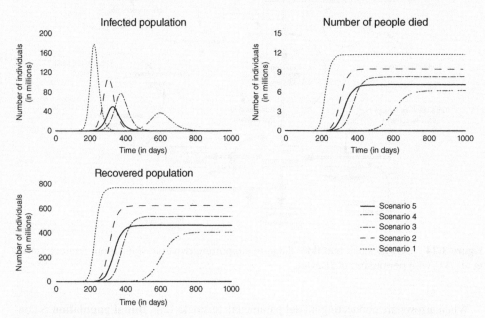

Figure 3.25 COVID-19 system behavior over time. Source: Kumar et al. [31]/with permission of Elsevier.

Several observations related to the dynamic interactions taking place are immediately evident that can inform policy decisions. For example, without intervention (scenario 1) the infected population level is substantially higher than any of the intervention options modeled, peaking at roughly 180 million 220 days into the horizon. Under the actual actions taken by the Indian government (scenario 5), the total number of individuals infected was the lowest and occurred latest in time. Similar observations can be made regarding the other stocks.

Note however the effect of a balancing loop on the **Number of People Died** (balanc-ing loop B2 in the causal loop diagram), leveling off in all five scenarios albeit at dif-ferent levels. Similarly, the **Recovered Population** represented by **People recovered** in the causal loop diagram in Figure 3.23 has both positive and negative correlated changes influencing its level. Both of these are examples of the unique dynamics able to be rep-resented, modeled and simulated with system dynamics as they influence system behavior over time.

Controlling a dynamic simulation and properly presenting quantitative results is left to online tutorials to discuss, although the simulation does adhere to the principles discussed in a section that follows.

Not all elements need be quantifiable to be useful. For one particular systems effort in 2020, a Systems Engineering team at the US Military Academy created a *Vensim Pro* model to help a client understand the dynamics involved with creating a new career specialty field containing a range of skill levels and several management layers. The causal loop diagram and its accompanying stock and flow model contained difficult-to-quantify variables such as morale, job satisfaction, and work stress levels and their influence on other system elements. For the causal loop diagram, the direction of causation these elements have on others is all that was required. Subsequently, their associated cause–effect levels could be represented in the stock and flow diagram and system dynamics simulation using relative estimates instead of exact amounts.

3.7   IDEF0 MODELS

Black box representations serve a useful purpose early on in the process of designing a system, when system concepts are being explored and stakeholder requirements are being identified based on their needs, wants, and desires. These stakeholder requirements are translated into system requirements in which specific system functions (or activities) are identified as simply boxes that "do" the function, but because no resource commitments are being made as to *how* each system function will be enabled, these boxes are black box representations.

As purely conceptual tools for thinking, these diagrams connected system functions to input resources, control features, associated mechanisms, and the expected output of the function. Once the major system functions have been diagrammed, subsystem, subsubsystem, and component functions are identified and diagrammed in the same manner, but only so far as a black box construct can be maintained because what is being diagrammed is generic rather than specific. It is too early in the design process to lock in any decisions on specific solutions. Once completed, these diagrams provide an organized, typically hierarchical, and effective basis for communicating ideas between stakeholders, systems engineers, and the various specialty engineering teams involved with the system effort.

IDEF0 is one member of a family of IDEF methods [34] that can be used to support the SDP during the early phases of a system design effort. IDEF0 models describe the functions that are performed by a system and what is needed to perform those functions. Table 3.2 shows the variety of methods and the purpose for which IDEF methods were designed [35].

An IDEF0 model is capable of representing the functions, decisions, processes, and activities of an organization or system. It is particularly useful for representing complex systems comprised of a host of processes. The top level diagram, called Level 0, is the highest level of system abstraction. Using a single box to represent the top level system function, it illustrates in equally high level terms the things that cross the system boundary as inputs and outputs, the physical mechanisms that enable the top level system function, and the controls that determine how this function will operate. Levels 1, 2, and so on proceed to decompose this Level 0 representation, successively exposing more and more detail concerning the interconnections and interactions of the various subfunctions supporting the overall system function.

Proceeding from Level 0 to Level 1, for example, is a bit like lifting the lid off of a black box representation for a system. The sequence of processes, activities, or functions linked together to successfully perform the top level function is unveiled and represented. Even though IDEF0 models are generated using a decomposition strategy, they tend to maintain a "big picture" orientation for

TABLE 3.2   Family of IDEF Methods.

Method	Purpose	Method	Purpose
IDEF0	Function modeling	IDEF8	User interface modeling
IDEF1	Information modeling	IDEF9	Scenario-driven IS design
IDEF1X	Data modeling	IDEF10	Implementation architecture modeling
IDEF2	Simulation model design	IDEF11	Information artifact modeling
IDEF3	Process description capture	IDEF12	Organization modeling
IDEF4	Object-oriented design	IDEF13	Three schema mapping design
IDEF5	Ontology description capture	IDEF14	Network design
IDEF6	Design rationale capture		

the desired system that other approaches such as functional flowcharts can lose as modeling detail increases. It is particularly useful when establishing the scope of a functional analysis as it forces the user to decide on the system boundary in order to display even the highest level of representation for a system.

IDEF0 uses a single box to represent each activity, combines activities to define a process, and then links system processes to describe a complete system. Creating IDEF0 models of a system generally proceeds by decomposing system functions into layers, the top layer being a system-level model resembling a black box that is based on information obtained during stakeholder interviews. In this sense then, it is helpful to decide whether an IDEF0 model is going to be used prior to interviewing stakeholders. Doing so insures that key information required for the IDEF0 model can be obtained without having to unnecessarily re-interview stakeholders.

Creating an IDEF0 model loosely follows a step-wise procedure. At the start, the overall model purpose and the particular stakeholder(s) viewpoint that is going to be represented by the IDEF0 must be identified on the Level 0 representation. This explicit statement of viewpoint orients a user of the IDEF0 model as to the perspective that should be assumed when interpreting the information presented. Next, using both stakeholder interviews and independent research, identify the information that becomes the top level IDEF0 model:

- the system;
- the system boundary;
- any material or information inputs and outputs;
- the top level system function that turns inputs into outputs;
- any regulations, laws, operating guidelines, and stakeholder desires that control or constraint system behavior; and,
- the physical triggers, actions, or environmental influences that cause the system to operate.

Following this, the major processes that are needed to turn the system inputs into outputs are indentified. For each major process, identify the objectives or purpose associated with it. These processes typically are sequentially linked at the highest level. Each of these processes will further break down into sequences of activities organized to achieve the objective(s) of the process. All three of these system structures: the system, its processes, and its activities, are represented as individual IDEF0 models.

Lastly, it is important to decide on the decomposition strategy that will be used. Four common decomposition strategies are [36]:

- *Functional decomposition* breaks things down according to **what** is done, rather than *how* it is done. This tends to be the most common decomposition strategy because it naturally aligns with the strategy used for constructing a functional hierarchy.
- *Role decomposition* breaks things down according to **who** does what with the system.
- *Subsystems decomposition* starts by breaking up the overall system into its major subsystems. If the major subsystems are relatively independent, this is a helpful strategy to initiate the IDEF0, and afterwards employing functional decomposition to further decompose the subsystems into processes.
- *Life cycle decomposition* is occasionally used when the stages of a system life cycle are relatively independent and subsystems and their processes generally align with the age of the system.

At the end of these steps, an initial IDEF0 system representation can be formally constructed. As with most system representations, IDEF0 diagrams undergo revisions during the SDP as new and more accurate information arises with regard to the needs, wants, and desires of stakeholders.

A basic IDEF0 model at any level consists of five possible components [36]:

1. *Activity, Process, or System.* A box labeled by "verb–noun" expression that describes the activity/function that the box represents (e.g. collect intelligence; weld joint; coffee making).
2. *Inputs.* Arrows entering the left side of the box represent "raw material" that gets transformed or consumed by the activity/function in order to produce outputs (e.g. information; welding rod, electric current, Tungsten Inert Gas (TIG); coffee grounds, water).
3. *Controls.* Arrows entering the top of the box are controls. These specify the conditions required for the function/activity to produce outputs, such as guidelines, plans, or standards that influence or direct how the activity works (e.g. US federal regulations; union safety standards; recipe, coffee machine directions).
4. *Mechanisms.* Arrows connected to the bottom side of the box represent the physical aspects of the activity/function that cause it to operate (e.g. agents; union welder, TIG welding torch, electricity; drip coffee machine, coffee person, electricity). These can point inward towards the box or outward away from the box. Inward pointing arrows identify some of the means that support the execution of the activity/function. These are also called *enablers*. Arrows pointing outward are *call* arrows, indicating a sharing of detail between models or between portions of the same model.
5. *Outputs.* Arrows leaving the box on the right are outputs, which are the result(s) of the activity/function transmitted to other activities/functions within the IDEF0 model, to other models within the system, or across the system boundary to the environment (e.g. intelligence reports, fused metallic bond, pot of coffee).

The upper left illustration in Figure 3.26 shows the generic structure of a basic IDEF0 model. The three other models are examples of IDEF0 models for each of the example activities noted in the description earlier. Constructing even the Level 0 representation of a system can be challenging.

Referring to the upper left illustration in Figure 3.26, it is helpful when building each block in a IDEF0 diagram to conceptualize the block as a function that "transforms inputs 1 and 2 into outputs 1 and 2, as determined by controls 1 and 2, using mechanism 1 and sending coordination information using Call 1." The verbs in this expression add clarity to the definitions of inputs, outputs, controls, and mechanisms.

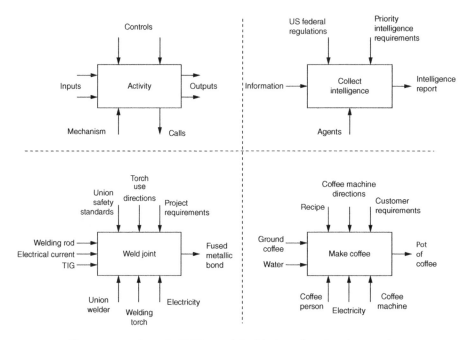

Figure 3.26   Generic IDEF0 model with three functional examples.

Creating an IDEF0 model of a system proceeds in a decomposition fashion similar to that used to create a hierarchy. The highest level model of the system—Level 0—communicates the system boundary in relation to its environment. This top-level representation on which the subject of the model is represented by a single box with its bounding arrows that is labeled as A-0 (pronounced "A minus zero"). The A-0 diagram at Level 0 sets the model scope, boundary, and orientation through the visualization of the box, the purpose and viewpoint expressed in text after the box, and the title of the A-0 diagram at Level 0. The Title block affords an opportunity to identify the name of the system. The Purpose statement communicates to a reader why they are looking at the IDEF0 model and whose viewpoint it represents.

Figure 3.27 shows a slightly more complicated A-0 diagram for the "Make Coffee" function introduced in Figure 3.26. The boundary of the system, purpose, and viewpoint are shown in the main diagram area. Along the bottom of the A-0 diagram are tracking information specified by the systems engineer who would create the diagram. The "ProjectID" (QA) and "NodeID" (A-0) are unique identifiers. The "Title" block is used to describe the overall activity in the context of the process, subsystem, or system it supports. The "C-number" is a combination of the author's initials (MSD) and document ID number (0001).

This Level 0 model assumes that a particular mechanism (electric coffee machine) is to be used in any systems solution that might result from the systems project. Given the perspective noted, this appears reasonable. However, for most applications of the SDP, it is best to avoid including solution elements (how to do something) early in the Problem Definition phase, which is when the IDEF0 representation is most likely to be used. Coffee can be made without either electricity or a coffee machine. If a department administrative manager (stakeholder) placed a high preference (value) on some functionality provided by an electronic coffee maker, it would be better to include this as stakeholder input for the next level of decomposition (Level 1) rather than as a hard mechanism

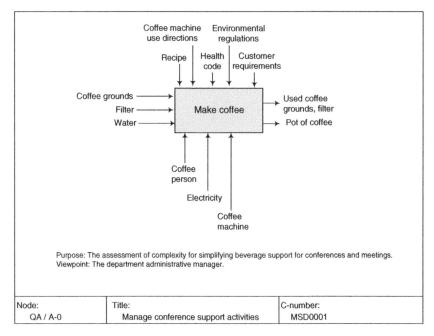

Figure 3.27   An A-0 diagram for the Make Coffee function.

at this modeling level (Level 0). In this way, solution alternatives are free to creatively satisfy this desired functionality using mechanisms other than an electric coffee maker, if feasible.

Second, even a simple process of making coffee for a meeting can take on complex interactions when viewed from a systems thinking perspective. The SDP has useful cues via its environmental factors for where to look to recognize these interactions. For example, health code and environmental regulations (legal factor) exert a nontrivial amount of control over this function when the output is to be served in a public forum. Thus, the Make Coffee function interacts with the legal system.

Finally, comparing the output of this IDEF0 model with that of Figure 3.26, notice that waste products (the unintended consequences) along with the designed product (the intended consequences) are shown as output of the system. In this way, the Make Coffee function as a system interacts with the environmental system existing outside of its system boundary. This interaction is easy to overlook, as some industrial companies operating in the United States have learned the hard way. (See http://www.epa.gov/hudson)

Although sequenced IDEF0 models like this one are commonly linked through inputs and outputs, they can also be linked by controls and mechanisms as well. In Figure 3.28, the professional systems engineering standards (ANSI/GEIA EIA-632 and IEEE 1220-2005) and the SDP activities act as control on each of the functions shown. Likewise, the SE team itself links the three functions by acting as a common physical mechanism enabling each of the functions to successfully occur. Each of the subsequent SDP phases can be represented by an IDEF0 diagram as well, which is left as an exercise for the reader.

Figures 3.29, 3.30, and 3.31 illustrate an example of three levels of IDEF0 models for a hypothetical fast food restaurant in the United States. The Level 1 model in Figure 3.30 presents the top level system function as a sequence of three subfunctions: "process customer order," "prepare

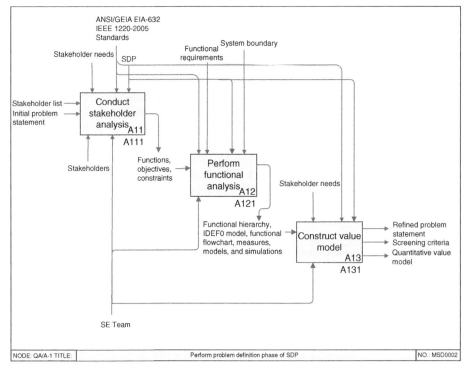

Figure 3.28 Level 2 representation of the Problem Definition phase of the SDP.

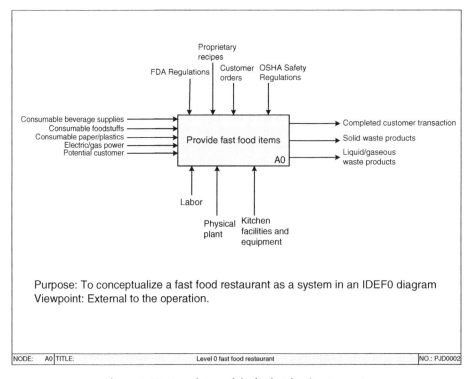

Figure 3.29 Level 0 model of a fast food restaurant.

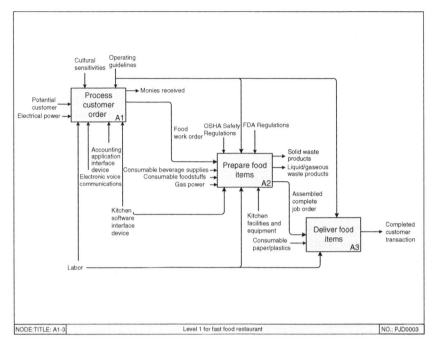

Figure 3.30   Level 1 model of a fast food restaurant.

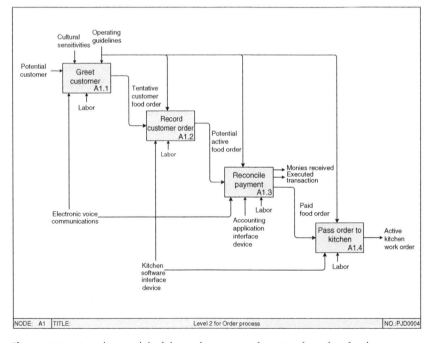

Figure 3.31   Level 2 model of the order process function for a fast food restaurant.

food items," and "deliver food items." Figure 3.31 then shows how the "process customer order" function is decomposed into a sequence of four functions. In turn at Level 2, similar models would be created for the "prepare food items" and "deliver food items" processes shown at Level 1. Notice how each level increases the amount of detail being presented concerning the system's operation, which has implications on the amount and quality of information needed from stakeholders in order to properly represent the system at these levels.

IDEF0 diagrams represent one modeling framework that has been implemented in a host of software applications. Since their introduction and with the explosive growth of interconnected systems, other tools strongly leveraging systems thinking have been developed. One such effort resulted in a modeling language based on the object-oriented analysis and design language Unified Markup Language (UML) called SysML.

The SysML (Systems Modeling Language) is a general purpose modeling language for systems engineering applications that supports the specification, analysis, design, verification and validation of a broad range of systems and systems-of-systems [37]. Introduced in 2003 by a group of partners interested in improving the precision and consistency of systems diagrams, the development effort split in 2005 into an open-source project (www.SysML.org) and a commercial software product (OMG SysML: www.sysmlforum.com) offered by the Object Management Group (OMG). Where UML is predominantly used for software development, SysML's charter extends into much broader classes of systems, many of which do not include software components.

TABLE 3.3   Open Source SysML Diagrams.

SysML Diagram	Primary Purpose
Activity Diagram	Show system behavior as control and data flows. Useful for functional analysis. Compare Extended Functional Flow Block diagrams (EFFBDs), already commonly used among systems engineers.
Block Definition diagram	Show system structure as components along with their properties, operations and relationships. Useful for system analysis and design.
Internal Block diagram	Show the internal structures of components, including their parts and connectors. Useful for system analysis and design.
Package diagram	Show how a model is organized into packages, views and viewpoints. Useful for model management.
Parametric diagram	Show parametric constraints between structural elements. Useful for performance and quantitative analysis.
Requirement diagram	Show system requirements and their relationships with other elements. Useful for requirements engineering.
Sequence diagram	Show system behavior as interactions between system components. Useful for system analysis and design.
State Machine diagram	Show system behavior as sequences of states that a component or interaction experience in response to events. Useful for system design and simulation/code generation.
Use Case diagram	Show system functional requirements as transactions that are meaningful to system users. Useful for specifying functional requirements. (Note potential overlap with Requirement diagrams.)
Allocation tables	Show various kinds of allocations (e.g. requirement allocation, functional allocation, structural allocation). Useful for facilitating automated verification and validation (V&V) and gap analysis.

As can be seen in Table 3.3, SysML contains a host of visualization tools that enable a user to represent a system in a number of ways depending on the need being addressed. Many of these tools can augment those introduced in Chapters 4–11 to support the SDP activities.

3.8 SIMULATION MODELING

Simulations are the natural follow-on to nearly all system representation efforts. It's just a case of when this will occur and what type of simulation is going to be used. And for this, an understanding of the general choices available is useful.

In its simplest form, a *simulation* is a model operated over time. In more mathematical terms, it is the numerical execution of a model to see the potential effect of the variables used on the model's output [38]. Often, vast amounts of data representing the states of a system need to be generated in order to establish statistical significance of change on the system.

3.8.1 Analytical Methods versus Simulation

It is appropriate to use simulation when a system is sufficiently complex that the possibility of a straightforward analytical method is unlikely [38]. Many times when starting a modeling effort, systems can appear simple. However, once variables and parameters change, the mathematical representation or model can become too complex to solve using a closed form analytical approach. The term "closed form analytical method" means a collection of mathematical expressions that can be solved for an exact solution.

In general, choosing to use a simulation is based on six factors [39]:

- An operational decision based on a logical or quantitative model is needed;
- The system being analyzed is well-defined and repetitive;
- System/model activities, variables, and events are interdependent and change over time or condition;
- Cost/impact of the decision is greater than the cost of developing the model, executing the simulation, and assessing the data;
- Experimenting with the actual system is more expensive than developing a model, executing the simulation, and assessing the data; and,
- System events occur infrequently, not allowing for the system to achieve a steady state of performance where multiple adjustments to the system events can be made and assessed in an attempt to create a more efficient system.

The first three factors address system characteristics and structures. The next two address resource concerns. The last factor deals with the frequency of system usage. The first five factors can be used to help determine if a simulation is appropriate for assessing the alternatives generated in the Solution Design phase of the SDP. The last factor is a possible mitigating factor used to balance the risk of making or not making changes to a system that is used infrequently.

Simulation tools are categorized in different ways depending on their intended use. Industry and military simulations both require careful scenario development, but the basic simulation engine typically exists, alleviating the need to program a theoretical model. Also, their user interfaces allow for a rapid development of a simulation scenario. The ProModel® simulation application discussed in this section is representative of a wide range of existing commercial products.

ProModel® is a discrete-event queuing simulation software application used to model manufacturing, transportation, logistics, and service-related systems. It allows systems to be represented as a series of queues (waiting lines) and servers in which an entity—typically a customer product being produced/processed—is either being serviced or awaiting service. Various alternative physical reconfigurations and service process designs can easily be tested prior to implementing a specific layout or process in the actual system. *ProModel*® has the fidelity to model "resource utilization, production capacity, productivity, inventory levels, bottlenecks, throughput times, and other performance measures." [39]

ProModel® is used by many industries to simulate their manufacturing and or transportation system(s). It has also been used to simulate military systems. Figure 3.32 is an example of a student-lead systems engineering project focused on identifying viable solution alternatives for a proposed missile defense system. Other simulation applications currently available on the market are *Arena*®, *SIMUL8*, and *AutoMod*.

There are four simulation typologies: live, virtual, augmented, and constructive. The right side of Figure 3.33 is a visual depiction of the relationship between the first three simulation typologies and games. Each typology can be considered in terms of people and environment. Each may be either real or synthetic, as shown in Figure 3.34.

Live simulations involve real people using real systems in a simulated environment. An example of a live simulation is an emergency response team conducting a full dress rehearsal on a launch pad prior to the launch of a manned rocket. **Virtual simulations** involve real people using simulated systems immersed in a computer generated environment. A person conducting early flight training in a simulator is an example of a virtual simulation. Virtual simulations use closed off headsets, audio elements, and mechanical effects that isolate a user from the natural surroundings of the simulation, such as a laboratory, classroom, or office.

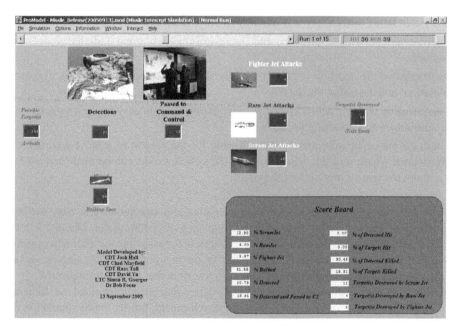

Figure 3.32 ProModel® anti-ballistic missile simulation example [40]. Source: ProModel Corporation.

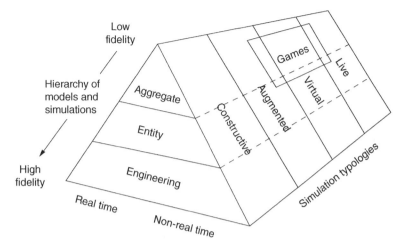

Figure 3.33 Simulation types [41].

	Environment	
	Real	Synthetic
People — Real	Live	Virtual
People — Synthetic	Augmented	Constructive

Figure 3.34 Simulation-reality relationships.

Augmented simulations add computer generated elements to the natural surroundings where the simulation is taking place, typically through goggles with pass-through lens and audio headsets. These are especially useful when safety is a consideration. For example, augmented reality simulations are used by aircraft maintenance personnel to quickly repair system components without needing to refer to printed or digital manuals. The repair steps and locations appear as tags and pointers to the person using the simulation.

Another common augmented reality technique is to display computer-generated people in optical systems through which real people look. This allows the use of real weapons against synthetic criminals or combatants in a training environment without the risk of bodily harm or death.

The fourth typology is **constructive simulation**. In this typology, simulated entities operate in a simulated environment. Constructive simulations are normally used to simulate activities in rapid succession in order to provide insight into emerging system behavior or possible outcomes based on changes in equipment or processes. Agent-based simulations of human behavior or multifaceted relationships between entities and which replicate hundreds, if not thousands, of entities interacting in a complex virtual environment are examples of constructive simulations. For example, NASA could use a constructive simulation to assess the effect(s) of asteroid activity on a space station.

It could use other constructive simulations to predict the oxygen exchange rate in a space station based on the predicted growth of vegetation in the station, air filtering capacity of the ventilation system and the number of personnel in the station.

Real-time versus Non-real-time Simulations. Simulations can be categorized based on their ability to provide "real-time" performance or "non-real-time" performance. *Real-time* simulations are usually associated with virtual simulations which provide human participants with timely information, reactions, and effects. *Non-real-time* simulations are usually associated with constructive simulations that run uninterrupted for their duration. During solution design and decision making phases of the SDP, systems engineers frequently use non-real-time simulations to generate data for use in analysis of alternatives. The use of non-real-time simulations allows users to conduct studies using the highest fidelity algorithms available with little concern for how long it takes to run the simulation because the system activities modeled in this type of simulation are not constrained to actual clock time. Non-real-time simulations can work faster or slower than actual clock time. A real-time simulation could be used to conduct flight training or to test the reaction times of emergency response teams. A non-real-time simulation could be used to identify the disturbance of the air flow (lift and drag) as it streams over the fins of a new rocket design.

Hierarchy of Models and Simulations. Military simulations are also categorized according to the simulation's level of *fidelity* (see left side of Figure 3.33). The greater the fidelity, the greater the detail of the item(s) being simulated. For example, a low-fidelity model of a rocket system might represent the rocket as a solid object where a higher fidelity model might include the fins, fuel system, guidance system, and load capacities of the rocket. Fidelity exists on a continuous scale but is routinely organized into smaller groupings to make it easier to group simulations into consistent hierarchy categories. Some organizations place simulations into a hierarchy consisting of five levels: campaign, theater, mission, engagement, and engineering [42]. Others combine theater and campaign into one level [43]. Yet others refer to these four levels as campaign or theater, battle or multi-unit engagement, single engagement, and phenomenological [44].

The front triangle of Figure 3.33 shows a three-tier hierarchy: aggregate, entity, and engineering. The *aggregate* level consists of simulations or models that combine entities into groups based on functionality or association. Aggregating entities helps to reduce the computational requirements for modeling and simulating large scale scenarios. Aggregate simulations routinely have less fidelity than is normally found at the entity and engineering level simulations. Aggregate simulations would represent a group of vehicles, such as a convoy, as it moves packaged goods from one side of a country to another.

Entity-level simulations reside between aggregate and engineering level simulations. Entity-level simulations represent individual systems, products, individuals, and platforms along with the effects created by or acting on them. As such, a "distinguishable person, place, unit, thing, event, or concept" simulation must maintain or track information about each entity in the model [45]. An entity-level simulation of an asteroid field would replicate each individual asteroid, its relevant behaviors and positional data as a rocket passes through the asteroid field.

Engineering–level simulations normally address components of one or two individual systems or subsystems. These simulations may go into more detail (higher fidelity) to model the physical aspects of a system. Organizations use this form of modeling and simulation prior to building new equipment or integrate new technologies into existing systems before testing the changes using live simulations.

Simulations versus Games. Military and industrial organization produce numerous simulations that provide training for their people or conduct analysis of operations/systems. The needs of the research and training communities place different constraints on the validity of the model or simulation. In the gaming industry, the overriding concern is to manufacture a product people are interested in purchasing and playing. A notable exception is the game America's Army™, which was originally built as a recruiting tool for the U.S. Army.

Games are "activit(ies) engaged in for diversion or amusement" [46]. As such, the focus of the gaming industry has been to produce simulations which deliver entertainment value to its customers; however, developing or adapting games for use in education or training is becoming more popular. The belief is that individuals will learn more if they are actively engaged in the learning activity is one of the fundamental reasons for using games. Most computerized games are simulations primarily designed for entertainment but may be used for learning, individual or team training, or analytical studies seeking to gain insight into human behavior. No matter which simulation category a game resides, game developers' primary concern is entertainment but with an eye towards achieving a fantasized version of reality during the design and coding of a game. This lack of realism can place games at the lower end of the fidelity spectrum (see Figure 3.33).

Simulation Behaviors. A simulation executes based on the prescribed set of behaviors defined for each modeling entity. These behaviors can be complex or very simple. They can be reactive or proactive in nature. Simulation behaviors are most often limited based on the model architecture used to represent these behaviors. Generally speaking, the five most popular cognitive model representations in use in the late twentieth and early twenty-first century are agent-based, Bayesian network, multi-agent system, neural-networks, and rule-based.

Rule-based Simulations. A rule-based (knowledge-based) simulation replicates human behavior using a catalog of actions with causal if/then association to select and execute an appropriate action [47,48]. This causal representation often requires an extensive effort to identify and code all relative possible conditions an entity may encounter along with viable entity actions for those conditions. Subject matter experts are routinely used to establish and validate this data prior to its use. Rule-based simulations are best used to model systems, which are physics-based, or for replicating systems with a relatively limited (countable) number of states and actions.

Agent-based Simulations. Agent-based simulations model intelligence through codified objects that perceive characteristics of the environment and act on those perceptions [47]. There are several types of agent-based cognitive architectures. Two of these are *reactive* and *rational* agents. A reactive agent bases its actions solely on the last set of sensory inputs. Often the approach uses a simple condition action rule (e.g. if this is my perceived state of world, then I choose this action). A rational agent uses sensors to perceive its environment and performs actions on the environment using effectors. Rational agents maintain a state of situational awareness based on their past knowledge of the world and current sensory inputs [47].

Multi-agent System Simulations. The multi-agent system (MAS) is a relatively new representation for modeling and simulating behaviors based on the complex adaptive system (CAS) theory. Developed in the late 1970s, MAS is a system with autonomous or semiautonomous software agents that produce adaptive and emergent behaviors. The model uses a bottom-up approach where software agents have independent micro decisions that generate group and system-level macro behaviors. A MAS can use any form of agent-based software technology (reactive, rational, goal-based, utility-based, etc.) that has agents characterized as possessing intentions that influence their actions. Multi-agent systems are used in large domains where nonlinearity is present [49]. A MAS, limited only by the physics constraints of the simulation boundaries, uses an indirect approach to search the large domain for viable results. Another feature of MAS is its ability to allow agents to evolve to create new agents which, in general, are better suited to survive or prosper in the simulated environment [50].

Agent-based and MAS simulations are often used to explore a wide spectrum of possible system effects based on an extensive range of variables inputs. This allows systems engineers to assess the likelihood of possible system-level behavior in the context of various system constraints. Agent-based tools often lack the higher fidelity levels found in most physics-based simulations. However, these lower fidelity agent-based models allow for more varied behavior interactions. This makes them highly useful for simulating system alternatives in which complex, nonlinear interactions can occur between entities that are difficult, if not impossible, to specify in the closed-form expressions required of physics-based models and simulations.

3.8.2   Check on Learning

Concepts:
  (a) What is the difference between a model and a simulation?
  (b) What is the difference between a game and a simulation? Can a game be a simulation? Why?
  (c) Would a systemigram be helpful for understanding public policy? What would be the mainstay for the systemigram be? What elements would be connected along the mainstay? What organizations would need to be added to create a full systemigram using the mainstay?

Comprehension:
  (a) What is the difference between a deterministic and a probabilistic model? Give an example of each using a fast-food restaurant as your system.
  (b) What are the four major steps in the modeling process?
  (c) Which of the three simulation hierarchies would be used to describe a model of traffic flow of individual vehicles down an interstate highway? Why?

Application:
  (a) List and describe the four qualities you feel are the most important for a model to be useful. Why did you pick these four?
  (b) A security checkpoint screens passengers entering the passenger terminal of an airport. List the probabilistic elements in the system. Describe how you could make these elements deterministic.
  (c) Create an IDEF0 level 0 diagram for operating a motor vehicle. Although the inputs and outputs may seem obvious, the controls and mechanisms may not be.

3.9   DETERMINING SIMULATION SAMPLE SIZE

A convenience of deterministic simulation models is that given a known set of inputs, the same output is assured. For example, using $E = mc^2$ with a given mass, the same energy calculation results. If the speed of light was unknown or uncertain and consequently represented by a random variable between 299 and 300 million meters per second (mmps), instead of a constant 299,792,458 mmps, an output distribution occurs containing some number of results, each with a different value. The nuances of this type of modeling are discussed in Chapter 10. These calculations, interchangeably called *replications*, *trials*, or *runs*, may significantly add to the cost of an experiment, so the modeler needs a mechanism to understand the trade-offs between replication cost and certainty. Deterministic models of complex systems may also benefit from testing only a sample of the possible combinations instead of the entire population.

Two methods are usually used to determine a reasonable number of replications, the *required sample size* on which to base an estimate. The first, called *power analysis*, is an approach that determines how much "power" a test has to detect a particular effect. It is often referred to as the *power of the test*. This approach is not explored in this chapter.

The second method is based on the logic of a statistical confidence interval (CI). In this case, the goal is to have a certain degree of confidence that the true population mean has been captured by determining the sample mean, given a certain number of observations and an acceptable probability of error. The formula for determining a confidence interval is shown in Equation (3.4) as:

$$CI_n = \bar{x}_n \pm t_{n-1,1-\alpha/2} \sqrt{\frac{s_x^2}{n}}. \tag{3.4}$$

This states that, with only an α probability of error, that the true mean is the same as the sample mean, $\bar{x}_n$, give or take some margin of error. The margin of error—everything to the right of the $\pm$ symbol—is made up of the variance of the sample, s_x^2, a desired level of confidence, $1 - \alpha$, and the t statistic for $n - 1$ degrees of freedom where n is the sample size.

For example, a health inspector may take 10 samples of drinking water to measure the amount of a contaminant and records the following levels, in parts per million (ppm): 29, 34, 20, 26, 20, 35, 23, 30, 27, 34. The mean, $\bar{x}_n$, is found to be 27.8, the variance, s_x^2, is 31.51, n is 10, and α is 0.10 for a 90% confidence interval. Inserting these numbers into Equation (3.4), the true mean value of contaminant in the drinking water is 27.8 ± 3.254, or an interval of between 24.546 and 31.054 ppm.

Since everything to the right of the $\pm$ symbol represents margin of error, the number of samples required, n, can be calculated if the modeler is willing to specify that error up-front. This is done routinely, for example, when someone declares some value, "give or take a couple." This is the same approach taken in power analysis when the modeler selects a level of effect to be detected. The modeler is saying, "I want to know how many samples/trials/replications/runs are required to detect a certain margin of error." These calculations can be done easily in a spreadsheet, although the modeler must rely on experience and judgment to avoid certain pitfalls. Specifically:

- Select a meaningful measure to use for sample size estimation.
- Generate a reasonable number of pilot runs to establish a solid mean and variance.
- Beware of the assumption that the pilot variance represents the true variance.
- Always round up the estimated n to the next higher number. Err on the side of caution.
- Generate an estimated n from the pilot runs, then incrementally increase the actual runs, rechecking the estimate for n, until the estimated n equals the actual n and your professional judgment is comfortable with the results and they are defensible to a decision maker.
- The larger the n, the greater the likelihood that the sample mean represents the true mean. Find the balance between replication cost and result accuracy.

Sample Size - Golf Club. Consider a golf club manufacturer interested in the performance of a new club. A swing machine hits 10 balls that fly the following distances, in yards: 220, 210, 189, 201, 197, 200, 205, 198, 196, and 200. Engineers want to use this series of pilot replications to determine how many balls need to be hit to find the mean distance, plus or minus two yards. By saying that, they acknowledge that they are willing to have a margin of error of two yards. Since it has been shown that the margin of error is represented in Equation (3.5), the engineers can set the margin of error equal to two and solve for n, as in:

$$\text{Margin of error} = t_{n-1,1-\alpha/2}\sqrt{\frac{s_x^2}{n}} \tag{3.5}$$

$$2 = 1.833\sqrt{\frac{72.27}{n}} \tag{3.6}$$

$$\Rightarrow 2 = \frac{(1.833)(8.5)}{\sqrt{n}} \tag{3.7}$$

$$\Rightarrow \sqrt{n} = \frac{(1.833)(8.5)}{2} \tag{3.8}$$

$$\Rightarrow n = \left(\frac{15.58}{2}\right)^2 \tag{3.9}$$

$$\Rightarrow n = 60.68 \tag{3.10}$$

Hitting 61 more golf balls is not likely to be a problem, unless they replace the swing machine with a professional golfer, whose per-swing fee may be very costly to the company. In that case, they may have the professional golfer hit another 10 balls and recalculate the required n. They can continue to incrementally move toward the 61-ball goal until the revised n equals the actual n. With each increment, the recorded variance approaches the true variance for the club and is therefore a better representation of reality. Although this approach provides only an estimate, it also provides the modeler with an easy and defensible tool for determining how many replications are required to achieve a desired result.

REFERENCES

1. Heylighen, F., Joslyn, C., Turchin, V. (2000) *The Principia Cybernetica Web*. Brussels: Principia Cybernetica. Available at: http://pespmc1.vub,ac.be/. (Accessed 24 Feb 2022).

2. Fidelity Implementation Study Group, SISO. (1998) *Fidelity ISG Glossary.* Version 3.0. Available at: https://vva.msco.mil/Special Topics/Fidelity/Fidelity-pr.pdf. (Accessed 24 Feb 2022).

3. Aaronson, S. (2005) 'NP-complete problems and physical reality,' *SIGACT News Archive*, 36(1), pp. 30–52.

4. (2003). *DoD Instruction 5000.61: DoD Modeling and Simulation (M&S) Verification, Validation and Accreditation (VV&A)*. Washington, DC: Department of Defense. Available at: https://www.esd.whs.mil/Portals/54/Documents/DD/issuances/dodi/500061p.pdf. (Accessed 24 Feb 2022).

5. Curedale, R. (2019) *Design Thinking Process & Methods*. Topanga, CA: Design Community College Inc.

6. Buede, D.M. (2009) *The Engineering Design of Systems: Models and Methods*, 2nd ed. New York: John Wiley & Sons.

7. Rechtin, E. (1990) *Systems Architecting*. New York, NY: Prentice Hall.

8. Omazaki Group (2022). *Types of Electric Cars and Working Principles*. Indonesia. Available at: https://www.omazaki.co.id/en/types-of-electric-cars-and-working-principles/. (Accessed 24 Feb 2022).

9. Sifaleras, A. (2013) 'Minimum cost network flows: problems, algorithms, and software,' *Yugoslav Journal of Operations Research*, 23(1), pp. 3–17.

10. Kennington, J.L. (1978) 'A survey of linear cost multicommodity network flows,' *Operations Research*, 26(2), pp. 209–236.

11. Bazarra, M.S., Jarvis, J.J., Sherali, H.D. (2009) *Linear Programming and Network Flows*, 4th ed. New York: John Wiley & Sons.

12. Charness, N., Boot, W.R. (2015) 'Technology, Gaming, and Social Networking,' in *Handbook of the Psychology of Aging*, 8th ed, K.W. Schaie and S.L. Willis, Ed. New York: Academic Press, pp. 389–407.

13. Suh, N.P. (2001) *Axiomatic Design: Advances and Applications*. New York: Oxford University Press.

14. Whitfield, R.I., Smith, J.S., Duffy, A.H.B. (2002) 'Identifying component modules,' in *7th International Conference on Artificial Intelligence in Design AID'02*, Cambridge, UK.

15. Steward, D. (1981) 'The design structure system: a method for managing the design of complex systems,' *IEEE Transactions on Engineering Management*, 28(3), pp. 71–74.

16. Steward, D.V. (1981) 'The design structure system: a method for managing the design of complex systems,' *IEEE Transactions on Engineering Management*, 28(3), pp. 71–74.

17. Pimmler, T.U., Eppinger, S.D. (1994) 'Integration analysis of product decompositions,' in *Proceedings of the ASME International Design Engineering Technical Conferences*, Minneapolis, MN.

18. Chen, S., Huang, E. (2007) 'A systematic approach for supply chain improvement using design structure matrix,' *Journal of Intelligent Manufacturing*, 18(2), pp. 285–299.

19. Fang, C., Marle, F., Vidal, L. (2010) 'Modelling risk interactions to re-evaluate risks in project management,' in *Proceedings of the 12th International Dependency and Structure Modelling Conference, DSM 10*, Cambridge, UK.

20. Charlesraj, V.P., Maheswari, J.U., Kalidindi, S.N., Varghese, K. (2004) 'Knowledge management for planning construction projects using dependency structure matrix,' in *20th Annual Conference of Association of Researchers in Construction Management*, Edinburgh, UK.

21. Eppinger, S.D., Browning, T.R. (2012) *Design Structure Matrix Methods and Applications*. Cambridge, MA: MIT Press.

22. Shea, G. (ed.) (2007) *Systems Engineering Handbook*, NASA/SP-2007-6105 Rev 2. Washington, DC: National Aeronautics and Space Administration.

23. O'Donovan, B.D. (2002) 'The input/output matrix method,' in *Proceedings of the 4th International Design Structure Matrix Workshop*, Cambridge, MA.

24. Mirshekarian, S. (2012) DSM Program, Version 2.1. Cambridge, MA: Massachusetts Institute of Technology (MIT). Available at: https://dsmweb.org/excel-macros-for-partitioning-und-simulation/. (Accessed 19 Jan 2022).

25. Hólttá-Otto, K., Suh, E.S., de Weck, O. (2005) 'Trade-off between modularity and performance for engineered systems and products,' in *Proceedings of International Conference on Engineering Design*, Melbourne, Australia, pp. 15–18.

26. Hólttá, K., de Weck, O. (2007) 'Degree of modularity in engineering systems and products with technical and business constraints,' *Concurrent Engineering: Research and Applications*, 15(2), pp. 113–126.

27. Hólttá, K. et al. (2012) 'Comparative analysis of coupling modularity metrics,' *Journal of Engineering Design*, 23(10–11), pp. 790–806.

28. Ledet, W., Himmelblau, D. (1970) 'Decomposition procedures for the solving of large scale system,' *Advances in Chemical Engineering*, 8, pp. 185–254.

29. Vorley, G. (2008) *Mini Guide to Root Cause Analysis*. Guildford, Surrey, UK: Quality Management & Training Ltd.

30. Danilovic, M., Browning, T.R. (2007) 'Managing complex product development projects with design structure matrices and domain mapping matrices,' *International Journal of Project Management*, 25, pp. 300–314.

31. Kusiak, A. (2002) 'Integrated product and process design: a modularity perspective,' *Journal of Engineering Design*, 13, pp. 223–231.

32. Kumar, A., Priva, B., Srivastava, S.K. (2020) 'Response to the COVID-19: understanding implications of government lockdown policies,' *Journal of Policy Modeling*, 43(1), pp. 76–94.

33. Holford, N.H. (1997) 'Clinical pharmacokinetics of ethanol,' *Clinical Pharmacokinet*, 13(5), pp. 273–292.

34. Beverton, J.H., Holt, S.J. (1993) *On the Dynamics of Exploited Fish Populations*. Dordrecht, GA: Springer.

35. Colquhoun, G.J., Baines, R.W., Crossley, R. (1993) 'A state of the art review of IDEF0,' *Journal of Computer Integrated Manufacturing*, 6(4), pp. 252–264.

36. Mayer, R.J., Painter, M.K., deWitte, P.S. (1992) *IDEF Family of Methods for Concurrent Engineering and Business Re-engineering Applications*. College Station, TX: Knowledge-Based Systems, Inc.

37. Straker, D. (1995) *A Toolbook for Quality Improvement and Problem Solving*. Englewood Cliffs, NJ: Prentice-Hall.

38. *Open source SysML project*. Available at: http://www.SysML.org. (Accessed 24 Feb 2022).

39. Law, A.W., Kelton, W.D. (2000) *Simulation Modeling and Analysis*, 3rd ed. New York: McGraw-Hill.

40. Harrell, C., Ghosh, B.K., Bowden, R.O. (2000) *Simulation Using ProModel*®, 2nd ed. New York: McGraw-Hill.

41. Foote, B.L., Goerger, S.R. (2005) 'Design considerations for simulating ABM systems,' in *Huntsville Simulation Conference*, Huntsville, Alabama.

42. Goerger, S.R. (2004) *Validating computational human behavior models: consistency and accuracy issues*. Doctoral dissertation. Monterey, CA: Naval Postgraduate School.

43. Fox, W. (2002) *Combat Modeling Overview*. Class notes, Introduction to Joint Combat Modeling (OA/MV4655), Monterey, CA: Operations Research Department, Naval Postgraduate School.

44. (2008) *Modeling and Simulation Guidance for the Acquisition Workforce*. Version 1.0. Office of the Deputy Under Secretary of Defense for Acquisition and Technology, Systems and Software Engineering, Developmental Test and Evaluation (ODUSD(A&T)SSE/DTE), Washington, DC. Available at: https://acqnotes.com/acqnote/tasks/modeling-simulation-planning. (Accessed 24 Feb 2022).

45. Hughes, W.P. (1997) *Military Modeling for Decision-making*, 3rd ed. Alexandria, VA: Military Operations Research Society (MORS).

46. Cole, J.L., Valentine, P. (1993) 'Joint data base elements for modeling and simulation,' in *Proceedings of the Winter Simulation Conference*, Institute for Operations Research and the Management Sciences (INFORMS). Available at: https://www.informs-sim.org/. (Accessed 24 Feb 2022).

47. Merriam Webster, Inc. (2022) *Merriam-Webster Online Dictionary*. Springfield, MA: Merriem-Webster. Available at: https://www.merriam-webster.com/. (Accessed 24 Feb 2022).

48. Russell, S., Norvig, P. (1995) *Artificial Intelligence: A Modern Approach*. Upper Saddle River, NJ: Prentice-Hall.

49. Dean, T., Allen, J., Aloimonos, J. (1995) *Artificial Intelligence: Theory and Practice*. Redwood City, CA: Benjamin/Cummings Publishing Company.

50. Holland, J.H. (1995) *Hidden Order: How Adaptation Builds Complexity*. Cambridge, MA: Perseus Books.

51. Freedman, A. (1999) *The Computer Desktop Encyclopedia*. Ver. 12.1. Point Pleasant, PA: Computer Language Company.

Chapter **4**

The Systems Decision Process

The decisions you make are a choice of values that reflect your life in every way.
—Alice Waters, Chef/Owner Chez Panisse Restaurant

4.1   INTRODUCTION

Systems engineering and systems decision support projects are complicated enough to require a repeatable process that can effectively guide one along the way. This is the purpose of the systems decision process (SDP) that we discuss in detail in this chapter. It is not a locked-in recipe that must have every step executed to succeed. The SDP guides activity, planning, and thinking. When coupled with systems thinking, it is a powerful approach to a broad array of challenges from conceptual design to retiring systems.

4.2   VALUE VERSUS ALTERNATIVE FOCUSED THINKING

The lead systems engineer guides the team in how it engages with the SDP. Two major philosophies dominate the approach strategies: *alternative-focused thinking* (AFT) and *value-focused thinking* (VFT), although hybrid strategies have been proposed. The SDP represents a VFT approach.

"Values are what we care about," Keeney notes in *Value-Focused Thinking* [1]. "As such, values should be the driving force for our decision-making." Values, he notes, are principles used for the evaluation of actual or potential consequences of action and inaction, of proposed alternatives, and of decisions. The VFT process differs from traditional AFT in that a clear

Decision Making in Systems Engineering and Management, Third Edition.
Patrick J. Driscoll, Gregory S. Parnell, and Dale L. Henderson
© 2023 John Wiley & Sons, Inc. Published 2023 by John Wiley & Sons, Inc.

React to Decision Problem		Identify or Create Decision Opportunity	
Alternative-Focused	**Value-Focused**		
1. Recognize a decision problem	1. Recognize a decision problem	1. Identify a decision opportunity	1. Specify values
2. Identify alternatives	2. Specify values	2. Specify values	2. Create a decision opportunity
3. Specify values	3. Create alternatives	3. Create alternatives	3. Create alternatives
4. Evaluate alternatives	4. Evaluate alternatives	4. Evaluate alternatives	4. Evaluate alternatives
5. Select an alternative	5. Select an alternative	5. Select an alternative	5. Select an alternative
Column 1	Column 2	Column 3	Column 4

Figure 4.1 Value-focused versus alternative-focused thinking sequences.

understanding of values drives the creation of alternatives, rather than the traditional approach in which alternatives are identified first, evaluated in some manner, ranked in terms of evaluation outcome metrics, and presented to decision makers for selection. This process can be applied not only to externally generated events, which largely characterize systems decisions affected by environmental elements and influences (aka "problems"), but also to internally generated events presenting unique *opportunities* to advance organizational goals, enhance the satisfaction of system output consumers, or improve system functionality.

The sequence of actions in VFT and AFT thinking is shown in Figure 4.1 from [1]. Columns 1 and 2 show that the major difference in reactive approaches under VFT and AFT is in the timing of when values are captured and codified. By understanding the decision maker's values before identifying alternatives, alternatives can be tailored to the context of the decision maker's unique needs. Keeney contrasts this with the alternative-focused approach that first identifies alternatives and then uses values to choose from among the alternatives that are available. To use an analogy involving purchasing a new electric vehicle, AFT would have you pick a vehicle from the existing inventory at a dealer location; VFT would have you build your ideal vehicle(s) online and then go shopping at the dealer that has it. While AFT does succeed in many cases, it does so in a somewhat serendipitous way.

The sequences shown to create decision opportunities enable more aggressive control of a situation. Column 3 is similar to Column 2 except that rather than reacting to a problem, the decision maker is alerted to opportunities. Keeney cites a situation in which a clothing manufacturer who observes fabric scraps identifies a decision opportunity and, by working through Steps 2–4, decides to open a new product line built from scrap material [1]. Decision opportunities can be created once strategic objectives and values are specified.

A conceptual model of the multi-criteria decision problem structure from both perspectives is shown in Figure 4.2. This figure, adapted from Buchanan et al. [2], shows the opposing approaches. Alternatives are defined here as courses of action that can be pursued and will have outcomes measured in terms of the criteria. The criteria reflect the values of the decision maker. Attributes are defined as the objectively measurable features of an alternative. This model separates the subjective from the objective components.

The greatest pitfall of a pure AFT approach is the danger of locking onto the list of alternatives and seeing only criteria that fit the alternatives while ignoring all others. Contrarily, a criticism of the VFT approach is that stakeholder values may not be sufficiently well-formed in the early

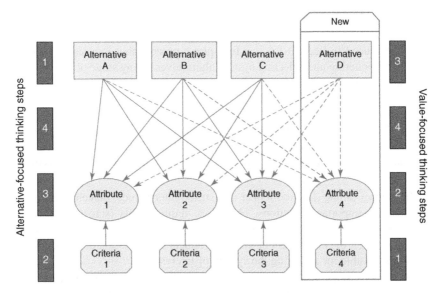

Figure 4.2   Flow of value-focused and alternative-focused thinking.

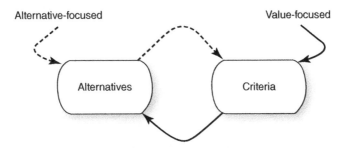

Figure 4.3   Dynamic approach to problem structuring. Source: Adapted from Corner et al. [5].

stages of the decision making process [3]. VFT is significantly different than AFT. First, the order is different. Second, VFT results in new criteria, new attributes, and new alternatives. Third, VFT changes the attribute ranges from local ranges to global ranges. Fourth, VFT takes additional effort to develop the value model, find new alternatives, and analyze the alternatives.

Finally, there is a "Which comes first: the chicken-or-egg?" dilemma that states that values are formed from experience with alternatives [4]. This leads some to argue that the starting point is not the issue. In their proposal for dynamic decision problem structuring, Corner et al. say, "What is important is that the decision maker learns about one (criteria or alternatives) from working with the other" [5]. Their concept is shown in Figure 4.3, where criteria and alternatives are shown as a causal loop, with entry through either an AFT (dashed line) or a VFT (solid line) approach. This suggests that by thinking about alternatives the solution designer helps identify criteria, and vice versa. This approach also recognizes the iterative nature of thinking about problems, so that both alternatives (or opportunities) and criteria can be refined during the problem definition and solution design phases.

4.3   THE SDP IN DETAIL

The SDP first introduced in Section 1.6 is a four-phase process that focuses on achieving high value return when evaluating and selecting system alternatives at any stage of a system life cycle. Figure 4.4 shows the complete SDP.

The SDP has five essential characteristics:

- It starts with efforts to understand the current system using systems thinking tools and systems representations introduced in Chapters 2 and 3. The current system, or baseline, is the foundation for assessing future needs and comparing candidate system solutions to meet those needs.

- The SDP focuses on the decision maker and stakeholder values. Stakeholders and decision makers identify important functions, objectives, requirements (screening criteria that all potential solutions must meet), and constraints that shape alternatives. Key stakeholders are the decision maker, the consumers of system products and services, the system owners, and the client responsible for acquiring the system of interest.

- The SDP focuses on creating value for decision makers and stakeholders and defines the desired end state that they are hoping to achieve. The value modeling task of the Problem definition phase plays an important role in defining an ideal solution that efficient alternatives try to achieve. The solution improvement task improves alternative design solutions. Once a choice set of efficient alternatives is identified, the SDP applies VFT to improve non-dominated solutions.

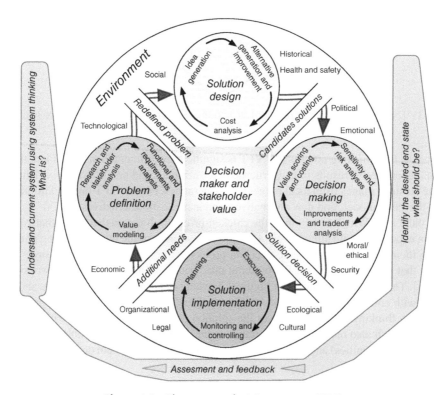

Figure 4.4   The systems decision process (SDP).

- It has four phases (Problem definition, Solution design, Decision making, and Solution implementation) and is highly iterative based on information and feedback from stakeholders and decision makers throughout the process.
- It explicitly considers the environment (historical, legal, social, cultural, technological, security, ecological, health and safety, and economic) that the system of interest will operate within and the political, organizational, moral/ethical, and emotional issues that arise with stakeholders and decision makers in the environment.

Although Figure 4.4 is not shown in color, colors are used to characterize each phase of the SDP when introducing it in classes or workshops. A full color version of the SDP is available upon request. The colors selected have a symbolic meaning for system engineers and engineering managers.

Problem definition. The most important task in any SDP is to identify and understand the actual problem or system challenge rather than the one that is initially presented to the team. Experience has demonstrated that being too familiar with the system of interest can cause stakeholders to overlook alternatives that take a fundamentally different approach toward meeting system requirements. For example, when a particular cellphone design becomes obsolete, cellphone companies pursue a new design that builds on previous features and capabilities. This is an example of contractive thinking to meet user communication requirements. Novel communications alternatives, perhaps even disruptive technologies, emerge as possibilities by using expansive thinking to understanding the same concerns, objectives, and constraints of the decision makers and stakeholders while being open to how these should be addressed. Failing to identify and fully understand the right problem can waste a lot of time and energy creating a great system solution to solve the wrong problem. For this very reason, the problem definition phase is colored **RED** to remind the team to **STOP** and make sure a clear understanding of the problem has been developed before designing any solutions.

Solution design. Having developed a clear understanding of the problem during the problem definition phase of the SDP, the team can go about the business of developing system solution alternatives. The complexity presented by internal and external interactions between system elements complicates solution design, and makes this setting different from other problem-solving settings. Despite the fact that the systems team might recognize the problem and be familiar with previous successful approaches, the team should resist the urge to quickly implement a solution from past experience. Core characteristics of stakeholders and system elements most certainly evolve over time, as does the system environment. Color-coding the solution design phase with a **YELLOW** circle is a reminder to **Proceed with Caution**. Each systems decision support engagement should be embarked upon with a fresh perspective and due diligence to develop new ideas while generating and improving alternative solutions to the problem.

Decision making. During the decision making phase of the SDP, all information and products from the previous phases of the SDP are leveraged to create materials that clearly showcase analytical features and results that inform decision making. For the SDP, these materials craft a rich tradeoff setting that highlights an array of important decision considerations. And, while the systems team can certainly provide recommendations, it is the decision maker who selects from among the choice set of system solutions based on their unique understanding of the situation. The decision making phase is colored **GREEN** to represent the **Green Light** the team is hoping to receive to proceed with implementing one of the final solution alternatives.

Solution implementation. Once a decision has been made, attention turns to implementing the system solution. This is often referred to as a decision handoff to whomever is responsible for managing continued system development and deployment. The solution implementation phase of the SDP is colored **BLUE** to represent **Blue Skies and Smooth Sailing** for the team implementing the system solution. Solution implementation is one of the most challenging phases of any decision support effort, including the SDP because it comes face-to-face with system integration, the most challenging aspect of systems engineering.

Decision maker and stakeholder values are positioned in the center of the SDP as a reminder that the entire process is grounded on creating system solutions that have significant value return imbedded in the SDP products being carried forward from one phase to the next: a redefined problem, a set of candidate system solutions, a solution decision, and additional needs as warranted. The cradle and arrows shown in the SDP indicate the iterative nature of the process that takes place between phases and within the tasks defining each phase.

4.3.1 The System Environment

The many factors affecting activities and products within the SDP and outside the boundary of the system of interest are called the system *environment*. The factors shown on the SDP are meant to illustrate a subset of these rather than being an exhaustive list because every systems effort is unique in some way. These factors represent systems that could in one way or another have cross-boundary interactions with the system of interest that will influence system solutions, and are briefly discussed in what follows.

Technological. System elements use technologies to perform functions that meet design requirements. Some technologies are commercial or government "off-the-shelf," meaning that they are developed and available in inventory for acquisition. Cutting edge, new technologies complicate matters because of technical, cost, and schedule risks that accompany them during research and development. Moreover, long term consequences of new technologies are not always understood early in their lifecycle. For example, while asbestos served as a very effective insulation material for many years, its health consequences as a human carcinogen were not identified until years later.

Economic. Economic factors are almost always major systems decision influencers both from a budget perspective and in terms of financial concerns. Most program managers have a constrained budget within which to complete a system development. Past this, however, is the reality that a new system imposes economic impacts on its environment as well. For example, when Microsoft® releases a new Windows operating system, computer hardware devices that were developed specifically for the previous OS may no longer function correctly, requiring code changes or design revisions. For example, as new requirements were introduced into various nations' health care systems because of COVID-19 and all its variants, a host of external systems that were dependent upon recreational and business travel suffered economic losses.

Political. Political factors come into play for many systems decisions. A system solution that has strong technical appeal may not be acceptable because of political reasons. Lobbying groups help influence system solution choices among private and government organizations that best align with their interest groups. Additionally, many public decisions require approval by U.S. government agencies and/or Congress, such as the recently passed U.S. infrastructure bill. Press coverage also has the potential to make any system development effort a major political issue, such as that seen when new nuclear power facilities are proposed.

Legal. Systems must comply with federal, state and community legal requirements. For example, automobiles must meet federal safety and emissions standards and also state regulations. Similarly, there are a good number of regulations, codes, and standards that must be adhered to when building a new home, putting up a new cellular telephone tower, flying a small unmanned aerial vehicle (UAV) near populated urban areas, and so on. These legal requirements should be included in the set of system requirements with the organization responsible for enacting and enforcing them listed as a stakeholder.

Health and Safety. The impact of a system on the health and safety of humans and other living creatures is an important consideration in all stages of the system life cycle. Health and safety issues can cause a system development effort to stop until these issues have been addressed sufficiently. Systems thinking and risk analysis are important tools to help identify and mitigate potential health and safety issues.

Social. Systems can have social implications as evidenced by the proliferation of social media use, which has changed the way that humans interact. Sometimes it is difficult to understand how a system will impact a society. For example, the city of Guangzhou, China has ongoing efforts to improve housing conditions for all of its citizens by moving them from their existing abodes that have a single floor of living space above a one car garage into beautiful multi-story apartments with modern utilities and features. In some cases, this has not been warmly received because the one car garage space is actually used as a family bodega, selling a wide variety of goods from auto hubcaps to prepared food. This activity cannot be accommodated in the apartment building design, which will disrupt important family financial and social systems.

Security. Systems, their products, and services must be secure from potential threats. Many organizations have minimum acceptable standards for system security that automatically become part of system requirements. Cybersecurity organizations thrive in today's world, and for very good reasons. In general there are three types of security controls that influence systems efforts: technical, administrative, and physical.

Ecological. Systems can have significant negative impact on a wide range of ecological elements, from disrupting mycelium growth in forests by logging, development, and recreational use to microplastic pollution in the oceans affecting undersea life and human health. Sometimes, systems have a positive impact as well, such as modern water treatment facilities with designed in counter-flood protection that prevents spillage into rivers and streams. And sometimes a system's impact on the environment is debatable, as in the case of nuclear power plants releasing warm water into rivers and zebra mussels finding ideal habitat near the outlets.

Cultural. In an isolationist economy, systems and products are designed to accommodate only national and local considerations. In a global economy, international cultures must be taken into consideration as well when designing and marketing systems. Cultural considerations also arise when an organization is faced with adapting to meet new challenges and desires to retain a set of cultural characteristics that define who they are or how they operate.

Historical. Some systems impact historical concerns. When the Jefferson Library project at the U.S. Military Academy was moving from the design into the build phase, the Office of Parks, Recreation, and Historical Preservation (OPRHP) had to approve the design because it called for the building to be placed 4 feet onto an area that was considered historically significant. Had they not approved, the project would have had to change the building's design or intended location. Most states have historical preservation societies that oversee potential changes that impact historical landmarks and facilities.

Moral/ethical. Moral or ethical issues are generally associated with system use, arising in response to the question: "Are we doing the right thing here?" Data packaging services collecting and selling subsets of personal data from online transactions, commercial logging ventures harvesting from the Amazon forests, open pit mining, animal use in science research, hydraulic fracking to gain access to underground natural gas reserves, and military use of drone technologies are example system settings that give birth to moral and ethical issues.

Organizational. Decisions are made within organizations, and organizations have their own way of doing things that has enabled them to be in the position they are in (good and bad). The key formal and informal organizational leaders can be important stakeholders in the decision process. Stakeholder analysis is the key to identifying and resolving organizational issues.

Emotional. Sometimes decision makers or key stakeholders have personal preferences or emotional issues regarding the system of interest or potential system solutions that will seem less than logical when first encountered by a systems team. These stakeholders may have risked their career or reputation on the current system design, or perhaps they have knowledge from a trusted source that one or more of the proposed designs has succeeded or failed in the past and are not willing to risk failing on a similar system effort despite the fact that circumstances are different. These are delicate matters that require careful consideration by the systems team if they are not to become project obstacles.

This list of factors constituting the system environment has several uses. Once a system boundary is defined, the list is often used as a system thinking tool to identify external dependencies by other systems on the system of interest, its components, its subsystems, and its input and output. This helps inform the project team when creating system representations such as those introduced in Chapter 3. Moreover, illuminating the breadth of dependencies and interrelationships that exist across these environment categories can also expose features that contribute greatly to system complexity, since complexity is frequently created because of interconnections and dependencies.

The environment factors also function as a very useful checklist early in a system project engagement when extensive research is ongoing and an effort is being made to identify all of the key system stakeholders. This is especially true for systems in which the project team has limited technical or operational knowledge and such knowledge is critical if the team is going to be successful.

Lastly, the environmental factors can guide feasibility studies when a new system is being proposed and the question: "How possible is this?" is posed. Depending on the setting, other factors such as market responses should be addressed. By addressing each of the factors while engaging in strengths, weaknesses, opportunities, and threats (SWOT) analysis and summarizing the overall effort in an effective display such as a stoplight diagram, a systems decision support team will touch on many, if not all of the concerns motivating such a study.

4.3.2   When to Use the Systems Decision Process

The SDP has broad applicability. Since the process is very general and grounded in sound principles, it may be useful for problem solving and solution design in settings where no one has been given the title "systems engineer." In some decision applications, only one or more of the SDP tasks may be required. For example, the stakeholder analysis techniques can be used to help define the problem in any public or private decision setting.

When considering whether or not to use the SDP, the engineering manager and lead systems engineer should consider three criteria: need, resources, and consequences. The SDP is needed if one or more of the project tasks meet the criteria listed in Table 4.1 for each of the four phases.

If the systems effort meets the criteria stated in Table 4.1, resource availability is next considered. The time it takes to analyze systems engineering data and provide reports and presentations to senior decision makers can be significant for large, complex systems. The full SDP process

TABLE 4.1 Criteria for When to Use Each Task in the Systems Decision Process.

Phase	Task	When needed	When not needed
Problem definition	Research and stakeholder analysis	Many research areas, multiple decision makers, and stakeholders with conflicting views about the system and system life cycle	Single decision maker and known stakeholder views
	Functional and requirements analyses	System functions and requirements not defined and are critical to system success	System functions and requirements are defined or not applicable
	Value modeling	System objectives and value measures not defined	Clear objectives, value measures, and value functions are known
Solution design	Idea generation	Concern about the quantity or quality of alternatives	Several high value alternatives are known or an established model or process is available to develop high value alternatives
	Alternative generation and improvement	Alternatives must be designed to ensure they perform system functions	Solution design is complete or simple to complete
		Alternatives need improvements to achieve the desired value	Solution optimization techniques are already available
	Cost analysis	Resources and costs are significant drivers for the decision	Costs and resources are not significant decision drivers
Decision making	Solution scoring and costing	Solution performance and costs are unknown	Solution performance and costs are known or not applicable
	Sensitivity and risk analyses	Important to understand the most sensitive assumptions or parameters and to assess the key risks	Impact of assumptions and risks are already known or not important
	Improvements and tradeoff analysis	Opportunity to improve the solution. Tradeoffs must be made between efficient solutions	Ideal solution is known or no opportunity to improve the solution
Solution implementation	Planning	Many complex tasks, significant resources, and many participants	Simple tasks, few resources, and few participants
	Executing	Critical to success of the decision	Not required or not critical to decision success
	Monitoring and control	Schedule and resource usage are important	No management oversight is required

described in this book takes time and resources. The amount of time spent on systems decision making should be proportional to the type of system and the potential consequences of the decision to the decision makers and stakeholders. The decision to select the airplane design for the next Boeing commercial airliner should require more SDP resources than the design of the next Nespresso™ coffee maker. The consequences of the next commercial airliner design may be much more significant to the future of Boeing (including its decision makers and stakeholders) and the global travel economy than the next coffee maker is to the future of Nestlé. The SDP requires access to senior leaders, decision makers, stakeholders, and subject matter experts. There may also be costs for developing tools to enable the process, for example, functional analysis, systems models, simulations, and life cycle cost models. In addition, depending on the experience level of the systems engineering team, there may be costs for education and training.

The SDP can be tailored to any stage of the system life cycle. For large, complex systems engineering and systems decision support projects all phases and at least one technique applying each of the common tasks may be required. However, for many projects, the SDP can be tailored to the size and scope of the project, and the particulars associated with the stage of the system life cycle that the project is addressing. In these situations, some SDP phases or common tasks may not be required. Based on the information provided in Table 4.1, the systems team should discuss which phases and tasks appear to be required and which do not based on the unique situation they face.

There are times when not all stakeholders are in agreement that the systems project should be undertaken. Possibly, there are organizational "turf wars" ongoing in which various divisions are competing for resources. Some of these resources would be consumed by the project and so the project can be seen as a threat. Or, perhaps there are differing opinions as to which direction the systems project should proceed, who should be in charge, and what outcomes are expected. In this case, stakeholder analysis plays a critical role in helping to focus the effort. In particular, the Findings, Conclusions, and Recommendations (FCR) matrix resulting from stakeholder analysis reveals stakeholder viewpoints and their logic to decision makers. This can provide a neutral means of opening a dialog among stakeholders that may result in a common consensus in support of the systems project. While typically each of the statements listed in Findings is credited to a source when presented to decision makers, there are times when a lead systems engineer will decide to make these statements anonymous to protect the participants while providing the decision maker with important information. This can be a wise decision.

The SDP requires systems engineers and systems decision support teams to work with key people associated with a system of interest. Key people are successes in their fields and positions, and they have strong beliefs as to how success is to be gained. Maintaining a neutral, objective, and calm demeanor with an attitude that the systems decision support team plus key stakeholders form the "us" and "we" who are working the effort goes a long way toward overcoming challenging situations during the process.

Table 4.2 gives an example of a systems engineering project that used the SDP. In some cases, the phases or tasks were not done or done by another group after the systems decisions support project was completed. For example, the Army Base Realignment and Closure (BRAC) study was done by the Army Basing Study team in 2002–2005. The solution implementation phase was performed in 2005–2015 by the Army's Installation Management Command after a successful decision handoff [6].

Table 4.3 compares the SDP with two other problem solving processes. Both of these problem solving processes are similar to the SDP. Athey's systematic systems approach is a more general approach than the others. The SDP provides more detail concerning structured process steps and

TABLE 4.2   Systems Decision Process Example.

Phase	Task	Army BRAC [6]
Problem definition	Research and stakeholder analysis	Many senior leader interviews and document reviews
	Functional and requirements analyses	Requirements analysis used to develop installation portfolio constraints
	Value modeling	Used for the ranking of installations and the evaluation of alternatives
Solution design	Idea generation	Performed by subject matter experts informed by modeling
	Alternative generation and improvement	Developed by mission and functional experts
	Cost analysis	Used many models in the analysis process
Decision making	Solution scoring and costing	Scoring data submitted and certified by each Army installation
	Sensitivity analysis	Significant sensitivity analysis at all parts of the process
	Improvements and tradeoff analysis	The value was to transform Army installations and save operations and support funds. Solutions were improved after analysis
Solution implementation	Planning	Performed by BRAC division on the Army staff
	Executing	Will be performed by major commands and the Installation Management Command
	Monitoring and controlling	Critical since execution is monitored by the US Government Accountability Office and US Congress

intended output than Athey's approach. The military decision making process (MDMP) goal is to produce a viable and effective course of action, which is similar to selecting among alternative system solutions.

4.3.3   Check on Learning

Concepts: Suppose that a decision maker was convinced that he knew the answer to a problem his organization's system was having but was willing to bring in a systems team to address the problem.

(a) Is this a case of expansive or contractive thinking?

(b) How would his belief affect the system team's actions during problem definition, solution design, and decision making SDP phases?

(c) Is the decision maker engaging in value focused thinking?

TABLE 4.3   Comparison of Problem-Solving Processes.

Systems decision process	Athey's systematic systems approach	Military decision making process
1. Problem definition	1. Formulate the problem	1. Receipt of mission
(a) Research and stakeholder analysis	2. Gather and evaluate information	2. Mission analysis
(b) Functional and requirements analyses	3. Develop potential solutions	3. Course of action (COA) development
(c) Value modeling	4. Evaluate workable solutions	4. COA analysis
2. Design solution	5. Decide the best solution	5. COA comparison
(a) Idea generation	6. Communicate system solution	6. COA approval
(b) Alternative generation and improvement	7. Implement solution	7. Orders production
(c) Cost analysis	8. Establish performance standards	8. Rehearsal
3. Decision making		9. Execution and assessment
(a) Value scoring and costing		
(b) Sensitivity and risk analyses		
(c) Improvements and tradeoff analysis		
4. Solution implementation		
(a) Planning		
(b) Execution, monitoring, and control		

Comprehension:

(a) If an inventor came up with a new, innovative approach to preventing restaurant tables from wobbling, would she need to apply the SDP to get her idea developed and on the market? Why?

(b) Suppose another inventor came up with a new, innovative approach to protecting law enforcement officers that would involve modifying their vehicle doors. Would he be best advised to use the SDP to get this idea developed? Again, why?

(c) Is there a fundamental difference between the two situations posed that is conditioning your answers?

Application: Suppose that a feasibility study is needed for a proposed new pipeline that would be used to transport hazardous liquids from a chemical production plant in Pennsylvania to a processing plant in Illinois.

(a) Using the SDP environmental factors as a checklist, identify and list the major concerns that would have to be analyzed under each environmental factor that applies to this situation.

(b) Use a green, yellow, and red colored matrix to indicate environment factor concerns that are good-to-go, of some concern, and are show-stoppers.

(c) Who are the major stakeholders for this situation? What stakeholder type would the CEO of the chemical production plant be? Why?

4.4 THE ROLE OF STAKEHOLDERS

Given that the SDP is needed and the potential resources are reasonable for the consequences of the systems decision, the final consideration is whether decision makers and stakeholders will support the process. If senior decision makers do not support the process, the resources (people and funding) will not be available to implement the process. If the decision makers and stakeholders do not participate in the process, any resulting recommendations may not be accepted.

What sets the SDP apart from other problem solving methods is that it requires frequent and consistent engagement with stakeholders. There are settings in which a client will sponsor an effort to resolve a challenging problem they are facing and then not see the team working the problem for many months. In these settings, a significant amount of discussion will take place among the project team regarding how the solution is going to need to be sold to the client. This is not the case with the SDP. By essentially drawing stakeholders into the process as collaborators, their involvement with SDP tasks and activities motivates a vested interest in the eventual results. When this happens, systems decision support teams will hear comments such as " … our value model … " and " … our alternatives … ," indicating that stakeholders have internalized ownership of the systems effort. This is an indicator of success.

Teams that are new to the SDP approach may be apprehensive to engage with key stakeholders early in the process because little progress has been made at that point and little or no results are in-hand. This is a misplaced concern. All projects should to be socialized with key stakeholders early on to begin a process of building trust. Having expert capability on a systems team is one thing; trusting that expert capability to deliver on expectations is quite another. At times, trust may appear to be personality dependent, but it is always established and maintained by meeting stakeholder expectations for professional behavior.

Stakeholders are important to system success because they have amazing talent within their organizations. If a systems project is worthwhile and stakeholders see benefits in its undertaking, they will make some of their talented people available to assist in the effort. Work priorities are set by management, and stakeholders represent management in some dimension.

Managing stakeholder expectations is a carefully thought out activity that affects the entire systems team. The goal in this regard is to deliver more value return during and at the end of the project than promised. This translates into the systems team keeping a fairly constant watch for places during the project at which doing a little bit more adds unexpected positive results for stakeholders.

Unless the systems team is part of the organization that owns the system of interest, the team members are outsiders from the stakeholders' viewpoint. However, there are common reasons why organizations appeal to outside sources for assistance. Here are a few:

- Fresh eyes on a problem can bring new perspectives that reveal new opportunities, alternatives, and approaches. Having exhausted internal options and ended up with similar decision alternatives, bringing on new talent with a holistic approach represented by systems thinking and the SDP might offer innovative and creative options.

- The situation is dire and frustrating management to a point that a scapegoat might be useful to blame the disaster on. This happens rarely, but it is a bad situation and a good one to walk away from.

- An engagement with outside help offers a way to spend a portion of budget funding on a problem that is minor in the big scheme of things but is nagging and persistent. Funding of this nature usually comes directly out of an organization's internal research and development (IRAD) budget. This can also occur when an organization has funds that are set to expire at the end of a fiscal year, a commonplace occurrence in government organizations. These are generally low-threat opportunities that should be captured.

- The talent that the outside team brings is unique and cannot be found within the organization or trained within the time horizon within which solutions need to be identified and implemented. This is a very common situation, and one that recognizes the limited duration that systems decision support is needed.

Finally, if stakeholders are concerned that an "all in" fully-funded project may not yield the value return they need because they are unfamiliar with the SDP process, it is sometimes helpful to suggest a smaller scale pilot effort that is lower cost and limited scope but will provide stakeholders with a better sense of what is possible and what is involved with engaging the SDP. In this situation, showing the decision maker or client an example of the SDP output, especially graphs that directly support systems decision-making, and explaining how these support the final decision will help them form an accurate assessment of the project potential. There is a good chance that stakeholders will be familiar with alternative thinking approaches because these may be dominating their practices. Explaining the differences between evaluating system alternatives based on technical performance scores and evaluating alternatives based on how these scores translate into value is another fundamental concept that will aid their understanding.

The following case study illustrates how a system arises out of need. It will be revisited at various points in succeeding chapters to show how system decisions are supported by the SDP. The system decision was regarding a system concept associated with the second stage in a system life cycle (see Figure 1.1). That decision requires commitment of department resources. The department will choose to buy (or not buy) system development software and hire (or not hire) people to do system design and development. The department employed techniques in each phase of the SDP to arrive at a system concept that best supported the department's stakeholders and their values.

Curriculum Management System (CMS): The Opportunity. Teaching undergraduate systems engineering disciplines to cadets is the core function of the United States Military Academy's Department of Systems Engineering. Teaching includes building and managing the curriculum, delivery of that curriculum to the cadets, and continuously assessing and adjusting that curriculum to maintain excellence. The department has processes in place for curriculum management, but they can be labor intensive, slow, and disjointed. Given the proliferation of information technology into education, there was an opportunity for the department to leverage information technology to improve its capability to manage the curriculum and to teach cadets.

The department has a complex, evolving curriculum that must be synchronized across four academic programs in accordance with Academy education goals and accreditation requirements. Advances in systems engineering, engineering management, systems management, and operations research require continuous curriculum changes at all levels. These include program goal updates, course additions or deletions, textbook changes, and lesson changes. Any one of these changes has the potential to disrupt the synchronization an academic program in a number of ways. They can jeopardize achievement of Academy or program goals, force cadets to use multiple texts for the same material, present duplicate material, or present material out of order from the students' perspective.

The department and the Academy prevent some of these problems through centralization and committee work. However, these processes are slow and laborious, and they do not support frequent lesson-level changes that should be synchronized across one or two courses. These low-level changes often occur outside of the purview of academic committees, but, over time, they have just as much potential to disrupt synchronization. The department's curriculum development process stands to improve flexibility and synchronization through the application of information management and decision support.

Teaching, by its nature, is a collaborative process. Instructors must develop and deliver content by a combination of textbook reading and problem assignments, in-class instruction, electronic files, and graded events. Ideally, these are well organized and stored in a structured manner that supports easy access by cadets and instructors and consistency across courses. In reality, the department employs a variety of methods to manage the curriculum. These include:

- Network drive storage for cadet access,
- Network drive storage for faculty access,
- Course Web sites maintained by faculty, and
- Academy-wide collaboration system to support teaching.

The Problem. Each faculty member selects the method or combination of methods to use based on his or her preferences. While this is not a problem within the context of a single course, it creates difficulties for cadets with multiple courses or for instructors who must collaborate across courses. People often cannot find needed information without directly contacting its originator. As a result, collaborative opportunities are lost, and the curriculum becomes disjointed. This also complicates archiving course information at the end of the semester.

Finally, the department faculty assesses and updates the curriculum at regular intervals. These assessments ensure responsiveness to a dynamic world, maintain accreditation, support educational goals, and improve teaching methods. Because they are so data intensive, the assessments require many man-hours to compile the necessary information. The input data is scattered across many systems:

- Cadet surveys
- Instructor assessments
- Course administrative documents
- External assessment reports
- Meeting notes
- Various internal and external Web sites

The department had an opportunity to use a structured information system and well-synchronized processes to streamline and improve the assessment process. This would ensure the curriculum remains current and responsive to its stakeholders.

The Opportunity. In order to better build and manage the curriculum, deliver material to cadets, and continuously assess against dynamic demands, the Department of Systems

Engineering proposed to build an integrated Curriculum Management System (CMS). This system should synchronize advanced information technology with internal management processes in order to provide leap-ahead improvements.

REFERENCES

1. Keeney, R.L. (1992) *Value-Focused Thinking: A Path to Creative Decisionmaking.* Cambridge, MA: Harvard University Press.
2. Buchanan, J.T., Henig, E.J., Henig, M.L. (1998) 'Objectivity and subjectivity in the decision making process,' *Annals of Operations Research*, 80, pp. 333–345.
3. Wright, G., Goodwin, P. (1999) 'Value elicitation for personal consequential decisions,' *Journal of Multi-Criteria Decision Analysis*, 8, pp. 3–10.
4. March, J.G. (2020) 'The technology of foolishness,' in *Shaping Entrepreneurship Research*, S.D. Saravathy, N. Dew, and S. Venkataraman, Eds. New York: Routledge.
5. Corner, J., Buchanan, J., Henig, M. (2001) 'Dynamic decision problem structuring,' *Journal of Multi-Criteria Decision Analysis*, 10, pp. 129–141.
6. Ewing, P., Tarantino, W., Parnell, G. (2006) 'Use of decision analysis in the Army base realignment and closure (BRAC),' *Decision Analysis Journal*, 13(1), pp. 33–49.

Chapter 5

Problem Definition

The last 10 percent of performance generates one-third of the cost and two-thirds of the problems.
—Norman R. Augustine, former President, CEO Lockheed-Martin Corp.

5.1 PURPOSE OF THE PROBLEM DEFINITION PHASE

The Problem Definition phase can and should be used to support systems decision making at any stage of the system life cycle. Properly executed, the investigation and problem structuring activities that the phase advocates result in a better understanding of the systemic and symptomatic conditions motivating the existing situation. With this in-hand, a problem restatement is possible that more keenly guides activities in the subsequent phases.

It is well-known in decision support that an initial problem as described by stakeholders is rarely the exact issue needing to be addressed by a system solution. This is because symptoms are easy to recognize and identify, especially those that are being actively experienced by stakeholders. Systemic causes, which are ones that system solutions are used to alleviate, require careful investigation along with expansive and contractive thinking in cycles to produce data that informs efficient and effective alternatives. These types of problems are subset combinations of evident symptoms combined with underlying issues affecting system performance that are hidden from direct observation, such as mismatches between designed functional behavior and changes that have occurred in environmental elements that influence system behavior.

Decision Making in Systems Engineering and Management, Third Edition.
Patrick J. Driscoll, Gregory S. Parnell, and Dale L. Henderson
© 2023 John Wiley & Sons, Inc. Published 2023 by John Wiley & Sons, Inc.

History is rife with examples of solutions developed to a problem incorrectly or incompletely defined by hard-working, well-intentioned individuals. For example:

- General Robert E. Lee (United States Military Academy Class of 1829) of the Army of Northern Virginia believed that the Confederacy's problem was to decisively defeat the Union Army in the Civil War to achieve the goals of the Confederate states. Lee's strategy to solve this problem was to invade the Union States to draw their Army into a decisive engagement. Ultimately this led to a disaster at the Battle of Gettysburg when Lee attacked the larger and better equipped Union Army who held ground favorable to the defense. Others in the Confederacy, including Lieutenant General James "Pete" Longstreet (United States Military Academy Class of 1842), believed the problem was to destroy the Union's will to continue the conflict by threatening the seat of government in Washington DC. Others felt the Confederate Army could capture Washington, DC and sue for a favorable peace to achieve their goals [1]. We will never know who correctly defined the Confederacy's problem but it is evident from history that destruction of the Union Army was not necessarily the complete problem facing the Confederacy in achieving their goals.
- The late 1970s and 1980s saw Japanese automakers gain a significant share of the U.S. auto market. U.S. auto manufacturers believed the problem was how to compete on cost against the smaller, more fuel efficient Japanese cars that were cheaper to purchase and operate. While true, this problem definition proved to be incomplete. Japanese auto manufacturers were successful then due to both the lower costs and higher quality of their cars. U.S. auto manufacturers were slow to recognize that they could realize a positive return on investment in improved quality control measures in producing cars [2]. As history has shown, Japanese automakers gained significant market share of the US auto market during this period.
- In 1983, IBM introduced the IBM PC Junior to compete in the home computer market against the then-dominant Commodore 64 and Apple II [3]. Apparently, IBM's plan to meet consumer needs in the home computer market was to build a scaled-down version of its popular IBM PC, which was then very successful for business consumers. Unfortunately the changes to the business IBM PC did not make the Junior easy to use at home and did not make it affordable. The IBM PC Junior suffered from an incomplete definition of the problem for IBM to successfully compete against Apple and Commodore in the home computer market.

These examples from history show that a thorough, complete definition of a problem is crucial when forming effective solutions. As with any good decision support process, the Problem definition phase requires a thorough research effort starting with the system of interest and expanding outwards into environmental systems to uncover important environmental influences and their connections to the system of interest. Performing a literature review of appropriate laws, organizational policies, applicable studies previously undertaken, and pertinent discipline-specific principles is necessary to effectively define a problem.

The concept diagram in Figure 5.1 shows the tasks involved in the Problem Definition phase: *research*, *stakeholder analysis*, *functional* and *requirements analyses*, and *value modeling*. While research into a systems decision problem continues throughout the SDP, it is particularly helpful early on for helping the systems team gain a more comprehensive understanding of the challenge, and to identify specific disciplines related to the problem whose expertise may need to be added to the team. Moreover, research helps to identify a more complete set of stakeholders who have a vested interest in any resulting solution.

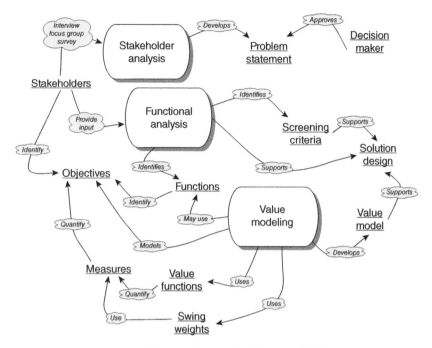

Figure 5.1 Concept diagram for Problem definition.

Stakeholder analysis enables systems engineers to identify objectives, functions, requirements, and constraints for a system or decision problem along with specific values held by decision makers that will influence how alternatives are crafted and scored. Because this is a holistic, fresh look at a system and its environment, stakeholder analysis can also uncover previously unidentified opportunities along with potential new research areas related to the system of interest.

A system is developed to perform specific functions. These functions should be designed to meet the purpose and objectives of the system. Systems must also meet stakeholder requirements to be considered feasible; how well they do so defines their effectiveness. An effective system solution is one that provides good value return to key stakeholders while satisfying as many of their expectations as practical. Despite meeting all requirements, a system solution will most likely fall a bit short in satisfying all stakeholder expectations or maximizing value return to each. The SDP places priority on the decision maker's values, then on any others who are identified as important stakeholders. The qualitative and quantitative models developed using the SDP as described in Chapter 6 do precisely this.

5.1.1 Comparison with Other Systems Engineering Processes

Beginning the systems decision process with deliberate, focused tasks for defining a problem is not unique. Axiomatic design, typified by architectural design, spends a significant amount of time and effort up-front to understand nuanced aspects of what a client is trying to achieve. It's rarely simply a matter of designing living space, office space, or infrastructure support. Most often, architects are seeking to match the "statement" that a client is trying to make by building a new structure. If this is missed, the build is not a success. In an analogous fashion, the initial problem or system need described by a client is not quite the whole picture [4].

Several systems engineering and problem solving processes naturally start with some form of problem definition [5]. Wymore, for example, defines a system life cycle in seven phases, the first of which develops requirements. During this phase, systems engineers work on tasks such as understanding the problem situation and the customer needs [6]. The SIMILAR process for the systems design starts with a "state the problem" function [7]. The International Council on Systems Engineering includes Plowman's model of the systems engineering process in their systems engineering body of knowledge (SEBoK). This process includes a function for understanding what a customer wants and how a system must perform [8]. This identifies just a few of the systems engineering processes and/or life cycles that incorporate a deliberate process for defining the problem.

The goal for the Problem definition phase is to have a clearly defined problem statement that gains approval by the key stakeholders, a set of systems requirements or constraints that guide alternative solution design, and an initial quantitative methodology for evaluating how well alternatives meet the values of stakeholders in solving the redefined problem.

Several common decision situations regarding electric vehicles (EVs) are being used in this chapter to illustration most of the key concepts associated with the Problem definition phase. A select number of these are carried forward into later chapters as well.

5.2 RESEARCH AND "WHAT IS?"

On first contact with a system of interest, an intense amount of activity occurs that is centered on understanding as much about the system and its environment as possible. This investigation delves into technical, operational, financial, and strategic performance over a limited past time horizon, touching on many if not all of the SDP environmental factors and more. In doing so, the process uncovers observable and subtle internal and external dependencies while allowing stakeholders to be identified and analyzed for their potential roles as the project moves forward.

The aggregate of this information is called the *current state of the system*, or in terms of the SDP, answers the question *"What is?"* Comparing this information to what the system was designed to do (its purpose) is an act of analysis. Comparing the present to the past in this manner illuminates gaps which, if performed sufficiently in-depth, should corroborate a good percentage of the client's problem description and more. These gaps between how the system performed upon deployment and operation and its current performance levels can naturally occur as the environment surrounding the system evolves. At some point, a system exhausts its ability to adapt to maintain performance and redesign, renovate, or replace the only options. The results from this initial analysis are not necessarily going to reveal root causes for any substandard or dissatisfying system performance, but they will substantiate or rebut a client's interpretation of the current situation.

Following this, the investigation next turns forward-looking in time, bringing client expectations and aspirations for the system into view by inquiring from stakeholders *"What should be?"* Resolving the difference(s) between *"What is?"* and *"What should be?"* defines potential objectives for a systems decision support project. Narrowing and focusing these possibilities to a subset that are achievable during the available project time and with all resources in-mind is called project *scoping*. Exactly which system aspects to include with the project and which to set-aside is a decision driven by priorities set by the client, available resources, and systems team expertise.

There are several ways to select which opportunities to pursue and which to suspend. Overall, any effort should focus on returning high value to stakeholders. One might cross-compare performance gaps with associated system behavior and select the 20% of system behaviors responsible for 80% of the performance gaps. This is called the "80/20 rule," or Pareto rule. Or, one might estimate the time and resources it might take to address each of the gaps noted, solicit a priority ranking

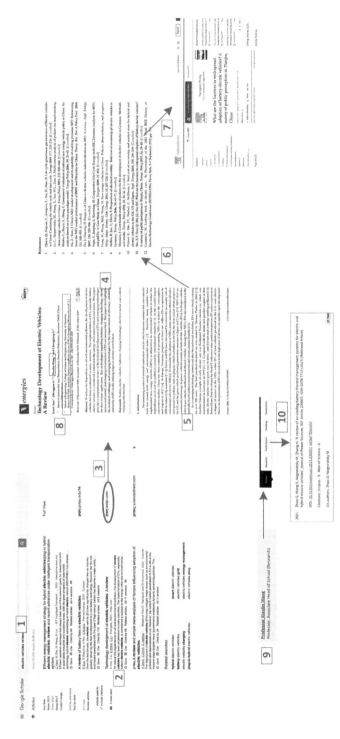

Figure 5.2 Online investigative pattern common to literature reviews. Source: Google LLC, MDPI, Elsevier.

from the client, and establish a project plan that accommodates sequential and parallel activities. In either case, selecting a small number of major objectives that can be finished in the time allotted and a number of smaller ones that can be completed in very short order or coincident with the main effort would a good strategy. These lesser intensive objectives are referred to as "quick wins." The major objectives chosen for the project are combined into a single statement which focuses the system decision support effort. This is called the *Fundamental Objective* for the project, which is displayed at the top of a qualitative value model discussed in Chapter 6.

The collection of activities during this initial investigation, which includes reviewing published technical articles and reports, conducting stakeholder interviews, engaging data collection surveys, and other problem structuring efforts described in Section 5.3 is referred to as *research*.

The technical nature of modern systems inevitably directs a good portion of research towards professional journals specialized in publishing recent developments related to and directly supporting the project's Fundamental Objective. Mining and categorizing these sources, briefly summarizing their potential contribution(s) to the project, and adding them to a growing list of formal references that will become part of a project's report known as the *literature review*.

A literature review for a systems project is considerably different than a humanities-based book review, and in many ways simpler. Book reviews are comprehensive summaries of a published work, illuminating story arcs, author's motivation, interpretation, prose style, and a host of other concerns. Literature reviews are much more surgical in nature, extracting only the facts, techniques, and results that are relevant to the project. Patterns for accomplishing this type of research are well-known. Figure 5.2 and the example that follows describes typical steps that have proven effective for researching information related to systems decision support efforts.

 When the systems team needs a refresher on a specific mathematical or modeling technique, it may appear logical to go first to published journals whose focus is specifically on the topic you are after. However, if a summary does appear in a resource such as this, the authors tend to assume that readers will be familiar with most background foundational material or that they are operating on the cutting edge of research in that area. This assumption affects the terseness and complexity of their presentation approach and may not be appropriate for the team's use. Consider instead where such a technique might be used as an application area and try to find articles in that context. The authors of articles in these journals assume that readers will need a brief reminder of foundational material in more conversational language, possibly more to the point of what the team needs.

Example Research Pattern: Electric Vehicles (EV). A systems engineering and systems decision support effort is underway that involves integrating EV support into the overall design and construction of a new Cyber & Engineering Academic Center (CEAC) at West Point (https://www.westpointaog.org/file/CEACbrochure.pdf). From a holistic perspective, the entirety of the design, build, operate, and maintain considerations is a complicated system requiring careful planning. How EVs are planned for affects many design choices, among them space allocation and flow for a multi-story parking garage that needs to accommodate both fossil fuel and EVs for staff, faculty, and visitors.

As part of investigating the existing system state, the team is performing research to uncover up-to-date credible facts and issues with EVs. Since this is an new area for most of the team, they start their investigation looking for a recently published *survey* article that would hopefully summarize current knowledge on the topic while perhaps listing emerging technologies, challenges, and ongoing research efforts. Figure 5.2 shows one small piece of this information mining effort, which adheres to a well-known pattern for conducting literature reviews.

1. Starting with a broad search tool, in this case Google Scholar®, the team starts a search for a survey article using the term "electric vehicle review" limiting results to those published "Since 2020" and including citations but not patents. Since the focus is on finding a survey article, results are initially sorted by relevance and not by date. In this case, 53, 500 sources are found.

2. Luckily, the third article displayed appears very promising and on-topic, and it appears to be available in PDF format. In years past, special subscriptions were needed to access full text articles in PDF form from publishers. This is no longer the case, and many publishers provide online full access to their articles without charge to the reader.

3. Following the link produces a full text article written by Sun et al. and published in the professional journal *Energies*.

4. The team reads the abstract, noticing that the authors discuss some information that they are looking for, which they highlight. They then scan through the article to read the section(s) addressing the material they are after. Assuming that the facts and results stated are useful, in a separate file they add a complete citation for this article to their growing list of references using the format that they intend to use for their technical report(s). Along with this citation, they add a brief note describing what is in this article and the information's potential use for their project. This use could be simply supporting facts they need to state, providing a useful modeling approach, stating technical parameters that may be useful, describing key current issues with EVs that have not been resolved, and so on. Once done, they save the PDF to an appropriate folder on a share site that all team members can access and continue their investigation.

5. Next, they read through the Introduction section looking for other work that the authors used to support their article that could be useful to the project. In this case, there is a sentence stating a major benefit of EVs in comparison to other non-fossil fuel vehicle options. This is a fact that they would like to state in their report. So like all statements of fact, they need a credible reference supporting it.

6. The citation link goes to the References section that lists the source article for the fact they state.

7. Clicking on the *CrossRef* link yields the article in the journal *Transport Policy* archived by the ScienceDirect®database service. They can repeat the investigative steps again with this article adding it to their growing list of references. Or, they can return back to the survey article by Sun et al. to follow another lead. Notice, however,

that each time they follow a References link concerning published material, they are stepping further back in time. If the team decides to only use material that is no older than 3 years, which seems reasonable given how fast EV manufacturing is developing, they will most likely be reiterating the previous 6 steps on multiple initial search terms.

8. Optionally, the team can decide to follow a path from the past to the present using an assumption that technical researchers who are actively publishing articles in professional journals will continue their work in a particular line while productive. These could include authors who are academic faculty, students, or industry members. Faculty websites often list recent publications so that graduate students and research sponsors can see their research interests. There is a possibility that this survey article was an early work in the field by Wang, and that more recent articles have been published that might be useful for the project. Noting that Wang appears associated with the College of Science and Engineering, University of Tasmania, the team visits that site looking for more recent work on EVs published by Wang.

9. Following the path down from the School of Engineering landing page: '*School of Engineering -> Research -> People -> Faculty*', yields a faculty listing for Professor Wang, who appears to be the Associate Head of School (Research). This link leads to Professor Wang's homepage, which offers several information tabs; among them being Publications.

10. Selecting the *Publications* link and examining the listed publications, the team sees that his interest in EVs continues and a more recent article in 2021 is available. If relevant, the same article scanning process as described earlier is applied, the citation is added to the list of references with a short note, and this more recent article becomes a place to begin the sleuthing process once again. This step forward in time technique can be used on any of the authors noted on a journal paper.

 The primary author or the most senior member of a research team is typically listed first among the authors on a journal article or technical report. Alternatively, if all authors contributed equally to a research article, it is common practice to list the authors alphabetically.

5.2.1 Check on Learning

Concepts:
   (a) Does the level of research needed for a system redesign depend on the life cycle stage that the system is in? Why? Can you give a system example to illustrate?
   (b) Does information appearing on commercial websites automatically make it credible information? Likewise, does information appearing in personal blog sites automatically render it useless because it did not go through a peer review process?

(c) Do you agree with the statement: "a technical report with a very small number of references is more trusted than one with a lot of references because it shows the intelligence of the people who created it." Why?

Comprehension: Suppose that a systems team was conducting research in support of a system improvement project for an existing telecommunications system. The improvement is substantial and will need a substantial number of new cell towers to be constructed.

(a) Using the SDP environmental factors, identify the major concerns that will have to be addressed and investigated by the systems team.

(b) The team locates a 4-year old report published online that contains a lot of the information they are looking for, but they are concerned that the information is a bit outdated. The company that created the report no longer exists. How might they go about locating any of the original analysts that worked on the report?

5.3 STAKEHOLDER ANALYSIS

Given the multi- and interdisciplinary nature of systems engineering, a systems team needs to be aggressive and inquisitive in order to uncover valuable topics that will be needed regarding the system of interest. The research and stakeholder analysis task is an important and iterative process. When introduced to a new problem, systems teams conduct research in order to understand the nature of the disciplines involved in the project. This research leads to identifying the stakeholders impacted by the problem. Stakeholders identify additional research sources for the systems engineering team to investigate. Thorough research is critical for developing a complete definition of the problem.

Systems teams use research and stakeholder analysis to understand the problem they face, identify the people and organizations relevant to the problem at hand, and to determine stakeholder needs, wants, and desires with respect to the problem and its system solution [9]. Stakeholders comprise a set of individuals and organizations that have a vested interest in the system of interest, its products, and its processes [10]. This group provides primary source information for identifying needed system requirements, system functions, objectives, measures, and constraints associated with a systems decision. Figure 5.3 shows a high level IDEF0 conceptualization for stakeholder analysis activities, the controls guiding these activities, the mechanisms that support them and their output using a slightly different format than described previously.

Besides decision makers, stakeholders can include the customers of the products and services output by the system, system operators, system maintainers, bill payers, owners, regulatory agencies, sponsors, manufacturers, and marketers, among others. Understanding who is affected by a system or potential system solutions to a systems decision problem provides a foundation for developing a complete definition of the problem. Diversity in this regard helps substantially. If the pool of stakeholders is limited to only those holding a common perspective or representing a small number of stakeholder types, important requirements can be overlooked. For the SDP, which bases its tradespace construction on individual solution alternatives' estimated value returns, this group provides the values against which solutions are designed, evaluated, and selected for implementation.

Stakeholder analysis also includes a thorough research into the environmental factors impacting the systems decision problem. By considering such relevant issues as the political, economic, social, ethical, and technological factors affecting the problem, many of the active and passive stakeholders within the project's scope can be identified.

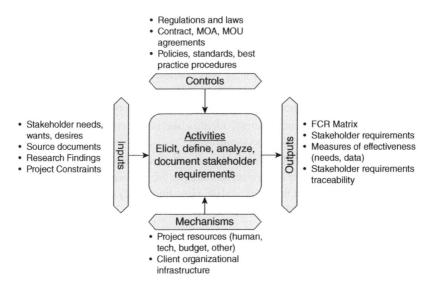

Figure 5.3 An IDEF0 conceptualization of stakeholder analysis.

In the very early part of a systems decision project, the team typically receives an initial description of the challenge that generated the project. Rarely is this initial problem statement representative of all the relevant considerations that the team needs to consider. Somewhere haunting most project starts is a concern that there is more to the problem than meets the eye. Stakeholder analysis and research are the activities used to determine the complete picture before the engagement commits resources in any one direction.

Example: EV Stakeholders. An early feasibility study commissioned in 2013 by the Mayor of New York City [11] created the Long Term Electric Taxi Task Force to bring together many of the stakeholders who could provide insight into the city's goal for complete replacement of internal combustion engine (ICE) taxis with EVs. Table 5.1 shows the organizations represented on the task force. Because it was an early feasibility study and not a systems design project, stakeholder representation was sufficient. However, had the focus of this effort been on the design and deployment of a new EV taxi system, the list of stakeholders would need to include many others that the system would affect, including passengers, fueling station owners and operators, and quite a few unions associated with the many types of system operators that would be needed.

Stakeholders can also include subcontractors and technical experts that may contribute to urban EV taxi system design and production. Performing an analysis of these stakeholders will provide insights useful for developing and evaluating candidate system solutions. This example will be carried forward as a notional systems decision support project to illustrate many of the SDP phase products that result from its application.

TABLE 5.1   Stakeholders Involved in NYC Taxi EV Study.

Stakeholder	Stakeholder
Con Edison	Empire Clean Cities
Mayor's Office of Long Term Planning and Sustainability	Metropolitan Taxi Board of Trade
Natural Resource Defense Council	New York Power Authority
New York State Energy Research and Development Authority	New York Taxi Workers Alliance
NYC Dept of City Planning	NYC Dept of Transportation
NYC Taxi and Limousine Commission	Port Authority of New York and New Jersey
Real Estate Board of New York	

Several familiar techniques exist for soliciting input from diverse stakeholders. The three techniques described in what follows are interviews, focus groups, and surveys.

5.3.1   Techniques for Stakeholder Analysis

Three general techniques are commonly used for stakeholder analysis: interviews, focus group meetings, and surveys. Each technique has characteristics that make them suitable for different settings. Five considerations that help identify which technique to use are: the time commitment of the participants, the ideal stakeholder group, activity preparation, activities need for execution, and the type and extent of analysis activities need to process, summarize, and present results. Table 5.2 provides a description and a comparison of the three techniques against each of the five characteristics. The number of interviews, number and size of focus groups, and number of surveys required depend on the problem and the diversity of the stakeholders. Statistical tests can be used to determine the minimum number of data samples needed, if appropriate.

Interviews.   Interviews are one of the best techniques for stakeholder analysis if the systems team intends to solicit information from each individual separately. Interviews are especially appropriate for senior leaders who do not have the time to attend longer duration focus group sessions or the interest in completing a survey. However, interviews are time-consuming for the interviewer due to the preparation, execution, and analysis time. The following are best practices for each phase of the interview process: planning, scheduling, conducting, documenting, and analyzing interviews.

Before the Interview. For interviews with senior leaders and key stakeholder representatives, it is important to prepare a questionnaire to guide the interview discussion rather than just ask questions as the discussion takes shape. The following are best practices for interview preparation:

- Unless the team has significant problem domain experience, research is essential to understand the systems decision problem domain and the key terminology associated with it. Once

TABLE 5.2   Stakeholder Analysis Techniques.

	Time commitment of participants	Ideal stakeholder group	Preparation	Execution	Analysis
Interviews	30–60 minutes	Senior leaders and key stakeholder representatives	Develop interview questionnaire(s) and schedule or reschedule interviews.	Interviewer has conversation with senior leader using questionnaire as a guide. Separate note taker.	Note taker types interview notes. Interviewer reviews typed notes. Team analyzes notes to determine findings, conclusions, and recommendations.
Focus groups	Shortest—60 minutes, Typical—4 to 8 hours	Mid-level to senior stakeholder representatives	Develop meeting plan, obtain facility, and plan for recording inputs. May use Group Systems software to record [12].	At least one facilitator and one recorder. Larger groups may require breakout groups and multiple facilitators.	Observations must be documented. Analysis determines findings, conclusions, and recommendations.
Surveys	5–20 minutes	Junior to mid-level stakeholder representatives	Develop survey questions, identify survey software, and develop analysis plan. Online surveys are useful.	Complete survey questionnaire, solicit surveys, and monitor completion status.	Depends on number of questions and capability of statistical analysis package. Conclusions must be developed from the data.

started, research is a continuous process, initially intended to capture a base understanding of the system, its environment, and the problem at-hand, research is used to refresh data to improve accuracy in every phase.

- Develop as broad a list of interviewees as possible. Diversity is key here. Identify one or more interviewees for each stakeholder group. Review the interview list with the project client to insure that all key stakeholders are on the list of potential interviewees.

- Begin the questionnaire with a short explanatory statement that describes the reason for the interview, the preliminary statement of the problem, and the stakeholders being interviewed in addition to the current one. This is a good way to solicit information from the interviewee regarding who might be missing from the list.

- It is usually useful to begin the interview with an unfreezing question that encourages the interviewee to think about the future and how that will impact the problem that is the subject of the interview.

- Tailor the questionnaire to define the problem and obtain information that will be needed to support known project tasks taking place in the future.

- Tailor the questionnaire to each category of interviewee. Make the questions as simple as possible. Rather than structuring questions with a long lead-in, it is often better to go right to the question and leave the interviewee an opportunity to ask refining questions.

- Do not use leading questions that imply you know the answer and want the interviewee to agree with your answer.

- Do not ask a senior leader questions as a replacement for doing research. When this is done, a senior leader will get the impression that the team is ill-prepared for a serious discussion, thereby diluting the senior leader's expectations for a valuable outcome for the time they have committed.

- End the session's questions with a closing question, for example, "Is there any other question we should have asked you?"

- Arrange to have an experienced interviewer and a recorder present for each interview.

- Decide if the interviews will be for attribution or not for attribution. Usually, the information obtained during interviews is not attributed to individuals.

 All interviews operate on stakeholder time. *Never* be the one to go over the scheduled time for a stakeholder meeting or interview! When no less than 5 minutes are remaining, tactfully remind attendees that the meeting endpoint is approaching. If they wish to extend meeting time, they will say so. If not, summarize the progress that has been made, describe the next steps, clarify primary points-of-contact and preferred means of communication, ask if any questions need resolving, and schedule the next meeting, as appropriate.

Schedule/Reschedule the Interview. Interviews with senior leaders require scheduling and, frequently, rescheduling. The following are best practices for interview scheduling:

- It is usually best to conduct interviews individually to obtain each interviewee's thoughts and ideas on the problem and the potential solutions. Additional attendees change the interview dynamics. Senior leaders are sometimes reluctant to express ideas in front of a large audience for a variety of reasons. If this is the case, they may defer to staffers to let them participate.

- Provide a brief problem statement and/or fundamental objective for the systems project to the interviewees when the interview is scheduled. This helps them understand why the team needs to discuss the project with them.

- Provide the interviewee with a short read-ahead document that clearly communicates the purpose of the interview and enables the interviewee to adequately prepare for the session. A typical read-ahead applicable for all meetings with stakeholders includes:
  - A short summary of the background of the problem/issue/system of interest being discussed. This could take the form of an abstract or executive summary. The individual(s)

or organization(s) sponsoring the systems project that motivated the interview should be clearly identified.
– A statement of the purpose of the interview (e.g., " … to identify all system linkages to outside agencies … ," " … to identify key stakeholders related to the system design, their vested interests, and points-of-contact for critical system requirements in support of the project … ," etc.).
– The proposed duration of the interview. If this is first contact with the interviewee's organization, don't overbook the session by having them block off more time than will actually be needed.
– A short list of desired outcomes if not clear from the purpose statement.
– Attachments that contain pertinent, *focused* materials supporting the interview. Plan on bringing along with you supporting materials that provide more extensive detail, as available.
– If slides are going to be forwarded as part of the read-ahead, then:
  * Use no more than two slides per page; less is inefficient, more challenges the eyesight of the interviewee.
  * Use the Storyline format (see Section 9.9.5) for slides to limit the interviewee's likelihood of misinterpreting the intended message on each slide. Remember: these slides will be present at the interviewee's location before you get a chance to conduct the interview in-person.
– A list of the key project personnel and their contact information, identifying a primary point-of-contact for the systems team among those listed. Once interviewees become connected with a project by an interview, the systems team should anticipate additional information and follow-on questions to ensue. Designating a single team member to have responsibility as the centralized contact keeps this information flow (both in-and-out of the team) controlled and organized while simultaneously creating a "familiar face" on the team for the interviewees.
- If possible, do not provide the interview questionnaire to the interviewees ahead of time. When a questionnaire is provided, the interviewee's staff may provide the answers to the questions instead of the principal person being interviewed. This can result in the interviewee reading "staff answers." If staff answers would be helpful, a separate focus group session should be considered.
- Many times it is best to have the stakeholder representatives assigned to your team (if this is the case) schedule the interview since they might have better access to the interviewee's and their schedules, limit interviews to 30–60 minutes in duration. If the interview unearths more information than can be discussed in that time frame, schedule a follow-up meeting.
- Interviews can be done in person, over digital meeting applications like Microsoft Teams and Zoom, or over the phone. In-person interviews are the most effective since interaction is easier, but sometimes they are not possible and the only practical choice one of the other means.
- The more senior the leader, the more likely scheduling will be a challenge.

One cautionary note is in order regarding advanced materials sent to the interviewee. As mentioned, it is usually *not* a best practice to provide detailed questions ahead of the interview for two reasons. First, remember that the purpose of the interview is to obtain information directly from the stakeholder and not an intermediary representative. If the interview questions are provided in a read-ahead packet, there is a likelihood that the stakeholder's staff will prepare responses to the questions, thereby defeating the purpose of the interview (as mentioned earlier). Secondly, the systems team conducting the interview should have the flexibility to add questions and/or follow-up on valuable information leads should they arise. If the stakeholder is pre-conditioned into knowing the questions (and responses) in advance, the team might not be able to 'stray from the script' without providing written questions to the stakeholder or staff.

During the Interview. The team's execution of the interview creates an important first impression with the senior leader about the systems team that will develop a solution to the problem. The goal of the interview is to obtain the stakeholder insights in a way that is interesting to the interviewee. Some thoughts for conducting interviews are as follows:

- The best number of people to conduct an interview is one interviewer and one scribe to take notes. An alternative to having a notetaker is to record the session. However, some interviewees may be reluctant to be recorded. If you think that recording is needed, request permission first.
- Conduct the interview as a conversation with the interviewee. Use the interview questionnaire as a guideline. Take the questions in the order the interviewee wants to discuss them. Keep track of what is not being asked.
- Make the interview interesting to the interviewee.
- Use an unfreezing question for the first question. An unfreezing question helps the interviewer focus on the problem in the future.
- Be flexible, following up on an interesting observation even if it was not on your questionnaire. Many times an interviewee will make only one important observation. It is critical to make sure you understand the observation and the implications.
- Ask simple open-ended questions that require the interviewee to think and respond. Avoid complex, convoluted questions that confuse the interviewee.
- Respect the interviewee's time. Stay within the interview time limit unless the interviewee wants to extend the interview period. (See earlier callout.)
- When the interviewee's body language signals that they have finished the interview (e.g., fold up paper, look at their watch), go quickly to your closing question, and end the interview as recommended.

After the Interview. Documentation of the interview is the key to providing the results of the interview to the systems decision support team. Best practices for documenting interviews are the following:

- As soon as possible after the interview, the scribe should formally type the interview notes into a document.
- The questions and the answers should be aligned to provide proper context for the answers.
- It is best to record direct quotes as much as possible.
- The interviewer should review the recorder's typed notes and make revisions as required.
- Once the interview notes are complete, they should be provided to the systems team.
- The documentation should be consistent with the decision to use the notes with or without attribution.

Analysis of the Interview Notes. The interview notes are a great source of data for the entire systems team. The key to interview analysis is binning (i.e., categorizing) the comments, summarizing observations, and identifying unique "nuggets" of information that only a few interviewees provide. The best practice for analyzing interview notes is the following:

- The most common analysis approach is to bin the interviewee responses by the questions being asked.
- The most challenging task is to identify unique "nuggets" of information that only one or two interviewees provide.
- The best way to summarize interviews is by using a findings, conclusions, and recommendations (FCR) matrix (see Section 5.3.2). Findings are listing of significant facts stated by the stakeholders or uncovered during research that are relative to the topics discussed during an interview. Conclusions are consolidated summaries of several findings after the findings are analyzed by the systems team. Recommendations are actions that the systems team is proposing in response to conclusions.
- It is important to integrate research findings with interview findings. Many times an interviewee will identify an issue that requires subsequent investigation and data collection.
- Identifying findings for a large number of interviews is challenging. One approach that mitigates this situation is a preliminary findings approach. Here is one way to do the approach:
  - Read several of the interview notes.
  - Form preliminary findings.
  - Bin quotes for the interviews that relate to the preliminary findings.
  - Add research information to the quotes.
  - Revise the preliminary findings to findings that are fully supported by the interview and research data.

As findings are being identified, it is important not to get distracted by potential findings that are interesting but unrelated to the purpose of the stakeholder analysis. If appropriate, these findings should be presented separately to the decision makers. For example, if stakeholder interviews were being conducted to identify significant external system dependencies and one stakeholder mentioned a potential insider threat, this threat information would not be presented in interview findings but would be recorded and reported to decision makers separately, respecting the agreed upon interview conditions regarding anonymity.

Follow up With Interviewees. Many times the interviewee will request follow-up information. The following are examples of appropriate follow-up products:

- Thank you note or e-mail to the interviewee and/or the stakeholder representative that scheduled the meeting.
- A revised statement of the systems problem after stakeholder analysis or the Problem Definition phase is complete.
- A copy of the findings, conclusions, and recommendations from interviews and related research.
- A briefing or copy of the final report at the end of the project.

Examples of Studies Using Interviews. These are studies done by the authors that have used interviews as a key technique in the stakeholder analysis task:

- Ewing et al. [13].
- Powell et al. [14].

- Parnell et al. [15].
- Parnell et al. [16].
- Trainor et al. [17].

Focus Groups. Focus groups are another technique for stakeholder analysis. Focus groups are often used for product market research. However, they can also be useful for quickly determining stakeholder opinions regarding a specific systems decision problem. While interviews typically generate one-way flows of information, focus groups create information through discussions between focus group participants who typically have a common background related to the problem being studied. For example, if the problem involved designing an efficient production plant, the team would form separate focus groups for plant management and for plant laborers. As a general rule, focus groups should comprise 6–12 individuals. Too few participants may lead to too narrow a perspective while too many will lead to some individuals not able to provide meaningful input. As with interviews, the focus group facilitation team needs to allot sufficient time for preparing and executing the focus group session, and analyzing the resulting data [12].

Preparing for the Focus Group Session. As with any stakeholder analysis technique, developing the goals and objectives of the focus group session is critical to success. A few best practices for preparing for a focus group session [18] include the following:

- Develop a clear purpose statement for the focus group session and a listing of anticipated results. This should be coordinated with the systems project client and provided to all focus group participants.
- Develop a profile of the type of participant that should be part of the session and communicate that to the project client. This profile should include requisite background knowledge, organizational employment level, recent experience, and professional skill type (e.g., software programmer, chemical engineer, human resources specialist, etc.). It might also include recommended interpersonal skills if relevant to the session.
- Select a participant pool in collaboration with the project client.
- Select and prepare systems team moderators who can facilitate a discussion without imposing their own biases on the group. If resources permit, hire a professional moderator.
- Schedule a time and location during which this group can provide 60–90 minutes of uninterrupted discussion. It is often helpful to create a secure cellphone temporary storage bin on-site so that participants can engage without distraction.
- Develop a set of questions that are open-ended and will generate discussion. Do not use "Yes/No" questions that will yield little discussion. The most important information may come out of a discussion about an issue ancillary to a question posed to the group.

Conducting the Focus Group Session. The most important components for a successful focus group session are the moderator and the recording plan. Here are some thoughts for conducting a focus group session [19]:

- The moderator should review the session goals and objectives, provide an agenda, and discuss the plan for recording the session with all participants. If non-attribution of source is an agreed upon condition with the client, the participants should be informed of this.
- The moderator should ask one question and allow participants a few minutes to discuss their ideas. The moderator should ensure equitable participation from the group to prevent a few individuals from dominating the group.

- A good technology solution for facilitating focus groups is GroupSystems software [20]. This application facilitates group participation in brainstorming activities and generating ideas from individual participants without requiring open discussion. Participants type their ideas on a computer in response to questions generated by the moderator. Software such as this helps mitigate adverse effects from individuals who tend to dominate discussions. It also automates the information recording process for the session and aids subsequent data analysis.

- Do a video and audio recording of the session if possible. If not, multiple note takers from the systems team should be used. Comments and ideas should be recorded with attribution initially and later removed if required.

- The moderator may steer the discussion to follow a particular issue brought up that impacts the problem being studied. The moderator must be careful to avoid diverting from the session plan in order to pursue a topic that, while interesting and potentially important to participants, only marginally contributes to the session objectives.

- On closing, tell the participants they will receive a record of the session to verify their statements and ideas. This is why attribution should initially be recorded by note takers.

- Follow up the session with an individual thank you note for each participant.

Analyzing the information. Focus groups participants can provide a great source of qualitative data for the systems analysis team, either by directly stating it during the session or suggesting reliable and credible sources from professional experience. The team should verify any data that was generated during the session before summarizing it in findings, conclusions, and recommendations format using the methods discussed in Section 5.3.2. If more than one focus group session is conducted, it may not be possible to correlate data between groups unless they were previously structured to have necessary common characteristics.

Surveys.   Surveys are a good technique for collecting information from large groups of stakeholders particularly when they are geographically dispersed. Surveys are appropriate for junior to mid-level stakeholders. If the problem warrants, surveys can be used to gather quantitative data that can be analyzed statistically in order to support conclusions and recommendations. A great deal of research exists on techniques and best practices for designing effective surveys. Surveys can be distributed and data responses collected via mail, email, secure login websites, or other technical means for many of the situations appropriate for surveys.

Surveys are perhaps the most challenging stakeholder elicitation techniques. While in-person interviews with stakeholders can be daunting for various reasons, there is an adaptability inherent in interview sessions that allow the systems team to change direction or modify questions that were prepared ahead of time. Not so with surveys. Very careful thought needs to be put into the wording and focus of the questions because it is a one-shot effort. Poorly crafted, confusing, or misdirected questions dramatically increase the non-response rate for surveys. With stakeholders, such content seeds doubt in their minds as to the competency of the survey team.

This section provides an overview of survey design and methods for conducting surveys. As with any stakeholder analysis technique, surveys require detailed planning to accomplish the team's goals. These steps can be followed to plan, execute, and analyze surveys [21]:

- Establish the goals of the survey.
- Determine who and how many people you will ask to complete the survey, that is, determine the sample of stakeholders you will target with the survey.
- Determine how you will distribute the survey and collect the survey data.

- Develop the survey questions.
- Test the survey.
- Distribute the survey to the stakeholders and collect data from them.
- Analyze the survey data.

Preparing an Effective Survey. Determine your goals, survey respondents, and means of distributing and collecting survey data. The stakeholder analysis team needs to clearly articulate the goals of the survey and the target sample of stakeholders whom they want to answer the survey. Often surveys for systems decision problems will be used to collect textual answers to a standard set of questions. However, if the team plans to collect and analyze data from questions with standard answer scales (e.g., "Yes/No" or multiple choice answer scales), it is important to determine the appropriate sample size needed to draw valid statistical conclusions from the survey data. Sample size calculations are described in basic statistics books, and online tools are available to do these calculations [22]. The team needs to work with the project client to determine the appropriate stakeholders to survey.

The method for implementing a survey needs to be selected before the survey is designed. Table 5.3 provides a listing of some of the advantages and disadvantages of these survey methods [21].

TABLE 5.3 Advantages and Disadvantages of Popular Survey Methods.

Survey method	Advantages	Disadvantages
Mail	<ul><li>Can include extensive supporting graphics</li><li>Respondents have flexibility in completing the survey</li></ul>	<ul><li>Takes a great deal of time</li><li>Hard to check compliance and conduct follow-up with respondents</li><li>Response data will have to be transformed by the analysis team into a format for analysis</li></ul>
Electronic mail	<ul><li>Fast to distribute and get responses</li><li>Low cost</li><li>Easy to check compliance and do follow-up</li></ul>	<ul><li>Need to obtain e-mail addresses for the survey sample</li><li>Cannot program automatic logic into the survey (e.g., "skip over the next set of questions if your answer is No to this question")</li><li>Respondent e-mail programs may limit the type of information that can be sent in the survey</li><li>Response data will have to be transformed by the analysis team into a format for analysis</li></ul>
Internet Web survey	<ul><li>Extremely fast</li><li>Can include special graphics and formatting</li><li>Can collect responses in a database to facilitate analysis</li></ul>	<ul><li>May be hard to control who responds to the survey due to world-wide Internet access</li><li>Respondents can easily provide only a partial response to the survey</li></ul>

The ability to collect survey responses in a database when using a web survey instrument can be extremely beneficial to the stakeholder analysis process. Several online programs exist to help teams design web surveys, collect responses, and analyze the results. Some popular programs include surveymonkey.com [23], InsitefulSurveys.com [24], and the SurveySystem.com [25].

Executing a Survey Instrument. Developing the survey questions, testing, and distributing the survey. Surveys should be designed to obtain the information that will help the stakeholder analysis team meet the goals of the survey. To maximize response rates, the survey should be short with clearly worded questions that are not ambiguous from the respondent's perspective. Start the survey with an overview of the purpose of the survey and the goals that the team hopes to achieve from the information provided by the respondents. Here are some general principles that can be followed in developing effective survey questions [26]:

- Ask survey respondents about their first-hand experiences. That is, ask about what they have done and their current environment so that they can provide experience-informed answers. Respondents should not be asked hypothetical questions, nor should they be asked to comment on things outside their working environment.

- Ask only a single question in each of the survey questions. Avoid using compound questions that may muddle the interpretation of responses.

- In wording questions, make sure that all respondents answer the same question. Editing questions between respondents will likely muddle interpretation of their responses. If the question includes terms that could be interpreted differently by respondents, provide a list of definitions to clarify any possible ambiguities. This list of term definitions should precede the questions.

- Articulate to respondents the type of acceptable answers to a question. For objective questions, the answer scales can be set up as multiple choice answers from a rating scale or level-of-agreement scale. For certain questions, it may be appropriate to provide benchmark examples for the answer scales. For example, the responses to a question regarding the respondent's level of effort on a project may include a benchmark statement like "full time effort equates to 40 hours of work per week." For open-ended text response questions, the question should be worded so that respondents provide information germane to the question. Close the survey with a statement allowing respondents to provide any additional information they believe is pertinent to the goals of the survey.

- Format the survey so that it is easy for respondents to read the questions, follow instructions, and provide their answers. For example, answer scales should follow a similar pattern in terms of the order in which they are presented (e.g., the least desirable answer is the first choice ascending to the most desirable answer).

- Orient the respondents to the survey in a consistent way. This can be accomplished with a set of instructions that describe the goals of the survey, the method for completing their responses, and the means for submitting the completed survey.

Once the survey questions are written, test the survey instrument with a few individuals outside the systems team. Ask them to complete the survey using the same medium that respondents will use (e.g., by e-mail, mail, or on the web). Ask them for feedback regarding the instructions and wording of the questions and answer scales. If a web survey is used, test the method for collecting responses to make sure it operates correctly. Use the feedback from the test group to improve the survey. Once improvements are made, distribute the survey to respondents using the method chosen. Develop a plan for monitoring the response rate and establish when reminders will be sent to respondents who have not completed the survey. The team should also have a standard way to thank respondents for their time and efforts.

Analyzing Survey Data. A key part of the analysis effort will be in formatting the survey data that is received. If a web survey is used, the team can program the survey instrument to put responses directly into a database file. This will allow the team to perform statistical analysis on objective-type questions relatively quickly. For text answer questions, a database file provides a means to bin the responses quickly. The goals of the analysis are the same as for interviews and focus group sessions. Similar to the process discussed earlier in this section, the team should bin the responses by survey question and analyze these responses to develop findings. These findings will lead to forming conclusions, which then will lead the team to form recommendations.

CMS Case Study—Research and Stakeholder Analysis. To determine the proper functions and performance measures for the new curriculum management system (CMS), the systems team had to first identify the system's stakeholders. These were as follows:

- Cadets (consumers) receive the entire curriculum from the department and must apply what they learned upon graduation in a dynamic world with proliferating technology.
- Instructors (users) prepare and deliver the program's curriculum to cadets.
- Program directors (users) synchronize curriculum across courses they oversee to support an academic major. They are also responsible for program assessment and accreditation.
- The department's accreditation officer (user) works with ABET, Inc. and various Academy committees to ensure their department academic majors meet accreditation standards and requirements.
- The department operations officer (user) synchronizes the delivery of the department's entire curriculum from semester to semester, ensuring that knowledge transfer regarding all course administration is preserved for future use.
- The department leadership (decision authority, owner) sets and enforces standards, allocates resources to the academic majors programs, ensures alignment with the Academy's overall academic program goals, and ensures that programs achieve and maintain accreditation.

The department used three stakeholder analysis techniques to elicit stakeholder needs, wants, and desires from the people represented by this list earlier.

Cadet Survey. The systems team designed and administered a Web-based survey to cadets. This method was selected based on the considerations in Table 4.1 and Table 4.2. This was a reasonably large group of very important stakeholders. The cadets targeted for the survey were enrolled in a junior year Computer Aided Systems Engineering course whose content was similar to the system of interest. The sample of 70 cadets represented about 35% of the total population of systems engineering majors. A total of 48 cadets completed the survey, besting the expected 10% return that is typical of survey responses. The primary goal for the cadet survey was to determine their needs for curriculum delivery. Questions asked them to compare and rank the various delivery methods being used by the department. They were also asked for suggestions regarding how to improve content delivery. Analysis of survey data produced the findings shown in Tables 5.4 and 5.5.

TABLE 5.4 Percentage of cadets who prefer different methods of electronic content delivery.

Content Delivery Method	Percentage of Cadets Who Ranked This Method 1st	95% Confidence Interval
Course website	56%	±12.3%
Course network folder	33%	±11.6%
Academy-wide portal	10%	±7.4%

TABLE 5.5 Percentage of cadets who would rank a newly developed portal against the current methods.

Ranking Against Current Methods	Percentage of Cadets Who Ranked This Rating	95% Confidence Interval
1st	58%	±12.2%
2nd	27%	±10.1%
No preference	15%	±8.8%

One survey question described a structured web-based portal to cadets and asked them to rank it with respect to the other methods currently used. Free text response questions asked cadets to describe the reasoning for their rankings and to provide suggestions as to how the department can improve content delivery. There were a few trends identified in their responses. Several cadets mentioned availability as a reason for ranking criteria. The Academy-wide portal experienced frequent access failures, especially from locations outside of the Academy's internal network. They also did not like having to perform a separate login to access content after logging into the system. They found electronic course folders very useful because it enabled them to deposit files into personal folders while in class and access them later from their rooms. Finally, they wanted consistency across courses, expressing frustration in having to work with different file structures.

The survey results were organized into an FCR matrix (See Section 5.3.2. From these findings, the systems team concluded with strong confidence that most cadets preferred web-based content delivery. However, cadets did not like the Academy-wide implementation of that delivery that existed. They showed a strong preference for a redesigned portal under a single CMS framework. However, they were concerned about system availability, extra login steps, ability to post content, and consistency as described earlier.

These conclusions yielded a recommendation to consider redesigning the department's content delivery system as a web-based portal that is reliable, easy to use, allows two-way communication, and is used consistently across the department.

Faculty Focus Groups. The primary users of the system were the Department of Systems Engineering faculty. To elicit needs, wants, and desires from this group, the design team brought them together as a focus group in the department's Systems Methodology and

Design Laboratory (SMDL). The SMDL was specially configured to use *GroupSystems*®
collaboration software. The *GroupSystems* software application enabled a more productive
focus group session because it allowed anonymous simultaneous input from participants,
avoiding the issues of a single person dominating discussions and lessening the potential for
"groupthink" to occur. The system automatically recorded all input and generated a report
for future analysis.

Before the focus group meeting, the lead systems engineer presented the agenda to participants to help shape their expectations:

1. Brainstorm functions in the Topic Commenter. This allows faculty to list functions in
   a brainstorming fashion. Other faculty can comment on the ideas.
2. Bin functions in the Categorizer. This develops related groups of functions.
3. Brainstorm values for this system in the Topic Commenter.
4. Bin values in the Categorizer.

The entire focus group took about 90 minutes to complete. Afterwards, the systems team
affinitized the input, which resulted in the following categories of system functions and stakeholder values:

- Functions   → Lesson management
                → Compatibility with other Academy and department IT systems
                → Scheduling
                → Resources
                → Course administration
                → Course project management
                → Interface
                → Accreditation

- Values   → Easy to use interface
                → Automatic administrative report generation
                → Compatibility and non-redundancy with other systems
                → Accessibility
                → Security and stability
                → Usability
                → Ad hoc query capability
                → Ease of maintenance

Note that there is some overlap between the aforementioned lists of functions and values.
As is usually the case, the focus group output cannot be directly translated into a functional
hierarchy and values hierarchy without analysis. However, the *GroupSystems* report was a
valuable resource to ensure that the needs, wants, and desires of the faculty are not lost in
subsequent project actions.

Stakeholder Interviews. Because of their unique positions and critical relationships with the CMS system of interest, interviews were limited to the following people:

- *Department leadership*—establishes department vision, mission, and objectives, allocates department resources. The results of this interview contributed to development of top-level values in the values hierarchy and approval of top-level functions for the functional hierarchy.
- *Department operations officer*—responsible for scheduling and execution of department courses. The results of this interview contributed to the development of the Integrate Department Academic Operations function.
- *Department accreditation officer*—responsible for coordinating accreditation for department programs. The results of this interview contributed to development of the Assess Program function. Results from these interviews were combined with those from the other stakeholder analysis techniques in preparation for functional and requirements analysis.

5.3.2   At Completion—FCR Matrix

When research and stakeholder analyses are completed, the systems decision support team should have a thorough summary recording and understanding of stakeholder values, objectives, facts, assumptions, constraints, screening criteria for potential solutions, and decisions needed for subsequent SDP phase activities. The team should also have a clear list of any needed or recommended follow-on actions. Stakeholder analysis should also assist the team in identifying key life cycle cost and risk factors that should be considered in any system solution.

Summarizing the variety of results produced by initial research efforts is the role of a findings, conclusions, and recommendations (FCR) matrix. The FCR matrix is an effective format for presenting research results to clients and decision makers, or stakeholders in general. In a single display typically created using a spreadsheet application such as Excel, an FCR matrix lists significant facts that were discovered during research and stakeholder interviews/surveys/focus groups (findings), the team's interpretation of the relevance of these facts (conclusions), and follow-on actions that the team intends to pursue or recommends be taken to advance the project towards achieving its fundamental objective (recommendations). Recommendations can include statements such as "record as a stakeholder requirement," "record as a system function," "record as a constraint," "perform additional research in classified sources," and so on.

Much like the categorization that is done when conducting an affinity diagramming session after brainstorming, findings and facts are grouped into broad categories that organize the FCR matrix. Figure 5.4 shows a small FCR matrix constructed after beginning research supporting a systems decision problem regarding options for internal combustion engine (ICE) vehicle replacement by EVs for an urban taxi service. This would be a typical and useful product for an interim progress review (IPR) briefing to a decision maker or other stakeholder. Among the category groups, two are shown: Public Opinion and Battery Manufacturing.

The Findings column presents brief statements of facts along with one of two typical citation methods. In one part of the matrix numerical references are shown. This method communicates to the decision maker that there is supporting evidence for the fact stated while keeping the source(s) from being revealed. The second section calls out the sources without using a full citation. The full

Topic	Findings	Conclusions	Recommendations
Public opinion	Conventional carbon fuel vehicles are a primary source of greenhouse gas (GHG) emissions [1, 3]		Team should continue to research BEV battery developments, especially for options other than lithium (see Denmark). Look for potential positive messaging already being used in Europe.
	Electric vehicles generate lower air polutants than conventional vehicles [1, 3, 4]		
	Battery electric vehicles (BEV) are the most prevalent electric vehicles		
	Recent research shows that the environmental performance of BEVs is strongly dependent upon battery size, energy consumed for battery recharging, and how this energy is produced. [5, 6, 7]	There is a risk to continued support of BEVs by the American public if sufficient disinformation is propagated because the facts can be used to support pro and con.	
	Life cycle assessment (LCA) is used to assess the energy and environmental impact of various vehicles [3]		
	Potential and existing BEV customers are not aware of lithium mining environmental issues [1]		
	Americans are closely divided over the idea of phasing out combustion engine vehicles by the year 2035, and many are on the fence about whether they themselves would purchase a chief alternative: an electric car or truck (Pew Research)		
	47% of Americans support phasing out gas-powered cars; 51% oppose it. (Pew Research)		
Battery manufacturing	Lithium ion batteries in large quantities inside fixed facilities pose significant facility risk (Kenexis)	Sufficient detrimental characteristics of lithium battery manufacturing exists in the public domain to warrant a comprehensive risk analysis.	Team should conduct a comprehensive risk analysis prior to any transportation system substantially investing in BEVs and their derivative products.
	Toxic gases can be a significant hazard for closed spaces without mitigation methods in-place (Kenexis)		
	Manufacturing Li batteries can emit 74% more CO_2 than conventional cars (Industry Week)		
	Batteries powering electric vehicles are forecast to make up 90% of the lithium-ion battery market by 2025 (World Economic Forum)	The impact of unregulated battery manufacturing could be significant if lithium continues to be relied upon for BEV.	
	BEV's can generate more carbon emissions over their lifecycle than diesel or petrol cars (World Economic Forum)		

Figure 5.4 Two categories for FCR matrix after BEV research.

185

citation would be listed in the references section for an ongoing draft report. Either method is acceptable as a best practice, but only one method should be used.

In the Conclusions section, summary statements are made relating the findings to the problem under consideration. A single summary conclusion statement appears regarding the Public Opinion findings. Two summary statements appear in the Battery Manufacturing conclusions section because the team considered both dimensions important to communicate to the decision maker. How many conclusion statements are needed is a judgment call made by the systems team. However, having one conclusion statement for each finding is discouraged because it misses the intent. In the example shown, shading is used to highlight the teams concerns regarding individual conclusions. The first conclusion statement for Battery Manufacturing is shaded dark, meaning a high-priority action is required. If color were used, red would be an appropriate choice.

As noted earlier, the Recommendations section is used to communicate the follow-on actions recommended by the team. These are either focused on actions the team should take, or actions that the stakeholder's organization should undergo. Depending on the nature of the conclusions, these actions could be intended for the near, mid, or far time horizon relative to the project. In Figure 5.4, both statements are recommendations for team actions as a consequence of the conclusions noted.

For most SDP applications, adding citation numbers or source identification to each finding will add strength to concluding statements and support recommended post-session activities. If non-attribution was an agreed upon condition with the client, sources should be recorded in session or survey data but not presented in an FCR matrix in any manner that could compromise their identity.

Stakeholder analysis helps to identify initial findings, system requirements, objectives, measures, and stakeholder values for developing candidate solutions to the systems decision problem. Functional analysis is used to identify the key functions and requirements that any acceptable solution must be designed to perform and to organize them in a logical fashion sufficient to support design. Functions are what the system does while attempting to achieve its purpose(s).

5.4   REQUIREMENTS ANALYSIS

Requirements analysis involves determining the essential attributes or characteristics of a system and is critical in designing an effective and cost efficient system solution. Requirements emerge in a purposeful manner during the initial Problem definition SDP phase as stakeholder analysis and research are consuming most of the systems team's efforts. As they are identified, requirements are recorded, organized, reviewed, and revised in collaboration with stakeholders. Products such as an FCR matrix directly support requirements analysis.

To be clear, writing requirements is not fun. It requires careful, organized, and deliberate interactions with stakeholders for the resulting list to be comprehensive, clear, and correct. There are a small number of principles to follow, and these we discuss here to give you a fundamental understanding of the process and outcome. This topic can be the subject of whole courses in universities, so we provide only a basic introduction to the topic sufficient to get started on the right path. For a more complete discussion see any of the excellent references by Martin [27], Wasson [28], Kossiakoff and Sweet [29], Maciaszek [30], Grady [31], or Hull et al. [32].

While it is not impossible to develop systems without first identifying to some level of detail what the system is expected to do for stakeholders who have a vested interest in the system existing, doing this is a *very* bad idea because the resulting system has no guarantee of meeting any expectations. When systems are developed and input from some stakeholder group is absent, in particular the intended users of the system, the likelihood of technology acceptance and adoption by that stakeholder group decreases significantly [33] and the risk of system failure as designed becomes a very real possibility. It's easy to diagnose when input from the intended users (often called end users) was not incorporated into system design because phrases like "Who thought that *this* was going to be a good idea?!?" and "There's no way I'm going to use this!" permeate the user population. And, it gets worse when other groups of stakeholders are left out of the process as well.

What stakeholders need, want, and desire of a system are called *requirements*. Early in a systems decision support effort, requirements are directly elicited from all the stakeholder types, mapped to system functions, and tracked throughout system development to make sure all requirements are being addressed and incorporated into design or discarded, as appropriate. Design engineers like to separate requirements into source (customer) requirements and derived requirements, which can be useful for engineering teams working on their development tasks. For systems decision support teams, this distinction is less helpful since all requirements stem from a system need.

For convenience and clarity, requirement statements can be partitioned into two groups based on the subject that a requirement is focused on: the *problem domain* and the *solution domain*. Requirement statements addressing the problem domain represent the stakeholders' views of what they want to achieve by using the system. These are generally the first type of requirements that will arise during discussions with stakeholders early in the systems decision process (SDP) during the period that the systems decision support team (or systems engineers) are defining the problem after receiving an initial problem statement from a client. Stakeholders familiar with the problem setting are typically trying to do something with the existing system and are frustrated that this cannot be done. So, they are looking for a solution that will improve the situation they face and give them the capabilities they think they need. But, while they are well-versed in the current situation, they may need assistance conceptualizing and framing the situation as a system with all its interconnections and dependencies emphasized, which is the point behind creating system representations based on systems thinking as discussed in Chapter 3.

As problem domain requirements are being discussed and recorded, requirements associated with the solution domain will start to emerge as the focus shifts from what the users will want to do with the solution (system) to what the solution (system) has to do by itself to be considered successful. Solution domain requirements are ones that address expectations for system behavior that will satisfy stakeholder needs, wants, and desires for the requirements in the problem domain to be met. The more inclusive the types of stakeholders that are included in this activity, the more comprehensive solution domain requirements become.

The functions, activities, or services that a system must do to be considered successful are called *functional requirements*. A *function* is a characteristic, task, or activity that must be performed by the system to achieve a desired outcome. For a product, it is a desired system behavior that supports the overall system purpose. A function may be accomplished by one or more system elements comprised of hardware, software, firmware, facilities, personnel, and procedural data. Functional requirements are statements of system behavior.

The second category of requirements called *non-functional requirements* identify constraints (restrictions) that the system must obey, such as the system's "look and feel," visual properties of the system, technical performance, cybersecurity restrictions, interface characteristics, usability specifications, reliability levels, efficiency levels, supportability constraints, and so on. Non-functional requirements, also called specification requirements, are not statements of system behavior, but rather specific bounds that any acceptable system design, development, and operation must obey. Non-functional requirements can also address cultural and political issues as well as legal requirements that the system must comply with. Constraints are requirements that must be met while a capability is a desired function, feature, trait or performance characteristic [27].

It may appear a bit confusing at first, but the language used to specify constraints makes it clear what is expected by stakeholders and allows for the system design space—how varied and creative the potential alternatives are—to be as large as possible. In general, requirements should avoid any reference to a specific system design or potential solution, because this anchors [34] potential solutions to a specific starting point in the overall design space, thereby losing opportunities for innovation and creativity that can lead to disruptive innovation and clear advantage.

The standard, and perhaps somewhat peculiar way that requirements are stated, avoids ambiguity and enables test and development teams to create test environments directly connected to functional and non-functional requirements. The word "shall" is used consistently as a best practice that leaves little room for ambiguity.

For example, suppose that a new night vision system was being designed for use by foot soldiers in a defensive position. A problem domain requirement takes the following form:

The <stakeholder type> shall be able to <capability>.

And, a requirement expressed by stakeholders in the problem domain for a night vision system might state:

The <untrained user> shall be able to <identify the type of shoulder-fired weapon being carried by a human>.

A more complete problem domain requirement also includes some aspect of performance constraint and operational condition within which the system functions, if these were known by stakeholders:

The <stakeholder type> shall be able to <capability> within <performance> of <event> while <operational condition>.

For example,

The <untrained user> shall be able to <identify the type of shoulder-fired weapon being carried by a human> within <10 seconds> of <detecting human presence at 400 meters> while <in a static, ground level defensive position>.

The additional information provided in this requirement leads directly to testing conditions and assessment criteria. For the SDP, such conditions support the screening of alternative solution designs prior to moving on to full evaluation.

In comparison, a solution domain requirement focuses on statements regarding the system as the subject of the sentence. A solution domain requirement regarding the same system as just noted might read:

The <night vision system> shall <operate in a passive light emission mode>.

And again, performance constraints are also a natural addition to this type of requirement:

The <system> shall be able to <operate in a passive light emission mode> for <4 continuous hours> after <being switched on> while <conducting surveillance during hours of limited visibility>.

If requirement statements exist that no system function addresses, then the solution design will fail to meet stakeholder expectations. If system functions exist that are not linked to requirements, a condition known as *function creep* has occurred and stakeholders end up paying for system features they did not ask for. Function creep also has an impact on schedule, especially when very new technology is associated with these extra functions that introduce various forms of uncertainty into planning. An effective way of checking whether either condition exists is to use two design mapping matrices (DMM) (see Section 3.5) to relate (1) stakeholders (row) to requirements (column), then (2) requirements (row) to system functions (column). The type of traceability these DMMs afford is called *longitudinal* traceability because of the evident paths leading backwards from system functions to stakeholder sources. They are often leveraged later during system development to support verification testing. When used in this fashion, DMMs are equivalent to requirements mapping matrices.

Requirements are not established randomly. The systems team should maintain records that trace requirements to objective information defining and describing the requirement. For the SDP, this involves the systems decision support team creating a concept requirements list (CRL) [31]. This is a simple document consisting of a cover page and as many pages of numbered and ordered requirements as needed. The cover page should list the project name or other specific identification label, the work breakdown structure (WBS) label (or chapter number for the requirements document), and the date and document number. As a minimum, the lead engineer or person responsible for creating the document should be listed on the cover page along with their signature and contact information.

Similar to functional hierarchies and work breakdown structures (WBS) in terms of their organization, requirements are typically listed starting at a top level viewpoint of the system. These top level requirements are then decomposed into lower level requirements so that each of the low level requirements can be directly traced back up through the structure as being part of some higher level requirement [28]. This type of traceability is known as *vertical* or *parent-child* traceability within the requirements set. For example, a set of hierarchical requirements supporting a telephone system for a non-profit organization could look like the following.

1. **The <automated answering system> shall <schedule the next incoming call on the fundraising agent's request>.**

    (a) **The <automated answering system> shall <activate Next Call push button upon entry to the fundraising agent's incoming call list>.**

        i. **The <Next Call push button> shall <illuminate when active>.**

    (b) **The <automated answering system> shall <archive the current call data prior to terminating the call>.**

    (c) **...and so on.**

Software products that can store and track requirements as a database, such as CORE®, exist to create and trace requirements hierarchies [35]. Low memory costs, improved networking, cross-platform compatibility, remote access and virtual private networks (VPN), computer literacy, and flexible output formatting have made these products commonplace in systems decision support and systems engineering work today.

It is the team lead or project manager's choice whether to separate the requirements into problem and solution domain sections or to list them in a continuous $1, \ldots, n$ fashion. If separated, then each section will have its own continuous listing such as $1.1, \ldots, 1.n$ and $2.1, \ldots, 2.n$, with lower level requirements organized and numbered under major ones, similar to the way that a book's chapter, sections, subsections, and subsubsections are organized. Either is acceptable so long as every requirement statement has a unique numerical identifier. Once identification numbers are assigned to each requirement statement and the CRL is published, the numbers *do not* change. If a requirement is deleted, the remaining requirements keep their original identifier, which means there will be gaps in the listing order but they will be traceable gaps.

Once the requirements document is complete, comparing the ordered listing of requirements against a similar listing of system functions resulting from Functional Analysis helps to ensure that requirements are being satisfied by the current design and that superfluous functionality with no links to stakeholder requirements has not crept into the design. This can be accomplished using a requirements traceability matrix (or DMM) that places requirements in rows and system functions in columns, a feature included in all specialty software designed to serve this purpose.

A key objective of requirements analysis is to transform problem domain requirements (also referred to as operational requirements or required outcomes of a system in use), into solution domain requirements (also called performance requirements) that can be defined as engineering characteristics of the system [29]. Again, doing this supports both design and subsequent testing and assessment events during development.

Wasson [28] provides a helpful list of questions that systems engineers can think about while performing requirements analysis:

1. Do the list of requirements appear to be generated as a feature-based "wish list" or do they reflect a structured analysis?
2. Do the requirements appear to have been written by a seasoned subject matter expert?
3. Do the requirements adequately capture user operational needs? Are they necessary and sufficient?
4. Do the requirements unnecessarily constrain the range of viable alternative solutions?
5. Are all the system interface requirements identified?
6. Are there any critical operational or technical issues that require resolution or clarification?

A final note on eliciting requirements. While stakeholder interviews and discussions are common and effective ways to elicit system requirements, system representations such as the ones introduced in Chapter 3 aid this process tremendously. Much like the saying that a "picture tells a thousand words," a system representation cues a thousand thoughts.

The human mind has a great affinity for visualizations because they are vehicles for expansive thinking that open mental boundaries restricting the scope and range of possibilities. Features in visualizations trigger considerations that are not immediately available in stakeholder minds, which quite often are preoccupied with factors causing issues in the problem domain. This is an important point for new system designs that have no existing system to reference from. Existing system improvement projects have the luxury of having a full up 3D system in operation to provide visual cues to requirements.

Once a stakeholder sees a representation, reactions such as: "The system can't have sharp corners like that because...," or "If the system looked like that, then it would have to have...", or "Our operators would never be able to work with a system like that because..." are common. Interestingly, rather than causing an anchoring effect on a suggested solution, representations tend to broaden a requirements discussion rather than restricting it, thereby leading to new requirements that might have been missed, especially those in the solution domain. Text listings can have this effect as well as seen in brainstorming sessions. But, in order to do so, a stakeholder must first map the text information to an image they create in their mind and then expand their thinking based on that image. Representations such as sketches, 3D renderings, architectural models, rapid prototypes,

Department of Defense Architectural Framework (DoDAF) views, graphs, and others provide a suggested image that works as mental scaffolding that aids the requirements analysis process.

5.4.1 Margins

Most modern systems, whether developed new or modified from a previous system, are blends of existing and new technologies. This it true even when generalizing the idea of a system to organizations, laws, and so on. There always is a blend of new and old system elements (objects, interactions, dependencies).

Staying with the case of hardware as an example, it is to a developer's advantage to leverage the technologies they have on-hand when creating system design alternatives because the costs and actual capabilities of these are known. In comparison, using new technologies with which a developer has little or no actual performance or cost data introduces uncertainty in cost and performance and makes meeting specification constraints and cost targets more challenging, especially if these technologies are still in a research and development state. To complicate matters more, even if a new technology demonstrates that it exceeds stakeholder performance requirements on its own, the challenge still exists to integrate it into a system with existing technologies without causing a reduction in their performance levels. And, there is always the possibility that stakeholders will interpret the added performance as a benefit they are not willing to underwrite and pay for, unless it is shown to be true value return—the topic of a later chapter.

Despite these cautionary notes, a blend of new and old technologies offers managers and engineers a useful opportunity they can leverage to meet requirements with system alternatives. The tool that capitalizes on this opportunity is called a *margin*.

Definition. A *margin* is an unallocated portion of a quantifiable, allocable requirement value that is used by design engineers and management to avoid and resolve problems that arise during system development.

Margins are buffers used to absorb overages or excesses with regards to bounds on performance requirements when a maximum acceptable value is specified, and underages when a minimum is specified. Margins are a tool used to deal with the natural direction that a specification level will head towards during system development. System weight is one specification that typically appears as a maximum acceptable value, so margins are allocated to absorb subcomponent upward weight variance before the overall system exceeds the acceptable level. This is also the case, for example, with component hardware that must fit together with other components into a common hardware slot.

Ideally, the means of documenting requirements would capture the required value, any margin established, and the current demonstrated capability [31]. An example will help.

Consider the hypothetical design architecture shown in Figure 5.5 in which System A is being developed. It consists of three subsystems (A.1, A.2, and A.3). Subsystem A.1 already exists and will be used in this design. Its 96 lb weight is known and will not change.

Suppose that the weight requirement for System A was specified as:

> **The complete <System A> shall <not exceed 235 lbs including all packing and transport materials>.**

and the project manager was concerned because two of the three subsystems in their proposed design (A.2 and A.3) involved new technologies under development in their organization. One subsystem (A.1) already exists and the weight is known at 96 lbs. One subsystem (A.3) includes a new component (A.3.2) still under development. The weight estimates provided to the project manager from each subsystem engineering team lead has some degree of uncertainty associated

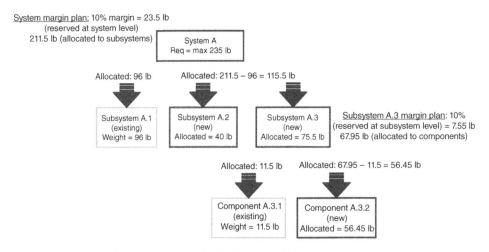

Figure 5.5   Hypothetical margin allocation example.

with them, mostly due to questions regarding part sources and materials used to build out the subsystem designs.

The company has a standing policy that a project manager should hold back 10% of the weight limit during design to handle any overages that might arise either with subsystem A.2 or A.3, or the new component A.3.2. So, rather than allocating $235 - 96 = 139$ lbs to the engineering teams for A.2 and A.3 development, she intended to allocate 211.5 lbs, withholding 23.5 lbs as a margin at the system level in case any of the actual completed subsystems exceed their target weight limit. In discussions with the lead engineers, she is allocating 40 lbs as a weight limit to subsystem A.2, and 75.5 lbs as a weight limit to subsystem A.3, which they agreed were achievable weight targets.

However, the lead engineer for subsystem A.3 also concluded that there is enough uncertainty regarding the final weight for Component A.3.2 that he was going to also apply the company's margin plan and holdback 10% of his subsystem's weight allocation (7.55 lbs) at the subsystem level and allocate 56.45 lbs as a weight limit to the component A.3.2 development team. Again, component A.3.1 already exists and has a known weight of 11.5 lbs.

If all goes according to design, the resulting total system weight will be 211.5 lbs, 23.5 lbs under the requirement limit. However, if some additional weight creeps into the actual build of subsystem A.2, subsystem A.3, or component A.3.2, the buffer of 23.5 lbs exists to hopefully keep the overall system below the requirement weight limit.

Margins for cost and other quantitative requirement constraints like reliability are handled in the same manner but with different considerations as to why some percentage could or should be held as a margin at some level of the system. This example suggests why a developer who constructs their system design using only existing technologies very rarely invokes margins except for costs: their existing system elements either do or do not meet the requirements as specified. But, for stakeholders, a design that uses existing technology instead of cutting edge research and development can weaken their competitive position in comparison to other company designs. Depending on the reputation of the company and the performance specifications of their existing system elements, this may or may not have an impact on whether their design gets adopted or not. Every system development effort is unique in this way. More often is the case that a company will use very new technology or new configurations of existing and new technology to meet critical system function requirements. Margin management offers one approach that helps reduce a company's risk in doing so, if the modified requirement limits passed on to subsystem development teams are practically achievable.

 No matter how familiar the systems team is with the system of interest and its functions, be very careful to not create requirements! Requirements come from stakeholders. If the team generates useful ideas of what the system could possibly do in a way that is cost-saving or creates a leap-ahead capability, these ideas should be discussed with key stakeholders for them to decide whether or not they should be part of system requirements. System requirements should not be created by members of the systems team.

5.5 FUNCTIONAL ANALYSIS

Functional analysis is a systematic process for identifying system functions and interfaces required to achieve the system purpose and objectives. The INCOSE Systems Engineering Handbook lists 13 functional analysis techniques [26]. This section introduces four of the most useful techniques. Table 5.6 summarizes the purposes, uses, and limitations of the four techniques. Each of these will be discussed in what follows.

5.5.1 Functional Hierarchy

A *functional hierarchy* is diagram that communicates the transformation of system requirements into essential functions (actions) that a system must perform to achieve its intended purpose(s). It illustrates a decomposition of major system functions into successive levels of subfunctions in a way that shows the number of decomposition levels, the breadth of each level of decomposition, and the overall number of essential functions from which the system design will be derived (Figure 5.6).

The number of decomposition levels can vary throughout the functional hierarchy, providing an initial indication of integration challenge that lies ahead. The breadth of each decomposition level, including the top level major system functions, implies the complexity of component integration and testing that lies ahead, because all functional elements on a single level must be integrated into a cohesive whole for a parent function to be performed by the system. The overall number of functional units on a functional hierarchy provides an initial indication of the number and type of development teams that will be needed along with the scope of their activities.

Functional hierarchies can be developed using affinity diagrams. An affinity diagram is a collection of ideas binned into logical groupings for a specific purpose (Figure 5.6) [36]. Affinity diagramming is a simple creative technique that has many valuable uses. Affinity diagramming is usually a group process used to generate ideas and provide new groupings of the ideas for a specific purpose. The affinity diagram is similar to the KJ Method originally developed by Kawakita Jiro [37]. The affinity diagram was made popular as a quality management technique. It is one of the most widely used Japanese management and planning tools.

Affinity diagramming can be done on any vertical or horizontal surface with Post-It™ notes (hence the nickname "the yellow-stickee" drill) or it can be done with specialized collaborative decision support software, for example, GroupSystems [20]. Affinity diagramming can be used for many systems engineering and systems decision support activities that require working with a group to generate new ideas and grouping the ideas into logical categories. Affinity diagramming can be combined with other techniques to determine priorities or actions for each group of

TABLE 5.6   Selected Functional Analysis Techniques.

Functional analysis techniques	Purpose	Uses	Limitations
Functional hierarchy	Identify the system functions and subfunctions.	Provides functional hierarchy to guide concept development, design, and help identify performance measures.	Does not define functional relationships and interfaces. Nor does it validate the system design.
Functional flow diagram	Identify and show the relationships of system functions and subfunctions.	Defines the relationship of functions and subfunctions to guide concept development, design and help identify performance measures.	Does not define or validate system interfaces. Nor does it validate the system design.
IDEF0	Model the decisions, actions, and activities of an organization or system.	Provides detailed information on the functions including inputs, outputs, mechanism, and controls to support the system design and development. Helps refine performance measures.	Does not validate system design.
Models and simulations	Model the system and/or its operation	Understand and support system design and evaluation. Helps refine performance measures.	Will not validate all aspects of system design.

ideas. Our interest in using affinity diagramming in functional analysis is to develop a functional hierarchy.

Steps for Affinity Diagramming for Functional Analysis. There are six steps involved with developing a functional hierarchy for a system. These are:

1. *Invite required stakeholders or their representatives to attend.* For the affinity diagramming exercise to be successful, stakeholders must participate in the process either directly or through a representative who can clearly articulate the viewpoint of the stakeholder. All key

Figure 5.6   Affinity diagramming in action.

stakeholder groups should be represented. If key stakeholders are not represented, important functions may not be identified.

2. *Define the system.* The scope of the system is critical for obtaining the appropriate functions. The following systems will have very different functions: the U.S. transportation system, an urban transportation system, an automobile, or a car engine. We recommend using a system boundary diagram (Figure 2.3) or an input–output diagram.

3. *Generate system functions.* Each function should be specified with a verb and an object. The verb defines the activity of the function. The object provides the context. Both are required! The function should be specified without specifying the system element that will perform the function. For a vehicle, some appropriate functions might be transport passengers, store luggage, avoid collision with an object, and so on. An inappropriate function would be "step on the brakes" since this function assumes that brakes will be an element and that the foot will be used to activate the brakes. The brainstorming can be done by individuals in the groups on the basis of their knowledge and experience. In some settings, it is appropriate (if not essential) to have the individual use organizational documents that provide required capabilities, functions, or requirements for the system. It is usually a good idea to get 10–20 functions from each individual.

4. *Rapidly group ("affinitize") similar functions.* Once the functions have been recorded they should be displayed. Next, a few individuals should bin the functions into logical groups. Usually the verbs are the most helpful for binning the functions. For example, the following functions might be binned together: relocate passengers, take family to the store, seat passengers, and transport kids to soccer practice. As the affinitizing process is being performed, participants should continue to add new functions as ideas come to their mind or the discussion keys an idea. These function groups will become the lowest tier in the functional hierarchy. At this point each function group should be named. The name should be the most general name that captures the activity of all the functions in the group. The functional group should be named with a verb and an object. You can use one of the function names or develop a new name. In our example, "transport passengers" might be a good function group name.

5. *Develop preliminary functional hierarchy.* The next step is to affinitize the function groups into the next higher level. Again, similar function groups will be binned together. The higher level function groups will need to be named with a verb and object that capture the meaning of the function groups below it in the hierarchy. For example, transport passengers and move material, might binned into transport people and objects. For some systems two levels may be sufficient. For complex systems, many levels may be required. This step would be repeated until the first tier of the hierarchy has about three to five functions. Three to five is a useful guideline since it is relatively easy to remember this number of functions. At each level of the hierarchy, the functions should be presented in the most logical order. For example, time sequencing may be appropriate. At this point the group activity is complete.

6. *Refine the functional hierarchy.* The lead systems engineer will need to refine the hierarchy and vet it with stakeholders who could not attend the affinity diagramming workshop and with system decision makers. During the process the function names on each tier may change as reviewers provide insights on a clearer or more acceptable way to name the functions.

Uses of Functional Hierarchy. Once the functional hierarchy is complete, it has several uses. First, the functional hierarchy can (should!) be used to provide a clear understanding of the intended system functions. This makes it useful for presentations to stakeholders and other participants in the system project. Second, the functional hierarchy is an important first step towards a more detailed functional analysis, which is required to identify and define subsystem and component interfaces. Third, the functional hierarchy can serve as a foundation for an assessment of candidate solution designs (See Chapter 6). Fourth, the functional hierarchy can be used to help develop models and simulations. The functional hierarchy should be updated throughout the system life cycle and especially at every application of the systems decision process. Finally, the functional hierarchy can be used to support system architecture and system design since both of these processes involve mapping system elements to system functions.

Affinity Diagramming & Functional Hierarchy for EV. A notional small taxi company is looking to modify its operational vehicle fleet with EVs. After assembling a group of stakeholders from both inside and outside the company, the systems team conducted a brainstorming session to elicit their input as to what the BEVs must do to be considered successful.

Prior to starting, the facilitator encouraged a general discussion regarding their concerns—pros and cons—with making EVs a part of their taxi company's fleet. Most of the ideas centered on the importance of selecting the right vehicle(s) while being prepared to change this selection with as little problems as possible in the event that unforeseen issues arose. It was not seen as a simple vehicle purchase or leasing venture, mostly because of the relatively limited experience EVs have had as part of a taxi fleet.

Several of the company's mid-level managers worried that "their necks would be on the line" if the wrong vehicle was selected because it would impact operations, maintenance, storage, and replacement once the vehicles are put into operation. They also placed a high priority on rider satisfaction to avoid a bad investment that had occurred years earlier when they tried to capitalize on a vehicle design fad.

Several stakeholders who had a holistic perspective on their company's operations realized that placing EVs into their taxi fleet operation would be analogous to replacing a major system component. They could envision what looked like a straightforward decision having a rippling disruptive effect throughout their organization, including human resources, training, maintenance infrastructure, vehicle security, insurance, profit sharing with employees, union concerns, and others. The facilitator used key words to widen their considerations so that they did not become overly focused on a small number of concerns early in the process (i.e., avoiding contractive thinking).

The first 30-minute session was facilitated by the lead systems engineer on the systems decision support team. After reminding stakeholders of the project's fundamental objective, the new EV's purpose, and that ideas needed to be free-flowing without judgment, the session began. Participants generated nearly 90 Post-It® notes of ideas, positioning them on a large whiteboard in the session room. The facilitators considered using a digital option like Windows Sticky Notes app on a large screen, but decided to use physical notes so that stakeholders would be more active, getting out of their seats and moving around, which worked well.

Following this, an affinity diagramming session was conducted by the systems team to group notes into categories that could be generalized into major system functions. Some of the major categories discussed were: passenger satisfaction, maintenance, financial costs, new training requirements, green initiatives, driver ease of use, driving time disruptions, and vehicle fit in an urban environment. Many of these will become objectives for the EV to achieve, such as minimizing greenhouse gas emissions and minimizing life cycle cost burden. Some become major system functions and supporting subfunctions, as shown in Figure 5.7.

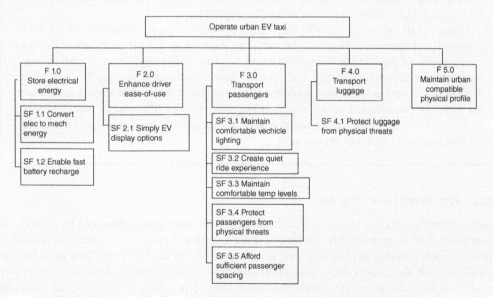

Figure 5.7 Example functional hierarchy for a battery electric vehicle (BEV).

The systems team and appropriate stakeholders will revise and expand upon this initial hierarchy in follow-on sessions. It serves as a starting point for continued research and stakeholder analysis to ensure that the hierarchy is as inclusive and complete as possible. This also supports the team when creating a multiple criteria value model (MCMV) used to support a tradeoff decision for this project. In this hierarchy, the term "Passenger" includes the driver where appropriate.

Limitations of Functional Hierarchy. A functional hierarchy is a first step towards identifying and adding structure to system functions. Additional information is required to identify the inter-relationships of functions and interfaces using system representations such as DSMs. A functional hierarchy can also help identify which functions may need to be modeled and/or simulated for analysis and performance purposes.

CMS: Functional Hierarchy. Once complete with research and stakeholder analysis, the systems team was able to develop a functional hierarchy for the proposed curriculum management system (CMS). Using the general trends from the stakeholder surveys, focus group, and interviews they conducted to identify high-level functions for the system. They then used relevant detailed information from each of the stakeholder analysis techniques to decompose each high-level system function into subfunctions. Many of the resulting subfunctions were further decomposed to achieve the appropriate level of system behavior definition. Once complete, the systems team presented the functional hierarchy to the department leadership for approval and possible revisions, as needed (Figure 5.8).

Figure 5.9 shows the first two levels of the functional hierarchy developed for the CMS system. It is important to note that the functions depicted in this hierarchy are not simply the functions of the CMS information system software application alone. It also includes functions that department faculty roles (actors) have to perform to manage the curriculum. A subset of these functions were intended to be performed by the CMS application itself, but were not consolidated or automated at that time. For a CMS system, including these additional functions helped to ensure that the CMS behaved as needed and was not simply another facility to exchange information.

5.5.2 Functional Flow Diagram

Once a system's top level functions have been identified, their relationships can be depicted in a functional flow diagram (FFD). An FFD is a diagram that expands on a functional hierarchy, chronologically ordering several levels of system functions in the order that they must be performed. As each functions is decomposed into subfunctions, the element interfaces become more specific and more complex. This functional decomposition is continued until discrete tasks can be defined that can be mapped (allocated) to specific system elements to perform (subsystems, assemblies, components). Trade studies are performed to allocate tasks to system elements.

Figure 5.8 illustrates an initial functional flow diagram for a National Aeronautical and Space Agency's Space Transportation System (STS) Flight Mission [26]. This diagram was based on three initial system functions: launch vehicle, perform mission operations, retrieve payload, and re-enter and land. Decomposition and chronological ordering produced specific functions as shown.

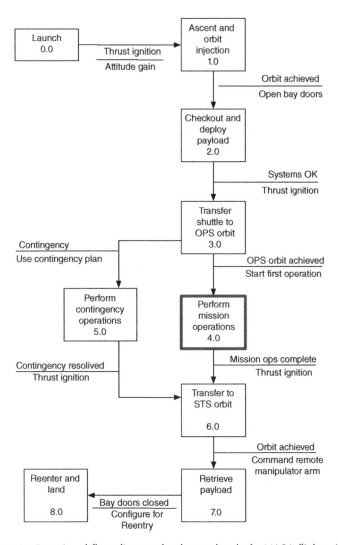

Figure 5.8 Functional flow diagram for the top level of a NASA flight mission.

Each of the top level functions in Figure 5.8 can be further decomposed into tasks that are required to perform each top level function. Figure 5.10 shows the functional decomposition for the system Function 4.0: Perform Mission Operations. It has been further decomposed into 10 tasks that provide further detail about their interfaces [26]. The functional decomposition of each of the tasks could continue to a next level as needed.

Uses of the Functional Flow Diagram. Functional flow diagrams (FFD) are most useful during system concept, design, and development stages of a systems life cycle. Once a functional flow diagram is complete it has several uses. First, the diagram provides a better understanding of the relationships of the functions and tools to support the identification of the requirements. The top level functions are useful for presentations to participants in the systems decision support or systems

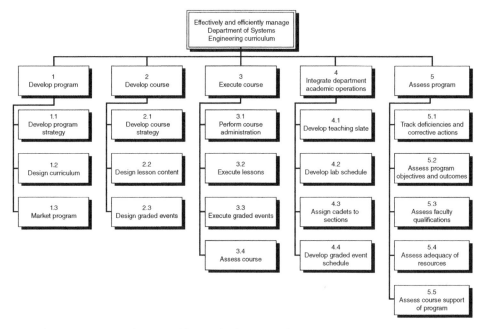

Figure 5.9 Partial functional hierarchy for curriculum management system (CMS).

engineering process, including decision makers and stakeholders. Second, the functions in the diagram can serve as a foundation for assessing alternative solution designs (see Section 6.2.1). Third, a functional flow diagram can be used to support system architecture and system design. Fourth, a functional flow diagram can be used to help develop models and simulations to design and evaluate systems.

Limitations of the Functional Flow Diagrams. A functional flow diagram defines the relationships of the functions but does not define the interfaces needed to complete the design. An FFD identifies the functions and the interrelationships among the functions but does not identify all the inputs, outputs, controls, and mechanisms that are required during system design or a detailed development of models and simulations. The next technique provides additional functional analysis data to help fill this gap.

5.5.3 IDEF0 Functional Modeling Method

IDEF0 models were discussed in detail in Section 3.7. These models can help a systems team to communicate with key stakeholders to identify the functions, inputs, outputs, mechanisms, and controls of the system. IDEF0 is a useful method for functional analysis. The simple graphical approach helps involve subject matter experts early in the system development process. IDEF0 can be implemented with widely available tools (e.g., Microsoft® Visio [38]) or can be implemented with specialized software. Figure 5.11 provides an example of a high level IDEF0 functional analysis for performing an engineering design of a system [39].

Uses of IDEF0. The model has several uses. First, the model can support the system design. IDEF0 helps identify and structure system functions to define "As-Is" and "To-Be" architectures.

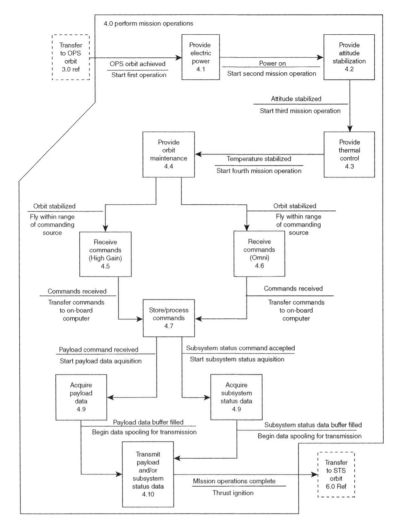

Figure 5.10   Functional flow diagram for Function 4.0: perform mission operations.

As-Is models are usually developed bottom-up and To-Be models are developed top-down. For each function inputs, outputs, controls, and mechanisms (ICOMs) are specified using a standard modeling language. The model is developed as a hierarchy of functions. The modeler can stop when functions are specified at the level of detail required for system decision making. Second, the functions in the diagram can serve as a foundation for assessing alternative solution designs (see Section 6.2). Third, the models can be used to help develop models and simulations to design and evaluate systems.

Limitations of IDEF0. These models provide detailed information to support system design and qualitative evaluation of candidate solutions. However, the models do not validate that the design will work in a system's environment or that the design has the capacity to provide all the inputs and outputs for each function to meet the quantitative system performance goals. Models, simulations, development tests, and operational tests are needed to overcome these limitations.

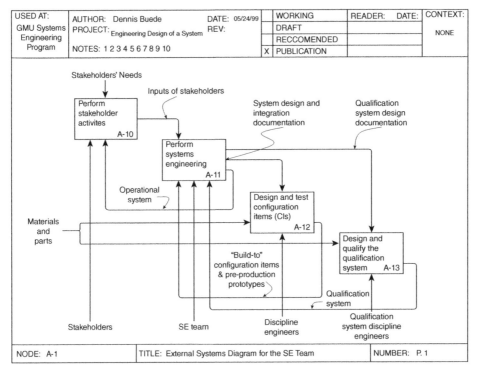

USED AT: | AUTHOR: Dennis Buede | DATE: 05/24/99 | WORKING | | READER: DATE: | CONTEXT:
GMU Systems Engineering Program | PROJECT: Engineering Design of a System | REV: | DRAFT | | | NONE
| | | RECCOMENDED | |
| NOTES: 1 2 3 4 5 6 7 8 9 10 | | X | PUBLICATION | |

NODE: A-1 — TITLE: External Systems Diagram for the SE Team — NUMBER: P. 1

Figure 5.11   IDEF0 Level 1 functional analysis example.

5.6   ASSESSING SYSTEM READINESS

During the early stages of a system life cycle when science and technology efforts are primary, basic prototypes are constructed to test concepts, confirm design feasibility, or to gain an initial understanding as to the difficulty associated with integrating various system elements into a system. As mentioned previously, most modern systems are a blend of existing and new elements. Each separate component, assembly, or subsystem can be described by its technology readiness level (TRL), indicating on a 1 to 9 scale where in the development process it is, otherwise known as its level of maturity. The TRL index is currently the only reported tracking scale used by the U.S. Department of Defense (DoD) Joint Capabilities Integration Development System (JCIDS).

Figure 5.12 shows the 1 to 9 TRL scale developed by the U.S. Department of Defense (DoD) to support science and technology acquisition and development. Notice that in keeping with best practices for creating constructed scales (see Chapter 6), each of the TRL scale values have specific definitions that enable system elements to be matched to scale levels. Supporting information for applying the TRL scale to system elements comes from the engineering teams responsible for developing them and *not* from the systems decision support team. Knowing the TRL for a system or its sub-elements helps focus assessments, experiments, and demonstrations designed to verify and validate the developer-assigned level. TRL also provides an indication of the challenges facing successful system development, thereby informing risk estimates for resource and budgeting purposes.

Although the TRL scale has been widely adopted and has proven its utility in acquisition and system development, it does not provide a semi-quantitative estimate of the state of integration between system elements. Systems often fail, experience development delays, or incur higher than estimated development costs because attention is given to the technology while knowledge of the linkages between system elements is overlooked. These linkages affect a system's architecture

Technology readiness level	Description
1. Basic principles observed and reported.	Lowest level of technology readiness. Examples might include paper studies of a technology's basic properties.
2. Technology concept and/or application formulated.	Invention begins. Examples are limited to analytic studies.
3. An analytical and experimental critical function and/or characteristic proof of concept.	Includes analytical and lab studies to physically validate predictions of separate elements of the technology. Examples include components not yet integrated.
4. Component validation in laboratory environment.	Basic technological components are integrated. This is relatively "low fidelity" compared to the eventual system.
5. Component validation in relevant environment.	Basic technological components are integrated with reasonably realistic supporting elements so it can be tested in a simulated environment.
6. Prototype demonstration in a relevant environment.	Representative prototype system tested in a relevant environment. Represents a major step up in a technology's demonstrated readiness. Examples include testing a prototype in a high-fidelity laboratory environment or in simulated operational environment.
7. Prototype demonstration in an operational environment.	Prototype near, or at, planned operational system. Represents a major set up from TRL 6, requiring demonstration of an actual system prototype in an operational environment.
8. System qualified through test and demonstration.	Technology proven to work in its final form and under expected conditions. Represents the end of true system development. Examples include developmental test and evaluation of the system.
9. System proven through successful mission operations.	Actual application of the technology in its final form and under mission conditions, such as those encountered in operational test and evaluation.

Figure 5.12 U.S. Dept of Defense technology readiness levels (TRL).

203

and communication channels with other elements within and outside of the system's boundary. If sufficient and timely attention is not given to element integration early on, project rework can result as the development team has to undo engineering decisions to accommodate integration needs.

Ontology metrics have been used in the computer industry to assess the coupling levels between modules and other software components [40]. Despite this, there are still few reasonable approaches to capturing the level of system element integration in a meaningful manner. Because of this, systems teams frequently must construct custom integration assessment tools that depend on the characteristics and specifics of the system of interest and the assessment context (e.g., live field experiment, laboratory demonstration).

One such integration assessment tool is illustrated in Figure 5.13, which was developed purely as a tracking and reporting tool to track the level of integration that individual sensor systems achieved with a command and control (C2) system during Technical Support and Operational Assessment (TSOA) experiments [41]. Notional results are shown for 9 of the 23 systems involved with the experiment. The integration scale was simply structured to capture 5 possible data flow conditions that were of primary concern for the experiment. Marginal percentages of integration were automatically calculated for rows and columns. As an assessment level was entered into the matrix, a corresponding circular image would appear whose fill proportion aligned with the integration level achieved. For example, an empty circle indicates level 0, with quarter circle filling corresponding to levels 1, 2, 3, and 4. With 23 systems represented in the full integration matrix, having a quick visual cue as to the individual integration levels was useful for daily planning. The main diagonal locations which correspond to a system's integration with itself are not used because systems must be at least fully-functioning prototypes in order to participate in TSOA.

In this way, this approach is equivalent to using numerical DSMs to track integration, availing it to further analysis using software such as Cambridge Advanced Modeller (CAM). While simple, it nonetheless provided a quick and accurate assessment of the experiment's integration progress and highlighted those systems needing a repeat engagement to achieve the desired two-way data flow. Such an approach could easily be tailored to track integration completeness within and across system boundaries.

A second option available for assessing integration is an integration readiness level (IRL) scale proposed by Gove et al. [42]. This IRL improved upon several previous research efforts [43–46]. Its nine levels are intentionally aligned with the nine TRL levels, which can be seen in the IRL level definitions shown in Table 5.7.

An interesting idea is to mathematically blend the IRL scale with TRL in a manner that captures both system and component (subsystem, assembly) progress towards systems readiness as was done by Sauser et al. [46, 47]. Individual component TRL levels are captured in a column vector. IRL levels are organized in a matrix similar to the TSOA integration tool setup, which allows bi-directional integration levels to be different.

By normalizing the readiness levels and applying matrix multiplication, the resulting system readiness level (SRL) yields an index on a [0, 1] interval for each component and one for the overall system (*composite SRL*) that align with specific system development phases formalized in DoD acquisition as shown in Table 5.8. In doing so, it provides a means to assess the state of a system or subsystem relative to where it should be based on historical data. The SRL approach directly addresses three questions every systems engineering team faces:

1. How complete is each individual element's development (TRL)?
2. To what extent does each system element have its required dependencies in-place and working (IRL)?
3. Considering both TRL and IRL, what stage of development are the system and its subelements with regard to the DoD systems acquisition timeline?

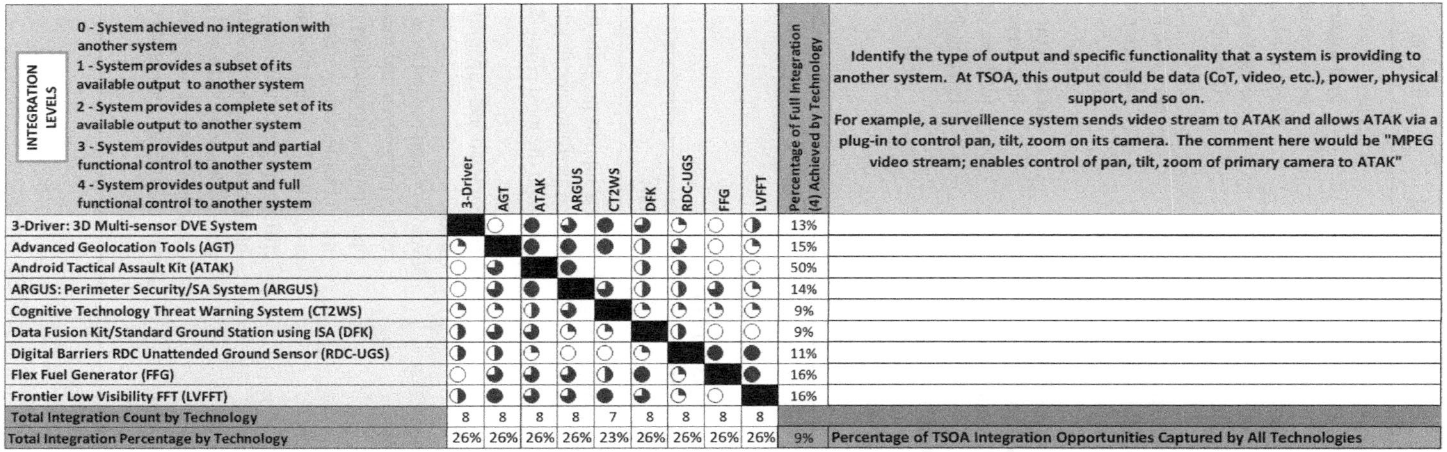

INTEGRATION LEVELS

0 - System achieved no integration with another system
1 - System provides a subset of its available output to another system
2 - System provides a complete set of its available output to another system
3 - System provides output and partial functional control to another system
4 - System provides output and full functional control to another system

Identify the type of output and specific functionality that a system is providing to another system. At TSOA, this output could be data (CoT, video, etc.), power, physical support, and so on.
For example, a surveillance system sends video stream to ATAK and allows ATAK via a plug-in to control pan, tilt, zoom on its camera. The comment here would be "MPEG video stream; enables control of pan, tilt, zoom of primary camera to ATAK"

	3-Driver	AGT	ATAK	ARGUS	CT2WS	DFK	RDC-UGS	FFG	LVFFT	Percentage of Full Integration (4) Achieved by Technology
3-Driver: 3D Multi-sensor DVE System										13%
Advanced Geolocation Tools (AGT)										15%
Android Tactical Assault Kit (ATAK)										50%
ARGUS: Perimeter Security/SA System (ARGUS)										14%
Cognitive Technology Threat Warning System (CT2WS)										9%
Data Fusion Kit/Standard Ground Station using ISA (DFK)										9%
Digital Barriers RDC Unattended Ground Sensor (RDC-UGS)										11%
Flex Fuel Generator (FFG)										16%
Frontier Low Visibility FFT (LVFFT)										16%
Total Integration Count by Technology	8	8	8	8	7	8	8	8	8	
Total Integration Percentage by Technology	26%	26%	26%	26%	23%	26%	26%	26%	26%	Percentage of TSOA Integration Opportunities Captured by All Technologies: 9%

Figure 5.13 Integration tracking tool for sensor field experiments.

TABLE 5.7 Integration Readiness levels [42].

IRL	Definition	IRL	Definition
9	Integration is **mission proven** through successful operations.	4	There is sufficient detail in the **quality and assurance** of the integration between technologies.
8	Actual integration completed and **mission qualified** through test and demonstration in the system's environment	3	There is **compatibility** between technologies to orderly and efficiently integrate and interact.
7	The integration of technologies has been **verified and validated** with sufficient detail to be actionable.	2	There is some level of specificity to characterize the **interaction** (i.e., ability to influence) between technologies through their interface.
6	The integrating technologies can **accept, translate, and structure information** for its intended application	1	An **interface** between technologies has been identified with sufficient detail to allow characterization of the relationship.
5	There is sufficient **control** between technologies necessary to establish, manage, and terminate the interaction.		

Source: Adapted from Gove et al. [42].

TABLE 5.8 System Readiness Levels (SRL) [46].

SRL Index	Acquisition Phase	Definitions
0.9 to 1.0	*Operations & Support*	Execute a support program that meets operational support performance requirements and sustains the system in the most cost-effective manner over its total lifecycle.
0.80 to 0.89	*Production*	Achieve operational capability that satisfies mission needs.
0.60 to 0.79	*System Development & Demonstration*	Develop system capability or (increments thereof); reduce integration and manufacturing risk; ensure operational supportability; reduce logistics footprint; implement human systems integration; design for production; ensure affordability and protection of critical program information; and demonstrate system integration, interoperability,, safety and utility.
0.40 to 0.59	*Technology Development*	Reduce technology risks and determine appropriate set of technologies to integrate into a full system.
0.10 to 0.39	*Concept Refinement*	Refine the initial concept; develop system/technology strategy.

Source: Adapted from Sauser et al. [46].

The SRL index level intervals shown in Table 5.8 were derived using sensitivity analysis with sample systems.

As an index, the SRL serves a very useful purpose to a systems engineering or systems decision support project, especially when it comes to making project/program management decisions. Like the TSOA integration tracker, the SRL assessment tool is easily implemented in a spreadsheet. The overall process is straightforward:

1. Collect current TRL levels from each of the n engineering teams responsible for component development and place these in a (nx1) column matrix (vector).
2. Assess bi-directional integration levels between the n components using the IRL scale. Record these integration levels in an (nxn) matrix, leaving the entries along the main diagonal blank.
3. Normalize the entries in both the TRL and IRL matrices by dividing each entry by 9.
4. Multiply the IRL matrix times the TRL matrix, resulting in an (nx1) column vector. Call this the *computed SRL*.
5. Divide each entry in the computed SRL column vector by the number of non-zero entries in its corresponding IRL row. This is a scaling adjustment to recognize the number of required integrations for each component. Call this column vector the *scaled SRL*.
6. Compare the scaled SRL values with the intervals shown in Table 5.8 to determine the current development state for each component.
7. Compute the average scaled SRL using the non-zero entries in the scaled SRL vector. This value represents a *composite SRL* index for the system.
8. Compare the composite SRL index value with the intervals shown in Table 5.8 to determine the current system development state considering both technology development and integration.

The information in the IRL matrix is interpreted as being directional relationships oriented row to column (right-and-up), in the same way as DSMs described earlier. This is important to preserve the correct directional relationships between components so that the results of the required matrix multiplication are correct after normalizing: $[IRL]_{nxn} \times [TRL]_{nx1} = [computedSRL]_{nx1}$.

Example SRL Calculation. For this example, suppose that a developing system is currently in the *Technology Development* phase of DoD acquisition, and it has six major subsystems requiring integration with every other subsystem. This assumption is just for illustration purposes. In practical settings, integration requirements vary. Each of the subsystem development teams reported their individual TRL levels, and the systems team entered these in a (6x1) column vector:

$$[TRL]_{6x1} = \begin{bmatrix} 5 \\ 4 \\ 5 \\ 5 \\ 6 \\ 5 \end{bmatrix} \tag{5.1}$$

Scaling this vector by dividing by 9 yields:

$$[TRL]_{6x1} = \begin{bmatrix} 0.56 \\ 0.44 \\ 0.56 \\ 0.56 \\ 0.67 \\ 0.56 \end{bmatrix}. \qquad (5.2)$$

The systems team assessed the required integration levels against the IRL scale shown earlier and entered their levels in a (6x6) matrix:

$$[IRL]_{6x6} = \begin{bmatrix} 2 & 3 & 5 & 6 & 5 \\ 2 & 4 & 6 & 7 & 4 \\ 5 & 3 & 6 & 5 & 4 \\ 6 & 6 & 5 & 6 & 4 \\ 2 & 5 & 4 & 8 & 3 \\ 7 & 4 & 6 & 3 & 5 \end{bmatrix} \qquad (5.3)$$

which, scaling by dividing by 9 yields:

$$[IRL]_{6x6} = \begin{bmatrix} 0.2 & 0.3 & 0.6 & 0.7 & 0.6 \\ 0.2 & 0.4 & 0.7 & 0.8 & 0.4 \\ 0.6 & 0.3 & 0.7 & 0.6 & 0.4 \\ 0.7 & 0.7 & 0.6 & 0.7 & 0.4 \\ 0.2 & 0.6 & 0.4 & 0.9 & 0.3 \\ 0.8 & 0.4 & 0.7 & 0.3 & 0.6 \end{bmatrix} \qquad (5.4)$$

Matrix multiplication then produces:

$$[IRL]_{6x6} \times [TRL]_{6x1} = [computedSRL]_{6x1} = \begin{bmatrix} 1.35 \\ 1.51 \\ 1.44 \\ 1.67 \\ 1.30 \\ 1.56 \end{bmatrix}. \qquad (5.5)$$

Dividing each [*computedSRL*] entry by the number of non-zero entries in its corresponding IRL row (in this case all are divided by 5), yields the scaled SRL column vector:

$$[scaledSRL]_{6x1} = \begin{bmatrix} 0.27 \\ 0.30 \\ 0.29 \\ 0.33 \\ 0.26 \\ 0.31 \end{bmatrix}, \qquad (5.6)$$

and a composite SRL for the system equal to 0.29.

Comparing these values to the DoD acquisition intervals to interpret results shows that although the system is in the *Technology Development* phase, the SRL index reveals that the state of every component along with the overall system are actually lagging. None of the individual component SRLs meet the minimum index level needed to be considered in the *Technology Development* phase (0.40), and neither does the system as a whole despite the fact that all component development teams reported that component validation has taken place in a relevant environment (minimum TRL 5).

This result should be interpreted in a diagnostic sense by the systems team in that some investigation appears necessary to determine why this development delay is presenting itself. Within the development teams, it could be that teams reported overly optimistic TRL levels, or that several low levels for needed integration are holding back system development. External to the project, budget reductions or reallocations, contract delays, supply chain issues, personnel losses, scheduling and coordination problems, and a host of other events beyond the engineering teams' control could be contributing to the delay. In any case, plans will need to be developed to get the system development project back on-track.

5.7 INITIAL RISK ASSESSMENT

As the complexity of systems and their environment increases, the number, type, likelihood, and impact of events that can occur to threaten the well-being of systems becomes increasingly more difficult to identify. For a systems engineering or systems decision support team, there are two basic risk categories that are of particular concern: those associated with the system of interest, and those associated with the systems project itself. Risks that can threaten some dimension related to the system of interest (e.g., degraded performance, purpose failures, cost overruns, etc.) are those most often discussed and are again so here. These are risks that are uncovered in collaboration with stakeholders.

Risks that can threaten success for the systems project include things like cancelled or reduced project funding, client dissatisfaction, damage to reputation, loss of key project personnel, and other events more closely aligned with project management than with systems engineering. These are risks handled internally within the systems project team. Both categories should be discussed as part of any systems project so as many relevant risks as possible can be identified, managed, mitigated, or eliminated.

A *risk* is a probabilistic event that, if it occurs, will cause unwanted change in the cost, schedule, or value return (e.g., technical performance) of an engineering system [48]. The goal of risk management is to identify and assess risks in order to enact policy and take action to reduce the risk-induced variance of system technical performance, cost, and schedule estimates over the entire system life cycle. In other words, risk management describes a collection of thoughtful and deliberate actions to protect the system from the adverse effects of specific events that have a non-zero probability of occurring in the future.

System complexity works against accomplishing this goal in an easy manner because by increasing the number and type of interconnections, vested interests, and uncertainty levels, it becomes more and more difficult to effectively apply risk management. This is especially true if risk management activities lack formal, repeatable organization. It is simply impossible to "fly by intuition" in this regard. Moreover, while risks associated with specific components, so-called *non-systemic* risks, might be identifiable by ad hoc procedures based on experience alone, the more subtle and elusive *systemic* risks—those inherent in the entire system (shared across components)—will routinely avoid detection without some organized, repeatable process. This latter group can, if left unattended to, take down an entire financial, communications, transportation, or other system when they occur [49].

Risk management is comprised of the three main activities: risk identification, risk assessment, and risk mitigation. It is an ongoing process applied throughout the life cycle of a systems engineering project. This section takes a broad view of risk management [50], focusing on core principles and concepts that set the stage for a more in-depth exploration in later chapters.

5.7.1   Risk Identification

The process of identifying risks consists of determining any sources of risk and the scenarios under which they may occur. Risk identification seeks to discover and categorize uncertain events or conditions whose occurrence will have a negative impact on any number of important measures such as system cost, schedule, value, technical performance, or safety. The focus of this effort often changes during a systems decision support project. The systems team could be initially concerned about the risks associated with having the project proposal approved, shifting then to possible risk impediments to the SDP effort, and finally to addressing threats to the successful implementation and sustained health of the selected system solution. Ideally then, techniques used to identify risks need to be flexible or general enough to apply throughout the duration of a systems decision support project and its resulting solution implementation.

Two convenient techniques for identifying possible risks to systems are *prompt lists* and *brainstorming*. Both techniques involve extensive interaction with system stakeholders. Their unique insights arising from stakeholder familiarity with a system's operating environment are critical information needed to develop comprehensive risk categories.

A *prompt list* is simply a listing of possible categories of risks that are particular to the current systems project. They function as word recall prompts during stakeholder interviews, helping to cue participants towards thinking of as many risks to its success as possible. As a technique, prompt lists can be used on an individual basis or in a group setting with a facilitator from the systems team in control.

For example, when identifying risk elements during a life cycle stage that focuses on establishing the need for a system, the team could use a prompt list consisting of SDP environmental factors: technological, health & safety, social, moral/ethical, security, cultural, ecological, historical, organizational, political, economic, and legal, in order to develop a preliminary list of major risks associated with developing a system to meet the needs of stakeholders. The risk elements emerge in subsequent discussions as the details required to document risks in a risk register are identified and recorded. Executive board objections to the overall decision support, potential financial problems with funding the effort to completion, knowledge deficiencies due to venturing into new competitive territory, political backlash from government administrators or the general public, and so on, are examples of the types of risk that can arise that are external to a system boundary.

As discussed earlier, brainstorming (see Section 5.3.1) works much in the same manner as a prompt list except that a neutral human facilitator from the systems team serves a similar purpose as the prompt list: to elicit without judgment from the stakeholders any possible risks to successful project completion they might identify from their experience. Brainstorming is also performed almost exclusively in a group setting. The facilitator might employ project schedules, graphical illustrations, data tables, or even a prompt list to help the participants identify risks.

A successful brainstorming session depends heavily on the participation of key stakeholders (see Section 5.3.1). As with many senior leaders of organizations who have constant demands on their time, these key stakeholders may not be able to assemble as a single group for any significant length of time. When stakeholder access is limited, prompt lists are a better technique to use to identify risks because they allow decentralized participation in the risk identification process while maintaining a common frame-of-reference provided by the logical structure of the list. In either instance, a good practice is to plan on at least two complete iterations of stakeholder interviews so that the first set of interview results might be leveraged as prompts for stakeholders participating in the second session.

There are six questions [51] that are commonly used to capture various dimensions of risk to a system during brainstorming sessions with key stakeholders. The answers to these questions provide the data needed to start analyzing risks and plan for their mitigation during the project. The six questions are:

1. What can go wrong?
2. What is the likelihood of something going wrong?
3. What are the consequences?
4. What can be done and what options are available?
5. What are the trade-offs in terms of risk, costs, and benefits?
6. What are the impacts of current decisions on future options?

To make an important point clear: identifying project risks is a demanding task that consumes a good deal of time, effort, and brainpower to get right. Using a structured, repeatable method that is easy to understand is a key ingredient to success. As an example of how important this process is to successful systems decision support projects and how systems engineers attempt to address this concern as comprehensively as possible, consider the listing of techniques used by NASA scientists and risk specialists to identify risks to the National Space Transportation System (NSTS) [52] shown in Table 5.9. These tasks represent thousands of work hours by a host of people across a broad range of system stakeholders.

As each risk is identified, it is categorized to ensure that risks are not double-counted and that the identification of risks is comprehensive. Similar to the affinity diagramming process earlier, the intent here is to group risks into mutually exclusive and collectively exhaustive categories. INCOSE recognizes four categories of risk that must be considered during a system decision problem: technical risk, cost risk, schedule risk, and programmatic risk [53, 54].

Technical risk is concerned with the possibility that a requirement of the system will not be achieved, such as a functional requirement or a specific technical performance objective, because of a problem associated with the technology incorporated into the system, used by the system, or interfacing with system input and output. Functional analysis can aid in this process because its functions illustrate what any feasible system solution must do to be considered successful. For a host of modern systems, technology is the main driver of these functions. By considering the risk to accomplishing each function, a comprehensive treatment of technical risk will occur.

Cost risk is the possibility of exceeding the planned design, development, production, or operating budgets in whole or in part. For any system, estimates of future life cycle costs are subject to varying degrees of uncertainty due to uncontrollable environmental factors, time, and the source of information used to develop these estimates. The further forward in time these costs are anticipated

TABLE 5.9 Techniques for the Identification of Potential Sources of Risk in the NSTS Program.

Hazard analysis	Design and engineering studies
Development and acceptance testing	Safety studies and analysis
FMEAs, CILs, and EIFA	Certification test and analysis
Sneak circuit analyses	Milestone reviews
Failure investigations	Waivers and deviations
Walk-down inspections	Mission planning activities
Software reviews	Astronaut debriefings and concerns
OMRSD/OMI	Flight anomalies
Flight rules development	Aerospace safety advisory panel
Lessons-learned	Alerts
Critical functions assessment	Individual concerns
Hot line	Panel meetings
Software hazard analysis	Faulty tree analysis
Inspections	Change evaluation
Review of manufacturing process	Human factors analysis
Simulations	Payload hazard reports
Real time operations	Payload interfaces

to occur, the more uncertainty is associated with their estimates. While objective cost data with similar systems decision problems is desirable, subjective expert opinion is often used to create cost estimates for items less familiar to the project team and stakeholders. This injects additional uncertainty that must be taken into account, as we show in Chapter 5. Cost risk planning is more complicated than simply accounting for program spending and balancing any remaining budget. Cost risk extends over the entire system life cycle. Decisions made throughout the system life cycle are assessed for their downstream impact on the total system life cycle costs. It becomes necessary to identify major cost drivers whose variability can cause the project to "break the budget" rapidly, thus causing a termination of the effort in the worst case. Properly eliciting the information needed to model and analyze cost uncertainty requires careful thought and consideration [55].

Schedule risk represents the possibility that a project will fail to achieve key milestones agreed upon with the client. Scheduling individual tasks, duration, and their interrelationships is critical to sound project planning. Doing so directly identifies those system activities that lie on a critical path to project success (see Chapter 13). Systems engineers and program managers should focus a large amount of their effort on these critical path tasks because when these tasks fail to achieve on-time start and completion times, the overall project schedule and delivery dates are directly affected. While the more common method of identifying critical path activities is deterministic, recent developments have demonstrated significantly improved benefits for analyzing cost, schedule, and risk *simultaneously* via Monte Carlo simulation [56].

Programmatic risk arises from the recognition that any systems decision problem takes place within a larger environmental context. Thus, it is an assessment of how and to what degree external effects and decisions imposed on the project threaten successful system development and deployment. This last form of risk is closely related to the concept of operational risk emerging from the banking industry [57]. Increased levels of critical suppliers, outsourcing specific engineering tasks, budget reductions, personnel reassignments, and so on are all examples of programmatic risk.

The INCOSE risk categories provide a useful framework for facilitating risk identification and ensuring a comprehensive treatment of risks. It should be noted that the aforementioned risk categories interact with each other throughout a system life cycle. While standard in a systems engineering environment, these are not the only grouping categories that are used. Commercial banks, for example, divide their risk categories into financial, operational, and more recently, systematic risks in order to track the most common undesirable future events they face.

The systemic risk category is worth emphasizing because of its recent realization in global securities markets. The Counterpolicy Risk Management Group [58] suggests an effective definition for our use. A *systemic risk* is the potential loss or damage to an entire system as contrasted with the loss to a single unit of that system. Systemic risks are exacerbated by interdependencies among the units often because of weak links in the system. These risks can be triggered by sudden events or built up over time with the impact often being large and possibly catastrophic.

Systemic risk is an interesting phenomenon gaining growing attention across all risk concerns with systems. Recently, the impact of unmitigated systemic risk events occurring within the financial markets was felt across the globe. The U.S. Congressional Research Service (CRS) describes systemic risk in the following manner:

"All financial market participants face risk-without it, financial intermediation would not occur. Some risks, such as the failure of a specific firm or change in a specific interest rate, can be protected against through diversification, insurance, or financial instruments such as derivatives. One definition of systemic risk is risk that can potentially cause instability for large parts of the financial system. Often, systemic risk will be caused by risks that individual firms cannot protect themselves against; some economists distinguish these types of risks as a subset of systemic risks called systematic risks. Systemic risk can come from within or outside of the financial system. An example of systemic risk that came from outside of the financial system were fears (that largely proved unfounded in hindsight) that the September 11, 2001 terrorist attacks on the nation's financial center would lead to widespread disruption to financial flows because of the destruction of physical infrastructure and death of highly specialized industry professionals. Systemic risk within the financial system is often characterized as contagion, meaning that problems with certain firms or parts of the system spill over to other firms and parts of the system [59]."

The CRS report emphasizes several characteristics of systemic risk that all systems experience: shared risk due to system interconnectivity of people, organizations, equipment, policy, and so on. Systems engineering teams should be aware that systemic risks loom large on complicated projects. As the system solution structure grows, so does the likelihood that the activities supporting its development within the SDP will be subdivided among groups of the team with specialized knowledge and experience. While both effective and efficient, the project manager (PM) must maintain an integrated, holistic perspective of the overall project. Without this perspective and sensitivity to systemic risk, the project could be doomed to failure. A recently release report of the World Economic Forum strongly emphasized this point by bringing together a wide range of systems thinking experts to assist the financial services industry to develop just such a perspective. During the financial crisis of 2007 and 2008, no one regulatory authority or organization in the financial services industry had system-wide oversight that might have identified the rising systemic risk of over-leveraging that occurred [49].

Risk Register A common and effective means of documenting and tracking risks once they are identified is through the use of a *risk register*. A risk register holds a list of key risks that need to

Risk	Category	Impact	Likelihood	Risk level	Current	Mitigation	Risk owner
Government failure to set aside contingency funds	Financial	Medium	Low	Amber	None	Monthly monitoring of contingency funds by design team	Client
Breach of legislation	Legal	Medium	Medium	Amber	Compliance audit	Peer review by legal	Team internal legal
Substandard composite material used in multiple component	Systemic	High	Low	Green	Periodic material sampling	Material engineering review during IPRs	Project lead engineer

Figure 5.14   Example risk register used during the SDP.

be monitored and managed. When used properly, it is reviewed and updated regularly and should be a permanent item on any project meeting agenda. Figure 5.14 shows an example risk register for the rocket problem using several of the risk categories noted earlier. The values shown in the impact, likelihood, and risk level columns are developed using the techniques described in what follows.

Once risks have been identified and categorized, the next challenge is to determine those risks that pose the greatest threat to the system. This *risk assessment* process involves assessing each hazard in terms of the potential, magnitude, and consequences of any loss from or to a system. When there exists historical data on these losses or the rate of occurrence for the risk event, risk analysis is directly measured from the statistics of the loss. Otherwise, the risk event is modeled and predicted using probabilistic risk analysis (PRA) techniques [60]. This latter option has become the norm in modern risk analysis because for complex systems, especially those involving new or innovative technologies, such historical loss data rarely exists. Because some of the hazards to the system may involve rare events that have never occurred, estimates of the probability of occurrence can be difficult to assess and often must be based on a subjective estimate derived from expert opinion. When this occurs, techniques such as partitioned multiobjective risk method (PMRM) that uses conditional risk functions to properly model and analyze these extreme events are employed [61].

The consequence imposed on system success when a risk event does transpire can involve increased cost, degradation of system technical performance, schedule delays, loss of life, and a number of other undesirable effects. With complex systems, the full consequence of a risk may not be immediately apparent as it might take time for the effects to propagate across the multitude of interconnections. These 'downstream' effects, often referred to second, third and higher order effects, are very difficult to identify and assess, and can easily be of higher consequence than the immediate ones.

The risks associated with the Tacoma Narrows Bridge on Highway 16 in Seattle collapsing can be assessed from structural engineering information and historical data existing from its previous collapse in 1940. However, suppose that when this bridge collapses, the express delivery van carrying human transplant organs does not make it to the regional hospital in time to save the patient because it has to find another route that it did not plan for. The patient happens to be a U.S. senator who is the current champion of a new bill to Congress authorizing direct loans to Washington State residents suffering under the collapse of the mortgage industry. The bill fails to pass and thousands of people lose their homes, and so on. The Middle English poet John Gower captured this domino effect in his poem *For Want of a Nail*, the modern nursery rhyme version of which goes:

For want of a nail, the shoe was lost;
For want of the shoe, the horse was lost;
For want of the horse, the rider was lost;

For want of a rider, the battle was lost;
For want of the battle, the kingdom was lost;
And all for the want of a horseshoe nail.

Probability-Impact Tables Probability-impact (P-I) tables [62], also known as probability-consequences tables, are a straightforward tool that can be used both to differentiate between and help prioritize upon the various risks identified and to provide clarifying summary information concerning specific risks. In concept, P-I tables are similar to the matrix procedure described in Military Standard (MIL-STD) 882 [63], elsewhere adapted to become a bicriteria filtering and ranking method [53].

P-I tables are attractive for use early in the system life cycle because as a qualitative technique they can be applied using only stakeholder input. Later, as risk mitigation costs become available, a third dimension representing the mitigation cost range can be imposed on the P-I table, thereby completing the trade space involved with risk management. Stakeholders are asked to select their assessed level of likelihood and impact of risks using a constructed qualitative scale such as very low, low, medium, high, and very high. If the actual probability intervals are difficult to assess at an early stage, a similar constructed scale can be used to solicit stakeholder input as to the likelihood of risks: unlikely, seldom, occasional, likely, and frequent [53]. The point is to start the risk management process early in the system life cycle and not to delay risk consideration until sufficient data are available to quantify risk assessments.

Typically, each of these qualitative labels is defined with a range specific of outcomes for the risks that helps the stakeholder to distinguish between levels. Using ranges, such as those illustrated in Figure 5.15 for five qualitative labels, helps normalize estimates among stakeholders. Ideally, what one stakeholder considers very high impact should correspond to what all stakeholders consider very high impact. When this is not possible to achieve, other methods such as swing weighting (see Chapter 6) become useful.

It is very important to understand what can go awry with subjective approaches such as that used in the P-I table approach, and nearly all of these considerations are based on the fact that stakeholders are involved [64]. Among these, three are important to highlight: stakeholders can have very different perceptions of risk and uncertainty [65]; qualitative descriptions of likelihood are understood and used very differently by different stakeholders; and, numerical scoring schemes can introduce their own source of errors. Straightforward techniques such as calibration tests [64] can help move stakeholders to a common scale while helping the systems team translate stakeholder input for use in risk modeling and assessment. The swing weighting technique introduced in later chapters can easily be modified and used for eliciting reasonably accurate stakeholder numerical

| | Scale | Prob | Impact on project | | |
			Schedule delay	Cost increase	Performance
Value ranges	Very high	40–50	>6 Days	>20%	Multiple major failures
	High	30–40	3–5 Days	15–20%	Limited major failures
	Medium	20–30	2–3 Days	10–15%	Single major failure
	Low	10–20	1–2 Days	5–10%	Multiple minor failures
	Very low	0–10	<1 Days	<5%	Limited minor failures

Figure 5.15 Example of constructed risk outcome range scales.

Probability impact table for project x risk elelments					
Impact	Very high	3				
	High				4	
	Medium					
	Low		1,2	6		
	Very low	5				
		Very low	Low	Medium	High	Very high
		Probability of occurrence				

Figure 5.16 Example P-I table for 6 risk elements.

scores. Its basis in decision analysis mitigates many of the scoring error concerns noted in the literature.

Since each risk element is characterized in terms of its likelihood of occurrence and subsequent impact should the event occur, a two-dimensional P-I table as shown in Figure 5.16 can be used to categorically match each risk with its pair-wise correlation to the two characteristics. The resulting table enables the systems team to prioritize its risk management efforts appropriate to the threat level posed by specific risk elements.

For example, risk 5 has been estimated by stakeholders to have a very low likelihood of occurring and, if it does occur, will have very low impact on the system. Although it would continue to be monitored and measured throughout the system life cycle stages in which it was present, it more than likely would receive very little mitigation effort on the part of the systems team. Risk 4 on the other hand, estimated by stakeholders to have a high likelihood of occurring and, if it does occur, will have a high (and serious) impact on the success of the project, would command a good degree of attention throughout the life cycle of the system.

Figure 5.17 shows that the stakeholders consider risk element 3 to have three different impacts on the system: schedule (S), technical performance (P), and cost ($), each with varying estimations on their likelihood of occurring and their potential impact should they occur. In this example, the likelihood of violating cost limits for the program is estimated to be very low, but if it does occur it has the possibility of potentially terminating the program because of its very high impact. This is an example of an extreme event described earlier. Its low probability of occurrence does very little to allay the fears associated with this risk, should it occur.

P-I tables provide an important perspective on the anticipated risks that a system or project will face. To form a comprehensive understanding, P-I table results should be combined with other methods as appropriate. These include: capturing the frequency of occurrence, estimating correlation to other risks, estimating "time to impact" if a risk were to come to fruition, using decision

Probability impact table for risk element 3					
Impact	Very high	$		S		
	High					
	Medium					
	Low		P			
	Very low					
		Very low	Low	Medium	High	Very high
		Probability of occurrence				

Figure 5.17 Specific P-I table for risk element 3.

analysis, and incorporating simulation experiments to assess the dynamic effects associated with risk. Generally, risk analysis proceeds through increasing levels of risk quantification, beginning with a qualitative identification of the risk, followed by an understanding of the plausible range of each parameter, a "best estimate" of each parameter, and finally an estimate of the probability distribution of each parameter and the effect on the overall program. The size of the system, the severity of the risks, and the time available will determine the appropriate degree of quantification.

Assessment of technical risk, which involves the possibility that a requirement of the system will not be achieved, is enabled by functional analysis, introduced in Section 5.5 and is further discussed with uncertainty considerations in Chapter 10. Through functional analysis, the systems engineer defines the functions that the system must perform to be successful. Technical risk is assessed by considering each function and the likelihood and consequence of hazards to that function.

It is important to consider any required interactions between functions and any risks associated with these interactions. Being sensitive to the connections between all elements of a systems solution forces a systems team to pay attention to the most common points of failure in complex systems: *the seams of a system*. These seams afford interface compatibility and sharing protocols between systems. They are system boundaries rather than system components. Because of this, they are easily overlooked during risk identification sessions with stakeholders who have not internalized a systems thinking perspective of their operational environment. Accounting for the importance of each function and the degree of performance required, enables a prioritization and comprehensive treatment of technical risk.

Assessment of cost risk, which involves the possibility of exceeding the design, development, production, or operating budgets in whole or in part, consists of examining the various costs associated with a system solution or project, their uncertainties and any possible risks and opportunities that may affect these costs. The risks and opportunities of interest are those that could potentially increase or decrease the estimated costs of the project. This includes decisions made throughout the system life cycle, which may have downstream effects on the total system life cycle costs. These risks are projected for all stages of the life cycle of a system project. Assessment of cost risk is enabled by an understanding of the uncertainty involved with the major cost drivers. The resulting analysis produces a projected system life cycle cost profile as shown in Figure 5.18. This profile varies by the type of system. A software program, for example, has high design and development costs, but generally lower production and deployment costs. These estimates are less certain and more likely to vary the more into the future they occur. Chapter 8 discusses life cycle costing in

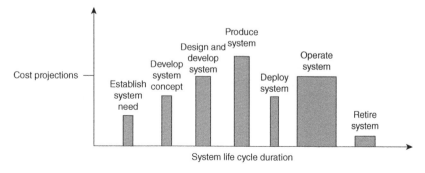

Figure 5.18 Example system life cycle cost profile.

detail. Chapter 10 expands further on this approach, introducing Monte Carlo simulation to link risks to specific cost elements.

Assessing schedule risk, which involves the possibility that the system or project will fail to achieve a scheduled key milestone, examines the time allotted to complete key tasks associated with the project, the interrelationships between these tasks, and the associated risks and opportunities that may affect the timing of task accomplishment. Schedule risk analysis relies on analytical methods such as Pert charts to unveil the sometimes complex logical connections existing between tasks. Chapter 12, which describes activities in the Solution Implementation phase of the SDP, addresses scheduling of program tasks, duration, and their inter-relationships, as well as identifying system activities that lie on a critical path to project success. These critical path tasks should be a primary focus of schedule risk assessment, because a delay in the completion of any of these tasks will result in a delay in the overall program schedule.

Programmatic risk assessment considers all threats to successful system development and deployment resulting from external effects and decisions imposed on the system or project. This assessment is informed by an understanding of the system and its relation to lateral systems and the metasystem within which it is spatially located. A thorough stakeholder analysis as discussed earlier in Section 5.3 will also enable an assessment of potential programmatic risks.

Borda Ranking Algorithm   The Borda algorithm [66] is an effective tool used to rank order risks after they have been identified. It was originally developed in the late 18th century by the French mathematician Jean-Charles Chevalier de Borda, and used to elect members of the French Academy of Sciences. The idea for its use for rank ordering risks is substituting risks for candidates and assigned risk impact levels for votes in the original approach. Each risk receives a certain number of points based on its probability likelihood level, and points for its impact (severity) level in each risk criteria category. Risks are then rank ordered based on the tally. Consider the following example adapted from [48].

Consider the five risk events shown in Table 5.10. Each risk was evaluated using constructed scales in terms of the probability of their occurrence (scale: 1 to 5) and severity impact should they occur in each of the risk categories (scale: 1 to maximum shown). If there are n risks, then the one with the highest level in each evaluation criteria receives $(n - 1)$ points; the second place receives $(n - 2)$ points; the third place receives $(n - 3)$ points and so on.

In Table 5.10, there are 5 criteria and 5 risk events. The rank ordering for risk events on each criteria is (highest wins):

$$\text{Prob Level } R2 > R1 > R3 > R4 > R5$$

$$\text{Cost Impact } R2 = R5 > R1 = R3 = R4$$

$$\text{Schedule Impact } R1 = R3 > R2 = R4 = R5$$

TABLE 5.10   Five risk events and their probability and criteria impact levels.

Risk Event	Prob Level	Cost Impact	Schedule Impact	Tech Performance	Program	Max Level
1	4	2	3	4	3	4
2	5	3	2	1	5	5
3	3	2	3	3	1	3
4	2	2	2	2	2	4
5	1	3	2	1	4	4

$$\text{Tech Performance } R1 > R3 > R4 > R2 = R5$$

$$\text{Program } R2 > R5 > R1 > R4 > R3$$

For 'Prob Level,' event $R2$ receives $(n - 1)$ points, or 4 points for this example. Event $R1$ receives $(n - 2)$ points (3 points); $R3$ gets 2 points; $R4$ gets 1 point, and $R5$ receives $(n - 4)$ points or 0 points in this case. The same point allocation happens for each of the other criteria. When ties occur, points are derived according the average of the point levels. For example, for the criteria 'Cost Impact,' risks $R2$ and $R5$ tied for positions that would receive $(n - 1)$ and $(n - 2)$ points had they not tied. So each of these risk events receive: $((n - 1) + (n - 2))/2 = 3.5$ points. The Borda counts are tallied in Table 5.11. The resulting rank order across all five criteria is:

$$R1 > R2 > R3 > R5 > R4$$

The Borda count ranking then provides a means for prioritizing mitigation efforts across all risk events. For a small example such as this, the ranking may be easily deduced without using the Borda algorithm. However, when the number of identified risk events is large, a straightforward and defendable approach afforded by this algorithm is helpful.

The nature and methods of risk assessment vary somewhat across the risk categories described. In addition to assessing the risks in each category, a systems engineer must consider the seams here as well: possible interactions between risk categories. These interactions can impose correlations that should be included in Monte Carlo simulation models [67]. For example, schedule delays could result in monetary fines for not meeting agreed upon contractual deadlines. Also, there may exist correlation between risks, with the occurrence of one risk increasing (or decreasing) the likelihood of other risk events taking place. These dependencies can again be modeled using simulation to analyze the effect of *simultaneous* variation in cost, schedule, and value (technical performance) outcomes. Dependencies between cost elements can be accounted for using correlation coefficients [68] or they can be explicitly modeled [69].

By assessing the relative likelihoods and consequences of each risk across and among each category, risks can be prioritized, policy can be set, and actions can be taken to effectively and efficiently monitor and mitigate risks.

5.7.2 Risk Mitigation

With the knowledge gained through risk identification and risk assessment, project managers and systems engineers are equipped to reduce risk through a program of *risk mitigation* designed to

TABLE 5.11 Borda algorithm point allotment and totals.

Criteria	Risk Events				
	R1	R2	R3	R4	R5
Prob Level	3	4	2	1	0
Cost Impact	1	3.5	1	1	3.5
Schedule Impact	3.5	1	3.5	1	1
Tech Performance	4	0.5	3	2	0.5
Program	2	4	0	1	3
Total	**13.5**	**13.0**	**9.5**	**6**	**8**

monitor, measure, and mitigate risk throughout the system life cycle. Risks should be continuously monitored once identified, even if their assessed threat to the success of the program is minor. Time and situational factors beyond the control of the systems team and stakeholders can dramatically increase (or decrease) the potential threat posed by risk factors. Maintaining a watchful eye on the system environment throughout a systems decision problem helps to identify these risks early, thereby reducing the likelihood of unwelcome surprises.

The goal of risk mitigation is to take action to decrease the risk-based variance on performance, cost, value, and schedule parameters over the entire system life cycle. Figure 5.19 shows a graphical illustration of the variance of a project's total cost estimate before effective risk management (A) and after (B). The spread between worst case and best case estimates is reduced earlier in the life cycle, yielding more accurate estimates of total system costs, and dramatically reducing the threat of cost overruns to project success. Effective risk management has a likewise effect on value, technical performance and schedule.

Once risks are identified, are actively being monitored, and are being measured, systems teams should be proactive and take action to mitigate the potential threats to the system or project. Simply being aware of potential system or project risks is insufficient to properly manage or control the degree of their presence or impact. The primary means of deciding how to do this is through a risk management plan that clearly prioritizes the risks in terms of their relative likelihoods and consequences. To be successful, the risk management plan must be supported by organizational and project leadership. By properly aligning incentives, technical expertise, and authority, these leaders can help facilitate the greatest likelihood of overall success.

Once a risk has been identified, assessed, and determined to require mitigation, there are several options available to mitigate system risk. It may be possible to *avoid* the risk, if the organization can take action to reduce the probability of occurrence to zero or completely eliminate the consequences of the risk. It may be appropriate to *transfer* the risk to another organization through a contract;

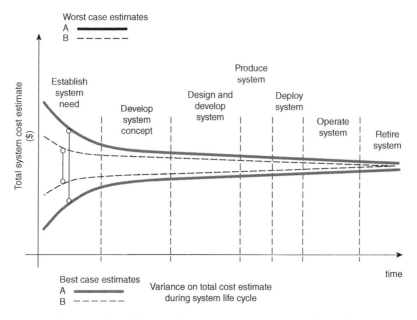

Figure 5.19   Estimate of system cost variance over life cycle.

an insurance policy is one example of this approach. An organization may *reduce* risk by taking action to reduce the likelihood of the hazard occurring or reduce the severity of consequences if the hazard does occur. Finally, an organization may choose to *accept* risk if it has little or no control over the risk event and the overall system threat is considered to be very low. Each risk should be considered individually and within the context of the larger system as management decides on the appropriate approach (avoid, transfer, reduce, or accept) and the subsequent actions to take as a result.

All system activities involve risk; therefore, risk management must be a continuous process applied throughout the system life cycle of any systems engineering project.

REFERENCES

1. Shaara, M. (1974) *The Killer Angels.* New York: Ballantine Books.
2. Reid, R.D., Sanders, N.R. (2005) *Operations Management: An Integrated Approach*, 2nd ed. New York: John Wiley & Sons, Inc..
3. Old Computers.com. IBM PC Junior. Available at: www.old-computers.com.
4. Sage, A.P., Rouse, W.B. (1999) *Handbook of Systems Engineering and Management.* New York: John Wiley & Sons, Inc.
5. Gaffney, G. (1999) 'What is Affinity Diagramming?' Information & Design. Available at https://infodesign.com.au/assets/AffinityDiagramming.pdf. (Accessed 20 June 2022).
6. Wymore, A.W. (1993) *Model-Based Systems Engineering.* New York: CRC Press.
7. Bahill, A.T., Gissing, B. (1998) 'Re-evaluating systems engineering concepts using systems thinking,' *IEEE Transactions on Systems, Man, and Cybernetics Part C: Applications and Reviews*, 28(4), pp. 516–527.
8. G2SEBoK. *Plowman's Model of the Systems Engineering Process.* INCOSE Guide to the Systems Engineering Body of Knowledge. Available at: http://g2sebok.incose.org/.
9. Department of Systems Engineering, United States Military Academy (2006) *Readings for Systems Engineering and Engineering Management*, 3rd ed. Mason, OH: Thomson Custom Solutions.
10. Sage, A.P., Armstrong, J.E. Jr. (2000) *Introduction to Systems Engineering.* New York: John Wiley & Sons, Inc..
11. Miller, D.M., Stiles, R., Kahn, A., Gordon, G., Quintero, O., Nussbaum, J., Klahr, D. (2013) *Take Charge: A Roadmap to Electric New York City Taxis*, NYC Long Term Electric Taxi Task Force. New York: NYC Taxi & Limousine Commission.
12. Proctor, C. (1998) *What are Focus Groups?* Section on Survey Research Methods, American Statistical Association. Available at: www.surveyguy.com.
13. Ewing, P., Tarantino, W., Parnell, G. (2006) 'Use of decision analysis in the army base realignment and closure (BRAC) 2005 military value analysis,' *Decision Analysis Journal*, l3(1), pp. 33–49 [about 40 interviews with senior Army leaders].
14. Powell, R., Parnell, G., Driscoll, P., Evans, D., Boylan, G., Underwood, T., Moten, M. (2005) 'Residential communities initiative (RCI) portfolio and asset management program (PAM) assessment study,' in *Presentation to Assistant Secretary of the Army for Installations and Environment, 15 December 2005* [72 interviews with Army senior leaders, installation leaders, and RCI personnel].
15. Parnell, G., Burk, R., Schulman, A., Westphal, D., Kwan, L., Blackhurst, J., Verret, P., Karasopoulos, H. (2004) 'Air force research laboratory space technology value model: creating capabilities for future customers,' *Military Operations Research*, 9(1), pp. 5–17 [about 50 interviews with senior Air Force leaders].

16. Parnell, G., Engelbrecht, J., Szafranski, R., Bennett, E. (2002) 'Improving customer support resource allocation within the National Reconnaissance Office,' *Interfaces*, 32(3), pp. 77–90 [about 25 interviews with senior leaders and key stakeholders].

17. Trainor, T., Parnell, G., Kwinn, B., Brence, J., Tollefson, E., Downes, P. (2007) 'Decision analysis aids regional organization design,' *Interfaces*, 37(3), 253–264 [about 50 interviews with senior Army leaders and key stakeholders].

18. Greenbaum, T.L. (1997) 'Focus groups: a help or a waste of time?,' *Product Management Today*, 8(7), Available at: www.groupsplus.com.

19. McNamara, C. (1999) Basics of Conducting Focus Groups. Free Management Library. Available at: www.managementhelp.org.

20. Group Systems Corporation. Collaborative Thinking and Virtual Meetings: The New Way to Work! Available at: http://www.groupsystems.com.

21. Creative Research Systems (2005) The Survey System—Survey Design. Available at: www.Surveysystem.com.

22. Creative Research Systems (2005). The Survey System—Sample Size Calculator. Available at: http://www.Surveysystem.com.

23. SurveyMonkey.com. Available at: http://surveymonkey.com.

24. Insiteful Surveys. Available at: http://insitefulsurveys.com/.

25. Creative Research Systems. The Survey System. Available at: www.Surveysystem.com.

26. INCOSE-TP-2003-016-02 (2004) *INCOSE SE Handbook*, Version 2a.

27. Martin, J.N. (1997) *Systems Engineering Guidebook: A Process for Developing Systems and Products.* Boca Raton, FL: CRC Press.

28. Wasson, C.S. (2006) *System Analysis, Design, and Development: Concepts, Principles, and Practices.* Hoboken, NJ: John Wiley & Sons.

29. Kossiakoff, A, Sweet, N.S. (2003) *Systems Engineering: Principles and Practice.* Hoboken, NJ: John Wiley & Sons.

30. Maciaszek, L. (2007) *Requirements Analysis and System Design.* Essex, England: Pearson Education Limited.

31. Grady, J.O. (2014) *System Requirements Analysis.* Waltham, MA: Elsevier.

32. Hull, E., Jackson, K., Dick, J. (2005) *Requirements Engineering.* London, UK: Springer.

33. Taherdoost, H. (2017) 'A review of technology acceptance and adoption models and theories,' *Procedia Manufacturing*, 22, pp. 960–967.

34. Tversky, A., Kahneman, D. (1974) 'Judgment under uncertainty: heuristics and biases,' *Science*, New Series, Vol. 185(4157), pp. 1124–1131.

35. CORE Software, Vitech Inc. Information about the CORE® software from Vitech, Incorporated is available online www.vitechcorp.com.

36. Affinity Diagrams, Basic Tools for Process Improvement. Available at: www.saferpak.com. (Accessed 1 June 2006).

37. SkyMark Corporation. Available at: www.skymark.com/resources/tools/affinity_diagram.asp. (Accessed 1 June 2006).

38. Lempke, J. (2003) *Microsoft Visio 2003, Step-by-step.* Redmond, WA: Microsoft Press. Available at: http://office.microsoft.com/visio. (Accessed 2 June 2006).

39. Buede, D.M. (2000) *The Engineering Design of Systems: Models and Methods.* Wiley Series in Systems Engineering. New York: Wiley-Interscience.

40. Orme, A.M., Yao, H., Etzkorn, L.H. (2006) 'Coupling metrics for ontology-based systems,' *IEEE Software*, 23(2), pp. 102–108.

41. Driscoll, P., Goerger, N., Ferreira, M., Klopfenstein, J. (2015) 'The ART of the Red Team,' Army AL&T, October-December, pp. 77–83.

42. Gove, R., Sauser, B., Ramirez-Marquez, J. (2007) *Integration Maturity Metrics: Development of an Integration Readiness Level*, SSE-S&EM-004-2007. Hoboken, NJ: Stevens Institute of Technology.

43. Mankins, J.C. (2002) 'Approaches to strategic research and technology (R&T) analysis and road mapping,' *Acta Astronautica*, 51(1–9), pp. 3–21.

44. Nilsson, E.G., Nordhagen, E.K., Oftedal, G. (1990) 'Aspects of systems integration,' in *Proceedings of the 1st International System Integration*, Morristown, NJ: IEEE.

45. Fang, J., Hu, S., Han, Y. (2004) 'A service interoperability assessment model for service composition,' in *Proceedings of the 2004 IEEE International Conference on Services Computing (SCC'04)*, Shanghai, China.

46. Sauser, B., Verma, D., Ramirez-Marquez, J., Gove, R. (2006) 'From TRL to SRL: the concept of systems readiness levels,' in *Proceedings of the Conference on Systems Engineering Research (CSER)*, Los Angeles, CA.

47. Sauser, B., Ramirez-Marquez, J.E., Magnaye, R., Tan, W. (2008) 'A systems approach to expanding the technology readiness level within defense acquisition,' *International Journal of Defense Management*, 1, pp. 39–58.

48. Garvey, P.R. (2009) *Analytical Methods for Risk Management*. Boca Raton, FL: Chapman & Hall/CRC Press.

49. Report of the World Economic Forum (2010). Rethinking Risk Management in Financial Services. New York. Available at: www.weforum.org. (Accessed 20 April 2010).

50. Vose, D. (2000) *Risk Analysis: A Quantitative Guide*. West Sussex, England: John Wiley & Sons.

51. Haimes, Y.Y. (1991) 'Total risk management,' *Risk Analysis*, 11(2), pp. 169–171.

52. The Committee on Shuttle Criticality Review and Hazard Analysis Audit, Aeronautics and Space Engineering Board (1988) *Post-Challenger Evaluation of Space Shuttle Risk Assessment and Management*. Washington, DC: National Academy Press.

53. Haimes, Y.Y. (1998) *Risk Modeling, Assessment and Management*. New York: John Wiley & Sons.

54. INCOSE-TP-2003-016-02. *Systems Engineering Handbook*. Seattle, WA.

55. Galway, L.A. (2007) Subjective probability distribution elicitation in cost risk analysis: a review, RAND Techical Report: Project Air Force. Santa Monica, CA: RAND Corporation.

56. Primavera Risk Analysis (2015). ORACLE Data Sheet. Available at: www.oracle.com. (Accessed 20 April 2010).

57. Operational Risk (2001). Report of the Basel Committee on Banking Supervision Consultative Document, Bank for International Settlements, January 2001.

58. Report of the Counterparty Risk Management Policy Group III (2008) Containing systemic risk: the road to reform. New York. Available at: www.crmpolicygroup.org, August 6, 2008.

59. Labonte, M. (2009) Systemic risk and the Federal Reserve. CRS Report for Congress R40877, Washington, DC, October 2009.

60. Modarres, M. (2006) *Risk Analysis in Engineering: Techniques, Tools and Trends*. Boca Raton, FL: CRC Press.

61. Haimes, Y.Y. (2004) *Risk Modeling, Assessment, and Management*. New York: John Wiley & Sons.

62. Simon, P. (1997) *Risk Analysis and Management*. London, England: AIM Group, Ltd.

63. Roland, H.E., Moriarty, B. (1990) *System Safety Engineering and Management*, 2nd ed. New York: John Wiley & Sons.

64. Hubbard, D.W. (2009) *The Failure of Risk Management*. New York: John Wiley & Sons.

65. Kahneman, D., Tversky, A. (1972). 'Subjective probability: a judgment of representativeness,' *Cognitive Psychology*, 3, pp. 430–454.

66. Saari, D.G. (2001) *Decisions and Elections: Explaining the Unexpected*. New York: Cambridge University Press.

67. New horizons in predictive modeling and risk analysis. ORACLE White Paper. Redwood Shores, California: ORACLE Corporation, 2008.

68. Book, S.A. (2001) 'Estimating probable system cost,' *Crosslink*, 2(1), pp. 12–21.

69. Garvey, P.R. (2000) *Probabilistic Methods for Cost Uncertainty Analysis: A Systems Engineering Perspective*. New York: Marcel Decker.

Chapter **6**

Value Modeling

When values are clear, decisions are easy.

—John Spence, Executive Coach

6.1 INTRODUCTION

In all system engineering and systems decision support projects, there are many options available for modeling the benefits that stakeholders hope to achieve with new or revised systems. Most commonly, this is done under a return-on-investment (ROI) notion using utility or value return constructs. The quantitative dimension of the systems decision process (SDP) takes a value return approach based on soliciting accurate representations of stakeholder values.

Value modeling explicitly recognizes that measures alone are insufficient for making systems decisions because while they may be accurate, stakeholders must individually translate the various measure level results into their value context while recognizing biases and applying priorities. This complicates decisions, especially when consensus or a balance of conflicting priorities is needed. The value modeling approach adopted for the SDP accommodates these considerations as part of decision support. Three other considerations further support taking a value modeling approach:

- Values differ among stakeholders for a system of interest. Consequently, while stakeholders from one organization may have common values, this may not be the case when the stakeholder pool is expanded to include multiple vested interests.
- Anticipated value return levels justify (or not) costs in the minds of stakeholders, more so when significant risk is involved with the systems decision.

Decision Making in Systems Engineering and Management, Third Edition.
Patrick J. Driscoll, Gregory S. Parnell, and Dale L. Henderson
© 2023 John Wiley & Sons, Inc. Published 2023 by John Wiley & Sons, Inc.

- Measure scales will differ, making it challenging to aggregate numerical measure scores into summary representations for competing alternatives a meaningful manner.

A common example illustrates the first two reasons. With apologies to vegan and vegetarian readers, there is a reason that organic meat products cost significantly more than the same non-organic products: they generally require more time, labor, land, and other resources per product than ones resulting from mass production. At the time of writing, an organically produced 16 oz NY strip steak costs US$ 25.00/lb, while the non-organic is US$ 14.49/lb. So, if a stakeholder values organic ranching techniques and their implications, the additional ten dollars per pound might be worth the increased cost. If not, then the same quantity of NY strip steak can be acquired for less cost. The two steaks measure the same 16 oz. Stakeholders decide which option to pick based on what they value. It is the same with investments, large purchase items, clothing, and especially systems.

The last consideration warrants a short discussion concerning scales. Translating all measure scores to a single, continuous scale such as value appears on the surface to automatically eliminate issues regarding differing measure scales. This is not quite the case. There is a subtlety present involving scales that require extra attention. There are mathematical rules associated with combining scales that impact the validity of results depending on the type of scales that are involved in the algebraic operation. The type of scale used either does or does not limit what can be done with them.

The four basic types of measurement scales and their mathematical limitations are defined as follows.

Definition: A *nominal* scale represents named variable categories without numerical significance or ordering.

A nominal scale is the weakest level of measurement and the most limited in terms of mathematics that can be applied to it. The only permissible mathematics with numbers on a nominal scale is counting. For example: {red, blue, black}, {male, female}; there are three members in the first set and two in the second.

Definition: An *ordinal* scale is one in which an ordering or ranking is defined, but the distance between measurement score levels on this scale has no meaning. It represents named and ordered variables. *Do not treat ordinal measures as interval data.*

Assigning numbers to ordinal levels is merely for convenience, if used. Mean, standard deviation, and parametric analysis based on a normal distribution should not be used. Non-parametric analysis based on rank, median, and range is appropriate, as are tabulations, frequencies, and contingency tables that do not assume distribution knowledge. Examples of ordinal scales are: order of merit ranking, star ratings on Amazon, frequency of occurrences (very often, often, occasionally, rarely, very rarely), degree of agreement (totally agree, agree, disagree, totally disagree).

Definition: An *interval* scale is one that possesses ordering, and distances between measurement score levels are equal and have meaning.

An interval scale is the minimum scale requirement for use in additive value models. Interval scales have direction and exact differences between numerical values but correlation and proportion statements are not allowed. Addition and subtraction are allowed, but not multiplication and division. The interval scale may have a zero value (e.g. 0°F), but it is not a true zero point. For example, a zero on the Fahrenheit scale does not mean the absence of temperature. Consequently, ratios are not allowed. So, computing the ratio of 90 to 30°F does not have the same meaning as the ratio of 60–20°F. A temperature of 30°F is not twice as warm as 15°F. Examples of interval scales are: Likert Scale, IQ test, calendar dates.

Definition: A *ratio* scale is one in which meaningful ordering, distances, decimals, and fractions involving numbers on this scale is possible.

An absolute zero exists for a ratio scale, communicating that a zero score means the absence of the measured quantity. All available mathematics can be applied to measures on this scale. Examples of ratio scales are: weight, height, sound volume, illumination levels.

When combining scales of different types, the mathematical rule states that the end result of a mathematical computation inherits the mathematical properties associated with the lowest scale in terms of allowable computations.

This rule is analogous to what happens with significant figures when manipulating numbers with decimals. If one data point has accuracy to two decimal places and all the others have accuracy to five decimal places, the results of calculations involving these data are limited to two decimal place accuracy.

In a value modeling approach such as the one used in the SDP, an additive value function expression combines value scores which are mapped from measure scores that have either ordinal, interval, or ratio scales. Value scores $v_i(x)$ arising from these value functions inherit their value measure (VM) x_i scale limitations based on the mathematical rule stated. Thus:

- Ordinal + Ordinal $\Longrightarrow$ Ordinal limitations.
- Ordinal + Ratio $\Longrightarrow$ Ordinal limitations.
- Ordinal + Interval $\Longrightarrow$ Ordinal limitations.
- Interval + Ratio $\Longrightarrow$ Interval limitations.
- Ordinal + Interval + Ratio $\Longrightarrow$ Ordinal limitations.
- Ratio + Ratio $\Longrightarrow$ Ratio limitations.

Unless care is taken when creating individual value functions, the additive value function results could be misleading. The concern for tradespace analysis lies with ordinal measure scales that limit value scores to having ranking interpretations at best. Tradespace analysis of the type used in the SDP and elsewhere requires the spatial separation (distances) between value scores—including total value scores—to have meaning. When this is not the case, a tradespace graph can be misleading.

Figure 6.1 illustrates this concern. It displays 10 deterministic system options presented to a decision maker for selection. Options 6, 8, and 10 are Pareto efficient and should be the three options in the choice set, barring any further stochastic analysis. In this model, a positive risk deviation is desirable in that it represents performance above stakeholder chosen threshold levels. An ideal option is shown in the upper right corner for reference only. Visually, the graph communicates to a decision maker that Option 6 has higher value but less risk deviation than Option 8. If some of the underlying value measure scales were Ordinal, then the vertical distance in value between Option 6 and Option 8 would be questionable if only direct methods were used to create value functions. The ordinal scale limits interpretation of vertical positioning to ranking only. When the lowest order scale among the value measures is Interval or Ratio, the mapped value distances automatically have meaning and the adage "what you see is what you get" is correct.

One might contend that a small number of ordinal scales among all the value functions in an additive total value expression has a minor influence on alternative positioning in a tradespace

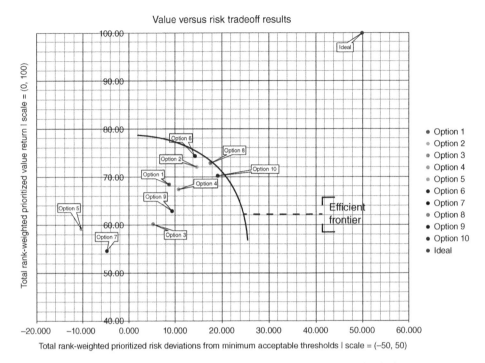

Figure 6.1   Example tradespace involving total value return and risk deviations.

graph. Furthermore, one might also contend that if all alternatives are evaluated in the same model, then any visual error present is affecting all alternatives equally so no alternative is penalized by ignoring this underlying condition. Several comments in response.

First, the number of value functions involved in an additive value models is usually under 20 and frequently between 10 and 12. As the number of value functions increases, it is well-known that the priorities created by linear weighting can become diluted in their influence on the total value score unless extreme high-weighting on a small number of value functions is done, with the residual allocated to all remaining value functions. This does not happen in practice because when stakeholders express their values, they are significant to the decision being made. Additionally, the swing weighting technique used for the SDP makes this type of practice very difficult to rationalize. Consequently, even a single ordinal scale-based value function will have a priority weight affecting results, and possibly a good deal of it.

Second, constructed ordinal scales are used quite frequently in systems decision support, especially for intangible values expressed by stakeholders that are modeled using discrete ordinal scales. Star-ratings and discrete scales such as the Department of Defense (DoD) technology readiness scale and integration readiness scale are good examples of three commonly used ordinal measure scales for systems. Properly accommodating these scales into value modeling ensures that subsequent graphs and mathematical analysis are valid.

Third, a similar contention might be said for a situation involving significant figures. In this case however, the global practitioner and educator Science, Technology, Engineering, and Mathematics (STEM) community universally recognizes the contention as wrong because violating the significant figure rule is bad mathematics.

Lastly, the contention raises an ethical issue regarding modeling due diligence on the part of the systems team. It is never good practice to obfuscate or intentionally hide from a decision maker model features that affect results, even if minor. Ignoring mathematical limitations associated with ordinal scales is akin to not calling out modeling assumptions: the decision maker is placed in a situation of misplaced blind trust in the systems team. It is a best practice to highlight considerations such as this, and to point out what was done to protect the validity of modeling results. In doing so, decision makers gain an appreciation for the knowledge base and integrity of the systems team.

The value increment method described in Section 6.3 fixes this situation by eliciting spatial separation meaning from stakeholders when creating value functions for measures whose scales are ordinal, thereby enabling proportional comparisons between discrete ordinal level differences. And, since value functions having ordinal domains (measure) are the only concern here, ordinal measures are the only ones that the value increment method or an equivalent method must be used to protect the validity of tradespace interpretation. Value functions involving interval or ratio scales can use any of the techniques for creating value functions without limiting tradespace interpretation.

Value modeling appears as an activity in Phase 1 of the SDP because it brings together all of the Problem definition results into a neat and tidy product that provides a foundation for activities supporting the SDP phases that follow. Done properly, the qualitative and quantitative models directly inform creative alternative design in Phase 2 and support tradespace analysis during Phase 3. Throughout the SDP, the value modeling products developed during Phase 1 are continuously refined until they are a comprehensive and reasonably complete representation of stakeholder values.

6.2 QUALITATIVE VALUE MODELING

Qualitative value modeling employs value-focused thinking (VFT) as discussed in Section 4.2 to yield a qualitative value model representing the most important functions and objectives for the system. When these functions and objectives are paired with measures designed to assess the degree to which system objectives are being achieved, the hierarchy representing this organization is called a *value hierarchy*. This qualitative model is used as a foundation for a quantitative value model that builds on a value hierarchy by adding decision maker-based value functions that translate value measure scores into value return estimates while imbedding decision maker priorities using a carefully constructed weighting technique. The quantitative value model then provides a means for evaluating how well candidate system-solution alternatives satisfy stakeholder values focused on the system's intended purpose. The underlying mathematical framework for this type of value modeling relies upon key concepts and techniques from multiple criteria value modeling (MCVM) and multiple objective decision analysis (MODA).

A key question that is often asked by practitioners new to value modeling is: "Whose values are represented in the value model?" The short answer is the values of important stakeholders, and *not those of the systems decision support or systems engineering team.* The most important values are those of the decision maker, but other stakeholder groups have values that should be considered as well: owners, users, and consumers. System owners benefit directly from returned value for their financial investment in the system and the ways it supports their organizational and operational goals. Users benefit when a system is perceived as returning value through ease-of-use and usefulness for the products and services they create. Collaborators are generally not directly included in this modeling activity unless they are formally linked to the system owner by way of contracts, operating memorandums, memorandums of agreement, and other legal mechanisms.

Kirkwood describes the criteria for a good value hierarchy as "completeness, non-redundancy, decomposability, operability and small size" [1]. The concept of completeness means that the value model, represented by all its objectives and value measures, must be sufficient in scope to support the fundamental objective of the systems decision project. This is often referred to as "mutually exclusive and collectively exhaustive." Non-redundancy means that functions or value measures on the same hierarchy tier should have mutual preferential independence and be uncorrelated, respectively. This means that value measures cannot measure the same thing; that is, the scores assigned to measures on a given level of the hierarchy should not impact the scores of any other measure on that level. Operability means that the value hierarchy is easily understood by all who use it. Finally, a value hierarchy should contain as few measures as possible while still meeting the requirement to be mutually exclusive and collectively exhaustive.

Constructing a value model in support of systems decisions requires a good deal of attention to detail and a sensitivity to what stakeholder groups are expressing during interviews, focus groups, and surveys. It is likewise important to define some of the key terminology used in value modeling.

Fundamental objective. The overarching objective that the stakeholders are trying to achieve with the systems project. This is the purpose of the project, *not* the system's purpose.

Value measure. A scale established to assess how well a candidate system alternative attains an objective associated with a system function. These are also referred to as evaluation measures, measures of effectiveness, performance measures, and metrics.

Qualitative value model. A complete description of the stakeholder qualitative values, including the fundamental objective, major functions and subfunctions, objectives, and value measures. Once complete and approved by a decision maker, a qualitative value model becomes the foundation for a quantitative value model.

Value hierarchy. A diagrammatical representation of the qualitative value model that shows associations between its elements. A value hierarchy consists of four tiers: a project fundamental objective, major functions and subfunctions, performance objectives, and value measures.

Tier. Levels in a value hierarchy numbered from the fundamental objective (tier 0) through the furthest subfunction decomposition into objectives and value measures. Much like requirements, this numbering scheme provides a convenient way of keeping track of these elements throughout the various analytical processes used by the SDP.

Weights. Numerical values assigned to each value measure that reflects the decision maker/stakeholder's priorities. When the preferred weighting method called *swing weighting* is used, the numerical weights represent a blend of the measure's importance and the impact of a complete range variability from low to high on the corresponding measurement scale. Weights are initially assigned as swing weights on a scale [0, 100], and then normalized to become convex *global weights* on [0, 1] for use in an additive total value expression. Other weighting techniques could be used, but are limited to single dimension interpretation (e.g. AHP: importance ranking only).

Value measure score. A position on a value measure scale that reflects the assessed performance of a candidate solution with regard to a particular value function. Value measure scales represent different measures of performances (MOPs), measures of effectiveness (MOEs), and technical performance measures (TPMs) with different units of measure. Value functions translate these scores into value units.

Value function. A function that maps a value measure score to a value score on [0, 100]. Value functions represent stakeholder/decision maker estimates for returns to scale over the domain of each value measure score.

Quantitative value model. A MCVM used to evaluate candidate system alternatives in support of tradespace analysis. Building directly upon a qualitative value model, it incorporates stakeholder value functions, weights, and measures along with a mathematical expression for estimating total value return. The stochastic version also imbeds any uncertainties associated with model inputs and parameters.

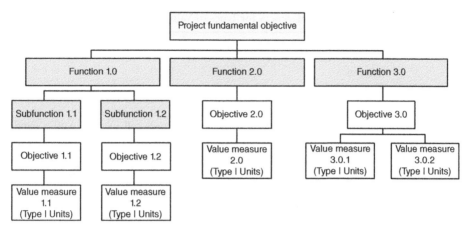

Figure 6.2 Qualitative value model general structure.

6.2.1 Developing a Qualitative Value Model

The information developed in the stakeholder and functional analysis tasks is used to determine major system functions, objectives, and value measures that make up a qualitative value model. A qualitative value model is a diagram that links stakeholder expectations for system behavior (functions), stakeholder intentions for these behaviors (objectives), and agreed upon measures to be used to indicate the extent to which a competing alternative system design achieves each objective. Figure 6.2 shows the general structure for a qualitative value model diagram with value measures appearing on the bottom tier of the hierarchy.

There are six basic steps for developing a qualitative value model [2]:

1. *Identify the fundamental objective.* This is a clear, concise statement of the primary reason for undertaking a systems decision project. It is a purpose for the project, not to be confused with the system of interest's purpose. A systems decision project for the U.S. Army concerned the organizational structure for a key mid-level Army unit. The fundamental objective of this project was to "develop the most effective and efficient organizational structure to support the Army's mission" [3]. This fundamental objective statement is focused on the project effort by the decision support team, not what the organization's purpose is, what it does as a mission or what it is intended to deliver to the Army.

2. *Identify major system functions and subfunctions.* These functions describe what a system of interest must do for stakeholders to consider it successful. Functions describe system behavior. Techniques for identifying major functions and subfunctions are discussed in detail in Section 5.5. For many systems, the functional hierarchy provides a basis for the value hierarchy. In Figure 6.2, the shaded boxes represent the items directly extracted from a functional hierarchy. Major functions are labeled with a short text label describing a system action, along with numbering scheme $1.0, 2.0, \ldots, n.0$. Subfunctions inherit their parent function numbering, expanding as needed.

3. *Identify objectives that define the direction for increasing value.* An objective provides a conditional stakeholder goal describing their directional preference for system behavior while it performs each system function. For example, "minimize spurious electrical emissions," "maximize passenger comfort," and so on. In addition to a short statement, objectives inherit the numbering labels of the functions/subfunctions they are associated with. There can be more than one objective assigned to a single function/subfunction.

TABLE 6.1   Preferences for Types of Value Measures.

Type of Measure	Direct	Proxy
Natural	1	3
Constructed	2	4

4. *Identify value measures for each objective.* Value measures tell us how well a candidate system alternative accommodates an objective. Value measures can be MOE, MoP, TPM, and others that rely on quantitative or limited types of qualitative scales. Value measures can be direct, proxy, natural, or constructed [1]. A natural measure for "maximize profit" would be dollars. A constructed measure for "maximize tech maturity" could be the technology readiness level (TRL) scale described in Section 5.6. Which type is used follows directly from objectives, although there is a preference ordering as shown in Table 6.1.

5. *Identify value measure scales.* Value measure scales can be ordinal, interval, or ratio scales. When an ordinal scale are used for a value measure, the value increment method or its equivalent must be used to construct its value function for use in the quantitative value model (See Section 6.1. Nominal scales are not used. For value modeling purposes, the measure scales must at least have an ordering property.

6. *Gain approval from key stakeholders.* A value model does not move forward without approval and agreement from key stakeholders. Since the entire value model construction process is a collaborative venture with stakeholders, gaining this approval should involve only potential editing. Typically an interim progress review (IPR) is used for this purpose. In an IPR, key stakeholders collectively or individually provide their concurrence, corrections, or additions to the various qualitative value model components. Past this point, what exists as the qualitative value model will be leveraged to create a quantitative value model that will be used to evaluate the total value return of each system alternative that passes established screening criteria. Accomplishing this task significantly contributes to keeping the project on-track.

While direct, natural, and constructed measures are straightforward, a note on proxy measures might be helpful. A proxy is an indirect measure of a desired outcome which is itself strongly correlated to that outcome. Proxy measures are commonly used when direct measures of the outcome are unobservable and/or unavailable. Proxy measures are "one off" or "once removed" from directly measuring a quantity. For example, a reasonable proxy measure for an objective such as "maximize environmental quality" might be the air quality index. Similarly, a homicide rate could serve as a reasonable proxy measure for the objective "maximize public safety."

6.2.2   Measures

The measures chosen to assess how well system alternatives achieve stakeholder objectives for system behavior represent input quantities for modeling and simulation within the SDP and motivate the type of modeling representation a systems team uses. These ultimately must be *based on stakeholder values*. A fatal flaw in systems analysis occurs when modelers force a system into their favorite analysis tools, observe dominant outcomes, and attempt to reverse engineer measures from outcomes. Almost always this identifies measures that do not reflect stakeholder values. Value models constructed in this way fail to provide meaningful support to a decision maker because foundational elements of such a model lack a logical connection to the decision maker's needs, wants, and desires for a system.

Measures are tied either directly or indirectly to every system objective identified during the Problem definition phase. Although most objectives can be evaluated directly, others such as "Maximize energy policy quality" can be assessed only in terms of percentage of fulfillment of other objectives [4]. Measures for value models can take several forms, but the most prevalent for systems are measures of performance (*MOP*) and measures of effectiveness (*MOE*) [5]. Technical performance measures (*TPM*) are most often used for system components.

Definition: A measure of performance (*MOP*) is a quantitative expression of how well the physical or functional attributes relating to system operation, measured or estimated under specific testing and/or operational environment conditions (i.e. how well the system meets its design specifications).

MOPs derive from the system developer or system designer's viewpoint. MOPs focus on ensuring that a system has the capability to achieve system objectives. MOPs are linked to or provide MOPs often map directly to system requirements and are expressed in terms of distinctly quantifiable performance parameters such as material stress levels, frequency, hardness, and so on. For example, the measure *miles per gallon* reflects the efficiency of engine performance on a bus. It is not directly related to the success of the greater system's mission, which may be to transport people across town.

Definition: A measure of effectiveness (*MOE*) is a quantitative expression of how well a system achieves its intended purpose in the intended operational environment under a specified set of conditions.

MOEs are stated from the stakeholders' points of view, and as such they represent stakeholders' overall operational success criteria for systems once the system is placed into operation. While a system can be technically performing exactly as designed (MOP), there is always concern among stakeholders about its ability to deliver value return by operating effectively.

For example, MOPs would indicate if a fighter aircraft meets all of its technical requirements, but a MOE would be used to determine how many aircraft would be needed to form a protective fighter cap for a hostile region. A military weapon system may meet a requirement specification of firing 1000 *rounds per minute* (a MOP), but if the *probability of hitting* a target with a single round (a MOE) is 0.9 and the *probability of destroying the target, given a hit* (a MOE) is 0.9, and then the measure of performance-rounds per minute-is not very helpful in evaluating the effectiveness of the greater system in its mission of destroying targets.

Definition: A technical performance measure (*TPM*) is a quantitative expression that measures attributes of a system or subsystem component to determine how well this element is satisfying or expected to satisfy a technical requirement or goal.

TPMs are measures used during subsystem and component development heading toward full system prototypes. They provide insights and information for establishing system-level MOPs. TPMs should be limited to critical technical thresholds or parameters that, if not met, will introduce cost, schedule, or performance risk. They are not intended to cover a full spectrum of measures needed to assess system or subsystem performance against requirements.

The primary stakeholders for MOEs are those who will own and operate the system, those responsible for developing the full system (typically referred to as the integrated product team (IPT), and those whose role is tracking system levels of quality. MOPs do not involve quality management, but they do involve the engineering teams responsible for developing all system elements. TPMs generally involve the engineering teams for component development and the IPTs. Systems engineers are involved with all three measures.

Measures are generally not all developed simultaneously during system projects because thinking about how a system will be evaluated occurs continuously as the system team's and stakeholders' understanding of the system evolves. Performance measures are developed by systems engineers during the Problem definition phase of the SDP. They are listed and described in a system specification document and carried forward for use in later test and evaluation events. Effectiveness measures are also based directly on stakeholder values, but these measures view the system in its larger operational context in its environment. Selecting meaningful MOEs early on can be challenging. Defining a good MOE has seven steps, two of which are optional. These are:

1. *Define the measure.* Include both a narrative description and an equation.
2. *Indicate the dimension of the measure.* Is it a ratio, an index, a time interval?
3. *Define the limits on the range of the measure.* Specify upper and lower bounds.
4. *Explain the rationale for the measure.* Why is this measure useful?
5. *Describe the decisional relevance of the measure.* How will this measure help the decision maker?
6. *List associated measures.* If any, create a group to put this measure in context (optional).
7. *List references (optional).* Link to definitions, give examples of where it has been used.

An example MOE developed using these steps is shown in the following example.

MOE Example: Time To Estimate Range.

1. *Definition of the measure.* Time to estimate range is the elapsed time from detection of a target to estimation of range. Input data are the moment of detection and the moment estimation of range is complete. Relation of output to input is:

$$\text{time to estimate range} = \text{time of estimation} - \text{time of detection}.$$

2. *Dimension of the measure.* Interval-elapsed time in terms of seconds. If the measure is taken at different times or under varying circumstances, it can be used in the form of mean time to estimate range or median time.

3. *Limits on the range of the measure.* The output can be zero or any positive value. The resolution of the measure is limited by the precision of taking start time and end time. The data cannot be disassociated from the definition of computed estimation used, whether it is the first estimate stated regardless of accuracy or is the final in a series of estimates which is used for firing.

4. *Rationale for the measure.* This measure addresses a component of target acquisition time. Problems in estimation are assumed to contribute to the length of estimation time.

5. *Decisional relevance of the measure.* This measure can be used to compare estimation times of means of range estimation (techniques, aids, range finders, trained personnel) with each other or a standard. It would not ordinarily be used alone, but would be combined with accuracy of estimation or accuracy of firing in most cases.

6. *Associated measures.*
   - Accuracy of range estimation
   - Firing accuracy
   - Time to detect
   - Exposure time
   - Time to identify

There are several characteristics of a good MOE [6]:

- A good MOE reflects and measures functional objectives of the system.
- A good MOE is simple and quantifiable.
- A good MOE measures effectiveness at echelons above the system (how it contributes).
- A good MOE involves aggregation of data.
- A good MOE can be used to determine synergistic effects of a system.

EV Qualitative Value Model. Starting with the functional hierarchy developed after an affinity diagramming session with a select group of stakeholders, the systems decision support team refined the functional hierarchy to include new system functions, objectives, and an initial set of value measures needed for a qualitative value model. This structure represents a value hierarchy for the system. A hierarchical listing and numbering is as follows:

Function 1.0 : Store Electrical Energy
             Objective 1.1: Minimize Charging Time
                Measure 1.1: Charging Time (hours)
             Objective 1.2: Maximize Single Charge Range
                Measure 1.2.1: Range (km)
                Measure 1.2.2: Energy Consumption (kWh)
Function 2.0 : Transport Passengers
             Objective 2.1: Maximize Passenger Carrying Capacity
                Measure 2.1: Total Passenger (count)
             Objective 2.2: Maximize Passenger Space
                Measure 2.2.1: Passenger Volume (cubic feet)
                Measure 2.2.2: Rear Seating Shoulder Room (inches)
Function 3.0 : Transport Luggage
             Objective 3.0: Maximize Luggage Capacity
                Measure 3.0: Cargo Volume (cubic feet)
Function 4.0 : Accelerate Vehicle
             Objective 4.1: Maximize Acceleration
                Measure 4.1: Acceleration (seconds) (0 to 100 km)
             Objective 4.2: Maximize Power
                Measure 4.2.1: Electric Drive Unit Power (Hp)
                Measure 4.2.2: Top Speed (km/h)

Figure 6.3 shows a qualitative value model diagram for this listing.

It is important to note that the systems decision here involves an EV purchase, which is similar to a consumer purchase rather than a design project. If the project was affecting EV design, then more detailed system functions would be part of the qualitative value model shown, along with their objectives and associated measures. These could be: convert electrical energy into mechanical energy, control energy flow, maintain comfortable compartment lighting, create quiet ride experience, maintain comfortable temperature levels, translate torque to wheels, Americans with Disabilities Act (ADA)-compliant features, enhance driver ease-of-use, and a host of others.

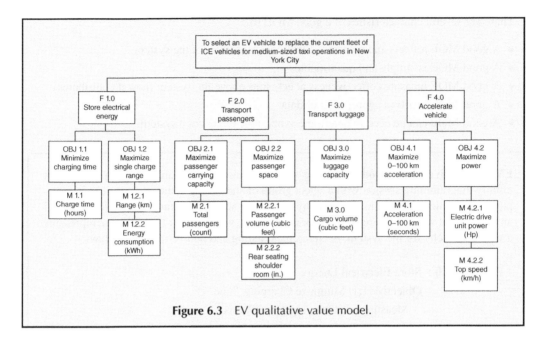

Figure 6.3   EV qualitative value model.

Rocket Design Example. As a second example, suppose that a systems engineering team assembled a group of stakeholders in support of a project whose fundamental objective was "to develop a small, mobile rocket capable of delivering payloads rapidly and accurately to the rocket's intended destination." The stakeholder group included representative users from military, commercial, and research organizations along with manufacturers. After providing a system purpose and description, the group used affinity diagramming to develop a list of initial requirements that would become system functions based on input such as:

- The launch platform should be mobile enough to traverse a variety of terrain.
- The support requirements for the launch platform should be a small as possible.
- The rocket should be able to carry heavy payloads.
- The rocket needs to be flexible enough to carry different types of payloads.
- The rocket needs to be as accurate as possible.
- The rocket should be able to carry payloads as far as possible.

During the session, the team constructed a simplified initial qualitative value model based on a subset of stakeholder input to illustrate the SDP framework being used. They created the value hierarchy shown in Figure 6.4 based on three major system functions: Launch rocket, Transport payload, and Achieve desired effect. The systems team explained that the diagram's organization represents a simple functional hierarchy that will expand to include all major functions and subfunctions as the project progresses. The objectives tier provides a means for encoding stakeholder preferences regarding system behavior. There is at least one objective associated with every system function or subfunction. The seven value measures provide a quantitative means to evaluate how well a candidate rocket system attains the stated objectives.

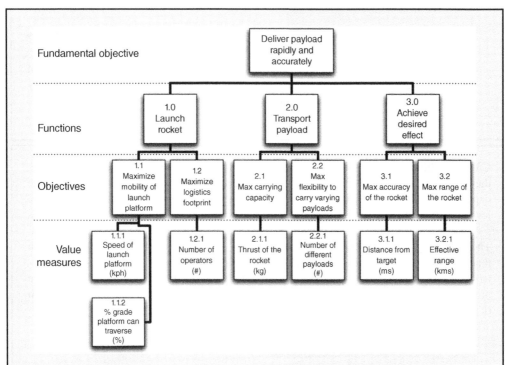

Figure 6.4   Simplified value hierarchy for the rocket example.

Each of the objectives and associated value measures were defined and recorded as they were identified. Objectives 1.1, 1.2, and 3.2 are examples of how this was done.

Objective 1.1 Maximize mobility of the launch platform. Mobility is difficult to directly measure with a single value measure. Consequently, two value measures were used to more completely assess an alternative system's degree of mobility: speed of the launch platform and the percent grade that the platform can traverse.

    Value Measure 1.1.1 Speed of the launch platform in kilometers per hour (kph). Speed of candidate solution platforms in kph is a natural measure for attainment of an associated objective (proxy) to maximize the speed of the launch platform.

    Value Measure 1.1.2 Percent grade of ground that the launch platform can traverse (% grade). This is a proxy measure since the mobility objective is not directly measured, this measure is classified as a "natural-proxy" measure. Modeling, simulation, and testing can provide data to support this value measure.

Objective 1.2 Minimize the logistics footprint of the launch platform. The quantity of total support required (aka: its logistic footprint) by the system will be difficult to directly measure, so candidate system solutions will be assessed in terms of the number of people needed to put the rocket into operation.

    Value Measure 1.2.1 Number of people required to operate the rocket system. Since attainment of the logistics footprint objective is not directly measured, this measure is also classified as a "natural-proxy" measure.

Objective 3.2 Maximize range of the rocket. The range of the candidate system solutions can be directly evaluated by data provided via live testing.

> **Measure 3.2.1** Effective range of the rocket (kilometers). Measuring kilometers that candidate rockets travel in testing is a natural measure that can be used to directly evaluate attainment of this objective; so this is an example of a "natural-direct" measure.

CMS Qualitative Value Model. Once the systems team completed functional analysis, they were able to align CMS functions with top-level department values solicited from the department head during stakeholder interviews. Once this alignment was accomplished, they leveraged it to identify supporting objectives that would facilitate proper CMS behavior as a system within stakeholder's expectations for success. Figure 6.5 illustrates this alignment. The team assigned importance values to each of the objectives based on the degree to which that capability supported the critical CMS functions in the diagram. These importance values were not intended to be used as weights but rather to document and reinforce objective priorities during development should it proceed. The value measures associated with each of the objectives are not shown on this diagram.

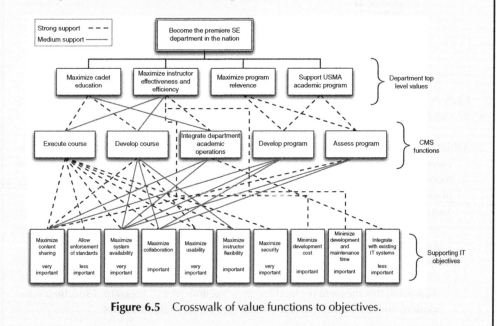

Figure 6.5   Crosswalk of value functions to objectives.

6.3   QUANTITATIVE VALUE MODEL

The quantitative value modeling approach used in the SDP is a type of multiple criteria value modeling (MCVM) that is a specialization of multiple criteria decision analysis (MCDM) and multiple objective decision analysis (MODA) designed to use value instead of utility as a beneficial return quantity. In utility modeling, a decision maker's risk preference is an integral part of the assessed utility. Not so with value modeling. Risk levels are addressed as a tradeoff dimension to value similar to cost, or integrated into cost or schedule considerations. Decision maker risk preferences are considered separately from value return when this is done.

If constructed properly, a quantitative value model captures in a single model all or most significant decision maker values with regard to the system of interest, along with decision maker accepted measures for estimating system performance objectives, value functions that translate measure scales to a common value scale, and a total value return estimate containing stakeholder priorities by way of linear weights that reflect levels of measure importance and the impact of measure variation across each measure's entire range.

In the SDP, as in any decision support approach, it is important to distinguish between *screening* and *evaluating* activities. A screening process applies a decision maker's minimally acceptable criteria levels to potential system solution alternatives. These minimally acceptable levels are called *thresholds*. Ideal levels of criteria are called *objective* levels, as they represent criteria levels that completely satisfy stakeholders' goals for a system solution. Potential alternatives that do not meet threshold screening criteria in one or more categories are eliminated (i.e. "screened out") from further consideration during the SDP. A simple matrix layout that portrays each alternative against screening criteria as red, yellow, and green is sufficient for applying a screening process.

Alternatives that meet all threshold screening criteria move on to a more in-depth evaluation. Within the SDP, value modeling is the primary approach used to evaluate potential system alternatives that meet stakeholder established screening criteria and are competing to be part of the final alternative choice set presented to a decision maker.

Since only alternatives that satisfy threshold screening criteria are evaluated in a quantitative value model, alternatives that are screened out of the process do not have a chance to be evaluated against stakeholder values, priorities, and objectives. Be careful *not* to screen to a solution! Always retain alternatives that appear promising except for a small number of close threshold failures because decision maker thresholds can sometimes change or be waived by a decision maker. Make sure these close alternatives are presented to a decision maker for discussion.

A quantitative value model defines the mathematical relationships supporting alternative ranking and tradespace analysis leading to a choice set of alternatives from which a decision maker selects. Tradespace analysis is the preferred method for accomplishing alternative evaluation because it separates cost (or risk) as an independent variable apart from value return. This separation is important for several reasons.

First, U.S. DoD acquisition regulations mandate cost be treated as an independent variable (CAIV) so that cost, schedule, and performance may be traded off within a tradespace between thresholds and objectives documented in a capability needs document [7]. Second, when a tradespace based on principles such as Pareto efficiency presents value versus cost as independent assessment dimensions on the same graph, more information is immediately available than in a pure ranking approach. Since the underlying mathematical scales for value and cost are at least interval and ratio, respectively, proportional increases or decreases in value for cost adjustments are evident. Moreover, stacked bar charts or similar disaggregation charts that rely on value being separate from cost reveal exactly why alternatives are positioned in a tradespace as shown and how they are achieving this positioning relative to the decision maker's stated values and priorities. Finally, while cost usually presents itself in the guise of a constraint in systems decision problems, it is a project dimension that can flex as financial and budgetary options become available.

A useful feature of quantitative value models is their ability to have both complementary and conflicting objectives in the same modeling construct. Properly constructed, the output of a quantitative value model can be traced back through the model to system requirements, stakeholder values, and the decision maker's priorities, functions, and objectives. This becomes critically important when results are presented to decision makers, especially if alternatives are positioned higher or lower in the tradespace than they anticipated. The ensuing discussions focus on sensitivity results and re-confirming priorities, values, objectives, and other modeling elements that were directly obtained from decision makers. The systems team facilitates this discussion and makes changes to modeling elements as desired to accommodate decision makers' "What if?" concerns. This again reinforces the point that the information supporting these major quantitative modeling elements originates with stakeholders, and *not the systems decision support team*. This critical condition can sometimes be overlooked in academic and workshop settings because of artificial limitations such as not having access to live stakeholders from whom input can be solicited.

6.3.1 Value Functions

With multiple criteria being used as assessment value measures for competing alternatives, the various value measures need to be aggregated into a single quantity that summarizes each system alternative's total estimated value return. Among the options available [1], the most common approach is an additive value model which incorporates a set of linear convex numerical weights as value score coefficients to properly represent decision makers' priorities.

An additive value model makes assumptions about the structure of the problem to which it is applied. Specifically, it assumes that a property called *mutual preferential independence* exists among measures so that value scores are not conditional. Given two value measures applied to a system, mutual preferential independence means that a decision maker can express preferences on either measure independent of the other. Preferential relationships are directional. Preferential independence would not exist if a decision maker was asked about his preferences on a particular design criteria and he needed the value of another criteria first in order to answer.

For example, suppose two measure criteria being considered were trouser material (wool, cotton) and hat style (bowler, driver's cap). If a decision maker was asked what material he preferred and he answered "wool" without regard to hat style, then trouser material would be preferentially independent of hat style. In the other direction, if asked which hat style he preferred and he needed to know which trouser material he was wearing to state his hat style preference, then hat style would not be preferentially independent of trouser material. These two criteria would not have mutual preferential independence. If two value measures are preferentially dependent, they often can be combined into a single measure, thereby allowing an additive value model to be used. Kirkwood [1] provides an excellent discussion of the concepts of mutual preferential independence, measurable value, and utility for the reader who wishes to gain a deeper understanding of this topic.

The mathematical expression for aggregating value scores into a total value return estimate for any of the $n = 1, 2, \ldots, N$ competing solutions surviving screening is given by

$$V_n = \sum_{m=1}^{M} w_m f_m(x_{n,m}) \tag{6.1}$$

where V_n is the total value of candidate solution n, $n = 1, \ldots, N$ and M equals the number of value measures. The variable $x_{n,m}$ is the score of the nth candidate solution on the mth value measure. The term $f_m(x_{n,m})$ represents the value score translated from the mth measure score by a value function $f_m(x)$, and w_m is the measure weight (normalized swing weight) of the mth value measure. Convexity of weights is achieved by requiring $\sum_{m=1}^{M} w_m = 1$.

A value function is a real-valued mathematical expression defined over an evaluation criterion (attribute, value measure) that represents an alternative's goodness (value return) across the levels of a value measure scale. Value functions translate value measure scores $x_{n,m}$ using different scales into value return levels (called *value scores*) $f_m(x_{n,m})$ all having the same [0, 1] or [0, 100] scale so that these can be aggregated into a total value return quantity V_n for tradespace analysis.

The common value score scale [0, 1] or [0, 100] must be at least interval to preserve meaning with separation distances presented in subsequent tradespace charts because discussions center on how much more (less) value is possible for incremental increases (decreases) in cost. For these comparisons to be valid, subtraction and addition must be supported by both the total value and total cost scales.

For systems decision support, the values used are most commonly those of the decision maker. The decision maker describes their value return expectations across each measure scale's full range, from the lowest possible measure level (category) to the highest. The results are then encoded using a value function.

Rather than presenting a decision maker with a listing or numerical table, a value function's general shape is most often used as a reference when soliciting value functions from stakeholders/decision makers because this visualization (e.g. chart, sketch) readily shows important effects such as linear returns to scale, diminishing returns to scale, or increasing returns to scale.

Value functions are most often represented by continuous linear or piecewise linear continuous functions so that the entire [0, 1] or [0, 100] value score scale is accessible when translating measure scores $x_{n,m}$ into value scores $f_m(x_{n,m})$. When a discrete measure scale is involved, the value increment method described in Section 6.3.2 is used to create a piecewise linear value function that ensures the associated value score scale is at least an interval scale.

The most common process used to solicit value function information from decision makers is called a *direct assessment* method. It starts with the systems team working with a decision maker to identify the general shape of the value function curve, and then proceeds to have the decision maker identify their increase (or decrease depending on the shape of the curve) in value moving across the measure scale from low to high. Doing this for multiple increments up to the maximum on the measure scale will lead to an appropriate shape for the value function.

The minimum information needed from a decision maker in order to accomplish a direct assessment are answers to the following questions:

- Does value monotonically increase across the value measure scale being used? That is, do the lowest and highest measure values correspond to the least and most valued measure scores, respectively?

- Does value monotonically decrease across the value measure scale being used? That is, do the lowest and highest measure values correspond to the most and least value measure scores, respectively?

- Does value return occur at a constant rate throughout the value measure score scale, or are there areas where value return increases or decreases slowly or quickly than the rest of the scale (i.e. increasing or decreasing returns to scale)?

- Is there an intermediate point on the value measure scale that defines the most valued or least valued measure score?

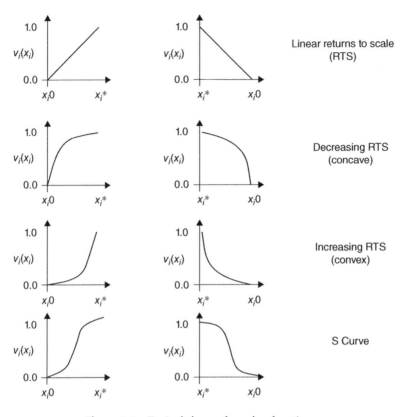

Figure 6.6 Typical shapes for value functions.

Figure 6.6 illustrates some of the common shapes for a continuous value function. The general pattern shown also applies to piecewise linear value functions. The curves on the left of the figure are monotonically increasing from a minimum to a maximum level of the value measures. The curves on the right are monotonically decreasing.

When a value function is monotonically increasing or decreasing, an exponential method [8] could be used to produce a closed-form mathematical expression for the value function, as could appropriate curve-fitting techniques when data is involved. Closed-form value function expressions are helpful when creating value models intending to be implemented in programming languages such as *R*. In these cases, a single mathematical expression can be more convenient than constructing tables, especially if the value model is intended for use as a back-end analytical engine for a web-deployed application.

For most value modeling efforts involving spreadsheet models, closed-form expressions for value functions are not needed. A simple two-column table that establishes value breakpoints is used in Excel along with one of two Visual Basic for Application (VBA) macros that perform linear interpolation on these table entries to yield a value score. (See Appendix B for macro code and installation steps). Creating a chart with this two-column table produces a piecewise linear value function that can be used as a visual tool when working with stakeholders/decision makers. Figure 6.7 shows an example of a two-column table along with its piecewise linear value function used for the rocket design example.

Number of people

Number of people	
X	**Value (Y)**
0	100
1	97
2	90
3	60
4	40
5	15
6	5
7	0

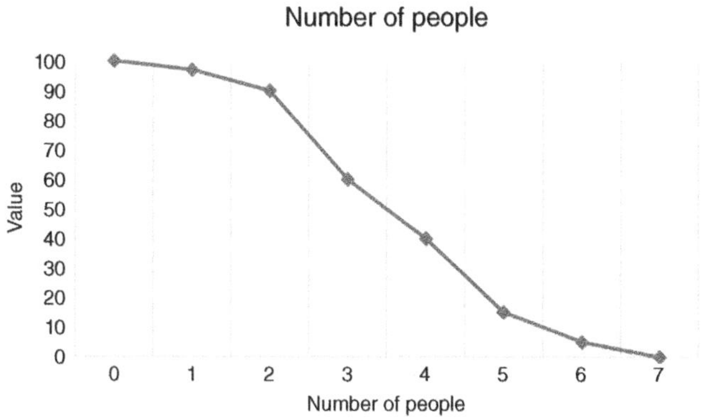

Figure 6.7 Value function for minimizing the logistical footprint value measure for the rocket example.

In Excel, a small two-column table is used to represent value functions; the value function plot is used for visual reference only. Typically, 3–10 breakpoints (x-values) are chosen to partition the value measure score scale (axis) into segments. These breakpoints are recorded in the table's first column, with the first and last x-values corresponding to the value score extremes 0 and 1 (or 100) in the 2nd column. The 0-level in the value score column corresponds to the minimally acceptable threshold screening value measure score when the value measure was used during alternatives screening.

The remaining value score entries in the table can be approximated directly from the shape of the curve when direct assessment is used or by using any of the other three options discussed in what follows. Two custom VBA macros– `=ValuePL()` [9] and `=ValuePL4()` —perform linear interpolation on these tables to return value score estimates for measure scores on each system alternative. (See Appendix B for the macro code.) Both macros perform the same linear interpolation. The `=ValuePL4` macro was created to handle value function tables that reversed the x-axis scale, and is now used more frequently.

There are three other methods used to create value functions: the *difference method*, the *bisection* method, and the *value increment method*. All three methods can be used when the measure score scale is either interval or ratio. The value increment method is used when the measure score scale is ordinal. Both the difference method and the bisection method assume that the value function is monotonically increasing or decreasing over the range of its associated value measure. When a decision maker identifies an intermediate point on the measure scale as the point where highest value return occurs, rather than modeling a non-monotonic value function, the measure criteria is typically split into two criteria: one criteria exhibiting monotonic increasing behavior and one criteria with monotonically decreasing behavior.

The *difference method* proceeds by first partitioning the value measure's range into a small number of segments (3–5) using either information inferred from decision maker statements or simply partitioning the scale into equal segments. Then, the decision maker is asked to rank order the value return of each segment as the measure score moves from the lower bound to the higher bound of each segment. The resulting ranking is then used to estimate how rapidly the value function increases or decreases on each interval, which informs the shape of the curve. The highest ranking (1) segment is one that returns the most value increase (decrease) as one steps from the segment's lower bound to upper bound. This equates to a region where the value function has its greatest slope (rise/run) or equivalently, the fastest rise (fall) in the value function curve. The least ranked segment corresponds to a region where the value function's slope (rise/run) is the least; that is, the region which will yield the smallest value return movement for increases in the measure score. A value function is drawn based on this information. The segment bounds become column entries in the small two-column table for the value function when building the value model in Excel.

The *bisection method* is similar to the difference method in that it involves segmenting the measure score scale into segments to help construct the value function. Here, however, the goal is to get the decision maker to identify specific measure scores that equate to 0, 25%, 50%, 75%, and 100% levels on the value score scale. These (x_i, v_i) quantities are used to build the two-column table in Excel.

Assuming that the measure score scale has bounds $[a, d]$, the process starts by bisecting the measure score scale into two segments: $[a, b]$ and $[b, d]$, and asking the decision maker if equal value return occurs when the measure score moves from each segment's lower to upper bound. If the answer is "yes," then b represents the point where 50% value return occurs on the vertical axis representing value score. The process is again applied to bisect $[a, b]$ and $[b, d]$ individually, resulting in four segments: $[a, c]$ and $[c, b]$; and $[b, e]$ and $[e, d]$, seeking the 25% (c) and 75% (e) points for value return. A piecewise representation for the value function curve is then plotted based on these breakpoints.

At any level of pairwise comparison, when a decision maker identifies a segment as having greater value return than the other, say it was $[c, b]$, then the bisection point for the higher value return interval is adjusted (e.g. to c_1 with $c_1 > c$) so that the new high value segment has smaller width: $[c_1, b]$, thereby reducing its value return while increasing the value return associated with the other segment: $[a, c_1]$. This adjustment process continues until the decision maker considers the value return for both segments to be equal. The last bisection point on the measure scale becomes the desired percentage breakpoint for plotting the value function.

Creating a Value Function (EV). As an example, consider value Measure 2.2.2: Rear Seating Shoulder Room (inches), which is being used to support Objective 2.2: Maximize Passenger Space. Suppose that this measure score's ratio scale was between [50, 70] inches. This was based on the decision maker's statement: "Anything less than 50 inches is considered below industry standards." So, 50 became a screening criteria threshold as a lower bound on shoulder room. Above that level, value return needs to be evaluated.

When asked about value return over the entire measure range, the decision maker stated:

- "Value return increases quickly from 50 inches to the industry average of 54.4 inches. In fact, about 75 percent of value return occurs by achieving the industry average. Then it begins to slow until around 59 inches."

- "After hitting the industry average, value return continues to increase but slows down. After about 59 inches, there's not much value return at all for sedans because to get that much rear shoulder room, the car width has to increase. This causes issues for parking garages and other fixed width parking spaces."

Using direct assessment, these statements appear to describe a value function with monotonically decreasing returns to scale, which could be modeled using an S-curve or a quick rising concave curve depending on how quickly the rise in value from zero occurs. An S-curve describes a value function with an "s" shape that starts close to zero, grows gradually until it reaches a relatively sudden increase, then levels off or decreases. The decision maker's first statement is contrary to the s-curve's gradual increase at the start.

Consequently, a concave curve similar to the one second down on the left of Figure 6.6 was sketched for the decision maker to confirm. It rapidly increases and then exhibits diminishing returns as the measure approaches 70. It would be inappropriate to use a linear curve in this situation because the decision maker's statements are contrary to the linear assumption of a constant return to scale.

Next, the sketched curve was adjusted with the decision maker using the difference method. The measure scale was partitioned into four segments: [50, 54], [54, 60], [60, 65], and [65, 70]. 54 in. was used as a segment breakpoint because of the decision maker's statement. The value return rankings assigned to these segments by the decision maker were:

Increase in Shoulder Room		Increase in Value (Ranking)
From	To	
50	54	1 $\longrightarrow$ Greatest increase
54	60	2
60	65	3
65	70	4

The decision maker's rankings reinforce using a concave value function because the greatest increase in value is occurring for lower values of Rear Seating Shoulder Room. The resulting value function and its two-column table for use in Excel is shown in Figure 6.8.

This same approach was used to create value functions for all of the other value measures since none of the measure scales associated with these value functions were ordinal, which would have required the value increment method to be used as described next. Most of the value functions have a different number of breakpoints depending on the value measure. Whatever number of breakpoints was easiest for the decision maker to describe how value changed across the value measure was used.

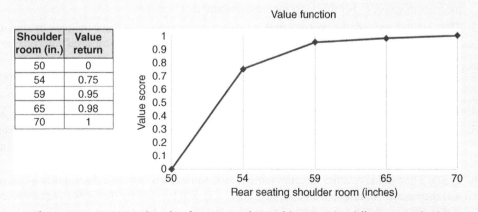

Shoulder room (in.)	Value return
50	0
54	0.75
59	0.95
65	0.98
70	1

Figure 6.8 EV example value function and 2D table using the difference method.

6.3.2 Value Increment Method

In deterministic tradespace analysis supporting systems decisions, Cartesian scatter plots of (Total Cost, Total Value) for each alternative are compared based on spatial separation of these points and how close they are to an ideal. For this to happen in a meaningful manner, the distances between alternative locations on both scales need to have meaning. The total cost scale aggregates lower level costs on ratio scales, all of which have no limitations with regards to scale. However, as mentioned earlier, for total value score differences to have meaning, all of the value functions feeding into it must at least be interval scales.

When a measure scale is interval or ratio, any method can be used to create value functions. When a measure scale is ordinal, which commonly occurs when constructed scales are needed, a value increment method for creating value functions must be used. Otherwise, its value score scale will inherit the measure's ordinal scale limitations, as will the additive value function expression once aggregation occurs. Under these conditions, the vertical separation of total value return between alternatives is limited to interpretation of ranking only; its spacing has no meaning other than the convenience of positioning for display. The cost dimension is typically a ratio scale and is not a concern in this vein.

The value increment method [8] for creating value functions solves this problem. The value increment method is a stakeholder interactive method that converts an ordinal measure scale into a cardinal interval value score scale in which spatial separation between value points on the scale has meaning. The resulting value score scale can then be aggregated into a weighted total value score without restricting the positioning of alternatives in a tradespace to ranking interpretation only. While the value increment method could be used for creating all value functions, it is especially helpful in this case.

Once a stakeholder establishes ordinal ranking preferences for the discrete measure levels, the procedure relies on a decision maker being able to identify the interval between measure levels that returns the smallest (Δ) increase to value, and to express all other measure level increase intervals as a multiple of Δ. Knowing this information and the fact that all stepwise value increments sum to 1, a piecewise linear value function can be constructed that has cardinal interval scale properties in which vertical spacing has proportional meaning.

The steps for applying the value increment method to an ordinal scale are (assuming that a value score scale [0, 1] is being used):

1. Have the decision maker identify the increase between measure levels that returns the least increase in value. Label this least increase amount Δ.
2. Then one-by-one, ask the decision maker to identify the amount of value increase by moving from lesser to higher preference levels for each of the other measure level intervals *as a multiple of* Δ.
3. Set the value return for the least preferred measure score level equal to 0, and the most preferred equal to 1.
4. Since the sum of all value increments must equal 1, create this expression and solve for Δ.
5. Substitute the value of Δ into each measure level expression to identify the value score return associated with each measure level. These become vertical coordinate breakpoints for a piecewise linear value function.
6. Create a two-column value function table for use in Excel, using the x_i breakpoint locations and their corresponding v_i value scores. This table will be used by the `=ValuePL4()` and `=ValuePL()` VBA macros (See Appendix B). Plot and label the piecewise linear value function on a line chart to support discussions with the decision maker.

Value Increment Method Example. A small technology startup company engaged a systems decision support team to assist in the design of their company's work environment, which they viewed as a system. The current CEO stated that all aspects of the work environment needed to be integrated together as a coherent system for the programmers, engineers, admin, marketing, and sales personnel to achieve the level of performance needed during the first three years of operating. Toward the end of the SDP Phase 1 they were using, the systems team was creating a quantitative value model in which one of the value measures requested by the CEO was clothing material that was to be used for corporate business casual wear. She stated that her favorite materials for business use, in order of her preference, were rayon, cotton, corduroy, linen, and wool, with wool being her favorite.

The lead systems engineer recognized that these discrete categorical values were on an ordinal scale because the CEO had an established preference for each material relative to the others, and that the value increment method needed to be used so that the value score scale could meet the minimum requirement for the tradespace analysis that would follow.

Using her material choices, he first asked the CEO which change in material from a lesser preferred option to a more preferred option would she get the least value return if that change was made. She stated that going from rayon to cotton represented the smallest value return for her. The lead engineer labeled this interval between rayon and cotton as Δ.

Next, stepping through each of the other intervals he asked what each value return increase would be relative to the rayon to cotton increase she said brought the least value return to her. She replied:

- The value return from cotton to corduroy was roughly 1.5 times that of going from rayon to cotton;
- The value return from corduroy to linen was approximately twice that of going from rayon to cotton;, and,
- The value return gained by moving from linen to wool (her most preferred material option) was about 4 times that of the value return going from rayon to cotton.

In equation form, this became:

$$\text{Value(rayon)} = 0$$

$$\text{Value(cotton)} = \text{Value(rayon)} + \Delta = \Delta$$

$$\text{Value(corduroy)} = \text{Value(cotton)} + 1.5\Delta = 2.5\Delta$$

$$\text{Value(linen)} = \text{Value(corduroy)} + 2\Delta = 4.5\Delta$$

$$\text{Value(wool)} = \text{Value(linen)} + 4\Delta = 8.5\Delta$$

Then, knowing that the Value(wool) = 1, he solved for Δ:

$$8.5\Delta = 1 \quad \rightarrow \Delta = \frac{1}{8.5} = 0.118$$

Substituting 0.118 for Δ produces each of the value scores corresponding the ordinal measure levels: Value(cotton) = 0.118, Value(corduroy) = 0.295, Value(linen) = 0.531, with

Value(rayon) = 0, and Value(wool) = 1. The value score axis now had cardinal interval properties in which the spacing between value score levels has defined meaning that will support proportional comparisons in a tradespace involving alternatives using this value function as part of their additive total value estimate. The resulting piecewise linear value function for Material Preferences is shown in Figure 6.9.

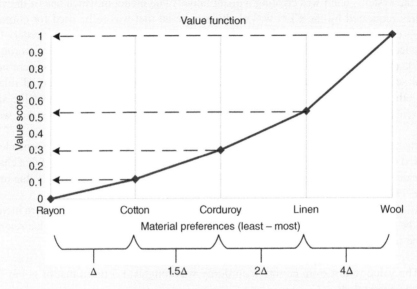

Figure 6.9 Value function for the example value increment method.

Figure 6.10 shows the remaining nine value functions for the EV Taxi example. The Rear Seating Shoulder Room value function was already illustrated in Figure 6.8. These piecewise linear value functions are very representative of the type used in value modeling. In contrast with the others, the "Passenger Volume" and "Total Passenger" value function curves extend beyond the point at which 100% value has been achieved. This was an intentional choice by the decision maker who intended to use these charts in discussions with EV competitors. He knew that some of the competitors were considering offering vehicles in the upper ranges of both value measure scales, and he wanted to illustrate to them that offering an EV that surpassed 100% value score was not going to improve their alternative's assessment.

6.3.3 Weighting Options

In practice, not all value measures are perceived as equal by stakeholders because values are tied to organizational and personal objectives regarding the system of interest and these are linked to outcomes stakeholders hope to achieve with the system solution. Properly representing estimated total value return for system alternatives requires individual value scores to be weighted by decision maker priorities and aggregated into a single number. The most common way of applying weights in this manner is by appending coefficients w_i to each of the n value functions $v_i(x_i)$ in the additive

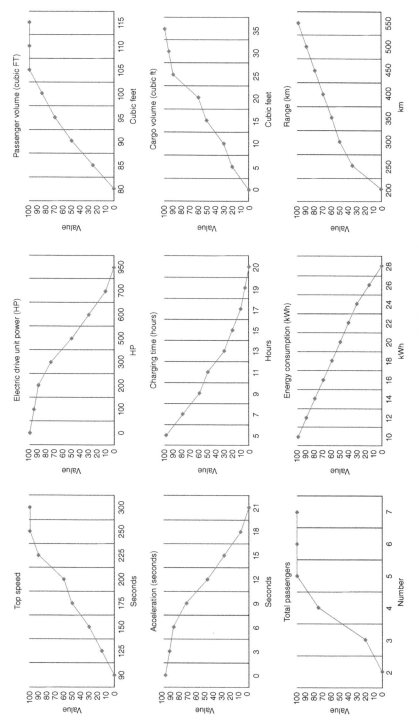

Figure 6.10 Value functions for the EV example.

249

total value expression shown previously in Equation (6.1) and repeated here for convenience:

$$V_n = \sum_{m=1}^{M} w_m f_m(x_{n,m})$$

As mentioned previously, linear convex weighting is standard practice in this setting. In addition to representing decision maker priorities, these weights quantify trade-offs between conflicting objectives by scaling the contributions made to total value by weighting their associated value functions. Altering these weights and examining the effects of reallocating weights is a primary focus when conducting sensitivity analysis on modeling results.

Kirkwood [1] and Clemen and Reilly [10] provide multiple methods to elicit weights from stakeholders. The two methods most often used in MCDM to identify linear weights for value functions are the *analytic hierarchy process* (AHP) [11] and *swing weighting* [12]. While both require decision maker interaction and both produce convex linear weights, the results obtained by the two approaches are not equivalent because of what their results represent and the effect that pairwise comparisons introduce into the logical consistency of AHP's weighting scheme. This bears discussion.

Analytic Hierarchy Process.   The AHP focuses solely on extracting a decision maker's level of importance assigned to each value function. The resulting weights represent a proportional allocation of total importance. The scale of relative importance shown in Table 6.2 is the most familiar scale used by AHP. As with all constructed scales, it consists of a verbal part and a numerical part. The verbal part expresses gradations of comparison judgments on the part of a decision maker. The numerical part digitizes these judgments to support weighting calculations. The basis for this scale is psychological: because of natural short-term memory limitations an individual cannot simultaneously compare more than 7 ± 2 objects without confusion [13]. This was the original scale developed for AHP.

The weights identified by AHP are the result of successive pairwise importance comparisons between all value measures (VM) that a systems team facilitates with a decision maker, assuming that each of the underlying importance relationships are bi-directional and logically consistent. The bi-directional assumption means that if VM_3 was determined to be five (5) times as important as VM_6, then VM_6 is one-fifth as important as VM_3. Logical consistency requires the relationship between measures to be *transitive*. For example, if VM_1 is twice as important as VM_2, and VM_2 is deemed three times more important than VM_3, then the importance relationship is transitive: VM_1 is 6 times more important than VM_3. This consistency aspect is where AHP has difficulty. If consistency was guaranteed using the five-level scale, some of the multiplication criteria would exceed the scale bounds.

Instead, the AHP technique addresses but does not negate this concern by including a computational step that checks for consistency by calculating a *consistency index (CI)* and comparing the

TABLE 6.2   AHP Relative Importance Scale.

Scale	Description
1	Equal (equally important)
3	Moderate (moderately/weekly/slightly more important)
5	Strong (strongly more important)
7	Very strong (very strongly important/demonstrably more important)
9	Extreme (extremely/absolutely more important)
2, 4, 6, 8	Intermediate values/compromises between values
1/2, 1/4, 1/6, 1/8, 1/9	Inverse comparison values

TABLE 6.3   Random Consistency Index (RCI) Values.

n	1	2	3	4	5	6	7
RCI	0	0	0.58	0.9	1.12	1.24	1.32

8	9	10	11	12	13	14	15
1.41	1.45	1.49	1.51	1.48	1.56	1.57	1.59

result to an average *random consistency index (RCI)*. The average *RCI* was computed by Saaty using 500 randomly generated AHP matrices of size $n \times n$, $n = 1, \ldots, 10$, with possible entries being $\{1/9, 1/8, \ldots, 1, \ldots, 8, 9\}$ and maintaining the bi-directional AHP importance relationship requirement. Table 6.3 shows the random consistency indices for $n = 1, \ldots, 10$. When the ratio $(CI/RCI) < 0.10$, the judgment consistency expressed in pairwise comparisons by the decision maker is considered acceptable. If not, the process is repeated by revisiting all the pairwise judgments and revising as necessary.

The basic steps for AHP are as follows. It is easily performed in a spreadsheet.

1. Create a square pairwise comparison matrix with $i = 1, \ldots, m$ rows and $j = 1, \ldots, n$ columns in which $m = n$. Row and column labels contain all of the value measures in identical order. So, if 10 value measures are being weighted, the comparison matrix will be 10×10. Each cell location (i, j) in this matrix will be used for comparisons except for those on the main diagonal where $i = j$. These matrix entries on the main diagonal are set to 1 because a value measure compared with itself is logically of equal importance.

2. Starting with the first row, ask the decision maker: "How important is value measure i (in a row) with respect to value measure j (in a column)?" Their answer determines the numerical value placed in cells (i, j) and (j, i). For example, if value measure i is strongly more important than value measure j, then a 5 is placed in cell (i, j) and cell (j, i) is assigned 1/5. If the decision maker's response was "somewhere between moderate and strong importance," then the intermediate value 4 is placed in cell (i, j) and cell (j, i) is assigned 1/4. This is the bi-directional characteristic of AHP's importance weighting. This step proceeds until all matrix entries are filled in. When finished, convert each fraction to its decimal equivalent, which automatically occurs for spreadsheet matrices.

3. In the cells below each column in the matrix, compute each column sum.

4. Normalize the entries in each column (including the main diagonal entry set to 1) by dividing them by their associated column sum. The resulting matrix entry values are typically referred to as criteria values. Each column now sums to 1.

5. In the cells to the right of each row, compute the average of its row entries (including the main diagonal entries). These row averages are the value measure weights used as coefficients for each value measure in the additive total value expression. For example, the value measure weight for the value measure associated with row 1 would be the computed row average of all the entries in row 1.

6. *Consistency check.* Using the AHP matrix created in Step 2 prior to normalizing, create a new matrix by multiplying each column entry in the non-normalized AHP matrix by the value measure weight corresponding to the row with the same label. For example, if the value measure weight for row $i = 4$ was calculated as 0.1450, then all the AHP matrix entries in column $j = 4$ would be multiplied by 0.1450; row 4 and column 4 have the same value measure label. This can also be accomplished using matrix multiplication with the Excel function `=MMULT(row, weights)`.

7. Using this new matrix, in the cell to the right of each row, calculate the row sum. Divide each row sum by the value measure weight for that row. Compute the average of these results. Label this ratio average as λ_{max}.

8. Compute the consistency index (CI): $CI = (\lambda_{max} - n)/(n - 1)$

9. Calculate the consistency ratio Cr by dividing the CI by the RCI for a size n matrix using Table 6.3.

10. If $Cr < 0.1$, the decision maker's judgment consistency is acceptable. If not, revisit the pairwise comparison matrix to resolve high violations of transitivity.

Since its introduction, at least five (5) alternative AHP scales have been proposed to remedy the AHP's issue with transitivity to some degree of success: the Ma-Zheng scale [14], the Donegan–Dodd–McMaster scale [15], the Lootsma scale [16, 17], the Salo-Hämäläinen scale [18], and the Ji-Jiang scale [19]. All of these approaches attempt to maintain a straightforward verbal scale for working with decision makers, recognizing a natural propensity to complicate matters as numerical scales and their associated computations increase in mathematical difficulty.

EV Value Measure Weights via AHP. The systems team engaged with the primary decision maker working the EV taxi replacement systems decision problem to continue their build of a quantitative value model having previously identified most of the required elements. It was now time to incorporate the decision maker's priorities regarding the 10 value measures being used to evaluate system alternative EVs. The team preferred to use swing weighting for this, but a decision maker's assistant suggested that the team first apply Saaty's AHP having used it previously when he was working at a different organization.

Figure 6.11a shows the results of pairwise comparisons made by the decision maker. The team facilitated these comparisons row by row. When the decision maker chose an importance level for a cell (i, j) according to Table 6.2, they entered a reciprocal entry in the AHP matrix for the cell location (j, i). Figure 6.11a shows these as decimal amounts.

Figure 6.11b shows the normalized AHP matrix along with each of the calculated value measure weights in the last column. These are convex weights required by the additive total value expression. With these weights, the coefficient represent the decision maker's priorities regarding value return. In decreasing order, the decision maker's most important value measures appear to be: Total Passengers (0.191), Rear Seating Shoulder Room (0.175), Range (0.166), and Passenger Volume (0.153).

Value measures

EV AHP matrix	Charging time	Range	Energy consumption	Total passengers	Passenger volume	Rear seating shoulder room	Cargo volume	Acceleration	Electric drive unit power	Top speed
Charging time	1.0	0.143	7	0.250	1	0.333	4	3	1	4
Range	7	1.0	5	0.333	1	0.333	5	5	5	3
Energy consumption	0.143	0.200	1.0	0.250	0.200	0.200	0.500	1	1	1
Total passengers	4	3	4	1.0	2	0.500	3	3	5	6
Passenger volume	1	1	5	0.500	1.0	1	3	7	5	5
Rear seating shoulder room	3	3	5	2	1	1.0	2	3	2	3
Cargo volume	0.250	0.200	2	0.333	0.333	0.500	1.0	3	3	4
Acceleration	0.333	0.200	1	0.333	0.143	0.333	0.333	1.0	1	1
Electric drive unit power	1	0.200	1	0.200	0.200	0.500	0.333	1	1.0	1
Top speed	0.250	0.333	1	0.167	0.200	0.333	0.250	1	1	1.0
Column sum:	17.976	9.276	32.000	5.367	7.076	5.033	19.417	28.000	25.000	29.000

(a) AHP matrix with DM input

Value measures

EV AHP matrix (Normalized)	Charging time	Range	Energy consumption	Total passengers	Passenger volume	Rear seating shoulder room	Cargo volume	Acceleration	Electric drive unit power	Top speed	Row average (measure Wts)
Charging time	0.056	0.015	0.219	0.047	0.141	0.066	0.206	0.107	0.040	0.138	0.103
Range	0.389	0.108	0.156	0.062	0.141	0.066	0.258	0.179	0.200	0.103	0.166
Energy consumption	0.008	0.022	0.031	0.047	0.028	0.040	0.026	0.036	0.040	0.034	0.031
Total passengers	0.223	0.323	0.125	0.186	0.263	0.099	0.155	0.107	0.200	0.207	0.191
Passenger volume	0.056	0.108	0.156	0.093	0.141	0.199	0.155	0.250	0.200	0.172	0.153
Rear seating shoulder room	0.167	0.323	0.156	0.373	0.141	0.199	0.103	0.107	0.080	0.103	0.175
Cargo volume	0.014	0.022	0.063	0.062	0.047	0.099	0.052	0.107	0.120	0.138	0.072
Acceleration	0.019	0.022	0.031	0.062	0.020	0.066	0.017	0.036	0.040	0.034	0.035
Electric drive unit power	0.056	0.022	0.031	0.037	0.028	0.099	0.017	0.036	0.040	0.034	0.040
Top speed	0.014	0.036	0.031	0.031	0.028	0.066	0.013	0.036	0.040	0.034	0.033
										Sum:	1.000

(b) Normalized AHP matrix with measure weights

Figure 6.11 EV AHP input matrix and normalized matrix with value measure weights.

EV AHP matrix (Consistency)	Value measures										Row sum	Measure weight	Consistency ratios
	Charging time	Range	Energy consumption	Total passengers	Passenger volume	Rear seating shoulder room	Cargo volume	Acceleration	Electric drive unit power	Top speed			
Charging time	0.103	0.024	0.218	0.048	0.153	0.058	0.289	0.104	0.040	0.132	1.170	0.097	12.083
Range	0.724	0.166	0.156	0.064	0.153	0.058	0.362	0.174	0.200	0.099	2.156	0.166	13.007
Energy consumption	0.015	0.033	0.031	0.048	0.031	0.035	0.036	0.035	0.040	0.033	0.336	0.029	11.425
Total passengers	0.414	0.499	0.125	0.191	0.306	0.088	0.217	0.104	0.200	0.198	2.341	0.200	11.724
Passenger volume	0.103	0.166	0.156	0.095	0.153	0.175	0.217	0.243	0.200	0.165	1.674	0.150	11.186
Rear seating shoulder room	0.310	0.499	0.156	0.382	0.153	0.175	0.145	0.104	0.080	0.099	2.103	0.179	11.774
Cargo volume	0.026	0.033	0.062	0.064	0.051	0.088	0.072	0.104	0.120	0.132	0.752	0.072	10.407
Acceleration	0.034	0.033	0.031	0.064	0.022	0.058	0.024	0.035	0.040	0.033	0.375	0.035	10.771
Electric drive unit power	0.103	0.033	0.031	0.038	0.031	0.088	0.024	0.035	0.040	0.033	0.456	0.040	11.381
Top speed	0.026	0.055	0.031	0.032	0.031	0.058	0.018	0.035	0.040	0.033	0.359	0.033	10.895

Ratio average (lambda max:)	11.465
Consistency index:	0.163
Consistency ratio:	0.109

Consistency ratio calculations

Figure 6.12 EV AHP consistency ratio matrix and results.

The team next checked the weights for judgment consistency as required by Saaty's AHP approach. The consistency ratio calculation results are shown in Figure 6.12. The calculated consistency ratio (0.109) was slightly above the recommended threshold (0.10), so further examination of the decision maker's importance assignments might need to occur.

Although these weights could be sufficient for use in the value model (especially as an initial weighting that could be changed), the team explained to the decision maker that AHP weights only represent his relative importance assessment. They said that it is possible that changes in a lower importance value measure such as "Charging Time" could actually affect his selection decision more than a high importance value measure if its increase or decrease was large enough. Using swing weighting would imbed this consideration into the weights along with importance. Moreover, if he was satisfied and confident in the rank ordering reflected by the AHP value measure weights already developed, these would provide a great start to swing weighting because his importance comparisons have already resulted in a numerical ranking. The decision maker agreed to participate in another session to see what results.

Swing Weighting. Swing weighting avoids AHP's issue of logical consistency by not engaging in pairwise comparisons. It is the preferred method for developing weights for MCVM and is also the primary method supporting value measure weighting during the SDP. Swing weighting considers each value measure separately from the others when constructing weights. Maintaining logical consistency between value measure weights is achieved by enforcing a two-dimensional ordering condition when assigning each value measure's initial swing weight prior to normalizing them. The two-dimensional characteristic occurs because swing weighting simultaneously extracts a decision maker's importance levels *and* a decision maker's estimate of the influence (impact) that changing each measure score across its entire measure scale (i.e. the "swing" in swing weighting) will have on the overall system decision they must make. This blend of weighting considerations is unique among weighting approaches, offering a more robust interpretation of value modeling results and subsequent sensitivity analysis interpretations.

The process uses a matrix approach involving a two-dimensional chart on a whiteboard rather than a spreadsheet. When interacting with a decision maker, this approach allows the decision maker to see a more holistic view of the weights as they are being developed, facilitating quick revisions if necessary. Figure 6.13 shows the layout of this two-dimensional chart. The column scale in this matrix (High, Medium, Low) defines a general value measure importance. The row scale represents the additional dimension captured by swing weighting: the impact that changes across a value measure's scale has on the decision being made. This chart is called a swing weight matrix.

As an example, a decision maker places Value Measure 1 in Figure 6.13 in the upper left corner block of the 3×3 matrix. This means that in addition to being considered of high importance to the decision maker, as Value Measure 1 changes across its measure scale it will have a high impact on the decision being made. That matrix location holds value measures corresponding to a (High, High) assessment. Similarly, Value Measure 2 is placed in the lower right corner block of the matrix, corresponding to a (Low, Low) assessment by the decision maker. Each value measure gets assigned to one of the matrix blocks until all value measures have been placed. While this is a fairly standard size matrix used in applications, the dimensions of the matrix could expand if a higher level of discrimination between value measures (e.g. 5×5) is required.

This additional consideration for weighting arose in practice in order to accommodate value measures with very large measure scale ranges being in a value model with ones possessing very small ranges. Changes in the one with a small range (e.g. VM_3 = number of aircraft carriers) had a high impact on the system decision being made while and changes in the one with a large range (e.g. $VM_1 2$ = number of service personnel) had small impact. Both were considered of high importance by the decision maker, but clearly there was a difference not being captured by importance alone. VM_3 was placed in the upper left block (High-High) in the swing weight matrix and $VM_1 2$ in the lower left block (High-Low), allowing for separation in numerical swing weights that would capture this difference.

The mathematical expression for obtaining value measure weights by normalizing swing weights is given by

$$w_m = \frac{SW_m}{\sum_{m=1}^{M} SW_i}$$

		Level of value measure importance		
		High	Medium	Low
Impact on decision if value measure swings across its scale	High	Value measure 1 SW = 100		
	Medium			
	Low			Value measure 2 SW = 11

Figure 6.13 Matrix for assigning value measure swing weights.

where SW_m is the non-normalized swing weight assigned to the mth value measure, $m = 1, \ldots, M$, and w_m are the corresponding measure weights.

The basic concept of this method for determining weights is relatively straightforward. A measure that is very important to the decision problem should be weighted higher than a measure that is less important. This feature coincides with AHP and other weighting approaches. A value measure that differentiates between candidate solutions for the decision being made, that is, a measure in which the changes in candidate solution scores across this value measure's scale range has a high impact on the decision, is weighted more than a measure that does not differentiate between candidate solutions. This is the idea associated with the second consideration integrated into swing weighting.

Since swing weights may be provided by different individuals, it is important to check for the consistency of the weights assigned. It is easy to understand that a very important measure with a high impact for changes in its range will be weighted more than a very important measure with a medium impact for changes in its range. It is harder to trade off the weights between a very important measure with a low impact on the decision for value measure range changes and an important measure with a high impact on the decision for changes in its range.

To insure consistency, an *upper left box rule* must be followed in which swing weights should decrease in magnitude moving from top left to bottom right in the matrix. Specifically, by isolating a single matrix block, say (High, High), and using this block as the upper left portion of a box drawn around its outer edges to the matrix bottom right corner, swing weights assigned to value measures in the (High, High) block must be strictly greater than all the others. Measures assigned to the same cell typically differ in small amounts while adhering to the upper left box rule as a group. This rule applies to every block in the swing weight matrix. Referring to the labeling shown in the 3×3 swing weight matrix in Figure 6.14, the following relationships must hold for swing weights to have judgment consistency using the upper left box rule:

- A measure placed in cell A has to be weighted greater than measures in all other cells.
- A measure in cell B_1 has to be weighted greater than measures in cells C_1, C_2, D_1, D_2, and E.
- A measure in cell B_2 has to be weighted greater than measures in cells C_2, C_3, D_1, D_2, and E.
- A measure in cell C_1 has to be weighted greater than measures in cells D_1 and E.
- A measure in cell C_2 has to be weighted greater than measures in cells D_1, D_2, and E.

		Level of value measure importance		
		High	Medium	Low
Impact on decision if value measure swings across its scale	High	A	B_2	C_3
	Medium	B_1	C_2	D_2
	Low	C_1	D_1	E

Figure 6.14 Value measure placement in swing weight matrix: upper left box rule.

- A measure in cell C_3 has to be weighted greater than measures in cells D_2 and E.
- A measure in cell D_1 has to be weighted greater than a measure in cell E.
- A measure in cell D_2 has to be weighted greater than a measure in cell E.

The idea of an upper left box rule is evident by selecting any of these constraints and drawing a box starting with and including the first mentioned cell (e.g. B_1 in the second constraint listed) to the lower right outside corner of the matrix (which would include cells C_2, D_2, C_1, D_1, and E). No other restrictions are used. These requirements extend to whatever size swing weight matrix is used.

EV Swing Weighting. Three weeks after the AHP weighting session, the EV project systems decision support team met with the decision maker in a follow-up session to go through the swing weighting process. The decision maker has a copy of the previous AHP results to use as a reference regarding his previous importance preference, if needed. Prior to starting, he told the team: "Things change over time, and some of my previous importance assessments might be slightly different than last session, but the rank ordering is still the same."

After explaining the swing weighting process, the decision maker placed each of the value measures into a single cell on the swing weight matrix first according to importance and then shifted its location based on the impact that a swing across the value measure scale would have on his decision. Once complete, the team walked him through assigning swing weights to each of the value measures based on the upper left box rule. Figure 6.15 shows the swing weighting results along with the AHP ranking and AHP weights from the previous session. The value measures shown are indexed by numbers assigned during the creation of the qualitative value model shown in Figure 6.3. Several differences became obvious immediately.

		Level of value measure importance		
		High	Medium	Low
Impact on decision if value measure swings across its scale	High	Total pass (100) Range (95)	Charging timo (89)	
	Medium	RSS room (85)	Cargo vol (60)	Elec Dr Pwr (50)
	Low	Pass vol (75)	Acceleration (35)	Top speed (25) Energy con (15)

Previous AHP ranking		
Importance	Value measure	Name
1	2.1	Total passengers
2	2.2.2	Rear seating shoulder room
3	1.2.1	Range
4	2.2.1	Passenger volume
5	1.1	Charging time
6	3	Cargo volume
7	4.2.1	Electric drive unit power
8	4.1	Acceleration
9	4.2.2	Top speed
10	1.2.2	Energy consumption

Figure 6.15   EV swing weighting results.

The Rear Seating Shoulder Room value measure was second in importance ahead of Range after AHP and consequently received a higher weight. With the additional consideration of decision impact resulting from value measure swings however, the decision maker concluded that while Rear Seating Should Room's importance was High, such swings would only have a Medium impact on his decision while Range was considered High under both considerations. Weights reversed as a consequence.

Passenger Volume retained an importance of High consistent with the input the decision maker provided during the AHP session, but its influence on the system decision was considered Low and the numerical weighting followed. Electric Drive Unit Power stayed Low importance along with Top Speed and Energy Consumption, but the decision maker was able to better differentiate between these as a result of the additional dimension. Similarly, Acceleration elevated slightly in weighting because of the decision maker now considered it of Medium importance with Low impact on his decision should the value measure swing across its range.

Figure 6.16 shows the differences in assigned value measure weights (also referred to as *global weights*) between the two weighting processes. It is clear from these results that the additional consideration beyond importance that swing weighting uses makes a difference in the weights used in the additive total value expression. The decision maker agreed with the systems team's recommendation to use swing weights.

	Previous AHP ranking			Swing weighting	
Importance	Value measure	Name	AHP value measure weight	Swing weight	SW value measure weight
1	2.1	Total passengers	0.191	100	0.159
2	2.2.2	Rear seating shoulder room	0.175	85	0.135
3	1.2.1	Range	0.166	95	0.151
4	2.2.1	Passenger volume	0.153	75	0.119
5	1.1	Charging time	0.103	89	0.141
6	3	Cargo volume	0.072	60	0.095
7	4.2.1	Electric drive unit power	0.04	50	0.079
8	4.1	Acceleration	0.035	35	0.056
9	4.2.2	Top speed	0.033	25	0.040
10	1.2.2	Energy consumption	0.032	15	0.024
		Sum:	1	629	1.000

Figure 6.16 AHP and swing weighting value measure weight results.

It is worth mentioning that an automatic ranking approach has occasionally been used to assign convex weights to value functions when access to a decision maker is very limited and schedule does not permit a more involved, interpersonal engagement [20]. The resulting weights are used as a proposed start point for interacting with a decision maker so that they can adjust weighting levels as desired. Automatic ranking is rarely, if ever, used as the final set of convex weights because they are statistically based and do not represent decision maker priorities until review and revision as appropriate.

CMS Quantitative Value Model. Building on the qualitative model they developed, the systems team next created value measures for each of the objectives. Because the project focused on concept development, they used a constructed scale to evaluate alternative CMS designs:

- **– 1** Worse than current system
- **0** Same as current system
- **+ 1** Marginal improvement to current system
- **+ 2** Some improvement to current system
- **+ 3** Significant improvement to current system

To ensure the resulting value score scales were interval scales, the value increment method was used to create all the value functions except two, which directly translated into the two-dimensional tables needed for their spreadsheet model.

The systems team next used swing weighting to identify convex weights for the additive total value expression being used. These swing weights were based on importance values determined by the values to functions to objectives crosswalk and the degree to which the alternatives varied with respect to these measures. Figure 6.17 shows the swing weight matrix for this systems decision which received input on value measure placement and numerical swing weights from the department chairperson. The convex global weights for value measures are shown on each objective block in Figure 6.18. The weights shown on each major system function are the sum of the value measure weights below it on the hierarchy, providing the systems team a sense of system function ranking according to the two dimensions used by swing weighting. The two highest priority system functions were *Information Sharing* (0.29) and *Usability* (0.25) which aligned with the needs expressed during stakeholder analysis.

		Level of value measure importance		
		High	Medium	Low
Impact on decision if value measure swings across its scale	High	Usability 100	Collaboration 75 Development time 75 Development cost 50	
	Medium	Content sharing 90 Availability 75	Instructor flexibility 40	Enforce standards 10 Integrate 5
	Low	Security 45		

Figure 6.17 Swing weight matrix for CMS concept decision.

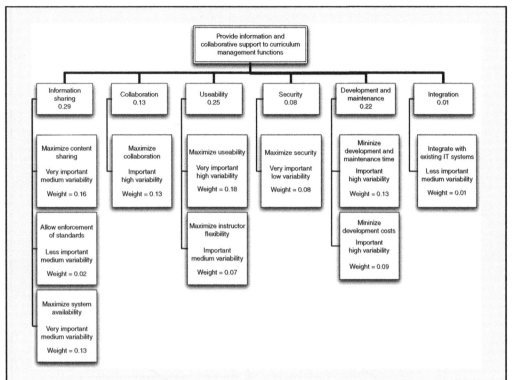

Figure 6.18 CMS qualitative value model with tiered weighting.

For two of the value functions–development cost and development time–the systems team used available data from similar in scope software development projects at the Academy. They had total cost estimates for each alternative. They also had estimates of the time required (in months) to achieve course-level functionality for each system. These two value functions were developed using the bisection method. The resulting value functions are shown in Figure 6.19.

Some of the criteria, such as content sharing, enforcement, and collaboration, have increasing returns-to-scale. This reflects the rapid increase in collaborative interactions as more and more people join a collaboration network. Some criteria, such as availability and security, have decreasing returns-to-scale. This reflects the negative consequences of not achieving at least a baseline performance level expected by stakeholders. Others, such as development cost and development time, have a linear return-to-scale as past data had indicated.

The requirements analysis conducted by the systems team also exposed several constraints for the system. The total development budget, including software and development effort was limited to US$ 250,000. The system also had to operate on the United States Military Academy information technology network, which being a government network at the time, introduced a host of limitations concerning access and security as technical requirements. To support an upcoming ABET accreditation visit, once the project began, the new CMS was required to achieve course-level functionality in five months and program assessment functionality by the project's 11th month.

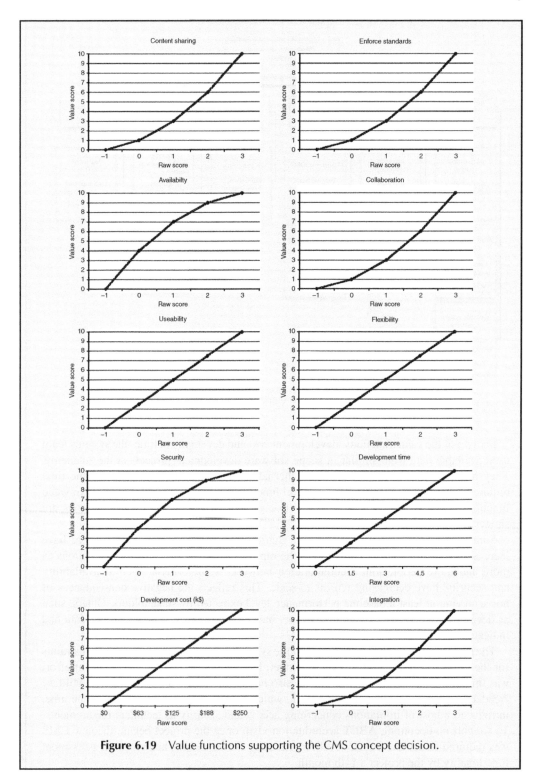

Figure 6.19 Value functions supporting the CMS concept decision.

Quantitative Value Model—Rocket Design. Figure 6.20 shows the value functions developed for each of the seven rocket design value measures minus the logistical footprint value measure depicted earlier in Figure 6.7. The systems team again used the preferred swing weighting method with the decision maker to elicit global weights for each value measure, resulting in the weights shown in Figure 6.21.

In this example, the value measures are shown indexed by numbers assigned while building the qualitative value model as an option to create linkages between models for the team. An additional option to help in this manner is to create summary tables such as Table 6.4.

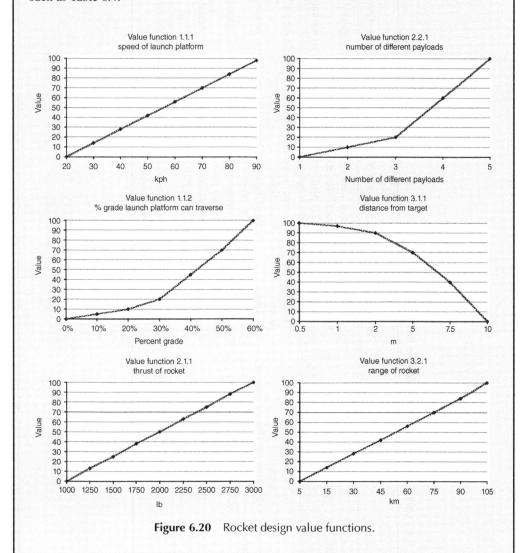

Figure 6.20 Rocket design value functions.

TABLE 6.4 Quantitative Value Model for the Rocket Example.

Function	Objective	Value Measure	Definition of Value Measure	Measure Type	Global Weight	Shape of Value Curve
1.0 Launch rocket	1.1 Maximize mobility of launch platform	1.1.1 Speed of platform	Speed of launch platform in kph (more is better)	Proxy, natural	0.23	Linear
		1.1.2 % Grade	% Grade platform can traverse (more is better)	Proxy, natural	0.01	Convex
	1.2 Minimize logistics footprint	1.2.1 Number of people	# of people to operate system (less is better)	Proxy, natural	0.06	S Curve
2.0 Transport payloads	2.1 Max carrying capacity of the rocket	2.1.1 Thrust	Thrust of the rocket in pounds force (more is better)	Proxy, natural	0.12	Linear
	2.2 Max flexibility to carry varying payloads	2.2.1 Number of payloads	# of different payloads rocket can carry (more is better)	Direct, natural	0.17	Convex
3.0 Achieve desired effects	3.1 Max accuracy of the rocket	3.1.1 Accuracy	Average distance from target in testing in meters (less is better)	Proxy, natural	0.27	Concave
	3.2 Max range of the rocket	3.2.1 Range	Effective range of the rocket in kilometers (more is better)	Direct, natural	0.14	Linear

Value Measures	Swing Weight	Measure Weight
1.1.1 Speed of platform	85	0.23
1.1.2 % Grade	5	0.01
1.2.1 Number of people	20	0.06
2.1.1 Thrust	45	0.12
2.2.1 Number of payloads	60	0.17
3.1.1 Accuracy	100	0.27
3.2.1 Range	50	0.14
Total =	365	1.00

Figure 6.21 Swing and global weights for the rocket design quantitative value model.

REFERENCES

1. Kirkwood, C.W. *Strategic Decision Making: Multiple Objective Decision Analysis with Spreadsheets.* Pacific Grove, CA: Duxbury Press; 1997.

2. SkyMark Corporation. Available at: http://www.skymark.com/resources/tools/affinitydiagram.asp. (Accessed February 2022).

3. Trainor, T., Parnell, G., Kwinn, B., Brence, J., Tollefson, E., Downes, P. (2007) 'The US Army uses decision analysis in designing its installation regions,' *Interfaces*, 37(3), pp. 253–264.

4. Sage, A.P., Armstrong, Jr. J.E. (2000) *Introduction to Systems Engineering.* Wiley Series in Systems Engineering. New York: Wiley-Interscience.

5. INCOSE Measurement Working Group (2005) *Technical Measurement*, INCOSE-TP-2003-020-01. San Diego, CA: INCOSE.

6. U.S. Army Combat Developments Command (1973) *The Measures of Effectiveness*, USACDC Pamphlet No. 71–1. Fort Belvoir, VA: U.S. Army Combat Developments Command.

7. Defense Acquisition Notes (2022) *Cost as an Independent Variable.* U.S. Defense Acquisition University. Available at: https://acqnotes.com/acqnote/careerfields/cost-as-an-independent-variable. (Accessed 1 Mar 2022).

8. Garvey, P.R. (2009) *Analytical Methods for Risk Management.* Boca Raton, FL: Chapman & Hall/CRC.

9. Kirkwood, C. (1997) *Strategic Decision Making: Multiobjective Decision Analysis with Spreadsheets.* Pacific Grove, CA: Duxbury Press.

10. Clemen, R.T., Reilly, T. (2004) *Making Hard Decisions with Decision Tools Suite.* Pacific Grove, CA: Duxbury Press.

11. Saaty, T.L. (1977) 'A scaling method for priorities in hierarchical structures,' *Journal of Mathematical Psychology*, 15, pp. 234–281.

12. Parnell, G.S. (2007) 'Value-focused thinking using multiple objective decision analysis,' in *Methods for Conducting Military Operational Analysis: Best Practices in Use Throughout the Department of Defense*, A.G. Loerch, L.B. Rainey, Eds. Military Operations Research Society.

13. Saaty, T.L. (1980) *The Analytic Hierarchy Process.* New York: McGraw-Hill.

14. Ma, D., Zheng, X. (1991) 'Scale method of AHP,' *Proceedings of the 2nd International Symposium on AHP*, Vol. 1, Pittsburg, PA: University of Pittsburg.

15. Donegan, H.A., Dodd, F.J., McMaster, T.B.M. (1992) 'A new approach to AHP decision-making,' *Statistician*, 41, pp. 295–302.

16. Lootsma, F.A. (1992) 'Scale sensitivity in the multiplicative AHP and SMART,' *Journal Multi-Criteria Decision Analysis*, 4, pp. 87–110.

17. Lootsma, F.A. (1999) *Multi-criteria Decision Analysis via Ratio and Difference Judgment*. Dordrecht: Kluwer Academic Publishers.

18. Salo, A.A., Hämäläinen, R.P. (1997) 'On the measurement of preferences in the analytic hierarchy process,' *Journal of Multi-Criteria Decision Analysis*, 6, pp. 309–319.

19. Ji, P., Jiang, R. (2003) 'Scale transitivity in the AHP,' *Journal of the Operational Research Society*, 54(8), pp. 896–905.

20. Alrares, H., Duffuaa, S.O. (2008) 'Determining aggregate criteria weights from criteria rankings by a group of decision makers,' *International Journal of Information Technology and Decision Making*, 7(4), pp. 1–13.

Chapter 7

Solution Design

It's so much easier to suggest solutions when you don't know too much about the problem.

—Malcolm Forbes, *Publisher Forbes Magazine*

7.1 INTRODUCTION

The solution to any well-formed problem exists, needing only to be found. Once decision makers' needs, wants, and desires have been identified and translated into requirements, and their values identified and modeled, the *solution design* process commences to develop a pool of feasible alternative system solutions within which a "best" solution will be selected. This candidate pool of alternatives is refined as the process proceeds, checking them against the problem definition and measured against stakeholder criteria until a much smaller *choice set* is identified from which the best solution will be selected by a decision maker. This process is fluid and may iterate often across the spectrum of define, design, and decide loops, as shown in Figure 7.1. Each alternative carries with it some degree of uncertainty and risk that needs to be identified and understood, with appropriate plans put into place that will eliminate or mitigate risks, and so the solution must include techniques to reduce these to make the decision maker's job easier.

Definition: Solution design is a deliberate process for composing a set of feasible alternatives for consideration by a decision maker.

Decision Making in Systems Engineering and Management, Third Edition.
Patrick J. Driscoll, Gregory S. Parnell, and Dale L. Henderson
© 2023 John Wiley & Sons, Inc. Published 2023 by John Wiley & Sons, Inc.

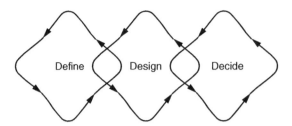

Figure 7.1 Define, design, decide loops.

The Solution design Systems Decision Process (SDP) phase includes techniques for identifying or creating innovative system solutions in a raw form, reducing the set of alternatives to most likely candidates (choice set), and presenting compelling evidence for how each alternative meets the needs of stakeholders and the decision maker as expressed by the quantitative value model and associated system requirements.

Identifying *who* contributes to a solution design process is a critical decision driven largely by the lead systems engineer. This task involves expansive thinking that delves significantly into functional and non-functional aspects of the system of interest and the environment within which the system does or will exist. The process results benefit greatly by the systems team adopting and maintaining a holistic approach when deciding who will participate because the decision depends not only on the skills they possess, but also in consideration of their motivation, availability, personality, and the degree of recent experience they have related to some aspect of the system project. Specialty skills that primarily focus on systems projects have always been in high demand, so generally making them available to the systems team requires careful budgeting. Figure 7.2 shows a Solution design Concept Map that illustrates the role of the system design teams within the context of ideation.

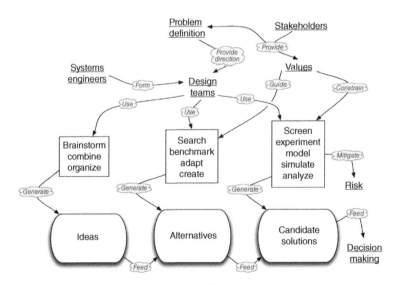

Figure 7.2 Concept map for the Solution design phase.

7.2   IDEATION TECHNIQUES

Innovative thinking is essential for successful solution design, but should not be confused with haphazard design, which more often leads to observations like Thomas Edison's: "I have not failed. I've just found 10,000 ways that won't work."

There is no single correct way to generate alternatives during a solution design effort. Much of the art of solution design is in knowing which tools to draw upon and who to include for a specific problem. However, all methods follow the basic model shown in Figure 7.3. The circular arrows indicate feedback and iteration loops, as necessary.

7.2.1   Brainstorming

Brainstorming capitalizes on the idea that a panel of creative thinkers can create a pool of ideas that will include the nucleus of a solution. It embraces the adage that two heads are better than one, or in what early operations researchers proclaimed as the *n-heads rule* [1]: *n heads are better than n heads minus 1*. The sole product of a brainstorming session is a comprehensive and inclusive list of ideas that are collected without judgment. No attempt at analysis is made except to reduce the total list of ideas to general categories by using techniques such as affinity diagramming, described later in this chapter.

The brainstorming concept was developed by advertising executive Alex Osborn in 1942, who observed that conventional business meetings were conducted in a way that stifled free and creative voicing of ideas. The term *brainstorming* evolved from his original term to *think up* for his new process [2]. In a series of later writings, he described brainstorming as "a conference technique by which a group attempts to find a solution for a specific problem by amassing all the ideas spontaneously by its members." Osborn became a prolific writer on the Creative Problem Solving (CPS) process in works including *Your Creative Power: How to Use Imagination* [3], in which he introduced the brainstorming term, *Wake Up Your Mind: 101 Ways to Develop Creativeness* [4], and *Applied Imagination: Principles and Procedures of Creative Thinking* [5].

Osborn developed the following four basic rules for guiding brainstorming sessions:

No criticism of ideas.   All judgment on ideas is deferred and participants feel free to voice all ideas without fear of judgment of the idea or themselves. This is why participant personalities matter.

Encourage wild and exaggerated ideas. Wild and crazy ideas often contain nuggets of unique insight that may be built upon. This is expansive thinking at its best. Wild ideas will be later refined and filtered during contractive thinking activities intended to evaluate concepts.

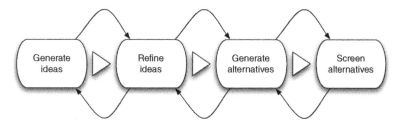

Figure 7.3   The ideation process.

Seek large quantities of ideas. Brainstorming sessions are fast-paced and spontaneous. Ideas may not only be useful in their own right, but also serve as catalysts for other ideas. Keeping accurate track of the many ideas that result from active, committed participants is challenging.

Build on each other's ideas. Ideas offered from one person's perspective often trigger wholly new ideas from others. Recognize that doing this engages contractive thinking that is locking onto a solution path. So, cycle back to ideas that are not in concert with the one(s) being pursued with vigor or they risk being lost.

Brainstorming sessions generally take one or more of three forms: *structured, unstructured* (free form), or *silent*. The main difference between the first two forms involves the level of control imposed by the facilitator(s), who may combine any of the three forms to meet needs as a session progresses.

A typical brainstorming session has six steps and lasts for about an hour. Ideal participants are those who can listen effectively, do not feel a need to dominate conversations, and are genuinely enthusiastic about participating. When possible, some subset of stakeholders or their representatives should be included in this process as long as their presence does not inhibit others from participating freely. When stakeholders are part of the genesis of potential system design solutions, they naturally have buy-in on potential alternatives that result and can explain to their organizations and organizational leadership how ideas originated. For the systems decision support team, this typically translates into increased project endorsement and support.

Groups generally consist of 5–10 creative participants. They should represent a broad range of experience with regards to the system, its purpose, or the problem of interest. A structured session may take the following form [6]:

1. *Problem definition.* The problem statement should be simple, often a single sentence, and identified in advance. The problem should be more specific than general, and complex problems should be split into functional subproblems that can be addressed in multiple sessions. Osborn recommends that a one-page background memo should accompany the invitation to participants, along with some sample ideas. For system solution design, problem statement takes the form of the fundamental objective with the one-page background memo focusing on intended system purpose(s) and any known functional requirements.

2. *Organization.* Seating participants around a round table is ideal for promoting interaction and for enabling the fast pace of the actual session. Distracters such as food and books should be avoided.

3. *Introduction.* Facilitators introduce the problem statement and context. The process is explained and any questions on the problem or process are answered.

4. *Warm-up.* A five-minute warm-up with sample problems may help energize participants towards a high-tempo level. Sample questions may include out-of-the-box examples such as: "What if restaurants had no food?", "What if pens wrote by themselves?" [7], "What if autos drove and fueled themselves?"

5. *Brainstorming.* Restate the problem and begin. Limit the session to 20–30 minutes. Pass a My Turn object around the table, with a 10-second time limit for the holder to offer an idea before passing it to the next person. This is similar to the idea of passing a "talking stick." The idea(s) offered by each individual is recorded on a 3-by-5 index card or Post-It® note by the object holder (good), a recorder (better), or the facilitator (best). Ideas should not exceed

approximately 10 words. If the stated idea motivates another one from another member of the group, the object passing goes out of sequence to this other person; if the holder cannot think of an idea, the My Turn object moves to the next person in sequence. Trends toward an exhaustion of ideas may be broken by radical ideas interjected by the facilitator. The session ends when time expires or no more ideas are offered. When the session is complete, idea cards are grouped into categories using affinity diagramming and central themes and core ideas are identified.

6. *Wrap-up*. Conduct a brief after-action review to identify strengths and weaknesses from the session. Use these comments to describe the environment in which ideas were made during the solution design process and how to improve upon the process for future sessions, if required.

Unstructured sessions use a more free-form approach, abandoning the "My Turn" object. Participants contribute ideas as they come to mind, cued by comments made by others or ideas appearing in written form.

Brainstorming critics soon emerged. By the 1950s, detractors declared that the effectiveness of brainstorming had been overstated and the tool simply did not deliver what it promised [8]. Much of the criticism, however, was based on poorly planned or conducted sessions, or focused not on brainstorming itself, but on the use of individuals or groups in brainstorming, as was the case of the report that became known as the Yale Study done in 1958 [9].

Critics generally agree on seven main disadvantages of Osborn's process, summarized by Sage and Armstrong [10] in the following text. Several of these factors contribute to what Yale social psychologist Irving Janis called *groupthink*, when group members' striving for unanimity overrides their motivation to realistically appraise alternative courses of action [11].

Misinformation/disinformation. There is no guarantee that incorrect or intentionally misleading information will not influence the process.

Social pressure. A group may pressure individuals to agree with the majority, whether they hold the majority view or not.

Vocal majority. A strong, loud, vocal majority may overwhelm the group with the number of comments they make, causing those not in the vocal majority to shut down.

Agreement bias. A goal of achieving consensus may outweigh one for reaching a well thought-out conclusion; don't rush to a solution.

Dominant individual. Active or loud participation, a persuasive personality, or extreme persistence may result in one person dominating the session.

Hidden agendas. Personal interests may lead participants to use the session to gain support for their cause rather than an objective result.

Premature solution focus. The entire group may possess a common bias for a particular solution.

The ensuing decades witnessed numerous variations on Osborn's technique, each seeking to overcome one or more of the identified flaws. Some of these are described next.

7.2.2 Brainwriting

Brainwriting is a form of silent brainstorming that attempts to eliminate the influence of dominant individuals and vocal majorities if there is concern that these disruptive elements might be included in the process participants. The two most popular variations are written forms of the structured and unstructured brainstorming techniques.

- In structured brainwriting, ideas related to the given problem are written on a paper that is passed from member to member in much the same way as the My Turn object. New ideas may be added or built from others.
- Unstructured brainwriting does not follow a sequential path. Ideas are written on note cards and collected in a central location.

7.2.3 Design Thinking

Design thinking is a CPS methodology [12] that blends many best practice techniques into a single approach facilitated in a small number of sessions. It is "a way of finding human needs and creating new solutions using the tools and mindset of design practitioners." It has a lot in common with the activity flow within the SDP, and like the SDP, design thinking places high value on holistic systems thinking (Figure 7.4).

Brainstorming leverages a combination of stakeholders acting in their own roles and leveraging their own experiences to ideate. The design thinking approach asks stakeholder participants to adopt system user roles. It then goes beyond ideation to create novel system prototypes and put them into use with stakeholders to collect immediate feedback. The feedback provided by stakeholders is then used to adapt any initial prototypes based on this information and repeat.

This rapidly executed process consists of five steps shown in Figure 7.4. The process is usually conducted as a two-day workshop, and is designed to be iterated through, either in part or in whole to generate as much learning as possible, as rapidly as possible. Focused on potential users, design thinking encourages iterative time periods of divergent and convergent thinking to generate numerous ideas and hyper-focus on a specific idea for rapid and iterative prototyping and testing with real users. The phases are defined as follows.

Empathize: understand the user. Because design thinking is focused on user perspectives, participants must initially assume a user state of mind without imposing personal assumptions or biases. Empathy is important because participants must understand and adopt user values for the system in order to objectively ideate. The goal of this stage is to gain deep insights into the users' needs

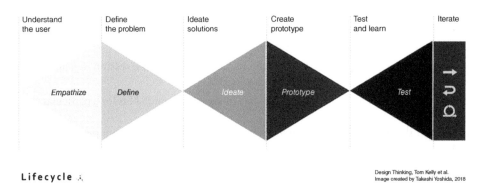

Figure 7.4 The design thinking process steps. Source: Adapted from Yoshida [13].

and wants. For system design and systems decision support projects, responses during this stage can inform requirements.

A session facilitator encourages this by prompting participants to [13]:

- Speak to the users, develop personas.
- Dig for user stories, feelings, and emotions.
- Find out what is important by asking "Why?" five times.
- Observe and infer.
- Suspend assumptions and challenge assumptions.
- Think complete thoughts embracing systems thinking.

Define the problem. Since the Solution design SDP phase follows from Problem definition, the systems decision problem has already been defined and approved by the decision maker. In general design thinking settings, this stage is used for accomplishing this task. The interesting feature embraced by design thinking is a belief that users do not express their real needs and wants right away because they often do not know them well enough for immediate recall. Using inputs from the *Empathize* stage, participants are encouraged to:

- Synthesize any learning and insights from the *Empathize* stage into user needs.
- Adopt personas because although different users have different needs, common patters can emerge that inform design requirements.
- Reframe the problem using the problem statement, tying it into leading questions as to "How might we … ?"
- Use noun-verb expressions to write user needs. For example: "User wants to … " and "User need a way to … " Participant responses to these translate directly into potential system functions.
- Add insights that were identified that more deeply explain the reasoning behind user needs.
- The problem statement, also called the *Point of View* (POV) should not contain any specific solution as to how the needs might be met. This is reserved for the *Ideate* stage.

Design thinking uses this stage as a replacement for in-depth research, preferring instead to mine information from stakeholder participants based on their knowledge and experience related to the system of interest, reframing the problem iteratively as new information is exposed.

Ideate. The previous two stages create user-focused conditions that this stage leverages using brainstorming techniques described in Section 7.2.1. *Ideate* encourages radical design alternatives, going wide with concepts and outcomes to explore a wide system solution space from which prototypes can be built and tested with users. In addition to the list-and-affinitize task common to brainstorming, design thinking also uses diagrams, arrows, stick people, and other representations to capture as many solution ideas as possible without concern about format. For supporting the SDP, the design thinking process could potentially end with this stage, re-engaging the other tasks associated with the Solution Design phase.

Prototype. This stage is primarily concerned with getting participants to engage with focused aspects of system solutions identified during activities in the *Ideate* stage. Not to be confused with system prototypes associated with Technology Readiness Level (TRL) 6, a design thinking prototype can be almost anything at any level of refinement. The systems team and participants can learn a lot from a sticky note and sharpie prototype of an app or a mock boardroom filled with "board members" played by the design team. A prototype is nothing more than a probe to engage with users, empathize, and learn. Prototypes need to focus on a single aspect of the system solution that will be tested among stakeholder participants.

Test. Testing is how the systems team learns from each prototyped solution. Facilitating this stage is primarily focused on users interacting with the prototype(s). The exact nature of testing changes and adapts over time depending on the prototype system solution resolution. Early in process iteration, testing is more focused on empathizing with the user and less about any specific solution. The prototypes created help stakeholder participants to gain a more tangible understanding of user needs for the system of interest. Later in the process, the systems team and participants spend significantly more time on each prototype to add specificity to potential system solutions. There are four guidelines for the system team during the *Testing* stage:

1. *Build/develop*. Narrowly create the prototype and testing scenario to focus on a single aspect of the solution you want to learn more about, but don't be discouraged by a "wandering" stakeholder user; they will still provide significant amounts of insight into what they want from a solution, thereby providing priceless feedback on how to execute better testing.

2. *Observe*. Allow users to interact with the prototype. The systems team should not have to provide participants with instructions as to how the prototype works. Identify and record emotions expressed by stakeholders (excitement, frustration, pain points, etc.) for later discussions during the post-testing interviews.

3. *Participate*. The testing stage is about active engagement both with the prototype by users and the systems team with stakeholders and prototypes.

4. *Interview*. The testing stage is complete after interviews with stakeholder participants take place. Rather than a typical question–answer session, the interviews should focus discussions on the emotions pinpointed during testing and seek stories from the user. For example, "You seemed really excited by ≪observation≫, why was that so exciting? Tell me about the last time something got you that excited." And so on. Interviews attempt to understand stakeholder motivations related to observation noted during the *Testing* stage. This helps to add rich context and understanding as it relates to potential system solutions, either to replicate some aspect of the prototype into a system solution or avoid it altogether.

7.2.4 Affinity Diagramming

This technique was introduced in Section 5.5. Affinity diagramming categorizes the ideas generated by brainstorming or brainwriting into groups that can then be rated or prioritized. This is also a silent process, with participants creating logical groups of ideas with natural affinity. When done using physical notes such as Post-It notes, duplicates are first removed from the collection, and notes are stuck to a wall or large board so that all participants can see them. Without speaking, participants move notes into unnamed groups using logical associations that they make until everyone is satisfied with the organization. This often results in notes being moved back-and-forth to different clusters many times until the solution design group reaches a reasonable consensus and the facilitator ends the activity. The idea groups are then labeled with summary descriptive headers. These often form the basis of alternatives by category, with the group header as an alternative name and the member ideas as desirable attributes.

7.2.5 Delphi

Delphi methods seek to minimize the biasing effects of dominant individuals, irrelevant or misleading information, and group pressure to conform. Delphi introduces three unique variations on the brainstorming concept [14].

1. Anonymous response—where opinions are gathered through formal questionnaires.
2. Iteration and controlled feedback—processing information between rounds.
3. Statistical group response—with group opinion defined as an aggregate of individual opinions on the final round.

Delphi methods also differ from traditional brainstorming techniques in their stricter reliance on subject matter experts. Development of the tool began in the mid-1940s shortly after General Henry H. "Hap" Arnold, Commanding General of the Army Air Forces, pushed for the creation of a Research and Development (RAND) project within the Douglas Aircraft Company of Santa Monica, California. Arnold, a 1907 graduate of West Point, who was taught to fly in 1911 by Orville Wright and rose to lead the Army Air Forces during World War II, wanted expert forecasts of technologies reaching decades into the future.

The Air Force's Project RAND, which became the RAND Corporation in 1948, developed a statistical treatment of individual opinions [15], and researchers evolved the process that became known as Delphi. By 1963, Dalkey and Helmer had introduced the idea of controlled feedback [14]. Their project was designed to estimate, from a Soviet strategic planner's view, the number of atomic bombs necessary to reduce United States' munition output by a given amount.

Delphi sessions typically follow 10 basic steps, described by Fowles [16]:

1. Form the team to undertake and monitor the session.
2. Select one or more panels of experts to participate.
3. Develop the first round questionnaire.
4. Test the questionnaire for proper wording.
5. Submit the first questionnaire to the panelists.
6. Analyze the first round responses.
7. Prepare the second round questionnaire.
8. Submit the second questionnaire.
9. Analyze the second round responses. Repeat steps 7 through 9 as necessary.
10. Prepare the report on the findings.

The 10 steps highlight another benefit of the approach in that panelists most likely are not assembled in a central location. However, this also suggests a danger inherent in this process. A Delphi session in which there is insufficient buy-in by participants or is poorly conceived or executed may suffer from participant frustration or lack of focus. Other critics of this technique note that the aggregate opinion of experts may be construed as fact rather than opinion, facilitators may influence responses by their selection and filtering of questions, and future forecasts may not account for interactions of other, possibly yet unknown, factors.

Selecting the right questions is key for Delphi success. The example that follows: *In Case of Nuclear War ...*, extracted from Dalkey and Helmer's reflections on applications of the Delphi method [1], shows questions from the first two of five rounds of their 1953 study. Panelists included four economists, a physical vulnerability expert, a systems analyst—precursor of the systems engineer—and an electronics engineer. The paper was published 10 years after the event for security reasons, and even then parts remained classified and were omitted.

In Case of Nuclear War—A Delphi Study:

Questionnaire 1. This is part of a continuing study to arrive at improved methods of making use of the opinions of experts regarding uncertain events. The particular problem to be studied in this experiment is concerned with the effects of strategic bombing on industrial parts in the United States.

Please do not discuss this study with others while this experiment is in progress, especially not with the other subject experts. You are at liberty, though, to consult whatever data you feel might help you in forming an opinion.

The problem with which we will be concerned is the following:

Let us assume that a war between the United States and one of its peer adversaries breaks out on 1 July 1953. Assume also that the rate of our total military production (defined as munitions output plus investment) at that time is 100 billion dollars and that, on the assumption of no damage to our industry, under mobilization it would rise to 150 billion dollars by 1 July 1954 and to 200 billion dollars by 1 July 1955, resulting in a cumulative production over that two-year period to 300 billion dollars. Now assume further that the enemy, during the first month of the war (and only during that period), carries out a strategic A-bombing campaign against US industrial targets, employing 20-KT bombs. Within each industry selected by the enemy for bombardment, assume that the bombs delivered *on target* succeed in hitting always the most important targets in that industry. What is the least number of bombs that will have to be delivered on target for which you would estimate the chances to be even that the cumulative munitions output (exclusive of investment) during the two-year period under consideration would be held to no more than one quarter of what it otherwise would have been?

Questionnaire 2. As the result of the first round of interviews, it appears that the problem for which we are trying with your help to arrive at an estimated answer breaks down in the following manner.

There seem to be four major items to be taken into consideration, namely:

A. The vulnerability of various potential target systems;
B. The ability of various industries and combinations of industries to recuperate;
C. The expected initial stockpiles and inventories; and,
D. Complementarities among industries.

Taking all these into account, we have to:

1. Determine the optimal target system for reducing munitions output to one-fourth; and,
2. Estimate for this target system the minimum number of bombs on target required to create 50% confidence of accomplishing that aim.

We would like to establish the background material consisting of A, B, C, D more firmly. With regard to A and B, the interviews have suggested two lists of factors related to vulnerability and an ability of the US to recuperate, respectively.

7.2.6 Groupware

This is increasingly popular for conducting brainstorming and other collaboration using networked computers. Applications such as *GroupSystems* mirror the brainstorming process and emphasize anonymity. Other groupware tools include e-mail, newsgroups and mailing lists, workflow systems, group calendars, server-based shared documents, shared whiteboards, teleconferencing and video teleconferencing, chat systems, and multi-player games.

7.2.7 Lateral and Parallel Thinking and Six Thinking Hats

These are unique creativity techniques for thinking about problems differently. "You cannot dig a hole in a different place by digging the same hole deeper," says concept developer Edward de Bono [17]. He insists that basic assumptions be questioned in lateral thinking. For example, he notes that chess is a game played with a given set of pieces, but challenges the rationale for those pieces. Lateral thinking, is concerned not with playing with the existing pieces, but with seeking to change those very pieces. Parallel thinking [18], focuses on laying out arguments along parallel lines instead of adversarial.

Techniques for accomplishing this are described in his Six Thinking Hats approach. In these sessions, participants display or wear one of six colored hats that determine the person's role in the session.

- *White hat*. Neutral, focused on ensuring that the right information is available.
- *Red hat*. Intuitive, applies feelings, hunches, emotion, and intuition.
- *Black hat*. Cautious, provides critical judgment and says why things cannot be done.
- *Yellow hat*. Optimist, finds ways that things can be done, looks for benefits.
- *Green hat*. Creative, encourages creative effort, new ideas, and alternative solutions.
- *Blue hat*. Strategic, organizes and controls the session.

7.2.8 Morphology

Morphology is defined as the form and structure of an organism or one of its parts. In a systems setting, it defines a process of exploring combinations of required system elements (e.g. components) to examine how well the resulting system structures perform against screening criteria. For solution design, morphology offers potential innovation and creativity options that might have been missed otherwise. This approach, called morphological analysis (MA), was developed by astrophysicist and aerospace scientist Fritz Zwicky in the mid-1960s for studying multidimensional, non-quantifiable complex problems [19]. Zwicky, a scientist at the California Institute of Technology (CalTech), wanted to find a way to investigate the total set of possible relationships between system components, then to reduce the total set to a feasible solution space. He summarized the process in five steps:

1. Concisely formulate the problem to be solved.
2. Localize all parameters that might be important for the solution.
3. Construct a multidimensional matrix containing all possible solutions.
4. Assess all solutions against the purposes to be achieved.
5. Select suitable solutions for application or iterative morphological study.

Zwicky proposed finding complete, systematic field coverage by constructing a matrix with all possible system attributes, then producing a feasible set by eliminating combined attributes that are inconsistent with the stated purposes of the system. These inconsistencies could be such items as:

- Logically inconsistent, such as "achieve Earth orbit in an underwater environment."
- Empirically inconsistent, based on improbability or implausibility, such as "build an aircraft carrier using personal savings."
- Normatively inconsistent, based on moral, ethical, or political grounds.

Solution designers should focus initially on the first two inconsistencies but they cannot ignore the third, which includes legal and regulatory constraints. The U.S. Department of Defense (DoD), for example, publishes DoD Directive 5000.01 (The Defense Acquisition System), DoD Instruction 5000.02 (Operation of the Adaptive Acquisition Framework) specifying processes for the Defense Acquisition System.

Although Zwicky's model is actually an *n*-dimensional matrix, his original illustration, shown in Figure 7.5, makes clear why it has become known as Zwicky's Morphological Box or simply Zwicky's Box. This figure shows a $5 \times 5 \times 3$ matrix containing 75 cells, with each cell containing one possible system configuration. Continuing the rocket design problem, solution designers might develop the 4×4 Zwicky Box shown in Figure 7.6 to conduct an MA. Columns are labeled with parameter names and rows with variable names. The matrix is filled in with possible values.

Figure 7.6 shows an alternative generation table for the rocket problem example. The systems engineers identified four system design decisions that will have to be made: the number of fins, the thrust, the seeker, and the type of guidance. On the basis of the number of options in each column (5, 4, 4, and 4), 320 alternatives can be developed. However, all of these may not be feasible. The system alternatives selected for further exploration and consideration should span the design space as widely as possible. Five designs are shown in the table.

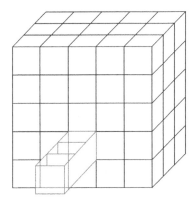

Figure 7.5 Zwicky's morphological box. Source: Zwicky [19]/ With permission of Springer Nature.

Solution design parameters			
Fins	**Thrust**	**Seeker**	**Guidance**
2	1000	Forward looking infared	Inertial
3	1667	Laser	Global positioning system
4	2334	Audio	Wire
5	3000	None	Optical

Morphological box

	Solution design parameters			
Strategy	**Fins**	**Thrust**	**Seeker**	**Guidance**
Global lightening	5	2334	Laser	Global positioning system
Hot wired	4	3000	None	Wire
Sight and sound	2	3000	Audio	Optical
Slow poke	3	1000	Forward looking infared	Inertial
Star cluster	3	1667	Forward looking infared	Global positioning system

Generated alternatives

Figure 7.6 From morphological box to alternatives.

7.2.9 Ends-Means Chains

Thinking about how means support goals challenges solution designers to think creatively by presenting a higher-level objective and seeking different means for achieving it. This is repeated for means—seeking means to achieve previously stated means—to generate lower level ideas. In this process, described by Keeney as a means-ends objectives network [20], lower-level objectives answer the question of how higher level objectives can be achieved. This differs from a fundamental objectives hierarchy in which lower level objectives identify aspects of higher level objectives that are important. The process of finding new ways to achieve successive levels of objectives assists solution designers in structuring alternatives. Such a chain for the rocket design is shown in Figure 7.7. Arrows in this figure indicate the direction of influence.

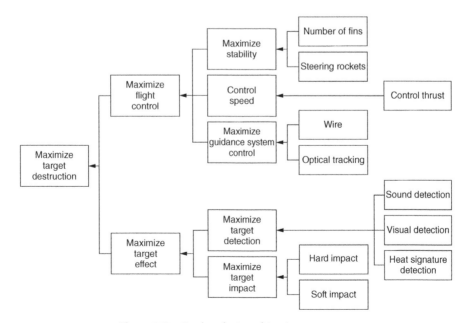

Figure 7.7 Rocket design objectives structure.

TABLE 7.1 Housing Upgrade Example [21].

Method	Housing Example
Existing system	Present house—three bedrooms new rug, new dishwasher.
Modified existing system	Remodel present house. Add-on a fourth bedroom. Repaint outside
Prepackaged design	
• Off-the-Shelf	• New housing tract
• Learn from Others	• Buy neighbor's four-bedroom house
• Influential People Suggest	• House mother-in-law suggests
New System Design	
• Idealized	• Design custom house
• Parallel Situation	• Build beehive house
• Morphological	• Consider house, apartments, condo, mobile home
• Cascading	• Select home by bedroom first, then family room, then back yard, etc.

Source: Athey [21]/Pearson Education.

Not all system solution ideas must be completely new. Choices for using new or existing options are summarized by Athey [21] in Table 7.1, focusing on a problem to buy or upgrade a residence.

7.2.10 Other Ideation Techniques

Other techniques are cited in MacCrimmon and Wagner's presentation on Supporting Problem Formulation and Alternative Generation in Managerial Decision Making [22]. These include the following:

Metaphoric connections to link disparate contexts by associating the problem with fragments of modern poems.

Loto modifications that alter existing ideas using modifiers such as "make it bigger, make it smaller."

Relational combinations and juxtaposition seek to create new ideas in ways similar to Zwicky's. The first technique applies sentences such as "[Process] by means of [Object 1] *relational word* [Object 2]." The latter technique uses up to three different problem elements at the same time.

Recently, a technique called *set-based design* or *set-based concurrent engineering* has been gaining popularity for use in systems design and acquisition [23]. Less of a design philosophy and more of an approach to arriving at a high value return system alternatives, it keeps requirements and design options flexible for as long as possible during system design and development. By retaining as many alternative designs as practical for as long as possible during system design and development, it allows a systems team to simultaneously explore multiple options while gradually allowing poorer ones to be eliminated.

7.3   SCREENING AND FEASIBILITY

Converting freewheeling ideas generated during ideation sessions into reasonable alternatives occurs during the conceptual design phase of a system life cycle. Here, ideas are compared with requirements and constraints and a feasible subset emerges for further analysis. Potential options are identified and then subjected to at least a preliminary evaluation to eliminate clearly unacceptable alternatives [24] due to substandard criteria merit. Alternatives that survive screening are then subjected to more detailed design effort, cost/value evaluation, and more complete architectures or specifications are obtained.

There is no clear line marking where idea generation ends and alternative screening begins. As seen earlier, this is built into many ideation techniques and the entire process normally cycles through several iterations. While the previous section focused on generating original ideas, practice shows that this represents only a fraction of the tactics used by organizations to uncover alternatives. A study of 376 strategic decisions showed that only about a quarter of the alternatives considered were developed using an original design tactic for generating alternatives [25]. In "A Taxonomy of Strategic Decisions and Tactics for Uncovering Alternatives," Nutt describes a study of 128 private, 83 public, and 165 private nonprofit organizations and the tactics they used to generate alternatives. Organizations ranged from NASA to Toyota and from Hertz-Penske Rental to AT&T. He distilled their tactics into six categories:

1. The *existing idea* tactic draws on a store of fully developed, existing solutions, and follows a solution-seeking-a-problem approach with subordinates on the lookout for ways to put their ideas and visions to use.

2. *Benchmarking* tactics, where alternatives are drawn from practices of others who are outside of the organization rather than inside, as with the original idea tactic. Nutt draws a distinction between *benchmarking*, which adapts a single practice used by another organization; and,

3. *Integrated benchmarking*, which uses a collection of ideas from several outside sources.

4. *Search* tactics outsource the process through requests for proposals (RFPs) from vendors, consultants, and others who seem capable of helping.

5. *Cyclical searches* use an interactive approach, while *simple searches* use a one-time RFP.

6. The *design* tactic calls for custom-made alternatives that stress innovation to achieve competitive advantage. These normally require more time and other resource commitment.

Of the decisions studied, either only 36 could not be classified using Nutt's taxonomy, or decision makers switched methods during the process. The remaining 340 decisions are categorized in Table 7.2. Examining these techniques from alternative-focused thinking (AFT) versus value-focused thinking (VFT) perspectives (see Section 4.2) shows that *design* and *search* techniques favor a VFT approach, while *benchmarking, integrated benchmarking*, and *existing idea* techniques use AFT. The *cyclical search* technique could use either or both, depending on circumstances in each iteration.

Feasibility screening techniques were introduced in the discussion of Zwicky's Box in Section 7.2.8. Several other techniques are also possible [26–28]. Their use in this setting is to reduce the number of alternatives that must be evaluated fully using a multiple criteria value model (MCVM) of the type described in this book by refining, combining, or eliminating those

TABLE 7.2 Remaining 340 Ddecisions.

Tactic	Number	Percent	How Alternatives Were Generated
Cyclical Search	9	3	Multiple searches in which needs are redefined according to who is available
Integrated benchmarking	21	6	Amalgamation of ideas from several outside sources
Benchmarking	64	19	Adapt a practice used by another organization
Search	69	20	A single search cycle with a decision after RFP responses received
Design	82	24	Develop a custom solution
Existing idea	95	28	Validate and demonstrate benefits of a preexisting idea known in the organization

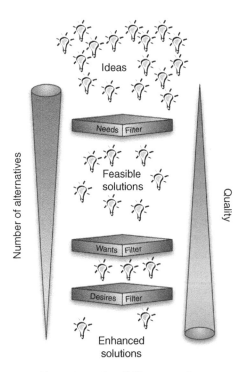

Figure 7.8 Feasibility screening.

alternatives that do not meet critical stakeholder requirements identified during the Problem Definition phase of the SDP (see Chapter 5).

The feasibility screening process can be thought of as a series of increasingly fine screens that filter out alternatives that fail to meet the stakeholders' needs, wants, and desires, as shown in Figure 7.8.

- *Needs* are those essential criteria that must exist for the alternative to be considered. These are "must have" requirements identified by stakeholders that must be incorporated into system design and performance. These are considered the minimum elements used in screening, and their lower bounds on associated measures are considered *threshold* criteria.

- *Wants* are additional features or specifications that significantly enhance the alternative, but do not cause an alternative to be rejected if missing. These are "should have" requirements identified by stakeholders. Oftentimes, these are also referred to as "objective" criteria in that they express what stakeholders want a system solution to be or to achieve in performance. Requirements in this category that are considered by the stakeholders or decision maker to be significant to the system's overall quality or to gain a competitive advantage. These could migrate to needs and be included in screening criteria. While not mandatory to meet requirement thresholds and pass screening, these requirements often distinguish between alternatives and provide opportunities for developers to capitalize on their particular design strengths, technical capabilities, and development skills, thereby increasing the likelihood their system alternative would be selected as the system solution.

- *Desires* are features that provide an increased margin of excellence. These are nice to have requirements identified by stakeholders and are frequently considered "targets of opportunity" for developers to keep in mind as they structure alternatives. It is worthwhile for system decision support teams to capture these desires and look for opportunities to accommodate them as alternatives undergo refinement as they do add value in some way to what stakeholders are looking for.

Solution designers may choose to initially screen at only the *needs* level, or may add screens for specific *wants* and *desires* at the start as well. In typical system solution settings, narrowing alternatives to a set of 10 or less alternatives is a workable number for subsequent analysis. However, the number of alternatives carried forward from screening can also be restricted by budget and regulatory guidelines specific to a client organization.

In all cases, screening is evaluated on a go or no-go basis—an alternative either passes through the screen or it does not. Before rejecting a no-go alternative, however, designers should examine it to see if the offending feature can be modified or deleted so that the otherwise feasible alternative can make it through a repeat screening. The concept of alternative reduction also may be enhanced by combining alternatives or ideas, as described by affinity diagramming in Section 7.2.4.

Rocket Design—Feasibility Screening. Revisiting the rocket design from Section 7.2.8, assume that the minimum standard for such a rocket is that it must have an effective range of 5 km, be launched from a standard four-wheel drive vehicle, and operate in terrain ranging from open fields to dense forest. A *feasibility screening matrix* with 6 of the 16 possible alternatives identified earlier versus criteria is shown in Table 7.3. Alternatives often take on descriptive names by this point, but in this case we list the parameters of *number of range criterion, mobility criterion, terrain criterion, and overall assessment*. This example shows that four of these alternatives met all of the minimum requirements. A single *no-go* for any criterion triggers an overall *no-go* assessment and the alternative is flagged for revision or rejection. For example, Sight and Sound fails the terrain criterion.

Not all threshold screening criteria originate from technical requirements related to major system functions. Because a system operates in an environment within which interactions and dependencies occur, screening criteria can also be affected by requirements originating in any of the

TABLE 7.3   Partial Rocket Design Feasibility Screening Matrix.

Alternative	Range Criterion (> 500 km)	Mobility Criterion (> med)	Terrain Criterion (all)	Overall Assessment
Global Lightening	Go (800)	Go (high)	Go (All)	Go
Hot Wired	Go (600)	Go (high)	Go (All)	Go
Sight and Sound	Go (700)	Go (high)	No-Go (limited)	No-Go
Slow Poke	Go (550)	Go (very high)	Go (All)	Go
Star Cluster	Go (600)	Go (high)	Go (All)	Go
5-fin, 2234# Thrust, None, Wire	No-Go (400)	Go (high)	No-Go (limited)	No-Go

SDP environmental factors: legal, cultural, ecological, security, moral/ethical, emotional, political, health and safety, social, historical, economic, and organizational. For this reason, if a feasibility study is needed as a precursor to pursuing a system solution, these environmental factors assume a primary role supporting the study and the four SDP phases are not used. The results of a feasibility study illuminate whether the system solution effort should begin or further work must be done before hand such as seeking legislative relief, permissions from historical preservation organizations, advise and consent from cultural groups, and so on.

Feasibility screening matrices support alternative generation by quickly eliminating ideas that are clearly not feasible. Recall that two of the four guidelines for brainstorming described in Section 7.2.1 are "encourage wild and exaggerated ideas" and "seek large quantities of ideas." This will naturally lead to many alternatives that are clearly not feasible. For example, a basic requirement for an aircraft is that it must be able to fly. Any alternative that does not meet this fundamental criterion is eliminated during the feasibility screening process.

Screening criteria should avoid targeting feasible but less desirable alternatives. Feasibility screening sifts out alternatives based on non-negotiable criteria. For all others, finding the best trade-offs will lead the preferred solution. For example, a raw value of 90 for variable A may be acceptable when variable B is 30, but not when it is 50. Setting a No-go criterion for A at 90, then, would unduly restrict the solution space.

EV Taxi—Feasibility Screening. Seven potential electric vehicles (EVs) were identified as possible ICE taxi fleet substitutions and were then screened against minimally acceptable value measure levels as set by the decision maker. Five (5) vehicles passed all 10 threshold minimums. Two (2) vehicles–Option F and Option G–failed to meet the minimum threshold for Cargo Volume. In discussions with the decision maker, the systems team pointed out that this was not a near-threshold failure. Both of the vehicles do not have designated trunk space for cargo. In order to accommodate any cargo such as passenger luggage, rear seating had to be folded down, reducing Total Passenger carrying capacity, which was the highest priority value measure (Figure 7.9).

Given that the remaining five (5) EVs represented a good span of the possible design space in terms of vehicle design and performance capabilities, the system team recommended that

Feasibility screening matrix (EV alternatives)								
Value measures		Option A	Option B	Option C	Option D	Option E	Option F	Option G
Total passengers		5.00	4.00	5.00	5.00	5.00	5.00	5.00
Rear seating shoulder room		52.50	53.60	52.76	55.10	57.70	53.90	54.70
Range		382.00	260.00	320.00	539.00	311.00	201.00	448.00
Passenger volume		92.40	84.00	93.90	100.00	106.50	93.50	97.10
Charging time (Full)		7.50	20.00	9.50	7.00	6.00	9.60	9.00
Cargo volume		14.80	9.20	17.00	31.60	12.60	0.00	0.00
Electric drive unit power		150.00	170.00	200.00	503.00	120.00	134.00	201.00
Acceleration		7.90	7.30	7.80	2.40	9.90	9.60	11.20
Top speed		90.00	160.00	146.00	260.00	172.00	150.00	166.00
Energy consumption		18.00	13.10	28.00	18.60	15.10	14.50	15.70

Figure 7.9 Feasibility screening for electric vehicle (EV) candidates.

Option F and Option G be eliminated from further consideration. The decision maker agreed. Options A through E moved on for cost and value return evaluation against the 10 value measures.

All feasible alternatives become solution candidates. Balancing trade-offs to find the preferred solution is accomplished by enhancing and measuring solution candidates. Quite often, system alternatives contain valuable sub-elements that will have high value return in one or more dimensions, and are lacking in others. This situation creates unique opportunities for merging alternatives in a way that can offer higher potential value return to stakeholders than any single system alternative in the screening set. The ideation techniques discussed here help make this possible.

 Be careful to *not* "screen to a solution" by using screening criteria so restrictive that only one or two alternatives survive. Also, take a very hard look at alternatives that fail screening criteria by only minor amounts, "minor" being a relative term. Although eliminating these close failures may shorten the process for arriving at a solution, remember that none of the alternatives eliminated by screening criteria will have been evaluated for potential value return by taking raw measure results and translating them into how stakeholders value these measures.

Cost constraints are vital considerations at all stages of a system's life cycle, a point reinforced in Chapter 8 in which life cycle costing, cost estimating techniques, and the life cycle stages appropriate for the various techniques are discussed. In previous phases of the SDP, the systems support team identified various component life cycle costs for the system under focus. Now, the systems decision support team must review these cost components and ensure that they completely encompass each candidate solution's costs.

Once detailed cost estimates are needed, a great deal more information about the candidate solutions must be present than was needed at the start of the SDP. What has changed? Are there hidden or higher costs, such as development costs, manufacturing costs, or operational costs? Does the cost model consider all components of the newly developed candidate solutions? Once the cost model is indeed complete, costs are computed for each candidate solution still under consideration. Although overall costs are needed for the next step, it is important to include all of the components in detail to sufficiently document the work and to answer any questions the decision maker may have about the analysis. As will be seen in Chapter 8, these facts are directly leveraged when Monte

Carlo simulation is used to examine how uncertainty affects each alternative's cost profile. At this Solution design phase, costs are typically assumed to be accurate as stated.

Although popular when shopping for major system items, starting with a hard budget limit and only examining potential alternatives that fall at or below this limit is another form of AFT that can over-restrict potential system solutions. Unless it is very clear that no wiggle room at all is available with regards to costs, screening out alternatives solely on the basis of cost is discouraged because the myriad of financial options available to stakeholders can quickly turn infeasible costs into feasible ones.

7.4   IMPROVING CANDIDATE ALTERNATIVES

The solution designer, armed with a list of feasible alternatives, must choose which of them to present to the decision maker for action. This choice is based on both qualitative and quantitative measures so that only the best alternatives make the cut to become final *solution candidates*—the best the solution design team can offer. Key tools at this stage are the models and simulations described in Chapter 3 and a deliberate experimental design strategy for analyzing alternatives.

Models have been used both directly and indirectly throughout the problem-solving process. Early in the problem definition stage, key stakeholder values were assembled into a value model that identified five key aspects of value:

1. Why is the decision being made (the fundamental objective)?
2. What has a value (functions and objectives)?
3. Where are objectives achieved?
4. When can objectives be achieved?
5. How much value is attained (the value function)?

The value modeling process identified many of the fundamental requirements used during feasibility screening. It continues to be used during this phase to assess the value of each feasible alternative as solution candidates emerge.

Feasible alternatives must also be evaluated using mathematical, physical, or event models developed for the system and assessed using measures of effectiveness or performance, as described in Chapter 3.

Complex systems with no closed-form solution or that have many interactive variables that change during operation often require simulations to generate effectiveness or performance values. As noted in Chapter 3, a simulation is a model of a system's operation over time.

Models and simulations provide solution designers and decision makers with insights into possible futures of a system given specific conditions. It is important that these conditions are well defined to support the study and its outcomes. In its Defense Acquisition Guidebook [29], the DOD's Defense Acquisition University recommends that modeling and simulation analyses specify the following at the beginning of any study:

- *Ground rules* that include operational scenarios, threats, environment, constraints, and assumptions.
- *Alternative descriptions*, including operations and support concepts.

- *Effectiveness measures* that show how alternatives will be evaluated.
- *Effectiveness analysis*, including methodology, models, simulations, data, and sensitivity analysis.
- *Cost analysis*, including the life cycle cost methodology, models and data, cost sensitivity, and risk analysis.

CMS Solution Design.

For the solution design phase for the CMS project, the system designers had to scan the environment for potential IT solutions for the problem identified in the previous chapter. On the basis of the unique constraints and challenges identified, they had to come up with a feasible subset of IT solutions that could be expected to solve the problem. This is truly a value-focused approach because they have defined a broad set of value-added functions that the system could support with limited understanding of the alternatives' abilities to achieve that functionality. They are asking the question, "What do we want the system to do?" as opposed to asking, "Which of these predefined alternatives helps us most?" With this approach, they are more likely to identify opportunities to improve curriculum management functions.

Once they had scanned the IT environment for potential software and development solutions, the team formulated the problem as a sequence of interrelated decisions. For this reason, they used Zwicky's morphological box shown in Figure 7.10 to represent these alternatives. Each column of the box represented one of the development decisions for the design team. The options for each decision are represented in the rows.

Although this box gives a possibility of 54 ($3 \times 2 \times 3 \times 3$) alternatives, system and administrative dependencies reduced this significantly. Other possible combinations that would form alternatives were not feasible or clearly inferior with no analysis required. The design team reduced the alternatives to a feasible set of five for which they would conduct additional analysis.

1. *Improve the existing system.* Department IT personnel work with department leadership to develop a set of structured templates, storage folders, and processes to be applied to the current system of curriculum management. This alternative does not require significant IT development. Instead it seeks to identify, standardize, and enforce best practices employed in the current system.

2. *Develop the system under external contract.* The department hires an external contractor to develop an enterprise-wide system using database and interface solutions determined by the contractor and approved by the department. This outsourcing approach removes the development load from the department's IT staff, but requires significant external coordination with a contractor who may not understand department processes.

3. *Develop web-data application.* Department IT personnel, supported when possible by capstone students (undergraduate students doing a two semester team research project), develop a web-data application to handle the curriculum management functions. They do this using Vendor A, web services, and a service-oriented architecture to maximize usability of services and integration with existing systems. This alternative provides excellent opportunities for flexibility and customization, but it places a heavy burden on the department IT staff.

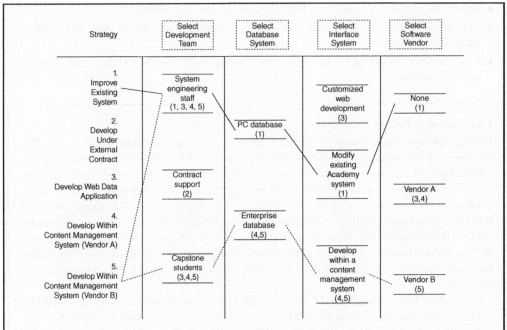

Figure 7.10 CMS morphology box application.

4. *Develop within a content management system (Vendor A).* Department IT person-nel, supported when possible by capstone students, performs development within the framework of a content management system from vendor A to integrate structured curriculum data into the portal. With this alternative, the content management system provides a significant portion of the required capabilities with limited or no develop-ment required. It does have some additional cost.

5. *Develop within a content management system (Vendor B).* This alternative is distin-guished from the previous one by a different vendor for the content management system. Vendor B's system has different functionality and cost. Given these alterna-tives, the design team must score each alternative against the value measures using a tradespace analysis approach discussed in Chapter 9.

Because this is a system concept decision, the team did not have sufficient design data to accomplish modeling and analysis of the alternatives. For supporting this systems decision, it was sufficient to research each alternative to subjectively assess the objectives in the values hierarchy.

7.4.1 Design of Experiments

Having identified alternatives that meet stakeholders' needs, wants, and desires, the solution design team must develop a plan for getting the most information about the operation of those alternatives with the least amount of effort. A mathematical process for accomplishing this is the *Design of Experiments* (DOEs), developed in the 1920s and 1930s by Ronald A. Fisher [30], a mathematician who worked at the Rothamsted Agricultural Experimentation Station, north of London (after whom the statistical *F-test* was named), wanted to understand the effects of fertilizer, soil, irrigation, and environment on the growth of grain. His technique, published in 1936, examined the main and interaction effects of key variables (factors) in a system design. The development of Fisher's process is chronicled in *Lady Tasting Tea: How Statistics Revolutionized Science in the Twentieth Century* [31].

Concepts. DOE provides solution designers with a way to simultaneously study the individual and interactive effects of many factors, thus keeping the number of experiment iterations (replications) to a minimum. The basic question addressed by DOE is, "What is the average outcome (effect) when a factor is moved from a low level to a higher level?" Since more than one factor is at play in a complex system, efficiencies can be gained by moving combinations of factors simultaneously.

Consider an experiment for the new rocket design developed in this text. The solution design team may have initially determined that the key factors are engine thrust and number of stabilizing fins. They also determined the constraints for each factor: the engine thrust must fall between 1000 and 3000 lb at launch, and competing concepts call for 3- and 5-fin designs. The primary measure of effectiveness is "distance from target impact point."

In this design, the two factors, *A* and *B*, are shown with both low (−) and high (+) levels, representing the upper and lower bounds on the constraints (Figure 7.11). Four conditions are possible in this design: point *a*, where both *A* and *B* are at their lower levels; point *b*, where *A* is low and *B* is high; point *c*, where both *A* and *B* are high; and *d*, where *A* is high and *B* is low. Table 7.4 shows

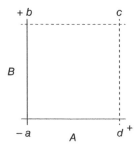

Figure 7.11   Two-factor, two-level design.

TABLE 7.4   A 2 × 2 Design Matrix.

Design Point	Factor 1	Factor 2	Response
1	−	−	R_1
2	+	−	R_2
3	−	+	R_3
4	+	+	R_4

a design in which each of these points can be tested. Experiments designed this way are called 2^k *factorial designs*, since they are based on factors and each factor has two possible levels. The k exponent refers to the number of factors being considered—in this case, two. This way of looking at designs tells the experimenter how many possible states—or design points—exist, and also lays the groundwork for determining the main and interactive effects of combining the factors.

The order in which the table is constructed is important for subsequent calculations. Notice that the column labeled Factor 1 alternates between − and +. This will always be the case, no matter how many design points there are. The second column, labeled in this case Factor 2, will always alternate between two minuses, followed by two pluses. Note that this is because the design moves one factor from its low to its high point while holding other factors constant.

Calculating Main and Two-Way Interaction Effects.   The *main effect* of a factor is the *average change in the response* (the performance measure) that results from moving a factor from its − to its + level, while holding all other factors fixed.

This is the effect that a particular factor has, without regard for possible interactions with other factors. In a 2^2 factorial design, this is calculated using Equation (7.1) for Factor 1 (e_1).

$$e_1 = \frac{(R_2 - R_1) + (R_4 - R_3)}{2} \tag{7.1}$$

Figure 7.12 shows the relationship between Table 7.4 and Equation (6.1).

Some designers prefer to use capital letters of the alphabet to label factors, while others use numbers. When letters are used, the *effect* nomenclature is the lower-case equivalent of the factor letter. So, the main effect for Factor A would be written e_a.

Assume that tests were run on the experimental rocket design and yielded the results shown in Table 7.5. These results show the distance, in meters, from the desired and actual impact points

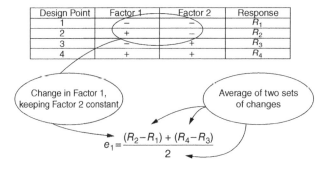

Figure 7.12   Calculating main effects.

TABLE 7.5   Rocket Example Initial Test Results.

Design Point	Factor 1	Factor 2	Response
1	−	−	13.6
2	+	−	13.0
3	−	+	17.6
4	+	+	14.8

for rockets built using the given constraints. Using Equation (6.1), the main effects of this rocket design can be calculated as follows:

$$e_1 = \frac{(13.0 - 13.6) + (14.8 - 17.6)}{2} = -1.7 \tag{7.2}$$

$$e_2 = \frac{(17.6 - 13.6) + (14.8 - 13.0)}{2} = 2.9 \tag{7.3}$$

This means that by changing from a 3- to 5-fin design and holding thrust constant, there should be an average decrease in error of 1.7 m. Increasing thrust alone should result in an average increase in error of 2.9 m. In the equation for e_2, the response for DP 3 is subtracted from that of DP 1, and DP 4 is subtracted from DP 2 before the sum is averaged.

A shortcut that achieves the same mathematical result is to apply the signs of the factor column to the corresponding result (R), sum them, then divide by 2^{k-1}, as shown in Equation (6.4) for calculating the main effect of Factor 2 (e_2).

$$e_2 = \frac{-R_1 - R_2 + R_3 + R_4}{2} \tag{7.4}$$

This method provides a simpler approach for achieving the same result, as shown next:

$$e_1 = \frac{-13.6 + 13.0 - 17.6 + 14.8}{2} = -1.7 \tag{7.5}$$

$$e_2 = \frac{-13.6 - 13.0 + 17.6 + 14.8}{2} = 2.9 \tag{7.6}$$

A strength of DOE is that it also allows the solution design team to understand the *interaction effects* between factors. These effects show the synergistic relationships between factors by measuring how the effect of one factor may depend on the level of another. It is defined as follows:

The two-way *interaction effect* of a two-level design is half the difference between the average effects of Factor 1 when Factor 2 is at its + level and when it is at its − level. All other factors are held constant.

A design matrix with interaction effects is created by adding an interaction column to the standard design. The "sign" values for this column are determined by multiplying the signs of the factors of interest. A matrix for the rocket example that includes the interactions of Factors 1 and 2 (labeled e_{12}) is shown in Table 7.6.

If letters are used to indicate factors, the interaction effect of AB would be written as e_{ab}. Using the definition for interaction effects, the equation for two-way interactions becomes

$$e_{12} = \frac{1}{2}[(R_4 - R_3) - (R_2 - R_1)] \tag{7.7}$$

$$e_{12} = \frac{1}{2}[(14.8 - 17.6) - (13.0 - 13.6)] = -1.1 \tag{7.8}$$

TABLE 7.6   DOE Matrix with Interactions.

Design Point	Factor 1	Factor 2	1 × 2	Response
1	−	−	+	13.6
2	+	−	−	13.0
3	−	+	−	17.6
4	+	+	+	14.8

This tells the solution designer that by combining both *treatments*, the overall effect is that the rocket hits 1.1 m closer to the aim point than without the higher level alternatives. Following the shortcut logic described earlier, the same result can be found by multiplying the signs of the inter-action column (1 × 2) by the response, as shown next:

$$e_{12} = \frac{R_1 - R_2 - R_3 + R_4}{2} \tag{7.9}$$

$$e_{12} = \frac{13.6 - 13.0 - 17.6 + 14.8}{2} = -1.1 \tag{7.10}$$

Designs with More Than Two Factors.   It is rare for complex systems to be dominated by only two factors. The solution designer must carefully balance the complexity of the design with an ability to find meaningful results. The earlier design could be represented as a two-dimensional square with four corners (design points). The addition of a third factor changes the design from a square to a cube, with 2^3, or eight design points, shown in Figure 7.13. The addition of Factor C results in the 2^k factorial design with eight design points shown in Table 7.7. Notice that the repetition of minuses and pluses for Factors 1 and 2 follows a similar pattern as with a 2^2 design. If there were four factors, the pattern of Factor 3 would repeat to fill the 2^4 (16) design points, and Factor 4 would have a series of eight minuses, followed by eight pluses, and so on for however many factors that are being considered.

Determining the main and interaction effects of 2^3 designs follows the same logic as for the 2^2 design, although the complexity of the non-shortcut method increases significantly. The two methods for calculating the main effect of Factor 1 described earlier are expanded next to consider

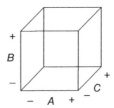

Figure 7.13   Three-factor, two-level design.

TABLE 7.7   2 × 3 Design Matrix.

Design Point	Factor 1	Factor 2	Factor 3	Response
1	−	−	−	R_1
2	+	−	−	R_2
3	−	+	−	R_3
4	+	+	−	R_4
5	−	−	+	R_5
6	+	−	+	R_6
7	−	+	+	R_7
8	+	+	+	R_8

three factors.

$$e_1 = \frac{(R_2 - R_1) + (R_4 - R_3) + (R_6 - R_5) + (R_8 - R_7)}{4} \tag{7.11}$$

$$e_1 = \frac{-R_1 + R_2 - R_3 + R_4 - R_5 + R_6 - R_7 + R_8}{4} \tag{7.12}$$

Notice that the denominator is now four, reflecting the four comparisons in the numerator. As before, this value will always be 2^{k-1} for full factorial designs.

When more than three factors are considered, the geometry of the design gets more complex, with the three-way cube becoming part of a larger shape known as hypercube. A four-factor design, for example, can be viewed as two cubes at either end of a line having minus and plus ends that provide for the 16 design points, as shown in Figure 7.14. All 16 design points have unique locations in this geometry. For example, the lower right corner of the right cube has these signs: A = +, B = −, C = −, D = +. Similarly, a 2^5 hypercube design has 32 design points and would appear to have cubes on the corners of a 2^2 (square) design.

Blocking and Randomization. A major concern facing solution designers as they consider their strategic approach is that of controllable and uncontrollable factors. This is more of a problem in physical experiments than in simulation-based experiments, where all factors are controllable. Physical experiments generally have an initialization period before reaching a steady operational state. Likewise, samples taken from different lots may show significant variation not found within a lot. Two methods for managing these variations are *blocking and randomization*.

A *block* is a portion of the experimental material that is expected to be more homogeneous than the aggregate [32]. Blocking takes known, unavoidable sources of variation out of the design picture. For example, a situation in which conditions are expected to be the same at a given time of day could be blocked on time-of-day, taking that out of the analysis. Another example might be an experiment comparing hand–eye coordination between dominant and non-dominant hands. An approach that focused on blocking on people would select 100 people at random, have each one throw 10 darts at a target using the right hand and 10 with the left. Then compare the difference in results for each person, thus taking individual skill, ability, and similar person-specific variables out of the mix. The result is an experiment isolated on the test issue and avoiding influence by *noise* factors. By confining treatment comparisons with such blocks, say Box, Hunter, and Hunter [32], greater precision can often be obtained.

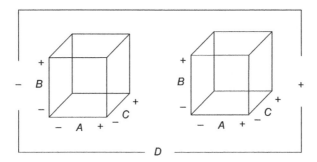

Figure 7.14 Geometry for a 2^4 factorial design.

The sequence in which trials are run within an experiment must also be planned by the systems solution design team. A single trial of an experiment that contains random variables is not sufficient to base findings upon. Concluding that a coin-flip will always result in "heads" based on a single flip (trial) is not supportable. The general rule in DOEs to "Block what you can and randomize what you cannot," [32] is a useful mantra for the solution designer.

7.4.2 Fractional Factorial Design

Factorial techniques explored so far are reliable ways to identify all main and interaction effects in solution designs when the number of factors is small. But even with increasing computing speed, designs quickly become unmanageable as the number of factors grows. A 2^5 design, for example, has 32 design points, while a 2^7 design has 128. It is not uncommon for designs to be affected by 15 or more factors, which would require 32,768 or more design points. Designs with random variables further increase complexity since they require multiple replications to determine central tendencies. A two-level design with 15 factors, with each design point requiring 10 replications, would require 327,680 separate iterations. Some designers use the terms *replications, runs, and design points* interchangeably. Care must be taken to differentiate between single design points, as used here, and *iterations*, which denote multiple trials to account for randomness.

Fractional factorial designs present two useful solutions to the problem of scale. First, they allow designers to achieve nearly the same results with a fraction of the effort, and second, they provide designers with a tool to further screen out factors that do not make a significant contribution to the outcome.

Fractional designs provide similar results as from a 2^k design, but with 2^{k-p} design points, where p determines what fraction of the total design will be used. We have seen that a full three-factor design requires $2^3 = 8$ design points. If p is set to 1, half as many design points are required, since $2^{3-1} = 4$. This is known as a half-fraction design. A p of 2 produces a quarter-fraction design that would require only a quarter as many design points to achieve nearly the same result.

Having fewer design points comes with a cost: precision is increasingly lost as the fraction increases. Solution designers must be aware of these trade-offs and balance the loss of precision with savings in resources (time, material, etc.).

Consider the full factorial design with two levels and four factors shown in Table 7.8. There is 1 mean effect, 4 main effects, 6 two-way effects, 4 three-way effects, and 1 four-way effect, for a total of 16 design points.

A half-fraction factorial design promises to provide nearly the same outcome with half as many design points. To do this, start with a full factorial design with $2^{k-p} = 2^{4-1} = 2^3 = 8$ design points, as shown in Table 7.9. Provide for the fourth factor by multiplying the signs of 1, 2, and 3.

The half-fraction matrix directly accounts for 8 of the 16 original effects: 1 mean effect (no contrast between design points—all values are minus), 4 main effects, and 3 two-way interaction effects. The missing effects—three two-way, four three-way, and one four-way—can be found by examining them separately, shown in Table 7.10.

Notice the relationships of the signs in the factor columns. The sequence for Factor 14 (shorthand for 1×4) is the same as that for 23 in Table 7.9. Comparing all the columns provides the data for Figure 7.15. A striking observation in Figure 7.15 is that every effect involving Factor 4 is algebraically the same as another effect not using Factor 4. These identical terms are said to be *aliases* of each other. They are also described as being *confounded* by one another, since the effect is calculated exactly the same way and therefore it is impossible to know which effect is producing the result. Notice that Figure 7.15 now accounts for all 16 main and interaction effects.

TABLE 7.8 Full 2^4 Factorial Design.

	1	2	3	4	12	13	14	23	24	34	123	124	134	234	1234
DP1	−	−	−	−	+	+	+	+	+	+	−	−	−	−	+
DP2	+	−	−	−	−	−	−	+	+	+	+	+	+	−	−
DP3	−	+	−	−	−	+	+	−	−	+	+	+	−	+	−
DP4	+	+	−	−	+	−	−	−	−	+	−	−	+	−	+
DP5	−	−	+	−	+	−	+	−	+	−	−	−	+	+	+
DP6	+	−	+	−	−	+	−	−	+	−	+	−	+	+	−
DP7	−	+	+	−	−	−	+	+	−	−	−	+	−	+	+
DP8	+	+	+	−	+	+	−	+	−	−	−	+	+	−	+
DP9	−	−	−	+	+	+	−	+	−	−	+	−	−	−	−
DP10	+	−	−	+	−	−	+	+	−	−	−	+	+	+	−
DP11	−	+	−	+	−	+	−	−	+	−	+	−	−	+	+
DP12	+	+	−	+	+	−	+	−	+	−	+	−	+	−	+
DP13	−	−	+	+	+	−	−	−	−	+	−	+	−	−	−
DP14	+	−	+	+	−	+	+	−	−	+	−	−	+	−	−
DP15	−	+	+	+	−	−	−	+	+	+	−	−	−	+	−
DP16	+	+	+	+	+	+	+	+	+	+	+	+	+	+	+

TABLE 7.9 2^{4-1} Design Matrix.

	1	2	3	4(123)	12	13	23
DP1	−	−	−	−	+	+	+
DP2	+	−	−	+	−	−	+
DP3	−	+	−	+	−	+	−
DP4	+	+	−	−	+	−	−
DP5	−	−	+	+	+	−	−
DP6	+	−	+	−	−	+	−
DP7	−	+	+	−	−	−	+
DP8	+	+	+	+	+	+	+

TABLE 7.10 The Lost 2^4 Effects.

	14	24	34	123	124	134	134	1234
DP1	+	+	+	−	−	−	−	+
DP2	+	−	−	+	−	−	+	+
DP3	−	+	−	+	−	+	−	+
DP4	−	−	+	−	−	+	+	+
DP5	−	−	+	+	+	−	−	+
DP6	−	+	−	−	+	−	+	+
DP7	+	−	−	−	+	+	−	+
DP8	+	+	+	+	+	+	+	+

	1	2	3	4	12	13	23	14	24	34	123	124	134	234	1234
DP1	−	−	−	−	+	+	+	+	+	+	−	−	−	−	+
DP2	+	−	−	+	−	−	+	+	−	−	+	−	−	+	+
DP3	−	+	−	+	−	+	−	−	+	−	+	−	+	−	+
DP4	+	+	−	−	+	−	−	−	−	+	−	−	+	+	+
DP5	−	−	+	+	+	−	−	−	−	+	+	+	−	−	+
DP6	+	−	+	−	−	+	−	−	+	−	−	+	−	+	+
DP7	−	+	+	−	−	−	+	+	−	−	−	+	+	−	+
DP8	+	+	+	+	+	+	+	+	+	+	+	+	+	+	+

Figure 7.15   Fully expanded 2^{4-1} matrix.

This suggests that the same result should be found using a 2^{4-1} design as with a full 2^4. This relies on the *sparsity of effects* assumption that states that if an outcome is possible from several events, the less complex event is most likely the cause. So, if faced with two identical outcomes, one resulting from a single main effect and one resulting from the interaction of several effects, this assumption claims that the single main effect is most likely the cause and the complex effect can be ignored. This assumption, though convenient, is a source of loss of precision and must be used with caution.

Another observation from Figure 7.15 is that the interaction effect 1234 is composed of all plus signs. Comparing this table with Table 7.8, it becomes apparent that the fractional matrix is identical to the full matrix design points 1, 10, 11, 4, 13, 6, 7, and 16. The annotated hypercube in Figure 7.16 confirms that the fractional design symmetrically targets half of the possible points of a full design. The corners not selected in Figure 7.16 represent the half fraction where factor 1234 is a column of all minus signs. Either half could be used, although the one shown uses the principal fraction (all pluses) and is most common. The column with all plus signs is also known as the *identity* column, and it has a number of unique attributes. Most obvious, it is the only column that does not have an equal number of plus and minus signs. But more importantly, it reflects the fact that any sign multiplied by itself results in a positive value. In the fractional design earlier, Factor 4 was determined by multiplying Factors 1, 2, and 3. Therefore, 4 = 123, which produced the identity column *I*, which equals 1234, or *I* = 1234. This is called the *design generator*, because it can be

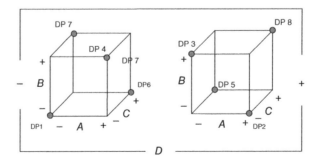

Figure 7.16 2^{4-1} design plot (principle fraction).

used to generate the entire aliasing structure for the design, eliminating the need for pattern-match tables of pluses and minuses.

To find the alias for a factor, simply multiply the factor times I. Finding the alias for Factor 2 in the previous design, for example, is accomplished as shown in the following steps:

- *Step 1.* $I = 1234$, establish the design generator
- *Step 2.* $I = 2 \times 2$
- *Step 3.* $2I = (2)1234$
- *Step 4.* $2(2 \times 2) = (2 \times 2)134$
- *Step 5.* $2 = 134$, which is verified in Figure 7.15.

A simplified rule of thumb for finding aliases is to drop the column in question from the *generating relation*. Therefore, in this example, $1 = 234$; $2 = 134$; $3 = 124$; $12 = 34$; and so forth. Higher order fractions (quarter, eighth, etc.) have more than one generator, but the fundamental process is the same.

Calculating main and interaction effects in fractional factorial designs is accomplished in the same way as with full factorial designs, except that the denominator is 2^{k-p-1} instead of 2^{k-1}. The main effect of Factor 1 for the half-fraction design shown earlier is developed in Equation (11.14).

$$e_1 = \frac{-R_1 + R_2 - R_3 + R_4 - R_5 + R_6 - R_7 + R_8}{2^{4-1-1}} \tag{7.13}$$

$$= \frac{-R_1 + R_2 - R_3 + R_4 - R_5 + R_6 - R_7 + R_8}{2^4} \tag{7.14}$$

Given a choice of conducting a full factorial experiment with many design points or a fractional design with many fewer, why would a solution designer consider anything but the one with the fewest? The answer is in the balancing of resources available and the loss of precision inherent in fractional designs. The key to achieving that balance lies in the concept of *design resolution*.

Definition: Design resolution is a measure of the degree of confounding that exists in a fractional factorial design.

Generally, and with notable exceptions, the highest resolution design the experimenter can afford to conduct is the preferred choice. Screening designs, discussed later, are the main exceptions to the rule.

The level of resolution is shown using roman numerals to distinguish it from other numbers in the design notation. The numeral indicates the level at which fractional designs are clear of confounding. Two effects are not confounded if the sum of their *ways* is less than the resolution of the design. Main effects are considered one-way effects, while interaction effects such as 12 and 34 are two-way, 134 and 234 are three-way, and so on. In a resolution IV design, no main effects are aliased with any two-way effect ($1 + 2 < 4$), but two-way effects are aliased with other two-way or higher order effects. ($2 + 2$ or more < 4).

Knowing that higher resolution designs have less confounding and therefore less precision loss, yet will require more design points, the solution designer can balance available resources against precision in constructing an experimental design. It is also important that the designer indicate this trade-off in discussing the design. The notation for fractional factorial designs is shown in Figure 7.17.

Tables for quickly determining which designs best meet the resolution criteria exist in much of the DOE literature, including *Statistics for Experimenters* [32] and *Simulation Modeling and*

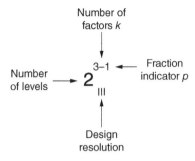

Figure 7.17   Fractional factorial design notation.

TABLE 7.11   Confounding in Fractional Factorial Design.

	Resolution		
k	III	IV	V
3	$2^{3-1}_{\text{III}} \rightarrow 3 = \pm 12$		
4		$2^{4-1}_{\text{IV}} \rightarrow 4 = \pm 123$	
5	$2^{5-2}_{\text{III}} \rightarrow 4 = \pm 12$ $5 = \pm 13$		$2^{5-1}_{\text{V}} \rightarrow 5 = \pm 1234$
6	$2^{6-3}_{\text{III}} \rightarrow 4 = \pm 12$ $5 = \pm 13$ $6 = \pm 23$	$2^{6-2}_{\text{IV}} \rightarrow 5 = \pm 123$ $6 = \pm 234$	
7	$2^{7-4}_{\text{III}} \rightarrow 4 = \pm 12$ $5 = \pm 13$ $6 = \pm 23$ $7 = \pm 123$	$2^{7-3}_{\text{IV}} \rightarrow 5 = \pm 123$ $6 = \pm 234$ $7 = \pm 134$	

Analysis [33]. The table of designs where $k \leq 7$, shown in Table 7.11, illustrates how greater confounding occurs at lower resolutions.

Lower resolution designs are particularly useful as *screening designs* to eliminate factors that do not contribute significantly to the system's operation. Caution and experience are necessary to prevent too low of a resolution from being selected and a resulting greater loss of precision leading to faulty conclusions.

While feasibility screening, described in Section 7.3, provides a *criteria-based* tool for narrowing alternatives, factorial screening provides a merit-based tool to further refine the solution space. Revisiting the rocket scenario described earlier, the solution designers' feasibility screening matrix shows that five factors pass the initial test, as shown in Table 7.12.

A full factorial design is developed and tested, with the response being a score of 0–100 where 100 is a bull's-eye target hit. The results are shown in Table 7.13.

Several statistical software packages, such as Minitab®, allow solution designers to construct and analyze factorial designs. Analysis of the responses reveals that only the *seeker type, guidance system*, and *thrust* main effects and the interactions of *seeker-guidance* and *guidance-thrust* have a statistically significant effect on system performance, given an alpha value of 0.05.

TABLE 7.12   Modified Rocket Design Factors.

Factor	Name	Low (−)	High (+)
1	Skin composition	Aluminum	Composite
2	Seeker	Forward-looking infrared	Laser guided
3	Fins	3	5
4	Guidance	Inertial navigation	Global positioning system
5	Thrust	1000 lb	3000 lb

TABLE 7.13   Rocket Design Test Results.

$R_1 = 61$	$R_2 = 53$	$R_3 = 63$	$R_4 = 61$
$R_5 = 53$	$R_6 = 56$	$R_7 = 54$	$R_8 = 61$
$R_9 = 69$	$R_{10} = 61$	$R_{11} = 94$	$R_{12} = 93$
$R_{13} = 66$	$R_{14} = 60$	$R_{15} = 95$	$R_{16} = 98$
$R_{21} = 59$	$R_{22} = 55$	$R_{23} = 67$	$R_{24} = 65$
$R_{25} = 44$	$R_{26} = 45$	$R_{27} = 78$	$R_{28} = 77$
$R_{29} = 49$	$R_{30} = 42$	$R_{31} = 81$	$R_{32} = 82$

Skin type and *number of fins* did not make a significant difference in rocket performance, as seen in the Minitab chart shown in Figure 7.18. The vertical line at 3.12 on the horizontal axis indicates the threshold for significance.

A 2_V^{5-1} design should produce essentially the same findings, but with half the physical testing and the associated time and material costs required by the full factorial experiment. Figure 7.19 shows the Minitab results. Once again, *seeker, guidance*, and *thrust* main effects and *seeker-guidance* and

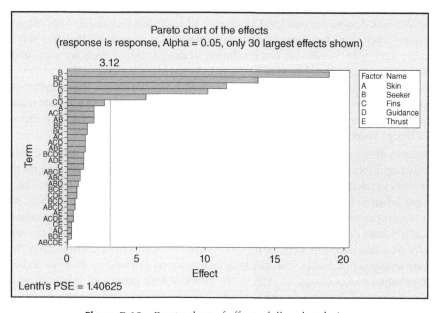

Figure 7.18   Pareto chart of effects, full rocket design.

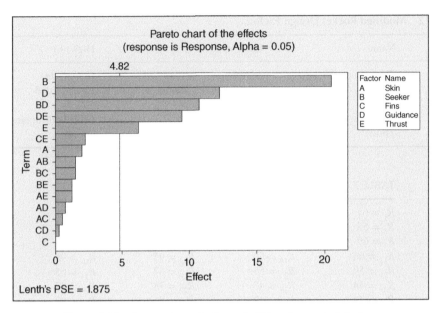

Figure 7.19   Pareto chart of effects, half-fraction rocket design.

guidance-thrust interaction effects are shown to be significant. *Skin type* and *number of fins* could be screened out of the design based on the rocket performance.

Other Design Strategies.   Full and fractional factorial designs as described earlier are common, general-purpose approaches to experimental design. However, many others are available to the solution designer, each designed to meet unique situations that may be encountered.

Plackett–Burman designs are two-level, resolution III fractional factorial designs often used for screening when there is a large number of factors and it is assumed that two-way interactions are negligible. Recall that in a resolution III design, main effects are confounded with two-way interactions ($1 + 2 \geq 3$). Introduced in 1946 [34], it is based on the number of design points being a multiple of 4 instead of a power of 2, as seen earlier. The number of factors must be less than the number of design points, so a 20 DP design can estimate main effects for up to 19 factors. In general, these designs will estimate main effects for n factors using $n + 1$ design points, rounded up to the nearest multiple of four.

Latin squares designs are used when there are more than two factors and there are assumed to be only negligible interaction effects. They are an offshoot of magic square designs that trace their roots to ancient Asia, and are the source of the popular Sudoku puzzles. The concept was published in Europe in 1782 by Leonhard Euler [35], and involved a square matrix of n-by-n cells containing n symbols, each of which occurs only once in each row and column. In Latin Square designs, one factor, or treatment, is of primary interest and the remaining factors are considered blocking, or nuisance, factors. Treatments are given Latin characters and are arranged in a matrix. The blocking factors are represented by the rows and columns. A modified rocket design to explore the effect of four propellant mixtures on thrust is shown in Figure 7.20. This design is blocked on two factors: seeker and guidance system. It is recognized that slight variations may exists between individual components, and this

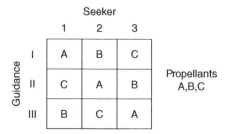

Figure 7.20   Latin Square rocket design focused on thrust.

TABLE 7.14   Three-level Latin Square Matrix.

DP	Row Blocking Factor	Column Blocking Factor	Treatment Factor
1	1	1	1
2	1	2	2
3	1	3	3
4	2	1	3
5	2	2	1
6	2	3	2
7	3	1	2
8	3	2	3
9	3	3	1

design will eliminate seeker-to-seeker and guidance-to-guidance differences to get a truer understanding of the primary effect being considered.

Table 7.14 shows the general matrix for a three-level Latin Square design that illustrates how this results in n^2 design points. The same approach is used for designs with more levels. The fundamental model for Latin Square and related designs follows the form where Y is the observation, η is the mean, R_i is the row effect, C_j is the column effect, T_k is the treatment effect, and ϵ_{ijk} is random error.

$$T_{ijk} = \eta + R_i + C_j + T_k + \epsilon_{ijk} \tag{7.15}$$

Graeco-Latin and Hyper-Graeco-Latin square designs are extensions of the Latin Square method for studying more than one treatment simultaneously. Graeco-Latin squares, also introduced by Euler, are constructed by superimposing two Latin Square designs into one matrix and differentiating them by using Greek letters for one of the treatments. This design uses three blocking factors, instead of two. A Hyper-Graeco-Latin Square design considers more than three blocking variables. A Graeco-Latin Square design for a rocket system experiment conducted over three days, the new blocking factor, is shown in Figure 7.21.

Response surface method (RSM) designs are used to examine the relationship between a response variable and one or more factors, especially when there is *curvature* between a factor's low and high values, which has been assumed to not exist in designs so far. The full and fractional factorial designs described earlier were assumed to follow a straight line between values. RSM designs reveal the *shape* of a response surface, and are useful in finding *satisficing* or *optimal* process settings as well as weak points.

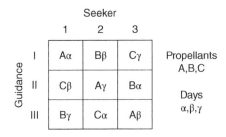

Figure 7.21 Graeco Latin rocket design.

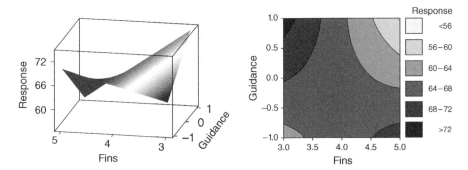

Figure 7.22 Response surface plots of the rocket design.

Figure 7.22, extracted from a Minitab run of the full factorial design responses from the rocket design, clearly shows a nonlinear relationship between the number of fins and the choice of guidance system. Both plots show the greatest response from the increase in guidance system technology, which is consistent with the Pareto analysis shown in Figures 7.18 and 7.19. What is particularly revealing in both the *surface plot* on the left and the *contour plot* on the right, however, are the spikes in responses when the number of fins is at low and high points. This suggests that if, for example, the higher technology guidance system is not available or is too expensive, the rocket should achieve better results with a 5-fin design than something less. Clearly, considering these interactions alone, a 4-fin design is least desirable using either guidance systems.

Other design techniques have been developed and are in use by solution designers. Though not as universally adopted as the techniques described earlier, these methods include modified factorial designs proposed by Taguchi in *System of Experimental Design* [36] and variations on Latin hypercubes, including nearly orthogonal designs by Cioppa [37].

7.4.3 Pareto Analysis

Pareto analysis further reduces the complexity of the solution space by critically examining factors that make up a solution and eliminating those that fail to make a meaningful contribution. It continues the drive to condense the problem to only the most essential factors.

The Pareto principle, also known as the *sparsity principle*, the *law of the vital few*, and the *80-20 rule*, was coined by quality management expert Joseph M. Juran in the 1951 edition of his *Quality Control Handbook* [38]. In a 1975 explanation described in *The Non-Pareto Principle; Mea Culpa* [39], Juran traces how in the 1930s he came to understand that a small number of factors usually make the greatest contribution to the whole. He confesses that he simply extended Italian economist Vilfredo Pareto's concepts on the unequal distribution of wealth beyond their intended scope described in *Cours d'économie politique* [40]. In it, Pareto noted that 80% of the wealth was owned by 20% of the people. Juran noticed that this ratio held true for many quality issues and used the term *Pareto principle* to describe his concept of the vital few and trivial many. Pareto analysis, regardless of the accuracy of the name, is now widely used to separate the *vital few* from the *trivial many* in many different applications. Common Pareto analyses use a combination of bar and line charts to visually identify the vital few. Raw values are typically displayed in a bar chart sorted in decreasing order from left to right.

A secondary *y*-axis shows a cumulative distribution using a line chart. Figure 7.23 uses this approach to display the results of the full factorial rocket design. A key to interpreting this kind of Pareto chart is to look for a *knee of the curve* for the cumulative distribution function. Inspecting the cumulative distribution function leads to identifying a point (x^*, y^*) where the curve's direction is changing rapidly from large slopes to small slopes. This location x^* is inferred to be the point at which diminishing returns for effort or investment of resources begins. Factors prior to x^* on the steeper slope making a greater contribution to what is being portrayed in the graph. Visual inspection is typically sufficient to approximate the location of the knee of the curve on a Pareto cumulative distribution. If more exact specification is required, it is possible to calculate the value of x^* using the concept of curvature from calculus and differential geometry [41].

In Figure 7.23, the knee of the curve occurs at about the 70% point. If there is no distinct change in the slope of the line, a conservative approach is to consider factors that contribute 60% of the total. This reinforces Juran's confession that the 80-20 rule is more of a rule of thumb and should not be interpreted as an absolute metric. Table 7.15 summarizes the factors contributing to this point. Figure 7.23 is strong supporting evidence for screening out the trivial many factors in this solution design.

The Minitab charts in Figures 7.18 and 7.19 show another method for conducting a Pareto analysis, with main and interaction effects plotted in decreasing order and a vertical line marking the boundary of statistical significance. In this case, the vital few are those that exceed the threshold for significance. Note that this figure reveals an identical conclusion as Figure 7.23: the five factors named in Table 7.15 are the most important vital few factors in this design.

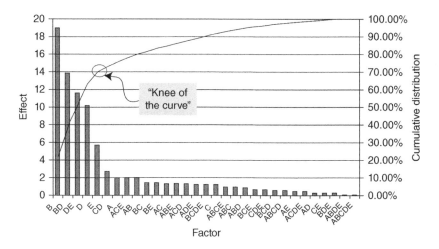

Figure 7.23 Pareto analysis of the rocket design experiment.

TABLE 7.15   The Vital Few Rocket Design Factors.

Factor	Factor name	Response	Total (%)	Cumulative (%)
B	Seeker	18.938	21.97	21.97
BD	Seeker* guidance	13.812	16.02	38.00
DE	Guidance* thrust	11.563	13.42	51.41
D	Guidance	10.187	11.82	63.23
E	Thrust	5.688	6.60	69.83

Pareto analysis can be used throughout the systems decision process whenever there is a large set of values to be prioritized. Other opportunities arise during brainstorming or stakeholder analysis, for example, to reduce the number of inputs to the vital few.

REFERENCES

1. Dalkey, N.C. (1969) *The Delphi Method: An Experimental Study of Group Opinion*. Santa Monica, CA: United States Air Force Project RAND.

2. Osborn, A.F. (1942) *How to Think UP*. New York: McGraw-Hill Publishing.

3. Osborn, A.F. (1948) *Your Creative Power: How to Use Imagination*. New York: Charles Scribner's & Sons.

4. Osborn, A.F. (1952) *Wake Up Your Mind: 101 Ways to Develop Creativeness*. New York: Charles Scribner's & Sons.

5. Osborn, A.F. (1953) *Applied Imagination: Principles and Procedures of Creative Thinking*. New York: Charles Scribner's & Sons.

6. Durfee, W.K. (1999) 'Brainstorming Basics,' ME 2011 Course Handout. Minneapolis, MN: University of Minnesota.

7. de Bono, E. (1992) *Serious Creativity: Using the Power of Lateral Thinking to Create New Ideas*. New York: Harper Business.

8. Isaksen, S.G. (1998) 'A review of brainstorming research: six critical issues for inquiry.' Monograph 302. Buffalo, NY: Creative Problem Solving Group.

9. Taylor, D.W., Berry, P.C., Block, C.H. (1958) 'Does group participation when using brainstorming facilitate or inhibit creative thinking?,' *Administrative Science Quarterly*, 3, pp. 22–47.

10. Sage, A.P., Armstrong, J.E. Jr. (2000) *Introduction to Systems Engineering*. New York: Wiley-Interscience.

11. Janis, I.L. (1983) *Groupthink: Psychological Studies of Policy Decisions and Fiascoes*, 2nd ed. Boston, MA: Houghton Mifflin.

12. Kelley, T., Kelley, D. (2013) *Creative Confidence*. New York: Currency.

13. Yoshida, T. (2018) *Try Design Thinking + Scrum: a powerful hybrid agile approach*. Available at: https://agile-od.com/. (Accessed 7 March 2022).

14. Dalkey, N., Helmer, O. (1963) 'An experimental application of the Delphi method to the use of experts,' *Management Science*, 9, pp. 458–467.

15. Girshick, M., Kaplan, A., Skogstad, A. (1950) 'The prediction of social and technological events,' *Public Opinion Quarterly*, 14, pp. 93–110.

16. Fowles, J., Fowles, R. (1978) *Handbook of Futures Research*. Westport, CT: Greenwood Press.

17. de Bono, E. (1967) *The Use of Lateral Thinking*. London, England: Jonathan Cape Ltd. Publishers.

18. de Bono, E. (1995) *Parallel Thinking*. New York: Penguin Press.

19. Zwicky, F. (1969) *Discovery, Invention, Research Through the Morphological Approach*. New York: MacMillan.

20. Keeney, R.L. (1992) *Value-Focused Thinking: A Path to Creative Decisionmaking*. Cambridge, MA: Harvard University Press.

21. Athey, T.H. (1982) *Systematic Systems Approach: An Integrated Method for Solving Problems*. Boston, MA: Pearson Custom Publishing.

22. MacCrimmon, K.R., Wagner, C. (1991) 'Supporting problem formulation and alternative generation in managerial decision making,' *Presented at 24th Annual Hawaii International Conference on System Sciences*, Honolulu, HI.

23. Singer, D.J., Doerry, N., Buckley, M.E. (2009) 'What is set-based design?,' *Naval Engineers Journal*, 121(4), pp. 31–43.

24. Sage, A.P. (1992) *Systems Engineering*. New York: John Wiley & Sons.

25. Nutt, P.C. (2001) 'A taxonomy of strategic decisions and tactics for uncovering alternatives,' *European Journal of Operational Research*, 132, pp. 505–527.

26. Chen, Y., Marc Kilgour, D., Hipel, K.W. (2008) 'Screening in multiple criteria decision analysis,' *Decision Support Systems*, 45(2), pp. 278–290.

27. Jahanshahloo, G.R., Lofti, F.H., Izadikhah, M. (2006) 'Extension of the TOPSIS method for decision-making problems with fuzzy data,' *Applied Mathematics and Computation*, 181, pp. 1544–1551.

28. Shahsavarani, A.M., Abadi, E.A.M. (2015) 'The bases, principles, and methods of decision-making: a review of literature,' *International Journal of Medical Reviews*, 2(1), pp. 214–225.

29. (2003) *Defense Acquisition Guidebook*. Fort Belvoir, VA: Defense Acquisition University. Available at: https://www.dau.edu/tools/dag.

30. Fisher, R.A. (1971) *The Design of Experiments*, 9th ed. New York: Haffner Press.

31. Salsburg, D. (2002) *Lady Tasting Tea: How Statistics Revolutionized Science in the Twentieth Century*. New York: Henry Holt and Company.

32. Box, G.E., Hunter, W.G., Hunter, J.S. (1978) *Statistics for Experimenters*. New York: John Wiley & Sons.

33. Law, A.M, Kelton, W.D. (2000) *Simulation Modeling and Analysis*. New York: McGraw-Hill.

34. Plackett, R.L., Burman, J.P. (1946) 'The design of optimum multi-factorial experiments,' *Biometrika*, 33, pp. 305–325.

35. Euler, L. (1782) 'Recherches sur une nouvelle espece de quarres magiques,' *Verhandelingen/ uitgegeven door het Zeeuwsch Genootschap der Wetenschappen te Vlissingen*, 9, pp. 85–239.

36. Taguchi, G. (1987) *System of Experimental Design*. Vols. 1 and 2. White Plains, NY: UNIPUB/Kraus International Publications.

37. Cioppa, T.M. (2002) 'Efficient nearly orthogonal and space-filling experimental designs for high-dimensional complex models,' Ph.D. Dissertation. Monterey, CA: Operations Research Department, Naval Postgraduate School.

38. Juran, J.M. (1951) *Quality Control Handbook*. New York: McGraw-Hill.

39. Juran, J.M. (1975) 'The non-Pareto principle; mea culpa,' *Quality Progress*, 8, pp. 8–9.

40. Pareto, V. (1896) *Le Cour d'Economie Politique*. London, England: Macmillan.

41. Thomas, C., Sheldon, B. (1999) 'The knee of a curve - useful clue but incomplete support,' *Military Operations Research*, 4(2), pp. 17–24.

Chapter **8**

Costing Systems

Creativity is great, but not in accounting.

—Charles Scott, American Football Player

8.1 INTRODUCTION

System elements include products (hardware, software, firmware), processes, people, information, techniques, facilities, services, and other support elements. As part of a system, these integrated elements have a system life cycle consisting of seven stages: establish system need, develop system concept, design and develop system, produce the system, deploy the system, operate the system, and retire the system. Throughout each of these seven stages various life cycle costs occur. Early stage costs involve a good deal of contracting, design activities, system demonstrations, laboratory and field-based prototype assessments, production costs, and other costs incurred getting the system ready to transition into deployment and use. Past that point, transportation, installation, field certification, operation and maintenance, security, repair, replacement, design modification, storage, shipping, disposal costs, and others dominate a system's cost profile.

Life cycle costing (LCC) is the best practice approach supporting all phases of system development. It is required for systems decision making. LCC is used by a systems engineering team to estimate whether a new system or a proposed system modifications will meet functional requirements at a reasonable total cost over the duration of its anticipated life. When successfully employed and managed, LCC is also a tool for systems decision making. Consequently, LCC is the process

Decision Making in Systems Engineering and Management, Third Edition.
Patrick J. Driscoll, Gregory S. Parnell, and Dale L. Henderson
© 2023 John Wiley & Sons, Inc. Published 2023 by John Wiley & Sons, Inc.

used within the systems decision process (SDP) for costing system alternatives in preparation for tradespace analysis and solution selection by a decision maker.

The Society of Cost Estimating and Analysis [1] defines a life cycle cost estimate in the following way:

> A life cycle cost estimate is an estimate that covers all of the cost projected for a system's life cycle, and which aids in the selection of a cost-effective total system design, by comparing costs of various trade-offs among design and support factors to determine their impact of total system acquisition and ownership costs.

The concept map in Figure 8.1 provides a pictorial overview of LCC. LCC centers around the development of a system cost estimate, which in conjunction with the schedules is used by a program manager to manage the system's acquisition, operation, or disposal. System design and operational concepts drive the key cost parameters, which in turn identify the data required for developing a system cost estimate. As part of a systems engineering or systems decision support team, cost analysts rely on historical data, subject matter experts (SMEs), system schedules, and budget quantities to provide data to use LCC techniques.

System risk depends on the life cycle stage of the system and this risk affects the key cost parameters that drive the system cost estimate. Cost estimating is a critical activity for successful public and private organizations. Cost estimates are required when developing a project budget for developing a new system, preparing bids on project proposals, negotiating a price for a system, and providing baselines from which to track and manage actual costs as a systems project progresses. In addition to threatening systems project success, major cost estimating errors can dramatically impact the credibility and long-term viability of the systems team and the organizations they represent.

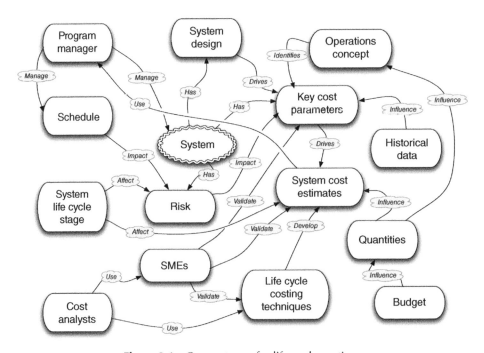

Figure 8.1   Concept map for life cycle costing.

Selecting the most appropriate LCC technique depends on the amount and type of available data and the perceived system risks that have been identified. As a system passes through each of its life cycle stages, more accurate information concerning system requirements, system design, system performance, and the environment surrounding the effort becomes available, and some dimensions of cost uncertainty are resolved. Therefore, which LCC technique is most useful depends on the stage of the system life cycle. Table 8.1 provides LCC technique recommendations along with suggested references for each technique.

Table 8.2 (Source: Adapted from [8]) shows the cost estimation classification system developed by the Association for the Advancement of Cost Engineering (AACE) International [10] generalized for applying estimate classification principles to system cost estimates. Under this classification system, the level of system definition is the primary characteristic for classifying cost estimates. Other secondary characteristics shown in include the estimate's end usage, the estimating methodology, the expected accuracy range, and effort to prepare the estimate.

Estimates are grouped into classes ranging from Class 1 to Class 5. Class 5 estimates are the least precise as they are based on the lowest level of system definition, while Class 1 estimates are the most precise being closest to full system definition and maturity. Successive estimates are prepared as the level of system definition increases until a final system cost estimate is developed.

The *level of system definition* provides ranges of typical completion percentages for systems within each class, which can provide information about the maturity and extent of available input data. The *end usage* describes the typical use of cost estimates generated at that level of system definition. Class 5 estimates are generally used only for system alternative low-level screening or feasibility analysis. The *methodology* contains the typical estimating methods that are employed to generate each class of estimate. The less knowledge is on-hand regarding the system, the more appropriate it is to provide a cost estimate range instead of a single number.

The *expected accuracy range* indicates the degree to which the final cost outcome for a given system is expected to vary from the estimated cost. The values in this column do not represent percentages as generally given for expected accuracy but instead represent an index value relative to a best range index value of 1. For example, if a given industry expects a Class 1 accuracy range of +15 to −10, then a Class 5 estimate with a relative index value of 10 would have an accuracy range of +150 to −100 percent. The final characteristic, *preparation effort* provides an indication of the cost, time, and other resources required to prepare a given estimate, which is again a relative index value.

Once definitions have been determined for all the cost elements forecasts to occur during a system's life cycle, the systems engineering team begins cost estimating—defined by Stewart, Wyskida, and Johannes [2] as "the process of predicting or forecasting the cost of a work activity or work output." This process is divided into 12 major steps discussed in more detail in the *Cost Estimator's Reference Manual* [2]. This manual is an excellent source for developing life cycle cost estimates. The book contains extensive discussions and numerous examples of how to develop a detailed life cycle cost estimate. The 12 steps are as follows:

1. Developing the work breakdown structure
2. Scheduling the work elements
3. Retrieving and organizing historical data
4. Developing and using cost estimating relationships
5. Developing and using production learning curves
6. Identifying skill categories, skill levels, and labor rates
7. Developing labor hour and material estimates

TABLE 8.1 LCC Techniques by Life Cycle Stage.

LCC techniques	Life cycle stages						
	Concept	Design	Development	Production	Deployment	Operation	Retirement
Expert judgment		Estimate by Analogy	Estimate by Analogy	Estimate by Analogy			
Cost Estimating Relationship [2]	Prepare Initial Cost Estimates	Refine Cost Estimates		Create Production Estimates			
Activity Based Costing [3]				Provides Indirect Product Costs		Use for Operational Trades	
Learning Curves [4, 5]			Provides Development and Test Unit Costs	Provide Direct Labor Production Costs			
Breakeven Analysis [6]			Use in Design Trades	Provides Production Quantities		Use for Operational Trades	
Uncertainty and Risk Analysis [7]	Use with CER Estimates	Use with Analogy or CER Estimates	Affects Development Cost	Affects Direct and Indirect Product Cost	Affects Deployment Schedules	Affects O&S Cost Projections	
Replacement Analysis [8]							Determines Retirement date

TABLE 8.2 AACE Cost Estimate Classification Matrix [9].

Primary characteristic		Secondary characteristic			
Estimate class	Level of System Definition expressed as % of complete definition	End Usage Typical Purpose of Estimate	Methodology Typical Estimating Method	Expected Accuracy Range Typical ± Range Relative to Best Index of 1a	Preparation Effort Typical degree of effort relative to least cost index of 1b
Class 5	0–2%	Screening or Feasibility	Stochastic or Judgmental	4–20	1
Class 4	1–15%	Concept Study or Feasibility	Primarily Stochastic	3–12	2–4
Class 3	10–40%	Budget authorization or control	Mixed but primarily stochastic	2–6	3–10
Class 2	30–70%	Control or Bid Tender	Primarily Deterministic	1–3	5–20
Class 1	50–100%	Check Estimate or Bid Tender	Deterministic	1	10–100

[a] If the range index value of "1" represents $+10 - 5\%$, then an index value of 10 represents $+100 - 50\%$.
[b] If the cost index value of "1" represents 0.005% of project costs, then an index value of 100 represents 0.5%.
Source: Origin Pro, OriginLab Corporation, Northampton, MA.

8. Developing overhead and administrative costs

9. Applying inflation and escalation (cost growth) factors

10. Computing the total estimated costs

11. Analyzing and adjusting the estimate

12. Publishing and presenting the estimate to management/customer

While all of these steps are important, the earlier steps are critical since they define the scope of the system effort, the appropriate historical data, and the appropriate cost models to use. In addition, identifying the technology maturity for each cost element is critical since many cost studies cite technology immaturity as the major source of cost estimating errors [11].

How these steps are used is dependent upon the stage of the life cycle, which impacts the level of detail required for the cost estimate. Many of these steps are by products of a properly executed systems engineering and management process. During the planning phase for system development, a work breakdown structure (WBS) for the systems is identified and documented. The low level activities in this WBS are then sequenced to provide a preliminary project schedule.

Once all the activities have been identified and scheduled, the next task is to estimate their costs. The best approach is to estimate the cost of the activities based on relevant past experience with similar systems in terms of technical characteristics, project scope, schedule, and costs. Finding this data and organizing it into a useful format is one of the most difficult challenges with cost estimating, and can be the most time consuming step in the process.

Because of this, cost analysts and cost engineers rely on software such as *ACEIT:ACE* to accomplish historically-based cost estimating [12]. *ACEIT:ACE* was developed in a collaboration between the U.S. Department of Defense and Tecolate Research, Inc. It is a powerful cost estimating software application that encompasses all cost estimating best practices. It can be linked to historical cost archives to automatically populate estimates with historical data specific to systems projects and programs, WBS cost structures, and a host of other information that makes this task less daunting.

Once data are found and organized, cost analysts must ensure that the collection is complete and accurate. Part of this accuracy check is to make sure that the cost data are normalized so that any comparisons being made are consistent and not "apples to oranges" comparisons.

Using proper inflationary/deflationary indices on estimates associated with future costs (Step 9) is one form of normalization. Once the data have been normalized, they are then used to develop statistical relationships between physical and performance elements of the system and cost. Steps 4 and 5 are used to establish baseline cost estimating relationships (CERs) and adjust the costs based on the quantities purchased. Steps 6, 7, and 8 are used when a detailed "engineering" level estimate (Class 2 or Class 3 estimate) is being performed on a system. This is a very time consuming task and these steps are necessary if one wants to build a "bottom-up" estimate by consolidating individual estimates of each of the work activities into a total project cost estimate. Like the earlier techniques in Steps 4 and 5, these steps are even more dependent on collecting detailed historical information on activities and their associated costs.

Finally, Steps 11 and 12 are necessary elements to cost estimating. Step 11 provides an analyst with an opportunity to revise and update their estimate as more information becomes available about the system. This may be an opportunity for cost analysts to revise or adjust the estimate based on the maturity of the technology [11]. Additionally, it provides an analyst an opportunity to assess the risk associated with the estimate. The analyst can account for any data uncertainty quantitatively by performing a Monte Carlo analysis on the estimate and creating a distribution for the systems life cycle cost in a similar fashion as is done for value measures in Chapter 10. Step 12 is one of the most important steps; it does not matter how good an estimate is if an analyst cannot convince the management that they have done a thorough and complete cost analysis.

All assumptions should be clearly articulated in a manner that provides insight on the data sources and key assumptions used. The foundation for a cost estimate is the basic list of ground rules and assumptions associated with that estimate. Specifically, all assumptions, such as data sources, inflation rates, quantities procured, amount of testing, spares provisioning, and so on should be clearly documented up front in order to avoid confusion and the appearance of an inaccurate or misleading cost estimate. Once the estimate is developed and approved, it can be used to develop a budget, create a bid on a project or proposal, establish the price, or form a baseline from which to track actual costs. Once archived, it can also be used as a reference for future system cost estimates.

The techniques discussed in what follows focus on developing and using CERs, learning, and cost progress curves. Developing a comprehensive and detailed cost estimate are extensive and cannot be given justice within a single textbook chapter. Interested readers are referred to Stewart, Wyskida, and Johannes [2] and Ostwald [4].

8.2 TYPES OF COSTS

Although most people think of costs in terms of dollars, the cost concept can refer to any entity that represents resources to an organization: hours, personnel years, facility space, political capital, and so on. Generalized cost measures such as these are an important factor in making meaningful trade-off decisions that affect a systems project and the organizations associated with it. Fortunately, generalized resource cost measures can often be converted to monetary units (dollars). In this way, decision makers, stakeholders, senior project management, and other engineering groups are provided with a unifying measure they can easily assess.

There are a variety of costs associated with developing new systems or modifying existing ones. These costs vary based on where in the system life cycle they occur and the type of system being developed, constructed, or acquired. Similar to using SDP environmental factors to help identify major system stakeholders, cost classifications provide checklists for identifying various sources of cost as well as the affect those sources have on the system life cycle cost.

Costs are partitioned into four classes [2]: acquisition, fixed and variable, recurring and nonrecurring, direct and indirect.

> *Acquisition cost.* The total cost to procure, install, and put into operation a system, a product, or a specific infrastructure element (e.g. buildings, bridges, cellular networks, electric vehicle (EV) charging stations, tunnels, rail transportation, airports, and so on). Acquisition costs are the costs associated with planning, designing, engineering, testing, manufacturing, and deploying/installing a system or process.
>
> *Fixed and variable costs.* Fixed costs are those costs that are independent of quantity or the life cycle stage being addressed in the estimate. Typical fixed costs include such items as research, lease rentals, depreciation, taxes, insurance, and security. Variable costs are those costs that change as a function of the number of systems or system output quantities. Variable costs increase or decrease as the amount of product or service output from a system increases or decreases. Typical variable costs include direct labor, direct material, direct power, and the like. In other words, any cost that can be readily allocated to each unit of system output can be considered a variable cost.
>
> *Recurring and nonrecurring costs.* Recurring costs are costs that repeat with every unit of product or every time a system process takes place. Like variable costs, they are a function of the

quantity of items output. Nonrecurring costs are those costs that occur only once in the life cycle of a system. For example, the costs associated with design, engineering, testing, and other nonproduction, activities would be normally classified as nonrecurring when developing a system cost estimate, because they are not anticipated to repeat once they occur.

Direct and indirect costs. Direct costs are those costs that are associated with a specific system, end item, product, process, or service. Direct costs can be further subdivided into direct labor, direct material, and direct expenses. Labor costs are those costs associated with the labor used directly on an item. Direct material costs are those costs associated with the bills of material purchased for the manufacture of the item and direct expense may be subcontracted work for part of the system or product. Indirect costs are those costs that cannot be assigned to a specific product or process. These are usually pooled into an overhead account which is applied to direct costs as a burden. Examples of indirect costs may include items like security, accounting and finance labor, janitorial services, executive management, training, and other activities and costs not directly related to the specific product or process but an integral part of the organization that is responsible for the product, process, or service. Activity-based costing is an LCC technique that can provide more accurate indirect cost analysis based on the premise that indirect costs should be allocated according to important functional activities that are performed during the system life cycle [3]. Indirect costs associated with these activities are identified and grouped into multiple cost pools based on similar cost drivers. Resulting system life cycle costs are thus based on a more detailed analysis than traditional indirect costing.

8.3 COST ESTIMATING TECHNIQUES

As mentioned earlier, a variety of tools and techniques are available to assist in developing a life cycle cost estimate for a system [13]. In order to begin, a cost analyst must have a very good understanding of the system's purpose, operational concept, system functions, hardware and software being used, the technology maturity, the quantities desired, and the system life cycle. All of these are developed in the course of applying the SDP during a life cycle stage. This information is necessary in order to develop a credible initial cost estimate.

Several effective techniques can be used to develop life cycle cost estimates. Expert judgment is useful when developing initial estimates for comparing system alternatives early in system concept development. CER provide more refined estimates of specific alternatives when selecting between alternatives and are often used to develop initial cost baselines for the system of interest. Learning curves are used in production cost estimating to analyze and account for the effect that quantity has on the cost of an item. This tool is often used in conjunction with CERs to build a life cycle cost estimate.

8.3.1 Estimating by Analogy

Cost engineers and analysts are often asked to develop cost estimates for products and services that are in the system concept stage. At this early stage, they may have nothing more than the system purpose, a preliminary set of functions and requirements, and a rough description of a feasible system concept. Given this very preliminary information, the program manager, the cost analyst, the systems engineer, and the system design team are often asked to develop a life cycle cost estimate for the proposed system as part of a funding approval process for the system project. Given the scarcity of information at this stage, many program managers and cost analysts will rely on their own experience and/or the experience of other stakeholders and experts to construct an initial cost estimate. Using expert judgment to construct an initial estimate for a system is not uncommon. It is often used when creating Class 4 and 5 estimates. Because these experts are typically stakeholders to the system of interest, this underscores yet another reason why a good deal of time and effort is dedicated to stakeholder analysis in the Problem definition phase of the SDP.

Technological advances create stakeholder requirements and/or market opportunities for new systems or for technology refreshments for existing systems. New developments in batteries, heating and cooling systems, solar panels, cybersecurity methods, CPU design, wireless antennas, satellites, subterranean tunnel construction, insulating materials, adhesives, electric vehicle power units, aircraft materials, and others introduce system elements whose costs are no longer reflected accurately in historical system costs. When this occurs, costs associated with the existing system or a system with very similar characteristics can serve as a reference point from which a baseline cost estimate for the new system of interest may be constructed. This method is called *cost estimating by analogy* [14].

The analogy method compares a new or proposed system with an analogous (similar) system that was successfully developed or acquired in the recent past, and for which there are accurate cost and technical data. There must be a reasonable correlation between the proposed and "historical" system. If historical cost and engineering data are available for an analogous system, then that system can serve as a useful baseline cost estimate from which modifications can be made based upon the complexity of the advances in technology and the increase in requirements for system performance.

Many times, an expert will be consulted to describe the increase in complexity by focusing on a single system element (e.g. the new CPU is three times as complex). A cost analyst translates this statement into a cost factor by referencing past experience. For example, "The last time we changed processors, it was two times as complex and it increased cost by 20% over the earlier generation." This equates 2× complexity to a 20% increase. So if the current system is 3× as complex as the past one, the cost factor would adjust by a 30% increase from the previous system.

These factors will be based on the expert's personal experience and historical precedent. In this example, the underlying assumption that the expert is making is that there is a linear relationship between the cost factor and the complexity factor so that the estimated increase or decrease is proportional to that existing previously. Given this assumption, if the baseline cost estimate without considering complexity was $10,000, then a baseline estimate with the new technology would be ($10,000 × 1.3 = $13,000). Estimating by analogy can be accomplished at the meta system level as well when the new system has proposed characteristics in common with existing systems. For example, the cost of high altitude unmanned aerial vehicles (UAVs) could initially be estimated by drawing analogies between missiles and these UAVs, because high altitude UAVs and missiles use similar technologies. By making appropriate adjustments for size, speed, payload, and other performance parameters, one could make an initial life cycle cost estimate based on historical missile data.

A major disadvantage associated with estimating by analogy is the significant dependency on the judgment of any expert(s) providing adjustment estimates and existing historical data. The credibility of the cost estimate rests largely upon the depth of expertise and experience of the person constructing the analogy. Estimating by analogy requires significantly less effort overall and therefore is not as costly in terms of time and effort as other methods. Therefore, it is often used as a check of the more detailed estimates that are constructed as the system description increases in detail.

8.3.2 Parametric Estimation Using Cost Estimating Relationships

Parametric estimates are used to create estimates of life cycle costs using statistical analysis techniques. They were first introduced in the late 1950s by the RAND Corporation for use in predicting costs for large-scale military systems. These techniques rely heavily on historical data.

A parametric, or statistical method uses regression analysis on a database of two or more similar systems to develop CERs which estimate cost based on one or more system performance or design characteristics (e.g. speed, range, weight, thrust). The parametric method is most commonly performed during the initial phases of system description beyond design and science and technology development. Estimating by parametrics is a method to show how parameters influence cost.

In general, parametric cost estimates are preferred to expert judgment techniques. However, if sufficient historical data are not available or the system and its associated technology have changed significantly since historical data were archived, then constructing a parametric cost estimate may not be possible.

The level at which parametric cost estimating is accomplished is largely dependent on the system life cycle stage. Parametric techniques can also be constructed and/or revised using detailed design and production information. Because they are designed to forecast costs into the future, they are often used to estimate operation and support costs after the system is deployed as well.

The end goal of this statistical approach is to develop a CER, which is a mathematical relationship between one or more system physical and performance parameters and the total system cost estimate. For example, the cost of a satellite may be estimated as a function of weight, power, and orbit. The cost of a house may be estimated by forming a relationship between cost and the square footage, location, and number of levels in a house.

As mentioned previously, when constructing a system life cycle cost estimate the baseline WBS for the system should be used. This is considered a best practice. Leveraging a WBS will help ensure that all the necessary elements of the system have been appropriately accounted for in the cost estimate. As an example, a three-level WBS for the air-vehicle portion of a missile system has been adapted from Mil-Hdbk-881a WBS-Missiles [15], and is presented in Table 8.3. The missile system has many more Level 2 components. For example, at WBS Level 2, one must also consider the costs of the command and launch components, the systems engineering and program management costs, the system test and evaluation costs, training costs, data costs, support equipment costs, site activation costs, facilities costs, initial spares costs, operational and support costs, and retirement costs. Each of these Level 2 elements can be further broken down into Level 3 WBS elements as has been done for the air vehicle. Additionally, when cost analysis shifts its attention from deterministic estimates to those involving uncertainty, uncertainty associated with low-level WBS element costs become distributions that contribute important budget risk information to higher-level system cost estimates.

A parametric CER can be developed at any of the WBS levels depending on the technological maturity of the system components, available engineering and cost data, and amount of time available to create the estimate. In general, the further along in the life cycle, the more engineering data available and the lower the WBS level from which an estimate can be constructed.

8.3.3 Common Cost Estimating Relationships (CER)

A CER is a mathematical function that relates a specific cost category to one or more system performance or design characteristics (variables). These variables must have some logical relationship to the system cost. Each of the four major CERs depend upon the underlying mathematical relationships between WBS elements and cost.

TABLE 8.3   Levels of Cost Estimating [6].

Level 1	Level 2	Level 3
Missile System		
	Air vehicle	
		Propulsion system
		Payload
		Airframe
		Guidance and Control
		Fuzing
		Integration and Assembly
	Command and Launch Components	
	Systems Engineering and Program Management	
	System Test and Evaluation	
	Training	
	Data	
	Support Equipment	
	Site Activation	
	Storage Facilities	
	Initial Spares	
	Operating and Support Costs	
	Retirement Costs	

Source: Park [6]/Pearson Education.

Linear CER with fixed and variable cost. Many WBS cost elements can be modeled reasonably well by a simple linear relationship, $Y = aX$. For example, facility cost can be modeled as a function of the floorspace area or total volume of the interior space. Personnel costs can be modeled by multiplying labor rates for individual skill levels by personnel hours. It is also possible to have a linear relationship that includes a fixed cost, denoted by b. For example, if the cost of a facility also included the land purchase agreement, then the CER would contain a fixed cost associated with the land purchase and a variable cost that is dependent on the size of the facility built on the land. The relationship is given by $Y = aX + b$. Both of these basic forms are shown in Figure 8.2.

Power CER with fixed and variable cost. Some systems may not have a linear relationship between cost and the selected estimating parameter or characteristic. This occurs when economy of scale affects are present. For example, as the size of a house increases, there can be a point at which the cost/ft^2 decreases. Also, when the scope or complexity of a systems project increases to a point that causes new rules, regulations, building code, worker skills, and other control factors to activate, it can cause the system of interest to fall into a new category with all new cost elements, imposing a discontinuous jump in costs. Similarly, cost estimating can encounter situations where there are dis-economies of scale. For example, large gemstones often have higher costs per unit size than smaller gemstones. Figure 8.3 illustrates the various shapes that a power CER can take as well as the functional form of the various CER.

Exponential CER with fixed and variable cost. Another functional form that is often used is the exponential CER. In this form, it is assumed that the relationship between the independent

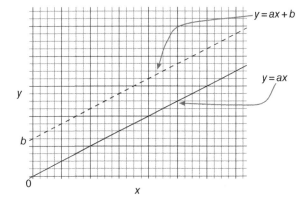

Figure 8.2   Linear CERs.

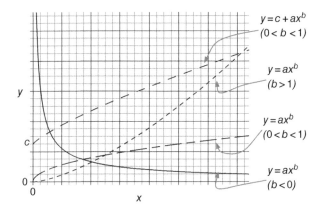

Figure 8.3   Power CERs.

variable and cost is such that a unit change in the independent variable causes a relatively constant percentage change in cost. Figure 8.4 illustrates the shape for an exponential CER for a variety of functional forms.

Logarithm CERs. Finally, one other common form that may be useful for describing the relationship between cost and a particular independent variable is the logarithm CER. Figure 8.5 illustrates the shape for a logarithm CER for a variety of functional forms.

Cost Estimating Relationships (CER)   Constructing a CER requires a sufficient amount of data to statistically fit a curve. What is sufficient for this purpose is a judgment decision that usually depends on the data that are readily available. For most CERs, a minimum of three or four data points would be sufficient to accomplish a curve fit, but it is likely to have a significant amount of error associated with the fit. Linear regression is most commonly used to accomplish this task because all of the functional forms discussed previously can be accommodated by linear regression by performing a transformation on the data. Table 8.4 adapted from Stewart, Wyskida, and Johannes [2], shows the relationship between the various CERs and their associated transformations.

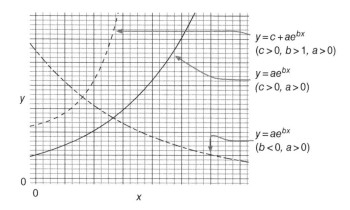

Figure 8.4 Exponential CERs.

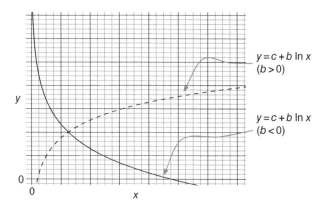

Figure 8.5 Logarithm CERs.

TABLE 8.4 Linear Transformations for CERs.

	Linear	Power	Exponential	Logarithmic
Equation form Desired	$Y = a + bX$	$Y = ax^b$	$Y = ae^{bX}$	$Y = a = b \ln X$
Linear Equation Form	$Y = a + bX$	$\ln Y = \ln a + b \ln X$	$\ln Y = \ln a + bX$	$Y = a + b \ln X$
Required Data Transform	X, Y	$\ln X, \ln Y$	$X, \ln Y$	$\ln X, Y$
Regression Coefficient Obtained	a, b	$\ln a, b$	$\ln a, b$	a, b
Coefficient Reverse Transform Required	None	$\exp(\ln a), b$	$\exp(\ln a), b$	None
Final Coefficient	a, b	a, b	a, b	a, b

Linear regression is a statistical method that fits a straight line through a set of data points with a goal of determining the coefficients for whatever linear model is being used. For a simple linear model such as $y = ax + b$, the two model parameters a and b of the linear equation would result. The parameters are determined by using the following formulas:

$$
b = \frac{\displaystyle\sum_{i=1}^{n} x_i y_i - \left[\frac{\displaystyle\sum_{i=1}^{n} x_i}{n}\right]\displaystyle\sum_{i=1}^{n} y_i}{\displaystyle\sum_{i=1}^{n} x_i^2 - \left[\frac{\displaystyle\sum_{i=1}^{n} x_i}{n}\right]\displaystyle\sum_{i=1}^{n} x_i}
\tag{8.1}
$$

$$
a = \frac{\displaystyle\sum_{i=1}^{n} y_i}{n} - b\left[\frac{\displaystyle\sum_{i=1}^{n} x_i}{n}\right]
\tag{8.2}
$$

Most of the time, especially when a reasonable sized data set exists, any software that can perform linear regression on data can be used as it is a common function incorporated into numerical analysis software. *Minitab* [16], *JMP* [17], *Origin* [9], and Excel are good examples of this type of software.

Estimating CERs Example. A systems cost analyst is using the data for labor hours and construction costs for highways shown in Table 8.5 to identify a CER between labor hours and cost. Intending to fit a simple linear model to the data, she created a scatter plot of the data shown in Figure 8.6. Using linear regression, she can estimate the parameters for a line that minimizes the squared error between the line and the actual data points. Because the regression line would be a straightforward 2-parameter model $y = ax + b$, she decides to simply substitute the data into the closed-form expressions for a and b from Equations 8.1 and 8.2.

TABLE 8.5   Labor Hours and Costs for Highway Construction.

Labor Hours (X)	Cost (Y)	Labor Hours (X)	Cost (Y)
940.87	252.87	1078.32	364.32
5814.28	4708.28	6961.21	5269.21
302.31	137.31	4174.96	1192.96
292.44	303.44	1277.78	813.78
149.46	149.46	1493.08	957.08
2698.94	1385.94	4731.84	2342.84
680.64	362.64		

Summarizing the data yields:

$$\sum_{i=1}^{13} x_i = 30,596.13$$

$$\sum_{i=1}^{13} y_i = 18,240.13$$

$$\sum_{i=1}^{13} x_i y_i = 87,361,422.71$$

$$\sum_{i=1}^{13} x_i^2 = 135,941,716.08$$

Using the summary data, coefficients a and b for the linear relationship are:

$$b = \frac{87,361,422.71 - \left(\dfrac{30,596.13}{13}\right) 18,240.13}{135,941,716.08 - \left(\dfrac{30,596.13}{13}\right) 30,596.13} = 0.695$$

$$a = \frac{1824.13}{13} - 0.695 \left(\frac{30596.13}{13}\right) = -232.61$$

Using *Minitab* to perform the regression on the same data produces the following output:

```
The regression equation is
Cost = -233 + 0.695  Labor Hours

Predictor        Coef    SE Coef      T          P
Constant       -232.6      253.8   -0.92      0.379
Labor hours   0.69499    0.07849    8.85      0.000

S = 627.579 R-Sq = 87.7%% R-Sq(adj) = 86.6%%

Analysis of variance

Source            DF     SS         MS          F        P
Regression         1     30880140   30880140    78.40    0.000
Residual error    11     4332404    393855
Total             12     35212544
```

The output indicates that the model is significant in that it accounts for approximately 87% of the total variation in the data. The intercept term has a *p*-value of 0.379 and therefore could be eliminated from the model. As part of the analysis, the underlying assumptions associated with the basic regression model need to be checked. The underlying assumption is that the errors are normally distributed, with a mean of zero and a constant variance. Examining the normal probability

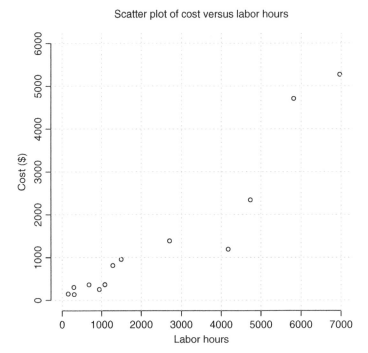

Figure 8.6 Scatter plot of the data.

plot shown in Figure 8.7 and the associated residual plot in Figure 8.8, the analyst concluded that the underlying assumptions might not be valid. The residual data does not fall along a straight line and therefore the errors are most likely not normally distributed. Moreover, it appears that the variance is not constant because for larger values of Labor hours the variance increases.

Given that the underlying assumptions are not met using a basic linear regression model, some other type of CER should be considered, such as a simple power CER. To do so, the data must be transformed according to Table 8.6, which shows the original data and the transformed data needed to fit a linear regression model to the transformed data. The data transformation is performed by taking the natural logarithm of the Cost data and the natural logarithm of the Labor hours data. Using this transformed data set, the coefficients for the transformed linear model can be calculated. Again, first summarizing the data:

$$\sum_{i=1}^{13} \ln x_i = 93.43$$

$$\sum_{i=1}^{13} \ln y_i = 85.64$$

$$\sum_{i=1}^{13} (\ln x_i) \ln y_i = 632.25$$

$$\sum_{i=1}^{13} (\ln x_i)^2 = 689.66$$

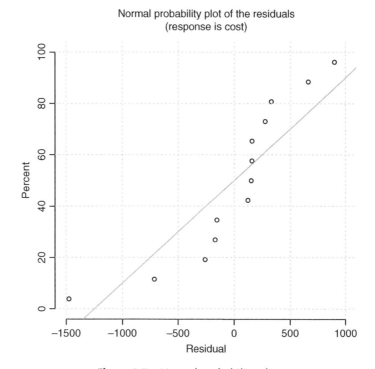

Figure 8.7 Normal probability plot.

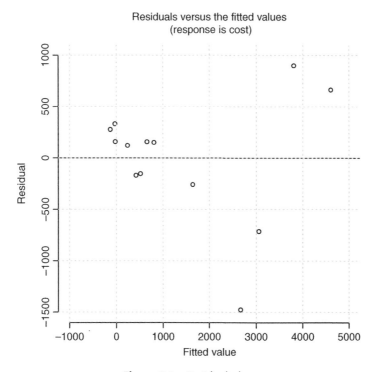

Figure 8.8 Residual plot.

TABLE 8.6   Transformed Data.

X	Y	ln(X)	ln(Y)	(ln(X))^2	(ln(X))(ln(Y))
940.87	252.87	6.85	5.53	46.88	37.88
5814.28	4708.28	8.67	8.46	75.14	73.31
302.31	137.31	5.71	4.92	32.62	28.11
292.44	303.44	5.68	5.72	32.24	32.45
149.46	149.46	5.01	5.01	25.07	25.07
2698.94	1385.94	7.90	7.23	62.42	57.15
680.64	362.64	6.52	5.89	42.55	38.44
1078.32	364.32	6.98	5.90	48.76	41.19
6961.21	5269.21	8.85	8.57	78.29	75.83
4174.96	1192.96	8.34	7.08	69.5	59.06
1277.78	813.78	7.15	6.70	51.16	47.94
1493.08	957.08	7.31	6.86	53.42	50.17
4731.84	2342.84	8.46	7.75	71.60	65.65

Next, substituting the summarized data into the coefficient expressions yields the transformed linear regression parameters:

$$b = \frac{632.25 - \left(\frac{93.43}{13}\right)85.64}{689.66 - \left(\frac{93.43}{13}\right)93.43} = 0.9209$$

$$a = \frac{85.64}{13} - 0.921\left(\frac{93.43}{13}\right) = -0.0313$$

Entering the same data set into *Minitab* yields the following output:

```
The regression equation is
LnY = -  0.031 + 0.921 lnX


Predictor   Coef      SE Coef     T        P
Constant -0.0313     0.7613    -0.04    0.968
LnX       0.9209     0.1045     8.81    0.000



S = 0.446321 R-Sq = 87.6%% R-Sq(adj) = 86.5%%



Analysis of variance
Source           DF        SS       MS       F       P
Regression        1    15.461   15.461   77.62   0.000
Residual Error   11     2.191    0.199
Total            12    17.653
```

Again the output indicates that the regression model is significant in that it accounts for approximately 87% of the total variation in the data. The intercept term has a *p*-value of 0.968 and therefore could be eliminated from the model at any level of significance less than or equal to $\alpha = 0.968$.

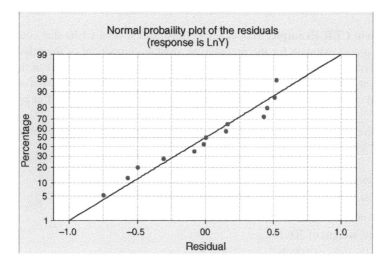

Figure 8.9 Normal probability plot.

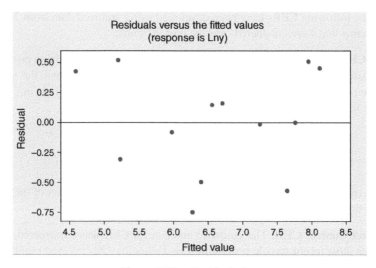

Figure 8.10 Residual plot.

Once again, however, the underlying assumptions associated with a linear regression model should be checked.

Examining the normal probability plot and the associated residual plot shown in Figures 8.9 and 8.10 respectively, the underlying assumptions appear to be valid. The residuals appear to be normal and have a constant variance with a mean of zero. Applying an inverse transformation puts the CER into a standard power form:

$$Y = e^{-0.031}X^{0.921}$$
$$Y = 0.97X^{0.921}$$

Missile System CER Example. This example illustrates several CERs that could be used to assemble a cost estimate for the notional air vehicle component of the missile system [18, 19] described in the WBS given in Table 8.3. The unit production cost of the air vehicle component is obtained by summing the first unit costs for the propulsion system, the guidance and control system, the airframe, the payload, and the associated integration and assembly.

Suppose that the first unit production cost for has the following engineering characteristics:

- Requires 15,000 lb of thrust
- Requires a 26 GHz guidance and control computer
- Has a 6-in. aperture on the antenna, operating in the narrow band
- Airframe weight of 300 lb
- Payload weight of 100 lb
- System uses electro optics
- System checkout requires seven different test procedures

Suppose the following CERs have been developed using archived data from 20 different missile programs that were conducted over the past 20 years:

Propulsion CER. The following CER was constructed using the propulsion costs from 15 of the 20 missile programs. Five of the programs were excluded because the technology used in those programs was not relevant for the missile system currently being estimated. The CER for the propulsion system is given by:

$$\text{Mfg \$ (FY 2022)} = (\text{Thrust (lbs)})e^{-0.1(\text{Yr}-2002)}$$

$$\text{Mfg \$ (FY 2022)} = (15000)e^{-0.1(2022-2002)} = 1114.10$$

The manufacturing cost in dollars for the propulsion system is a function of thrust as well as the age of the motor technology (current year minus 2002).

Guidance and Control CER. The guidance and control CER was constructed using data from the three most recent missile programs. This technology has evolved rapidly and it is distinct from many of the early systems. Therefore, the cost analysts chose to use the reduced data set to come up with the following CER:

$$\text{Mfg \$ K (FY 2022)} = 7.43(\text{GHz})^{0.45}$$

$$\times (\text{Aper (inches)})^{0.35}e^{0.7(\text{Wide/Narrow})}$$

$$\text{Mfg \$ K (FY 2022)} = 7.43(26)^{0.45}(6)^{0.35}e^{0.7(1)} = 121.36$$

The manufacturing cost in thousands of dollars for the guidance and control system is a function of the operating rate of the computer, the diameter of the antenna for the seeker, and whether or not the system operates over a wide band (0) or narrow band (1).

Airframe CER. Suppose the following CER was constructed using the airframe cost data from the 20 missile programs. The CER for the airframe is given by:

$$\text{Mfg \$ (FY 2022)} = 5.575(\text{Wt. lbs})^{0.85}$$

$$\text{Mfg \$ (FY 2022)} = 5.575(300)^{0.85} = 710.88$$

Thus, the manufacturing costs in dollars for the airframe can be estimated if the analyst knows or has an estimate of the weight of the airframe.

Fuzing System. The following CER was established using data from five of the previous missile programs. The proximity fuse in the system being estimated is technologically similar to only five of the previous development efforts.

$$\text{Mfg \$ (FY 2022)} = 15(\text{payloadwt.lbs})e^{0.3(\text{EO/RF})}$$

$$\text{Mfg \$ (FY 2022)} = 15(100)e^{0.3(0)} = 150$$

The manufacturing cost for the fuzing system in dollars is a function of the weight of the payload and the type of technology used. The term EO/RF is equal to 0 if it uses electro-optic technology and 1 if it uses radio frequency technology.

Payload. The payload CER is given by the following relationship in dollars:

$$\text{Mfg \$ (FY 2022)} = 150(\text{payloadwt.lbs})$$

$$\text{Mfg \$ (FY 2022)} = 150(100) = 15,000$$

Integration and Assembly. This represents the costs in dollars associated with integrating all of the air vehicle components, testing them as they are integrated, and performing final checkout once the air vehicle has been assembled. Letting n represent the number of system test procedures:

$$\text{Mfg \$ (FY 2022)} = 1.25 \left(\sum \text{Hardware costs} \right) e^{-(n)}$$

$$\text{Mfg \$ (FY 2022)} = 1.25(15,000 + 150 + 710.88 + 121.36 + 1114.10)$$

$$\times e^{-(7)}$$

$$\text{Mfg \$ (FY 2022)} = 157.68$$

Air Vehicle Cost. Using this information, the first unit cost of the air vehicle system is constructed next:

$$\text{Mfg \$ (FY 2022)} = 15,000 + 150 + 710.88 + 121.36$$

$$+ 1114.1 + 157.68$$

$$\text{Mfg \$ (FY 2022)} = 17,254.02$$

This cost is in fiscal year 2022 dollars and it must be inflated to current year dollars (2006) using the methods discussed in Section 5.4.2. Once the cost has been inflated, the initial unit cost can be used to calculate the total cost for a purchase of 1000 missiles using an appropriate learning curve as discussed in section 8.3.4.

8.3.4 Learning Curves

Learning curves are an essential tool for adequately modeling the costs associated with the development and manufacture of large quantities of systems [5]. Many studies have shown that human performance improves the more times a task is performed, supporting the old adage that "practice makes perfect!". This *learning effect* was first noticed by Wright [20] when he analyzed aircraft data in the 1930s. Empirical evidence from a variety of other manufacturing industries has shown that human performance improves by some constant amount each time the production quantity is doubled [21]. This concept is especially applicable to human labor intensive products. Each time the production quantity is doubled, the labor requirements necessary to create a unit decrease by a fixed percentage of their previous value. This percentage is referred to as the *learning rate*.

Learning effects typically produce a cost and time savings of 5–30% each time a production quantity is doubled [7]. By convention, the 10–30% labor savings equates to a 90–70% learning rate. This learning rate is influenced by a variety of factors, including the amount of pre-production planning, the system design maturity, the production force training levels, the manufacturing process complexity, as well as the length of the production runs. Figure 8.11 shows a plot of a 90% learning rate and a 70% learning rate for a task that initially would take 100 hours. As evidenced by the plot, a 70% learning rate results in significant improvement of unit task times over a 90% curve. Delionback [2] defines learning rates by industry sector. For example:

- Aerospace—85%
- Repetitive electronics manufacturing—90–95%
- Repetitive machining—90–95%
- Construction operations—70–90%.

Unit Learning Curve Formula The mathematical formula used to describe the learning effect shown in Figure 8.11 is given by:

$$T_X = T_1 X^r \tag{8.3}$$

where T_X = the cost or time required to build the Xth unit, T_1 = the cost or time required to build the initial unit, X = the number of units to be built, and r = negative numerical factor which is

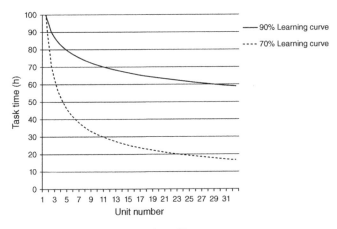

Figure 8.11 Plot of learning curves.

TABLE 8.7   Factors for Various Learning Rates.

Learning rate (%)	r
100	0
95	−0.074
90	−0.152
85	−0.235
80	−0.322
75	−0.415
70	−0.515

derived from the learning rate and is given by:

$$r = \frac{\ln \ (\text{learning rate})}{\ln(2)} \tag{8.4}$$

Typical values for r are given in Table 8.7. For example, with a learning rate of 95%, the resulting factor is $r = \frac{\ln(0.95)}{\ln(2)} = 0.074$.

The total time required for all units of production run of size N is:

$$\text{total time} = T_1 \sum_{X=1}^{N} X^r \tag{8.5}$$

Examining the previous equation, and using the appropriate factor for a 90% learning rate, we can calculate the unit cost for the first eight items. Assuming an initial cost of $100, Table 8.8 provides unit costs for the first eight items as well as the cumulative average cost per unit required to build X units. Figure 8.12 plots the unit cost curve and the cumulative average cost curve for a 90% learning rate for 32 units.

Note that the cumulative average curve is above the unit cost curve. When using data constructed with a learning curve, the analyst must be careful to note whether they are using cumulative average data or unit cost data. It is easy to derive one from the other, but it is imperative to know what type of data one is working with to calculate the total system cost correctly.

TABLE 8.8   Unit Cost and Cumulative Average Cost.

Total Units Produced	Cost to Produce Xth Unit	Cumulative Cost	Cumulative Average Cost
1	100	100	100
2	90	190	95
3	84.6	274.6	91.53
4	81	355.6	88.9
5	78.3	433.9	86.78
6	76.2	510.1	85.02
7	74.4	584.5	83.5
8	72.9	657.4	82.175

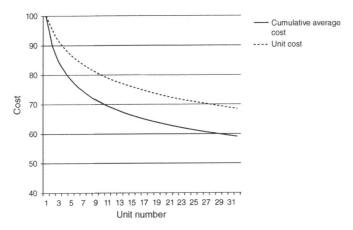

Figure 8.12 90% learning curve for cumulative average cost and unit cost.

Assembly Time with Learning 1. Suppose it takes 40 minutes to assemble the fins for a rocket motor the first time, and 36 minutes the second time it is attempted. How long will it take to assemble the eighth unit?

First, that task is said to have a 90% learning rate because the cost of the second unit is 90% of the cost of the first. If we double the output again, from two to four units, then we would expect the fourth unit to be assembled in (36 minutes) × (0.9) = 32.4 minutes. If we double again from four to eight units, the task time to assemble the eighth fin assembly would be (32.4) × (0.9) = 29.16 minutes.

Assembly Time with Learning 2. Suppose we wish to identify the assembly time for 25th unit, assuming a 90% learning rate.

First, we need to define r:

$$r = \frac{\ln (0.9)}{\ln (2)} = -0.152$$

Given r, we can determine the assembly time for the 25th unit as follows:

$$T_X = T_1 X^r$$

$$T_{25} = (40 \text{ minutes})(25)^{-0.152}$$

$$T_{25} = 24.52 \text{ minutes}$$

Figure 8.13 plots a 90% learning curve for the fin assembly.

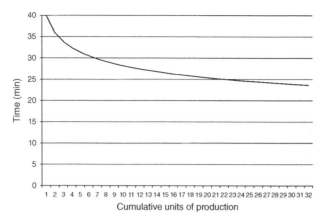

Figure 8.13 90% learning curve for fin assembly.

Assembly Time with Learning 3. It is common for organizations to define a standard of performance based on the 100th or 1000th unit. Suppose your organization sets a target assembly time for the 100th unit of 50 hours. Suppose that your company has historically operated at an 80% learning rate, what is the expected assembly time of the first unit?

$$T_X = T_1 X^r$$

$$T_X x^{-r} = T_1$$

$$T_1 = 50(100)^{-(-0.322)}$$

$$T_1 = 220.20 \text{ hours}$$

Composite Learning Curves Frequently, a new system will be constructed using a variety of processes, each of which may have its own learning rate. A single composite learning rate can be constructed that characterizes the learning rate for the entire system using the rates of the individual processes. One approach used to do this [2] weights each process in proportion to its individual dollar or time value. The composite learning curve is given by:

$$r_c = \sum_p \left(\frac{T_p}{T} \right) r_p$$

where r_c = composite learning rate, r_p = learning rate for process p, T_p = time or cost for process p, and T = total time or cost for the system.

Composite Learning Example. Suppose our rocket has a final assembly cost of $50,000 and the final assembly task has a historic learning rate of 70%. Suppose that the rocket motor construction has a total cost of $100,000 and that it has a historic learning rate of 80%. Finally, the guidance section has total cost of $200,000 and a historic learning rate of 90%. Calculate the composite learning rate for the rocket?

$$r_c = \left[\frac{50,000}{350,000}\right](70\%) + \left[\frac{100,000}{350,000}\right](80\%) + \left[\frac{200,000}{350,000}\right](90\%)$$

$$r_c = 84.29\%$$

Cumulative Average Formula The formula for calculating the approximate cumulative average cost or cumulative average number of labor hours required to produce X units is given by:

$$T_c \approx \frac{T_1}{X(1+r)}[(X + 0.5)^{(1+r)} - (0.5)^{(1+r)}]$$

This formula is accurate to within 5% when the quantity is greater than 10.

Cumulative Average Example. Using the cumulative average formula, compute the cumulative average cost for eight units, assuming an initial cost of $100 and a 90% learning rate.

$$T_c \approx \frac{100}{8(1 - 0.152)}[(8.5)^{(1-0.152)} - (0.5)^{(1-0.152)}]$$

$$T_c \approx 82.31$$

Note that this value is very close to the actual cost found in Table 8.8.

Constructing a Learning Curve from Historical Data The previous formulas are all dependent upon having a value for the learning rate. The learning rate can be derived for specific tasks in a specific organization by using historical cost and performance data. The basic data requirements for constructing a learning rate for an activity include the dates of labor expenditure or cumulative task hours, and associated completed units. The learning rate is found by comparing the total hours expended at the end of a given date and the corresponding number of units completed.

By computing the natural logarithm of both sides of the learning curve function discussed in Section 8.3.4, a linear equation can be constructed that can be used to find the learning rate as follows:

$$T_X = T_1 X^r$$

$$\ln(T_X) = \ln(T_1) + r \ln(X)$$

The intercept for this linear equation is $\ln(T_1)$ and the slope of the line is given by r. Given r, the learning rate can be found by using the following relation:

$$\text{learning rate\%} = 100(2^r)$$

Learning Rate Example. Suppose the data in Table 8.9 was obtained from a manufacturing company's accounting system. Transforming the data by applying the natural logarithm to the cumulative units and associated cumulative average hours yields Table 8.10. Figure 8.14 shows a plot of the transformed data along with a regression line fit to the data, which yields the following values for the slope and intercept of the linear equation:

$$\text{Slope:} \quad r = -0.2196$$

$$\text{Intercept:} \quad \ln T_1 = 4.633$$

$$\text{Coefficient of determination:} \quad R^2 = 0.962$$

Thus, the learning rate is:
$$100(2^{-0.2196}) = 85.88\%$$

TABLE 8.9 Accounting System Data.

Week	Cumulative Hours Expended	Cumulative Units Complete	Cumulative Average Hours
1	40	0	
2	100	1	$100/1 = 100$
3	180	2	$180/2 = 90$
4	250	3	$250/3 = 83.33$
5	310	4	$310/4 = 77.5$
6	360	5	$360/5 = 72$
7	400	6	$400/6 = 66.67$

TABLE 8.10 Natural Logarithm of Cumulative Units Completed and Cumulative Average Hours.

Cumulative Units Completed X	In X	Cumulative Average Hours TX	In TX
1	0	100	4.60517
2	0.693147	90	4.49981
3	1.098612	83.33	4.42281
4	1.386294	77.5	4.35028
5	1.609437	72	4.27667
6	1.791759	66.67	4.19975

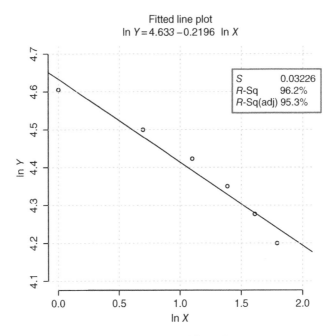

Figure 8.14 Fitted line plot.

8.4 TIME EFFECTS ON COST

Section 8.3 described how system costs could be calculated using expert judgment, cost estimating relationships (CER), and learning curves. The resulting cost estimates typically are associated with different months or years as system development projects proceed. Economic inflation, interest rates, and other phenomena affect the real value of these costs because buying power is diminished as time goes on. A monetary unit's value today is worth more than the same amount at a later date and this affect increases according to known mathematical relationships the further into the future cost estimates extend. Simply summing a stream of constant costs over time will not provide an accurate estimate of costs. This effect is known as the *time value of money*.

8.4.1 Time Value of Money

Life cycle costs must be identified in terms of timing as well as amount, because a dollar today is not the same as a dollar five years from now because of inflation and other economic effects. Two costs at different points in time are equivalent if they are equal to each other at some point in time for a given interest rate. For example, at a 10% annual interest rate, $500 today is equivalent to $605 two years from now. Comparing costs that occur over the duration of a system's life cycle requires annual and future life cycle costs to be converted into their equivalent in present time. Costs incurred today (present time) can also be converted into future costs as well as analyzing present and future costs as equal annual payments, depending on the specifics of the situation. Well-established equivalence formulas for converting costs in terms of time are shown in Table 8.11

TABLE 8.11 Equivalence Table [4].

Conversion	Formula	Example
Find F when given P	$F = P(1+i)^N$	A firm borrows $1000 for 10 years. How much must it repay in a lump sum at the end of the 10 year? $i = 5\%$ $F = 1000(1 + 0.05)^{10} = \$1628.89$
Find P when given F	$P = F\left[\dfrac{1}{(1+i)^N}\right]$	A company desires to have $1000 seven years from now. What amount is needed now to provide for it? $i = 5\%$ $P = 1000\left[\dfrac{1}{(1+0.05)^7}\right] = \$710.68$
Find F when given A	$F = A\left[\dfrac{(1+i)^N - 1}{i}\right]$	If eight annual deposits of $1000 each are placed in an account, how much money has accumulated immediately after the last deposit? $i = 5\%$ $F = 1000\left[\dfrac{(1+0.05)^8 - 1}{(0.5)}\right] = \$9549.11$
Find A when given F	$A = F\left[\dfrac{i}{(1+i)^N - 1}\right]$	How much should be deposited each year in an account in order to accumulate $5000 at the time of the sixth annual deposit? $i = 5\%$ $A = 5000\left[\dfrac{0.05}{(1+0.05)^6 - 1}\right] = \$735.09$
Find P when given A	$P = A\left[\dfrac{(1+i)^N - 1}{i(1+i)^N}\right]$	How much should be deposited in a fund to provide for 10 annual withdrawals of $500 each? $i = 5\%$ $P = 500\left[\dfrac{(1+0.05)^{10} - 1}{0.05(1+0.05)^{10}}\right] = \$3860.87$
Find A when given P	$A = P\left[\dfrac{i(i+1)^N}{(1+i)^N - 1}\right]$	What is the size of 10 equal payments to repay a loan of $10,000? $i = 5\%$ $A = 10000\left[\dfrac{0.05(1+0.05)^{10}}{(1+0.05)^{10} - 1}\right] = \$1295.05$

Source: Ostwald [4]/Pearson Education

along with an example for each conversion. These formulas are presented using the notation as follows:

- i = Effective interest rate per period
- N = Number of compounding periods
- P = Present life cycle cost
- F = Future life cycle cost
- A = Annual life cycle cost

8.4.2   Inflation

It is possible and likely that data available to support system LCC has been collected and archived from system projects extending over many different years. To perform LCC on a related or analogous system of interest, these historical cost data must be converted from *actual dollars*, which are the actual dollars spent at the time that the cost incurred, into *constant dollars* that represent adjusted amounts to capture purchasing power at some common reference point in time. This conversion is referred to as an *inflation adjustment*. Inflation refers to a steady rise in prices measured against a standard reference level of purchasing power.

 While inflation is the common effect addressed by time value of money, deflation can also occur in which prices drop over time. Both inflation and deflation are inextricably tied to supply and demand levels. The economy is by definition a complex system due to the vast number of inter-relationships that exist and adapt between internal and external system elements.

Annual inflation rates vary across different types of goods and services and over time. To create system life cycle cost estimates, economic assumptions must be made concerning how inflation is going to occur in the future. The approach presented here relies on a single, credible best estimate regarding inflation. Later, in Section 10.6, the uncertainty associated with this is addressed in a more robust manner by modeling a possible range of values with a distribution and leveraging simulation to arrive at cost estimates.

The consumer price index (CPI) is a measure of the average change in prices over time of goods and services purchased by households [8]. The CPI is commonly used to convert actual dollars to constant dollars. Table 8.12 provides the end of year (EOY) CPI for years 2000 through 2006 and the corresponding year-by-year change rates as provided by the US Bureau of Labor Statistics [8].

Constant dollars ($C\$$) at any time n of purchasing power as of any base time k can be converted to actual dollars ($A\$$) at any time n by using the equivalence formula for finding F given P.

$$A\$ = C\$_n^{(k)}(1 + f)^{n-k}$$

where f = average inflation rate per period over the $n - k$ periods.

A cost $C\$10,000$ that incurred in the past, say, 2002, can be converted to later time dollars, say, 2005, in the following manner:

$$f = \frac{f_{2003} + f_{2004} + f_{2005}}{3} = \frac{0.0188 + 0.0326 + 0.0342}{3} = 2.85\%$$

$$A\$ = \$10,000_{2005}^{(2002)}(1 + 0.0285)^{2005-2002}$$

$$A\$ = \$10,879.59$$

TABLE 8.12 Consumer Price Index and Yearly Inflation Rate for 2000–2006.

Year (i)	CPI (EOY)	Inflation Rate % (f_i)
2000	174	—
2001	176.7	1.55
2002	180.9	2.38
2003	184.3	1.88
2004	190.3	3.26
2005	196.8	3.42
2006	201.8	2.54

Converting Past to Present Dollars. An air vehicle unit cost estimate was developed in Section 8.3.2. In that estimate, the unit cost for producing the first air vehicle was estimated to be \$138,492.58 in base year 2000. Suppose that 2006 was the year that a system cost estimate was being performed, which means this cost needs to be converted into 2006 dollars as follows. Using the inflation rates listed in Table 8.12:

$$f = \frac{f_{2001} + f_{2002} + f_{2003} + f_{2004} + f_{2005} + f_{2006}}{6}$$

$$f = \frac{0.015 + 0.0238 + 0.0188 + 0.0326 + 0.0342 + 0.0254}{6} = 2.51\%$$

$$A\$ = \$138,492.58(1 + 0.0251)^{2006-2000} = \$160,702.9$$

8.4.3 Net Present Value

Systems decision making naturally relies on a tradespace in which costs and value comparisons must be made between competing alternative system solutions. The life cycle costs associated with these alternatives should consider both time value of money and inflation when being estimated. This analysis assumes that the following conditions exist [6]:

- Candidate system solutions must be mutually exclusive in that choosing one alternative excludes the choice of any other alternative.
- All candidate system solutions must be considered over the same length of time. If system alternatives have different expected total life cycles, the time period should equal the lowest common multiples of their lives or the length of time the selected system will be used.

These assumptions allow for cost adjustments and clear cost comparisons to be made between system alternatives. For completeness, it is worth mentioning that it is possible that system developers could negotiate contractual partnerships and other agreements with competing companies in the event that their alternative is not selected as the system solution. On face value, this runs contrary to the first assumption. However, arrangements such as these are typically not visible to the decision maker responsible for the system decision unless disclosed prior to the decision and was made in keeping with acquisition regulations.

Net Present Value—Rocket Example. An automated assembly system is being considered to assist in the production of the rocket system introduced in previous examples. The initial purchase and installation cost is assumed to be $300,000. The life of the system is assumed to be seven years with annual operating and maintenance costs of $65,000. It is expected that an annual increase of $100,000 in revenue will be obtained by increased production, and the system can be salvaged for $175,000 at the end of its seven year life. The interest rate (also known as the *minimum attractive rate of return*) is 7%, and an inflation rate of 3% is assumed.

Given these cost parameters, the net present value (NPV) of the assembly system can be computed to determine if the system should be purchased. The first step is to adjust the annual net cash flows for inflation as shown in Table 8.13. Once the adjusted annual net cash flows are estimated, a NPV can be computed using the equivalence formulas provided in Table 8.11. The system will be selected as economically justified if the NPV is greater than zero.

$$NPV = -\$300,000 + \$36,050 \left[\frac{1}{(1+0.07)^1}\right] + \$37,132 \left[\frac{1}{(1+0.07)^2}\right]$$

$$+ \$38,245 \left[\frac{1}{(1+0.07)^3}\right] + \$39,393 \left[\frac{1}{(1+0.07)^4}\right]$$

$$+ \$40,576 \left[\frac{1}{(1+0.07)^5}\right] + \$41,794 \left[\frac{1}{(1+0.07)^6}\right]$$

$$+ \$258,279 \left[\frac{1}{(1+0.07)^7}\right]$$

$$NPV = \$45,018.57$$

The resulting NPV of the assembly system is positive: $45,018.57, supporting a recommendation that the company approve the system for purchase and implementation.

TABLE 8.13   Inflation-Adjusted Annual Net Cash Flows.

EOY	Cash Outflows ($)	Cash Inflows ($)	Net Cash Flow ($)	Inflation Conversion Factor	Cash Flow in Actual ($)
0	−300,000.00		−300,000.00	$(1+0.03)^0$	−300,000.00
1	−65,000.00	100,000.00	35,000.00	$(1+0.03)^1$	36,050.00
2	−65,000.00	100,000.00	35,000.00	$(1+0.03)^2$	37,132.00
3	−65,000.00	100,000.00	35,000.00	$(1+0.03)^3$	38,245.00
4	−65,000.00	100,000.00	35,000.00	$(1+0.03)^4$	39,393.00
5	−65,000.00	100,000.00	35,000.00	$(1+0.03)^5$	40,576.00
6	−65,000.00	100,000.00	35,000.00	$(1+0.03)^6$	41,794.00
7	−65,000.00	275,000.00	210,000.00	$(1+0.03)^7$	258,279.00

| | Purchase | Ownership costs | | | | | | Total cost of ownership |
| | | Year | | | | | | |
	cost	NPV	1	2	3	4	5	Sum
Option A	$35,180.00	$28,699.08	6,384.00	6,228.00	6,069.00	6,790.00	7,321.00	**$61,619.12**
Option B	$44,450.00	$41,524.00	10,539.00	7,974.00	7,652.00	6,585.00	8,774.00	**$87,663.10**
Option C	$36,620.00	$29,629.00	8,096.00	5,004.00	4,752.00	5,391.00	6,386.00	**$67,640.56**
Option D	$74,490.00	$42,837.81	10,536.81	9,380.00	8,064.00	7,529.00	7,328.00	**$120,158.43**
Option E	$52,940.00	$34,817.08	9,733.59	6,455.12	6,139.12	5,841.12	6,648.12	**$89,768.80**

| | Financed | | Purchase and finance costs | | | | |
	20% Down	amount	NPV	1	2	3	4	5
Option A	$7,036	$28,144.0	$25,884.04	$5,896.17	$5,896.17	$5,896.17	$5,896.17	$5,896.17
Option B	$8,890	$35,560.0	$37,249.10	$7,449.82	$7,449.82	$7,449.82	$7,449.82	$7,449.82
Option C	$7,324	$29,296.0	$30,687.56	$6,137.51	$6,137.51	$6,137.51	$6,137.51	$6,137.51
Option D	$14,898	$59,592.0	$62,422.62	$12,484.52	$12,484.52	$12,484.52	$12,484.52	$12,484.52
Option E	$10,588	$42,352.0	$44,363.72	$8,872.74	$8,872.74	$8,872.74	$8,872.74	$8,872.74

Figure 8.15   Electric vehicle five-year total cost of ownership.

NPV—Electric Vehicle Cost Analysis. The systems team conducted a life cycle cost analysis for each of the five EV options using a total cost of ownership approach that in addition to purchase-related costs, included tax credits (if any), insurance, maintenance, repairs, taxes and fees, depreciation, and fuel (all types including electric power). The costing horizon considered a five-year useful life for each of the vehicles. NPVs were calculated for estimated yearly ownership costs and finance costs on any remaining purchase costs after a 20% initial downpayment was made in year 0. A 4.75% discount rate was used for NPV calculations. The results are shown in Figure 8.15.

8.4.4   Breakeven Analysis and Replacement Analysis

Two additional system selection techniques warrant discussion in this chapter due to their applicability to LCC: *breakeven analysis* and *replacement analysis* [4]. In breakeven analysis, the system output quantity required to earn a zero profit (breakeven) is determined as a function of the sales per output unit (revenue), variable cost per output unit, and total fixed cost. Past this breakeven point, profit becomes positive. Once the required breakeven output quantity is determined, a judgment as to whether or not this level of output is reasonable determines if the system should be selected.

Rocket Breakeven Point. A relatively new systems manufacturer is considering whether or not to compete for the rocket system development contract. Their design is quite modern, involving a host of technologies currently in research but estimated to be available in time if they were to win the contract. As part of their analysis, their systems cost analysis team calculated the company's fixed costs for producing rocket systems, the variable costs that were dependent upon the number of rocket systems they manufactured, and the total sales revenue they would make based on the number of rocket systems produced and sold. Figure 8.16 shows a chart of the results.

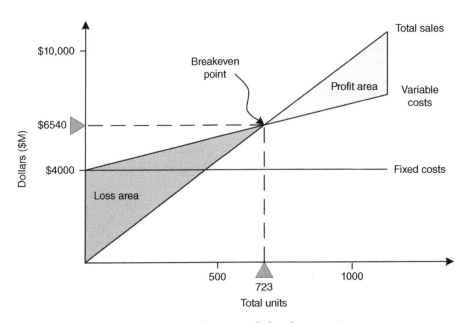

Figure 8.16 Rocket example breakeven point.

When their rocket system production and sales level is below 723, the Total Sales revenue is less than the total costs (fixed plus variable) and they will be operating at a loss as indicated by the Loss Area shading in Figure 8.16. Above 723 rockets, the Total Sales revenues exceed the total costs and the rocket system production and sales activity becomes profitable as indicated by the shaded Profit Area. At exactly 723 rocket systems, Total Sales ($ 6540M) equals total costs ($ 6540M) and zero profit (or loss) occurs. This is the breakeven point for their company's rocket system production and sales activity. Whether or not they decide to compete rests upon an internal decision regarding how feasible it is for them to produce 723 rocket systems.

Replacement analysis is generally performed using the equivalence formulas presented in Table 8.11. The primary decision involved with replacement analysis is whether an existing system (called the *defender*) should be retired from use, continued in service, or replaced with a new system (called the *challenger*). Accurate replacement analysis is very important when making systems decisions in the retirement stage of the life cycle.

REFERENCES

1. SCEA. *Glossary*. Vienna, VA: Society of Cost Estimating and Analysis. Available at: www.sceaonline .org. (Accessed 25 March 2022).
2. Stewart, R., Wyskida, R., Johannes, J. (1995) *Cost Estimator's Reference Manual*. 2nd ed. New York: John Wiley & Sons.

3. Canada, J.R., Sullivan, W.G., Kulonda, D.J., White, J.A. (2004) *Capital Investment Analysis for Engineering and Management*, 3rd ed. Upper Saddle River, New Jersey: Pearson Education.

4. Ostwald, P. (1991) *Cost Estimating*, 3rd ed. Upper Saddle River, New Jersey: Pearson Education.

5. Lee, D. (1997) *The Cost Analyst's Companion*. McLean, VA: Logistics Management Institute.

6. Park, C. (2004) *Fundamentals of Engineering Economics*. Upper Saddle River, New Jersey: Pearson-Prentice-Hall.

7. Kerzner, H. (2006) *Project Management*. 9th ed. New York, NY: John Wiley & Sons.

8. U.S. Bureau of Labor Statistics, Division of Consumer Prices and Price Indexes. Available at: http://www.bls.gov/CPI. (Accessed 25 March 2022).

9. OriginLab Corporation. *Origin Pro*. Northampton, MA. Available online: https://originlab.com. (Accessed 3 March 2022).

10. AACE, Inc. (2003) *Cost Estimate Classification System*. AACE International Recommended Practice No. 17R-97. Available at: https://www.anvari.net. (Accessed 8 Mar 2022).

11. GAO-07-406SP. Defense acquisitions: assessment of selected weapon systems, United States Government Accountability Office. Available at: http://www.gao.gov/new.items/d07406sp.pdf. (Accessed 19 Jan 2022).

12. Tecolote Research, Inc. (2020) *Automated Cost Estimating Integrated Tools (ACEIT:ACE)*. Version 8.0. Santa Barbara, CA: Tecolote Research.

13. Farr, J.V., Faber, I. (2021) *Engineering Economics of Life Cycle Cost Analysis*. Upper Saddle River, Florida: CRC Press.

14. DAU (2022). *Cost Estimation Techniques*. Washington, DC: Defense Acquisition University (DAU). Available at: https://www.dau.edu/acquipedia. (Accessed 9 Mar 2022).

15. AcqNotes (2005) *Work Breakdown Structures for Defense Material Items*. Mil-Hdbk-881a. Available at: https://www.acqnotes.com/Attachments/MIL-Hand%20Book-881.pdf. (Accessed 25 March 2002).

16. Minitab Statistical Software. Available at: http://www.minitab.com. (Accessed 25 Feb 2022).

17. JMP Statistical Software. Available at: http://www.jmp.com. (Accessed 25 Feb 2022).

18. Brown, C., Horak, J., Waller, W., Lopez, B. (1997) *Users Manual for TBMD Missile Cost Model*. TR-9609-01. Santa Barbara, CA: Technomics.

19. Shafer, W., Golberg, M., Om, N., Robinson, M. (1993) *Strategic System Costs: Cost Estimating Relationships and Cost Progress Curves*. Washington, DC: IDA Paper P-2702.

20. Wright, T. (1936) 'Factors, affecting the cost of airplanes,' *Journal of Aeronautical Sciences*, 3, pp. 122–128.

21. Thuesen, G., Fabrycky, W. (2000) *Engineering Economy*, 9th ed. Upper Saddle River, New Jersey: Pearson.

Chapter 9

Decision Making via Tradespace Analysis

There are no solutions. There are only tradeoffs.

—Thomas Sowell, Author

9.1 INTRODUCTION

Among the various methodologies specifically developed to address challenges associated with systems decision making exists a broad class whose members include multiple attribute value theory (MAVT) [1], multiple criteria value modeling (MCVM) [2], stochastic MCVM [3, 4], multiple criteria decision analysis (MCDA) [5, 6], multiple objective decision analysis (MODA) [7], multi-attribute decision theory (MADT) [8], and stochastic multicriteria acceptability analysis (SMAA) [9, 10] and their extensions. While not equivalent in their specific modeling elements and results, all assess a subset of viable alternatives guided by a set of preferences, criteria, and ideals that retain consistency throughout each method's model building process.

In MCVM in particular, a Cartesian plot that displays each alternative's total costs and total value return in a two-dimensional *tradespace* within which each alternative's geometric positioning relative to one another defines dominance conditions that help identify a *choice set* of efficient alternatives. From this choice set, a decision maker selects a best "bang-for-the-buck" alternative given the expressed cost and value structures underscoring each alternative's position. Reducing the set of competing system alternatives to a smaller choices set accommodates the cognitive limits

Decision Making in Systems Engineering and Management, Third Edition.
Patrick J. Driscoll, Gregory S. Parnell, and Dale L. Henderson
© 2023 John Wiley & Sons, Inc. Published 2023 by John Wiley & Sons, Inc.

of human working memory whose ability to contrast, combine, or manipulate elements has been shown to be no more than two to four elements at a time [11–13]. Notably such a display does not make use of ratios as they can mask important information in MCVM [14].

Not all MCVM efforts involve tradespaces as a primary artifact, seeking instead to produce a 1 to *n* ranking by combining all criteria into a single dimensional representation. For U.S. Department of Defense applications, which primarily motivated the MCVM approach presented herein, acquisition regulations mandate "[d]efining costs and benefits so they are mutually exclusive" [15] to help decision makers judge when additional benefits are worth additional costs and to make more explicit any risks associated with alternative selection [14]. Tradespaces naturally accommodate this requirement in a manner that ranking alternatives does not.

For decision makers, choosing among viable alternatives is a difficult task that evokes anxiety in pre-decision and post-decision settings [16, 17]. This response is associated with *cognitive dissonance*, a long studied in psychology literature [18]. In the field of psychology, cognitive dissonance is the perception of contradictory information stemming from a person's actions, feelings, ideas, beliefs, values, and things in the environment. Cognitive dissonance is typically experienced as psychological stress when people participate in an action that goes against one or more of those things [19].

Tradespace analysis within MCVM explicitly recognizes that stakeholders in general and decision makers in particular are likely to experience cognitive dissonance when making system decisions and has accommodations in its approach to alleviate this to the extent possible in several ways.

First, the closer that system alternatives are in their desirability—and truly competitive alternatives have this characteristic—the more difficult it is to make an exclusive choice between them [16, 20, 21]. Subtle distinctions between alternatives that otherwise might be overlooked take on elevated roles. MCVM exposes and emphasizes these subtle differences using value-focused thinking (VFT) graphs such as a cost-value tradespace and stacked bar charts in a deterministic setting and cloudplots, risk-value, risk-cost, and realization analysis when uncertainty is present. Alternative selection via ranking leaves these details out of sight rather than directly addressing conflicting values and objectives.

Second, as the number of competing alternatives increases, post-decision cognitive dissonance increases in response, resulting from mismatches in a decision maker's mind between what was expected as an outcome and what actually occurs. The systems decision process (SDP) and its MCVM approach are explicitly structured around a decision maker's expectations for system behavior (functions), what they hope to achieve by a system performing this way (objectives), the values they hold that contextualize their choices (value measures, value functions), their priorities (swing weights), their uncertainty regarding any data or information critical to the decision (stochastic MCVM), and their concerns about their personal exposure to regret having made a decision (Realization analysis). All these facilities are available with tradespace analysis. Additionally, these products expose decision information that also appeals to complex situations in which a decision maker has tacit constraints that are not shared with the systems decision support team but will nonetheless affect the choice they make among alternatives.

Moreover, the SDP is a constant engagement process with stakeholders and decision makers that can tailor client interactions to meet the specific needs of any decision maker. Decision makers grow ownership in the systems decision process and any models supporting it, understanding not only what was done but why it was done and how it supports the decision they have to make. This goes a very long way toward helping decision makers manage their expectations in an effective, realistic manner.

Lastly, when essential elements of uncertainty are appropriately incorporated into decision support models in this setting, communicating analytical insights becomes more challenging directly in response to increased mathematical sophistication. Realization analysis in MCVM, discussed in Chapter 10.1, shifts the discussion to focus on targeted simulation results that, while maintaining mathematical sophistication in the background, clearly expose the nuances that uncertainty has created as a result of its presence and the ramifications it has on the decision being made.

A tradespace requires that some measure of efficiency applies so that tradeoff comparisons can be made that logically and mathematically separate promising system alternatives from others. An MCVM tradespace does this by using Pareto efficiency as its foundation.

The concept of Pareto efficiency is widely leveraged in portfolio investment decisions that seek to achieve a maximum return level for a constrained investment amount and a fixed level of risk. When a theoretical maximum is calculated at all levels of risk, a curve called a *Pareto frontier* extends across the tradespace indicating optimal portfolio combinations. Higher or lower levels of risk and return are possible by altering the combination of portfolio investments being considered.

System solution alternatives in a systems decision making setting are analogous to alternative portfolio constructions. A similar Pareto frontier is created when alternative system designs involve value and cost tradeoffs: cost equates to risk (and sometimes risk itself is represented) while value equates to investment returns. System alternatives that position themselves along the Pareto frontier are efficient.

In a practical sense, when developers craft their system design, they face physical, technical, and financial constraints that limit the amount of stakeholder value their designs are able to achieve. Within these constraints, they leverage their organization's resources (skills, dollars, time, people, equipment, knowledge, experience, networks, etc.) to create what they think will maximize value from the decision maker's perspective for the dollars that their system will cost. Stakeholder values are based on their needs, wants, and desires, the total combination representing an ideal system. At a limited resource level, system developers can meet needs, a majority of wants, and a subset of desires, but not all. Consequently, developers must prioritize their efforts and in doing so, their system alternatives will fall short against some decision maker value measures and excel in others.

System integration and safety considerations further constrain designs, naturally preventing over-investing in needs, wants, and desires. For example, automobile drivers *need* night illumination to safely drive during periods of limited visibility. They *want* to be able to see as far as possible. They *desire* this to be unlimited. A good proxy measure for this night visibility is lumens, which is a measure of the total quantity of visible light emitted by a source per unit of time by the vehicle headlights.

Achieving the ideal value return would require a level of electrical power that exceeds the physical limits for a vehicle that are defined by lane dimensions, passenger compartment size, electrical wiring limits, and other measures whose objectives conflict with maximizing illumination. Moreover, even if such an output level were possible, safety concerns involving approaching drivers constrain the max design level. Integration prevents sub-optimizing on this measure because it would over allocate total electrical power available and shut down other needed features such as dashboard illumination, break lights, stereo, heating and cooling, computer and commutations equipment, and others.

The resulting design alternative coupled with its total cost uniquely positions it in the MCVM tradespace, enabling comparisons to be made. The underlying optimization creating Pareto efficient conditions in the trade space occurs when decision makers attempt to optimize value returns as expressed by the objectives in the qualitative value model.

9.2 TRADESPACE PROPERTIES

After eliminating alternatives that fail to meet critical requirements using the screening process introduced in Section 7.3, each of the $n = 1, 2, \dots, N$ surviving alternatives are evaluated against a set of $m = 1, 2, \dots, M$ value measures whose objective or subjective estimates (measure scores) $x_{n,m}$ are input to value functions $f_m(x_{n,m})$ discussed in Section 6.3.1. These value functions convert disparate measure units into common units of value, mapping to a scale of $[0, 100]$. Values are, in turn, aggregated into a total value return estimate V_n for each of the N alternatives using stakeholder-elicited preference weights w_m to impose priorities within an additive model:

$$V_n = \sum_{m=1}^{M} w_m f_m(x_{n,m}) \tag{9.1}$$

where $0 < w_m \leq 1$, and $\sum_{m=1}^{M} w_m = 1$.

A similar representation is developed for V's opposing tradespace axis, typically total cost being modeled as an independent variable (C). Thus, each of the N alternatives in this decision tradespace D are represented as $A_n = [C_n, V_n] \in D$.

The presence of an ideal alternative, $A_{ideal} = [C_{ideal}, V_{ideal}]$, is useful to value modeling despite the fact that system alternatives cannot achieve an ideal positioning in the tradespace. System developers will, however, make system design choices that create an alternative they believe will provide the highest levels of value return on the highest priority measures for the cost at which they are willing to offer it. Requirements, objectives, and other guidance provided to them attempt to communicate accurate information in this regard without codifying decision maker and stakeholder value model elements.

Known also as a *utopia point* [22], the ideal establishes a partial preference ordering on D such that for any two alternatives $A_i, A_j \in D$ with $i \neq j$, A_i is preferred to A_j, denoted by $A_i \succ A_j$, whenever $C_i \leq C_j$ and $V_i \geq V_j$ unless equality holds for both which yields indifference. This preference structure exists so long as any two points are comparable and no intransitive relationships exist [5]. In Figure 9.1, the ideal alternative A_{ideal}, which corresponds to maximum value and minimum cost, is shown in the upper left corner of the graph. Superimposed on the graph is an example Pareto frontier defined by non-dominated alternatives from among the set of five that were evaluated for total cost and total value.

This feature imposes Pareto efficiency properties [23, 24] on the tradespace D involving the ordinal positioning of alternatives [5]. Each alternative's ordinal positioning is directly leveraged for pairwise comparisons that expose *dominance* relationships between alternatives [2]. These dominance relationships can be visually and computationally identified by comparing their geometric positioning relative to each other and the A_{ideal} because spatial separation has meaning under the requirement that all value and cost scales be interval as a minimum and ratio at best. In Figure 9.1, alternatives A and C are dominated. The set of all non-dominated alternatives is referred to as a *choice set*.

Mathematically, dominance conditions are defined relative to each alternative's *polar cone*. In particular, for each alternative A_n, construct two linearly independent generating unit vectors: $\vec{uc}_n = [-1, 0]$ and $\vec{uv}_n = [0, 1]$, originating from translated origins centered on each A_n (see Figure 9.2).

Definition. The cone $K_n \subseteq D$ of A_n is the set of all alternatives $A_i \in D$ such that $A_i = A_n + \lambda_1 \vec{uc}_n + \lambda_2 \vec{uv}_n$, with $\lambda_1, \lambda_2 \geq 0$.

The cone definition states that any alternative lying in the cone K_n of A_n is a nonnegative linear combination of the generating unit vectors $\vec{uc}_n$ and $\vec{uv}_n$. Figure 9.3 shows A_4 being contained in the cone of A_5, $A_4 = [C_4, V_4] = A_5 + \lambda_1 \vec{uc}_5 + \lambda_2 \vec{uv}_5$ with $\lambda_i \geq 0$, $i = 1, 2$.

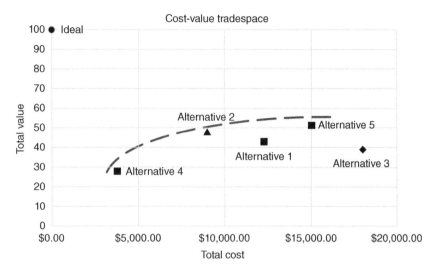

Figure 9.1 Example Pareto-based tradespace.

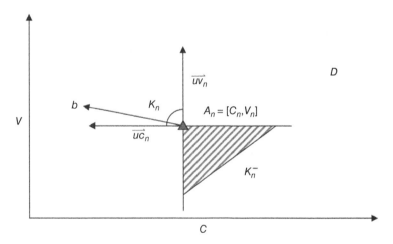

Figure 9.2 The cone K_n and polar cone K_n^- of alternative A_n.

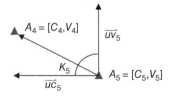

Figure 9.3 Alternative 4 (A_4) is contained in the cone K_5 of alternative A_5.

Definition. Given a cone $K_n \subseteq D$ of A_n, the *polar cone* of A_n, denoted by $K_n^- \subseteq D$ is the set of all points $k \in D$ such that $k = A_n - \lambda_1 \vec{uc}_n - \lambda_2 \vec{uv}_n$, with $\lambda_1, \lambda_2 \geq 0$.

Equivalently, the polar cone can be defined using the inner product $\langle k, b \rangle = \|k\| \|b\| \cos \theta$ as $K_n^- = \{k \in D : \langle k, b \rangle \leq 0 \,\forall\, b \in K_n\}$. Thus, the polar cone accounts for all points in D whose vectors extending from the translated origin on alternative A_n make an angle $90^\circ \leq \theta \leq 180^\circ$ with any vector corresponding to points within or on the boundary of cone K_n [25]. There exists a need to define dominance between alternatives in this tradespace D, as it is the basis for both deterministic and stochastic tradespace analysis discussed in this book.

Definition. An alternative $A_i \in D$ *dominates* alternative $A_j \in D$, $i \neq j$, (equivalently: A_j is *tradespace inferior* to A_i) if and only if $A_i \in K_j$ with $\lambda_1 > 0$ or $\lambda_2 > 0$, but not both.

Definition. An alternative $A_i \in D$ *strictly dominates* alternative $A_j \in D$, $i \neq j$, (equivalently: A_j is *strictly tradespace inferior* to A_i) if and only if $A_i \in K_j$ with both $\lambda_1 > 0$ and $\lambda_2 > 0$.

A consequence of the aforementioned definitions is that an alternative A_i dominates A_j ($A_i \succ A_j$) if $A_i \neq A_j$ and A_j lies in the polar cone of A_i. Similarly, A_i strictly dominates A_j ($A_i^* \succ A_j$) if $A_j \in K_i^-$ but does not lie on its boundary. This derivation, while seemingly obvious, supports the pairwise comparisons used in Pareto efficiency-based tradespace analysis.

Finally, we define the notion of *tradespace efficient* and *choice set* that are fundamental to tradespace analysis.

Definition. $A_i \in D$ is *trade space efficient* if no other alternative A_j, $i \neq j$ lies in its cone except A_{ideal}.

Definition. The *choice set* is the set of all trade space efficient alternatives. In the example tradespace shown in Figure 9.1, Alternative 2 strictly dominates Alternatives 1 and 3 (they both lie in the polar cone of Alternative 2). Alternative 5 strictly dominates Alternative 3. Although Alternative 1 strictly dominates Alternative 3 because Alternative 3 lies in Alternative 2's polar cone, the dominance of Alternative 1 by Alternative 2 prevents it from being tradespace (Pareto) efficient. Alternatives 4, 2, and 5 are non-dominated alternatives defining a Pareto frontier for this set of alternatives. Consequently the choice set would consist of these three alternatives.

9.3 SCORING SOLUTION ALTERNATIVES

As a matter of semantics, feasible system alternatives that successfully pass screening are also referred to as candidate system solutions, or candidate solutions because these will receive a full value return and life cycle cost tradespace analysis. They are still system alternatives in consideration of the systems decision being made, but because one of these alternatives is destined to be selected by the decision maker for implementation, it is fair to say that these represent potential solutions. In this section, the terms are used interchangeably.

Before the systems team begins scoring solution candidate alternatives (those passing screening) using the quantitative value model, it is helpful to review the products supporting alternative scoring to ensure they are complete. If any revisions, additions, or deletions are required, they should be performed prior to scoring. These include:

- *Revised problem statement.* Recognizing that time has passed since the Problem Definition phase, does the statement still capture the stakeholders' needs, wants, and desires? Does it still address the "real" system problem? Is it still relevant? If the answer to any of these is no, then more work should be applied to revising and properly structuring the problem statement. If "yes," then continue.

- *Value model.* System requirements developed during Problem Definition are used to reduce the number of competing alternatives to a set that only meet threshold measure levels. Have requirements changed? Has anything changed since screening was performed that might add or delete alternatives? Are the value measures (and hence value functions) complete? Are they still relevant? Have the decision maker's priorities changed, affecting the swing weights used in the value model?

- *Candidate solutions.* Does each candidate system solution have sufficient detail to score them on each value measure and assess their cost? Are the costs comparable between alternatives? Have they changed since the initial cost model was developed?

- *Modeling and simulation results.* Are the modeling and simulation results obtained during Solution design still valid? Do any of these need to be re-run using updated information? Are all the models and simulations properly stored so that they can potentially be used to analyze and improve system solution alternatives?

- *Confirm value measure ranges and weights.* Finally, this is a good time to reconfirm the ranges on the value measures and analyze their impact on the weights in the swing weight matrix. Does any new information suggest that the range of any value measure needs to be altered? Has anything happened since the quantitative value model was built that might cause the decision maker to change the shape of any value function?

Once checks are complete, system solution candidates are ready to be scored. There are five main information categories that support scoring alternatives against each value measure: operations, focused testing, modeling, simulation, and expert opinion.

9.3.1 Operations

The best data for scoring alternatives in a quantitative value model is that obtained by observing the alternative system during actual operations in its environment. Unfortunately, this is usually only possible for the existing baseline system that is being replaced or for system alternatives that are already deployed or are being used as advanced prototypes during operations similar to that of the system of interest. It will usually be cost and schedule prohibitive to obtain operational data on all candidate solutions, meaning that some other source of value measure data support must be used.

9.3.2 Focused Testing

Focused system tests generally fall into two types: development testing and operational testing. Development testing is performed on system alternatives by the organization that owns them, typically during a science and technology development phase which takes place at the developer's site. The system is represented in prototype with design accommodations that will allow development teams (engineers, scientists, computer scientists, organization and process specialists, etc.) uncomplicated access to the system elements they are responsible for. Consequently, many of the system's form factors could be different than the actual design. For example, the system's containment enclosure might be larger to allow the engineering team quick access to cables, power units, and so on so that they can replace, repair, or make alterations and adjustments to various parts and settings.

The system and its elements are only exposed to a limited subset of their environmental influences, enough to gather data on various measures of performance (MoP) and technical performance measures (TPM), making sure that the system, its subsystems, and components are behaving as designed. The system developer employs its own people to act as the intended system users. A good proportion of development testing can be performed in an isolated setting such as a laboratory or access-controlled field facility. Developers try to mimic the real life setting as much as practical.

Operational testing places a system in contact with its real-world environment and its actual intended users, maintaining developer presence to note and correct any deficiencies or anomalies regarding system behavior. A near final design is used, including final form factors and human interfaces. Operational testing takes place after one or more full-scale prototypes of the system are available.

In terms of accuracy and replicating results, this is probably the best method to gather information to score alternatives. It directly measures system performance against decision maker value measures and reduces the number of assumptions required by the other methods. The drawback of this method are the resource costs associated with running the test, data collection and scoring. That said, focused testing certainly has an important role in the design and evaluation process and is required prior to fielding any system.

9.3.3 Modeling

Modeling usually refers to mathematical and computer-based models as opposed to physical models, although physical models are uniquely beneficial when tactile contact is relevant to design. Mathematical models are useful because they are based on sound mathematical principles, are accurate, and can be easily modified, replicated, or replaced. Physics-based mathematical models are often used when scoring sensor, communications, medical diagnostic, quantum computing, nuclear power, electric infrastructure, and other systems that rely on the laws of physics in their design. Queuing models are important when determining service times for system alternative designs regarding facilities layouts. Often such problems lend themselves to a closed-form mathematical expression that can generate accurate scoring data and information. As a system of interest becomes more complex, and especially if its structure involves stochastic elements, system simulation becomes the model of choice.

9.3.4 Simulation

Simulation has become increasingly more important to system alternative scoring as computing power increases with lower unit costs have accompanied simulation applications that have become more accessible due to enterprise and open source licensing. Commercial simulations have graphical user interfaces (GUI) and option controls that make modeling building simpler and rapid. Simulation is not limited to computer simulation, however. Simulation simply means using a representation of the system to determine its performance characteristics. Using this definition, simulation includes computer simulation and also physical representations of the candidate solutions.

Simulation is a very powerful tool for any systems team because it can be used to evaluate nearly any candidate system solution. For example, a computer simulation could be built to assess the throughput of an assembly line layout, the physical security of a facility, and others. A vehicle model could be manufactured similar to a candidate system solution and placed in a wind tunnel or used in a physics-based virtual simulation to determine value measure scores required for the analysis regarding fuel efficiency.

Simulation has a relatively low cost when compared with developmental or operational testing. However, there are some significant limitations. One of the most significant is that the representation of a candidate system solution may be biased by the analyst building the simulation. In other words, what is put into a simulation greatly affects the results that come out. As a result, model transparency has become an important feature to systems engineering and systems decision support projects.

9.3.5 Expert Opinion

During any system development stage, subject matter experts (SME) are a part of system assessment. Education, experience, and objectivity are key determinants when selecting SMEs for system alternative scoring input. While it might seem to be a natural choice, developer personnel are typically not used for this purpose because of perceived or actual conflicts of interest. Expert opinion is often considered the simplest means for obtaining value measure score data regarding system alternatives. By its nature, expert opinion lends itself to more subjective analysis than the other methods described, which may motivate the systems team to incorporate accommodations and modeling adjustments for uncertainty earlier than intended. (See Chapter 10.)

Expert opinion does not necessarily mean having a SME physically present when scoring is being performed. With phenomenal access to credible information afforded by the internet and networks, expert research tends to play a very big role in candidate scoring for some very practical systems decision making applications. The results of any and all of the five major information categories may actually be published and verified by credible online sources such as professional trade publications, journals, watchdog organizations, accreditation and regulation authorities, and other organizations whose vested interests lie in objective and accurate data and information reporting. The key terms here are *objective*, *accurate*, and *credible*. If any of these characteristics are in question, the source should not be used for scoring input.

Expert opinion can be very valuable depending on the time available for analysis and the level of fidelity required to support the system decision being made. For example, if the decision timeline precludes modeling, simulation, and focused testing, then this is a very sound approach to determining value measure scores. Sensitivity and uncertainty analyses take on additional importance in this setting.

 "No value model ever survives first contact with the system alternative value measure scores." –Greg Parnell

Once an initial scoring of alternatives takes place, the system team should and will revisit each value measure to ensure it is sufficiently assessing its associated objective. For consistency, the team should use the same methodology to measure each value measure against each candidate system solution. This is not always possible. An example would be if a candidate solution is so early in the development stage that it cannot be fully modeled or operationally tested, but all other candidate solutions can be operationally tested.

If there are value measure scales that are not allowing for full measurement of each candidate solution, either the scale or the value measure must be changed. This will affect the overall value model. Both value measures and swing weights often require slight modifications once value modeling results are observed.

When the systems decision involves replacing an existing system comparable in functionality to the new alternatives, the existing system is scored against all value measures as well, thereby yielding a *baseline* alternative that can be compared with all of the new options being offered by developers. Despite the possible attractiveness of new technologies and functional implementations offered by new system alternatives, until they are evaluated against the decision maker's values and priorities, the extent to which these new features translate into value return is unknown. Consequently, the existing baseline system is included as an alternative because there is a possibility that it may outperform the new system alternatives once total value return is calculated and weighted by decision maker priorities, and combined with total costs.

9.4   SCORING OPTIONS

There are two main approaches for assessing the total value return for competing feasible system solutions: scoring candidate system solutions and scoring candidate components. The latter holistically scores each candidate system solution using value measures intended to assess system behavior in toto. Component scoring uses value measures designed to assess major subsystems and/or components.

Component scoring is useful when system configuration changes, technology refresh or upgrades, or subsystem replacements are being considered and their effects on total system value return and costs are driving decision maker concerns. This approach is more detailed than system scoring because it scores all of the possible component or subsystem combinations that could compose system alternatives.

Component scoring considers all feasible systems designs using the list of component types to perform each system function, assuming that only one component type contributes to each value measure's score. It next applies weights to value measures in the same manner as system scoring. However, rather than proceeding immediately to tradespace analysis, component scoring applies optimization to determine a candidate system configuration that yields the highest value subject to compatibility and cost constraints. The compatibility constraints—possibly driven by integration requirements—may eliminate a subset of component combinations that are not feasible.

The system candidate scoring approach is more common than component scoring but both are equally beneficial when supporting systems decisions using MCVM.

9.4.1   Candidate Systems Scoring

Spreadsheet models are commonly used to accomplish MCVM alternative scoring either at a system or component level. This is a sensible choice for several reasons. Spreadsheets are ubiquitous as either stand-alone applications or as part of any number of office suites available for Windows®, Apple O/S®, or Linux®platforms. These are usually cross-compatible with each other, providing a capability for model sharing and co-development as needed. For this reason, and reasons associated with network security, spreadsheets are the tradespace analysis environment of choice for most businesses and organizations today.

Client familiarity with spreadsheets aids their understanding of the models built by systems teams because spreadsheets are perceived less of a "black box application" than other commercial software alternatives. Spreadsheets do not require clients to pay for additional commercial software licenses in order to collaborate on modeling building with systems teams, or to use and modify these models for their own purposes after a system decision has been made and the systems project completed.

For the systems analyst responsible for building the model, having to construct each piece of a spreadsheet model builds a level of familiarity with the details and assumptions going into the model that can be useful in a decision briefing. This is also why spreadsheet modeling is commonplace in academics. With the availability of software designed to accommodate uncertainty modeling as a spreadsheet Add-in, such as *@Risk* and the *SIPmath* application used in this book, modifying quantitative value models in this way is quickly accomplished.

The main disadvantages of spreadsheet modeling lie in practical considerations: the time it takes for analysts to design and structure each modeling element and in the increased computational time required by spreadsheets as table and cell lookups increase with model size. Experience mitigates the first affect. Spreadsheet models involving a large number of worksheets with interconnected referencing and calculations will experience delays on output response at some point. This affect is, however, also dependent upon the capability of the computer running the model.

Lastly, while it is relatively straightforward to change a quantitative value model implemented in a spreadsheet, such as revising value functions, changing weights, or changing scores when the model is reasonably small, making these changes becomes more demanding and time consuming as modeling size increases. To be fair, depending on the commercial software application used, this disadvantage may not be unique to spreadsheet models. Where specialty software typically gains an advantage over spreadsheet models is in time. Many are pre-programmed to rapidly generate sensitivity analysis, statistical analysis, and custom charting results which would otherwise require additional effort, importing Add-in macros, or writing custom VBA programming in spreadsheets.

As of this writing, the magazine published by the Institute for Operations Research and Management Sciences (INFORMS) called *OR/MS Today*, publishes an annual survey of decision analysis software relevant to MCVM efforts [26]. Thirty-four of the packages mentioned are capable of performing tradeoffs among multiple objectives. Several of these packages allow an analyst to use some MODA techniques, but few can do all the MCVM analyses described in this book. Logical Decisions™ exemplifies a typical MODA package with several built-in analysis techniques [27]. The disadvantages associated with these packages include their cost and the time needed to learn them.

Scoring Candidate EV System Solutions. Resource constraints made it impractical to test all of the EV system alternatives using anything other than expert opinion. Fortunately, ample objective, accurate, and credible research sources publish their findings and results for electric vehicle ratings and reviews online. These were used to gather the information needed to score each EV against the 10 value measures supporting the qualitative and quantitative value models for this systems decision. An Excel spreadsheet was used for the entire MCVM. The scoring results are shown in Value Measure Scores table in Figure 9.4.

As with a large majority of MCVM models, the value model was constructed in Excel, leveraging the custom VBA function `=ValuePL4` to convert each value measure score into value scores. The resulting value scores on the interval [0, 100] were then multiplied by their associated global weights (normalized swing weights) on [0, 1] to yield a total value return estimate for each candidate EV system solution. The results are shown in the Value Return Assessment table in Figure 9.4. This table is often referred to as a *value matrix*.

The calculations were performed as follows. Value measure scores for each EV Option were entered directly in cells `E53:I62`. A value matrix was constructed below it using the same format and alignment as the Value Measure Score table above it, both for organization and ease of setting up computational formulas. The three value function tables that appear above the Value Measure Scores table are for reference purposes here, but should be

	B	C	D	E	F	G	H	I
4	Charging Time (hrs)			Range (km)			Energy Consumption (kWh)	
5	X	Value (Y)		X	Value (Y)		X	Value (Y)
6	5	100		200	0		10	100
7	7	80		250	35		12	90
8	9	60		300	50		14	80
9	11	50		350	60		16	70
10	13	30		400	70		18	60
11	15	20		450	80		20	50
12	17	10		500	90		22	40
13	19	5		550	100		24	30
14	20	0					26	15
15							28	0

51			Value Measure Scores (raw data matrix)					
52	Value Measures			Option A	Option B	Option C	Option D	Option E
53	Total Passengers			5.00	4.00	5.00	5.00	5.00
54	Rear Seating Shoulder Room			52.50	53.60	52.76	55.10	57.70
55	Range			382.00	260.00	320.00	539.00	311.00
56	Passenger Volume			92.40	84.00	93.90	100.00	106.50
57	Charging Time (full)			7.50	20.00	9.50	7.00	6.00
58	Cargo Volume			14.80	9.20	17.00	31.60	12.60
59	Electric Drive Unit Power			150.00	170.00	200.00	503.00	120.00
60	Acceleration			7.90	7.30	7.80	2.40	9.90
61	Top Speed			90.00	160.00	146.00	260.00	172.00
62	Energy Consumption			18.00	13.10	28.00	18.60	15.10

		Global Weights						
63								
64			Value Return Assessment (value scores using ValuePL4)					
65	Values	Global Weights	Option A	Option B	Option C	Option D	Option E
66	Total Passengers	0.159	100.00	75.00	100.00	100.00	100.00
67	Rear Seating Shoulder Room	0.135	46.88	67.50	51.75	79.40	89.80
68	Range	0.151	66.40	38.00	54.00	97.80	52.20
69	Passenger Volume	0.119	59.60	20.00	65.60	85.00	100.00
70	Charging Time (full)	0.141	75.00	0.00	57.50	80.00	90.00
71	Cargo Volume	0.095	49.20	28.40	54.00	96.60	40.40
72	Electric Drive Unit Power	0.079	92.50	91.50	90.00	49.40	94.00
73	Acceleration	0.056	80.50	83.50	81.00	96.00	67.50
74	Top Speed	0.040	0.00	38.00	27.60	100.00	47.60
75	Energy Consumption	0.024	60.00	84.50	0.00	57.00	74.50
76	Estimated Total Value Return	1.000	67.94	47.32	64.91	86.67	79.33

Figure 9.4   Candidate system solution scoring for the EV example.

organized in this way in the MCVM to make the value function conversion process easy to accomplish.

The same `ValuePL4` macro function was used in cells `E66:I75` to convert value measure scores into value scores. Using the value measure "Charging Time" for Option A as an example, the formula: `=ValuePL4(E57,$B$6:$B$14,$C$6:$C$14)` was entered into cell `E70`. The absolute references to cells indicated by adding a symbol $ before each row and column label in the formula locks in the reference. In this way, copy-pasting the formula or drag copying the formula to each of the other "Charging Time" cells `F70:I70` will allow the value measure score reference `E57` to change automatically to `F57` through `I57` while maintaining a lock onto the "Charging Time" value function table. This same process was applied row-by-row to all the other cells in the Value Return Assessment table.

Next, to compute a weighted additive total value return estimate for each option, it is necessary to multiply each Option's value score with its associated global weight and sum them together. This is accomplished using the `=SUMPRODUCT()` function. Using Option A as an example, the formula: `=SUMPRODUCT($D$66:$D$75,E66:E75)` was entered into cell `E:76`. This function performs vector multiplication equivalent to a matrix inner product (dot product) in mathematics that performs the required multiplication by entry and summing automatically. Again, the absolute reference symbol $ as shown locks in a link to the global weights. Drag-copying cells `E66:E75` to the other Option columns in the value matrix will create the appropriate references by allowing the Option cells to change while keeping the reference to global weights fixed.

The numerical Total Value (TV) return on the interval [0, 100] for each Option is shown in cells `E76:I76`. These represent the vertical axis values for each option. When coupled with their horizontal axis Total Cost (TC) estimates, they become $(x, y) = (TC, TV)$ Cartesian coordinates in the subsequent tradespace analysis. For completeness, the function `ValuePL` could have been used in this example without an issue.

Scoring Candidate Rocket System Solutions. A combination of Focused Testing, Modeling, and Simulation were used to collect scoring data for the systems decision involving rocket design alternatives. The scores were directly entered into the Value Measure Scores table shown in Figure 9.5. The measure scales, related information, and data sources were recorded on a separate worksheet in the spreadsheet to document this information.

Value Measure Scores (raw data matrix)							
Value Measures		Baseline	Global Lightning	Hot Wired	Star Cluster	Slow Poke	Ideal
Speed of Platform		30.00	75.30	66.20	44.70	29.60	90.00
Percent Grade		20.00	28.62	53.63	32.46	42.33	60.00
Number of People		6.00	6.00	3.00	4.00	2.00	0.00
Thrust		800	1546	2818	2993	1138	3000
Number of Payloads		2.00	5.00	4.00	3.00	2.00	5.00
Accuracy		10.00	1.97	4.65	3.50	7.77	0.50
Range		20.00	99.50	14.20	55.40	36.50	105.00

Value Return Assessment (value scores using ValuePL4)							
Values	Global Weights	Baseline	Global Lightning	Hot Wired	Star Cluster	Slow Poke	Ideal
Speed of Platform	0.233	15.00	77.95	64.09	34.70	14.40	100.00
Percent Grade	0.014	10.00	18.62	80.89	26.15	50.83	100.00
Number of People	0.055	5.00	5.00	60.00	40.00	90.00	100.00
Thrust	0.123	0.00	27.76	92.72	99.72	8.28	100.00
Number of Payloads	0.164	10.00	100.00	60.00	20.00	10.00	100.00
Accuracy	0.274	0.00	90.15	72.33	80.00	35.68	100.00
Range	0.137	20.00	94.50	13.80	50.40	34.33	100.00
Estimated Total Value Return	1.000	8.29	76.19	62.37	55.03	26.12	100.00

Figure 9.5 Candidate system solution scoring for the rocket system example.

The existing system, called the Baseline, along with each of the five rocket system design candidate solutions and an Ideal are listed as column labels, with the value measures appearing as row labels. This is the same organization as was used for the EV system scoring example. The matrix was duplicated next to create the Value Return Assessment table (value matrix). The left side of this table shows the individual global weights (normalized swing weights) established by the decision maker to indicate both the relative importance of each measure and the impact that swings across their individual scales would have on the rocket system selection decision. These are shown previously along with their swing weights in Figure 6.21.

Using the `ValuePL4` macro function and the Excel `=SUMPRODUCT()` function as described in the EV system scoring example, the total weighted value score for each rocket system alternative appears in the cells at the bottom row of the table. Once each alternative's Total Value (TV) is combined with its Total Cost (TC), they become $(x, y) = (TC, TV)$ Cartesian coordinates in the subsequent tradespace analysis to support the systems decision being made.

9.4.2 Candidate Components Scoring

The candidate system solutions scoring approach introduced in the previous section holistically scores each candidate solution on each of the value measures. Candidate components scoring applies optimization to determine the best system solution configuration subject to compatibility constraints as described earlier. The approach assumes that only one component affects each value measure. For most hardware and software systems this assumption is reasonable. However, when the system of interest involves more diverse systems, such as organizations seeking to restructure, collateral influences may make this assumption have a greater effect on which alternative configuration is identified as optimal. In settings such as this, sensitivity analysis takes on an even greater importance than normal to test the robustness of the system solution. This assumption can be relaxed with more sophisticated optimization approaches beyond the scope of this book.

Before performing component scoring, the individual value measures must be uniquely aligned to one component type that groups competing components. In the reverse direction the assignment from component to value measures can be many-to-one, allowing the possibility for several value measures to be aligned with a single component which allows for some degree of modeling flexibility. The rocket system design example will be used to illustrate the component scoring approach in this section.

Continuing the rocket problem analysis, consider the component raw data matrix shown in Figure 9.6. The five component types are mobility, logistics, rocket, number of payloads, and guidance. Mobility is shown with five candidate components (A through E) competing for selection while each of the rest has four candidate components. Scores are provided for each component on the measure(s) they affect. To illustrate an earlier point, notice how, for example, the component type "Rocket" affects two value measures (thrust and range), but each value measure is aligned with a single component. The same is true for the component type "Mobility."

Value functions and their 2D tables were developed for each value measure using the techniques described in Chapter 6. These were used to convert value measure scores into the value scores shown in the value matrix in Figure 9.7. Since components are competing for selection and not systems, each candidate component's weighted total value was calculated using only the value measures affected by the component. For example, in the Mobility component type, the component "Vehicle A's" total component value was obtained by multiplying each value score by its global weight shown above each column and summed across the row: $14(0.23) + 10(0.01) = 3.32$. An ideal component value was computed by summing the weights of the value measures affected and multiplying by 100.

The ideal component value is a useful analytical tool for examining the *value gap* associated with any one component. Comparing the maximum component value with that of an ideal component

Component Type	Value Measure:	1.1.1 Speed	1.1.2 % Grade	1.2.1 Number of People	2.1.1 Thrust (lbs)	2.2.1 Number of Payloads	3.1.1 Accuracy (m)	3.2.1 Range (km)
	Global Weight:	0.23	0.01	0.06	0.12	0.17	0.27	0.14
Mobility 0.23	Vehicle A	30	0.2					
	Vehicle B	75.3	0.5					
	Vehicle C	66.2	0.5563					
	Vehicle D	44.7	0.32446					
	Vehicle E	29.6	0.4233					
Logistics 0.01	Concept A			0				
	Concept B			3				
	Concept C			4				
	Concept D			6				
Rocket	Rocket A				1000			20
	Rocket B				1500			40
	Rocket C				2000			60
	Rocket D				3000			100
Payloads	Two					2		
	Three					3		
	Four					4		
	Five					5		
Guidance	Inertial						7.77	
	GPS						1.97	
	Wire						4.65	
	Optical						3.5	

Figure 9.6 Rocket component value measure score matrix (raw data).

	A	B	C 1.1.1 Speed	D 1.1.2 % Grade	E 1.2.1 Number of People	F 2.1.1 Thrust (lbs)	G 2.2.1 Number of Payloads	H 3.1.1 Accuracy (m)	I 3.2.1 Range (km)	J Component value	K Ideal
36	Component Type	Value Measure:									
37		Global Weight:	0.23	0.01	0.06	0.12	0.17	0.27	0.14		
38	Mobility 0.23	Vehicle A	14	10						3.32	
39		Vehicle B	77	70						18.41	
40		Vehicle C	65	87						15.82	24
41		Vehicle D	35	26						8.31	
42		Vehicle E	13	51						3.5	
43	Logistics 0.01	Concept A			100					6	
44		Concept B			60					3.6	
45		Concept C			40					2.4	6
46		Concept D			5					0.3	
47	Rocket	Rocket A				0			19	2.66	
48		Rocket B				25			37	8.18	
49		Rocket C				50			56	13.84	26
50		Rocket D				100			95	25.3	
51	Payloads	Two					10			1.7	
52		Three					20			3.4	
53		Four					60			10.2	17
54		Five					100			17	
55	Guidance	Inertial						36		9.72	
56		GPS						90		24.3	
57		Wire						72		19.44	27
58		Optical						80		21.6	

Figure 9.7 Rocket component value matrix.

provides information to help decide if the systems team should continue to search or continue designing for higher value component candidates or not. For example, in "Mobility," the highest value Vehicle B component currently achieves is 18.41. Compared with the ideal vehicle component value of 24, the value gap of 5.59 could motivate a search for an additional alternative component that could potentially close the value gap.

Once the component value for each component is calculated, optimization is applied with the goal of maximizing the total value return across the five component type categories subject to any incompatibility, cost, or other constraints that would prohibit or discourage specific component combinations. For the rocket design problem illustrated, the constraints were budget, weight limitations, and the restriction that only one component could be selected for each component category. The particular Excel spreadsheet-based optimization technique discussed here is adapted from a project selection methodology [28].

Figure 9.9 shows the standard format for an optimization table that is used to calculate the value and cost of any optimal component configuration. Since the component scoring technique here involves a small, binary linear program, the Excel Solver Add-in is more than sufficient to perform the needed optimization. A simple online search will reveal quite a few credible and helpful information sources that walk through the use of Excel Solver. (e.g. See http://www.solver.com.)

The left side of the table in Figure 9.9 is used to optimize the configuration value. The five component types are shown on the left and repeated at the top of the table. Each of the non-greyed out cells in each column represent decision variables for the optimization. These are called "Changing Variable Cells" in the Solver interface window shown in Figure 9.8. The approach described here assumes that only one component will be selected from each of the component types. A binary decision variable (0 or 1) is used to indicate whether a particular component is selected for the

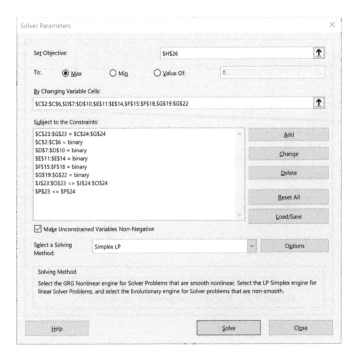

Figure 9.8 Excel Solver interface window. Source: Microsoft Corporation.

	A	B	C	D	E	F	G	H	I	J	K	L	M	N	O	P
1			Mobility	Logistics	Rocket	Payloads	Guidance	Value	NPV	Cost Year 1	Cost Year 2	Cost Year 3	Cost Year 4	Cost Year 5	Production Cost	Weight
2	Mobility	Vehicle A	0					3.32	$4.39	1	1	1	1	1	1	
3		Vehicle B	1					18.41	$8.78	2	2	2	2	2	2	
4		Vehicle C	0					15.82	$12.21	2	3	3	3	3	3	
5		Vehicle D	0					8.31	$16.60	3	4	4	4	4	4	
6		Vehicle E	0					3.5	$20.99	4	5	5	5	5	5	
7	Logistics	Concept A		1				6	$8.78	2	2	2	2	2	0	
8		Concept B		0				3.6	$13.17	3	3	3	3	3	0	
9		Concept C		0				2.4	$17.56	4	4	4	4	4	0	
10		Concept D		0				0.3	$26.34	6	6	6	6	6	0	
11	Rocket	Rocket A			0			2.66	$20.72	3	3	6	6	6	3	
12		Rocket B			0			8.18	$24.54	4	6	7	7	4	6	
13		Rocket C			0			13.84	$33.36	7	8	8	8	7	9	
14		Rocket D			1			25.3	$22.02	4	6	6	6	3	12	
15	Payloads	Two				0		1.7	$9.58	2	2	2	2	3	3	4
16		Three				0		3.4	$17.56	4	4	4	4	4	6	6
17		Four				1		10.2	$15.12	4	4	4	3	2	9	8
18		Five				0		17	$13.97	3	3	3	3	4	12	10
19	Guidance	Inertial					0	9.72	$12.33	2	4	3	3	2	10	4
20		GPS					1	24.3	$5.31	1	2	1	1	1	2	1
21		Wire					0	19.44	$15.92	3	6	3	3	3	5	1
22		Optical					0	21.6	$18.40	4	3	5	6	3	15	3
23		System Total:	1	1	1	1	1			13.00	16.00	15.00	14.00	10.00	25.00	9
24		Required:	1	1	1	1	1			20	18	20	20	15	50	10
25																
26							Total System Value	84.21					Legend			
27							Max possible value with no component limits:	91.01					Binary Decision Variable			
28													Calculation			
29							Total Configuration Cost	94.00								
30							Discount rate:	0.045								

Figure 9.9 Component optimization scoring table.

configuration solution (1) or not (0). For example, the component Vehicle B is selected by the optimization (1), the rest are not (0). This restriction is accomplished by constraining the decision variables in each block to be binary, as shown in the Solver constraint window.

The "System Total" row cells `C23:G23` at the bottom each contains an expression representing the sum of the column cells not greyed out. For example, the expression at the bottom of the "Mobility" column is `=SUM(C2:C6)`. These cells `C23:G23` become the left hand side expressions for the component type constraints created in the Excel Solver shown in the top of the Solver constraint window. The "Required" row entries immediately below these expressions are numerical values limiting this sum. For the rocket problem, these are set equal to 1, indicating that only one component can be selected for each component category. These "Required" values shown in `C24:G24` become the right hand side values for the component constraints for the Excel Solver as shown.

 Entering mathematical expressions or constants directly into the Excel Solver is bad practice because even when Excel allows it, it inhibits model changes. Instead, create links to cell locations on a worksheet that hold what is being asked for (e.g. left hand and right hand sides of expressions, coefficients, and so on).

An optimization needs an objective expression (function) to maximize or minimize. In this case, it is the Total System Value cell `H26`. The value column provides the component values calculated earlier in Figure 9.7. These act as objective function coefficients for each of the binary decision variables for creating the target cell objective function for the Excel Solver. The individual component values are included in the total system value being maximized only if their corresponding component is used in the design, meaning their decision variable equals 1. This is accomplished in cell `H26` by using a `=SUMPRODUCT()` to combine blocks of decision variables with their values, for example,' `=SUMPRODUCT(C2:C6,H2:H6))`, and then summing these 5 expressions to yield Total System Value. Cell `H26` becomes the "Set Objective" cell in the Solver.

The right side of the table is used to calculate the system costs and the weight of "Payloads" and "Guidance" components that must be launched by the rocket. The five-year research and development (R&D) costs and a single production cost are included for each component. The production cost is assumed to occur in year 0. A net present value (NPV) function is used to bring the series of future costs in years 1 to 5 into Year 0 dollars. For example, the NPV expression for the Vehicle A Mobility component is `=NPV($H$30,J2:N2)`, where cell `H30` contains the 4.5% discount rate used. Where possible in all expressions, absolute reference links are used when a reference location is not changing, as in `H30`. A `=SUMPRODUCT()` expression was again used in the same way as with component values so that a component's NPV would only contribute to the Total Configuration Cost if its decision variable equaled 1 after optimization.

Cells `J24:P24` each contain five `=SUMPRODUCT()` expressions being summed together to yield yearly total costs depending on which component was selected by the optimization. For example, the expression in cell `J24` is:

```
= SUM(SUMPRODUCT($C$2:$C$6,J2:J6)+ SUMPRODUCT($D$7:$D$10,J7:J10)
    + SUMPRODUCT($E$11:$E$14,J11:J14)+ SUMPRODUCT($F$15:$F$18,J15:J18)
                                    + SUMPRODUCT($G$19:$G$22,J19:J22)))
```

Cells `O24` and `P24` have similar expressions. The expressions in these seven cells become the left hand side expressions for budget constraints shown in the Solver window. The right hand side values are the fixed annual budget limits, production budget, and weight limits entered into cells `J24:O24`.

Many additional constraints may arise in optimizing a system design. For example, Vehicle B is not compatible with logistics concept D, or perhaps Rocket A can only launch two payloads. Kirkwood [28] and Ragsdale [29] provide examples of additional constraints that may be appropriate for systems design constraints and many others.

Finally, the appropriate `Simple LP` solving method is chosen from the drop down menu, and the optimization solved. The results are shown in Figure 9.9. The components selected to be included in the design are "Vehicle B," "Concept A," "Rocket D," "Payload Four," and "GPS" guidance, for a Total System Value of 84.21 and a Total Configuration Cost of 94.00.

The candidate components scoring approach has advantages and disadvantages compared with the candidate system solutions approach. The candidate system solutions scoring approach tends to be simpler and quicker because configuration options have already been decided, requiring a systems team to develop a small number of candidate solutions using the SDP technique. If, however, system configuration choices have not yet been made and various developers are offering potential candidate components, then the candidate components scoring approach will identify a configuration that maximizes total value return while meeting constraints, if one exists.

Moreover, because the technique's yields a wide perspective across all available components, the results can inform potential collaborations between developers that were not seen as valuable beforehand. This is an especially useful feature when the optimal component configuration is added to existing system configurations for tradespace analysis, as discussed in the following section.

Once the highest value candidate solution is identified, additional VFT can be applied to improve the solution. The candidate components approach requires more effort to obtain information on all of the component alternatives competing to be included in the system configuration. A major advantage of the candidate system solutions approach is that it will identify the highest value system solution possible given the components being considered and the constraint limitations within which all system configuration solutions must lie.

VFT can be used to change constraints and add better performing or less expensive components, if required by either the candidate components or candidate solutions approach. The systems team should select the best scoring method to use based on availability of data and time to perform the analysis.

The remaining sections of this chapter and the subsequent chapter addressing uncertainty will use the candidate solutions approach to illustrate and discussion various systems decision support modeling and analysis techniques. Discussions and examples will focus on analyzing results for candidate system solution alternatives via tradespace analysis, recognizing that each of these sections would be similar if they instead focused on a candidate components approach. Optimal and near-optimal candidate component configurations and their total cost estimates would position them in the tradespace. These would constitute the choice set from which a decision maker would select.

9.5 TRADESPACE ANALYSIS ON SCORING RESULTS

Deterministic tradespace analysis and the key charts that accompany it serve an important role in systems decision making support. As a precursor to the uncertainty modeling and analysis that necessarily follows, the cost-value tradespace provides a decision maker with clear information regarding the system alternatives that are competing for selection. Perhaps more importantly, the tradespace maintains and leverages VFT as opposed to alternative focused thinking (AFT) because it continues to seek high value system solutions even if they are not present in the set of alternatives being examined.

The tradespace created exposes the ramifications stakeholder and decision maker choices made throughout the SDP with regards to their stated values, approved value measures, representative value functions, accessible data sources, and priorities. This is possible because when properly applied, the SDP approach establishes and maintains traceability from end results to the very first discussions with system stakeholders. Consequently, it is not uncommon for a decision maker to ask the systems team to revisit some of these foundational MCVM elements once the results are displayed in a tradespace.

For tradespace analysis in support of systems decision making, there are two main VFT products that inform the decision. The first is a cost-value tradespace chart that has the Pareto efficiency properties described earlier in Section 9.2. The second main decision support product in support of systems decision making is a stacked bar chart that partitions the total value return estimates into their value measure components.

The cost-value tradespace directly facilitates relative comparisons between competing system solution alternatives based on their total costs and total value return estimates. The point estimates shown on this chart:

- Identify system alternatives or component configurations that are Pareto efficient and should be considered for selection. These constitute the *choice set* for the decision maker.

- Identify system alternatives or component configurations that are dominated by Pareto efficient alternatives. Unless there is relevant decision information outside of the criteria and costs modeled, these should not be considered for selection as alternatives.

- Reveal the competitiveness (or not) of the final alternatives based on the proximity of their location relative to others.

- Provides a "bang for buck" (value for cost) estimate for each alternative indicated by the slope of a straight line to each alternative when (0, 0) is used.

- Show the impact of current budget limitations regarding solution alternatives that might be included in the choice set if the decision maker's budget could flex upward. Similar to the discussion regarding alternatives that are close to threshold screening levels (see Section 6.3), attractive alternatives that exceed budget limits and are Pareto efficient should never be eliminated without further discussion with the decision maker.

- Begin to expose elements of decision risk. High quality, competitive alternatives tend to cluster toward the Pareto efficient frontier. Recognizing that actual value return and costs could end up being different from those estimated in the quantitative value model and the lifecycle cost model, especially for system designs that have not achieved a high level of prototyping, there is a chance that a logically supported selection can result in less system performance than expected, thereby exposing the decision maker to buyer's remorse. Sensitivity analysis on priority weighting explores the impact of changing priorities on the decision. Realization analysis discussed in Chapter 10 more directly engages this concern.

Electric Vehicle Tradespace Analysis. After completing a systems scoring for total value return of each EV option (Section 9.4) and a life cycle cost analysis using a total cost of ownership approach (Section 8.15), the systems team plotted both results in a cost-value tradespace chart shown in Figure 9.10. An Ideal Option was plotted at $45,000 instead of $0 dollars to orient stakeholders toward the direction of Pareto efficiency and to keep the chart focused appropriately on the options' positioning. The team also superimposed the taxi company's stated per vehicle total cost of ownership budget ($102,500) on the chart to support further discussion, if warranted.

Several important information elements are evident. Options A, E, and D are non-dominated system solution alternatives and therefore should be considered the choice set of alternatives from which the decision maker should pick. Option A strictly dominates both Option C and Option B; it offers higher value return for less cost than either of these two. Option C and Option B would not typically be included in the choice set.

While the choice set contains 3 out of 5 alternatives, Options A and C appear to be clustering with respect to cost and value return and may motivate keeping Option C until more analysis can be performed. Option E's higher cost could discourage its selection. However, since a total cost of ownership approach was used to develop all cost estimates, there are many cost categories being used that could potentially be negated or reduced depending on the capability and resources of the taxi company. If this were the case with Option E's developers, then Option E would move to the left in closer proximity to Options A and C, as typical of competitive solution alternatives. However, unless these reductions were specific to Option E, such adjustments would also decrease the other alternatives' costs. The end result would simply be a shift to the left for all alternatives.

Superimposed on the EV tradespace is the stated planning budget provided to the systems team early in the project. As it exists, Option D would be eliminated from the choice set as it is at least $15,000 over-budget. Even if the per vehicle budget could flex to accommodate Option D, the increase in value may not be worth the increase in cost, a judgment left to the decision maker. The decision maker concurred, allowing Options C, B, and D to be eliminated from further consideration.

However, the clustering of Options A and C appear to indicate that their value return and cost estimates are in relative close proximity. Given that these are estimates based on stakeholders and decision maker beliefs that could possible change over time, selecting one or the other could expose the decision maker to buyer's remorse if the non-selected alternative actually out-performed the selected one. A stacked bar chart will identify exactly how each of these two options achieved their total value return by category, potentially providing sufficient information to further justify one or the other's selection. This underscores a VFT principle that it's not just the total estimates that matter. Understanding how they achieved the levels they did is equally as important. If the non-selected alternative ultimately out-performs the chosen one but did so by achieving proportionally higher value return for lower priority values, then the risk posed by buyer's remorse will be reduced or mitigated.

The systems team next intended to create a stacked bar chart for these options to better understand their value return. They also recommended that they perform realization analysis on these three options to better understand how uncertainty might affect the decision maker's choice, once made.

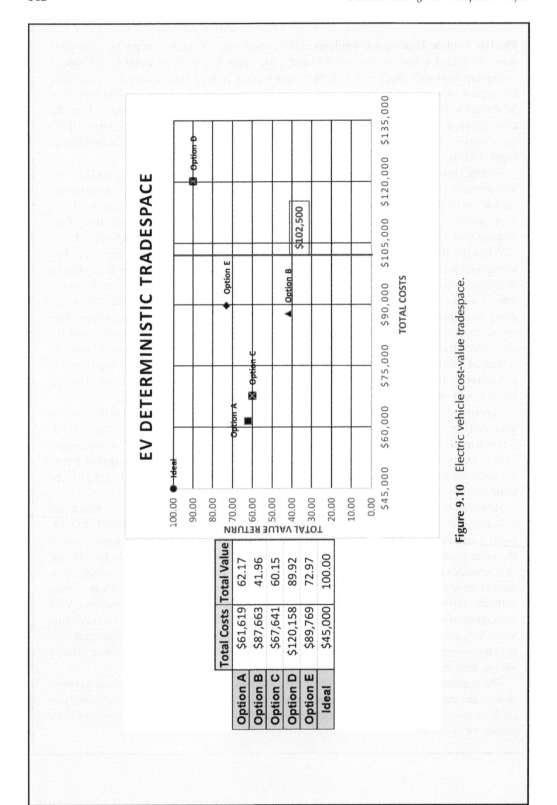

	Total Costs	Total Value
Option A	$61,619	62.17
Option B	$87,663	41.96
Option C	$67,641	60.15
Option D	$120,158	89.92
Option E	$89,769	72.97
Ideal	$45,000	100.00

Figure 9.10   Electric vehicle cost-value tradespace.

The decision maker agreed with this course of action, stating at this time, he is considering Option E as the system solution because its increased cost is still over $10,000 under budget and the value increase between the two closely clustered Options A and C and Option E appears to be significant enough to potentially justify its selection.

Rocket Design Tradespace Analysis. The systems team supporting the rocket design systems decision created a cost-value tradespace for discussion with the project's decision maker overseeing and guiding the rocket design selection process. Because the decision maker's organization had access to a number of independent component developers offering new technology for rockets, the systems team chose to include their component scoring results with their system scoring results to understand how an optimized configuration might compete with the others. They also felt that if the evidence for developer collaboration was strong enough in this regard, the decision maker would need to consider this possible project option. An Ideal alternative, which achieves a theoretical (but not achievable) levels for cost and value is again plotted to orient the decision maker to the directional pull towards Pareto efficiency motivating a Pareto frontier.

Figure 9.11 shows the rocket design deterministic tradespace with all alternatives. The low total value score achieved by the Baseline system illustrates stakeholder motivation for pursuing a new design. This is not suggesting that the Baseline system is failing in its purpose. Rather, it is more indicative of the evolutionary nature of stakeholder values in response to an aging system that can no longer adapt to a changing environment. Baseline is deficient in its ability to deliver value return for values expressed by the current group of stakeholders and the decision maker.

Interestingly, despite its low value return, Baseline is still Pareto efficient because the only alternative dominating it is the Ideal. The systems team included Baseline in the choice set along with Star Cluster, Global Lightning, and the Component optimization configuration. All lie in alignment with a Pareto frontier oriented on the Ideal in the tradespace. Global Lightning and Component alternatives strictly dominate Hot Wired. All design alternatives except for the Baseline strictly dominate Slow Poke and do so at a substantial difference in cost and value levels. Based on these results, the team recommended that Slow Poke should not be considered for selection. The decision maker agreed with these recommendations.

The systems team mentioned that it is interesting but not surprising that the optimized Component configuration scored as high in value as it did. As discussed previously, assuming that all components included in this system alternative are available, this is another illustration of VFT in action. It suggests to a decision maker that a high value design is possible assuming that reasonably comprehensive integration, performance, and other requirements were modeled in the optimization constraints.

The Component alternative's close proximity to Global Lightning does cause concern because any underlying uncertainty could alter and reverse their positioning. Decision risk is evident here. Depending on how Star Cluster, Global Lightning, and Component

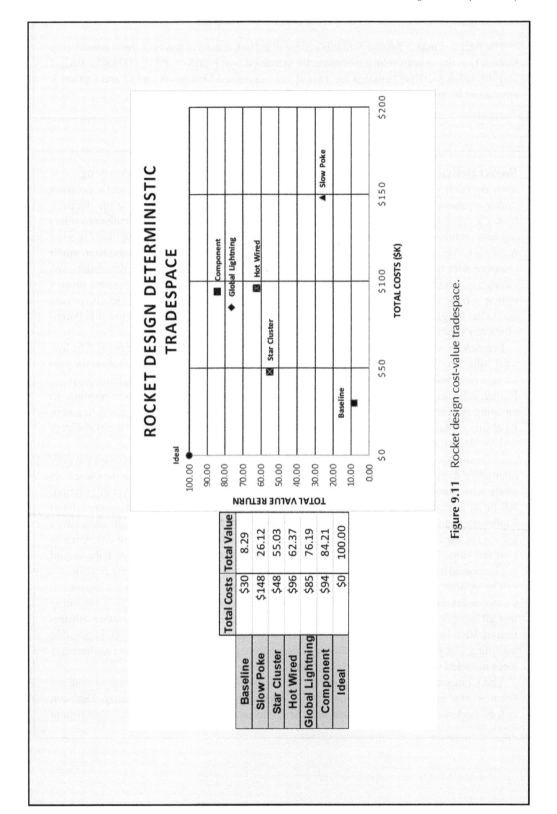

	Total Costs	Total Value
Baseline	$30	8.29
Slow Poke	$148	26.12
Star Cluster	$48	55.03
Hot Wired	$96	62.37
Global Lightning	$85	76.19
Component	$94	84.21
Ideal	$0	100.00

Figure 9.11 Rocket design cost-value tradespace.

achieved their total value returns, the Hot Wired design alternative could be held until any significant uncertainty is modeled and realization analysis performed on it, Star Cluster, Global Lightning, and Component. There appears to be enough competition among these alternatives that could cause the decision maker concern regarding buyer's remorse. Or, if the decision maker had additional considerations outside of the systems project that might motivate keeping it in consideration past this tradespace result, then it would be subjected to further analysis.

Drawing a straight line from the origin (0, 0) to each alternative indicates that Star Cluster currently yields the highest value for cost ("bang for buck") than any of the other alternatives. Consequently, despite its lower total value return, this value for cost return coupled with an alignment with the Ideal as to how Star Cluster achieved its total value by value measure, could make it a strong candidate for selection. Moreover, it offers significant value return increase over the Baseline while avoiding potential buyer's remorse due to alternative clustering. This will not be an easy decision to make.

A budget line was not provided to the systems team for this project, so budget flexing considerations relative to closely positioned alternatives such as that mentioned in the EV tradespace analysis would not apply at this point.

9.5.1 Analyzing Sensitivity on Weights

When supporting systems decisions in a tradespace context, it is important to not only summarize results for a decision maker, but also to explore the robustness of these results. Modeling results depend on the assumptions that support the model. In an MCVM approach such as this, value measure scores (raw data) have been weighted to reflect a decision maker's perspective of their individual importance and the impact that changes on their scale will impact the overall selection decision. The concern for deterministic tradespace analysis is whether the results would change significantly if a different weight allocation was used when aggregating total value scores. Exploring this possibility is called *sensitivity analysis*.

The purpose of sensitivity analysis is to see if a change in a modeling assumption changes the preferred solution. A parameter is sensitive if the decision maker's preferred solution changes as the parameter is varied over a range of interest. The most common sensitivity analysis is sensitivity to the allocation of weights by a decision maker. The concern here is not weight uncertainty because the sole arbiter of these values are the decision makers themselves; it is that the decision maker could be unsure of what weight to assign knowing his/her priorities, or that they are exploring priority alternatives in anticipation of challenges to the weights he/she assigned. This is accomplished by plotting weight versus value for the range of interest for all solutions. If the solution value lines do not intersect, then the selection made by the decision maker is not sensitive to weights. If the lines crossover, the solution is sensitive to the assigned weighting.

The standard approach for analyzing weight sensitivity is to vary one weight and hold the other weights in the same proportion so the weights continue to sum to one as the weight under focus increases and decreases from its current value. Since many factors are involved in realistically large value models (weights, value functions, and scores), the Pareto rule usually applies and less than 20% of the weights will be sensitive for realistic ranges of interest.

There are several ways to perform weights sensitivity. The first is to vary the weight of each value measure across its extremes from 0 to 1. This approach is shown in some MODA books [1] for illustrative problems with only a few value measures. This approach is not very useful for analytical purposes if there are a large number of value measures and little disagreement about the weights assessment.

A second approach when the weight allocation is not controversial is to vary each of the weights by 10%. This is a reasonable approach for determining if small changes in the weights will change the preferred solution.

When assigning weights is controversial and key stakeholders disagree on one or more weight allocations, they are more than likely interpreting the weights as importance indicators only, which is the case with analytic hierarchy process (AHP) and other weighting approaches. Consequently, it is easily the case that a subset of stakeholders possess a vested interest better reflected in a different set of weights than those observed influencing tradespace results. With swing weighting blending importance with the decision maker's consideration of value measure change impact on the decision, the weights shown represent more than just importance, making it more difficult to advocate specific weight changes simply to accommodate differences of opinion.

A third approach addresses this conundrum by varying the weight(s) involved in the disagreement across the range of interest as expressed by the stakeholders. For example, if the current value measure weight is 0.28 and a stakeholder suggests that this should be lower from their perspective to 0.13, then this range could be changed in sensitivity analysis. A more practical approach for this third approach is to vary the weight across the entire range from 0 to 1.0. Crossover points will become apparent if they exist, and if the preferred solution does not change (no crossover), then a disagreement between stakeholders regarding weight allocation is moot. If the preferred solution changes across the range of interest, then further discussion among the decision maker and stakeholders is warranted with the hope of the systems team receiving is warranted we need to present this to the key stakeholders and decision maker(s) for resolution.

When swing weighting is used, there are two options for weights sensitivity analysis. The first option is to perform the sensitivity analysis using the original swing weights as assigned by the decision maker before scaling to global weights has occurred. This approach has the advantage that sensitivity analysis is done directly on the weighting judgment. A disadvantage is that the measure weight variation depends on the swing weight sum and hence, the other swing weights. For example, suppose that a swing weight assigned to a value measure is 85 and the swing weight sum is 365 (equivalent to a global weight of 0.23). Varying this swing weight across the entire range from 0 to 100 (the highest swing weight) while holding the other weights constant will vary the sum from 280 to 380, causing the value measure's global weight to vary from 0 to 0.26.

Applying sensitivity analysis to the global weight 0.23 would vary the global measure weight 10% (± 0.1), causing it to span the interval 0.13–0.33, which is equivalent to a swing weight assignment of 47–120. The advantage of this approach is that is achieves the full range of ± 0.1. The disadvantage is that the equivalent swing weight range from 47 to 120 may be unrealistic if there is agreement among stakeholders that the value measure assigned a swing weight equal to 100 indicates the highest importance and highest range variation impact on the systems decision, which is what swing weighting assumes.

Applying weight sensitivity analysis directly on swing weights for any controversial value measure weights is the better approach. The swing weight sum used as a denominator to normalize swing weights into global weights automatically adjusts for each simulation iteration thereby maintaining their convexity characteristic summing to 1. Time permitting and for completeness, the team should consider varying the non-controversial value measures' global weights ± 0.1 to examine if crossover occurs.

9.5.2 Sensitivity Analysis on Weights Using Excel

Weights sensitivity can easily be performed using the table function and graphical plots in Excel. As an example, consider the swing weights assigned to the value measures supporting the rocket design systems decision as shown in Figure 9.12. In this example, the optimal component configuration alternative is not being used.

Suppose that the decision maker prefers the Global Lightning solution because of its high value return versus cost, and that stakeholders had difficulty assigning a swing weight for the "Speed of the launch platform" during modeling. Some stakeholders thought that the weight was too high and should be much less, and some thought it could be as highly weighted as the value measure "Distance from Target (Accuracy)." Suppose the swing weight is varied from its current value 85 out of 365 (= measure weight of 0.23) from 0 to 100 (the highest swing weight). The measure weight would then vary from 0 to 0.26.

This analysis can be accomplished in six steps using Excel. First, use the weights in the swing weight matrix in Figure 9.12 that were used to estimate each candidate solution's value on a worksheet in the MCVM spreadsheet. Second, construct the table in the middle of Figure 9.12. Across the top of the table link each cell reference to the swing weight name being analyzed. In the second row, enter a swing weight range from 0 to 100 in several increments. Since the plots will be straight lines, the actual increment numbers are not critical to the insights that sensitivity analysis will produce. Third, in the left hand side of the table link cell references the candidate system solution names and the cells used to calculate the solution value using the swing weight matrix assessments and the additive value model. Fourth, select the Excel menu item "Data," "What If Analysis," and then "Data Table." Fifth, create a cell reference to the swing weight matrix cell with 85 in the Row Input cell in the Data Table and click on "OK." The Data Table generates the table in the bottom of Figure 9.12. Finally, plot the swing weight range versus solution value as shown in Figure 9.13.

The results in Figure 9.13 show that Global Lightning is always the highest value alternative regardless of the targeted swing weight changing from 0 to 100. Therefore, the preferred solution is not sensitive to the weight assessment of the speed of platform value measure. However, suppose that Global Lightning was not an alternative, and the original swing weight assigned to the targeted value measure was 10 instead of 85. In this hypothetical case, the preferred solution would be Star Cluster for swing weight values below approximately 5 and Hot Wired for swing weight above 5 because of the crossing of the two alternative plots at 5. In this case, the preferred solution is sensitive to the weight assessment of the speed of platform value measure and the measure weighting should be revisited to resolve any further disagreement.

9.6 APPLYING VALUE-FOCUSED THINKING

The VFT framework affords a unique basis for differentiating among the members of the choice set C^* in a way that is consistent with the underlying trade space logic. The bar chart shown in Figure 9.14 illuminates both the total estimated value return associated with each solution alternative and the specific manner in which each alternative achieves its total, thereby providing a means of ascertaining the degree to which each choice set alternative aligns with the itemized value distribution of A_{Ideal}. Having originated with the decision maker, the distribution of A_{Ideal} represents in terms of value measures the ideal proportion of total value return that is desired from any feasible solution.

The practical concern in this regard is that some competing solution alternatives may achieve relatively high total value return estimates yet do so in a manner out-of-alignment with the

Swing Weight Matrix with swing weights link to calculation of value:

Range of variation		Level of importance of the value measure								
		Very Important			Important			Less Important		
		Value Measure	Swing Weight	Measure Weight	Value Measure	Swing Weight	Measure Weight	Value Measure	Swing Weight	Measure Weight
High		Accuracy	100	0.27	Range	50	0.14			
Medium		Speed of Launch Platform	85	0.23	Thrust of Rocket	45	0.12	Percent Grade Platform can Traverse	5	0.01
Low		Number of Different Payloads	60	0.16	Number of Operators	20	0.05			

Total 365

Data Table with cell referencing of Solution Value calculation cells:

Sensitivity Analysis on Speed of Platform

	0	25	50	85	100
Baseline	10				
Global Lightening	76				
Hot Wired	62				
Star Cluster	56				
SlowPoke	26				
Ideal	100				

Data Table completed by referencing Speed of Platform swing weight of 85:

Sensitivity Analysis on Speed of Platform

	0	25	50	85	100
Baseline	10	9	10	10	10
Global Lightening	76	76	76	76	76
Hot Wired	62	62	62	62	62
Star Cluster	56	60	58	56	55
SlowPoke	26	28	27	26	25
Ideal	100	100	100	100	100

Figure 9.12 Performing weight sensitivity analysis.

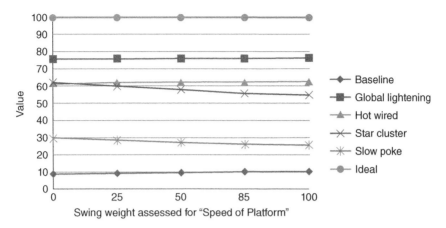

Figure 9.13　Swing weight sensitivity for Speed of Platform.

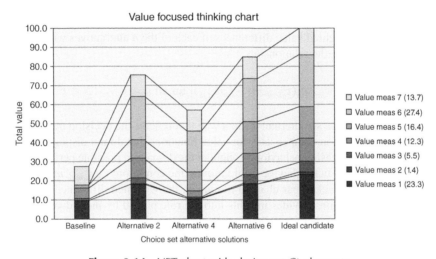

Figure 9.14　VFT chart with choice set C^* elements.

distribution of Ideal value as expressed by the decision maker. In such cases, it is possible that a less costly, yet less total value return alternative may be attractive to the decision maker because it better represents either a scaled-down version of the Ideal or its value return on value measures better represents high priority system behavior. A preference of this type arises in value modeling applications in which a "best fitting" candidate feasible alternative solution is sought, such as, for example, in strategic resource allocation, or competitive personnel hiring actions.

Figure 9.14 displays the VFT bar chart for each alternative in an example choice set C^*. Due to the underlying swing weighting, the height of each value measure element in the Ideal candidate is directly proportional to the decision maker's encoded importance and the impact that value measure chances across their scales will have on the system decision being made. It is apparent that A_6 has gained superior value return over A_2 principally because of its return on value measure 5, the third most heavily weighted value measure from the perspective of the decision maker.

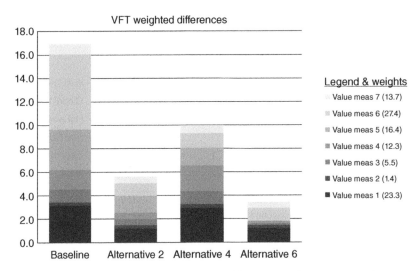

Figure 9.15 VFT chart with weighted differences and measure weights.

Computing the total weighted value differences of each of the n alternatives with m value measures against the ideal using the relationship

$$WD_n = \sum_{m=1}^{M} w_m \cdot |f_m(x_{ideal}, m) - f_m(x_{n,m})| \text{ for all } n = 1, \ldots, N \in C^* \qquad (9.2)$$

differentiates between choice set alternatives in a way that reflects the decision maker's priorities. The absolute value expression compensates for value functions that do not display monotonically non-decreasing or non-increasing behavior throughout the domain of possible performance scores, x_{nm}. Although uncommon, such behavior would impose the condition: $f_m(x_{ideal}, m) < f_m(x_{n,m})$.

Figure 9.15 exploits a stacked bar chart to illuminate the weighted differences between alternatives in a manner that again provides insights into the role played by individual value measure estimates. The greater the height of a particular value measure difference, the less it is aligned with the Ideal, either in total or by value measure component. This chart shows that A_2 has a greater misalignment with the Ideal than does A_6. Thus, if "best fit" was an important criteria for selection by the decision maker, the weighted difference results could be used to justify an increased cost of A_6 should that be the case. One can also easily infer from this hypothetical example a motivation to replace the baseline simply by observing the degree to which $A_{Baseline}$ is out of alignment with the desired Ideal.

EV Stacked Bar Chart Analysis. Continuing their analysis, the systems team created the stacked bar chart shown in Figure 9.16 to examine how each EV option achieved its total value in comparison to each other and the Ideal. Option D attains the highest total value with Option A coming in second, agreeing with earlier tradespace analysis results.

Examining the height of each stacked block in comparison with the Ideal shows each option's degree of alignment with the value profile expressed by the decision maker via swing weighting. Option D is very closely aligned with the Ideal on each value measure,

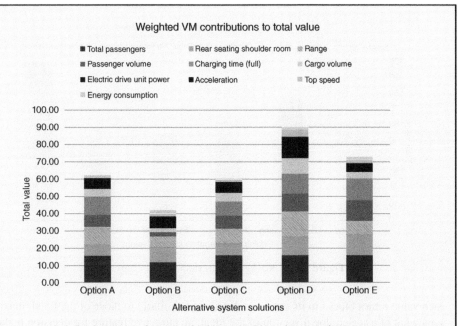

Figure 9.16   Electric vehicle stacked bar chart results.

appearing to be a scaled down version of the Ideal. Despite its high cost, this characteristic reinforces the reason that it is an attractive "high cost solution" if the budget could allow for it. Unfortunately, it does not.

Option E appears to deliver better value return on "Rear Seating Shoulder Room," "Passenger Volume," and "Electric Drive Unit Power" than Option A, while Option A offers better value return than Option E on "Range" and "Cargo Volume." Given that Option A was less cost than Option E, depending on the decision maker's priorities, either could be a contender for selection.

Option A's dominance over Option C appears less so when cast in this stacked bar analysis. The difference separating the two in terms of value appears to be in a single category: "Charging Time." With this evidence, the systems team decided to keep Option C in the decision maker's choice set along with Option A and Option D, and to apply uncertainty modeling to Options A and C to better understand the risks involved with selecting either of these. The decision maker agreed. Based solely on the deterministic tradespace analysis and bar charting, the decision maker could turn this selection into a cost-driven decision.

Rocket Design Bar Chart Analysis. After charting each alternative's value profile on a stacked bar chart, several interesting observations were possible (Figure 9.17). Global Lightning achieves the highest total value return in comparison to the other design alternatives, synchronizing with earlier tradespace analysis results. With the exception of "Thrust" and "Percent Grade," its value profile appears to be in proportional alignment with the Ideal;

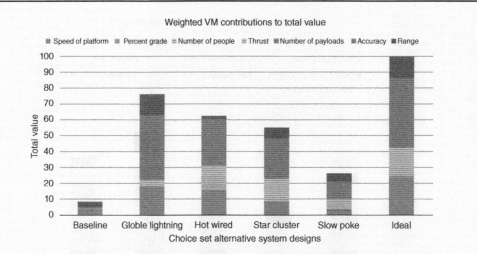

Figure 9.17 Rocket design stacked bar chart results.

each value return blocks in its stack are distributed similarly to those of the Ideal, making it somewhat of a scaled-down version of the Ideal, an attractive feature for decision makers.

Hot Wired, and less so Star Cluster, significantly out-perform Global Lightning on "Thrust," while delivering high value return on "Accuracy." If the decision maker placed special emphasis on these value measures for either reasons imbedded in the swing weights assigned or outside of the systems decision posed to the systems team, these two alternatives could be contenders for selection. Coupled with the tradespace results, Star Cluster again represents a return to value that, while less in overall alignment with the expressed Ideal, does offer significant value return in some categories as noted. Slow Poke has neither of these characteristics, further underscoring its elimination from further consideration.

This chart clearly reinforces the inference made earlier regarding the Baseline alternative: it significantly fails to satisfy any of the values expressed by stakeholders and decision makers for a system solution. A result such as this provides significant support to the systems project as it is obvious why the engagement was needed.

There appears to be a sizable value gap between Global Lightning's total value return and the Ideal. Whether or not this gap could be reduced given the evidence shown, would be dependent upon the feasibility of substituting other alternatives' functional system solutions (e.g. Star Cluster's thrust solution) for the one Global Lightning is current using. These considerations are discussed in Section 9.8.

9.6.1 Improving non-Dominated Alternatives

Solution designers are often presented with an opportunity to reassess and possibly restructure their "best and final" offer in a way that better addresses the ideal solution sought by the decision maker. This is true for both dominated and non-dominated feasible alternative solutions. The deterministic trade space characteristics coupled with VFT offer a means of informing strategies for doing so.

Improving the competitive position of a non-dominated choice set member $A_k \in C^*$ to some A'_k better situated in the trade space implies a shift in its position to improve its ratio-value efficiency, increase its total value estimate TV_k, or decrease its total cost estimate TC_k. While these options imply the expected, to wit: increase value by incurring a corresponding increase in cost, the trade space also illuminates the less obvious.

Consider A_4 in Figure 9.19 which is currently non-dominated as a member of C^*. It will be one of the alternatives logically considered viable as a solution. We can see that its competitive position can also be improved by sacrificing value to reduce cost, thereby moving closer to the constant returns-to-value line driven by A_2. Doing so requires a clear perspective of how value is currently being delivered by A_4 relative to A_{ideal} so that it is possible to increase TV_k without a corresponding increase in TC_k by aligning A_k to better fit the value distribution of A_{Ideal}. In Figure 9.14 for example, the value components in which A_4 is disadvantaged are clearly seen in its under-estimated returns on value measures 1, 3, and 4.

9.6.2 Improving Dominated Alternatives

Dominated alternatives pose a slightly more complicated challenge. Again however, successful strategies are clearly indicated in a combination of the trade space diagram and VFT bar charts.

There often ensues a discussion with decision makers concerning how and to what extent dominated alternatives should improve in order for them to be included in the choice set C^*. This question plagues a host of unsuccessful competitive bidding companies seeking to be awarded a prime contract in support of some systems development major activity. The definition for trade space efficiency suggests that a dominated solution A_l must achieve a trade space positioning in which A_{ideal} is the only alternative within K_l in order to become a choice set member. Therefore, A_l must adopt a modification strategy that moves it to a position in the trade space outside of the polar cone K_{m^-} of all $A_m \in C^*$. This is not necessarily equivalent to moving to an efficient ratio-value frontier.

Interestingly, when driven by resource constraints affecting cost and value, moving outside of the polar cones of C^* affords a possibility for improving the competitive position of an alternative solution by reducing total value return while simultaneously lowering cost. This could be an attractive option for any severely resource-constrained company looking to improve its alternative's standing in the trade space. Moreover, if the improvement strategy is not intended to spark direct competition with an existing alternative by dominating it in the trade space, which is what we consider first next, one should not enter a cone K_m for all $A_m \in C^*$.

For example, consider the situation shown in Figure 9.18 in which alternatives 3 and 5 are dominated and therefore excluded from membership in C^*. We assume for simplicity that an improvement strategy herein is one-sided so as to prevent a dynamic competition ensuing in which elements of game theory are called for [30]. We also assume in this example that $A_{Baseline}$ represents the existing system for which improvement is sought and its existence sets acceptance thresholds for total cost and total value.

To be included in C^*, A_3 must move to one of the three regions outside of the polar cones associated with members of C^*. Doing so incurs changes in cost and value return as shown in Table 9.1. Moving to Region III offers A_3 the ability to become trade space efficient and thus become a member of C^* by lowering its estimated total value return without incurring additional cost. Region II offers similar opportunity by requiring an increase in total value return. The lower rectangles of Regions II and III allow for A_3 to become a member of C^* without requiring A_3 to dominate an existing member of C^*, thus avoiding direct competition.

In either of these regions, one can further increase A_3's competitive attractiveness by improving its ratio value efficiency. Achieving parity with the most efficient alternative, A_2 in this example, is a matter of adopting a strategy to position A_3' on the constant returns-to-value line superimposed on Figure 9.18. This insight informs a targeting strategy for overcoming the advantages offered by a

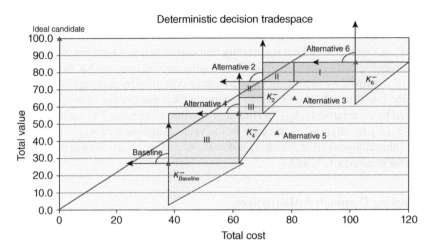

Figure 9.18 Improvement regions for non-dominated alternatives.

TABLE 9.1 Example Competitive Improvement Strategies for Dominated Solution Alternatives.

Region	ΔTC	ΔTV	Typical System Implementation
I	+	+	Add competitive functionality
II	−	+	Invoke redesign via VFT and efficiency
III	−	−	Remove non-competitive functionality via VFT

competing alternative solution improve the efficiency of A_3 while simultaneously moving into the cone K_m of the targeted alternative $A_m \in C^*$ so that A_m becomes trade space inefficient and drops from the choice set. Within the desire for accepting no diminution in cost or value for A_3, there is opportunity to target A_4 and/or A_6 in Figure 9.18 by a move to the appropriate area(s) of Region II shown.

9.7 SUPPORTING THE TRADESPACE DECISION

The alternative solutions in the choice set C^* are all trade space efficient in the sense we have defined them herein, thereby reducing the number of feasible alternative solutions to only those that should be considered by the decision maker given the underlying preference ordering supporting the trade space. This benefit notwithstanding, the challenge remains for the decision maker to select a solution from among these alternatives. While it appears tempting to select the highest value or lowest cost alternative outright doing so is generally discouraged because of ready access to much richer information stemming from this approach. VFT and applying ratio value efficiency are two ways of uncovering this information that we next describe.

Viewing the deterministic trade space in an aggregated input-output setting, it is straightforward to apply a ratio value efficiency concept [31] to distinguish the choice set alternatives by superimposing a constant total value returns-to-total cost line on the trade space as shown in Figure 9.19. In this example, A_2 is the most ratio value efficient alternative in terms of a simple value-to-cost

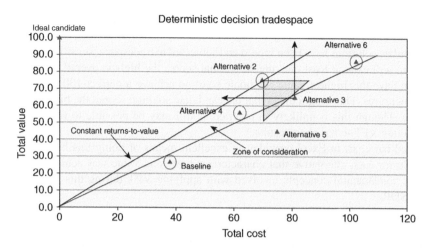

Figure 9.19 Improvement regions for non-dominated alternatives.

ratio. It subsequently becomes a basis of comparison for the other members of C^* by applying the measure

$$0 \le \rho = \frac{\frac{TV_m}{TC_m}}{\max\{\frac{TV_m}{TC_m}\}} \le 1, m \in M \subseteq N, \quad \text{for all } A_m \in C^* \tag{9.3}$$

It is interesting to note in the results presented in Table 9.2 that $A_{Baseline}$ attains only 66% of A_2's efficiency. Assuming that the underlying data supporting value and cost estimates are reasonably accurate, selecting A_2 as a solution would yield a 151% increase in ratio-value efficiency over $A_{Baseline}$. In comparison, incurring the additional cost for selecting A_6 would yield a substantially less (119%) increase in ratio-value efficiency over $A_{Baseline}$. Ordering the choice set alternatives $A_m \in C^*$ in terms of the underlying preference of the decision-maker for ratio-value efficient solution alternatives yield $1 = A_2 \succ A_m \succ A_m \succ A_{Baseline}$.

When considered *a priori*, this efficiency measure can further restrict the number of choice set alternatives by imposing a zone of consideration on the trade space that specifies the maximum amount of degradation the decision maker is willing to accept within the choice set when alternatives are compared with the most ratio-value efficient alternative. With a maximum 25% degradation acceptance, the choice set consists only of alternatives 2, 4, and 6, as illustrated in Figure 9.19.

TABLE 9.2 Efficiency Calculations for Alternatives in Figure 9.19.

	$A_{Baseline}$	A_2	A_4	A_6
Cost	38	70	62	102
Value	27	75	56	86
Value/Cost	0.71	1.07	0.90	0.84
ρ	0.66	1.0	0.84	0.79

9.8 USE VALUE-FOCUSED THINKING TO IMPROVE SOLUTIONS

After all candidate solutions have been scored and subjected to tradespace, sensitivity, and bar chart analyses, there will exist at least one alternative that scores the highest overall. It would be very rare indeed to have this highest value candidate solution achieve a perfect 100 total value return on all value measures. That would mean that the candidate solution scored the highest possible for each measure. Though this is unlikely in practice, it still may be possible to further increase its value by applying VFT to bar chart results.

The stacked bar chart in Excel provides an excellent means of doing this because it displays a value profile for each alternative that characterizes how total value was achieved. Figure 9.20 illustrates the fundamental concepts involved with applying VFT during this Decision Making phase of the SDP.

In the hypothetical situation shown, the Baseline is being compared with three candidate solutions and the Ideal, thereby motivating several questions. What value measure dimension(s) and what candidate solution(s) come closest to achieving the stakeholder Ideal scores? VFT first attempts to improve the best candidate solution by observing what is possible in the existing alternatives. Assembling the maximum value measure scores into a single new alternative produces an *improved* candidate solution. Is it possible to combine the known system elements from the different candidate solutions in this manner? What would this improved system solution look like? If it is not possible to combine the known elements generating the observed measure value levels in this manner, is there a new way of achieving a similar level of performance?

In a similar manner as described in Section 9.6, even this improved candidate solution falls short of the Ideal levels as expressed by the stakeholders. Closing this gap will quite possibly require new design activities focusing on any candidate solution improvements that would need to be made in order to attain a better score for each measure.

It is also valuable to examine the individual measure value gaps when trying to improve candidate system solutions. Returning to the rocket design problem, Figure 9.17 shows the candidate solution stacked bar chart comparison without an improved solution. As a concept check, try assembling an improved candidate solution for this systems decision problem. Figures 9.17 and

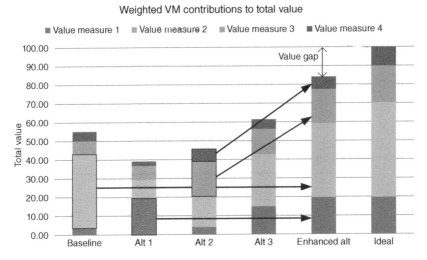

Figure 9.20 Value-focused thinking within the SDP.

TABLE 9.3   Fin Material Performance Uncertainty.

Fin Material	Probability	Range Score	
		Global Lightning	Star Cluster
Durable	0.7	99.5	55.4
Erosion	0.3	80.0	40.0

9.5 show that improving the Global Lightning design scores for "Percent Grade," "Number of People," and "Thrust" could be promising.

Attaining an ideal score on the "Percent Grade" value measures requires 60% grade measure score. What would the platform have to be to traverse a 60% grade? Can the existing platform be modified to achieve this? Does this require an entirely new platform be designed? Applying VFT in this manner requires all value measures be examined in this manner, seeking to find ways to move the best candidate solution closer to the Ideal. Once having identified the improved score for each measure, the systems project team works through the trade-offs required to make any improved solution feasible. Armed with the new improved solutions, the scoring and analysis process would be repeated.

9.8.1   Decision Analysis of Dependent Risks

In Chapter 10, techniques for modeling and analyzing input and parameter uncertainty are discussed. Apart from these, two other major sources of uncertainty in systems development are technology development challenges and the potential actions of competitors or adversaries. Suppose for the rocket problem that two concerns are identified late in the solution design phase that could impact operational performance. The first concern is a technical concern and the second concern is a potential adversary threat.

Suppose that the development engineering team identifies a technical concern with the new fin material that is planned to be used for both the Global Lightning and Star Cluster system solutions. This is a dependent uncertainty since the durability of the fins during flight has a direct impact on the range of the two candidate solutions. After working with the material and missile performance engineers, the systems engineer assesses the data shown in Table 9.3. If the fin material is durable the range will achieve the original score. However, if there is some flight erosion of the fins, the range could decrease for both solutions.

Suppose that the intelligence agencies identify a potential future adversary threat that could result in degraded accuracy of guidance systems that use the Global Positioning System (GPS). Again, this is a dependent uncertainty since the accuracy of Global Lightning and Star Cluster will depend on the outcome of this event. After working with the navigation and missile performance engineers, the systems team assesses the data shown in Table 9.4.

A decision tree can be used to analyze the risk of dependent (and also independent) uncertainties. For this example, a Microsoft Excel Add-in called *Precision Tree* ® is used to perform the analysis. Decision trees are described in most decision analysis texts (e.g. [32]), but they are typically used for single objective value and single objective utility. For MCVM, decision trees can be used with multiple objectives to determine the impact of the uncertainties on the preferences for Global Lightning and Star Cluster.

In Figure 9.21, the first node in the decision tree is a decision node, the second node is the Fin Material uncertainty, and the third node is the GPS Degrade uncertainty. Figure 9.22 shows

TABLE 9.4   Global Positioning System (GPS) Performance Uncertainty.

GPS Degrade	Probability	Accuracy Score	
		Global Lightning	Star Cluster
No Degrade	0.6	1.97	3.5
Degrade	0.4	4.0	7.0

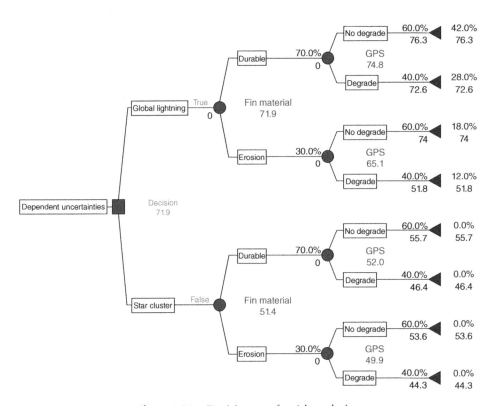

Figure 9.21   Decision tree for risk analysis.

the value calculations that are appended to the eight final branches of the decision tree. The value calculations are unchanged for the first five value measures. The value calculations for the last two value measures use the scores from Tables 9.3 and 9.4. The best decision is still Global Lightning but the solution's expected value is now reduced from 76.3 to 71.9.

Figure 9.23 shows the cumulative risk profiles for this situation. With two dependent uncertainties considered, a more complete picture of the risk of the two solutions is revealed. Since the cumulative risk profile of Global Lightening is down and to the right of Star Cluster, Global

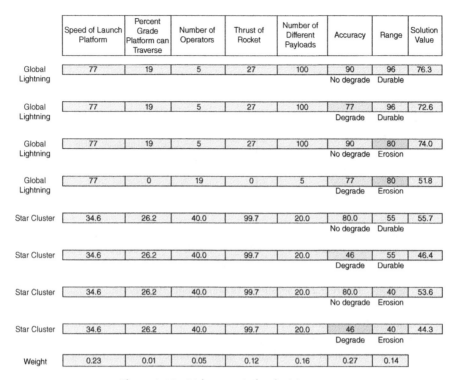

	Speed of Launch Platform	Percent Grade Platform can Traverse	Number of Operators	Thrust of Rocket	Number of Different Payloads	Accuracy	Range	Solution Value
Global Lightning	77	19	5	27	100	90 No degrade	96 Durable	76.3
Global Lightning	77	19	5	27	100	77 Degrade	96 Durable	72.6
Global Lightning	77	19	5	27	100	90 No degrade	80 Erosion	74.0
Global Lightning	77	0	19	0	5	77 Degrade	80 Erosion	51.8
Star Cluster	34.6	26.2	40.0	99.7	20.0	80.0 No degrade	55 Durable	55.7
Star Cluster	34.6	26.2	40.0	99.7	20.0	46 Degrade	55 Durable	46.4
Star Cluster	34.6	26.2	40.0	99.7	20.0	80.0 No degrade	40 Erosion	53.6
Star Cluster	34.6	26.2	40.0	99.7	20.0	46 Degrade	40 Erosion	44.3
Weight	0.23	0.01	0.05	0.12	0.16	0.27	0.14	

Figure 9.22 Value matrix for decision tree.

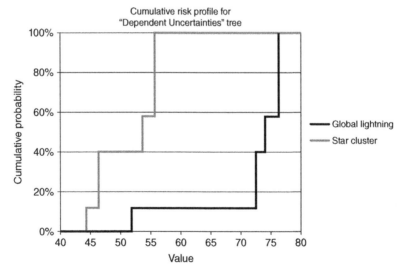

Figure 9.23 Cumulative risk profiles.

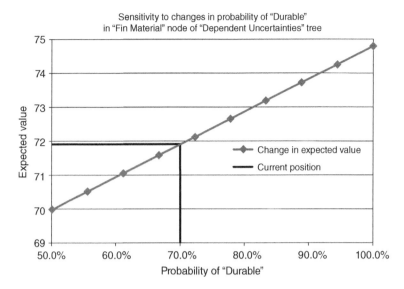

Figure 9.24   Sensitivity of dependent uncertainties.

Lightning stochastically dominates Star Cluster (see Chapter 10). However, from the decision tree (and the cumulative risk profile) it is evident that there is a 12% probability that Global Lightning will have a value of 51.8 which is less than the original value of Star Cluster before considering the two dependent uncertainties.

A decision maker would now be interested in knowing the impact of our assumptions about the two uncertainties. By varying the probability that the Fin is durable from 50% to 100%, the expected value of Global Lightning ranges from 70 to 75 as shown in Figure 9.24. The decision trees, cumulative risk profiles, and sensitivity analysis are easily generated using *Precision Tree* ®. Additional sensitivity analysis techniques, for example, two way sensitivity, are also available in the within the software application.

9.9   REPORTING AND DECISION HANDOFF

After all the painstaking work to identify choice set solution alternatives and develop a recommendation, it is now time to put it all together in a report or a presentation for the decision maker and stakeholders. This is a very critical step in the SDP process. Outstanding analytical work can be quickly dismissed by a decision maker when the presentation is overly complicated or too simplistic. The perceived professionalism of a written report or oral presentation can convince a decision maker of the validity of a recommendation, confuse the decision maker into inaction, or motivate them to find a better systems decision support team.

There is no one set order for developing the report or making a presentation. Though some decision makers request a decision briefing and then want a follow-up report that includes the decision and implementation plan, most decision makers request any final decision briefing to be accompanied by a detailed report. The implementation plan is then developed separately. This latter case is assumed in what follows. While several specific suggestions concerning the format of a presentation are discussed to increase its usefulness to the decision maker, the primary objective here is to provide general guidance on important factors that give a report and presentation the greatest chance at success.

9.9.1 Developing the Report

Organizations will often establish a standard format for written technical reports. Standardizing content and format lessens the burden on an analyst who has to prepare the report and makes it easier for decision makers to locate specific items of interest in the report. Regardless of the existence or absence of a specific format, there are some basic principles for developing a technical report for a decision maker. Reports should include an executive summary, a main body, and appendices (as necessary). The key to a successful technical report is a clear, concise executive summary.

An executive summary is designed to provide a brief overview of the content of the report for someone who does not have the time to read the entire report, a typical characteristic of many senior decision makers. It provides a decision maker with enough supporting facts and analysis results to make a decision without having to read the entire report. It should include the objective of the report (often to obtain a decision), the most compelling evidence to support a decision, and a quick overview of the methodology used. The best executive summaries can be crafted to fit on a single page. It should very rarely be longer than 10% of the overall length of the main body or over five pages, whichever is less. Additional details are provided in the body of the technical report.

The main body of a technical report is designed to be a much more detailed explanation of the study, assuming that persons reading the full technical report have the time, experience, education, and motivation to do so. Here, the details matter. Here the systems team must explain what any and all analysis results means in the context of the systems decision. The writing should be very concise and restricted to the important parts of the analysis which support the recommendation.

The report should be organized to allow the decision maker and key stakeholders to follow the analysis from the initial problem statement until the recommended decision. Rarely should the systems team include steps not taken. For example, if the analysis did not lend itself to operational testing, the analyst should not include a paragraph on operational testing even if the organization's standard report format calls for such a paragraph. The only exception would be if the absence of this step has a significant impact on the recommendation (e.g. in risk mitigation).

The appendices of the report should include detailed formulations of models, simulation code, and data. These are rarely of interest to the decision maker, unless he or she has a very strong technical background, or there are questions directed to them in the analysis. Appendices are very useful to other analysts or stakeholders, especially those interested in reproducing the team's results. A decision maker may ask other analysts to comment on the full report, in which case, these appendices are very important.

The final crucial part of any written work is documentation and references to any support received or researched in the analysis. Proper documentation accomplishes two things. First, it provides credibility to the work by showing that techniques and data sources used are supported by credible experts and peer review. Second, and most importantly, it reinforces the integrity of the systems team. Nothing destroys an analysis as quickly as questionable documentation and even experienced systems engineers cannot recover from integrity violations.

9.9.2 Developing the Presentation

The single most important consideration when developing a presentation is understanding what the decision maker needs in the presentation in order to make a decision. Written reports are commonly tailored to the type of problem being addressed and accepted report format of an organization. Oral presentations must be tailored to the decision maker. They must include any detail required to make a decision and to capture and hold the interest of the decision maker throughout the presentation. There are some general guidelines to follow when constructing a presentation in support of systems decision making.

Assuming that digital slides are being used, every detail on every slide matters. With the key team members present, the team should review every slide to ensure that there are no spelling errors, font size differences, and awkward illustrations. Every chart, graph, or table needs to be labeled completely (axes, title, citations). Special effect slide transitions should not be used. This process is known as "murder boarding the presentation." The team should do this three to four days in advance of the meeting with the decision maker so that any needed changes can be made in sufficient time to provide an accurate read-ahead copy to the attendees.

It is not uncommon for there to be more slides than time to present them. When this happens, carefully construct a single slide that summarizes a set of others. This slide will be included in the presentation deck. The other slides are hidden and labeled as back-up slides in case more detail is asked for during the presentation.

Timing the presentation is critical to success. If the decision maker has provided 30 minutes for the presentation, the team should plan on using 25 minutes and reserving 5 minutes for post-presentation discussions, or to accommodate ad hoc questions should they occur. Not counting the cover and finish slide, allotting two minutes per slide is a good guide to stay within the time limit. If there are specific, key analysis results being presented that most likely will spark a response from the decision maker, three minutes should be allotted to each of these slides.

The opening should set the tone for the remainder of the presentation. The presenter should introduce the members of the systems team present, indicating their role on the project. The presenter should immediately state the purpose of the presentation, focusing the decision maker's expectations. In this case, the purpose is to obtain a decision. Immediately following the purpose, the presenter should provide the decision maker with enough background on the problem to frame and focus their attention on the topic being presented. Although the topic may be fresh in the mind of the presenter, the decision maker may have just left a situation involving a topic entirely different that the one at-hand. The presenter should explain why the problem and the current presentation are important to the decision maker.

The final part of the opening is the recommendation. This is known as "the Bottom Line Up Front" or BLUF. This provides the decision maker with both a good idea of where the presentation is heading and the recommended solution decision. Knowing the final recommendation helps the decision maker focus on the questions critical to the decision he or she will make.

When the team is satisfied with the presentation, a PDF copy of the slides are sent to the decision maker's representative no later than two days prior to the meeting for their review and preparation.

9.9.3 Presenting Analysis Results

Which members of the system team present at a decision briefing is largely personnel dependent. Every systems team will have a number of key people who lead various activities within the SDP. It is not necessary, nor recommended, that the entire systems decision support group brief a decision maker. A good presentation typically has one or two presenters who are the most talented at this task. If the presentation is scheduled for more than 15–20 minutes, using two people—known as a "Mutt and Jeff" approach—is effective for holding the audience attention and altering the presentation voice being used. The remaining key team personnel take notes and are present to answer questions on the activities they had responsibility for when the presenter directs the question to them.

One or two people should be dedicated to taking notes. They will be responsible for summarizing and documenting the major discussion points, decision maker reactions, decisions, unresolved questions, and follow-on tasks. These are sent to the decision maker's representative as soon as practical after the presentation, usually the next day.

The presenter(s) should start the description of the analysis from an accepted point of common knowledge. This might be a summary of the previous meeting or even going back to the original problem statement. This orients all attendees and allows the decision maker to feel knowledgeable and comfortable at the start of the discussion of the analysis.

From there, the briefing should take the decision maker through the process at a detail required to maintain his or her interest and understanding until the recommendation is reached. Some decision makers are very detail-oriented and want the formulations and the data. Some want only highlights. In the absence of prior knowledge, the presenter should present limited details and have backup information ready to address specific questions.

The presentation should logically flow from the start point until an ultimate conclusion. This keeps the decision maker knowledgeable and comfortable. A knowledgeable and comfortable decision maker will be much more likely to support an analysis and make a decision at the end of a presentation than a decision maker who is overwhelmed with information and confused. This decision maker is more likely to put off a decision rather than make a wrong decision.

A good presenter will know exactly how much time the presentation has used and how much is remaining throughout the presentation with the goal of keeping the briefing shorter than the time allotted. This allows more time for questions and a busy decision maker will appreciate the extra time as their days are consumed moving from one meeting to another. Do not assume that the decision maker will allocate extra time for this presentation as he or she may leave prior to making a decision. Always have a one chart summary if the decision maker has to shorten the time.

9.9.4 Concluding the Presentation

After presenting a concise and convincing argument, the presenter should restate the recommendation and ask for a decision. When a presenter states at the start of the presentation that the purpose is to obtain a decision, the decision maker will be prepared for this request. The read-ahead slides presented to the decision maker's representative clearly communicate this as well. The decision maker might want to put off the decision and, if so, the presenter should politely ask when a decision might be forthcoming. Though some decision makers do not like to be pressed, when the timing of the decision is critical (e.g. in the progress of a manufacturing or development process), it is worth the effort to press the issue.

Whether the decision maker makes a decision or not, the presenter should continue with the future actions required based on the decision or lack thereof. Since the decision may significantly change the information prepared in advance of the presentation, the presenter should be prepared to adjust the plans as necessary.

Some final thoughts on briefings:

- *Do not read the slides.* Nothing detracts from a presentation and infuriates an audience as quickly. Summarize the slide or the chart in the presenter's own words, referencing text only as appropriate.

- *Have simple slides and quick thoughts.* A slide or concept in a presentation that tries to convey too much information often loses the audience and conveys little.

- *Transition the decision maker to focus on the problem topic very early in the presentation.* Yours is not the only problem on their mind, which is why orienting the attendees as noted previously is important.

- *Be careful with the use of pointers.* These can often distract the audience from the presentation, especially if the presenter is nervous!

- *Keep text font size consistent throughout the presentation.* Using larger font sizes has a similar effect as capitalizing letters in e-mail: giving the impression of yelling.

- *Dress professionally.* The presenter should always be more formal than the decision maker, but not overly so.

- *Speak professionally.* Do not use quaint or colloquial phrases or try to be funny. The briefing is designed to obtain a decision, not audition for stand–up.

- *Stay on message.* Do not introduce tangential material that is not essential to the decision.

- *Finish in control.* End the presentation in a ways that informs the decision maker of the project's status, what the next steps are, when deliverables should be expected, and what actions are required of the decision maker or his/her organization to make the project a success. It is a parting shot to reframe the presentation content before you lose the decision maker's attention.

9.9.5   Using a Storyline Approach

One straightforward method for organizing information and presenting it effectively is called a *storyline* method. There are two principles for creating a presentation using this approach: horizontal integration of the story and vertical integration of support. Conceptualizing each presentation slide as a single page of a book, the area at the top of the slide typically reserved for a slide title is used to "tell the story" of the presentation content from start to finish using a single sentence on each slide. Done correctly, the decision maker should be able to read across the top of every slide and understand the main messages that the system team wants to convey. This effect is known as achieving *horizontal integration* in the sense that if all the slides were laid out on a table in order, the presentation storyline could be read by reading horizontally across the slides.

The main body of each slide is then used to present key evidence (e.g. text, graphics, mathematics, simulation results, etc.) supporting the storyline sentence present in the slide title area. This is known as achieving *vertical integration*. It is "vertical" in the sense that the typical audience member will logically look to the title area first, encountering the storyline statement, and then "drill down" into the supporting evidence on the slide to understand the logical basis for the statement. Figure 9.25 illustrates a comparison between the storyline approach and a typical default presentation format that uses simple labels as slide titles in Microsoft® PowerPoint.

One attractive feature of this method is that it forces a presenter to clearly address the salient points needing to be made, the logic connecting these points, and the key elements of convincing evidence that the statement is factually based on in its claim. This frees the presenter to add value during the presentation by providing the audience with insights and reasoning that complement what they are seeing instead of reading the content of the slides to the audience, which is considered bad practice.

The storyline method delivers two additional benefits that add to its appeal for presentations supporting systems decision making. First, it is not uncommon for decision briefings to be circulated widely throughout an organization before the presentation using the PDF read-ahead slides that the team sent or after the presentation concludes. Vertical and horizontal integration helps prevent readers from misinterpreting results because the main points are clearly present along with their supporting evidence. Similarly, the storyline method enables slide handouts to function as stand-alone references for the presentation at a later date.

Secondly, slides created using this method tell the intended story. The resulting presentation can serve as a logical template for creating a technical report on the content as well. Each slide is first placed on a single page in a document. Next, the text following the slide focuses on the storyline statement, describing to the reader the content and conclusions providing vertical integration support to the storyline. Important graphics, charts, or images are retained as figures and charts in

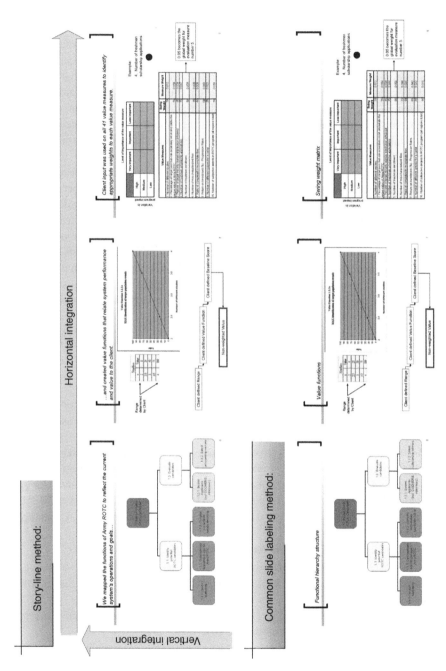

Figure 9.25 Two methods for organizing and presenting information in slideshows.

the technical report. Slides that contain purely textual information such as bullet lists are deleted, replaced by the expanded discussion following it. Adding any necessary references and section organization nearly completes the report.

A storyline approach is very helpful to "story board" the flow of the presentation prior to building it in software. One way of doing this when classroom or conference facilities are available is as follows. Estimating as a rule of thumb that every slide will consume approximately two minutes of presentation time on average, draw an empty box (placeholder slide) for each two minute segment of the presentation. Following each slide, identify a general group title that structures the presentation: title slide/team identification, agenda, current project timeline, bottom-line-up-front (optional but encouraged), problem background and description, methodology, modeling, results and analysis, conclusions, recommendations, areas for further improvement, updated timeline, and references (optional). The logical organization of these placeholder slides aligns with the horizontal integration of the slides when the presentation is complete.

Identify the content of each blank slide (in general terms, not specific detail) needed to support the storyline. The idea here is to see the presentation from a single, macroscopic perspective in the hope that by doing so any gaps in logic, analysis, content, and so on will be revealed. Finally, by examining the information the team actually possesses to support the storyline, the team's workflow can be adjusted as necessary to fill-in any missing information prior to the presentation being given.

Presentation software is not the only option for conducting effective presentations. Very successful briefings can be conducted using butcher charts, simple paper slides, or even chalk. The key is that the presentation is professional and it is concise. Many experts suggest that slides or charts should include no more than three ideas and have fewer than four very short lines per slide, chart, or board space.

REFERENCES

1. Eisenfuhr, F., Weber, M., Langer, T. (2010) *Rational Decision Making*. New York: Springer.
2. Parnell, G., Driscoll, P., Henderson, D. (2012) *Decision Making in Systems Engineering and Management*, 2nd ed. New York: John Wiley & Sons.
3. Celik, E., Gul, M., Yucesan, M., Mete, S. (2019) 'Stochastic multi-criteria decision-making: an overview to methods and applications,' *Beni-Suef University Journal of Basic and Applied Sciences*, 8(4), pp. 1–11.
4. Caddell, J., Dabkowski, M., Driscoll, P.J., Dubois, P. (2020) 'Improving stochastic analysis for tradeoffs in multi-criteria value models,' *Journal of Multi-Criteria Decision Analysis*, 27(5–6), pp. 304–317.
5. Keeney, R.L., Raiffa, H., Meyer, R.F. (1993) *Decisions with Multiple Objectives*. Cambridge, UK: Cambridge University Press.
6. Belton, V., Stewart, T. (2002) *Multiple Criteria Decision Analysis*. New York: Springer.
7. Brownley, C.W. (2013). *Multi-Objective Decision Analysis*. Business Expert Press.
8. Ishizaka, A., Nemery, P. (2013) *Multi-Criteria Decision Analysis*. Chichester, West Sussex, UK: John Wiley & Sons, Ltd.
9. Lahdelma, R., Hokkanen, J., Salminen, P. (1998) 'SMAA –Stochastic multiobjective acceptability analysis,' *European Journal of Operations Research*, 106(1), 137–143.
10. Lahdelma, R., Salminen, P. (2001) 'SMAA-2: Stochastic multicriteria acceptability analysis for group decision making,' *Operations Research*, 49(3), 444–454.
11. Miller, G. (1956) 'The magical number seven, plus or minus two: some limits on our capacity for processing information,' *Psychological Review*, 63, 81–97.
12. Simon, H. (1972) 'Theories of bounded rationality,' *Decision and Organization*, 1(1), 161–176.

13. Simon, H.A. (1982) *Models of Bounded Rationality: Empirically Grounded Economic Reason*, vol. 3. Cambridge, MA: MIT Press.

14. USGOV (2017) *Defense Acquisition Guidebook*. Washington, DC: Defense Acquisition University.

15. USGOV (2017) *Economic Analysis for Decision-making*, Change 1 Edition. Washington, DC: Department of Defense.

16. Festinger, L. (1962) *A Theory of Cognitive Dissonance*. Stanford, CA: Stanford University Press.

17. Festinger, L. (1964). *Conflict, Decision, and Dissonance*. Stanford, CA: Stanford University Press.

18. Harmon-Jones, E. (2019) *Cognitive Dissonance: Reexamining a Pivotal Theory in Psychology*. Washington, DC: American Psychological Association.

19. Dawson, L.L. (1999). 'When prophecy fails and faith persists: a theoretical overview,' *Nova Religio*, 3(1), pp. 60–82.

20. Brehm, J. (1956) 'Post-decision changes in the desirability of choice alternatives,' *Journal of Abnormal and Social Psychology*, 52, pp. 384–389.

21. Shultz, T., Léveillé, E., Lepper, M. (1999) 'Free choice and cognitive dissonance revisited: choosing "lesser evils" versus "greater goods,' *Personality and Social Psychology Bulletin*, 25(1), 40–48.

22. Kaliszewski, I. (2016). 'On variant selection mechanisms in interactive MCDA - engineering versus reverse engineering,' *Journal of Multi-Criteria Decision Analysis*, 23, pp. 40–48.

23. Fitzgerald, M.E., Ross, A.M. (2013) 'Guiding cooperative stakeholders to compromise solutions using an interactive tradespace exploration process,' *Procedia Computer Science*, 16, pp. 343–352.

24. Grierson, D.E. (2008) 'Pareto multi-criteria decision making,' *Advanced Engineering Infomatics*, 22(3), pp. 371–384.

25. Rockafellar, R.T. (1996) *Convex Analysis*. Princeton, NJ: Princeton University Press.

26. Maxwell, D. (2004) *Decision Analysis: Aiding Insight VII: Decision Analysis Software, OR/MS Today*. Marietta, GA: Lionheart Publishing.

27. Logical Decisions (2005) Available at: http://www.logicaldecisions.com. (Accessed 1 Mar 2022).

28. Kirkwood, C.W. (1997) *Strategic Decision Making: Multiple Objective Decision Analysis with Spreadsheets*. Pacific Grove, CA: Duxbury Press.

29. Ragsdale, C. (2017) *Spreadsheet Modeling and Decision Analysis*, 8th ed. Independence, KY: Cengage Publishing.

30. Dixit, A.K., Skeath, S., Reiley, D.H. (2014) *Games of Strategy*. New York: W.W. Norton & Company.

31. Charnes, A., Cooper, W.W., Rhodes, E. (1978) 'Measuring the efficiency of decision making units,' *European Journal of Operational Research*, 2, pp. 429–444.

32. Clemen, R.T.. (1997) *Making Hard Decisions*, 2nd ed. New York: Duxbury.

Chapter **10**

Stochastic Tradespace Analysis

The only thing that makes life possible is permanent, intolerable uncertainty; not knowing what comes next.

—Ursula K. Le Guin, Author

10.1 INTRODUCTION

In practice, nearly all multiple criteria value modelling (MCVM) tradeoff applications involve three primary decision support efforts: down-selecting post-screening alternatives, reducing the choice set to isolate Pareto efficient alternatives, and selecting a single alternative that maximizes value return against a tradeoff dimension. Both deterministic and stochastic tradespace analysis adhere to this pattern, the difference between them being an explicit treatment of uncertainty.

A satisfactory selection decision could be made on deterministic tradespace results alone, and certainly has been in the past. Stochastic tradespace analysis provides a more robust understanding of the complications associated with the decision that uncertainty imposes, taking what appears to be a straightforward decision from a deterministic analysis to one that introduces risk both with respect to system performance and to the decision maker.

As discussed in Chapter 9, the Decision Making phase of the systems decision process (SDP) places an even heavier emphasis on the decision maker who must choose among competing system alternatives. There, the discussion centered on using a deterministic approach in which cost and value data and model parameters were assumed to be known with certainty, even if this was not the

Decision Making in Systems Engineering and Management, Third Edition.
Patrick J. Driscoll, Gregory S. Parnell, and Dale L. Henderson
© 2023 John Wiley & Sons, Inc. Published 2023 by John Wiley & Sons, Inc.

case. The end result of deterministic MCVM is an effective tradespace based on Pareto efficient properties that nonetheless supply a decision maker with improved clarity and understanding of the decision that must be made. The relative positioning of each alternative after being subjected to systems scoring and life cycle cost analysis, coupled with a stacked bar chart that decomposes total value into its supporting sub-components, enables dominant alternatives to be identified and sequestered into an efficient choice set from which the decision maker should pick. These become candidate system solutions exhibiting a high degree of alignment to value and cost goals.

For deterministic modeling efforts, sensitivity analysis is performed on key parameters such as attribute weights to explore the implications of potential priority shifts or changes to input parameters for cost and value models. However, when internal or external uncertainty in its various forms [1] exists in data, measures, parameters, or value/utility functions, MCVMs must adapt to accommodate representations of this uncertainty while maintaining the same decision support principles embraced by its deterministic counterpart. Uncertainty significantly increases the challenge of communicating analytical results to a decision maker [2].

Uncertainty effects a host of modeling elements in systems decision making supported by MCVM: data input, value measures, parameters, and weighting strategies, requiring these models to be modified to represent as best as possible the real world problem facing a decision maker. Various approaches have been developed over time to address this challenge [2] such as the theory of probability [3], fuzzy set theory [4–6], vague sets [7], theory of interval mathematics [8, 9], intuitionistic fuzzy sets [10], rough set theory [11], evidential reasoning [12], stochastic multi-criteria acceptability analysis [13], and more recent approaches leveraging spreadsheet and other software modeling tools [14, 15].

Imbedding uncertainty distributions in both cost and value elements of MCVMs changes the tradespace from point estimates to multiple bivariate distributions of potential outcomes that are generated using simulation, such as those shown in Figure 10.1 for six alternatives. Their resemblance to clouds motivates naming this chart a *cloudplot*. A cloudplot reveals uncertainty's influence on the tradespace. For any alternative, the more spread out the potential realizations, the greater the level of uncertainty associated with input and model parameters, and vice-versa. The more that alternative clouds overlap, the greater the likelihood that a decision based on the earlier deterministic tradespace will result in disappointment because *any of the 1000 (TC, TV) point estimates appearing on the cloudplot is a potential outcome for a system alternative after a selection has been made.* Typically, a sampling size of $K = 1000$ is sufficient for accomplishing the goals for analyzing uncertainty. This stochastic tradespace becomes the focus of uncertainty analysis for systems decision support.

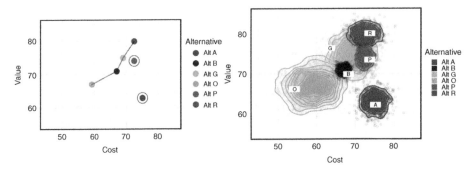

Figure 10.1   Deterministic and stochastic tradespaces.

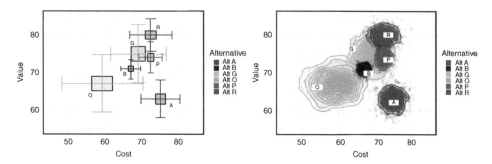

Figure 10.2 Stochastic tradespace examples: boxplot and cloudplot.

Given that random sampling is used, alternative expectations $\overline{A_n} = [\overline{C_n}, \overline{V_n}]$ representing average cost and value return results could be plotted, thereby reducing the stochastic problem to point estimates similar to deterministic modeling. The downside associated with using average costs and average values as surrogates for uncertainty far outweigh the conveniences they offer. While leveraging the deterministic tradespace's principles and constructs to guide decision maker choices, an expectation-based tradespace obscures information such as the degree to which a bad outcome might result from a good decision. This well-recognized possibility can incite decision maker regret or remorse after they commit to a particular alternative and its system performance may not be the realization that ultimately occurs. Such a situation poses very real personal risk for a decision maker, especially when the resources committed to the chosen system solution alternative and the internal and external dependencies on its operational behavior are significant.

As a result, this practice is discouraged because of the needless loss of valuable information that is incurred (see Section 10.3). The preferred alternative to expected value point estimates is working with full uncertainty distributions leveraging the power of simulation to accomplish the needed analysis.

One alternative in this direction would be to plot quartile boxplots to further expose variation in cost and value as shown in the lefthand chart in Figure 10.2. This option has statistical support that can be used to produce meaningful metrics regarding the underlying uncertainty.

Several interesting approaches have been developed to-date that have experienced success in unveiling meaningful insights regarding uncertainty's implications to the decision maker prior to the decision being made [16]. All these methods construct realistic representative distributions to embed uncertainty in their particular modeling approach while avoiding over-dependence on point estimate displays containing statistical expectation and sample averages. As will be discussed in Section 10.3, this is a best practice for systems decision making.

10.2 UNCERTAINTY CONCEPTS

Every systems decision support project involves uncertainty in one form or another that should be contended with and incorporated into modeling, analysis, and results interpretation in a meaningful manner, as was illustrated in Figure 1.9. It reveals itself naturally, oftentimes in discussion with stakeholders in the course of doing research to answer "What is?" and "What should be?" questions posed within the SDP. The degree to which uncertainty is accommodated is a choice made by the systems team, recognizing that ignoring it altogether is foolish at best and negligent at worse.

When considering uncertainties with systems, it can be helpful to think in terms of source, presence, and affects in broad categorical terms to aid in identifying them. For example, what uncertainties are associated with features internal to the system of interest versus external? What uncertainties are controllable by the design and development team versus uncontrollable? What is the degree of presence (trivial, moderate, substantial) and influence (inconsequential, significant) on design, development, and deployment of the system?

With system modeling, uncertainties arise as a model begins to take shape when the inputs, controlling parameters, and mechanisms needed for the type of modeling being used are being decided. Early in the SDP, it's possible that many of these unknowns/uncertainties can be resolved with investigation and research. Others cannot. Sets of these uncertainties affect various aspects of system design, build, test (and measure) and performance.

When building models, it is important to distinguish between the effects that uncertainty imposes and the effects of variability as a function of randomness. They are related, but more like cousins than siblings. Random events introduce variability in outcomes by way of stochastic processes. Variability is an effect of chance and is an inherent characteristic of a system that has random elements whose modeling and analysis are tightly coupled to the laws of probability. These elements could involve counting, selection, errors introduced by physical influences, and other actions. Also known as aleatory uncertainty, stochastic variability, and inter-individual variability, this type of effect is an inherent feature of the system of interest. Having a complete knowledge of the random element or its process will not resolve or reduce the potential variability in outcomes. The good news is that random elements can be readily modeled and analyzed using probability theory once they are accurately identified.

On the other hand, root causes for uncertainty lie with knowledge deficiency in humans. As such, there is a temporal dimension to uncertainty. Given enough time, talent, and resources, uncertainty indicated by a level of ignorance concerning system parameters and inputs can be eliminated, reduced, or mitigated by gathering more accurate information, if it is available. Failing this, epistemic uncertainty could be overcome by events as time goes on, but perhaps not in time to support the systems project appropriately. This type of uncertainty is also known as fundamental uncertainty, epistemic uncertainty, and degree of belief.

Knowing which modeling elements involve variability and which involve uncertainty enables a systems team to make wise choices during a project, particularly where resources are concerned. If time allows, and the talent is on-hand, and adequate resources (e.g., budget dollars) are available, gathering more information to reduce uncertainty by increasing the stakeholder pool, increasing the depth of investigation on elements where uncertainty exists, and accommodating new information into modeling parameters and inputs will affect designed alternatives, affording new or more focused options to a decision maker. Figure 10.3 illustrates a taxonomy showing the major sources of uncertainty encountered during a systems project.

Context uncertainty is specific to each project, recognizing that although the SDP provides a common framework that can guide all systems decision support efforts, each system has unique considerations that introduce novel uncertainties into the process. These subdivide into endogenous sources that arise from within the project team itself (e.g., skill levels, experience, motivations) and hence are under the team's control, and exogenous sources that are outside of the team's control (e.g., stakeholder biases, environmental factor dynamics, and interactions).

Data uncertainty has long been recognized as a major contributor to project outcomes. The saying that "garbage in equals garbage out" is one common way that teams have expressed concern over data in this sense. Data uncertainty has three major sources: data incompleteness, data inaccuracy, and data variation. Missing, withheld, and censored data create gaps in available data that prevent systems teams from eliminating assumptions and thereby increasing the fidelity of

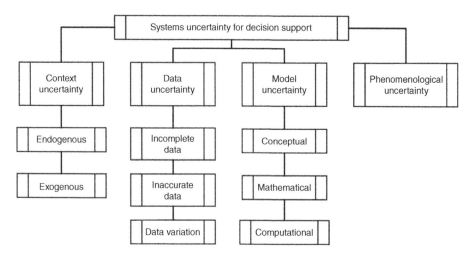

Figure 10.3 Sources of uncertainty in systems decision support projects. Source: Adapted from [17].

modeling results. More recently, the adverse effects introduced by using data averages in models instead of data representations via distributions has been recognized, and is discussed in detail in the section that follows.

Data inaccuracy is typified by inexact or unreliable data stemming from outdated, lagged, or error laden data sources. Data variation uncertainties result from source choices that inevitably must be made when alternative data sources are available.

Model uncertainty has three major uncertainty sources: conceptual, mathematical, and computational. Uncertainties in the conceptual model (e.g., systemigram relationships) that are not resolved will propagate to later modeling steps. Mathematical uncertainties result from expression simplifications and other choices that are made for practical reasons such as available references, software, team education, experience, and so on. Computational uncertainties are introduced either by not understanding software computational limits or by simplifications made to make computations tractable.

Phenomenological uncertainty directly stems from unknown future events that affect inputs, models and alternatives, and results. Some of these are recognized as risks and treated accordingly. Other future uncertainties are caused by evolution in the system's environment as the project proceeds. That is, the moment that input data, model parameters, and stakeholder information is collected and recorded, it is frozen in-place; it begins to age and its relevancy to the project's fundamental objective begins to erode. In recent times, the uncertainty introduced by this consideration can be effectively reduced by building analytical tools and models that leverage real time data feeds that allow users to make 'changes on-the-fly,' as it is described.

Expert opinion is a valuable part of every systems decision support effort, as are technical reports, published journal papers, databases, and experimental measurements. When model parameters and data input are based on these sources, it is considered best practice to explicitly use as much information as each possesses. With current computational software and spreadsheets, this means using uncertainty distributions to represent these modeling elements because doing so propagates critical information (e.g., variance, extreme value incidence rates, etc.) through a model to its output. The important numerical results become distributions, facilitating a host of statistical and graphical analyses that expose features such as risk that better inform the decisions being made.

The main approaches for accomplishing this in practice today are error propagation, decision trees, scenario analysis, and Monte Carlo and Latin Hypercube simulation.

Error propagation provides estimates of the output relative error based on the relative error of the inputs (i.e. ratio of standard deviation to mean). This approach works well for simple models involving mathematically smooth (i.e. continuous and differentiable) functions with small relative errors, producing reasonable approximations. As models become complicated with step functions, discontinuities, and dynamic elements, error propagation loses its appeal as an analysis option. Instead, most error propagation techniques model errors as distributions on stochastic variables, relying on powerful computational techniques and simulation to carry the workload [18, 19].

Probability trees, or decision trees, model each uncertain quantity by a small number of discrete outcomes typically as low, median and high values each with an assigned probability estimate of occurrence. In this way, the value of each outcome can be estimated. The overall model resembles a tree in which each uncertain quantity branches out with these outcomes. This method is often combined with decision variables, each represented as a small number of options. This decision tree approach has been adapted to include elements of fuzzy mathematics for modeling uncertain quantities on various branches throughout the tree structure. Commonly referred to as *soft decision trees* because of its ability to avoid fixing estimates as single numbers, it has demonstrated improved variance in its output [20]. In both the standard and soft decision tree approaches, the growth in the number of outcomes increases exponentially as the number of decision variables increases, making this approach intractable for larger models.

A third option frequently used in support of strategy development and futures forecasting is scenario analysis [21]. *Scenario analysis* creates a small number of scenarios by assigning values for each uncertain quantity and decision and computing the corresponding results. Fixing the future in this way essentially resolves the environmental conditions motivating uncertainty and allows for intuitive interpretation by decision makers. This value fixing faces the challenge of computational complexity as the number of value combinations (high, med, low) regarding each uncertain variable grows. Thus, in typical applications the number of scenarios is limited to under 10. Despite its usefulness, a drawback exists for uncertainty modeling because of the lack of information concerning the relative probability of each fixed scenario and its inability to provide a sense of parameter space coverage or variable interaction.

10.3 FLAW OF AVERAGES CONSIDERATIONS

Software applications used to lack an ability to imbed fully-analytical or simulation-based distributions into the various computations they were using. A variety of practices emerged as a consequence, none perhaps as fraught with potential difficulties as the decision to use averages in place of full data arrays or distributions.

Using an average to represent an uncertain number directly leads to two computational deficiencies popularized by Savage [22] as flaws of averages: unnecessary under-representation of information, and erroneously assuming that by providing a data sample average as input to a mathematical function, the output represents the average of the function. Savage calls the first of these the Weak form of the Flaw of Averages, and the latter as the Strong Form of the Flaw of Averages.

The Weak form sacrifices data spread patterns and risk information for computational efficiency. Software applications such as *SIPmath* [23], *Risk* [24], *Crystal Ball* [25], and *Analytica* [26] have the ability to manipulate sample distributions as objects similar to numbers. Simple to complex calculations, table lookups, and most all spreadsheet functions accept uncertainty distribution as they would numerical input and model parameters. The functions and expressions manipulating these inputs propagates forward their results in terms of distributions as well, an invaluable asset when performing risk, value, cost, and other uncertainty based analyses important to supporting systems decisions.

The Strong Form of the Flaw of Averages is known as Jensen's inequality [27], expressed in mathematical form as the inequality:

$$f(E[x]) \neq E[f(x)] \qquad \text{when } f(x) \text{ is purely convex or concave}$$

Here, $E[x]$ represents an input average calculated as a sample average or provided by expert opinion as an estimate, and $f(x)$ represents a nonlinear function whose output is being used for planning (e.g., project scheduling, cost estimation, revenue models, etc.). When $f(x)$ is linear, Jensen's inequality is satisfied as an equality and the Strong Form does not apply. Similarly, if $f(x)$ is not purely convex or concave then Jensen's inequality does not apply to $f(x)$ over the domain of x-values. It would however apply to intervals in which $f(x)$ was purely concave or convex.

Figure 10.4 illustrates the three cases that Jensen's inequality applies to. In each, a data sample x appears in the first column, the corresponding function values $f(x)$ appear in the second column, and a representative convex ($f(x) = x^{1.8}$), concave ($f(x) = x^{1/1.8}$), and linear ($f(x) = 10x$) function is used to illustrate the effect of Jensen's inequality on the output of $f(x)$.

In the convex case, when the sample average $E[x] = 75$ is substituted into the function $f(x)$, the resulting output underestimates the actual average of the convex function: $f(75) = 2371.98 < 2990.14 = E[f(x)]$. When the sample average is input to the concave function $f(x) = x^{1/1.8}$, the result overestimates the average of $f(x)$: $f(75) = 110.08 > 102.63 = E[f(x)]$. Finally, when $f(x)$ is linear, as is shown in the third chart, $f(E[x]) = E[f(x)]$ and Jensen's inequality does not apply.

The concern here is with input to nonlinear value functions in MCVM models and avoiding any misconceptions regarding input and output. Using distributions makes this concern moot as the full range of possible values are being used as input.

10.4 UNCERTAINTY DISTRIBUTIONS

From a modeling standpoint, uncertainty distributions are patterns that represent concentration locations and potential spread for input measures and parameter values. These distributions are the fundamental means available for incorporating uncertainty into decision support models and analysis. In the early days, select statistical numbers such as average estimates, high, medium, and low values, or percentage increases and decreases were used to examine the impact of input or parameter changes on important output results. Now, software applications such as Probability Management's *SIPmath*, Lumina's *Analytica* platform, Oracle's *Crystal Ball*, and Palisade Software's *@Risk* allow a user to substitute entire distributions for uncertain numbers in formulas, effectively propagating their pattern of uncertainty through a model to the affected outputs. This is a game-changer when it comes to systems decision support.

If accurate and appropriate data exist, histograms can be created directly from the sample data. These histograms are called *empirical distributions*. Distributions can also be fit to sample data and checked using statistical techniques. Both approaches carry with them an assumption that the present and future will perform much like the past, which could cause undesirable issues depending on the system of interest. One could argue that such is the case with expert opinion as well since it is based on past experience as well. The difference in most cases is how recent the information is that is being used.

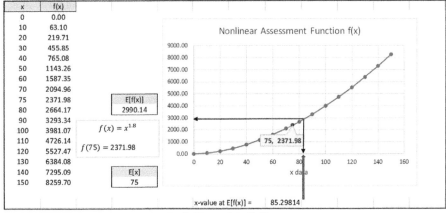

$$E[f(x)] > f(E[x])$$

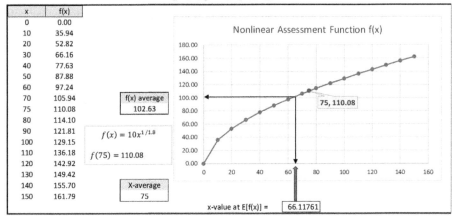

$$E[f(x)] < f(E[x])$$

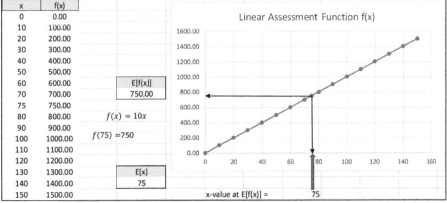

$$E[f(x)] = f(E[x])$$

Figure 10.4 Jensen's inequality applied to three cases.

Data fitting distributions could represent outdated information in another vein in that it does not reflect stakeholders' and subject matter experts' (SMEs) current knowledge. More importantly, their projected knowledge would be based on many information signals not coming from the current system. Potential new competitors, emerging technologies, changing costs due to supply chain threats, manufacturing and political instability, and many other disruptors to the system environment that introduce uncertainty will inform and affect stakeholder estimates in a way not possible with historical data. With only a limited knowledge of a specific system behavior, such as minimum and maximum, average, or behavior tendencies, it's possible to express recent relevant stakeholder knowledge as uncertainty distributions as an entry point for creating effective system models such as MCVMs.

Depending on the context, these distributions are also referred to as probability density functions (PDFs), probability mass functions (PMFs), and histograms. In simplest terms, PDFs and PMFs are distributions whose shapes reveal where potential numerical values are concentrated and how they are spread out over their possible values. The higher the pattern shape over a particular value, the higher the density of occurrence for that value and the more often it has/will occur. Thus, the vertical axis for a plot of an uncertainty distribution indicates the density, or concentration of potential values assigned to a measure over its domain of interest. It *does not* indicate the probability of a specific value occurring.

Histograms are uncertainty patterns displayed as vertical bar charts that typically result from sorting, ordering, and binning data into discrete intervals that subdivide the potential range of values for an uncertain quantity. The resulting graph is shown as a bar chart whose columns indicate density of occurrence over each interval. The vertical axis display raw counts of data falling into each interval once sorted. If the sample size is large enough, the patterns displayed in histograms are reasonable approximations to those of a PDF, which makes them ideal for uncertainty modeling purposes. They are the default display for distributions created in simulation software. When referring to uncertainty distributions, it is generally with a PDF or PMF shape in-mind.

PMFs are the discrete analog to continuous PDFs, but are like histograms in appearance being displayed as vertical bar charts. Because a PMF's columns count or stack numerical occurrences into discrete columns over specific single numerical values and there are no continuous intervals between these values, the vertical axis can represent counts, percentage density, and probability.

Distributions are also constructed using subjective information to guide the type, shape, and location of the pattern of behavior or belief regarding data, and for that reason they work well for modeling input and parameter uncertainty in MCVMs with the goal of exploring their impact on output results.

Their individual characteristics guide the choice of which to use in a specific situation:

- *Min/max bounds.* When only upper and lower bounds can be identified for an uncertain parameter or input data quantity, a Uniform distribution is warranted. Most likely, a bounded Uniform distribution will be used to shift and re-scale the Uniform(0,1) distribution to represent the desired interval.
- *Mode.* The mode of a distribution is a location on the value measure scale at which the strongest belief, the most recurring quantity, the most likely estimate, or the most frequently occurring data value occurs. When only one such location exists, the distribution will be unimodal, meaning it has only one mode over its possible domain. For subjective distribution building, this is typically expressed as the "most likely" value of the parameter being estimated. When a mode exists, a Uniform distribution is inappropriate.

- *Mean.* For symmetric distributions, the mean (or sample average) serves the same purpose as the mode for positioning a distribution. For asymmetric uncertainty distributions, it retains its role as the balance point for the distribution but is of less use for positioning.
- *Scale parameter.* For two-parameter distributions, the scale parameter helps to position the distribution along its domain. Most helpful in this regard is the scale parameter for the Weibull distribution used in reliability analysis. It represents the 63rd percentile for this distribution. It is the point at which 63% of outcomes occur to its left.

For most MCVM applications, a small number of distributions are used most of the time, especially for representing subjective uncertainty. These are the uniform, bounded uniform, triangular, normal, and project evaluation review technique (PERT)-beta distributions. Information regarding each of these uncertainty distributions is readily available on the Internet (see, for example, https://en.wikipedia.org/wiki/PERT_distribution).

10.5 MONTE CARLO UNCERTAINTY SIMULATION

Assuming that all key uncertain measures, criteria, input data, and parameters have been appropriately modeled using distributions [28], a standard Monte Carlo simulation can be used to generate a requisite number of two-dimensional output data. An equally effective approach using Latin hypercube sampling could also be used if a forced stratification of the sample space were called for [29].

The most effective approach for understanding uncertainty implications with regard to system decisions is to use probabilistic computer simulation, which is why it is considered a professional best practice among all disciplines affected by uncertainty. Because this type of simulation directly models uncertainty distributions associated with inputs and parameters, it makes use of the full range of information that uncertainty distributions represent, propagating this information to a model's output throughout its numerical computations.

During its developmental years (1960–1990), engaging in this type of modeling required an analyst to write and construct original code. It was largely seen as a modeling alternative for calculations too difficult or impossible to perform analytically [30]. Today, commercial software programs and online code repositories are readily available, making simulation the first choice for uncertainty modeling and analysis regardless of the associated problem's computational difficulty. This was another game-changer for systems decision support efforts.

All reliable computer simulations use high quality pseudo-random number generators (PRNGs) involving mathematical formulas to produce number sequences on the interval [0, 1] that approximate key properties of random numbers: the numbers generated are independent and possess an infinite sequence period (the length of the numerical sequence before it begins to repeat). PRNGs produce sequences that are near independent with periods much longer than any sequence or sampling used in any one calculation. How well they accomplish this is a topic of ongoing interest [31].

For practical purposes, the resulting PRNG sequences are treated as random numbers. For this reason, we'll refer to the practice of sampling from specific uncertainty distributions as *random sampling*, even though a PRNG is not truly random. When a true random number sequence is required, quantum random number generators (QRNGs) can be used used [32]. Once the tool of only the most sophisticated needs, online QRNGs are now available to the public free of charge [33] (https://qrng.physik.hu-berlin.de/).

All random sampling methods use cumulative distributions $F(x)$ to create the desired sample size n of data that will represent an uncertainty distribution $f(x)$. Specifically, PRNGs use the inverse

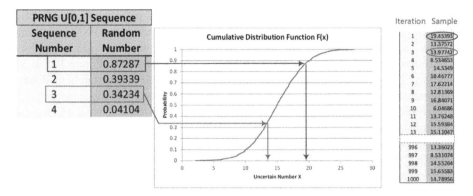

Figure 10.5 Random sampling using cumulative distribution for a $N(15, 4)$ uncertainty distribution.

cumulative distribution $x = F^{-1}(y)$ because the desired random samples are domain values $x \subset X$. Figure 10.5 illustrates how this is accomplished.

Suppose that 1000 random samples were needed from a normal uncertainty distribution $f(x)$ of an uncertain variable X with a mean of 15 and variance equal to 4 ($N(15, 4)$) and whose cumulative distribution function (CDF) is given by $F(x)$.

First, a PRNG formula generates a sequence of 1000 pseudo-random numbers on the scale $[0, 1]$ starting with an initial number r_0 used to initiate the sequence. This input value is known as a *seed* value. After the first pseudo-random number r_1 is generated, this number is used as input to the PRNG formula to create the second pseudo-random number r_2. This feedback process is continued until the number of pseudo-random numbers in the sequence n is the same as the desired sample size n. Once all 1000 are created, sampling starts by substituting the first pseudo-random number ($r_1 = 0.87287$) into the inverse CDF $F^{-1}(r_1)$ to produce the first random sample $x_1 = F^{-1}(0.87287) = 19.45393$ from the $N(15, 4)$ uncertainty distribution. The upper arrows in Figure 10.5 show this step graphically. The lower arrows illustrate this sampling using the third pseudo-random number from the sequence ($r_3 = 0.34234$), resulting in the random sample $x_3 = 13.97742$. The process stops when 1000 random samples have been created. As the type of distribution changes, say to a Weibull distribution instead of a normal distribution, the shape of the cumulative distribution function (CDF) changes – stretching or compressing along the x-axis – and the random sample result for any particular vertical axis value on $[0, 1]$ changes in response.

Microsoft Excel uses a linear congruential generator (LCG) for creating pseudo-random numbers for its =RAND(*) function. An LCG uses a recurrence relationship defined by:

$$r_{n+1} = (ar_n + c) \bmod m$$

where $n \geq 0$ is an integer sample size, m is an integer modulus ($m > 0$), a is a multiplier ($0 < a < m$), c is the increment ($0 \leq c < m$), and r_0 is the seed value. Pseudo-randomness is achieved by performing modulo arithmetic on the number produced within the parentheses. In addition to its long period, an LCG is fast and the sequence it generates can be reproduced simply by using the same seed value. As an Excel add-in application, *SIPmath* inherits the qualities of this PRNG for the modeling and simulation functions it performs. Other PRNG are based on the Kolmogorov–Anosov theory of mixing in classical mechanical systems.

There are two dominant random sampling methods in use that differ only in the manner in which they sample from a cumulative distribution: Monte Carlo sampling and Latin Hypercube sampling. The discussion that follows is for the one-dimensional case, but the principles apply to higher dimensional cases as well. Both techniques use an analytical inversion method involving a distribution's inverse CDF to produce samples. A Monte Carlo method uses a PNRG Uniform(0,1) value to draw one sample from the full domain for the targeted uncertain quantity during each iteration, terminating at the desired sample size. The process illustrated in Figure 10.5 is Monte Carlo sampling. This is the dominant random sampling method used in uncertainty modeling.

It is important to note that Monte Carlo sampling is not guaranteed to produce random samples across all possible x values. The degree to which it does depends on the shape of the CDF $F(x)$ and the desired sample size n. As n gets larger, say, $n = 100,000$ samples instead of $n = 1000$, the PRNG sequence length increases. Because this sequence closely approximates random numbers drawn from a distribution in which all values are equally likely (Uniform(0,1)), the resulting sampling increases the chances of using numbers toward the extremes of the interval [0, 1], thereby producing random samples from the tails of $f(x)$ and better representing the intended uncertainty distribution's values. However, if the uncertainty distribution has narrow, long tails, its associated CDF $F(x)$ has extreme [0, 1] values that are pinched closely to the horizontal making it more difficult for the sampling to result in x values associated with these tails. This can be observed in Figure 10.5 for x values from 3 to 7 and from 23 to 28, approximately. The steeper the rise of $F(x)$, the more concentrated the random samples will be around the center point of the steep rise, corresponding to the mode of $f(x)$ (which is close to the mean of $f(x)$ for symmetric or near-symmetric uncertainty distributions).

Latin Hypercube sampling, also called *stratified sampling*, is used when a more representative set of random samples is desired, especially for the case when n is not large. It attempts to produce an equal number of samples from sample space partitions in the following way. Latin Hypercube sampling first partitions the $U(0, 1)$ vertical axis into m equally sized intervals $\frac{1}{m}$. It then draws one random sample sequentially in turn from each partition using Monte Carlo sampling until the desired sample size n is met.

For example, suppose the uncertain quantity's sample space consists of the horizontal axis (domain) $x \in [5, 25]$ shown in Figure 10.5. Latin Hypercube sampling first divides the vertical axis into 4 equally sized intervals: [0, 0.25], [0.25, 0.50], [0.50, 0.75], and [0.75, 1.0]. The PRNG sequence $r \in [0, 1]$ then uses Monte Carlo sampling once per each interval during each iteration rather than once from the entire $r \in [0, 1.0]$ interval during each iteration. This continues until n random numbers were produced. In this way, the sampling is forced to pull equally from each partition, increasing the representation of the uncertainty distribution's tail values. When the simulation's output is being used to inform decisions that should take extreme values into consideration, Latin Hypercube sampling is useful for this purpose, particularly so when n is small.

10.6 COST UNCERTAINTY MODELING

Monte Carlo analysis is a useful tool for quantifying the uncertainty in a cost estimate. The Monte Carlo process creates a probability distribution for the total cost estimate by aggregating all uncertainty representations into a single distribution that represents the potential system costs. Once this distribution has been constructed, the systems team can provide a decision maker with meaningful insight about the probability that the total systems project cost exceeds a certain threshold, or that a schedule is longer than a specific target time. In general, there are five steps for conducting a Monte Carlo analysis for cost and schedule models [34]. These steps are as follows:

1. Identify the appropriate work breakdown structure (WBS) level for modeling; this level will be dependent upon the stage in the system life cycle that the estimate is being conducted. In general, as a system matures in its development, lower level WBS elements can be modeled.

2. Construct an initial estimate for the cost or duration for each of the WBS elements in the model.

3. Identify those WBS elements that contain significant levels of uncertainty. Not all elements will have uncertainty associated with them. For example, if part of the system of interest has existing off-the-shelf components with firm-fixed price quotes for the material, then there would be no uncertainty with the costs for those elements for the WBS.

4. Quantify the uncertainty for each of the WBS elements with an appropriate uncertainty distribution.

5. Aggregate all of the lower level WBS uncertainty distributions into a single WBS estimate by using Monte Carlo simulation. This step will also yield a CDF for the system cost. This distribution can be used to quantify the cost risk as well as identify the cost drivers in the system estimate.

Like all models, Monte Carlo simulation results are only as good as the data used to construct the model, the old adage that "garbage in, yields garbage out" applies to these situations. The specific distributions used to model uncertainty in WBS elements depend on the information known about each estimate. Many cost analysts default to the use of a Triangular distribution to express uncertainty because of minimum, most likely, and maximum estimates being available. The choice of a Triangular distribution is often a matter of convenience rather than the result of analysis. The uncertainty distribution selected should resemble in some way historical cost data for the WBS element being modeled. A Triangular distribution will often be used for early life cycle estimates where minimal information is available (lower and upper bounds) and an SME can provide a most likely cost estimate. When only upper and lower bounds for a WBS element's cost are available, a Uniform distribution is frequently used in a Monte Carlo simulation to allow all values between the bounds to occur with equal likelihood.

Software Cost Estimating Example. Suppose a cost estimate for software nonrecurring costs for a Department of Defense (DoD) satellite system is needed. The following cost estimating relationships (CERs) (see Section 8.3.3) have been developed to estimate the cost of the ground control software, the system support software, and the mission embedded flight software during the conceptual design phase of the life cycle.

Application and system software: Person-months = $4.3(\text{EKSLOC})^{1.2}(1.4)^{\text{DoD}}$

Support software: Person-months = $5.3(\text{EKSLOC})^{0.95}$

Space mission embedded flight software: Person-months = $8.7(\text{EKSLOC})^{1.6}(1.6)^{\text{DoD}}$

The DoD parameter equals 1 if it is a DoD satellite, and 0 otherwise. EKSLOC is a measure of the size of the software coding effort. It is the estimated size measured in thousands of source lines of code, but the engineers still need to estimate these sizes for their project.

Suppose that it is early in the design process and the engineers are uncertain about how extensive the coding effort will be. The cost analyst has chosen to use a Triangular distribution to estimate the EKSLOC parameter. The analysts ask the expert to provide a most likely estimate for the needed number of lines of code, m, which becomes the mode of the uncertainty distribution, and two other estimates: a pessimistic estimate (upper bound), b

and an optimistic estimate (lower bound), a. The estimates of a and b would be selected based on a belief that the actual size of the source lines of code will never be less than a or greater than b. These become the lower and upper bound estimates for the Triangular distribution. Law [35] provide computational formulas for a variety of continuous and discrete distributions.

The expected value and variance of the triangle distribution are calculated as follows:

$$\text{Expected value} = \frac{a + m + b}{3} \tag{10.1}$$

$$\text{Variance} = \frac{a^2 + m^2 + b^2 - am - ab - mb}{18} \tag{10.2}$$

Table 10.1 shows the EKSLOC values provided by the SME for each of the software components.

TABLE 10.1   EKSLOC Values by Software Component.

Software Type	Lower Bound	Most Likely	Upper Bound	Mean	Variance
Application	5	10	35	16.67	43.05
Support	70	150	300	173.33	2272.22
Embedded Flight	7	25	80	37.33	241.06

Using these values and the associated CERs a Monte Carlo analysis is performed using Oracle® *Crystal Ball* [25] software designed for use with Excel. The PDF for the embedded flight software is shown in Figure 10.6. The PDF for the estimated labor hours is given in Figure 10.7 for $K = 10{,}000$ simulation runs.

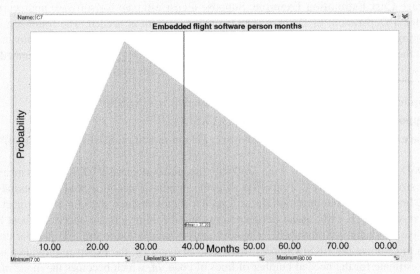

Figure 10.6   Triangular distribution for embedded flight software.

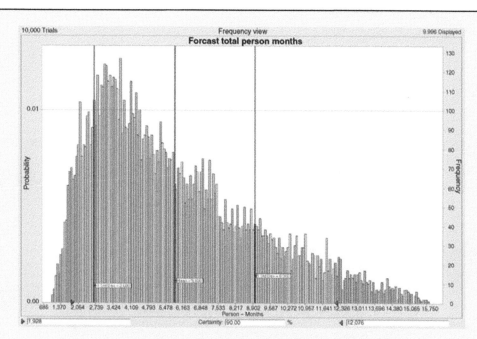

Figure 10.7 PDF for software person months.

Finally, suppose that management believes the labor cost is distributed as a normal random variable with a mean of $20 per hour and standard deviation of $5. This estimate assumes that engineers work 36 hours in a week on coding and that there are four weeks in a month. Figure 10.8 shows the PDF for the software development costs.

The primary observation to take away from Figure 10.8 is the spread in possible software development costs due to the uncertainty assumptions imposed on the WBS elements when the Monte Carlo simulation is constructed. For this example, while it is more likely that the actual software development costs will clump around $12 million, it is possible for them to be up to four times as much or as little as one-tenth as much because of the represented uncertainty. In the former case, the project could be threatened; in the latter, the project would continue well within budget. The probability of these events taking place can be computed directly from the applicable CDF which is easily done in applications such as *Crystal Ball* and spreadsheets. Based on the CDF in Figure 10.9, there is a 50% probability that the software development costs will be less than $15.96 million. Similarly there is a 20% probability that the software development costs will exceed $26.59 million.

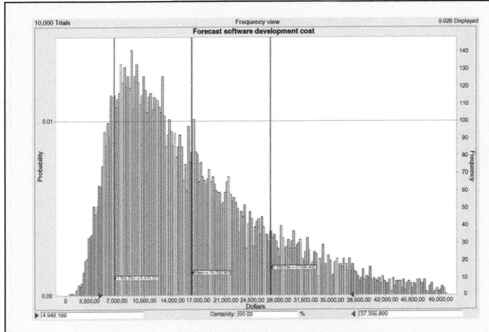

Figure 10.8   PDF for software development cost.

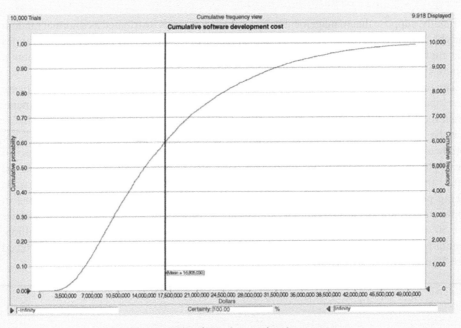

Figure 10.9   CDF for software development cost.

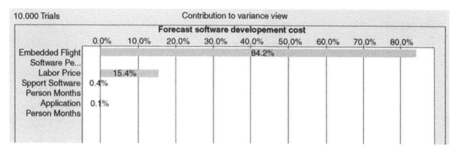

Figure 10.10   Variance contributor tornado chart.

Once cost uncertainty is modeled, the results can then be analyzed to identify those elements that are the most significant cost drivers. In the software cost estimating example, it is relatively easy as the total cost is only a function of three cost elements and one other factor. Realistic cost estimates may have on the order of 25–100 cost elements/factors and choosing the cost drivers from this set is not so easy. Fortunately, some applications such as *Crystal Ball* provide a tornado diagram (named for the shape) that analyzes the relative contribution made by each of the uncertain components to the overall cost and variance for the system cost estimate. Figure 10.10 shows the sensitivity output for this example.

Figure 10.10 indicates that the uncertainty associated with "Embedded Flight software person months" is the main contributor to the output spread of uncertainty (variance) in the cost estimate, followed by the uncertainty in "Labor Price for software engineers". To reduce this spread, the cost analyst, the systems team, or the supported organization should consider spending more time getting a better estimate for the "embedded flight software person months" cost factor, since reductions in the uncertainty associated with this WBS element will have the greatest impact on reducing the uncertainty in the total cost estimate seen in Figure 10.8.

10.7   REALIZATION ANALYSIS

When simulation is used for uncertainty modeling and analysis as it is in many systems decision support projects, then likelihood estimates for opportunity, disappointment, and regret are actually available prior to an alternative being selected from among the choice set. The full range of possible system outcomes, opportunities and threats, are simply outcomes lurking amongst the multitude of potential random sampling realizations. This is the insight that gave birth to *realization analysis* [36]. Realization analysis directly leverages simulation output in a way that differentiates it from previous work that extend the results of stochastic dominance approaches.

Realization analysis explicitly recognizes Monte Carlo simulation output as potential realizations for every candidate system solution alternative. By adopting a direct pairwise comparison approach using the same Pareto efficiency criteria as in a deterministic tradespace and remaining in the space of output realizations, realization analysis quantifies the magnitude of differences between alternatives. It produces accurate probability estimates for four types of potential outcomes that can realistically shape a decision maker's expectations and reduce or eliminate surprise as a ramification of their decision, providing them with an opportunity for proactive planning rather than reacting in recourse [37]. When informative, first-order stochastic dominance results are available, they are integrated into the overall analysis as well to augment decision support.

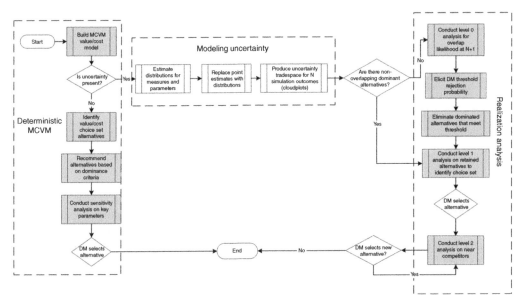

Figure 10.11 Full tradespace analysis decision support process. Source: Caddell et al. [36]/John Wiley & Sons.

Figure 10.11 shows the process flow for a full tradespace analysis that includes uncertainty modeling and realization analysis. It directly leverages the cost and value models created during deterministic tradespace analysis, adding uncertainty elements as needed and assuming that any underlying uncertainty distributions have been properly identified and represented in the MCVM without depending on parametric assumptions regarding these representations, making it a superb option for accommodating objective and subjective uncertainty estimates. These data are then propagated through the mathematical expressions performing and linking calculations and transformations in the deterministic MCVM, resulting in total cost and total value estimates represented as distributions, as shown in Section 10.5.

 There is a difference between applying uncertainty distributions directly to system cost elements—for example, WBS cost element totals—and incorporating a risk layer when modeling uncertain costs in Monte Carlo simulation. Directly tagging WBS elements brings into account the probability of various levels of cost taking place. Adding a risk layer introduces an additional uncertainty that the event might or might not occur; the cost increase (and its level) is dependent on the risk event taking place. In a model, this enables *probabilistic branching* to occur. Simulation results for a mixed cost and risk model will be different than one with just cost uncertainty.

As with the case with deterministic tradespace analysis discussed in Chapter 9, readily available spreadsheet Add-ins and other macro environments coupled with their proliferation across industry and government have made them the tool of choice for accomplishing stochastic tradespace analysis. When possible, these Add-ins have been translated into statistical *R* code to expand their accessibility and applications.

The first step in the realization analysis block, called *Level 0 analysis*, estimates the likelihood that alternatives are dominated using order statistics coupled with a multivariate generalization of the Chebyshev inequality [38]. The purpose of this step is to address the question whether or not additional simulation runs could produce a realization that was no longer strictly dominated, thereby encouraging further analysis. Based on this information, weak performing, likely dominated alternatives can be eliminated, leaving a revised choice set of alternatives competing at or near the Pareto front that have maintained their desirability in the face of uncertainty. Level 0 analysis is a more refined basis by which to reject dominated tradespace alternatives than doing so in the deterministic manner described Chapter 9. However, in practice, deterministic tradespace analysis serves as a reasonable approximation for this approach to eliminate dominated alternatives that do not have significant cloudplot overlap with other Pareto efficient ones. Uncertainty analysis typically proceeds directly to Level 1 analysis because alternative system solutions concerning the systems of interest tend to lie in close proximity to each other in the deterministic tradespace because they are highly competitive, producing cloudplot overlap in the stochastic tradespace.

When cloudplot overlap exists, *Level 1 analysis* uses Monte Carlo simulation to compare all the realizations generated by the choice set alternatives, quantifying the likelihood that any alternative dominates, is dominated by, or is Pareto optimal with any other alternative. This analysis reveals quantifiable information that is hidden when using expectations for total cost and total value, thereby facilitating a rich dialogue with the decision maker and further clarity regarding the systems decision being made. More importantly, it provides explicit probability estimates for post-decision outcomes that represent potential reassurance, opportunity, or disaster, informing a decision maker about their personal decision risk exposure. This is especially important for system acquisition projects where system solution alternatives exist and performance differences can be observed over time. This is the most used aspect of realization analysis, especially if spreadsheet models are employed because of the ease at which it can be performed.

The final step in the block called *Level 2 analysis* compares the ordinal positioning of the selected system solution chosen to the decision maker's next best alternative. The goal here is to characterize degrees of satisfaction with the decision maker's selection in comparison to what this second best alternative was expected to yield. Level 2 analysis performs pairwise comparisons between every realization for the selected alternative and the point estimate defined by $\overline{A_n} = [\overline{C_n}, \overline{V_n}]$. This is based on the assumption that since the next best alternative was not selected to be developed, the only logical performance level to compare with is its expected performance level with respect to cost and value.

Level 2 analysis exposes a selected alternative's attractiveness relative to options foregone by not selecting the next best alternative. In doing so, the results help a decision maker to understand more clearly the possibilities of experiencing decision regret or remorse. This is a different and perhaps less frequently encountered situation than that addressed by Level 1 analysis. Both Level 0 and Level 2 analysis are discussed in Appendix A as extensions for the Level 1 example discussed in Section 10.7.1.

Overall, realization analysis produces easily understandable charts and graphs supporting the underlying logical processes. A decision maker gains a practical benefit by understanding how and why outcomes might occur given the embedded uncertainty propagated throughout the model, regardless of whether first or second order stochastic dominance analyses produces conclusive results [39–43].

As mentioned elsewhere [28], directly comparing alternatives enhances a decision maker's understanding of the risk tradeoffs at the time of the decision while decreasing the likelihood of an unfortunate (or fortunate) surprise afterwards. In this, realization analysis adheres to a decision support philosophy that believes *transparency* in multi-criteria value models of all types contributes strongly to a decision maker's understanding of what is taking place mathematically based on what could occur in reality. Or, as Stewart puts it, "[E]legant mathematical models which are inaccessible to such participants are of very little practical value" [1].

In a majority of systems decisions projects, the choice set of alternatives emerging from the deterministic MCVM block produce overlapping cloudplots. Consequently, applying a check for first order stochastic dominance, examining expected total cost and expected total value against their respective standard deviations to estimate risk and opportunity, and applying Level 1 analysis subsequent to deterministic tradespace results is a complete treatment of uncertainty within the SDP as represented in Figure 1.9. These three techniques will be illustrated in what follows.

10.7.1   Level 1 Analysis—Choice Set Reduction

Level 1 realization analysis attempts to reach beyond the decision in time to help a decision maker understand the impact of a systems decision on what ultimately could result in terms of system cost and value given the uncertainty involved in the project as captured by the MCVM. Although not shown on the flowchart in Figure 10.11, it is worthwhile to conduct a cursory examination for first order stochastic dominance as part of the overall analysis. Despite its low likelihood actually occurring for systems decisions, it can provide supporting information regarding comparisons between alternatives (Figure 10.12) when such stochastic dominance is present.

First order stochastic dominance between alternatives exists when an alternative's CDF lies completely to the right (value) or left (cost) of other alternatives, indicating that its density of outcomes is positioned to provide higher probabilities of preferred outcome occurrence than other alternatives. Typically, these plots are most informative when plotted along with their PDF/histograms as shown in Figure 10.13.

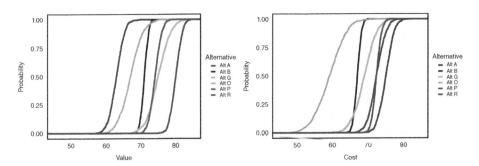

Figure 10.12   Six alternative stochastic dominance plots.

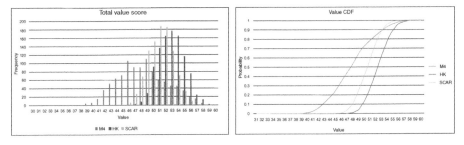

Figure 10.13   PDF and CDF plots for three alternatives.

Definition. A CDF $F(x)$ has first order stochastic dominance over another CDF $G(x)$ if and only if:

$$F(x) \leq G(x)(\text{cost})$$

$$F(x) \geq G(x)(\text{value})$$

for all x with a strict inequality over some interval.

Recalling that a CDF shows the probability of x being less than or equal to any designated value, being positioned to the right means that the probability of achieving any value greater than or equal to $x(1 - CDF(x))$ is greater for alternative HK than for either of the others, hence the high scores with respect to value return.

In the right-hand chart of Figure 10.13, alternative HK exhibits first order stochastic dominance in value over both alternatives M4 and SCAR as its value CDF lies completely to the right. Examining a plot of the three alternatives' PDF/histograms reveals what this means: Alternative HK's density of outcomes are concentrated toward high value return more so than the other two. Since a CDF rolls up or accumulates density moving from left to right, the CDF for Alt HK does not even begin to accumulate value until a value level of 47 is reached and then concentrates its possible outcomes (realizations) right of this mark. Not so for the other alternatives. The same insights apply to total cost CDFs, only the orientation is to the left (i.e. lower costs).

For the six alternative stochastic tradespace example illustrated in Figure 10.2 that will be used to step through the three levels for realization analysis, the CDFs for each of the six alternatives can be plotted to examine whether any of them exhibit clear stochastic dominance over the others. Because these have significant overlap in the cloudplot earlier, it is not likely. Figure 10.12 shows the results. Alt R stochastically dominates the other alternatives with respect to value, while Alt O does so with respect to cost, yielding an informative but inconclusive result, as suspected. This motivates a Level 1 analysis.

EV Cloudplots. After initial deterministic results narrowed the possible electric vehicles to Options A, C, and E, the systems team adapted their MCVM to include several uncertainties that were of concern to the decision maker, mostly because of the sources used to obtain value measure data: "Charging time" (SW = 89) and "Range" (SW = 95). The decision maker was also concerned with potential inaccuracies for total cost of ownership because of changing economic conditions in the U.S. influencing "discount rate", "Tax credit" upon purchase and "Taxes and fees" associated with first year operations. The decision maker was confident in the weights assigned to the individual value measures.

The team identified uncertainty distributions for each of the uncertain elements depending on the information supplied to them and suspected changes (see Table 10.2). *SIPmath* was then used to create distributions for each of these elements affecting Options A, C, and E where they occurred in the MDVM and to generate 1000 Monte Carlo simulation realizations. The resulting tradespace cloudplot shown in Figure 10.14 reinforces the separation between Options A and C and Option E. The overlap in realizations with Option A and Option C underscores the decision maker's concerns regarding uncertainty. There is no clear separation between the two that would allow a Level 0 realization analysis to invoke deterministic dominance.

TABLE 10.2   EV Uncertainty Distributions Used in the MCVM.

Model Uncertainty	Distribution Type	Parameters
Charging Time	Triangular	ML = current, Min/Max ±15%
Range	Normal	Mean = current, SD = 30 miles
Acceleration	PERT(Beta)	ML = current, Min = −1, Max = +2 s
Discount Rate	PERT(Beta)	ML = current, Min = −1.2%, Max = +3.1%
Tax Credit	Triangular	ML = current, Min = −40%, Max = +3%
Taxes and Fees	Triangular	ML = current, Min = −5%, Max = +35%

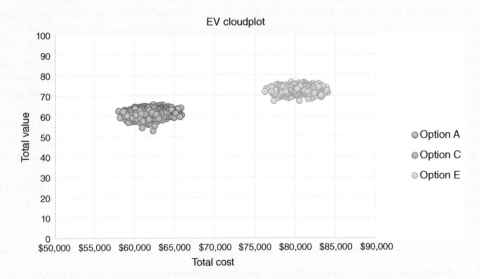

Figure 10.14   EV choice set cloudplot.

Next, the team plotted the cumulative distributions for total cost and total value for all three options to examine if first order stochastic dominance might untangle Options A and C. The results are shown in Figure 10.15. Option E clearly exhibits stochastic dominance over Options A and C with respect to value with its cumulative distribution lying to the right of both. This indicates that all of its possible realizations are distributed over higher total value scores. On the other hand, it carries the worst likely outcomes with respect to total cost. Option C stochastically dominates Options A and E with respect to total cost with Option A stochastically dominating Option E as well. Between Option A and C, A stochastically dominates C in value, but the reverse is true for cost. This inconclusive result is typical with strongly competing system solution alternatives, motivating both realization analysis and other mathematical extensions as noted.

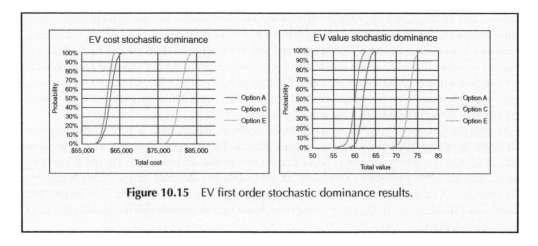

Figure 10.15 EV first order stochastic dominance results.

Continuing with the six alternative example, suppose that a decision maker narrows the selection preference to alternatives R and G and is leaning toward choosing Alt R for the system solution. However, the overlap between the two causes a concern that choosing Alt R introduces the possibility that Alt G will actually outperform Alt R in cost and/or value, posing personal decision risk to the decision maker. Level 1 analysis quantifies these possibilities using probabilities in the following way.

Considering Alt R and Alt G, suppose that a single realization of Alt G is selected and compared with every realization of Alt R to identify Alt R's location relative to the cone of Alt G, K_G. Recalling Figure 9.2, this comparison introduces four potential outcomes for a given Alt R-Alt G pair: (1) the Alt R realization dominates the Alt G realization (upper-left quadrant, $A_R \in K_G$), (2) the Alt R realization is dominated by the Alt G realization (lower-right quadrant, $A_R \in K_G^-$, (3) the Alt R realization is more expensive and more valuable than the Alt G realization (i.e. it is Pareto optimal (+), upper-right quadrant: "pay more, get more"), or (4) the Alt R realization is less expensive and less valuable than the Alt G realization (i.e. it is Pareto optimal (−), bottom-left quadrant: "pay less, get less"). Repeating this process for each of Alt G's remaining realizations yields $l = 1,000,000$ comparisons, which are summarized in Table 10.3.

Since the $l = 1,000,000$ comparisons are being conducted on possible realizations for these two system alternatives, the "% of Total" amounts shown in the fourth column of Table 10.3 represent probabilities. This novel result of Level 1 analysis reveals decision risk in the following way.

TABLE 10.3 Outcome Comparison for Every Alt R and Alt G Realization Pair.

Category	Outcome	Count	% of Total (prob)
A	Alt R dominates Alt G	160,262	16%
B	Alt R is Pareto optimal (+)	772,668	77%
C	Alt R is Pareto optimal (−)	13,351	1%
D	Alt G dominates Alt R	53,719	5%
E	Alt R and Alt G are equivalent	0	0%

Suppose that the decision maker selects Alt R. Category A indicates that among all possible simulation outcomes, there is a 16% probability that Alt R will dominate Alt G. This result, if it occurs, represents a good decision with a good outcome and not a personal decision risk to the decision maker. Categories B and C, while potentially disappointing, again are not personal decision risks to the decision maker because they are rational commonplace market effects: one gets more or less value return depending on how much cost is incurred. Alt R and Alt G are expected to be Pareto optimal with respect to each other the majority of time (78%).

In contrast, Category D represents a risk to the decision maker: there is a 5% probability that Alt G will dominate Alt R in cost and value performance. This category describes a good decision with a bad outcome which introduces buyer's regret or remorse after the system decision has been made. Whether a 5% probability represents an acceptable risk depends on the decision maker's risk tolerance. As a minimum, a rationale decision maker seeing Level 1 results with unfavorable probabilities in categories B, C, and D would be well-advised to institute risk mitigation steps after the systems decision is made.

Based on the deterministic result in Figure 10.1 and the boxplots in Figure 10.2, Alt R and Alt G are expected to be Pareto optimal the majority of time, and Table 10.3 confirms this. Providing this general insight is not novel; traditional approaches will lead to the same conclusion. That said, quantifying the likelihood of Alt R and Alt G's Pareto optimality, as well as revealing the substantial probability that Alt R could dominate Alt G (16%) is new information as it highlights a potential ramification of selecting Alt G that was previously absent in discussions with a decision maker.

While 1,000,000 comparisons may seem computationally burdensome, it is actually performed very quickly in a spreadsheet model for this purpose, which is illustrated in the EV example that follows. In fact, far fewer than that many comparisons are necessary to yield sufficiently precise estimates of the likelihoods in Table 10.3. After all, the rows of Table 10.3, along with the unlikely occurrence that Alt R and Alt G realizations have identical values and costs (known as *indifference points*), can be viewed as five mutually exclusive and collectively exhaustive bins.

Framed in this way, the number of comparisons necessary becomes a well-known sampling problem for multinomial proportions p_i, $i = 1, \dots, P$, subject to $p_i \geq 0$ for all i, $\sum_i p_i = 1$. Among the possible approaches in this vein, Thompson's [44] method is attractive, as it requires (a) no prior information about the p_i, which is realistic, and (b) equivalent desired half-width intervals (d_i), which is reasonable.

For example, constructing 95% confidence intervals for each of the five p_i with half-widths $d_i = 0.005$ and leveraging Thompson's method, the necessary sample size is $1.27359/0.005^2 = 50,944$, provided at least three of the five estimated p_i are non-zero. Alternatively, softening the restriction such that only two versus three of the p_i need to be greater than 0 decreases α_i to 0.025 and lengthens d_i to 0.01, yielding $1.55963/0.01^2 = 15,597$ comparisons. Simply put, 1,000,000 comparisons for each alternative pair appears extravagant; as few as 15,600 would likely suffice.

If Level 1 analysis was applied to all six alternative pairs, 15 pairwise comparisons yielding 15 similar tables would result because given N alternatives $\binom{N}{2} = N(N-1)/2$ tables are required. When the number of alternatives is small as in the case of a choice set narrowed down to 3 or so solution candidates, examining each of the tables is a reasonable approach. On the other hand, as the number of alternatives increases, this detailed, pairwise investigation quickly could become unwieldy.

To address this, an aggregating metric known as the *average dominance score* (ADS) is used [36], which is calculated for each of the N alternatives. Determining the *ADS* for alternative i starts by calculating a *dominance score* for alternative i over each of the remaining alternatives j ($DS_{i,j} \; \forall j \in n, j \neq i$) that are competing in the choice set.

TABLE 10.4   Average Dominance Score (ADS) Matrix for Six Alternative Example.

Alt	G	R	O	B	P	A	ADS
G	—	−0.107	−0.005	0.163	0.468	0.956	0.295
R	0.107	—	0.002	0.012	0.498	0.811	0.286
O	0.005	−0.002	—	0.080	0.020	0.874	0.195
B	−0.163	−0.012	−0.080	—	0.048	1.000	0.159
P	−0.468	−0.498	−0.020	−0.048	—	0.869	−0.033
A	−0.956	−0.811	−0.874	−1.000	−0.869	—	−0.902

Given l comparisons between randomly selected realizations of i and j, $DS_{i,j}$ is given by:

$$DS_{i,j} = \frac{\sum_l X_{i>j} - \sum_l X_{j>i}}{l} \tag{10.3}$$

where $X_{i>j}$ and $X_{j>i}$ are indicator variables for $i > j$ and $j > i$ respectively. Armed with its resulting dominance scores, alternative is ADS is calculated as:

$$ADS_i = \frac{\sum_{j=1, j \neq i}^{N} DS_{i,j}}{N-1} \tag{10.4}$$

Applying this to each of the alternatives in Figure 10.2 yields the ADS matrix seen in Table 10.4.

Ignoring the ADS column, Table 10.4 is antisymmetric, meaning entries are a negative refection of each other across the main diagonal, which is expected since multiplying $DS_{i,j}$ by −1 yields $DS_{j,i}$. Computationally, this antisymmetry provides some efficiencies, as only the upper (or lower) triangular portion of the ADS matrix must be calculated to obtain the results noted. Although different in computation and meaning, this metric is similar in spirit to an outranking degree most notably used in ELECTRE-III software [45], which seeks to aggregate partial concordance results with preference weighting in order to identify favorably attractive alternatives [46].

If a decision maker is confronted with a large number of alternatives, the ADS matrix provides a screening tool to potentially reduce the number of alternatives that should be considered further. In particular, if alternative i's ADS is greater than zero, alternative i is more likely to dominate its competing alternatives than be dominated by them and should be retained for further analysis. Conversely, if alternative i's ADS is less than zero, there are likely higher value and lower cost options, and it can reasonably be eliminated. Applying this logic to the six alternative example ADS Table 10.4, only the Alt G, Alt R, Alt O, and Alt B alternatives should be retained.

EV Level 1 Realization Analysis. The decision maker narrowed selection choices down to two: Options A and C. Given the inconclusive stochastic dominance results, the team then examined the expected total cost and expected total value in light of their standard deviations, a commonly used indicator of risk and conversely, opportunity. Figure 10.16 shows the results. Under the uncertainty parameters modeled, Option E possesses the highest risk/opportunity in both categories. Option C has less of a downside cost risk than

Option A. Option A has less variation for total value, limiting its upside potential along with its downside risk. Option C has greater variation with respect to total value, indicating both greater risk and opportunity than Option A in this regard.

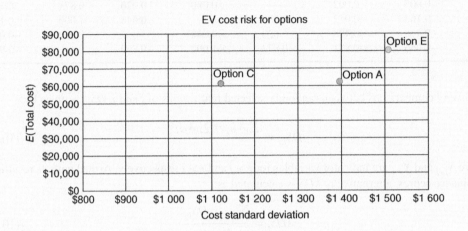

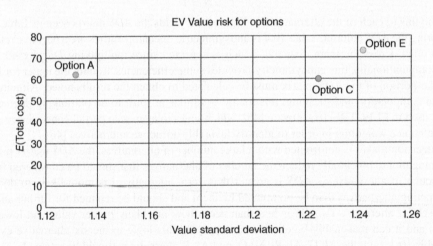

Figure 10.16   EV choice set total cost and value versus risk.

Finally, the team applied Level 1 realization analysis to Option A and C to better illuminate the decision makers risk for selecting either option. Figure 10.17 shows both the count table and a slice of the pairwise comparison table used in Excel. With a sample size of $n = 1000$, 1,000,000 pairwise comparisons are performed. As described earlier, relative positioning in this stochastic tradespace leverages the same Pareto efficient properties that drive a deterministic tradespace. The percentage results shown indicate occurrence probabilities for each category as well as count ratios. An *ADS* table approach was not necessary because of the very small number of alternatives being analyzed.

		Count	Percent
C Dominates	**A**	76299	7.6%
C PO(+)	**B**	30418	3.0%
C PO(-)	**C**	616433	61.6%
C Is Dominated	**D**	276850	27.7%
Alts. Are Equal	**E**	0	0.0%

	U	V	W	X	Y	Z	AA
		C cost	C value				
3							
4	A cost			61376.6	61715.8	61772.8	65049.6
5	A value			62.1341	63.7763	60.9186	60.7624
6		59812.2	59.8493	C	C	C	C
7		60589.8	57.3173	C	C	C	C
8		60512.7	60.7844	C	C	C	A
9		63190.1	60.1392	D	D	D	C
10		62083.5	61.2459	D	D	B	A
11		60637.7	60.7331	C	C	C	C
12		61021.8	59.9036	C	C	C	C
13		59991.9	61.5942	C	C	A	A

Figure 10.17 EV Level 1 realization analysis results (Options A and C).

The Level 1 analysis comparison table in Excel shown in Figure 10.17 is set up in the following manner. *SIPmath* stores random sampling results in a hidden XML file when uncertainty distributions are created on **Input**. Designating and naming these same cells as **Output** writes the numerical results to a spreadsheet worksheet titled `PMTable`. The 1000 simulation random sampling results for total cost and total value for Option A were copied from columns on the `PMTable` worksheet and pasted into the rows shown using `Paste Special` -> `Transpose`. Data samples for Option C were pasted directly into columns as shown.

The logical expression used to perform comparisons in this case is a nested `=IF()` statement that addresses the five possible comparison outcomes:

=IF(AND($W6=X$5,$V6=X$4),"E",IF(AND($W6>=X$5,$V6<=X$4), "A",

IF(AND($W6>X$5,$V6>X$4),"B",IF(AND($W6<X$5,$V6<X$4),

"C",IF(AND($W6<=X$5,$V6>=X$4),"D")))))

which, because of the absolute references caused by the symbol $, only is carefully entered once in the top left corner of the comparisons table—here it is cell `X6` and then drag-copied to the right and then down to fill the entire table with the correct comparison logic. The table shown to the left in Figure 10.17 counts the occurrences of each category in the comparison table using the expression: `=COUNTIF($X$6:$AMI$1005,O8)` where `$X$6:$AMI$1005` contain the 1,000,000 comparison cells and cell `O8` contains the category label `A` to its left. A similar expression was entered following this for each of the other four categories.

Given the uncertainty modeled, realization analysis results indicate that there is a 7.6% probability that Option C will dominate Option A. However, there is also a 27.7% chance that Option A will dominate Option C. If the decision maker prefers Option C, this represents a 27.7% chance of a realizing a good decision with a bad outcome, the source of buyer's regret and a direct decision risk. Whether this is a high level or not is a matter of decision maker risk tolerance. Selecting Option A has only a 7.6% probability of this result, reducing the decision risk to the decision maker by over 20%.

The other two categories (B and C) represent the cases "pay more, get more" and "pay less, get less" which place them in non-dominated relationships along the Pareto frontier in the stochastic tradespace. If Option C is selected, it has a 61.6% chance of delivering lower value at a lower cost than Option A, while only a 3% chance of actually achieving higher value at a higher cost.

In all, if value return is the decision maker's higher priority, Option A stochastically dominates Option C with respect to value, it has an 89.3% chance of either dominating Option C (27.7%) or realizing greater value at higher cost (61.6%). Since both Options A and C are well below the budget as indicated by Figure 9.10 earlier, Option A appears to be a better choice.

REFERENCES

1. Stewart, T., Durbach, I. (2016) 'Dealing with uncertainties in MCDA,' *International Series in Operations Research & Management Science*, 233, pp. 467–496.

2. Durbach, I.N., Stewart, T.J. (2012) 'Modeling uncertainty in multi-criteria decision analysis,' *European Journal of Operational Research*, 223(1), pp. 1–14.

3. Kolmogorov, A.N. (2018) *Foundations of the Theory of Probability*, 2nd ed. Mineola, NY: Dover Publications, Inc.

4. Prade, H., Dubois, D. (1980) *Fuzzy Sets and Systems Theory and Applications*. London, UK: Academic Press.

5. Zadeh, L.A. (1965) 'Fuzzy sets,' *Information and Control*, 8, pp. 338–353.

6. Zimmerman, H.J. (1996) *Fuzzy Set Theory and its Applications*. Boston, MA: Kluwer Academic Publishers.

7. Gau, W.L., Buehrer, D.J. (1993) 'Vague sets,' *IEEE Transactions on Systems, Man, and Cybernetics*, 23, pp. 610–614.

8. Atanassov, K. (1994) 'Operators over interval valued intuitionistic fuzzy sets,' *Fuzzy Sets and Systems*, 64, pp. 159–174.

9. Gorzalzany, M.B. (1987) 'A method of inference in approximate reasoning based on interval-valued fuzzy sets,' *Fuzzy Sets and Systems*, 21, pp. 1–17.

10. Atanassov, K. (1986) 'Intuitionistic fuzzy sets,' *Fuzzy Sets and Systems*, 20, pp. 87–96.

11. Pawlak, Z. (1982) 'Rough sets,' *International Journal Information and Computer Science*, 11, pp. 341–356.

12. Yang, J.B, Wang, Y.M., Xu, D.L., Chin, K.S. (2006) 'The evidential reasoning approach for MADA under both probabilistic and fuzzy uncertainties,' *European Journal of Operational Research*, 171(1), pp. 309–343.

13. Lahdelma, R., Salminen, P. (2001) 'SMAA-2: Stochastic multicriteria acceptability analysis for group decision making,' *Operations Research*, 49(3), pp. 444–454.

14. Kirkwood, C.W. (1997) *Strategic Decision Making*. Belmont, CA: Brooks/Cole.

15. Parnell, G.S., Johnson, E.R., Parnell, G.S., Tani, S.N., Bresnick, T. (2013) *Handbook of Decision Analysis*. New York: John Wiley & Sons, Inc.

16. Greco, S., Ehrgott, M., Figueira, J.R. (eds) (2016) *Multiple Criteria Decision Analysis: State of the Art Surveys*, Vol 233. New York: Springer-Verlag.

17. Kreye, M.E., Goh, Y.M., Newnes, L.B. (2011) 'Manifestation of uncertainty - a classification,' *International Conference on Engineering Design, ICED11*, 15–18 August, Denmark: Technical University of Denmark.

18. Gopal, S. (2009) 'Error (Propagation and Modeling),' *International Encyclopedia of Human Geography*. Edinburgh, UK: Elsevier Ltd., pp. 586–594.

19. Gardenier, G.H., Gui, F., Demas, J.N. (2011) 'Error propagation made easy - or at least easier,' *Journal of Chemical Education*, 88, pp. 916–920.

20. Olaru, C., Wehenkel, L. (2003) 'A complete fuzzy decision tree technique,' *Fuzzy Sets and Systems*, 138, pp. 221–254.

21. King, A.J., Wallace, S.W. (2012) 'Scenario-tree generation: with Michal Kaut,' in *Modeling with Stochastic Programming*. New York: Springer.

22. Savage, S.L. (2012) *The Flaw of Averages*. New York: John Wiley & Sons.

23. Probability Management Inc. (2022) *SIPmath* Modeler Tools. https://www.probabilitymanagement.org/tools.

24. Palisade Software (2022) *@Risk* Software. Ithaca, NY. https://www.palisade.com/risk/.

25. Oracle (2022) *Crystal Ball* Software. Redwood City, CA. https://www.oracle.com/applications/crystalball/.

26. Lumina Decision Systems, Inc. (2022) *Analytica* Software. Campbell, CA. https://lumina.com/support-2/analytica-downloads/.

27. Needham, T. (1993) 'A visual explanation of Jensen's inequality,' *The American Mathematical Monthly*, 100(8), pp. 768–771.

28. Tzeng, G., Shen, K. (2017) *New Concepts and Trends of Hybrid Multiple Criteria Decision Making*. Boca Raton, FL: CRC Press.

29. Mckay, M.D., Beckman, R.J., Conover, W.J. (2000) 'A comparison of three methods for selecting values of input variables in the analysis of output from a computer code,' *Technometrics*, 42(1), pp. 55–61.

30. Knuth, D.E. (1997) *The Art of Computer Programming*, Volume 2: Semi-Numerical Algorithms, 3rd ed. Reading, MA: Addison-Wesley.

31. James, F., Moneta, L. (2020) 'Review of high-quality random number generators,' in *Computing and Software for Big Science*, Vol 4. Springer.

32. Ma, X., Yuan, X., Cao, Z., Qi, B., Zhang, Z. (2016) 'Quantum random number generation,' *npj Quantum Information*, 2, 16021.

33. Miszczak, J.A. (2013) 'Employing online quantum random number generators for generating truly random quantum states in *Mathematica*,' *Computer Physics Communications*, 184(1), pp. 257–258.

34. Kertzner, N. (2006) *Project Management*, 9th ed. Hoboken, NJ: John Wiley & Sons.

35. Law, A. (2014) *Simulation Modeling and Analysis*, 5th ed. New York: McGraw-Hill.

36. Caddell, J., Dabkowski, M., Driscoll, P., Dubois, P. (2020) 'Improving stochastic analysis for tradeoffs in multi-criteria value models,' *Journal of Multi-Criteria Decision Analysis*, 27(5–6), pp. 304–317.

37. Morton, D.P., Romeijnders, W., Schultz, R. (2018) 'The stochastic programming heritage of Maarten van der vlerk,' *Computational Management Science*, 15(3), pp. 319–323.

38. Stellato, B., Van Parys, B.P.G., Goulart, P.J. 'Multivariate Chebyshev inequality with estimated mean and variance,' *The American Statistician*, 71(2), pp. 123–127.

39. Fishburn, P.C. (1964) *Decision and Value Theory*. New York: John Wiley & Sons.

40. Hadar, J., Russell, W.R. (1969) 'Rules for ordering uncertain prospects,' *American Economic Review*, 16, pp. 25–34.

41. Hadar, J., Russell, W.R. (1971) 'Stochastic dominance and diversification,' *Journal of Economic Theory*, 3, pp. 288–305.

42. Hanoch, G., Levy, H. (1969) 'The efficiency analysis of choices involving risk,' *Review of Economic Studies*, 36, pp. 335–346.

43. Whitmore, G.A., Findlay, M.C. (eds) (1978) *Stochastic Dominance*. Lexington, MA: Heath Publishing.

44. Thompson, S.K. (1987) 'Sample size for estimating multinomial proportions,' *The American Statistician*, 41(1), pp. 42–46.

45. Tzeng, G., Huang, J. (2011) *Multiple Attribute Decision Making*. New York: Chapman and Hall.

46. Ishizaka, A., Nemery, P. (2013) *Multi-Criteria Decision Analysis*. Chichester, UK: John Wiley & Sons, Ltd.

Chapter 11

System Reliability

There is no finish line when it comes to system reliability and availability, and our efforts to improve performance never cease.

—Source: Marc Benioff, CEO Salesforce

11.1 MODELING SYSTEM RELIABILITY

Modeling and measuring the effectiveness of a proposed system solution is a necessary component for assessing system performance that is specified in various ways within system requirements and reflected in the value measures used within both deterministic and stochastic tradespace analysis. Soban and Mavris [1] define *system effectiveness* as "a quantification, represented by system level measure, of the intended or expected effect of the system achieved through functional analysis." [1].

For systems of all types including complex systems, the key system level measures appearing most often in functional and value models are reliability, availability, and capability, because all three address aspects of how well a system can perform its purpose [1, 2].

Definition: System *reliability* is probability of a system or system element performing its intended function under stated conditions without failure for a given period of time [3].

Definition: System *availability* is the probability that a repairable system (RS) or system element is operational at a given point in time under a given set of environmental conditions [3].

Definition: System *capability* is the ability of a system to execute a particular mission or course of action to achieve a desired effect under a specified set of conditions.

Capability is a system specific measure that captures the overall performance objectives associated with the system. This measure used to be applied to isolated systems in controlled test

Decision Making in Systems Engineering and Management, Third Edition.
Patrick J. Driscoll, Gregory S. Parnell, and Dale L. Henderson
© 2023 John Wiley & Sons, Inc. Published 2023 by John Wiley & Sons, Inc.

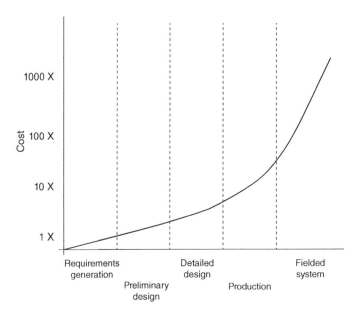

Figure 11.1   Cost of reliability improvement versus time. Source: Dietrich [4].

environments. The demand on systems to perform interconnected complex tasks has led to the concept of *capability sets*, that is, combinations of different systems that each contribute some amount of their functionality towards achieving a desired effect. Capability is used as a design criterion.

Reliability and availability are measures that apply to all types and levels of system analysis. Both of these measures are relevant to system design, development, and operations. Today, more than ever, system reliability is not only expected, but is in demand in the market. The current global economic environment is forcing system designers to find creative ways to make cost-effective, reliable systems that meet or exceed the performance expectations of their consumers and users. To maintain their competitiveness, system designers must design for reliability and make those system level trades early in the designing process. Attempting to improve reliability after the system has been designed is a costly endeavor as illustrated in Figure 11.1.

By definition, reliability is the probability that an item (component, subsystem, or system) or process operates properly for a specified amount of time (design life) under stated use conditions (both environmental and operational conditions) without failure. What constitutes failure for a component, subsystem, system, or process must be clearly defined as the item or process is developed. In addition, proper operating and environmental conditions must be adequately defined so that the designers and operators have a common understanding of how, when, and where the item or process should be used. In simple terms, reliability is nothing more than the probability that the system under study operates properly for a specified period of time.

11.2   MATH MODELS IN RELIABILITY

For it to be useful in systems decision support projects, the definition of reliability has to be precisely constructed. Mathematical models of reliability focus on items that can be in one of the two states: working ($X(t) = 1$) and not working ($X(t) = 0$). These models are often constructed by analyzing test data and using these data in conjunction with applicable rules from probability theory to characterize an item's reliability.

Ironically, the focus of system testing to develop reliability data is on system or component failures over time. The data collected record when specific systems or components fail for the first time. In this way, the data can be used for reliability analysis of both systems that cannot be repaired and systems that can be repaired in response to failures. The pattern of failure events over time constitutes a *failure distribution*, also referred to as a *lifetime distribution*. In mathematical terms, these patterns are described by probability density functions (PDFs) denoted by $f(t)$.

Suppose that N_0 identical items are subjected to testing at time $t = 0$, assuming that each item is functional at the start, that is $X_i(0) = 1$, for all $i = 1, \ldots, N_0$ items. Further suppose that each item has the same failure distribution $f(t)$.

Let $N_s(t)$ be the number of items that have survived to time t. Let $N_f(t)$ be a random variable representing the number of items that have failed by time t, where $N_f(t) = N_0 - N_s(t)$. Thus, the reliability at time t can be expressed as the ratio

$$R(t) = \frac{E[N_s(t)]}{N_0}$$

Recalling that reliability represents the probability that the item is working at time t, let T be a random variable that represents the failure time for an item. Since the PDF $f(t)$ represents how many items fail at specific times (density), its cumulative distribution function (CDF), denoted by $F(t)$, describes the probability that an item i will fail by a specific time T:

$$F_i(t) = P_i(T \leq t).$$

$F(t)$ can also be expressed as

$$F(t) = \frac{E[N_f(t)]}{N_0}$$

The CDF is referred to as the *unreliability* function for an item, so that a reliability function expressing the probability that an item will be operational at time T is

$$R_i(t) = P(T > t) = 1 - P(T \leq t) = 1 - F_i(t)$$

which can also be expressed as

$$R(t) = \frac{E[N_s(t)]}{N_0} = \frac{E[N_0 - N_f(t)]}{N_0} = \frac{N_0 - E[N_f(t)]}{N_0} = 1 - F(t)$$

Figure 11.2 shows an unreliability function $F(t)$ and a reliability function $R(t)$ for an arbitrary system. Given the relationship expressed, it is not surprising that $R(t)$ and $F(t)$ are a mirror image of each other.

Given the CDF of failure $F(t)$, the PDF describing the pattern of failures $f(t)$ is given by

$$f(t) = \frac{d}{dt} F(t)$$

Thus,

$$f(t) = \frac{d}{dt}(1 - R(t)) = -\frac{d}{dt} R(t)$$

The *hazard function* is another important mathematical entity. The hazard function is also called a *hazard rate* function and a *failure rate* function. The information that it represents is a conditional probability estimate that an item will fail in the next time period given that it is operational in the current time period. The hazard rate depends on the size of the time increments being used to track failures. For example, if time was being modeled in time steps of 1, then the hazard rate calculated

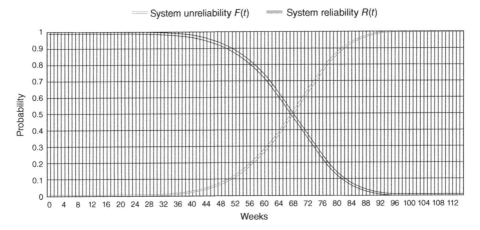

Figure 11.2   The unreliability $F(t)$ and reliability $R(t)$ relationship.

in time period 24 yields the probability that the item will fail in time period 25 given that it is operational in period 24. If time increments were in steps of 5, then a hazard rate calculated in time period 30 would provide the probability that the item will fail in the next time period (30, 35].

Formally, the hazard function is represented mathematically by the following equation:

$$h(t) = \lim_{\Delta t \to 0} \left\{ \frac{1}{\Delta t} \Pr[T \le t + \Delta t | T > t] \right\}$$

$$= \lim_{\Delta t \to 0} \left\{ \frac{1}{\Delta t} \frac{F(t + \Delta t) - F(t)}{R(t)} \right\}$$

$$= \frac{f(t)}{R(t)}$$

The hazard function provides another way of characterizing the failure distribution of an item. Hazard functions are often classified as increasing failure rate (IFR), decreasing failure rate (DFR), or constant failure rate (CFR), depending on the behavior of the hazard function over time. It is easy to accept an assumption that an item has an IFR. Items that have an IFR exhibit "wear-out" behavior so that the older the item, the greater the chance that a failure will occur in the next time period. CFRs are a characteristic of random failures. DFRs would seem to correspond to some physical improvement with age so that the longer an item survives the less the chance of failure in the next period. However, DFRs have also been attributed to an item having a mixture of distributions having a non-IFR [5].

A general relationship between the reliability function $R(t)$ and the hazard function $h(t)$ can be established as follows:

$$h(t) = \frac{1}{R(t)} \left[\frac{-dR(t)}{dt} \right]$$

$$h(t)dt = \frac{-dR(t)}{R(t)}$$

integrating both sides

$$\int_0^t h(u)du = \int_{R(0)}^{R(t)} \left[\frac{-dR(t)}{dt} \right]$$

$$\int_0^t h(u)du = \int_1^{R(t)} \frac{-dR(t)}{dt}$$

$$-\int_0^t h(u)du = \ln(R(t))$$

$$R(t) = \exp\left[-\int_0^t h(u)du \right]$$

and therefore

$$F(t) = 1 - \exp\left[-\int_0^t h(z)dz \right]$$

The most common form of the hazard function is the bathtub curve (see Figure 11.3). The bathtub curve is most often used as a conceptual model of a population of items rather than a mathematical model of a specific item. Early on, during the development of an item, initial items produced will often times be subject to manufacturing defects. Over time, the manufacturing process is improved and these defective units are fewer in number, so the overall hazard function for the remaining population decreases. This portion of the bathtub curve is referred to as the "infant mortality" period. Once the manufacturing system matures, fewer items will fail early in their life-time and items in the field will exhibit a constant hazard function. This period is known as the "useful life" period. During this time, failures are purely random and usually caused by some form of unexpected or random stress placed on the item. At the end of its useful life, items in the field may begin to "wear out" and as a result the hazard function for the population of items remaining in the field will exhibit a rapidly increasing rate of failure.

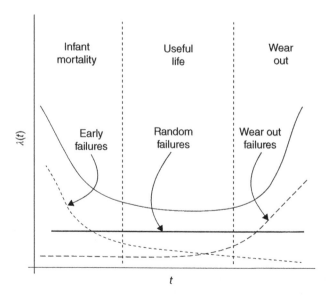

Figure 11.3   General bathtub-shaped hazard function. Source: Adapted from [6].

An example of the bathtub curve applying to a system is an automobile with an internal combustion engine (ICE). ICE vehicles exhibit bathtub curve behavior that is useful to know when crafting maintenance warranties in a way that minimizes corporate costs. If a company can avoid having to pay for high cost repairs and replacements typical of the wearout period, it is in its best interest to do so. If, for example, the wearout period for an automobile was known to start at year 8 of its lifetime, then lower-cost extended warranties could be constructed to cover up to year 6, more expensive ones to year 7, and the highest priced warranties would begin to reach into the known wearout period. For a consumer sensitive to repair costs, a helpful strategy would be to sell or trade-in a vehicle before it enters the wearout stage.

To remain competitive, most product developers attempt to reduce or eliminate the infant mortality period and the associated quality related failures by using a variety of quality control tools and initiatives. For high reliability items, many manufacturers may use environmental stress screening (ESS) or "burn-in" to enhance their quality initiatives and further reduce or eliminate a customer seeing this infant mortality period. ESS subjects the items to a variety of stresses (i.e. temperature, vibration, voltage, humidity, etc.) to cause the "weak" components to fail before they are released to customers. Burn-in is used to filter out the defective items by having each item operate for some predefined period of time, often at an increased temperature. Ideally, to maximize reliability, items need to operate successfully during the useful life period for as long as possible. Many organizations develop maintenance strategies that allow their products to remain in an operational state for a very long time. The goal of scheduled maintenance strategies is to replace items before they enter the wear-out period or fail while being used.

One final measure that is often used to characterize the reliability of an item is its mean time to failure (MTTF). The MTTF is nothing more than the expected value of the failure time of an item. Mathematically, the MTTF is calculated as follows:

$$\text{MTTF} = E[T] = \int_0^\infty tf(t)dt$$

or

$$\text{MTTF} = E[T] = \int_0^\infty R(t)dt$$

The variance for the time to failure T is given by the following relationship:

$$\text{Var}[T] = E[T^2] - E[T]^2 = \int_0^\infty t^2 f(t)dt - \left[\int_0^\infty tf(t)dt\right]^2$$

11.2.1 Common Continuous Reliability Distributions

As was mentioned previously, reliability is a function of time, and time is a continuous variable on a ratio scale. Thus, most items that operate over continuous periods should be modeled using continuous time-to-failure distributions. There are many continuous time-to-failure distributions that can be used to model the reliability of an item. Some of the well-known distributions include those listed in Table 11.1.

Most reliability books (see Refs. [7, 8]) cover in detail many of these distributions. Leemis [9] has done an exceptional job by describing each of the aforementioned distributions and their relationships with each other. An excellent online resource called *Reliawiki* that was created by the ReliaSoft Corporation to support their reliability analysis software provides explanations and examples for all these distributions and more [10]. Despite this large number of possible failure distributions, the two most widely used continuous failure distributions are the exponential and Weibull distributions.

TABLE 11.1   Common Continuous Reliability Distributions.

Continuous Reliability Distributions			
Exponential	Beta	Extreme value	Inverse Gaussian
Weibull	Gamma	Logistic	Makeham
Normal	Rayleigh	Log logistic	Hyperexponential
Lognormal	Uniform	Pareto	Muth

Exponential Failure Distribution. The exponential distribution is probably the most used and often abused failure distribution. It is a single parameter distribution that is easily estimated for a variety of data collection methods. Its mathematical tractability for modeling complex combinations of components, subsystems, and systems make it attractive for modeling large scale systems and system-of-systems. Empirical evidence has shown that systems made up of large numbers of components exhibit exponential behavior at the system level.

The exponential distribution has a CFR or hazard function. It is most useful for modeling the useful life period for an item. The exponential distribution possesses a unique property called the memoryless property. It is this property that often results in this distribution being used in inappropriate situations. The memoryless property states that if an item has survived until a specific time t, the probability that it will survive for the next time period $t + s$ is independent of t and only dependent on s. As a result, this distribution should not be used to model components that have wear-out failure mechanisms characterized by an IFR. The PDF, CDF, reliability function, and hazard function for the exponential distribution are

$$f(t) = \lambda e^{-\lambda t}$$

$$F(t) = 1 - e^{-\lambda t}$$

$$R(t) = e^{-\lambda t}$$

$$h(t) = \lambda$$

Figure 11.4 illustrates the PDF $f(t)$, hazard function $h(t)$, and reliability function $R(t)$ for an exponential distribution with $\lambda = 0.0001$.

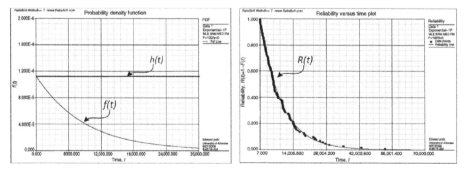

Figure 11.4 Failure distribution($f(t)$, hazard function($h(t)$), and reliability function($R(t)$) for an exponential distribution $\lambda = 0.0001$.

The MTTF for this distribution is

$$\text{MTTF} = E[T] = \int_0^\infty t\lambda e^{-\lambda t} = \frac{1}{\lambda}$$

Once the MTTF is identified, the constant hazard rate (λ) for an exponential failure distribution is known. There are several methods available to estimate the hazard rate for an exponential distribution. Techniques include the method of moments, maximum likelihood, and rank regression.

The *method of moments* estimator is found by equating population moments with sample moments once appropriate random sample data is available. Let $T_1, T_2, \ldots, T_n$ denote a random sample of failure times for n items from the total population of items. The sample mean (average) and sample variance are given by:

$$\overline{T} = \sum_{i=1}^n \frac{T_i}{n-1}$$

$$S^2 = \sum_{i=1}^n \frac{(T_i - \overline{T})^2}{n}$$

Equating the population mean, the true MTTF, to the sample mean and solving for MTTF yields

$$\text{MTTF} = \frac{1}{\lambda} = \overline{T} = \sum_{i=1}^n \frac{T_i}{n}$$

$$\hat{\lambda} = \frac{1}{\overline{T}} = \frac{n}{\sum_{i=1}^n T_i}$$

A second approach and the one that is most often used, especially for medium to large samples, is the method of maximum likelihood. Caution should be exercised for small samples as the maximum likelihood estimation (MLE) has been shown to be biased for small samples. *Maximum likelihood estimators* are found by maximizing the likelihood function. The likelihood function is derived by observing the status of all the items in the sample. This technique accounts for censored data. Censoring occurs when the exact failure time of an item on test is unknown. The most common situation occurs when n items have been put on test for s hours, p items have failed, and the remaining $n - p$ items have not failed, by time s. These $n - p$ items have been censored (i.e. the test has been terminated before they were allowed to fail). The general form of the likelihood function is given as

$$L(T; \lambda) = \prod_{i \in \text{failed}} f(T; \lambda) \prod_{j \in \text{censored}} R(s; \lambda)$$

$$L(T; \lambda) = \prod_{i=1}^p \lambda e^{-\lambda T_i} \prod_{j=1}^{n-p} e^{-\lambda s}$$

For the case where no censoring has occurred (i.e. every item was run to failure in the sample), the likelihood function is calculated by:

$$L(T; \lambda) = \prod_{i=1}^n \lambda e^{-\lambda T_i}$$

It is often easier to maximize the log-likelihood function. This is accomplished by setting the first partial derivatives equal to zero and solving for the parameter:

$$\ln L(T; \lambda) = n \ln \lambda - \lambda \sum_{i=1}^{n} T_i$$

$$\frac{\partial}{\partial \lambda} \ln L(T; \lambda) = \frac{n}{\lambda} - \sum_{i=1}^{n} T_i = 0$$

$$\hat{\lambda} = \frac{n}{\sum_{i=1}^{n} T_i}$$

Radar System MLE Example. The next generation over the horizon radar system is currently under development. As part of the development process, seven systems have been tested for 2016 hours. Two systems failed, one at 1700 hours and the other at 2000 hours. The remaining five systems were still operating at the end of the test period. Given this test data, what is the probability that the system will operate 24 hours a day, seven days a week for 30 days? Assume that the time to failure is adequately modeled by the exponential failure distribution.

To answer this question, first estimate the parameter for the exponential distribution by deriving the likelihood function and then constructing the MLE.

$$L(T; \lambda) = \prod_{i=1}^{2} \lambda e^{-\lambda T_i} \prod_{j=1}^{5} e^{-\lambda s} = \lambda^2 e^{\sum_{i=1}^{2} T_i} e^{-\lambda \sum_{j=1}^{5} s}$$

$$\ln L(T; \lambda) = 2 \ln \lambda - \lambda \sum_{i=1}^{2} T_i - 5\lambda s$$

$$\frac{\partial \ln L(T; \lambda)}{\partial \lambda} = \frac{2}{\lambda} - \left[\sum_{i=1}^{2} T_i + 5s \right]$$

$$= \frac{2}{\lambda} - [1700 + 2000 + 5(2016)] = 0$$

$$\hat{\lambda} = \frac{n}{\sum_{i=1}^{2} T_i + 5s} = \frac{2}{13,780} = 1.4514 \times 10^{-4}$$

Once λ is known, the probability that the system can work continuously for 30 days without failure is calculated by

$$R(t) = e^{-\hat{\lambda} t}$$

$$R(5040) = e^{-(1.4514 \times 10^{-4})5040} = 0.6937$$

Weibull Failure Distribution. The Weibull distribution is commonly used for reliability analysis because of its flexibility in modeling a variety of component failure patterns and other situations. It has also been shown to fit a wide variety of empirical data sets, especially for mechanical systems. The most common form of the Weibull distribution is a two-parameter distribution. The two-parameters are the scale parameter, η, and the shape parameter, β. An interesting fact that helps position a Weibull distribution when using it as an uncertainty distribution, is that the scale parameter η represents its 63rd percentile, the point at which 63% of component failures will have taken place.

When the shape parameter $\beta < 1$, the hazard function $h(t)$ for the distribution exhibits a DFR. When $\beta > 1$, the hazard function for the distribution exhibits an IFR. Finally, when $\beta = 1$, the hazard function is CFR. The PDF ($f(t)$), CDF ($F(t)$), reliability function ($R(t)$), and hazard function ($h(t)$) for the Weibull distribution are given by the following relationships:

$$f(t) = \frac{\beta}{\eta}\left(\frac{t}{\eta}\right)^{\beta-1} e^{-\left(\frac{t}{\eta}\right)^{\beta}}$$

$$F(t) = 1 - e^{-\left(\frac{t}{\eta}\right)^{\beta}}$$

$$R(t) = e^{-\left(\frac{t}{\eta}\right)^{\beta}}$$

$$h(t) = \frac{\beta}{\eta}\left(\frac{t}{\eta}\right)^{\beta-1}$$

Figures 11.5–11.7 illustrate the various shapes of the PDF and hazard function when the shape parameter β is varied. Notice that when $\beta \cong 3$ the PDF takes a shape similar to a normal distribution.

The MTTF for this distribution is

$$\text{MTTF} = E[T] = \int_0^\infty t\frac{\beta}{\eta}\left(\frac{t}{\eta}\right)^{\beta-1} e^{\frac{t^\beta}{\eta}} = \eta\Gamma\left(1 + \frac{1}{\beta}\right)$$

where the Γ function is

$$\Gamma(n) = \int_0^\infty e^{-x} x^{n-1} dx$$

A three-parameter version of the Weibull distribution is sometimes used and has the following PDF, CDF, reliability function, and hazard function:

$$f(t) = \frac{\beta}{\eta}\left(\frac{t-\gamma}{\eta}\right)^{\beta-1} e^{-\left(\frac{t-\gamma}{\eta}\right)^{\beta}}$$

$$F(t) = 1 - e^{-\left(\frac{t-\gamma}{\eta}\right)^{\beta}}$$

$$R(t) = e^{-\left(\frac{t-\gamma}{\eta}\right)^{\beta}}$$

$$h(t) = \frac{\beta}{\eta}\left(\frac{t-\gamma}{\eta}\right)^{\beta-1}$$

where γ is the location parameter for the distribution. The location parameter γ is sometimes called the "guaranteed life" parameter because it implies that if $\gamma > 0$, then there is zero probability of failure prior to γ. This is often a difficult assumption to prove and one of the reasons that the two-parameter model is used more often.

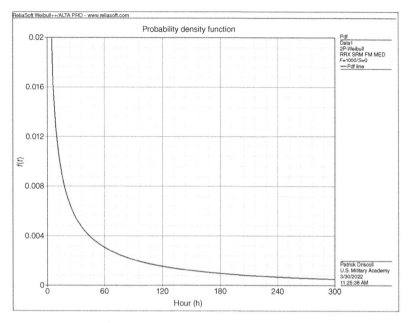

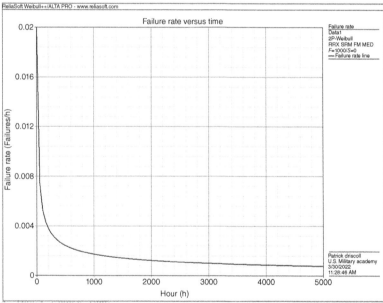

Figure 11.5 Weibull PDF and hazard function, $\beta = 0.5$.

The MTTF for the three-parameter Weibull failure distribution is given by the following relationship:

$$\text{MTTF} = E[T] = \int_0^\infty t \frac{\beta}{\eta} \left(\frac{t - \gamma}{\eta} \right)^{\beta - 1} e^{-\left(\frac{t-\gamma}{\eta} \right)^\beta} = \gamma + \eta \Gamma \left(1 + \frac{1}{\beta} \right)$$

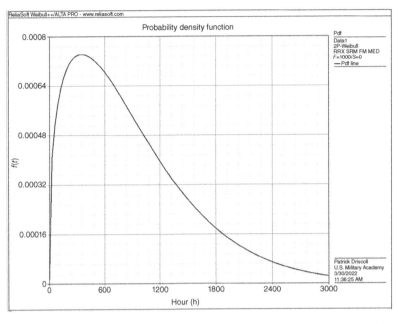

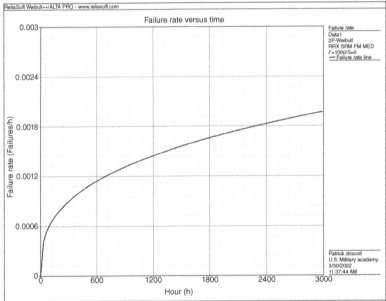

Figure 11.6   Weibull PDF and hazard function, $\beta = 1.32$.

Like the exponential distribution, there are a variety of techniques available for estimating the distribution parameters. The method of moments and maximum likelihood techniques are both reasonable techniques and constructed in the same manner as was demonstrated earlier on the exponential distribution. Kececioglu [11] provides a detailed description of each of these techniques for the Weibull distribution as well as several others.

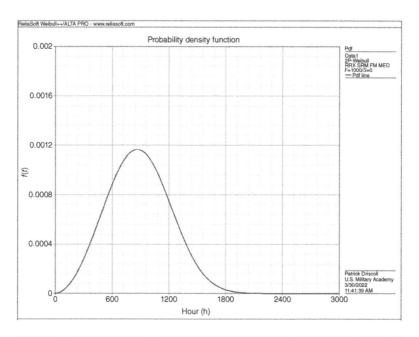

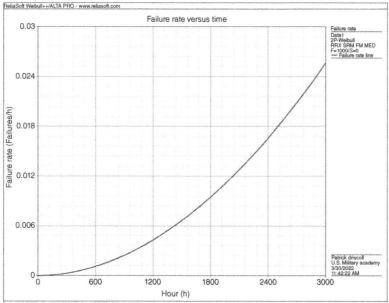

Figure 11.7 Weibull PDF and hazard function, $\beta = 2.95$.

11.2.2 Common Discrete Distributions

Certain components or systems may have performance characteristics that require them to be modeled using a discrete distribution. For example, a switch's performance may be better characterized by the number of cycles (on/off) rather than the amount of time it is operated. Another example is a satellite launch vehicle. It either launches successfully or does not. Time to failure is not an adequate measure to describe the performance of the launch vehicle. Two of the common discrete distributions used for measuring system performance are discussed in what follows, along with the method of moments and MLE approaches for estimating parameters for these distributions.

Binomial Distribution. The binomial distribution is a distribution that characterizes the sum of n independent Bernoulli trials. A Bernoulli trial occurs when an item's performance is a random variable that has one of two outcomes; it either works (success) or fails (failure) when needed. The probability of success, p, is constant for each trial. Mathematically, the PDF for a Bernoulli random variable is

$$f(x) = p^x(1 - p)^{1-x}$$

The mean and variance of the distribution are

$$E[x] = p$$

$$Var\ [x] = p(1 - p)$$

The PDF for the binomial distribution is given by

$$f(x) = \binom{n}{x} p^x(1 - p)^{n-x}$$

where

$$\binom{n}{x} = \frac{n!}{(n - x)!x!}$$

The mean and variance for the binomial distribution are

$$E[x] = np$$

$$Var\ [x] = np(1 - p)$$

Binomial Distribution Example. Suppose that a next generation aircraft is designed with three engines and that for the aircraft to fly, at least one of its engines must operate. If the probability that an engine fails during flight is $(1 - p)$ and each engine is assumed to fail independently, then a binomial distribution can be used to estimates the probability that the aircraft maintains its flight.

Since each engine is assumed to fail independently, then the number of engines remaining operational can be modeled as a binomial random variable. Hence, the probability that the three-engine next-generation aircraft maintains its flight is calculated:

$$= \binom{3}{1} p(1 - p)^2 + \binom{3}{2} p^2(1 - p)^1 + \binom{3}{3} p^3$$

$$= \frac{3!}{2!1!} p(^1 - p)^2 + \frac{3!}{1!2!} p^2(1 - p) + \frac{3!}{0!3!} p^3$$

$$= 3p(1 - p)^2 + 3p^2(1 - p) + p^3$$

Geometric Distribution. The geometric distribution is commonly used to model the number of cycles to failure for items that have a fixed probability of failure, p, associated with each cycle. For the case of component testing, this distribution is used to model the distribution of the number of trials until the first success. The PDF for this distribution is given by

$$f(x) = (1 - p)^{x-1} p$$

The mean and variance for the geometric distribution are given by

$$E[x] = \frac{1}{p}$$

$$\text{Var} = \frac{1 - p}{p^2}$$

Geometric Distribution Example. A manufacturer of a new dipole light switch conducted bench testing on 10 switches, recording the number of on/off cycles until failure for each switch. The results are shown next:

Switch	# Cycles	Switch	# Cycles
1	30,000	6	75,000
2	35,000	7	80,000
3	40,000	8	82,000
4	56,000	9	83,000
5	70,000	10	84,500

The marketing department believes they can improve market share if they are able to advertise this new switch as a high reliability switch. They would like to state that the new switch has a reliability greater than 98% for a five-year period of use, assuming that a consumer would cycle the switch three times a day, 365 days a year during the five-year period. By estimating a value for p, the manufacturer is able to calculate a point estimate for the reliability for the new switch during this period:

$$\hat{p} = \frac{n}{\sum_{i=1}^{10} C_i} = \frac{10}{63,550} = 1.5736\text{E} - 05$$

$$E[C] = \frac{1}{\hat{p}} = 635,500$$

$$P[C > (3 \times 365 \times 5)] = P[C > 5475] = 1 - P[C \le 5475]$$

$$= 1 - \sum_{x=1}^{5475} (1 - p)^{x-1} p$$

$$= 1 - 0.0826 = 0.9174$$

11.2.3 Check on Learning

1. Do any of the four professional societies mentioned in this chapter have programs and resources specifically designed for students? If so, provide a brief summary of the services or products they provide that you might find valuable now.

2. Answer the following questions regarding a concept map.

    (a) How would you define a concept map? Is there a standard positioning of nouns and verbs on a concept map?

    (b) Is a concept map different from Checkland's LUMAS model? Explain. Draw the LUMAS model that is associated with its definition.

    (c) Where on the spectrum of Figure would you position a concept map as a model? Why?

11.3 RELIABILITY BLOCK DIAGRAMS

Most systems are composed of many subsystems, each of which can be composed of hundreds or thousands of components. In general, reliability analysis is performed at the lowest levels and the results then aggregated into a system level estimate. This is done to save time and money during the development process. System level testing cannot be accomplished until the entire system is designed and assembled. Waiting to test components and subsystems until the entire system is assembled is not time or cost-effective. Consequently, as component and subsystem testing is accomplished, their data can be used to estimate the system level reliability. These reliability estimates are then updated as development continues and more accurate performance and failure data become available.

A *reliability block diagram* (RBD) is a block diagram used to describe the interrelations between system elements in a manner that defines the system. These are the backbone of reliability analysis for systems, especially during the early stages of development when failure estimates drive engineering choices, scheduling forecasts, integration plans, scheduled system maintenance plans, and a host of others. Usually, a system's functional and physical decompositions are used to help construct a system level RBD. This system RBD represents a functional or physical configuration for the system, As this configuration changes, as components and subsystems are replaced, and as newer technologies are integrated into the developing system of interest at various levels, the system reliability will change in response.

There are a number of possible configuration types that RBDs can represent [10]. The discussion in what follows focuses on the five most common component level RBD configurations and their characteristics:

- Series configuration
- Parallel configuration
- Combined series and parallel configuration
- k-out-of-n configuration
- Complex configuration

Each of these RBD configurations have mathematical rules that guide how individual component reliability functions $R_i(t)$ can be combined to form subsystem reliability functions $R_{ss}(t)$ and system reliability functions $R_s(t)$. Once the appropriate higher level reliability expression is created, the tools for conducting reliability analysis at all system levels become available.

Spreadsheets can be used to perform system reliability analysis in a straightforward manner for non-repairable systems. Doing so first requires that n random samples from each component failure distribution $(f_i(t))$ be created using Monte Carlo simulation. These n data represent random failure times for the component that match the failure distribution pattern. Typically, $n = 1000$ to $n = 10,000$ samples are sufficient. When binned into time segments over the lifetime of a component, these data can then be used to create histograms approximating the component's failure distribution ($f_i(t)$), unreliability function ($F_i(t)$), reliability function ($R_i(t)$), and hazard function ($h_i(t)$). Once this information block is completed for each component, system and subsystem level approximations can be created by using the closed-form mathematical reliability rules for the various configuration types to link individual component reliability functions together to form system and subsystem reliability functions.

Figure 11.8 shows an example of a component reliability information block in Excel. The component being modeled has a Weibull failure distribution with shape and scale parameters $\beta = 3.2$ and $\eta = 18.5$, respectively. *SIPmath* was used to generate the necessary $n = 1000$ random samples.

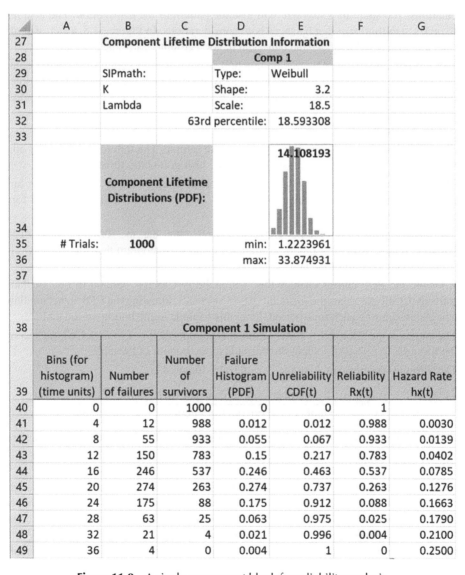

Figure 11.8 A single component block for reliability analysis.

Cell `E34` was selected to `Generate Input` to create the random samples that are automatically written to an underlying XML file. By designating this cell as `Output` and assigning a name, the data samples are automatically written to a labeled column on a separate worksheet in the back of the workbook. *SIPmath* automatically shows a sparkline histogram for this distribution in the cell.

The key to understanding and interpreting this approach is to think of the data as representing n components being simultaneously turned on and tested. The failure time data is then recorded when individual components fail. The information block is created in the following way:

1. By calculating the minimum and maximum values for the sample data, a bin size is chosen that leaves a bit of buffer at the upper bound to allow for changes in the component's failure distribution parameters. There is a bit of judgment required. Choosing too large of step size will result in lower level resolution for any plotted charts and less precise estimates for calculations. Too small of a step size will lose the pattern of the distribution. The goal here is to pick a step (bin) size that balances both considerations. In Figure 11.8, a step size of four time units was used to create the entries in the first column.

2. The Excel `=FREQUENCY()` vector function is next used to create the failure count histogram in the "Number of failures" column. To do so, select the cells next to the time step bins: `B40:B50`. Begin typing the formula: `=FREQUENCY(data array, bins array)` while the cells are still selected. For the required entry `data array`, select the sample data, and for `bins array` select the time step bins. Hit `CTRL-Shift-Enter` to tell Excel this is a vector function that should process the entire sample. The failure count density appears with a shape somewhat like that of the sparkline histogram only turned sideways.

3. The "Number of Survivors" starts at n and decreases each period by the number of failures that occur in that period. The expression in cell `C41` is `=C40 - B41`. Drag this formula to the bottom of the table.

4. The "Failure Histogram (PDF)" starts at 0. Cell `D41` has the formula: `=B41/1000`. Dividing by the number of random samples n creates a histogram that sums to 1. Drag this formula to the bottom of the table.

5. Knowing the PDF entries enables the "Unreliability CDF(t)" column to be calculated. It starts at 0. Cell `E41` has the formula: `=E40 + D41`, allowing the CDF to accumulate the new failures during each time period. Drag this formula to the bottom of the table.

6. The entries in the "Reliability Rx(t)" column are simply $R(t) = 1 = F(t)$. Cell `F40` contains the formula: `=1 - E40`. Drag this formula to the bottom of the table.

7. The formula for approximating the hazard (rate) function is

$$h(t) \approx \frac{\text{number of failures in period } t}{\text{number of survivors from period } t - 1} \cdot \frac{1}{\text{time step}}$$

There is no entry for the first cell because there are no failures at the start. The formula entered in cell `G41` is: `= (B41/C40)(1/4)`.

Creating a system (or subsystem) level reliability information block and generating reliability estimates is discussed using an example of a small series configuration. This spreadsheet approach works well for small (under 10 blocks) to medium sized (10–30) RBDs. Although it could be used on larger ones, at some point the layout and data samples begin to get unwieldy. When this happens, or when complex configurations are involved that complicate deriving system reliability

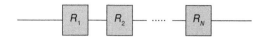

Figure 11.9 Series system.

functions, specialty software applications such as ReliaSoft's *BlockSIM* [12] are better employed to accomplish this task.

11.3.1 Series System

A set of N functionally independent components, each with individual measures of reliability $R_i(t)$ $R_1, R_2, \ldots, R_N$ for some specified period of performance in a specified environment constitutes a series system if the success of the system depends on all of the components operating simultaneously. If a single component fails, then the system fails. The RBD for this situation is shown in Figure 11.9.

The general form of a series system reliability function, which estimates the probability of system success at any time t, is given by

$$R_s(t) = R_1(t) \cdot R_2(t) \cdot \cdots \cdot R_n(t) = \prod_{i=1}^{N} R_i(t)$$

It should be noted that the system reliability for components in series is always smaller than the worst component. Thus, the worst component in a series system provides a loose upper bound on the system reliability. For example, suppose that four identical components form a series system. If the desired system reliability is supposed to be greater than 0.90 for a specified period, then the minimum reliability for each of the components would be calculated as:

$$R_s = R_1 \cdot R_2 \cdot R_3 \cdot R_4 = R^4 \geq 0.90$$

$$R \geq (0.90)^{1/4} \geq 0.974$$

Building a System Level Info Block – Series Example. Consider the four component series configuration shown in Figure 11.10 along with their individual data. Each has an

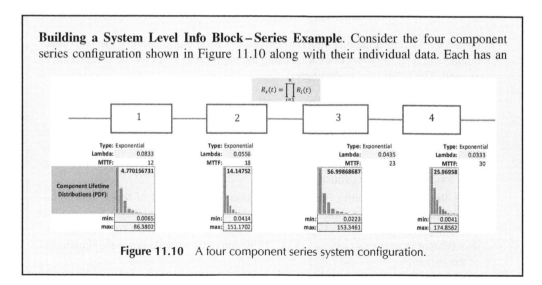

Figure 11.10 A four component series system configuration.

exponential failure distribution $f(t)$. The system reliability function in this case can be found easily using the laws of exponents:

$$R_s(t) = R_1(t)R_2(t)R_3(t)R_4(t)$$
$$= e^{-\lambda_1 t}e^{-\lambda_2 t}e^{-\lambda_3 t}e^{-\lambda_4 t}$$
$$= e^{-(\lambda_1+\lambda_2+\lambda_3+\lambda_4)t}$$
$$= e^{-0.2157t}$$

Its simplicity makes it a good example for illustrating how to create a spreadsheet system model added functionality for reliability analysis. As in the previous example, this relies on generating n random samples from each component failure (lifetime) distribution $f_i(t)$. The steps described apply to all configurations. The system level reliability function $R_s(t)$ is all that changes. The layout used for this spreadsheet full system reliability model is shown in Figure 11.11.

It is important to note that while each of the component information blocks are constructed on simulation data samples, no such data exist for the system. The key to assembling the system reliability information block is to use the system reliability expression that applies to the RBD to jump from component or subsystem level to system level. Here that expression is: $R_s(t) = R_1(t)R_2(t)R_3(t)R_4(t)$.

SETUP: To start, decide on the number of random samples to be used. Again, $n = 1000$ is commonplace; more if desired. Build individual component reliability information blocks as shown in Figure 11.8, all having the same number of bins and the same time step size. Calculate the minimum and maximum failure times for each individual component. Choose an appropriate bin size and time steps as described earlier. Create a blank reliability information block next to the last component block to hold all the system level information using the same bin size and time steps. Exactly where this block is positioned on a worksheet is a personal modeling choice. However, experience has shown that it is easier to construct the needed system level expressions if all the rows are lined up according to time step.

For the system level reliability information block:

1. Create the system reliability function expression $R_s(t)$ that combines the individual component reliability functions $R_i(t)$ using the appropriate rules for the configuration at-hand. The series rule applies here:

$$R_s(t) = R_1(t)R_2(t)R_3(t)R_4(t)$$

This expression acts as a bridge to go from component level, which relied on random sample data to create the various functions, to system level which has no random sample data to work with. The idea is to reverse engineer the information needed starting with a systems reliability function.

2. Enter the system reliability function expression in the top cell of the system reliability function column by linking to each of the component reliability function cells. For example, for the model in Figure 11.11 the starting cell is in cell `AI24`, the expression entered is: `=F24*M24*T24*AA24`. Drag copy this formula down the remainder of the column.

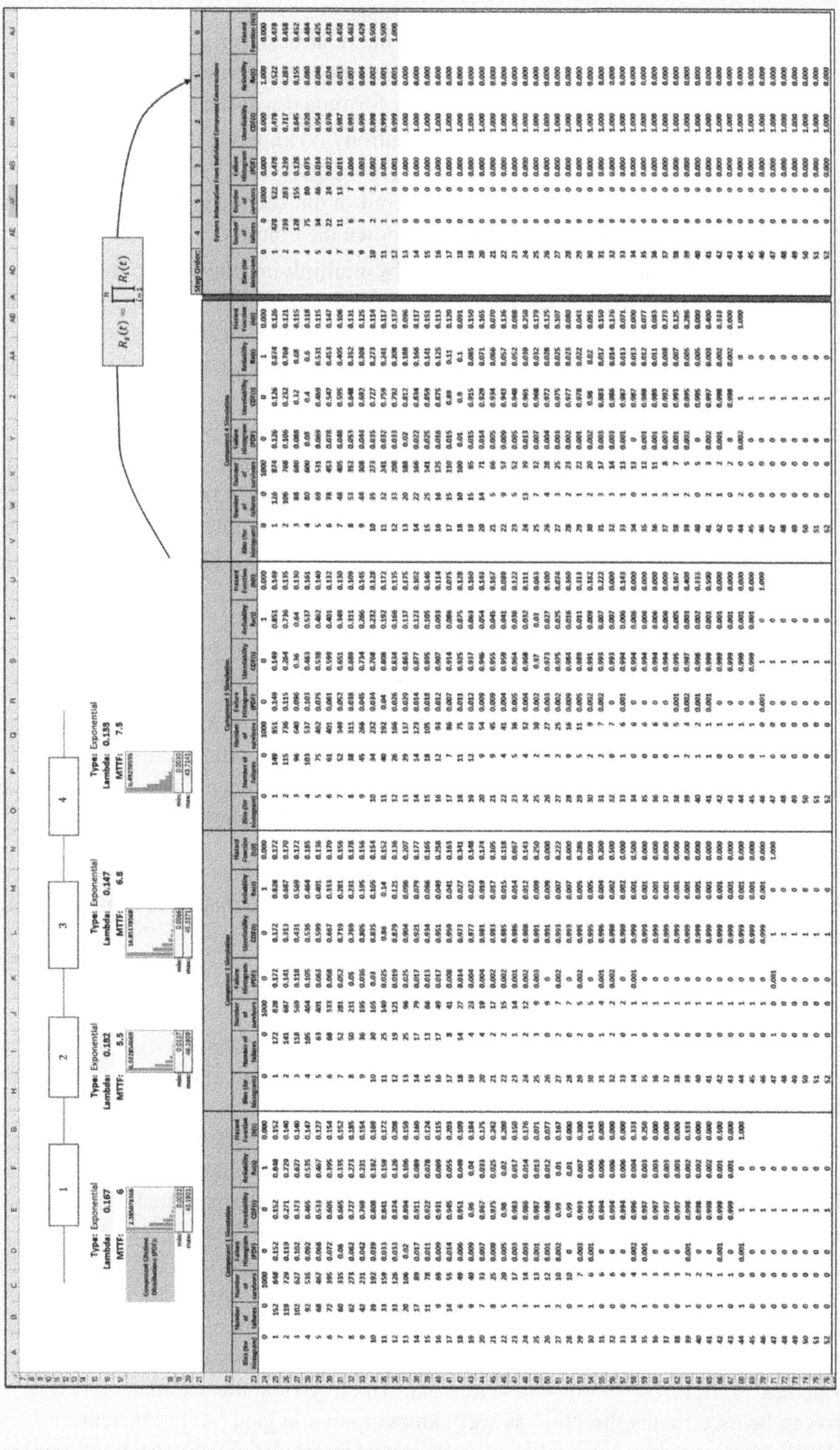

Figure 11.11 Complete spreadsheet reliability model for series configuration.

3. Create the unreliability column data using the relationship $F_s(t) = 1 - R_s(t)$ and starting with the top cell equal to zero. For this example, the formula entered in the second cell down is `= 1 - AI25`. Drag copy the formula down the column.

4. Next, create the system level failure distribution $f_s(t)$ knowing that the CDF rolls up the failure distribution from start to finish ($F_s(t) = F_s(t-1) + f_s(t)$) starting at zero, then $f_s(t) = F_s(t) - F_s(t-1)$. The formula entered in the second cell down this column is `= AH25- AH24`. Drag copy the formula down the column.

5. Create the "Number of failures" entries by multiplying the failure distribution $f_s(t)$ entries by the number of random samples used: $failures_s(t) = n \cdot f_s(t)$ and rounding the result. The formula entered in cell AE24 is `=ROUND(AG24 * 1000, 0)`. Drag copy the formula down the column. Rounding is necessary because of needing integer system failures.

6. Create the "Number of survivors" column entries starting at the number of random samples n. Then, in the second cell, subtract the "Number of failures" occurring in period t from the number of survivors coming into period t from period ($t-1$). Here, the formula entered is `=AF24-AE25`. Drag copy the formula down the column.

7. Create the hazard rate function column entries starting a 0. Then the hazard rate function can be approximated by the expression:

$$h_s(t) = \frac{\text{failures}(t)}{\text{survivors}(t-1)} \cdot \frac{1}{\text{time step}}$$

The formula entered in the second cell of this column is `=(AE25/AF24)` because the time step is equal to 1. Drag copy the formula down the column. At some point, Excel will report the error `#DIV/0!` because the approximation is dividing by zero when no survivors exist. It does not affect the results and can be ignored.

At this point, the system level model is complete and questions regarding reliability can be answered. The system level MTTF is estimated in the same manner a sample average is calculated when a histogram is involved:

$$\text{MTTF} \approx prob(\text{failures}(t)) * \text{number of failures}(t)$$

This is accomplished using the Excel function `=SUMPRODUCT(bins, PDF)`. For the series system in Figure 11.11, the system MTTF is calculated using the formula `=SUMPRODUCT(AD24:AD76,AE24:AE76)`.

Plotting each of the major system level functions: $f_s(t)$, $F_s(t)$, $R_s(t)$, and $h_s(t)$ enables easy approximations for various questions of interest. If intermediate estimates are needed that are between time steps, they can be visually approximated from the curves in Figure 11.12.

Or, the Excel macro `=ValuePL4` (see Section 6.3.1) can be used to perform a linear interpolation between the entries shown in any chart. For example, if the reliability for the series system at time $t = 8.5$ was of interest, the value 8.5 is entered into any cell outside of the model, say `U10`, and the estimate is obtained using the formula `=VALUEPL4(U10,AD24:AD36,AI24:AI36)`, which yields the estimate 0.00529. This macro can be used in any direction as well, knowing that in general it represents:

VALUEPL4(target value, enter table column, report interpolated value from column).

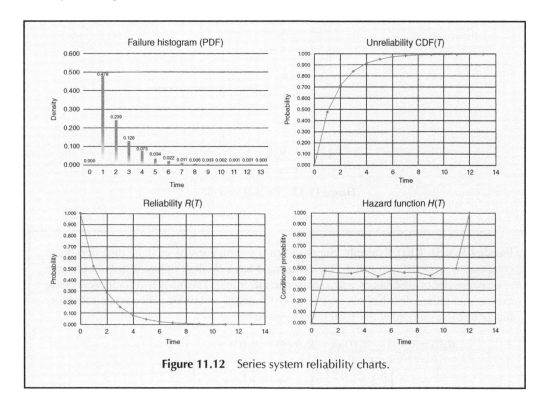

Figure 11.12 Series system reliability charts.

The spreadsheet modeling approach can accommodate changes in the system or subsystem configurations, adding or removing components, changing the reliability characteristics of individual components due to replacement or improvement, and so on. Again, the RBD size eventually becomes a limiting factor for this approach mostly for convenience sake (Figure 11.12).

11.3.2 Parallel System

Assume that a system consists of N functionally independent components, each with individual measures of reliability $R_1, R_2, \ldots, R_N$ for some specified period of performance in a specified environment. The set of components constitute a parallel system if the success of the system depends on one or more of the components operating successfully. If a single component survives, then the system succeeds. The general RBD for this situation is shown in Figure 11.13.

The reliability for a parallel system can be expressed as the probability that at least one component in the system survives. Mathematically, this can be expressed as one minus the probability that all of the components fail. The system reliability for a parallel set of components is given by

$$R_s(t) = 1 - [(1 - R_1(t))(1 - R_2(t)) \ldots (1 - R_N(t))]$$

It should be noted that the system reliability for a parallel system is always larger than the reliability of the best component. Thus, the reliability of the best component in a parallel system provides a loose lower bound on the system reliability (Figure 11.13).

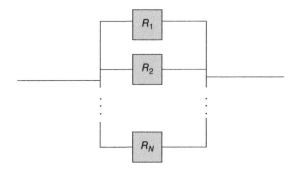

Figure 11.13 Parallel system.

Parallel System RBD Example. Suppose that a system consists of three time dependent components arranged in parallel. One component has a Weibull failure distribution with a scale parameter of 1000 hours, and a shape parameter of 2. The other two components have exponential failure distributions with $\lambda_1 = 0.005$ and $\lambda_2 = 0.0001$. The system reliability function $R_s(t)$ evaluated at $t = 1000$ hours is given by:

$$R_s(t) = 1 - (1 - R_1(t))(1 - R_2(t))(1 - R_3(t))$$

$$= 1 - \left[\left(1 - e^{-\left(\frac{t}{\eta}\right)^{\beta}}\right)(1 - e^{-\lambda_1 t})(1 - e^{-\lambda_2 t})\right]$$

$$= 1 - \left[\left(1 - e^{-\left(\frac{1000}{1000}\right)^2}\right)(1 - e^{-0.005(1000)})(1 - e^{-0.0001(1000)})\right]$$

$$= 0.94025$$

To reinforce a point made earlier, if the four component series system illustrated in the previous example was changed to a parallel configuration, the only cell in the entire model shown in Figure 11.11 that would need to be changed is the first reliability expression entered at the top of the "Reliability" function column. Instead of a series expression, the formula entered would be that for a parallel configuration: `= 1- (1-F24)*(1-M24)*(1-T24)*(1-AA24)`, and it would be drag copied to the bottom of the column. All other changes would propagate automatically to the other system level entries and any charts used.

11.3.3 Combined Series and Parallel RBD

A system typically has a combination of series and parallel component arrangements when redundancy is needed somewhere in the design or multiple components with the same performance and reliability characteristics are needed, such as multiple capacitors used in LED television sets. These clusters of parallel or series arrangements often represent subsystems. To obtain a system $R_s(t)$ or subsystem $R_{ss}(t)$ reliability function, the strategy is to iteratively collapse all parallel arrangements into subsystem expressions until all that remains is arranged in series, then multiply these together to identify the desired reliability function.

Combination Series and Parallel System $R_s(t)$. Consider the series-parallel system configuration shown in Figure 11.14. Creating the system reliability function $R_s(t)$ can be done by collapsing parallel arrangements into subsystem expressions until a series arrangement is all that remains. Then, $R_s(t)$ is obtained by multiplying these together. The expression needed to create system level links is obtained by substituting the individual component reliability functions for the subsystem terms.

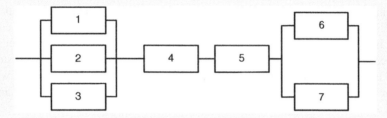

Figure 11.14   Series–parallel system.

Starting with components 1, 2, and 3 and denoting this block as subsystem 1, and then components 6 and 7 as subsystem 2:

$$R_{ss1}(t) = 1 - (1 - R_1(t))(1 - R_2(t))(1 - R_3(t))$$

$$R_{ss2}(t) = 1 - (1 - R_6(t))(1 - R_6(t))$$

The remaining arrangement involving these single subsystem blocks and components 4 and 5 is pure series, so:

$$R_s(t) = R_{ss1}(t)R_4(t)R_5(t)R_{ss2}(t)$$

$$= (1 - (1 - R_1(t))(1 - R_2(t))(1 - R_3(t)))R_4(t)$$

$$R_5(t)(1 - (1 - R_6(t))(1 - R_6(t)))$$

11.3.4   *K*-out-of-*N* Systems

K-out-of-N systems provide a very general modeling structure. It includes both series systems and parallel systems as special cases. In this structure, we assume that a system consists of N functionally independent components each with identical measures of reliability, for some specified period of performance in a specified environment. The set of components constitute a K-out-of-N structure if the success of the system depends on having K or more of the components operating successfully. If less than K components are operating, then the system has failed. The reliability for a K-out-of-N system can be expressed as the probability that at least K components in the system survive. Mathematically, this can be modeled as an application of the binomial distribution. The system reliability for a K-out-of-N system is given by

$$R_s = \sum_{i=k}^{N} \binom{N}{j} R^j (1 - R)^{N-j}$$

An N-out-of-N system is equivalent to a series system and a 1-out-of-N system is equivalent to a parallel system.

11.3.5 Complex Systems

Most systems are complex combinations of series and parallel system structures of components and subsystems. Consider the bridge network of functionally independent components with individual reliability functions $R_1(t)$, $R_2(t)$, $R_3(t)$, $R_4(t)$, $R_5(t)$ shown in Figure 11.15. The components are arranged in what is commonly called a *bridge network*. The system reliability for this structure can be constructed by the method of system decomposition. Decomposing the system around component 3 and using conditional probability produces the following expression in which C_3 is the event that component 3 is working, $\overline{C_3}$ is the event that component 3 has failed, and S is the event that the system is working:

$$R_s = P(S|C_3)P(C_3) + P(S|\overline{C_3})P(\overline{C_3})$$

If component 3 is working, then the system structure reduces to the series arrangement of parallel systems as shown in Figure 11.16.

The reliability for the system is given by the following:

$$R_s(t)|C_3 = \{1 - [(1 - R_1(t))(1 - R_2(t))]\} \cdot \{1 - [(1 - R_4(t))(1 - R_5(t))]\}$$

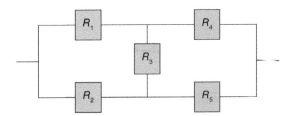

Figure 11.15 Bridge network.

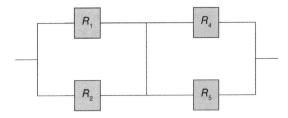

Figure 11.16 System structure when C_3 is working.

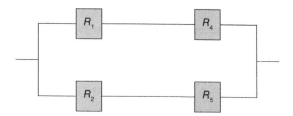

Figure 11.17 System structure when C_3 has failed.

If component 3 fails, then the system structure reduces to a parallel arrangement of series components as shown in Figure 11.17. The reliability for this system is given by the following:

$$R_s(t)|\overline{C}_3 = 1 - [(1 - R_1(t)R_4(t))(1 - R_2(t)R_5(t))]$$

Thus, the unconditional system reliability is given by the following relationship:

$$R_s(t) = 1 - [(1 - R_1(t))(1 - R_2(t))]\} \cdot \{1 - [(1 - R_4(t))(1 - R_5(t))]\}$$

$$+ R_3(t) + (1 - [(1 - R_1(t)R_4(t))(1 - R_2(t)R_5(t))])(1 - R_3(t))$$

Bridge Network $R_s(t)$ Example. Suppose all five components in the bridge structure are identical. Assume that the components have a Weibull distribution with a scale parameter of 10,000 hours and a shape parameter of 3. What is the 5000 hour reliability for the bridge system?

The first step is to calculate the component reliability for a 5000 hour period:

$$R_1(5000) = e^{-\left(\frac{5000}{10,000}\right)^3} = 0.8825$$

Substituting this probability into the system reliability equation yields:

$$R_s(5000) = \{1 - [(1 - 0.8825)(1 - 0.8825)]\} \cdot \{1 - [(1 - 0.8825)(1 - 0.8825)]\}(0.8825)$$

$$+ (1 - [(1 - (0.8825)(0.8825))(1 - (0.8825)(0.8825))])(1 - 0.8825) = 0.970$$

11.4 COMPONENT RELIABILITY IMPORTANCE MEASURES

Once a system design configuration achieves the desired level of reliability, keeping the system operational long enough to match or exceed that level becomes a concern. Maintenance activities such as code refreshes, updates, and security patches need to be anticipated and planned for rather than ignored and reacted to. The same is true for hardware systems. Component upgrades, swap-outs, improvements, and technology refresh actions make adjustments to systems that continue their ability to meet their design purpose in the face of an evolving environment and aging components.

Unless a complete system retire and replacement is called for, these tasks are planned for at the component and subsystem levels, requiring in some way that the element(s) most likely to be driving system failure the earliest be identified. This element (component) should be improved first as resources become available, and should be prioritized appropriately in any scheduled maintenance activities [13].

As was the case for configuration reliability analysis, RBDs again serve as the foundation upon which to accomplish this. Leveraging the appropriate system reliability function, and assuming component functional independence, a Birnbaum importance measure is used for this purpose [14]. This measure was recently extended to address the case for systems with dependent components as well [15].

The Birnbaum importance measure $I_i(t)$ is a time-dependent numerical value calculated by taking a first partial derivative of the system reliability function $R_s(t)$ with respect to each of the N component reliability functions $R_i(t)$ for $i = 1, 2, \ldots, N$ in the configuration.

$$I_i(t) = \frac{\partial R_s(t)}{\partial R_i(t)} \qquad \forall \quad i = 1, 2, \ldots, N$$

This suggests that the most important component R_{i*} is the component that has the largest importance measure. Thus,

$$\frac{R_s(t)}{R_{i*}} = \max \frac{R_s(t)}{R_i(t)}$$

$$R_{i*} = \min R_i(t)$$

To improve the reliability of a series system, the design of the least reliable component should be improved. The component with the highest Birnbaum measure is the most important component as it is the one that, according to its reliability characteristics will be the first to cause system failure. It is important to note that this measure is a function of time, which means that depending on the component reliability characteristics and the system configuration the most important component could and most likely will change as time proceeds.

11.4.1 Importance Measure for Series System

Maintaining the same assumptions as earlier, calculating individual component importance measures for a series configuration is straightforward: calculate the importance index expression for each component and either substitute specific values for times of concern t, or plot these expressions over the anticipated lifetime of the system.

For a system consisting of N functionally independent components, each with individual reliability functions $R_1(t), R_2(t), \ldots, R_N(t)$ for some specified period of performance in a specified environment, and arranged as a pure series system as shown in Figure 11.9, the component importance measure for component i is given by

$$I_i(t) = \frac{\partial R_s(t)}{\partial R_i(t)} = \frac{\partial}{\partial R_i(t)}[R_1(t)R_2(t) \ldots R_i(t) \ldots R_N(t)] = \prod_{\substack{j = 1 \\ j \neq i}}^{N} R_j(t) = \frac{R_s(t)}{R_i(t)}$$

Notice that component i's importance measure is a function of the reliability of all the other components but itself; a partial derivative treats all terms not involving $R_i(t)$ as constants. The most important component $R_{i*}(t)$ is the component that has the largest importance measure. And, since

$$\frac{R_s(t)}{R_{i*}(t)} = \max \frac{R_s(t)}{R_i(t)}$$

$$R_{i*}(t) = \min R_i(t)$$

the most important component for a series system at any time t is the one with the lowest reliability at that time.

Importance Measure—Series Configuration As an example, in a three component series configuration, the importance measure expressions would be:

$$I_1(t) = \frac{\partial R_s(t)}{\partial R_1(t)}$$

$$= \frac{\partial}{\partial R_1(t)}[R_1(t)R_2(t)R_3(t)]$$

$$= R_2(t)R_3(t)$$

$$I_2(t) = \frac{\partial R_s(t)}{\partial R_2(t)}$$

$$= \frac{\partial}{\partial R_2(t)}[R_1(t)R_2(t)R_3(t)]$$

$$= R_1(t)R_3(t)$$

$$I_3(t) = \frac{\partial R_s(t)}{\partial R_3(t)}$$

$$= \frac{\partial}{\partial R_3(t)}[R_1(t)R_2(t)R_3(t)]$$

$$= R_1(t)R_2(t)$$

which yields the same result as the calculation:

$$I_1(t) = \frac{R_s(t)}{R_1(t)}$$

$$I_2(t) = \frac{R_s(t)}{R_2(t)}$$

$$I_3(t) = \frac{R_s(t)}{R_3(t)}$$

In these product expressions, it is clear that for any time t, any product involving a low reliability component will result in an importance measure less than those not involving this component. The highest importance measure will result from a product involving the

---

highest reliability components. Suppose at time $t = 15$ weeks, $R_1(15) = 0.25$, $R_2(15) = 0.1$, and $R_3(15) = 0.4$. Then,

$$I_1(15) = R_2(15)R_3(15) = (0.1)(0.4) = 0.04 = \frac{R_s(t)}{R_1(t)} = \frac{0.01}{0.25}$$

$$I_2(15) = R_1(15)R_3(15) = (0.25)(0.4) = 0.1 = \frac{R_s(t)}{R_2(t)} = \frac{0.01}{0.1}$$

$$I_3(15) = R_1(15)R_2(15) = (0.25)(0.1) = 0.025 = \frac{R_s(t)}{R_3(t)} = \frac{0.01}{0.4}$$

The example confirms what is known about a pure series system: similar to a chain, its survival depends on the weakest link. In this case, the component with the worse reliability, component 2.

11.4.2 Importance Measure for Parallel System

Consider a system consisting of N functionally independent components, each with individual measures of reliability $R_1(t), R_2(t), \ldots, R_N(t)$ for some specified period of performance in a specified environment, and these components are functionally arranged as a parallel system configuration as shown in Figure 11.13. The Birnbaum component importance measure for component i is

$$I_i(t) = \frac{\partial R_s(t)}{\partial R_i(t)} = \frac{\partial}{\partial_i(t)} \left[1 - \prod_{i-1}^{N}[1 - R_i(t)] \right] = \prod_{\substack{j=1 \\ j \neq i}}^{N} (1 - R_j(t)) = \frac{1 - R_s(t)}{1 - R_i(t)}$$

Again, the most important component, R_{i*}, is the component that has the largest importance measure:

$$\frac{(1 - R_s(t))}{(1 - R_{i*})} = \max \left(\frac{1 - R_s(t)}{1 - R_i(t)} \right)$$

$$R_{i*} = \max R_i(t)$$

This tells us that for a pure parallel system (or subsystem) configuration we should improve the design of the most reliable component because the system will keep functioning until the last parallel component fails.

Importance Measure—Parallel Configuration As an example, in a three component parallel configuration, the importance measure expressions would be:

$$I_1(t) = \frac{\partial R_s(t)}{\partial R_1(t)}$$

$$= \frac{\partial}{\partial R_1(t)}[1 - (1 - R_1(t))(1 - R_2(t))(1 - R_3(t))]$$

$$= 1 - R_2(t) - R_3(t) + R_2(t)R_3(t)$$

$$I_2(t) = \frac{\partial R_s(t)}{\partial R_2(t)}$$

$$= \frac{\partial}{\partial R_2(t)}[1 - (1 - R_1(t))(1 - R_2(t))(1 - R_3(t))]$$

$$= 1 - R_1(t) - R_3(t) + R_1(t)R_3(t)$$

$$I_3(t) = \frac{\partial R_s(t)}{\partial R_3(t)}$$

$$= \frac{\partial}{\partial R_3(t)}[1 - (1 - R_1(t))(1 - R_2(t))(1 - R_3(t))]$$

$$= 1 - R_1(t) - R_2(t) + R_1(t)R_2(t)$$

which yields the same result as the calculation:

$$I_1(t) = \frac{1 - R_s(t)}{1 - R_1(t)}$$

$$I_2(t) = \frac{1 - R_s(t)}{1 - R_2(t)}$$

$$I_3(t) = \frac{1 - R_s(t)}{1 - R_3(t)}$$

Using the same component reliability estimates at time $t = 15$ weeks, $R_1(15) = 0.25$, $R_2(15) = 0.1$, and $R_3(15) = 0.4$, the components' importance measures in this pure parallel configuration would be:

$$I_1(15) = 1 - R_2(15) - R_3(15) + R_2(15)R_3(15) = 1 - (0.1) - (0.4) + (0.1)(0.4)$$

$$= 0.54 = \frac{1 - R_s(15)}{1 - R_1(15)}$$

$$I_2(15) = 1 - R_1(15) - R_3(15) + R_1(15)R_3(15) = 1 - (0.25) - (0.4) + (0.25)(0.4)$$

$$= 0.45 = \frac{R_s(15)}{R_2(15)}$$

$$I_3(15) = 1 - R_1(t) - R_2(t) + R_1(t)R_2(t) = 1 - (0.25) - (0.1) + (0.25)(0.1)$$

$$= 0.675 = \frac{R_s(t)}{R_3(t)}$$

The example confirms that to improve a system in parallel configuration, the component with the best reliability should be improved; the system's survival depends on the last component functioning. Here, that is component 3.

11.4.3   Check on Learning

1. Do any of the four professional societies mentioned in this chapter have programs and resources specifically designed for students? If so, provide a brief summary of the services or products they provide that you might find valuable now.

2. Answer the following questions regarding a concept map.
   (a) How would you define a concept map? Is there a standard positioning of nouns and verbs on a concept map?
   (b) Is a concept map different from Checkland's LUMAS model? Explain. Draw the LUMAS model that is associated with its definition.
   (c) Where on the spectrum of Figure would you position a concept map as a model? Why?

11.5   ALLOCATING AND IMPROVING RELIABILITY

Birnbaum's importance measure can be used to identify which component should be improved to maximize system reliability. Unfortunately, system designers generally do not operate in an unconstrained environment. Often, depending on the system, there are costs associated with improving a component's reliability. Costs can take a variety of forms such as dollars, weight, volume, quantity, and so on. Letting the cost per unit reliability of the ith component be C_i, then the incremental cost to improve the reliability of component i is given by

$$R_i(t) + \Delta_i = C_i \Delta_i$$

Assuming that the system of interest is a series system, then the improvement in system reliability as a result of the improvement in component i is given by

$$R_s^*(t) = \prod_{\substack{j=1 \\ j \neq i}}^{N} R_j(t)[R_i(t) + \Delta_i] = R_s(t) + \frac{R_s(t)}{R_i(t)}\Delta_i$$

If we assume that $R_s^*(t)$ can also be obtained by increasing the reliability of one of the other components by an incremental amount Δ_j at a cost of $C_j\Delta_j$, then the reliability of the improved system is given by

$$R_s^*(t) = R_s(t) + \frac{R_s(t)}{R_j(t)}\Delta_j = R_s(t) + \frac{R_s(t)}{R_i(t)}\Delta_i$$

Therefore,

$$\frac{\Delta_j}{R_j(t)} = \frac{\Delta_i}{R_i(t)}$$

Multiplying both sides by the associated costs for the incremental improvement in reliability and rearranging terms yields

$$C_i\Delta_i = \frac{C_i}{C_j}\frac{R_i(t)}{R_j(t)}C_j\Delta_j$$

Now, for $C_i \Delta_i < C_j \Delta_j$ to be true, the following relationship must hold:

$$\frac{C_i}{C_j} \frac{R_i(t)}{R_j(t)} < 1$$

$$C_i R(t) < C_j R_j(t)$$

Therefore, to improve the system reliability for a series system to $R_s^*(t)$ at minimum cost, the component that should be improved is the component that satisfies the following relationship:

$$C_{i*} R_{i*}(t) = \min C_i R_i(t)$$

Improving Series System Reliability. An advanced optical package has been designed for the next generation weather satellite for the National Weather Service. The basic optical package can be modeled functionally as a three-component series system. Each component has a five-year mission reliability of 0.99, 0.995, and 0.98, respectively. Due to the design constraints, there is a weight constraint for the optical package of 1000 lb.

Suppose that the reliability of the system can be improved by adding redundant components to the optical package. The goal would be to determine the optimal combination of components that maximize reliability at minimal cost subject to the 1000 lb weight constraint. Suppose the weight of each component is given by 150, 200, and 300 lb, respectively, and the initial system reliability at time $t = 0$ is given by

$$R_s(0) = R - 1(0)R_2(0)R_3(0) = (0.99)(0.995)(0.98) = 0.9653$$

For this example, the effectiveness of the satellite is measured by its reliability. Let n_1, n_2, and n_3 represent the number of each type of component used in the recommended optical package. The initial weight for the system is given by: $150 + 200 + 300 = 650$ lb. To proceed, the cost in terms of weight per unit of reliability improvement for each of the components needs to be determined. Starting with component 1, if a redundant component is added to it in parallel, then the reliability of this small parallel subsystem would be:

$$R_1^* = 1 - (1 - 0.99)(1 - 0.99) = 0.9999$$

The improvement in the contribution to the reliability for component 1 is 0.0099 at a cost of 150 lb. Therefore,

$$C_1 = \frac{150}{0.0099} = \frac{15,151.51 \text{ lb}}{\text{unit of reliability}}$$

Similarly, calculating the same costs for components 2 and 3 gives:

$$C_2 = \frac{40,201 \text{ lb}}{\text{unit of reliability}}$$

$$C_3 = \frac{15,306.12 \text{ lb}}{\text{unit of reliability}}$$

These results indicate that a redundant component should be added to component 1. This increases the optical package's weight to 800 lb. The option remaining is to compare the cost of adding a third component 1 or a second component 2. Since there is only 200 lb available, it prevents adding an additional component 3.

$$R_i^{**} = 1 - (1 - 0.99)(1 - 0.99)(1 - 0.99) = 0.999999$$

$$C_1^{**} = \frac{150}{0.000099} \frac{1,515,151.51 \text{ lb}}{\text{unit of reliability}}$$

Given this enormous cost associated with adding a third component 1 in parallel to the configuration, the best solution is to add an additional component 2, creating two parallel subsystems. The reliability for the final configuration is given by

$$R_s^* = (0.9999)(0.999975)(0.98) = 0.979877$$

11.5.1   Check on Learning

1. Do any of the four professional societies mentioned in this chapter have programs and resources specifically designed for students? If so, provide a brief summary of the services or products they provide that you might find valuable now.

2. Answer the following questions regarding a concept map.
   (a) How would you define a concept map? Is there a standard positioning of nouns and verbs on a concept map?
   (b) Is a concept map different from Checkland's LUMAS model? Explain. Draw the LUMAS model that is associated with its definition.
   (c) Where on the spectrum of figure would you position a concept map as a model? Why?

11.6   MARKOV MODELS OF REPAIRABLE SYSTEMS

The previous sections addressed techniques for analyzing non-repairable systems. Here, the focus shifts onto using continuous-time Markov chains (CTMCs) to model *repairable systems* [16]. A *repairable system* (RS) is a system that, after failure, can be restored to a functioning condition by some maintenance action other than replacing the entire system [17]. A CTMC is a stochastic process that transitions from state to state according to a discrete-time Markov chain (DTMC). It differs from a DTMC in that the amount of time it spends in each state before it transitions to another state is exponentially distributed [18]. Like a DTMC, it has the Markovian property whereby the "future is independent of the past, given the present."

This section addressed the case in which the CTMC has stationary (homogenous) transition probabilities (i.e. $P[X(t + s) = j | X(s) = i]$ is independent of s).

Definition. A CTMC is a stochastic process where each time it enters state i, the amount of time it spends in state i before it transitions into a different state is exponentially distributed with a rate v_i, and when the process leaves state i, it will enter state j with some probability p_{ij}, where $\sum_{j \neq i} P_{ij} = 1$ [19].

11.6.1 Kolmogorov Differential Equations

In the discrete-time case, $p_{ij}(n)$ represents the probability of going from state i to j in n transitions. In the continuous case we are interested in $p_{ij}(t)$ that represents the probability that a process currently in state i will be in state j in t time units from the present. Mathematically, we denote this by

$$p_{ij}(t) = P[X(t + s) = j \mid X(s) = i]$$

The intensity at which transitions occur for the continuous time case can be defined by examining the *infinitesimal transition rates*:

$$-\frac{d}{dt}p_{ij}(0) = \lim_{t \to 0} \frac{1 - p_{ij}(t)}{t} = v_i$$

$$-\frac{d}{dt}p_{ij}(0) = \lim_{t \to 0} \frac{p_{ij}(t)}{t} = q_{ij}$$

where v_i represents the rate at which we leave state i, and q_{ij} represents the rate at which we move from state i to state j. However, for small Δt, $q_{ij}\Delta t$ can be interpreted as the probability of going from state i to state j in some small increment of time Δt, given we started in state i. Using the transition intensities, as well as making use of the Markovian property, one can derive the Kolmogorov differential equations for $p_{ij}(t)$. The backward and forward Kolmogorov equations are given by Equations (11.1) and (11.1). These equations can be used to derive the transient probabilities of a CTMC. This is best illustrated through the use of an example.

$$\frac{d}{dt}p_{ij}(t) = \sum_{k \neq i} q_{ik}p_{kj}(t) - v_i p_{ij}(t)$$

$$\frac{d}{dt}p_{ij}(t) = \sum_{k \neq j} q_{kj}p_{ik}(t) - v_i P_{ij}(t)$$

11.6.2 Transient Analysis

Consider a single-component system that fails according to an exponential failure distribution with rate λ and whose repair time is exponentially distributed with rate μ. This system can be in one of the two states. It can be working (state 0) or can fail and be undergoing repair (state 1). The state transition diagram for this system is shown in Figure 11.18, which also shows the states and the associated transition rates between the states.

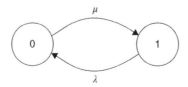

Figure 11.18 Single-component transition rate diagram.

Using the transition rate diagram and the Kolmogorov forward equation, Equation (11.1), the transition probabilities for the CTMC can be derived:

$$\frac{d}{dt}p_{ij}(t) = \sum_{k \neq j} q_{ik}p_{ik}(t) - v_i p_{ij}(t)$$

$$\frac{d}{dt}p_{00}(t) = \sum_{k \neq j} q_{10}p_{01}(t) - v_0 p_{00}(t)$$

$$\frac{d}{dt}p_{00}(t) = \mu p_{01}(t) - \lambda p_{00}(t)$$

$$\frac{d}{dt}p_{00}(t) = \mu[1 - p_{00}(t)] - \lambda p_{00}(t)$$

$$\frac{d}{dt}p_{00}(t) = \mu - (\mu + \lambda)p_{00}(t)$$

$$\frac{d}{dt}p_{00}(t) + (\mu + \lambda)p_{00}(t) = \mu$$

Solving this differential equation yields:

$$e^{(\lambda+\mu)t}\left[\frac{d}{dt}p_{00}(t) + (\mu + \lambda)p_{00}(t)\right] = \mu e^{(\lambda+\mu)t}$$

$$\frac{d}{dt}[e^{(\lambda+\mu)t}p_{00}(t)] = \mu e^{(\lambda+\mu)t}$$

$$e^{(\lambda+\mu)t}p_{00}(t) = \frac{\mu}{\lambda+\mu}e^{(\lambda+\mu)t} + c$$

$$\text{since } p_{00}(t) = 1, \quad c = \frac{\mu}{\lambda+\mu}$$

Therefore, $p_{ij}(t)$ for $i = j$ are given as follows:

$$p_{00}(t) = \frac{\lambda}{\lambda+\mu}e^{(\lambda+\mu)t} + \frac{\mu}{\lambda+\mu}$$

$$p_{11}(t) = \frac{\mu}{\lambda+\mu}e^{(\lambda+\mu)t} + \frac{\lambda}{\lambda+\mu}$$

Notice that $p_{00}(t)$ represents the probability that the system is operating at time t. This is also known as the *system availability* $A(t)$. If we take the limit of $p_{00}(t)$ as t goes to infinity, we get the limiting or steady state availability. The limiting availability is given as follows:

$$\lim_{t \to \infty} A(t) = \lim_{t \to \infty} p_{00}(t) = \frac{\mu}{\lambda+\mu}$$

In general, a set of N first order differential equations that characterize the probability of being in each state can be identified in terms of the transition probabilities to and from each state. Mathematically, the set of N first order differential equations is summarized in matrix form in the first equation, and the general form of the solution to this set of differential equations is given by the second equation [20].

$$\frac{d\underline{P}(t)}{dt} = [T_R]\underline{P}(t)$$

$$\underline{P} = \exp[T_R]t \cdot \underline{P}(0)$$

In these expressions, T_R is the rate matrix. For this simple single-system example, using Figure 11.18 yields the following rate matrix.

$$T_R = \begin{pmatrix} -\lambda & \mu \\ \lambda & -\mu \end{pmatrix}$$

To solve the set of differential equations one must compute the matrix exponential. There are several different approaches to computing the matrix exponential. Two such methods include the infinite series method and the eigenvalue/eigenvector approach. Such routines are readily available in many of the commercially available mathematical analysis packages (Maple™, Mathematica®, and MATLAB®). In many instances, as the problem complexity increases, the Kolmogorov differential equations cannot be solved explicitly for the transition probabilities. In such cases, a numerical solution techniques must be used. One option would be to use simulation (see [21]), or for a variety of reasons, focus attention on the steady state performance of the system instead.

11.6.3 Steady State Analysis

For many systems, it is the limiting availability (aka, steady state availability), $A(\infty)$, that is of interest. Another common name for the steady state availability is the *uptime ratio*. For example, the uptime ratio is of critical importance in a production facility. Similarly, for a communication system, the average message transfer rate will be the design transfer rate times the uptime ratio. Knowing the uptime ratio is essential for analyzing the performance of many systems.

The steady state probabilities can be computed by making use of the following:

$$\text{let } \rho_j = \lim_{t \to \infty} p_{ij}(t)$$

so that

$$v_j \rho_j = \sum_j p_i q_{ij} \quad \forall\, j = 0, 1, 2, \ldots, N \tag{BalEqns}$$

$$\sum_j \rho_j = 1 \tag{SysState}$$

Expression *BalEqns* is called the *balance equations* for the system. The balance equations state that the rate into each state must be equal to the rate out of each state for the system to be in equilibrium. Equation *SysState* states that the system must be in some state, and the sum of the probabilities associated with each state must be equal to 1. Using $(N-1)$ of the balance equations and Equation *SysState*, the steady state probabilities for each state can easily be derived.

11.6.4 CTMC Models of Repairable Systems

This section focuses on how to model and analyze a variety of repairable systems using CTMCs for the single machine cases. Consider a single repairable machine. Let T_i denote the duration of the *i*th interval of machine function, and assume that $T_1, T_2, \ldots$ is a sequence of independent identically distributed exponential random variables having failure rate λ. Upon failure, the machine is repaired. Let D_i denote the duration of the *i*th machine repair, and assume $D_1, D_2, \ldots$ is a sequence of independent identically distributed exponential random variables having repair rate μ. Assume that no preventive maintenance is performed on the machine.

Recall that $X(t)$ denotes the state of the machine at time t. Under these assumptions, $\{X(t), t \geq 0\}$ transitions among two states, and the time between transitions is exponentially distributed. Thus, $\{X(t), t \geq 0\}$ is a CTMC having the transition rate diagram shown in Figure 11.18.

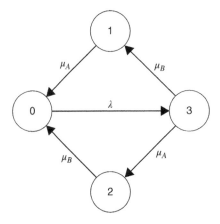

Figure 11.19 Transition rate diagram for multiple repair process.

To analyze the steady state behavior of the CTMC, let ρ_j denote the long-run probability that the CTMC is in state j. Balance equations can be used to identify these probabilities. Each state of the CTMC has a balance equation that corresponds to the modeling relationship "rate in" = "rate out." For the transition rate diagram in Figure 11.18, the balance equations are

$$\text{state 0: } \lambda\rho_1 = \mu\rho_0$$

$$\text{state 1: } \mu\rho_0 = \lambda\rho_1$$

These balance equations are equivalent, so an additional equation is needed to solve for ρ_0 and ρ_1, which is available recalling that the steady state probabilities must sum to 1.

This produces a set of two with two unknowns:

$$\rho_1 = \frac{\mu}{\lambda + \mu}$$

$$\rho_2 = \frac{\lambda}{\lambda + \mu}$$

Notice that ρ_1 is equivalent to the steady state availability found from taking the limit of the transient probabilities in the limiting availability expression earlier.

Consider another single-machine example. Just like the first example, let T_i denote the duration of the ith interval of machine function, and assume $T_1, T_2, \ldots$ is a sequence of independent identically distributed exponential random variables having failure rate λ. Upon failure, the machine is repaired. But this time, each repair requires two distinct repair operations, A and B. Assume that the duration of repair is exponentially distributed with rate μ_j where $j = (A, B)$. For this example, assume that there are enough resources available so that the repairs can be done concurrently.

This problem differs significantly from the first in that the machine now has four different states. State 0 is when the machine is operating; State 1 is when the machine is down and we are awaiting the completion of repair process A; State 2 is when the machine is down and we are awaiting the completion of repair process B; and State 3 is when the machine is down and is awaiting the completion of both repair processes. The transition rate diagram for this model is shown in Figure 11.19.

Using the rate diagram, a set of balance equations can be written as

$$\mu_A \rho_1 + \mu_B \rho_2 = \lambda \rho_0$$

$$\mu_B \rho_3 = \mu_A \rho_1$$

$$\mu_A \rho_3 = \mu_B \rho_2$$

$$\lambda \rho_0 = (\mu_A + \mu_B)\rho_3$$

Using these balance equations in conjunction with the total probability equation, the individual steady state values for each of the states can be solved for. The state of interest is state 0, as it represents the system steady state availability. Suppose the system described earlier has a mean time between failure of 100 hours, and the mean repair time for process A is 10 hours and for process B it is 5 hours. To determine the system steady state availability, the balance equations can be used to derive the equation in the following text and determine that the system has a steady state availability 0.96 (Figure 11.20).

$$\rho_0 = \frac{\mu_A + \mu_B}{\lambda} \left(\frac{\mu_A + \mu_B}{\lambda} + \frac{\mu_A}{\mu_B} + \frac{\mu_B}{\mu_A} \right)^{-1} = \frac{0.1 + 0.2}{0.01}(32.5)^{-1} = 0.9231$$

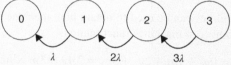

Figure 11.20 Partial transition rate diagram when $m = 3$.

11.6.5 Modeling Multiple Machine Problems

Suppose the repairable system of interest actually consists of m identical machines that correspond to the assumptions of Section 11.6.4. To model this situation using a CTMC, the definition of the system state $X(t)$ must be modified. Let $X(t)$ now represent the number of machines functioning at time t. However, $\{X(t), t_0\}$ is still a CTMC because the number of states is discrete and transition times are exponentially distributed.

A partial transition rate diagram for the case in which $m = 3$ is constructed in Figure 11.20. Notice that the repair rates on the diagram depend on s, the number of maintenance technicians in the system, and assume each repair requires exactly one technician.

Suppose $m = 3$, $s = 2$, $\lambda = 2$ failures per day, and $\mu = 10$ repairs per day. The completed transition rate diagram for the resulting CTMC is given in Figure 11.21. Notice that the transition rate from state 3 to state 2 is 6. This is because three machines are functioning; each has a failure rate of 2, so the total failure rate is 6. Note also that the transition rate from state 1 to state 2 is 20. This is because two machines have failed. This implies that both technicians are repairing at a rate of

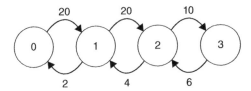

Figure 11.21   Completed transition rate diagram example.

10, so the total repair rate is 20. The corresponding balance equations are

$$\text{state 0: } 2\rho_1 = 20\rho_0 \rightarrow \rho_1 = 10\rho_3$$

$$\text{state 1: } 20\rho_0 + 4\rho_2 = 22\rho_1 \rightarrow \rho_2 = 50\rho_0$$

$$\text{state 3: } 10\rho_2 = 6\rho_3 \rightarrow \rho_3 = \frac{250}{3}\rho_0$$

The solution to these equations is

$$\rho_0 = \frac{3}{433}$$

$$\rho_1 = \frac{30}{433}$$

$$\rho_2 = \frac{150}{433}$$

$$\rho_3 = \frac{250}{433}$$

Now the steady state probabilities can be used to obtain both machine and technician utilization. For example, the average number of machines functioning is

$$\text{AVG M} = 0\rho_0 + 1\rho_1 + 2\rho_2 + 3\rho_3 = 2.49 \ (83\% \text{ utilization})$$

and the average number of busy technicians is

$$\text{AVG S} = 2\rho_0 + 2\rho_1 + 1\rho_2 + 0\rho_3 = 0.50 \ (25\% \text{ utilization})$$

   At this point, a reasonable question is "How many technicians should be assigned to maintain these machines? Should $s = 1, 2,$ or 3?" The CTMC must first be modified for the cases in which $s = 1$ and $s = 3$. Then, the steady state probabilities and utilization measures for each case can be computed. An economic model can be used to determine the optimal value of s in the following way. Let c_s denote the cost per day of employing a technician, let c_d denote the cost per day of machine downtime, and let C denote the cost per day of system operation. Then

$$E(C) = c_s S + c_d(m - \text{AVG M})$$

Multiple Machine Example. Suppose $c_s = \$200$ and $c_d = \$2500$. Then, $E(C) = \$1664.25$. For $s = 1$, the transition rate diagram is shown in Figure 11.22.

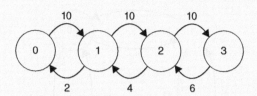

Figure 11.22 Example transition rate diagram with $s = 1$.

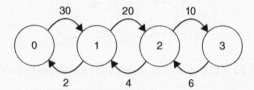

Figure 11.23 Example transition rate diagram, $s = 3$.

The resulting steady state probabilities are $\rho_0 = 0.0254$, $\rho_1 = 0.1271$, $\rho_2 = 0.3178$, and $\rho_3 = 0.5297$. Furthermore, AVG M $= 2.3518$ and $E(C) = \$1820.50$. For $s = 3$, the rate diagram is provided in Figure 11.23.

The resulting steady state probabilities are $\rho_0 = 0.0046$, $\rho_1 = 0.0694$, $\rho_2 = 0.3472$, and $\rho_3 = 0.5787$. Furthermore, AVG M $= 2.4999$ and $E(C) = \$1850.25$. Thus, $s = 2$ is the optimal staffing level.

Nonidentical Machine Problems. An interesting variation of the multiple-machine problem is the case in which the machines are not identical. For example, suppose a system contains two machines of different types that are repaired upon failure (no PM), and suppose two equally trained technicians maintain these machines. Let λ_i denote the failure rate for machine i, and let μ_i denote the repair rate for machine i. Modeling this problem using a CTMC requires a more complex definition of the system state.

$$X(t) = \begin{cases} 1,1 & \text{both machines are functioning} \\ 1,0 & \text{machine 1 is functioning, machine 2 is down} \\ 0,1 & \text{machine 1 is down, machine 2 is functioning} \\ 0,0 & \text{both machines are down} \end{cases}$$

The corresponding transition rate diagram is provided in Figure 11.24. For example, suppose $\lambda_1 = 1$, $\mu_1 = 8$, $\lambda_2 = 2$, and $\mu_2 = 10$. Solving the balance equations for this system yields $\rho_{1,1} = 0.7407$, $\rho_{1,0} = 0.1481$, $\rho_{0,1} = 0.0926$, and $\rho_{0,0} = 0.0185$. The steady state probabilities can then be used to compute machine availability

$$\text{machine 1: } \rho_{1,1} + \rho_{1,0} = 0.8889$$

$$\text{machine 2: } \rho_{1,1} + \rho_{0,1} = 0.8333$$

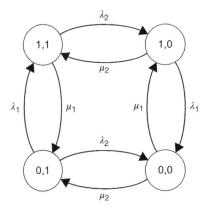

Figure 11.24 Transition rate diagram for two different machines.

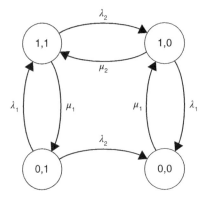

Figure 11.25 Transition rate diagram, multiple-machine, single technician, prioritized repair.

and machine and technician utilization

$$\text{AVG M} = 2\rho_{1,1} + \rho_{1,0} + \rho_{0,1} = 1.7222 \ (86\%)$$

$$\text{AVG S} = \rho_{1,0} + \rho_{0,1} + 2\rho_{0,0} = 0.2778 \ (14\%)$$

Another interesting variation occurs if only one technician is available. Suppose that in addition to only having one technician, that machine 1 has higher priority than machine 2. Thus, if machine 2 is being repaired and machine 1 fails, the technician will leave machine 2 to go work on machine 1. Once machine 1 is repaired, the technician will resume work on machine 2. The transition rate diagram for this situation is given in Figure 11.25.

Notice that the transition rate diagram for this situation is similar to the previous example. The key difference is that when the system is in a state $(0, 0)$, it can only transition to state $(1, 0)$ because of the fact that machine 1 has a higher priority than machine 2 and therefore the technician must repair machine 1 as soon as it fails.

Multiple Machines Single Technician. Assume that the system parameters have the same values as in the previous example; therefore $\lambda_1 = 1$, $\mu_1 = 8$, $\lambda_2 = 2$, and $\mu_2 = 10$. Solving the balance equations yields $\rho_{1,1} = 0.72859$, $\rho_{1,0} = 0.16029$, $\rho_{0,1} = 0.07285$, and $\rho_{0,0} = 0.03825$. The steady state probabilities can then be used to compute machine availability

$$\text{machine 1: } \rho_{1,1} + \rho_{1,0} = 0.8889$$

$$\text{machine 2: } \rho_{1,1} + \rho_{0,1} = 0.8015$$

and machine and technician utilization

$$\text{AVG M} = 2\rho_{1,1} + \rho_{1,0} + \rho_{0,1} = 1.69 \ (84.52\%)$$

$$\text{AVG S} = \rho_{1,0} + \rho_{0,1} + \rho_{0,0} = 0.2714 \ (27\%)$$

These results indicate that despite the fact that there is only one technician, machine 1s steady state availability can be maintained at the same level as if two technicians were available by giving it priority when it fails. As expected, machine 2s steady state availability is reduced from 0.8333 to 0.8015.

Another important point is that the technician utilization increases from 14% to 27%. Depending on the costs associated with an increase in downtime for machine 2, using a priority maintenance process may be more cost-effective than having two technicians available to perform maintenance.

Using Markov chains as an analysis tool for reliability and maintainability has both advantages and disadvantages, depending on the complexity of the system. A key advantage is the modeling flexibility that Markov chains give to an analyst to perform relatively quick analysis. As demonstrated in most of the examples, Markov chains are particularly well suited for modeling repairable systems. They are also often used to model redundancy (hot and cold standby), system dependencies, and fault tolerance systems. For most of these systems, Markov chain models are mathematically tractable, and thus avoiding the necessity of using simulation (see [22]). The biggest disadvantage of Markov chain models is the "curse of dimensionality [21]." For complex systems, the number of states required can be quite large, resulting in excessively long solution times. Fortunately, there are many commercial software tools available that help with the modeling and analysis of complex systems using Markov chains, such as *RELYENCE* [23] and *ITEM* [24].

REFERENCES

1. Soban, D., Mavris, D. (2000) Formulation of a methodology for the probabilistic assessment of system effectiveness, Research Report AIAA-MSC-2000-DS. Atlanta, GA: Georgia Institute of Technology.

2. Blanchard, B. (1998) *Logistics Engineering and Management*, 5th ed. Upper Saddle River, NJ: Prentice-Hall.

3. What is reliability? ASQ. Available at: https://asq.org/. (Accessed 22 Mar 2022).

4. Dietrich, D. (1993) Class Notes, SIE 608, Large Scale Systems, University of Arizona.

5. Proschan, F. (1963) 'Theoretical explanation of observed decreasing failure rate,' *Technometrics*, 5(3), pp. 375–383.

6. Fuqua, N. (1987) *Reliability Engineering for Electronic Design.* New York: Marcel Dekker.

7. Barlow, R.E., Proscan,F. (1965) *Mathematical Theory of Reliability.* New York: John Wiley & Sons, Inc.

8. Kapus, K., Lamberson, L. (1977) *Reliability in Engineering Design.* New York: John Wiley & Sons, Inc.

9. Leemis, L. (1995) *Reliability: Probabilistic Models and Statistical Methods.* Englewood Cliffs, NJ: Prentice-Hall.

10. ReliaWiki. Reliasoft Corporation. Available at: https://www.reliawiki.com. (Accessed 20 Feb 2022).

11. Kececioglu, D. (1993) *Reliability & Life Testing Handbook.* Englewood Cliffs, NJ: Prentice-Hall.

12. BlockSIM. Reliasoft Corporation. Available at: https://www.reliasoft.com. (Accessed 22 Feb 2022).

13. Nachlas, J. (2005) *Reliability Engineering: Probabilistic Models and Maintenance Methods.* Boca Raton, FL: Taylor & Francis.

14. Birnbaum, Z. (1969) 'On the importance of different components in a multicomponent system,' in *Multivariate Analysis*, P. Krishnaiah, Ed. New York: Academic Press, pp. 581–592.

15. Miziula, P., Navarro, J. (2019) 'Birnbaum importance measure for systems with dependent components,' *IEEE Transactions on Reliability*, 68(2), pp. 439–450.

16. Maillart, L., Pohl, E. (2006) 'Markov chain modeling and analysis,' *Tutorial Notes of the Annual Reliability and Maintainability Symposium.*

17. Ascher, H., Feingold, H. (1984) *Repairable Systems Reliability.* New York: Marcel Dekker, Inc.

18. Ross, S.M. (1989) *Introduction to Probability Models*, 7th ed. San Diego, CA: Harcourt Academic Press.

19. Ross, S.M. (1996) *Stochastic Processes*, 2nd ed. New York: John Wiley & Sons, Inc.

20. Minh, D.L. (2001) *Applied Probability Models.* Pacific Grove, CA: Duxbury Press.

21. Fuqua, N. (2003) 'The applicability of Markov analysis methods to reliability, maintainability, and safety,' *Select Topics in Assurance Related Technologies*, 10(2), pp. 1–8.

22. Pohl, E.A., Mykytka, E.F. (2000) Simulation modeling for reliability analysis. *Tutorial Notes of the Annual Reliability and Maintainability Symposium.*

23. RELYENCE. Relyence Corporation. Available at: https://relyence.com/relex/. (Accessed 20 March 2022).

24. ITEM. Item Software. Available at: https://itemsoft.com/. (Accessed 20 March 2022).

Chapter **12**

Solution Implementation

The focus of a project manager during a solution implementation is to do everything possible to ensure the system delivers the value expected, on-time, and within cost.
—Niki Goerger, U.S. Army Engineering Research & Development Center

12.1 INTRODUCTION

Once a decision occurs, focus adjusts toward implementing the chosen solution design. Simply deciding to implement the selected solution does not equate to solution success in implementation. The engineering manager hopes to encounter "blue skies and smooth sailing" as indicated by a blue color depicted on the systems decision process (SDP) when implementing the solution. Traditional or agile/adaptive project management approaches to solution implementation each remain grounded in delivering business and/or stakeholder value through productive working relationships [1].

Even the best of solution designs, if poorly implemented, can fail to meet the needs of a client. Successfully implementing a solution depends on the emphasis and consideration given to the eventual solution implementation during the three phases that precede it: Problem definition, Solution design, and Decision making. Planning for implementation must begin during Problem definition, continue throughout the design of alternative solutions, and be a consideration in the Decision making phase of the SDP. However, many of the implementation tools in this chapter can also be used to lead interdisciplinary and possibly geographically dispersed teams during the preceding three phases. As more and more trans-national systems engineering projects become commonplace,

Decision Making in Systems Engineering and Management, Third Edition.
Patrick J. Driscoll, Gregory S. Parnell, and Dale L. Henderson
© 2023 John Wiley & Sons, Inc. Published 2023 by John Wiley & Sons, Inc.

leveraging international talent in new ways, the likelihood that and entire systems team would be co-located is diminishing.

> Successful solution implementation depends on the preparation during the three phases that precede it. That preparation must address the life-cycle, cadence, phasing, and development approach of the system being implemented [1].

The phases of the SDP are highly interdependent as are the stages of a system life cycle. How one defines a problem certainly impacts the available solution design space. Similarly, the solution design selected by a decision maker will shape the plan developed in the Solution implementation phase. This same interdependence occurs between life cycle stages. For example, the design choice made early on in the Design and Develop the System life cycle stage will strongly influence the decisions and flexibility available to a project manager (PM) responsible for manufacturing the system in the Produce the System life cycle stage. For this reason and others, it is imperative that neither the designer nor the PM carry out his or her role independently of the other. Both should work toward the same set of objectives, focused on ensuring that the system solution chosen during the Decision making phase is met with success. In this sense, making decisions and implementing them are essentially indistinguishable, except in terms of their chronological order.

A concept map of the solution implementation phase is shown in Figure 12.1. The map depicts the interrelationship of the activities and tasks as well as the inputs and outputs within this phase. Agile project management approaches applied to the activities in this concept map would iterate frequently across many of the relationships shown to adapt to uncertainties and the volatility of the environment [1].

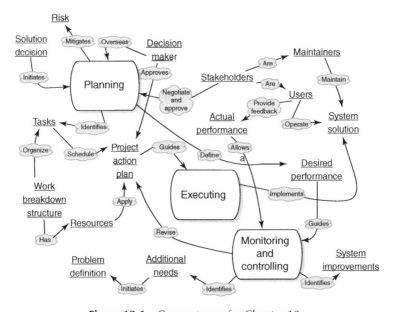

Figure 12.1 Concept map for Chapter 12.

This chapter focuses on the activities and elements that contribute to a successful implementation of a system solution. It begins with a discussion of the Solution Implementation phase and its relationship to specific stages of the system life cycle introduced in Section 1.4. While much of the preceding chapters introduce and discuss unique activities and techniques in the context of a systems project, it is worth noting that implementing a system solution tends to be a project in it of itself, largely relegated to the skills of engineering management and project management professionals who share many of the same interests.

12.2   SOLUTION IMPLEMENTATION PHASE

The Solution implementation phase is the fourth final phase of the SDP, engaged with only after a decision maker has selected a system solution from among the many competing alternatives. It is one of the more difficult phases to accomplish because the activities of this phase focus on turning a client's expectations for the system into reality while facing the many uncertainties that earlier tradespace modeling and analysis attempted to accurately integrate into the systems decision being made.

As mentioned earlier, there always exists the possibility of returning to an earlier phase of the SDP based on evolving project conditions, although doing so post-selection tends to be a costly endeavor. Engaging the SDP is an iterative, cyclical process, which is represented by the circular nature of the SDP diagram. Additionally, the Solution Implementation phase can be used in full, or in part during any one of the seven life cycle stages listed in Table 12.1.

The first step towards success for a systems team is conceptualizing the action of "implementing a solution" as a project. By doing so, the complete arsenal of project management principles are available to help plan, execute, monitor, and control the conversion of the system solution into reality.

Definition: A *project* is a temporary endeavor undertaken to create a unique system, product, service, or result [1].

As a temporary endeavor, a systems project has a definite beginning and end but this does not mean that it is short in duration. On the contrary, many systems projects may last for years making the concept of "temporary" less rigid than it may appear. Conceptualizing the Solution implementation phase as a system project means that a new fundamental objective for this engagement could be written in alignment with the intended outcome of Solution implementation phase. However, in most instances, the original fundamental objective also includes implementing a solution, if one is identified.

Properly moving a systems project through to completion requires expertise in project management capabilities. Project management encompasses the knowledge, skills, tools and techniques applied to activities in order to meet the project objectives [2]. It applies project management principles and performance domains to a valued system across the life cycle [1]. Traditional project management processes follow six major processes: initiating, planning, executing, monitoring and controlling, and closing. Initiating defines and authorizes the project; planning defines scope, objectives and the course of action; executing integrates people and resources to execute the project management plan; monitoring and controlling track progress and identify shortcomings requiring action; and closing is the formal acceptance of the product, service or outcome that brings the project to an end [1].

A complete treatment of all the skills, best practices, and nuances associated with project management exceeds the scope of this chapter. Thankfully, the Project Management Institute's PM Body of Knowledge (PMBoK), 7th Edition, and American Society for Engineering Management's

TABLE 12.1   Life Cycle Stages.

Life Cycle Stage	Purpose
Establish System Need	• Define the problem • Identify stakeholder needs • Identify preliminary requirements
Develop System Concept	• Refine system requirements • Explore concepts • Select concept
Design and Develop the System	• Develop preliminary and final designs • Build development system(s) for test and evaluation • Test for performance, integration, robustness, effectiveness, etc. • Assess risk, reliability, maintainability, supportability, life cycle cost, etc.
Produce the System	• Acquire long-lead-time components • Develop production plan and schedule • Perform low-rate initial production (LRIP) • Perform full-rate production (FRP) • Monitor and test production items for conformance to specifications
Deploy the System	• Identify deployment locations • Provide training for installation, maintenance, and operation • Transport to chosen locations • Plan and execute logistical support
Operate the System	• Operate system to satisfy user needs • Gather and analyze data on system performance • Provide sustained system capability through maintenance, updates, or planned spiral developed enhancements
Retire the System	• Store, archive, or dispose of system

EM Body of Knowledge, 5th Edition, serve as detailed repositories of technical approaches, knowledge, and skills for a systems team requiring a greater depth of domain understanding during implementation. The focus of this chapter is to highlight select portions of project management principles and domains in sufficient detail to enable a systems team to successfully complete the Solution Implementation phase.

There is more than one way to manage a project to successful completion, and one could argue that project management is more of an art than a strict science. Successful PMs tailor the six project management processes to fit the characteristics of a particular system solution.

Figure 12.2 depicts a model that illustrates how these different project management processes relate to one another. Viewing the model from left to right, the model begins with the initiating process. The *initiating process* develops a project charter and a scope statement. These two items

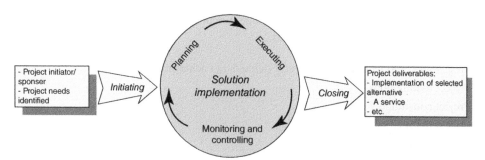

Figure 12.2 The project management process.

establish the breadth of the project and the objectives that need to be accomplished by the project end. From the initiating process, the model flows into the *planning process* which requires a systems project team to collect and consolidate information from many sources to identify, structure, and finalize the project scope, cost and schedule. These three items along with a plan as to how, when, why, and where the available people, tools, and resources are going to be used define a complete systems project action, or management plan.

The *executing process* that naturally follows consists of activities used to complete the work identified in the project management plan. The planning process and the executing process are iterative, allowing a PM to reassess the plan as new information arises or as the project scope requires adjusting. The *monitoring and controlling process* observes project execution so that any potential problems and challenges may be identified as early as possible. Once challenges/issues are identified, corrective action is taken to avoid schedule slippage, cost overruns, and other detrimental effects imposed by deviations from the plan. Monitoring and controlling activities must be performed frequently enough to allow a PM sufficient awareness of the project's status so that any corrective action required may be taken prior to events having an adverse impact on the project's cost, schedule, or performance. For systems decision problems, the performance element of the project plan is comprised of the total system value returned by properly implementing system functions of the qualitative and quantitative value models. The closing process employs techniques to formally terminate the activities of project management plan and verify project completion [1].

 An anecdote familiar to project managers is that a client can have it: "good, fast, or cheap; pick two." This speaks highly of the challenges associated with turning a system solution into reality.

12.3 THE INITIATING PROCESS

Initiating defines and authorizes the project by creating a project charter and a scope of work statement. The *project charter* is a document that provides authorization for the project. Using the project charter and the project statement of work, a preliminary project scope statement is developed in which traditionally is generally more rigid in nature than that of an agile project management approach. The project scope statement defines what needs to be accomplished and generally includes the following items [1, 3]:

- Project and product objectives (clearly defined and achievable)
- Project assumptions
- Project constraints
- Project requirements and deliverables
- Project boundaries
- Solution requirements and characteristics
- Initial project organization
- Initial project risks (risk register update)
- Initial work breakdown structure (WBS)
- Schedule milestones
- Project configuration management requirements
- Order and magnitude cost estimate
- Solution acceptance criteria

Each project scope statement will vary and not all of the listed items are needed for every Solution implementation effort. The project scope statement may also be redefined as the situation dictates. However, changing the project scope requires a PM to review each of the subsequent processes as well, since the project scope statement is the basis from which subsequent activities unfold. If a project is large or complex enough, it may need to be decomposed into phases to be properly managed. This should again appear in the scope statement. Finally, a feasibility analysis is conducted during the initiating process to assess the practicality of completing the project as planned.

As noted in the project scope statement list, identifying risks that might threaten the solution is vital to success. This activity's importance cannot be overemphasized. Identifying and analyzing project risks specific to this phase of the SDP in concert with the active risk register from earlier phases continues a common thread of vigilance through the project management process (see Section 5.7.1). By reviewing previously identified risks and adding new ones as needed specific to cost, schedule, logistics, liability, laws, regulations, and so on, the PM achieves a greater understanding of the impact of uncertainty going forward.

As discussed in Chapters 8, life cycle cost analysis continues into the Solution Implementation phase. An updated cost estimate that now includes many new elements specific to this phase will become part of the project scope statement. The PM uses this cost estimate to develop a realistic projected budget sufficient to carry the overall effort through to completion. This budget serves as a primary indicator for tracking progress in comparison to schedule and performance.

12.4 PLANNING

The Planning process is critical to setting conditions for overall success. Inadequate planning is a primary contributor to projects failing to achieve their schedule, cost, and performance objectives. The Planning process lays out a course of action to attain the scope and objectives for the project. There are several techniques and approaches to assist the systems engineer in this planning effort.

The first step in the Planning process is to analyze the preliminary project scope statement and project management processes to develop a *project management plan*. The project management plan uses all the necessary subordinate plans and integrates them into a cohesive effort to accomplish the project. The project management plan includes activities needed to identify, define, combine, unify, and coordinate the various processes to successfully accomplish the project. The 6th Edition of the PMBoK discusses subordinate plans that include but are not limited to [1–3]:

- Project scope management plan
- Schedule management plan
- Cost management plan
- Quality management plan
- Process improvement plan
- Staffing management plan
- Communication management plan
- Document control management plan
- Risk management plan
- Procurement management plan

Each one of these subordinate plans includes a number of project management techniques that help implement and monitor specific plans. For example, the project scope management plan is used to ensure all required work needed to complete the project successfully is identified. It is just as important to identify what is not included in the project. The WBS is one of the more effective techniques to help in this scoping effort.

Similar to the logic of describing and defining a functional structure for a system, the WBS is a hierarchical representation of all the tasks that must be accomplished in order to successfully complete a project. Four rules are used when developing a WBS. These are:

1. Each task that is broken down to a lower level must have at least two subtasks.
2. If it is difficult to determine how long a task will take or who will do the task, it most likely requires further decomposition.
3. Any task or activity that consumes resources or takes time should be included in the WBS.
4. The time needed to complete an activity at any level of the hierarchy should be the sum of the task times on branches below it.

Properly completed, the WBS ultimately serves as the basis for identifying and assigning appropriate task responsibilities to the systems team members. The WBS defines the exact nature of the tasks required to complete the project. While a hierarchical structure diagram or listing is certainly helpful, the WBS is not limited to one particular format. A WBS can appear as a tree diagram (Figure 12.3) with level one tasks directly below the overall project objective followed by level two tasks [3].

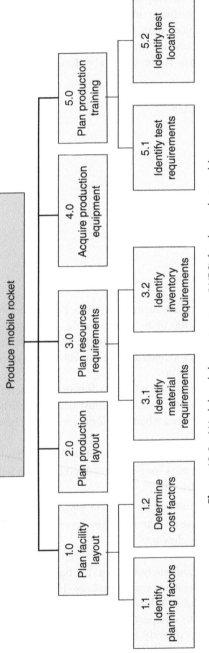

Figure 12.3 Work breakdown structure (WBS) for the rocket problem.

TABLE 12.2   Tools and techniques supporting the planning process.

- Linear responsibility charts
- Scheduling
  - Schedule milestone list
  - Activity sequencing
  - Activity resource estimating
  - Activity duration estimating
- Project configuration management requirements
- Order and magnitude cost estimate
- Resource allocation
  - Critical path method
  - Resource loading
  - Resource leveling
  - Constrained resource scheduling
- Staffing management plan
- Earned value analysis

- Schedule baseline
- Cost baseline
- Quality baseline
  - Quality assurance
  - Quality control
- Risk
  - Risk identification
  - Qualitative risk analysis
  - Quantitative risk analysis
  - Risk response
- Critical path method
- Value engineering
- Stakeholder communication plan
- Document control register
- Change control system

Rocket Example WBS. Considering the earlier rocket example, Figure 12.3 illustrates a classic WBS. The overall objective of this project to implement the decision maker's chosen system solution for a mobile rocket resulting from tradespace analysis. Under the hierarchy's first level task #5—Plan production training—the two subtasks include "Identify test requirements" and "Identify test location." This logical breakdown allows the systems team developing the project scope management plan to accurately identify the requirements associated with every task supporting the production of the mobile rocket objective. Although this example may seem simplistic, the WBS tool is highly effective for supporting much more complicated systems projects.

Other effective tools and techniques identified during the planning process include but are not limited to those shown in Table 12.2 [1–7].

The linear responsibility chart is an excellent technique used in conjunction with the WBS. When complex tasks are broken down to basic tasks, a linear responsibility chart takes those tasks and assigns responsibility for each one to specific people and organizations. A linear responsibility chart shows the critical interfaces between tasks and organizations/individuals and highlights areas that require special management attention [3]. Such a chart is illustrated in Figure 12.4 which takes the rocket WBS shown in Figure 12.3 and assigns a number of tasks to different individuals and teams.

A number of implied tasks are not listed on the WBS, such as for "Establishing Project Plan" and "Establish Project Budget." Associated generic managers and teams are added to illustrate the complexity of the overall organization and the interfaces between departments that can exist and be captured on a linear responsibility chart. For example, "Establishing Project Plan" is the responsibility of the lead planner and her planning team. Moving from left to right in the chart, certain relationships between particular individuals and teams are evident. Obviously, the plan is exceptionally important because it is the foundation for executing the overall project. Therefore,

	Senior vice president for programs	Program manager	Project manager	Lead planner	Planning team	Engineering manager	Engineering team	Operations manager	Operations team	Logistics manager	Logistics team	Lead budget analyst	Budget team	Resource manager	Resource team
Establish project plan	5	6	2,4	1,2	1	3	4	3	4	3	4	3	4	3	4
Establish project budget	5	6	2,4	4	4	3	4	3	4	3	4	1,2	3	3	4
Plan facility layout	5	6	1,2	3	4	1,2	1	3	4	3	4	3	4	3	4
- Identify planning factors		5	6	6,2	3	3	4	3	4	3	4	3	4	3	4
- Determine cost factors		6	6	3	3	3	3	3	3	3	3	1,2	3	3	3
Plan production layout		6	6,2	3	4	1,2	3	3	3	4	4	4	4	3	3
Plan resource requirements		5	6,2	3	3	4	4	3	3	4	4	4	4	1,2	3
- Identify material requirements		5	6	3	4	4	4	3	3	4	4	4	4	1,2	3
- Identify inventory requirements		5	6	3	4	4	4	3	3	4	4	4	4	1,2	3
Acquire production equipment		6	6,2	3	4					3	3	3	3	1,2	3
Plan production training		5	6,2	3	4	3	3	3	3			3	4	1,2	3
- Identify test requirements		5	6	3	4	3	3	3	3			3	4	1,2	3
- Identify test location		5	6	3	4	3	3	3	3			3	4	1,2	3

1 Responsible   4 Consultation possible

2 Supervision   5 Must be notified

3 Consultation madatory   6 Formal approval

Figure 12.4   Example linear responsibility chart.

formal approval is most likely needed throughout the project leadership from the PM, through the program manager, to the senior vice-President (VP) for programs.

The linear responsibility chart in Figure 12.4 also shows the relationships between the lead planner, the team, and the other departments. For planning purposes, it is important to consult each department because they have valuable information that the planner uses. As a minimum, a lead planner needs to consult each department manager. A "3" is used to identify a mandatory consultation requirement on the part of the lead planner. The lead planner has a mandatory requirement to consult with the systems team as well but that is not necessarily how every project organization sees their responsibilities. In this case, it is assumed that the department managers are the "gatekeepers" to their departments and that the lead planner needs to consult with them versus going directly to the department team they manage.

Many projects fail, regardless of size, when project planning is left to individuals who have limited practical experience. A successful plan must include experienced PMs on the planning team. Their expert advice brings a level of practical experience which equates to time and money savings when the final project management plan moves to execution. Ideally, a PM should be identified to lead the project during the planning phase. It is not required that a PM be brought in this early, but it should be viewed as a best practice effort to improve the overall quality and efficiency of the project.

Figure 12.2 illustrates the planning process as an iterative process which includes the two processes: executing, monitoring and controlling. As execution begins, there are inevitable changes that occur, such as information updates, challenges with resource allocation, scheduling delays, value engineering, and so on. These changes and information updates are identified during either the executing or the monitoring and controlling processes. Once identified, the change or information is fed back into the planning phase to allow the project management plan to be updated accordingly. These changes are for the most part unpredictable. Close integration of the planning, execution, and monitoring and controlling processes is essential for success. The PM must constantly seek this type of feedback in order to adjust the plan and execute accordingly.

12.5 EXECUTING

The *Executing* process requires a systems team to perform a myriad of actions to put the project management plan into action. As discussed, the project management plan is made up of specific management plans that employ various techniques and tools to execute the overall management plan. The systems team must orchestrate the integration, sequencing, and interfacing of these plans. Additionally, the systems team must track the deliverables (products, results, and/or services) from each of the subordinate plans. The communications plan becomes exceptionally important here as well because distributing accurate information keeps all team members informed of the project's progress and status.

Equally important is managing the expectations of stakeholders. The stakeholder involvement during this process can be troublesome at times. The PM should be aware of the type and amount of information that is passed along to stakeholders. Most projects do not proceed smoothly at all times because of natural occurring and frequently uncontrollable variation in project components affecting scheduling milestones. However, in the end these same projects are successful. Exposing stakeholders to a complete view of this variation may cause unwarranted celebration (upside variation), concern (downside variation), or over-reaction. Communicating information to stakeholders can be problematic if not properly overseen and personally accomplished by the PM. Effective execution in delivering the scope and quality of the project will lead to the following outcomes [1]:

1. Projects that contribute to business objectives and advancement of strategy.
2. Projects that realize the outcomes they were initiated to deliver.
3. Project benefits realized in the time frame they were planned.
4. A project team that has a clear understanding of requirements.
5. Stakeholder acceptance and satisfaction with the project deliverables.

It is vital to ensure information that affects the project management plan be updated as quickly as possible to ensure appropriate corrective/improvement action can be implemented in a timely manner. Most systems project deliverables take the form of tangible items such as roads, buildings, systems, software, reports, devices, and so on. However, intangible deliverables such as professional training, information, professional image enhancement, and security, among others, can also be provided [1].

12.6 MONITORING AND CONTROLLING

The monitoring and controlling process serves the purpose to track, review, and regulate the project's performance while identifying areas in which the plan might change, and ultimately initiative those changes [1]. One of the first steps to proper monitoring is identifying those essential elements requiring control, which for typical systems projects are performance, schedule, and cost. The PM must establish clear boundaries for control and identify the level of importance for each category. It is safe to say that the boundaries and level of importance are not the same for each project and are driven by the project's overall scope statement and stakeholder input [3, 8, 9]. Continuous monitoring in each of the subordinate plans (Section 12.4) allows the systems team to

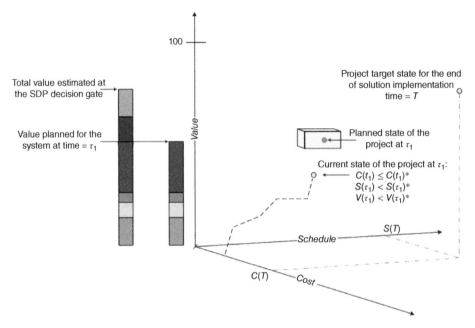

Figure 12.5   Conceptualization of project management during implementation.

keep current with the changing dynamics of the project and to register the project's health through the prism of performance, time, and cost.

The linear responsibility chart shown in Figure 12.4 underscores a need for good monitoring. Figure 12.5 demonstrates how continuous monitoring of a project motivates confidence for a PM that the project is on-track or that it requires action to restore it to this status. This diagram represents a three-dimensional "snapshot" of a project's status at time τ_1 in comparison to the cost, schedule, and value estimates provided to the decision maker prior to entering the Solution implementation SDP phase. The dot inside the box represents the coordinate for the project plan's ideal state of these three project elements by time τ_1. The box imposed around this ideal location represent acceptable levels of variation for these elements at time τ_1 under conditions in which "normal" (planned for) variation in these three elements occurs. If the current monitoring for these three planning elements locate the project state within this box, then for all practical purposes the project is on-track at time τ_1 to deliver the total system value (typically represented by functionality or performance) at the end of the Solution Implementation phase indicated by the solid dot further out on-time and under or at-cost by the end of project.

The dotted line shown in the figure illustrates a hypothetical development path that the project proceeded along up to time τ_1. Note that in this situation, the initial cost outlay for the project at the start of the Solution implementation phase was greater than zero. Unfortunately for the PM, the current state of the project at time τ_1 indicated by the dot below the box means that the project implementation has issues that must be addressed to close the gap. While the project is a bit ahead of schedule ($S(\tau_1) < \tilde{S}(\tau_1)$, and cost is less than or equal to the planned estimate ($C(\tau_1) \leq \tilde{C}(\tau_1)$), the system is not achieving the value return planned for ($V(\tau_1) < \tilde{V}(\tau_1)$) at this time. Thus, some corrective or controlling action is required.

An example of a corrective action taken when the schedule is behind is called "crashing the schedule." Crashing the schedule is a technique used in the critical path method (CPM) to bring a project back on schedule if a particular task is going over the schedule time allowed. This technique requires placing money and/or resources (personnel and/or equipment) against the task to reduce its duration. The obvious outcome of using this technique is increasing the cost of resources which increases the overall project cost.

Another method for monitoring a project is called *earned value (EV) analysis*. EV analysis is a commonly used method for measuring the overall performance of a project [1, 3]. It involves analyzing the physical work accomplished as compared with the projected budget and actual expenditures.

Figure 12.6 illustrates an EV graph representing the facility layout portion of for rocket project WBS shown earlier in Figure 12.3. In this case, the EV is lagging behind the budgeted amount and the actual expenditures. This leads the PM to conclude the project is behind schedule. The money spent on the project to-date exceeds the value accumulated by the system for the work performed. An EV graph and presents the PM with an effective means of monitoring critical project elements in a way that clearly highlights the links existing between cost, schedule, and value (performance). EV calculation metrics include [3]:

- EV–Actual Cost (AC = Cost Variance (CV, where overrun is negative)
- EV– Planned Value (PV = Schedule Variance (SV, where behind is negative)
- Scheduled Time (ST – Actual Time (AT = Time Variance (TV, where delay is negative)
- EV/AC = Cost Performance Index (CPI, where higher is more efficient in budgeted cost of work)
- EV/PV = Schedule Performance Index (SPI, where higher is more efficient for scheduled work performed)

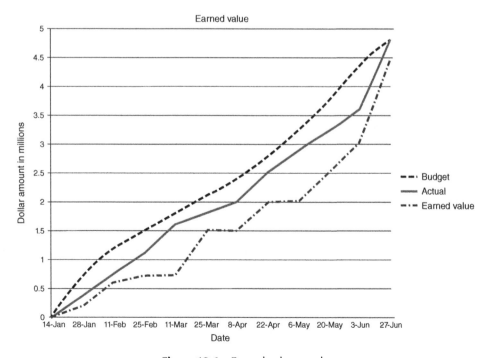

Figure 12.6 Earned value graph.

- (BAC−EV)/CPI = Estimated Cost to Completion (Estimated Cost at Completion [ETC] where BAC is the budget at completion)
- ETC+AC = Estimate at Completion (EAC)

There is more information in the EV chart shown in Figure 12.6 than simply a summary of goals being achieved or not. The stair stepping pattern of the EV line indicates surging by a contractor. While there are several reasons this pattern can occur, it often indicates challenges with a contractor. At the 11 February date, the contractor is stagnant (EV does not increase). The PM in this case responds with an increase in actual budget expenditure. More than likely, there is a possible cash flow problem with the contractor and he required more money to get the work done. Even though the EV is below what the PM would want, there are situations where paying the contractor ahead of the EV is the best course-of-action for project success. This occurs most often when a good working relationship and reasonable trust is established between the contractor and the PM. Working with the contractor to keep maintaining progress instead of, for example, dismissing the contractor and his organization from the project and pursuing litigation is probably the best course-of- action for the PM in this case.

The data past 11 March shows that the contractor responded with an upsurge in the EV. However, on 25 March, the contractor slows down again and EV begins to plateau. In this instance, the PM reacted differently and lowers the payment to the contractor in order to get him to respond. Notice also that near the end of the facility layout portion of the project, there is great gain in EV for the overall project. This is a very typical pattern for systems implementation projects. Engineers have a tendency to estimate a concave shape over the project planning period, indicating optimism in terms of how quickly value (functionality, performance) can be realized. In reality, the EV curve assumes a convex shape because of re-work imposed by test failures, unforeseen schedule delays and response surges in activity, and cost-conserving measures put in-place to mitigate the threat of running out of budget before the expected (or required) value has been delivered.

Overall, the measurement performance domain, which includes activities and functions associated with assessing project performance and actions to maintain performance, is concerned with but not limited to the following list of outcomes [1]:

- A reliable understanding of the status of the project.
- Actionable data to facilitate decision making.
- Timely and appropriate actions to keep project performance on track.
- Achieving targets and generating business value by making informed and timely decisions based on reliable forecasts and evaluations.

12.7   CLOSING

The *closing process* involves all the necessary administrative and contractual closing procedures to ensure proper project closeout. This process includes all the subordinate project plans as well as any phases (for complex/large projects) that are associated with the project. The administrative closing procedures are those procedures and project relationships dealing with different aspects of the project [1].

A major portion of the administrative work required in this process includes archiving project documentation for future reference and use (see Section 12.4). This process is exceptionally important for possible future legal inquiries. Many contracts start out with good intentions on the part of all parties, but more often than not, there are lawsuits brought against a company by a contractor for numerous reasons. A good document control plan and register assists the PM and the systems team to respond to litigation. The contract closure procedure includes those activities needed to complete contractual obligations including all the documents that a contractor is responsible to complete and deliver. For example, near the end of most projects, the daily requirements of progress reports sometimes get overlooked in the last couple of weeks especially if a contractor is nearly 100% paid. If a PM fails to hold the contractor to full compliance for contractual requirements such as progress reporting, the PM is technically liable for this deficiency. It is imperative that the PM team ensure all aspects of close out procedures are adhered too and followed.

12.8 IMPLEMENTATION DURING LIFE CYCLE STAGES

After careful analysis of the Solution implementation phase, it is important to understand its role during all stages of a systems life cycle. The life cycle is a dynamic living model that requires thorough understanding of the SDP and how it is used in every stage of the life cycle. As such, the Solution implementation phase uses different approaches to meet the particular needs as dictated by the solution and the life cycle stage. The guidelines presented in the previous sections are still relevant here as well but are adjusted to meet the unique circumstances presented by each situation. The following sections will focus on the implementation phase as it applies to the Produce the System, Deploy the System, and Operate the System stages of the system life cycle.

12.8.1 Implementation in "Produce the System"

An inherent and necessary objective during the Design and Develop stage is to create a design that enables the system and all of its elements to be produced effectively and efficiently. For most physical systems, the primary objective of the production stage is to turn the system solution into reality. During this time, the systems team handles any design changes justified by requirements or by market demands [6]. Inspection and testing of the product occurs in this stage. The PM team is required to validate that the product meets the specifications identified in the requirements. Project management techniques discussed earlier can be integrated with the SDP and systems engineering procedures and practices to organize and implement a production or manufacturing requirement. This can be an exceedingly complex set of activities requiring an excellent PM team [10].

Planning for "Produce the System" To achieve success during the produce the system life cycle stage, detailed planning must precede the execution of production. Planning the implementation of the system solution helps ensure that the system solution does get implemented in such a way that the expected performance is realized [11]. For the producing the system life cycle stage to be successful, specific planning actions such as those discussed in Section 12.4 must occur. The purpose of planning is not to eliminate uncertainties, but rather to prepare the team as much as possible for anticipated events and to adjust when unexpected events occur. Preparing a plan allows a common baseline from which to coordinate activities. Detailed planning is essential for the producing the system stage because it minimizes the risk inherent in projects.

The systems team must realize that although focus is on producing the system, the majority of planning for deploying and operating the system also occurs in this stage. That is to say that the planning of one stage is performed in relation to other life cycle stages. For example, how the system solution is deployed is taken into consideration when planning for how the system solution will be produced. Likewise how the system solution operates is considered when planning how the system solution will be deployed. Planning must occur not in a vacuum but concurrently and with the end state in mind.

Executing for "Produce the System"   When planning the production of the system solution is complete, the next step is to execute the production plan. Resources are required to execute the plan as well as supporting the deployment and operation of the system solution. Execution includes resource management for implementation of the system solution. Attention is now given to defining resource requirements for production to begin. Resources include everything needed to accomplish each task during production: people, money, supplies, inventory, equipment, facilities, infrastructure, external services, and technology to name a few. Spreadsheets and cost-estimating models are techniques that help organize and layout resource requirements (amount and time).

Microsoft® Project has the ability to display all of this information. This enables the PM to identify a task, its duration, start and finish dates, resources, resource requirements, and when those resources are required. The products of this stage are successfully executed if resources are available. As this stage is carried out, assessment and control of the stage must occur. During the execution of this stage, the key tasks of monitoring and controlling are critical to ensure that the system will function as expected and executed as planned.

Monitoring and Controlling for "Produce the System"   The SDP includes measures and methods that allow for monitoring and controlling system solution performance during all life cycle stages. A feature of Microsoft Project is that it may be used to measure progress in terms of time, budget, and project performance. Since Microsoft Project does not monitor progress in terms of system performance, other methods (simulations and testing) are used to assess system performance.

The project action plan allows the PM team to compare actual and planned task durations, resource usage, and expenditures at any level of activity. The project action plan is used as a control document by measuring comparisons. These comparisons dictate what project performance information is monitored. This gives the PM team the ability to control the project and take corrective action if the project is not proceeding according to plan [5]. The elements that are controlled during the produce the system stage include but are not limited to:

- Cost
- Schedule
- Risk
- System performance requirements
- Design changes
- Production and manufacturing process
- Quality
- Reliability
- Safety of product and personnel

Additionally, there may be others as required by the PM and/or stakeholders.

12.8.2 Implementation in "Deploy the System"

At the end of the produce the system life cycle stage, the system solution enters the fifth life cycle stage: Deploy the System. The PM team must receive prior approval from the decision maker that the system is ready to proceed to the next life cycle stage. Upon approval, the manufactured system solution becomes the deployment system, which delivers fully operational system solutions to users.

Planning for "Deploy the System"   The purpose of the Deploy the System stage is to transfer the system solution from the development facility to the operational location and to establish full operational capability. Distribution facilities, marketing, and sales organizations are required to support the implementation of this stage. Use of these and other resources are planned in great detail. In this section, the planning elements and methods for successful deployment of the system are addressed.

Deploying the system solution is a process that must also be planned for in order to meet stakeholder objectives. Elements of the development process requiring planning include but are not limited to:

- Geographical distribution
- Deployment schedule
- The type and number of system components at each location
- Logistical support
- Type training required (e.g. installation, maintenance, and operation)
- Resource requirements to support the required training
- Testing

Marketing, user, and consumer considerations largely determine the best locations to deploy a system solution. The strategy for deployment and support requirements are identified. Acceptance testing or a full operational testing occurs prior to moving the system solution into the next life cycle stage. Acceptance testing often results in minor adjustments to system operation [12]. This testing is conducted with stakeholders present. Stakeholders ensure that the system solution continues to operate as intended according to desired preferences. Risk is always present, and it is possible that the events and activities inherent in the deployment process may affect the system's operational performance. As such, a risk management plan is developed and contains elements as outlined earlier.

An operational test or demonstration is another type of test that is very useful to communicate the operability of a system. Before testing is complete, operational testing in the environment and under conditions in which the system solution operates is performed. Another critical activity in this stage that requires planning is training. Training produces installers, operators, and maintainers with the necessary skills to support the system solution's operation. Training resources are planned and phased into the project as required. The process planning methods described during the Produce the System stage are applied in this stage as well.

Executing for "Deploy the System"   Deploying a system solution requires excellent documentation concerning how to install the system in its operational environment. In some cases, special analysis and testing is carried out so as to ensure field operability. Training is also designed and delivered in formal well-developed programs. The required training is scheduled, not only in this stage but also in the Operate the System stage. Subsequently, training specialists are part of the team of personnel required to execute the project.

Upon completion of planning for deployment, the plan is carried out. Resources are present to execute the deployment process. Many products are late to market simply because of being starved for resources. When this occurs, the costs are enormous. To execute the deployment plan correctly, timing and resources are critically important. The right kind and the right amount of resources are required and on time when needed. When an increase or adjustment in resources is needed, senior leaders must prepare to respond quickly. Some examples of resource requirements in this stage are listed but not limited to:

- Competent trainees
- Users to perform operational testing
- Tentative user locations
- Transportation assets
- Training equipment

Monitoring and Controlling for "Deploy the System" The need to exert proper control over deploying the system mandates the necessity for monitoring and controlling the proper activities and elements during this stage. According to Table 12.1, the system solution is verified as having met system performance measures. In order for the system solution to perform during full operational capacity as intended it is monitored and assessed and controlled. The details of the deployment plan identify additional elements to control commensurate to the unique deployment requirements. As the system performs outside of its intended functions, corrective action is taken to bring performance in conformity with stakeholder preferences.

The fundamental items controlled are schedule, cost, and performance which were discussed earlier. It is prudent and necessary to perform testing of the system functions prior to the deployment process, during the deployment process, and upon arrival at user location if possible. These efforts ensure that the system operates as intended upon reaching the end user.

12.8.3 Implementation in "Operate the System"

A system is not considered successful until it is successfully implemented and is passed on to the owner. A full-scale operation generally occurs in the sixth life cycle stage: Operate the System. This stage begins as users receive the first operational systems. The objective of the operation stage is to fulfill the stakeholder's need. The stakeholders' needs are fulfilled when the system solution is realized. Planning, execution, and assessment and control during this stage are critical to ensure that the system solution is successfully implemented into full-scale operation. It is hoped that the events and activities preceding this stage were conducted thoroughly.

Planning for "Operate the System" In the Operate the System stage, the system has attained full operational capability. This means that the system solution operated and maintained in conformance with user requirements. This also includes satisfying the user, gathering data on system performance, sustaining and maintaining operability, adding enhancements to the system solution and identifying improvements for future implementation. During this long period in which the system is operational in the field, emphasis is placed on the continuous measurement of the system's performance.

The planning performed in this stage centers on operating and maintaining the system and identifying system improvements. Preliminary planning for retiring the system also occurs here. Since emphasis during this stage is on system performance, data is gathered to assess system performance. Measurement procedures range from simple manual data sheets to automated sensors that record operational status continuously [2]. Some companies try to maintain contact with consumers through hot lines, reports of satisfaction, and online usage monitoring.

To support these methods, it is important that procedures on how to install and sustain a performance measurements program be explicitly defined. Emphasis should be placed on maintaining the system solution to ensure that it continues to function in accordance to its operational requirements. Maintainability is the ability of the system solution to be retained in or restored to a performance level when prescribed maintenance is performed [5].

Executing for "Operate the System"   The system operators and maintainers execute the functions of operating and maintaining the system solution. The resources are adequately planned and acquired when needed. These individuals are involved in the collection of data to assess whether the system functions in accordance with its intended design. This is unlikely. Instead, trained individuals are assigned to perform periodic evaluations of the system as it operates in its natural environment and to perform the necessary maintenance needed to sustain system performance. Some examples of resource requirements include, but are not limited to, the following:

- Data collection methods
- Data collection equipment
- Personnel resources

Monitoring and Controlling for "Operate the System"   Once a system is operating, it is controlled; that is, its operation is regulated so that it continues to meet expectations [11]. Continual operational evaluation and testing of the system is a method used to identify what is controlled. System audits are also performed. This method is used after the recommended alternative is implemented to see how the actual system performs, whereas an operational evaluation can occur prior to operational implementation and during actual implementation. System improvement relies on the identification of deviations between the actual operation of the system and what is termed as normal or standard. After these deviations are pinpointed, their causes are identified in order to correct malfunctions. Feedback is another valuable tool. Users and maintainers provide feedback about what they like and do not like, which is used during refinement to make changes in the design, leading to upgrades of the system [13].

A set of specific evaluation test requirements and tests are evolved from the objectives and needs determined in the final requirements specifications. Each objective and critical evaluation component is measured by at least one evaluation test instrument. If it is determined that the resulting system product can no longer meet stakeholder needs, the problem enters phase one of the SDP, problem definition, and repeats the procedure set forth in this text.

Curriculum Management System (CMS)—Implementation. When a curriculum management system (CMS) solution was selected by the decision maker (department chair) as a result of earlier analysis, the focus shifted to Solution Implementation. This example describes some of the considerations taken into account by the systems team from a looking forward perspective. The system was successfully implemented on a cloud-based Amazon Web Services (AWSs) platform and was retired from use in 2021, replaced by an enterprise system solution acquired by the Academy.

The CMS project example introduced earlier in the book encompasses the design, development, deployment, training, use, maintenance, improvement, and retirement of the CMS system for the Department of Systems Engineering. The department's Chief Information Officer (CIO) has oversight of this project, and development will take place using a combination of internal IT staff and capstone students. The CIO, with approval from the department head, will schedule a phased development and deployment of the system to support the teaching calendar and ABET accreditation requirements. The goal is to have all components of the system deployed within 13 months in order to support ABET data collection beginning in August 2007.

Deployment during the 2006–2007 academic year will allow the department faculty to learn the system, use it, and provide feedback to the development team as to how it can better support their needs. The development team created a phased project plan using project management software. Their first step was to load all of the functions from functional analysis into the project plan. The next step was to break those functions into phases so that development could proceed in accordance with the academic calendar and ABET requirements. In addition, some functions naturally precede others. For example, the Develop Program function relies on the use of course data. Therefore, it made sense to sequence the Develop Course and Execute Course functions before the Develop Program function.

The Integrate Department Academic Operations function was least critical to ABET assessment, so it was sequenced last. Figure 12.7 shows a breakdown of the project by phases. Once the development team had developed a project plan, they took a detailed look at the Phase I activities and developed a WBS using project management software. They first had to look at each function and identify any additional development tasks needed in order to support implementation of each function. For example, the function Develop Course Strategy required the addition of two supporting tasks: Develop Course-Level Data Tables and Develop Course-Level Portal. Once all tasks were added, they had to be scheduled in order to meet Phase I deployment timelines—to include an acceptance test at the end of Phase I on 1 August 2006. In addition, some tasks required other tasks to be completed before they could be started. In order to implement the task "Develop Interface for Course Objectives," the Develop Course-Level Data Tables task had to be completed so that the objectives could be stored in the database.

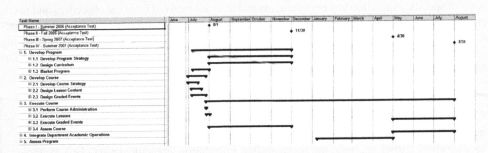

Figure 12.7   CMS project plan by phase.

In order to begin execution of the project plan, the team identified available development resources from the department's internal IT staff and assigned development engineers to the identified tasks. A portion of the resulting WBS with tasks assigned to different developers is shown in Figure 12.8.

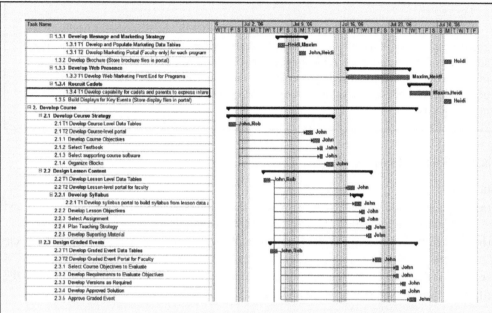

Figure 12.8   Detailed work breakdown structure for Phase I tasks.

The purpose of monitoring and control is to ensure that the system enables execution of the supported functions in accordance with the system design goals and expectations of the stakeholders. In order to monitor the performance of the CMS across all phases of the system life cycle, the development team incorporated three different techniques:

Acceptance testing. At the end of each phase of the development process, the program directors will do acceptance testing of the system to ensure it meets the design requirements specified in the needs analysis. Deficiencies will be noted and corrected. If serious enough, these deficiencies could delay deployment of the system until its performance is acceptable.

Online feedback. The development team will incorporate an online feedback capability for users of the CMS system. At any time, users of the system, including cadets, instructors, and program directors, can follow a link to a free text feedback page that allows them to provide feedback about how the system meets their needs. This feedback will be stored in the system database and reviewed monthly by the development team. Based on that feedback, they can change and update the CMS as required.

Focus groups. At the end of each semester, the development team will conduct a focus group with CMS users in order to get a more structured assessment of how the system is performing in accordance with stakeholder needs. The results of these focus groups will be integrated into the development and maintenance plan.

As the department continues to develop and use the CMS, the assessment feedback will guide decisions about maintaining or upgrading the system. They will also be able to assess adequacy of user training. At some point during the life cycle, information from the assessment process will indicate that the system is beyond its useful life. This will lead to retirement of the CMS and possible development of a new system to perform the curriculum management function.

12.8.4 Check on Learning

Concepts:

(a) Can a system-level solution be a solution that simultaneously addresses subsystems and components needs as well? Can you give an example of this?

(b) Explain the relationship of the Solution Implementation phase and the project life cycle stages.

(c) Why is the Solution Implementation phase considered the most difficult phase of the SDP?

(d) Why is the Initiating Process so important?

Comprehension:

(a) During the Solution Implementation phase, what signifies the completion of the project?

(b) What is a work breakdown structure? Why is it important to a PM?

(c) What is a work breakdown structure? Why is it important to a PM?

(d) What is linear responsibility chart? Why is it important to a PM?

Application:

(a) There are several techniques used to assist in the project manager in developing a project plan. List one method and explain how it works.

REFERENCES

1. (2021) *A Guide to the Project Management Body of Knowledge*, 3rd ed. Newtown Square, PA: Project Management Institute, Inc.

2. Kerzner, H. (2006) *Project Management: A Systems Approach to Planning, Scheduling, and Controlling*, 9th ed. Hoboken, NJ: John Wiley & Sons, Inc.

3. Meredith, J.R., Mantel, S.J. (2018) *Project Management*. New York: John Wiley & Sons, Inc.

4. van Gigch, J.P. (1991) *System Design Modeling and Metamodeling*. New York: Plenum Press.

5. Mantel, S.J., Jr., Meredith, J.R., Shafer, S.M., Sutton, M.M. (2001) *Project Management in Practice*. Hoboken, NJ: John Wiley & Sons, Inc.

6. Forsberg, K., Mooz, H., Cotterman, H. (2000) *Visualizing Project Management*, 2nd ed. New York: John Wiley & Sons, Inc.

7. Smith, P.G., Reinertsen, D.G. (1998) *Developing Products in Half the Time*, 2nd ed. New York: John Wiley & Sons, Inc.

8. Fisk, E.R., Rapp, R.R. (2004) *Engineering Construction Inspection*. Hoboken, NJ: John Wiley & Sons, Inc.

9. Palmer, D. (2006) *Maintenance Planning and Scheduling Handbook*, 2nd ed. New York: McGraw-Hill.

10. Eisner, H. (2002) *Essentials of Project and Systems Engineering Management*, 2nd ed. New York: John Wiley & Sons, Inc.

11. Athey, T.H. (1992) *Systematic Systems Approach: An Integrated Method for Solving Problems*. Boston, MA: Pearson Custom Publishing.

12. Sage, A.P., Armstrong, J.E. Jr. (2000) *Introduction to Systems Engineering*. New York: John Wiley & Sons, Inc.

13. Buede, D.M. (2000) *The Engineering Design of Systems: Models and Methods*. New York: John Wiley & Sons, Inc.

Chapter 13

Epilogue-Professional Practice

The system votes last.

—Jack Clemons, Lockheed Martin Corp.

13.1 INTRODUCTION

Systems Engineering as a discipline was introduced in Section 1.2 with many of the tasks and responsibilities as a member of a systems team described throughout the book. Given the proliferation of systems in today's world, all engineered to provide some function for humans or the things that humans value, it is becoming difficult to pigeonhole what a systems engineer (SE) is, and indeed, what a systems project team gets involved with on a day-to-day basis. This chapter is focused on the system engineer in practice: his or her place in the organization, responsibilities, and specific activities and tasks, so as to convey what it is like to be an SE. There are also some useful references addressing important aspects of an SE's job that are beyond the scope of this book. This section discusses the job in general, including the title and the organizational placement.

 The typical job for a professional systems engineer is technical integrator supporting a Program Manager who is developing a complex system.

Decision Making in Systems Engineering and Management, Third Edition.
Patrick J. Driscoll, Gregory S. Parnell, and Dale L. Henderson
© 2023 John Wiley & Sons, Inc. Published 2023 by John Wiley & Sons, Inc.

Typically, a professional SE works for a Chief SE, who in turn works for a Program Manager. The SE is the technical interface with clients, users, and consumers, and is often the one responsible for building a systems team to support a systems project. The team will without question adopt an attitude concerning the challenge (good or bad) that usually lasts throughout the team's life cycle. A good attitude regardless of the challenge is a big contributor to success because of the vast array of stakeholders the systems team, and in particular the lead SE, must interact with (Figure 13.1).

The SE has roles and responsibilities, and ideally has certain personal characteristics that contribute significantly to success. The specific activities that an SE performs are distributed (non-uniformly) over the system life cycle. Throughout this chapter, the acronym "SE" will be used to describe both a systems engineer and the discipline of systems engineering. The distinction will be clear from the context within which the acronym is used.

The systems engineering job. Anyone in any walk of life can use systems thinking to find good solutions to complex problems in a technological setting. To some extent, any professional engineer will use systems considerations to determine the requirements for a system that he or she is designing, to define its interfaces with other systems, and to evaluate how well it is performing. However, in professional practice some people are given specific big-picture engineering responsibilities for a system or group of systems. These people have "SE" in their job title or job description, and they are responsible for making sure that the technical efforts of everyone involved work together to produce an operational system that meets all requirements.

For instance, a team developing a new helicopter will include mechanical engineers to make sure all the moving parts work together, aeronautical engineers to make sure the vehicle

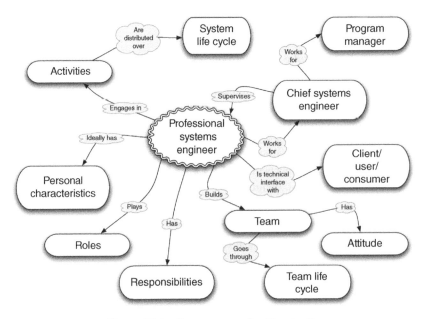

Figure 13.1 Concept map for Chapter 7.

flies, electrical engineers to make sure the control systems work, software engineers to make sure the onboard computer systems operate properly, and many other discipline or specialty engineers: reliability engineers, test engineers, human factors engineers, and so on. It is the SE who takes the overall view and is responsible for ensuring that all these engineers work together at the technical level to produce a system that meets the customer's needs. This chapter is about what these professional SEs actually do.

The International Council on Systems Engineering (INCOSE) has produced a *Systems Engineering Handbook* [1] that covers much of the material of this chapter in more detail, but in condensed handbook form for practitioners.

Three systems engineering perspectives. There are three perspectives on the practice of systems engineering: the organization's, the system's, and the individual's. The organization is interested in the process and what people do, and in meeting customer needs and expectations. However, equally as important is the point of view of the system: the product and its development throughout its life cycle. This is a long-term point of view, concerned with the design, manufacture, test, deployment, and operation of the system, regardless of the developing organization. Finally, the individual SE has a different perspective, concerned with the here and now, tasks and responsibilities, and getting the job done. This chapter stresses the organizational perspective and also describes the system and individual perspectives as they relate to the engineering organization.

Organizational placement of systems engineers. A civil or mechanical engineer sometimes works on his or her own, doing small design projects for individual customers. Such an engineer can also work for a small engineering company that takes on contracts to build bridges, levees, industrial facilities, and so on. In contrast, most SEs work for larger companies, because those are the companies that take on complex projects that cannot be done without a systems approach. The SE will be a part of a team developing a complex system such as an aircraft or a telecommunications network, or perhaps he or she will be in a systems engineering staff overseeing a number of smaller projects. If an SE works for a small company, it is generally a consulting firm whose clients are large companies or government agencies seeking advice on how to develop or acquire major complex systems.

The organizational placement of SEs can vary widely based on the scale and complexity of the system involved and on the technical practices of the organization. For a major system such as an enterprise software system, a global positioning satellite (GPS) system, an aircraft, or a spacecraft, where the development cost is hundreds of millions of dollars or more, there will often be a dedicated chief SE who reports to the program manager (PM). This chief SE may have a staff of SEs working for him or her, especially early in system development when key decisions about system architecture and system requirements are made. In this case, SE can refer to a functional organization. The chief SE may also be given responsibility for technical specialists, such as configuration management (CM) personnel. For a smaller system, there may be a chief SE working with a smaller staff, or even working alone as an advisor to the PM on overall technical integration of the program. Sometimes the PM him or herself is also designated as the program SE. If the organization is responsible for a family of relatively small systems, such as a set of communications or electronic devices, there may be a single SE with technical oversight for all of them.

13.2 SYSTEMS ENGINEERING ACTIVITIES

 An SE coordinates technical efforts over the lifetime of the system, but he or she is usually busiest toward the beginning, when he or she helps to define system requirements, develop the system concept, and coordinate and integrate the efforts of the other design engineers.

Whether a system is large or small, its development will go through a series of system life cycle stages (described in Chapter 1). The execution of the fundamental SE tasks (described throughout the book) will be distributed in a sequence of activities during these stages. The distribution is not uniform. A task such as "Use an interdisciplinary approach ... " applies constantly throughout the system life cycle, but "Convert customer needs ... " is predominantly in the early stages, and "Lead the requirements analysis ... " has peaks of activity both early, when system requirements are established, and later, during systems test, when proper function at the system level is verified. The SE's changing set of activities during these life cycle stages can be described as follows. Table 13.1 summarizes them.

TABLE 13.1 Summary of Systems Engineering Activities during a Systems Life Cycle.

Life Cycle Stage	Major SE Activities
Establish System Need	Stakeholder interaction (especially users)
	Requirements definition
	Functional analysis
Develop System Concept	Stakeholder interaction (especially users)
	Team building
	Requirements analysis and management
	Architectural tradeoff studies
	Definition of system architecture, elements, boundaries, and interfaces
	Creation of systems engineering master plan
Design and Develop the System	Stakeholder interaction (especially users)
	Interface control
	Overall design coordination
	Requirements analysis and management
	Configuration control
	Specialty engineering
	Coordinating major design reviews
	System testing
Produce System	Coordination with production engineers
	System development and testing
Deploy System	Coordinating deployment with users and other stakeholders
Operate System	Gathering data on system performance and user feedback
	Coordinating problem resolutions and system upgrades
Retire System	Coordinating hand-off of mission to replacement system
	Coordinating system disposal

Establish system need. Stakeholder interaction is a key role for SEs during this stage. The SE will talk to the stakeholders, paying special attention to consumers of the system's products and services, the system users, and to the system owner, in order to understand and document the needs that are driving the system development. For instance, if the system is a passenger aircraft, the consumer is the airline passenger, the user is the aircrew, and the owner is the airline. The SE will use the needs to identify the system functions and define the specific technical requirements for the system. The SE often acts as an interface between the consumer or user and the designer. He or she translates between "consumer-speak" or "user-speak" and "engineer-speak" and makes sure they understand each other correctly. The result is usually a formal statement of the system's form, fit, and function, agreed to in writing by all parties. After this stage, the SE continues to manage the requirements, ensuring no change without sufficient cause and agreement by all parties.

Develop system concept. At this point, the need is established and a project initialized, and the SEs play perhaps their most important role. In the organizational dimension, this is a time of team building, organization, and planning. This is when people are recruited, background research in the problem area is done, key tasks identified, and a preliminary schedule created. At the technical level, the SE continues to manage and refine the system requirements. The SE also examines different candidate system architectures and helps make the selection of the one to be pursued. This crucial process is described in more detail in Section 13.5; it includes identifying system functions, system boundaries, and major system elements, and defining their interfaces. A Systems Engineering Management Plan (SEMP) may also be written during this stage, to plan SE activities for the rest of the system's life cycle. A Test and Evaluation Master Plan (TEMP) may be written to describe how testers will ensure that the finished system meets requirements.

Design and develop the system. Detailed design is primarily the responsibility of discipline-specific engineers, but the SE also has a role to ensure system-level requirements are met. The SE maintains technical cognizance over the whole program to ensure that all elements will work together as they should. The SE often coordinates interfaces between system elements and between the system and its environment. Often these interfaces will be defined in a set of interface control documents (ICDs), which will be under configuration control, meaning that they can be changed only after review by the SE and approval by a Configuration Control Board (CCB). The ICDs will define the interfaces exactly, often in mind-numbing detail. For instance, the ICD for a data exchange will identify each data field, the type of data in it, the units of measurement, the number of characters, and so forth. An SE is also often involved in specialty engineering such as reliability, maintainability, and usability (see Section 13.5 and Chapter 8 for more on specialty engineering and its role in SE). When it is time to integrate the various elements and test them at the system level, the SE is usually in charge. He or she will be involved in planning, executing, and evaluating operational tests, in which test personnel not involved in system development use the system under field conditions. This is the second peak of activity for fundamental systems engineering Task 3 as described in Chapter 6: the time when the SE ensures system validation and successful system realization.

Produce system. The SE may be involved in the production plan and in monitoring performance to ensure that the system is built as designed. During this stage, the SE plays a key role in the analysis and approval of engineering change proposals and block upgrades.

Deploy system. The SE will help plan the deployment to ensure that all operability needs are met.

Operate system. The SE examines how well the system meets the consumers' needs, users' needs, and the client's expectations. This often involves gathering data and feedback from the consumers and users after the system is deployed. These provide input for deciding on modifications for future systems, problem fixes or upgrades for systems already in use, and improvements on systems engineering practices.

Retire system. The SE ensures that system retirement and disposal are properly planned for and executed.

13.3   WORKING WITH THE SYSTEMS DEVELOPMENT TEAM

Because of their wide responsibilities, SEs often find themselves working with a wide variety of other professionals, who may have widely varying engineering expertise. The following sections sketch out how an individual SE typically works with other professionals. Of course, people do not always fill these roles as a full-time job, though the larger the program, the more likely that they will. These relationships are summarized in Table 13.2.

The SE and the program manager. Broadly speaking, every project or program will have a manager who has overall responsibility for both technical and business success. In private organizations, the PM is responsible for making sure that the program makes money for the company. In public organizations, the PM is responsible for making sure the program provides the product or service for a given budget. This is the most responsible job in the program. The chief SE is the PM's chief advisor on overall technical aspects of the program, and the SE staff provides system integration for the PM. Table 13.3 compares the responsibilities of the PM and the SE.

The SE and the client, the user, and the consumer. The client pays to develop the system, the user operates it, and the consumer receives products or services from it. These may not be the same individuals, or even in the same organization. For instance, in Army acquisition the customer is a PM in Army Material Command stationed at a place like Redstone Arsenal in Alabama, whereas the user and the consumer may be soldiers in the field. For an information technology (IT) system, the client may be an IT organization within a company, whereas the consumers may be the clients of the company and the users may be distributed throughout the company's other divisions. Clients, users, and consumers are all critically important, but by definition the client has control over the acquisition process. The PM is responsible for relations with the client and the SE is the PM's primary advisor on technical issues in that relationship. The SE is also responsible for coordinating relationships with consumers and users, especially developing system requirements that take into account consumer and user needs and desires. This process is much easier if the client has good relations with the consumers and users.

The SE and the CTO or CIO. A company oriented toward research, technology, or systems development may designate a high-level executive to have responsibility for technical issues such as research and development and strategic technical direction. This person is often called the chief technology officer (CTO). The CTO is responsible for using technology to achieve the organization's mission. The exact scope of responsibilities varies widely from company to company, and some high-tech companies do not use this title. The CTO's role is somewhat like that of an SE for the entire company as a single enterprise. Other companies designate an executive as chief information officer (CIO), who will be responsible for the company's information strategy and for information technology systems to achieve the organization's mission.

TABLE 13.2   Summary of Program Roles in Relation to the Systems Engineer.

Individual	Basic Responsibility	Provides to SE	Receives from SE
Program Manager (PM)	Business and technical management of program	Program direction	Technical advice
Customer	Acquire the best system for his or her organization	System requirements	Technical information and recommendations
User	Operate the system	System requirements	Technical information and recommendations
CTO or CIO	Coordinate a company's technology policy and/or information systems	Guidance and cooperation	Technical information
Operations Researcher or System Analyst	Mathematical modeling to support decision making	Well-supported technical recommendation	Tasking for trade studies and analyses
Configuration Manager	Ensure no changes occur without agreed level of review	Assurance	Cooperation
Life Cycle Cost Estimator	Estimate system costs	Cost information	Technical information
Engineering Manager	Appropriate engineering processes	Well-managed discipline engineering	Cooperation
Discipline Engineer	Detailed design	Sound design and interface requirements	System architecture
Test Engineer	Ensure materials, components, elements, or systems meet specifications and requirements	Test results	Requirements
Specialty Engineer	Ensure system meets requirements in area of specialization	Specialized expertise	Requirements
Industrial Engineer	Technical operation of industrial plant	Efficient plant	Coordination
Quality Assurance	Ensure that manufacture and test is performed as intended	Assurance	Cooperation

TABLE 13.3   Comparison of the Program Manager and the Systems Engineer [2].

Domain	Program Manager	Systems Engineer
Risk	Manages risk / Sets guidelines	Develops risk management process / Analyzes risk
Changes	Controls change	Analyzes changes / Manages configuration
Outside Interfaces	Primary customer interface	Primary user interface
Internal Interfaces	Primary internal management interface	Primary internal technical interface
Resources	Provides and manages resources	Delineates needs / Uses resources

Source: Harris and Moran [2]/John Wiley & Sons.

The SE and the operations researcher or system analyst. These specialties involve studying existing or proposed systems and environments and evaluating system performance. They are sometimes regarded as part of systems engineering, though their emphasis is on mathematical and computer-based modeling and simulation (see Chapter 4) and not on such SE activities as managing user interfaces, requirements definition and allocation, and system performance verification. These individuals specialize in answering quantitative questions about complex systems, and they are often invaluable in making a sound and defensible decision when there is a lot at stake and the best course of action is not clear.

The SE and the configuration manager. CM is the process of ensuring that things do not change without due review and approval and without all stakeholders being aware of the change and its implications. This includes key documents, such as those that describe system requirements, design, and interfaces, as well as the actual physical configuration of the system being built. Experience has shown that without strong CM discipline, people will have good ideas that cause them to introduce small changes into the system, and these changes will accumulate and cause chaos later when everyone has a slightly different version of the system. Typically, detailed configuration is under the control of the design engineer early in the design process. At some point the design is brought under configuration control, and after that any change requires paperwork, reviews, signatures, and approval by a CCB that is often chaired by the PM. The configuration manager administers this paperwork process. It is not a romantic job, but it is absolutely essential in developing a system of any significant complexity. In some organizations CM is part of the SE shop; in others it reports independently to the PM.

The SE and the life-cycle cost analyst. The PM is deeply concerned with system costs in both the near and far terms, because costs help determine system viability and profitability. The total cost of a system over its entire life cycle is especially important. This includes costs to design, build, test, deploy, operate, service, repair, upgrade, and finally dispose of the system. Cost analysts have their own methods, models, and databases that they use to help estimate total life-cycle cost (see Chapter 8). Some of these methods are empirical or economic in nature; others are technical, and the SE can expect to be involved in them. Since life-cycle cost is a system-level criterion of great interest to the PM, the SE will want to use life-cycle cost as a key consideration in all systems decisions.

The SE and the engineering manager. An engineering manager (EM) is in charge of a group of engineers. He or she is concerned with ensuring that sound engineering methods are used, as well as performing the usual personnel management functions. To the extent that sound engineering always involves some element of a systems perspective, an EM will also be involved in promoting systems engineering. However, an EM's basic responsibility is sound discipline-specific engineering. When a functional or matrix organization is used, the EM may be in charge of engineers working on many different programs and systems, so his or her system perspective may be weaker than the cognizant SE. In contrast, the SE is primarily a technology leader, integrator, coordinator, and advisor.

The SE and the discipline engineer. The term "discipline engineer" refers to a focused engineering professional working as a mechanical engineer, civil engineer, electrical engineer, aerospace engineer, software engineer, chemical engineer, environmental engineer, information security engineer, and so forth. These engineers design things, and they are responsible for every detail of what they design. In contrast, an SE is responsible for the high-level structure of a system, and at some level of detail he turns it over to the appropriate discipline engineer for completion. Frequently an SE starts out professionally as a discipline engineer and moves into systems work as his or her career progresses. This provides a useful background that enables the SE to work with other engineers, particularly in his or her original discipline. However, the SE must have (or develop) the knack for dealing with experts in fields other than his or her own. He must convince them that he can grasp the essentials of a sound argument in the expert's field. Also, the SE often spends a great deal of time translating what the user or consumer says into precise language that the design engineer can use, and translating what the design engineer says into language that the user or consumer can understand.

The SE and the test engineer. Testing can occur at the material, component, element, system, or architecture level. System test is usually considered a systems engineering responsibility, and elements that are complex enough to be treated as systems in themselves may also be given to SEs to test. An engineer who specializes in system test is a specialized SE; other test engineers specialize in material or component testing, and they are considered specialty engineers.

The SE and the specialty engineer. Specialty engineers are those who concentrate on one aspect of design engineering, such as human factors, reliability, maintainability, or information assurance (see Section 13.5 for a longer list). Sometimes these specialties are collectively referred to as *systems effectiveness* or "the ilities." These specialties require a systems outlook, though they are narrower in focus than general systems engineering. An SE should have a basic understanding and appreciation of these specialty engineering disciplines. In a large program, there may be one or more engineers specializing in each of these areas, and they may be organized separately or within a systems engineering office.

The SE and the industrial engineer. An industrial engineer (IE) can be regarded as an SE for an industrial operation, such as a manufacturing plant. An IE's responsibilities might include facility layout, operation scheduling, and materials ordering policies. Other IEs design efficient processes for service industries; yet others deal with human factors in commercial operations. A program SE can expect to interact with a plant IE when working out producibility and related issues. Industrial Engineering as an academic discipline predates the emergence of SE, and many universities teach both in the same department because of the related history and substantial overlap in material.

The SE and quality assurance. Quality assurance (QA) means making sure an item is produced exactly as it was designed. In many organizations, there is a separate QA organization that reports directly to a high-level manager. QA personnel are not concerned directly with engineering, but with process. They ensure that all checks are made, that all necessary reviews are completed, and that all required steps are executed. QA personnel provide an important independent check to ensure that the fabrication and test process was executed exactly as the engineers intended. A QA person may carry a personal stamp to apply to paperwork to verify that it has been reviewed and that all necessary signatures are on it. That QA stamp will be required before work can proceed to the next step.

13.4 BUILDING AN INTERDISCIPLINARY TEAM

Systems engineers often form and lead interdisciplinary teams to tackle particular problems.

Because of their role as both leader and integrator, SEs often find themselves in the organizational role of assembling teams of people from various backgrounds to work on a particular task or project. The SE must identify early on the people with the best mix of skills to work the given problem. The team membership will vary by the nature of the problem. The team may include electrical, mechanical, and civil engineers; it can also include architects, computer or political scientists, lawyers, doctors, and economists. Technical skills are only a part of the mix.

13.4.1   Team Fundamentals

Figure 13.2 shows the key ingredients and products of a successful team. The vertices of the triangle show the products of a successful team. The sides and inner triangles describe what it takes to make the results happen. In *The Wisdom of Teams* [3], Katzenbach and Smith stress that the performance ethic of the team, comprising accountability and commitment, is essential for team success. They build on this to create a definition that distinguishes a team from "a mere group of people with a common assignment."

13.4.2   Definition

A team is a small number of people with complementary skills who are committed to a common purpose, performance goals, and approach for which they hold themselves mutually accountable.

Each member of the team must understand and be committed to the answers to three fundamental questions:

1. Why are we here?
2. What are we to accomplish?
3. What does success look like, and how will we know when we get there?

The answers to these questions will differ based on the type of team assembled.

Figure 13.2   Fundamentals of a successful team. Source: Katzenbach and Smith [3].

13.4.3   Team Attitude

It is vital that team members have an attitude that "only the team can succeed or fail." This is difficult to foster in an ad hoc team drawn from many sources. Members not fully assimilated into the team may have a loyalty to their home organization and seek what is best for their constituency. A key to building an effective SE team is to assemble the complete team early, rather than adding members over the life of the project. This encourages cooperation, buy-in, and a sense of ownership early by everyone. A common occurrence is the addition of expertise such as finance or marketing during later stages, when their contribution is more directly related. However, this often leads to a feeling of outsider-ship that can result in lackluster enthusiasm, if not outright sabotage.

13.4.4   Team Selection

Building and managing a successful team requires several up-front decisions by the lead systems engineer [4]:

- What is the right mix of skills and power level? Should members represent a spectrum of rank and authority to promote varied viewpoints, or should the power level be the same to avoid undue influence by superiors?
- What attitude toward collaboration and problem solving is required?
- How much time is available?
- How well defined must the problem be to fully engage team members?

Team life cycle. The SE must evaluate the impact of the team as it works through the problem. Katzenbach and Smith [3] designed the team performance curve shown in Figure 13.3 to illustrate how well various teams achieve their goals.

A working group relies on the sum of the individual "bests" for their performance. Members share information, best practices, or perspectives to make decisions to help each individual perform within his or her area of responsibility. Pseudo-teams are teams in name only and are not focused on the collective performance. Katzenbach and Smith rate their performance impact below that of work groups because their interactions detract from other individual performances without delivering any

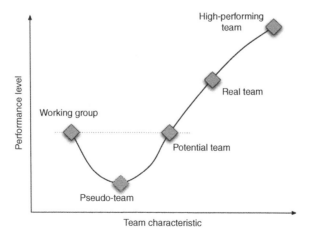

Figure 13.3   Team performance curve. Source: Katzenbach and Smith [3].

joint benefit. Potential teams have significant incremental performance and are trying to improve their impact. However, they have not yet established collective accountability. Their performance impact is about the same as a working group. Real teams are those that meet the definition of a small number of people with complementary skills who are equally committed to a common purpose, goals, and a working approach for which they hold themselves mutually accountable. Teams with the highest performance impact, high-performance teams, are those that are *real teams*, and their members are also deeply committed to one another's personal growth and success. That commitment usually transcends teams.

13.4.5   Cross-cultural Teams

A word is in order about the special problems of teams with members from different ethnic, national, or religious cultures. Such teams are becoming more and more common as professionals from all countries become more mobile, as more international projects are undertaken, and as "virtual teams" that interact only electronically become more common. Even men and women from the same culture can sometimes have different behavioral expectations. If team members are not used to working with people from the other cultures on the team, misunderstandings can arise that interfere with team formation. Different cultures have different customs governing how business is done, including norms on very basic things, such as the following:

- How close two people should stand when speaking together?
- What physical contact is appropriate between colleagues of the same or of the opposite sex?
- How one should dress in the workplace?
- How much privacy one should expect?
- How much organizational structure is needed?
- How many pleasantries must be exchanged before getting to business?
- How frank or tactful one should be when expressing dissatisfaction?
- How much deference should be shown to those in authority?
- How much individual ambition it is appropriate to express?
- What kind of humor is acceptable?
- How diligent one must be when on the job?
- How scrupulously honest one must be in matters small and great?

Cultural norms like these generally operate in the background. At first, many people are hardly aware that they are only the customs of the people they grew up with and not the universal rules of decent behavior. They can be unaware of how behavior that seems to them entirely normal and ordinary can be considered offensive according to other cultural norms. This is certainly true of some Americans, and it is equally true of some from Asia, Africa, Europe, Latin America, and every other place in the world.

Fortunately, if one is aware of the potential for misunderstanding and has a little bit of goodwill, these problems are not too hard to avoid, especially among the well-educated people likely to be on engineering teams. The important point here is to be aware of the potential problems due to cultural differences, to maintain a spirit of forbearance and understanding, and to be a good listener. Also, keep in mind that there is a lot of variation between individuals from the same culture, so not everyone will behave as one might expect based solely on their background. Harris and Moran [2] provide a text for those who want to better understand cultural issues and develop cross-cultural teamwork skills.

13.5 SYSTEMS ENGINEERING RESPONSIBILITIES

 Common specific assigned responsibilities of SEs include writing a systems engineering management plan, external technical interface, requirements analysis, requirements management, system architecting, interface control, writing a test and evaluation master plan, configuration management, specialty engineering, coordinating technical reviews, and system integration and test.

From the point of view of the individual, the following are the specific responsibilities that are often assigned to an SE. From the point of view of the organization, these are the tasks that the systems engineering office will accomplish.

13.5.1 Systems Engineering Management Plan (SEMP)

In a major project, an SEMP (often pronounced as one syllable: "semp") should be written when the system concept is defined but before design starts. This document describes how the ideal systems engineering process is going to be tailored for the problem at hand, and it is the basis for all technical planning. It relates technical management to program management, provides a technical management framework, sets coordination requirements and methods, and establishes control processes. It is a communication vehicle that lets the client, users, consumers, and everyone on the project know how systems engineering will be carried out. The SEMP is a living document that can be modified from time to time as circumstances change. A typical SEMP might contain the following:

- Description of the envisioned development process and system life cycle
- SE activities in each envisioned phase
- Participants and involved organizations
- Planned major system reviews, audits, and other control points, including success criteria
- Products and documentation to be produced by the SE
- Risk management plan
- System requirements, including method of testing
- Identification of key measures of technical progress
- Plan for managing internal and external interfaces, both physical and functional
- Description of any trade studies planned
- Integration plan for CM, QA, system effectiveness engineering, and other specialties, as required

13.5.2 Technical Interface with Users and Consumers

SEs will usually be charged with user and consumer relationships as described earlier. The SE will meet with the user and consumer, travel to their locations, conduct interviews, focus groups, or surveys, and do whatever else is required to ensure that the users' and consumers' needs and desires are captured. The SE will be responsible for ensuring that the written system requirements truly describe what the user and consumer need with sufficient precision to design the system, and with sufficient accuracy that a system that meets the requirements will also meet the needs. The SE also has to interpret engineering constraints for nontechnical stakeholders, so that they can understand when a particular requirement should perhaps be relaxed because of its disproportionate effect on system cost, reliability, or other criterion.

13.5.3   Analysis and Management of Systems Requirements

In any major system development, the SE should be in charge of the system requirements, and those requirements should be written down in a document that only the CCB can change. These requirements define what the system needs to do and be in order to succeed. They can determine whether or not a billion-dollar contract has been properly executed and how much (if anything) the contractor will be paid.

There is an important tradeoff in determining requirements. Typically, if the performance requirements are set at the high level that users and customers would like, the resulting system will be too expensive, unreliable, or both. If the requirements are set too low, the system may not perform well enough to be worth building. Ultimately, it is the PM's responsibility to make a requirements tradeoff between cost and performance while remaining cognizant of schedule. It is the SE's responsibility to make sure the PM understands the consequences and risks of the decision. A common approach is to establish both *threshold* requirements, which must be met to have a worthwhile system, and *goal* (or objective) requirements, which represent a challenging but feasible level of higher performance.

Requirements development should start with customer requirements that describe what is expected from the system by the operator, the client, and other stakeholders. These requirements should cover where and how the system will be used, in what environments, what its minimum performance should be, how long the system life cycle should last, and so forth. Requirements can start with a high-level objective such as, "We're going to land a man on the moon and return him safely to Earth." Analysis of such high-level requirements will produce *functional requirements* for such things as rocket propulsion, temperature control, breathable atmosphere, and communications. *Non-functional requirements* may specify criteria that will be used to judge the system but are not related to specific functional behaviors, for instance color, finish, or packaging. *Performance requirements* will specify how well or to what level functional requirements have to be performed, for instance speed in knots, availability in percent, or reliability as a probability.

Further analysis of a moon mission requirement will produce requirements for a launch vehicle, a command module, a lunar lander, and so forth. At the lowest level there will be *design requirements* describing exactly what must be built, coded, or bought. High-level requirements should not vary with the implementation, but as detail increases the requirements become more and more dependent on the particular technical design chosen. For instance, a lunar mission going directly to the Moon's surface without a rendezvous in lunar orbit would not have separate requirements for a command module and a lander. The value measures identified in the systems decision process (see Chapter 10) are natural bases for system-level requirements, if they are direct and natural measures suitable for formal testing.

Requirements that come from an analysis of other requirements, rather than directly from an analysis of what the system must do and be, are called *derived requirements*. One kind of derived requirement is an *allocated requirement*, which is laid upon a subsystem to partially

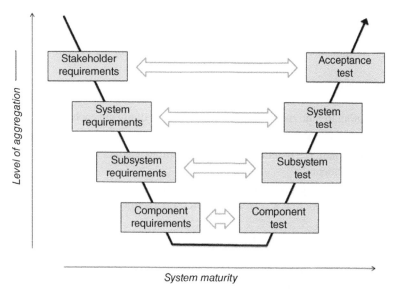

Figure 13.4 A systems engineering "V". Source: Hull et al. [5]/Springer Nature.

fulfill a higher-level requirement. For instance, two subsystems may have allocated reliability requirements of 0.9 and 0.8 in order to meet a system reliability requirement of 0.72.

The SE has the job of documenting both high-level and derived system requirements, at least down to a certain level of detail. One common way to visualize the process is the "Systems Engineering V," an example of which is shown in Figure 13.4. The highest level requirements should be written in language that the important stakeholders can readily understand, and they may be tested in an acceptance test. From these the SE may derive system requirements that are in engineering language and which will be tested at the system level. Further analysis may derive subsystem requirements, or may allocate system requirements directly to subsystems, and the subsystems will be tested in integration tests. At the lowest level are component requirements and testing. Thus, a requirement to go to the Moon leads to a requirement for a booster with a certain performance, which leads to a requirement for a rocket motor of a certain power, which leads to a requirement for a rocket nozzle with certain characteristics. At the lower levels, the design and requirements allocation will be in the hands of discipline engineers, but the SE will have oversight of the integrity of requirements traceability.

Requirements can be of different types (sometimes overlapping):

- Customer requirements, which describe what the client expects
- Functional requirements, which define what the system has to do
- Non-function requirements, which specify criteria not related to system behavior
- Performance requirements, which specify in engineering units how well the functions have to be performed
- Constraint requirements, which describe the constraints under which the performance needs to be demonstrated
- Design requirements, which specify in detail what is to be built, coded, or bought
- Derived requirements, which are developed from higher-level requirements

- Allocated requirements, which are derived from a higher-level requirement and assigned to a subsystem
- Physical requirements, which give the form, fit, and finish of the system

The SE should ensure all requirements are:

- Unique, meaning that no two requirements overlap or duplicate each other
- Unambiguous, so that there can be no misunderstanding of exactly what is required
- Testable, so that there is a practical way of determining whether the delivered system actually meets the requirement
- Traceable, so that every high-level requirement is met by one or more low-level testable requirements, and every low-level requirement supports a documented high-level requirement

Once set, requirements should be changed only with extreme reluctance. Fluctuating requirements typically waste effort by requiring redesigns; they also promote integration problems when the full implications of the change are not grasped at first. It is also common for stakeholders to come late to the process with new requirements, leading to "requirements creep" that accumulates until the system becomes unaffordable or unworkable. The resulting schedule and cost impacts have led to the demise of many programs. Later chapters in this book present techniques for requirements analysis and trade studies. These techniques include functional analysis (for functional requirements), screening criteria (for performance requirements), and value modeling (for goal requirements). These are described in Chapters 10 and 11 and their use is illustrated in Chapter 12. For the most complicated systems, requirements engineering can become a discipline of its own. See Hull, Jackson, and Dick [5] and Laplante [6] for in-depth treatments of requirements analysis.

13.5.4   System Architecting

This is the first stage in establishing the design for a complex system. For example, in the Apollo program, the decision to use one launch vehicle to put an entire mission into Earth orbit, rather than two launches with an Earth orbit rendezvous, was an architectural decision. So was the decision to have a separate lander to go from lunar orbit to the surface and back, rather than landing the entire spacecraft. These crucial decisions have to be made early in the design process. Making them wisely requires the participation of the best SEs, supported by the best discipline engineers and other specialists to provide expertise in their particular areas.

The first step in deciding on a system architecture is a functional analysis (see Chapter 10). A function is a task, action, or activity that the system must perform in order to accomplish its purpose. For a complex system, the SEs will be tasked to identify all system functions, analyze them to identify all required subfunctions, and develop a hierarchical functional architecture that documents them all. A function is identified using a verb and object. This may require block diagrams, data flow diagrams, state transition diagrams, and so forth, depending on the nature and complexity of the system.

The second step is to define the major elements or subsystems of the system. This is the point where a particular solution starts to be defined. The decisions made here will have a fundamental effect on the outcome of the design, so they should be made very carefully. The SE defines the system boundary (see Chapter 2), that is, what is to be regarded as part of the system being designed and what is part of the environment. For instance, in designing a cargo ship, the freight handling in ports could be defined as part of the system and subject to redesign, or as part of the environment that constrains the ship design. The SE defines the interface between the system and its environment, for instance, by defining the port facilities a ship must be able to use.

The SEs help conceptualize and analyze various system concepts to meet the need. Tools for conceptual systems design are described in Chapter 5. SEs, along with relevant discipline engineers, can expect to put much effort into architectural design trade studies during this step. In these studies, they will develop models of different system architectures and evaluate how well they will be able to meet system requirements. A complex system may consist of many different physical elements in different locations, as a spacecraft system might include ground stations, communications relay stations, a mission control center, a satellite, and a launch vehicle. In other cases, a system may contain subsystems or elements that are primarily the domain of one engineering discipline, as a helicopter might have a power system, flight control system, electrical system, and data processing system. The SE is responsible for identifying such major elements and defining their relationships. To the greatest extent possible, the architecture should be selected such that each system requirement can be allocated to exactly one element. The final architecture is often documented in a hierarchical diagram called a work breakdown structure (WBS), which provides the framework for subsequent breakouts of tasks on the project.

The third and final step in system architecting is functional allocation. The system requirements are allocated to the architecture elements. Element interactions and interfaces are defined. External interfaces (between system elements and the environment) are also defined. System elements are turned over to discipline engineers for further design work, or to SEs for elements that themselves are unusually complex or require the integration of different engineering disciplines. Architecting has become a subdiscipline of its own. There are several good texts that give extended advice on how to do it, including Maier and Rechtin [7].

13.5.5 Systems Engineering Tools and Formal Models

Some projects use standard description and documentation models, sometimes software-based. An SE will usually be responsible for creating and maintaining such models. Some projects use a standard format, such as the Department of Defense Architecture Framework, or DoDAF [8]. Such a standard framework eases communication and defines several standard ways to view the system description, e.g. from the point of view of capabilities, operations, functions, or schedules. Many projects use a commercial software product to manage requirements and system models; examples are *CORE*® [9] from Vitech Corporation and *Rational DOORS*® [10] from IBM. These tools can be complicated to use and require a good deal of training and experience, but they automate much of the tedious record keeping and consistency checking that the SE would otherwise have to do by hand. They keep track of dependencies and interaction, making it easier to determine the effect of a change in one part of the system. They ensure that a requirements of configuration change made in one place is also reflected everywhere else. They can produce a draft of a System Requirements Document and other standard documents, while ensuring that they are all consistent with each other.

13.5.6 Interface Control Documents (ICDs)

The interactions between system elements and between the system and its environment are recorded in ICDs, which are the responsibilities of SEs and configuration managers to write and to update as required, as described in Section 13.2. This is often one of the SE's major tasks during much of the system development period, after system architecting is complete and before system test starts, when much of the technical effort is in the hands of discipline engineers.

13.5.7 Test and Evaluation Master Plan (TEMP)

This document is sometimes assigned to the SE to write, and sometimes to a separate test organization. It describes all testing to be done on the project, from part and component test, to development testing of new element designs to evaluate how well they work, to systems testing of the entire system under field conditions to demonstrate that it meets user needs (see Figure 13.4). The more complex the system, the earlier it should be written.

13.5.8 Configuration Management (CM)

The role of CM has been described previously in Section 13.3. CM gains control of the major documents described earlier, the SEMP, the TEMP, and the ICDs, after the SE has written the initial versions and they are accepted by the CCB. The CCB will control many other documents, some of which will be written by SEs and some of which will only be reviewed by SEs.

13.5.9 Specialty Engineering

It is common for specialists in the some or all of following areas to be part of the systems engineering organization, reporting to the chief SE. They are responsible for reviewing the entire design and development process for the impact on their areas of responsibility, and for recommending areas for improvement.

- *Risk management.* Systems that have a significant chance of total failure commonly have one or more engineers dedicated to risk management. Such systems include spacecraft, high-tech military systems, and complex systems using cutting-edge technology. Risk cannot be completely eliminated from systems like these. Risk management involves identifying and tracking the sources of risk (e.g. piece part failure or extreme environmental conditions), classifying them by likelihood of occurrence and severity of effect, and guiding risk-reduction efforts into areas with the highest expected payoff.
- *Reliability, maintainability, availability (RMA).* Engineers who specialize in reliability, maintainability, availability (RMA) are focused on producing a system that is working when the user needs it. Reliability refers to the likelihood of malfunction, maintainability to the ease with which the system can be serviced and repaired, and availability to the overall level of readiness for use (the result of reliability, maintainability, and spare parts availability). RMA engineers use models to calculate expected availability and recommend efforts to improve it.
- *Producibility.* This is the attribute of being relatively easy and cheap to manufacture. Producibility engineering involves selecting the right design, materials, components, piece parts, and industrial processes for manufacture.
- *Quality.* The role of the QA function was described earlier (Section 13.3). Quality engineers design engineering processes that produce high-quality output (i.e. items having few defects), and they design systems so that they tend to develop few defects.
- *Integrated logistics support (ILS).* This function encompasses the unified planning and execution of system operational support, including training, maintenance, repairs, field engineering, spares, supply, and transportation. Integrated logistics support (ILS) is particularly important in military systems, which often have dedicated ILS engineers from the very beginning of system development, when they are responsible for establishing logistics-related requirements.
- *Human factors.* This specialty focuses on how the system interacts with people, particularly with users and consumers. It includes both cognitive and perceptual factors (man-machine

interface, situational awareness) and ergonomics (fit, comfort, controls, etc.). Other areas of concern are workload, fatigue, human reliability, and the impact of stress. Human factors engineers specialize in the human elements of the system and their interfaces.

- *Safety.* Safety engineers are concerned with preventing not only injury and death from accidents during system manufacture and test, but also mishaps that damage high-value equipment or result in long schedule delays. Because of the importance of safety and the natural human tendency to take more and more risks when behind schedule, it is common to have a separate safety office reporting directly to the PM or to another high-level officer.

- *Security and information assurance.* Engineers in these areas are responsible for ensuring that information about the program does not get to people the customer does not want to have it, for either commercial or national security reasons. They also provide systems and procedures to protect privacy data and to protect computer systems and data from attack. Finally, they assist in designing a system so that it can operate without having information about it obtained or tampered with by others. This is a particularly important function for financial and for military systems.

- *Environmental impact.* Major government projects often cannot be done without an environmental impact statement, and that statement is often a major hurdle. Environmental engineers will help write it and then ensure that the system is developed, built, and operated in accordance with it so that environmental impact can be kept as low as possible.

- *Independent verification and validation (IV&V).* Verification is ensuring that the system was built as designed; validation is ensuring that the system as designed and built meets the user's needs. An independent verification and validation (IV&V) engineer is a disinterested authority (not involved in the original development) responsible for ensuring that the system is correctly designed and built. The function is especially important in software system testing. The military services also have IV&V organizations to ensure new systems meet requirements.

13.5.10 Major Program Technical Reviews

Chapter 1 described the various life cycle models that are used in system development. Regardless of the model, usual practice is to hold a formal review as a control point (or gate) when moving from one stage to the next. The purpose of these reviews is to allow inspection and assessment of the work, to gain concurrence and approval, and to educate the staff, the management, the customer, and the user. These reviews go by such names as system requirements review, preliminary design review, critical design review, design readiness review, and full rate production readiness review, depending on the life cycle model used and the stage of the project. Design engineers, specialty engineers, testers, QA personnel, and others present the status of their work and any important open issues, as appropriate to the project stage.

An SE will often be tasked with organizing and emceeing the review, as well as presenting such SE topics as requirements, risk management, and systems test. For a major system, these reviews can be lengthy affairs. An auditorium full of people will look at slide after slide of Microsoft® PowerPoint for several days. The major program decision makers (PM, chief SE, etc.) will sit through the whole thing; others may come and go based on their involvement in each topic. People often find these reviews to be of compelling interest when the topic is in one's own area of responsibility, and crushingly boring at other times.

The review will result in a list of action items that identify areas that need clarification or further work. These can range from minor points like small discrepancies between two presentations of the same data to "show-stoppers" that threaten the development. Successful completion of the review (as judged by the PM or customer) is required to enter the next stage.

13.5.11 System Integration and Test

When the element development work is done, it is time to put the system together and test it to make sure that all the elements work together as intended, that the system interacts with its environment as it should, and that it meets client, user, and consumer needs. These are the activities on the upper right-hand side of the "Systems Engineering V" (Figure 13.4). It is normally an SE's responsibility to coordinate these efforts. In acceptance testing, the customer or user should be closely involved, and sometimes runs the testing.

13.6 ROLES OF THE SYSTEMS ENGINEER

 Systems engineers can play a number of roles that may or may not align closely with their formally assigned responsibilities.

—Adapted from Sheard [11]

These are short statements of the roles often played by a designated SE, whether or not they are really part of systems engineering and whether or not they are formally assigned. This is a more subjective account of the different roles an SE as an individual may play.

Technical client interface. The PM often relies on the SE for dealing with the client on technical issues, when no business matters are at stake.

User and consumer interface. This is a primary SE job; it is part of translating possibly inchoate needs into engineering requirements.

Requirements owner. The SE investigates the requirements, writes them down, analyzes them, and coordinates any required changes for the lifetime of the project.

System analyst. The SE builds models and simulations (Chapter 4) and uses them to predict the performance of candidate system designs.

System architect. The SE defines system boundaries, system interfaces, system elements, and their interactions, and assigns functions to them.

Glue among elements. The SE is responsible for integrating the system, identifying risks, and seeking out issues that "fall through the cracks." He or she is the technical conscience of the program, a proactive troubleshooter looking out for problems and arranging to prevent them. Since many problems happen at interfaces, the SE carefully scrutinizes them to ensure that the elements do not interfere with each other.

Technical leader. SEs frequently end up as the planners, schedulers, and trackers of technical work; sometimes the role is formally assigned by the PM.

Coordinator. SEs coordinate the efforts of the different discipline engineers, take charge of resolving system issues, chair *integrated product/process teams* (IPTs) assembled to provide cross-disciplinary oversight of particular areas, and head "tiger teams" assembled to resolve serious problems.

System effectiveness manager. SEs oversee reliability, availability, human factors, and the other specialty engineering areas that can make the difference between a usable and a worthless system.

Life cycle planner. SEs provide for such necessities as users' manuals, training, deployment, logistics, field support, operational evaluation, system upgrades, and eventual system disposal.

Test engineer. SEs are usually in charge of overall test planning and evaluation, and of execution of system-level tests.

Information manager. SEs often write key program documents, review all important ones, control document change, and manage system data and metrics.

13.7 CHARACTERISTICS OF THE IDEAL SYSTEMS ENGINEER

A good SE has a systems outlook, user orientation, inquisitiveness, common sense, professional discipline, good communication skills, a desire to cooperate, and a willingness to stand up for what's technically right.

—Adapted from SAIC [12]

As a final look at systems engineering practice, it is helpful to consider the personality traits that make an individual a good SE. Like any other job, some people fit more naturally into it than others. While anyone with the necessary technical skills and discipline can become a good SE, people with the following characteristics will find themselves easily falling into the role, liking the job, and doing well.

Systems outlook. A natural SE tends to take a holistic, systems-level view on problems. Other engineers may gravitate toward looking at the details and making sure that all the crucial little things are done right; many people tend to be most concerned with organizational relationships and personalities. A good SE looks at the system as a whole, considering both technical and human factors, and is comfortable leaving element details to other experts.

Client, user, and consumer orientation. The ideal SE has field experience relevant to the system being worked on, or at least can readily identify with the user's and customer's perspectives. The SE should feel or develop a strong affinity with the user and customer, since one of the SE's key jobs is facilitating the consumer–user–designer interfaces.

Inquisitiveness. An SE should have a natural curiosity, and should indulge it by inquiring into areas that "just don't look right." He or she wants to know as much about the system as can be absorbed by one person, and also about the design and development process. When the SE comes across something that does not seem to make sense, he or she presses the inquiry until the doubt is resolved. In this way, the SE gains a better systems-level understanding and also often uncovers problems that had escaped notice by others with more narrow responsibilities.

Intuition. A good SE has the ability to quickly grasp essentials of an unfamiliar field, and has a good feel for what level of detail he or she should be able to understand. He has good judgment on when it is necessary to press a question and when it is safe to hold off and leave it to other experts.

Discipline. A good SE adheres to engineering processes, knowing that they are essential for imposing structure on the formless and that they enable both understanding of the state of progress and control of the development. This includes objectivity: the SE maintains an objective and systems-level view of the project, and does not let him or herself become identified with any other group working on the project. A good SE will be accepted as an honest broker when there are internal disagreements.

Communication. This is essential to the SE's role as glue among the elements. It has three parts. The SE is ready to listen to everyone involved in the project, especially the users and others not in the same chain of command. The SE is also ready to talk to everyone, to make sure everyone has a common understanding of the big picture. Finally, the SE is ready to act on what he or she finds out, bringing problems to the attention of the appropriate people and getting them working together to find a solution.

Cooperation, but not capitulation. A natural SE is cooperative and eager to get everybody working together toward a common goal. The SE works to get buy-in from all parties. However, he or she knows when not to give in to resistance. If the issue seems important enough, the SE will insist on an appropriate explanation or investigation and is willing to take the problem to the PM (or perhaps to the Chief Technology Officer) if necessary. That is what the SE is paid for.

13.8 SUMMARY

This chapter has focused on the realities of those who have "SE" in their job title. These SEs can have a great variety of jobs, but perhaps the most typical is as the technical leader and integrator supporting a PM who is building a complex system like an aircraft or a telecommunications system. The SE will be responsible for coordinating technical efforts over the lifetime of the system, but he or she will probably be busiest toward the beginning, when he or she is in charge of defining the system requirements, developing the system concept, and coordinating and integrating the efforts of the other design engineers.

The coordinating role of SEs means that they will work with a wide variety of other professionals and specialists, including discipline and specialty engineers, analysts, testers, inspectors, managers, executives, and so on. The SE will often have the task of forming and leading interdisciplinary teams to tackle particular problems. Other specific tasks assigned to SEs will vary with the organization and the project; they often include defining the top-level system architecture, performing risk analysis and other specialty engineering, coordinating major technical reviews, and analyzing and maintaining system requirements, system and element interfaces, and the system test plan.

Besides accomplishing these tasks, SEs may find themselves playing many different roles during system development, such as external and internal technical interface, requirements owner, system analyst and architect, system effectiveness manager, and overall technical coordinator and planner, again depending on the organization and what the PM desires (or allows). The person most likely to enjoy and succeed at this kind of professional systems engineering is a person who naturally has a systems outlook, user orientation, inquisitiveness, common sense, professional discipline, good communication skills, desire to cooperate, and willingness to stand up for what is technically right. The SE is the one responsible to the PM for making sure that all the elements work together in a system that meets the needs of the client, user, and consumer.

REFERENCES

1. Haskins, C. (ed.) (2006) *Systems Engineering Handbook: A Guide for System Life Cycle Processes and Activities*, Version 3 INCOSE-TP-2003-002-03, San Diego, CA: INCOSE.

2. Harris, P., Moran, R. (1996) *Managing Cultural Differences*, 4th ed. Houston, TX: Gulf Publishing.

3. Katzenbach, J.R, Smith, D.K. (1993) *The Wisdom of Teams*. New York: HarperCollins.

4. Aranda, L., Conlon, K. (1998) *Teams: Structure, Process, Culture, and Politics*. Upper Saddle River, NJ: Prentice-Hall, Inc.

5. Hull, E., Jackson, K., Dick, J. (2005) *Requirements Engineering*, 2nd ed. London: Springer.

6. Laplante, P.A. (2009) *Requirements Engineering for Software and Systems*. Boca Raton, FL: CRC Press.

7. Maier, M.W., Rechtin, E. (2009) *The Art of Systems Architecting*, 3rd ed. Boca Raton, FL: CRC Press.

8. DODAF. U.S. Department of Defense. Available at: http://cio-nii.defense.gov. (Accessed 14 Feb 2022).

9. CORE software. Vitech Corporation. Available at: http://www.vitechcorp.com. (Accessed 15 Feb 2022).

10. DOORS software. IBM Corporation. Available at: http://www-01.ibm.com/software. (Accessed 12 March 2022).

11. Sheard, S.A. (2000) *Systems Engineering Roles Revisited*. Herndon, VA: Software Productivity Consortium.

12. SAIC (Science Applications International Corporation) (1995) Systems Engineering Definitions & Scene Setting [briefing].

Appendix **A**

Realization Analysis Levels 0 and 2

The detail contained in this appendix is and extension of the Level 1 application discussed in Section 10.7.1. It is an adaptation of the authors' work [1] is presented here for completeness regarding realization analysis. As noted in Chapter 10, Level 0 and Level 2 realization analysis steps are used to address specific concerns that are not in common to all systems decision support projects involving uncertainty. Consequently, they appear here rather than in the primary Chapter 10. The figure below is repeated from the chapter for convenience.

A.1 LEVEL 0 ANALYSIS—REFINED CHOICE SET IDENTIFICATION

Consider the Monte Carlo simulation output for the six alternatives shown in the righthand image of Figure A.1, which displays $n = 1000$ realizations of each alternative and significant overlap between the cloudplots. This notion of "overlap" is broader than the obvious commingling of realizations between alternatives. In Figure A.1, even though Alt B's realizations do not intertwine with Alt A's, several of Alt A's least cost realizations are cheaper than Alt B's most expensive ones.

Similarly, despite Alt B's generally higher value, several of Alt A's best-performing realizations produce greater value than Alt B's least valuable ones. In both cases, there is a non-zero probability that a randomly selected pair of realizations from the Alt B and Alt A cloudplots will be Pareto optimal. Applying first order stochastic dominance analysis does not appear to help in this regard as this possibility is effectively hidden by the cumulative distribution functions (CDFs) in Figure A.2, despite Alt B's stochastic dominance over Alt A in cost and value.

Neither non-overlapping cloudplots nor stochastic dominance is sufficient for identifying a choice set in this case.

Recalling the earlier discussion of dominance, alternative A_i deterministically dominates alternative A_j in a given dimension if A_i's worst possible outcome is better than alternative A_j's best:

Decision Making in Systems Engineering and Management, Third Edition.
Patrick J. Driscoll, Gregory S. Parnell, and Dale L. Henderson
© 2023 John Wiley & Sons, Inc. Published 2023 by John Wiley & Sons, Inc.

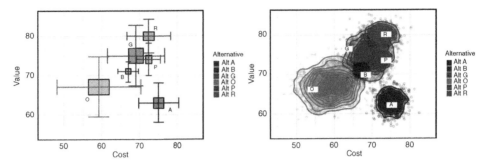

Figure A.1 Stochastic tradespace examples: (a) boxplot and (b) cloudplot.

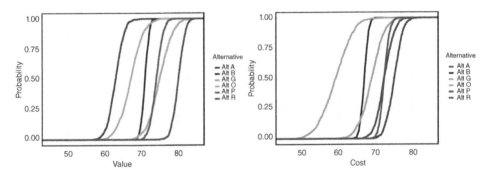

Figure A.2 Stochastic dominance results for the six alternative example. Source: Adapted from Caddell et al. [1].

$A_i \neq A_j$ and A_j lies in the polar cone of A_i. In terms of their value CDFs, this implies there is a V^* such that $F_j(V^*) = 1$ and $F_i(V^*) = 0$, while for cost there is a C^* such that $F_j(C^*) = 0$ and $F_i(C^*) = 1$. Figure A.3 depicts a situation in which alternative A_i (shown in black) deterministically dominates alternative A_j (shown in gray) in both value and cost.

In this case, V^* and C^* are defined by A_i's least valuable and most expensive realizations, respectively. With no evidence that A_j is capable of outperforming A_i in either dimension, dropping A_j from further consideration seems prudent. However, considering that Figure A.3's cloudplots are built from a sample of $K = 1000$ realizations from each alternative, there is a possibility that additional realizations might nullify A_i's apparent dominance. Put another way, if there is a reasonable likelihood that additional realizations of A_j are more valuable/less expensive than its current most valuable/least expensive realizations, then eliminating A_j would be ill-advised.

To address this concern probabilistically, a non-parametric result from the statistical sub-discipline of order statistics can be leveraged. Specifically, using a result from David and Nagaraja [2], given K independent and identically distributed realizations of A_j's value ($V_{j,k}$, $k = 1, \ldots, K$), the probability that one or more of Q future realizations of A_j's value ($V_{j,q}$, $q = 1, \ldots, Q$) is greater than its largest current realization ($V_{j,(K)}$, the Kth order statistic) is:

$$\eta_q(K, Q) = \sum_{q=1}^{Q} \frac{\binom{K+Q-q-1}{K-1}}{\binom{K+Q}{K}} \tag{A.1}$$

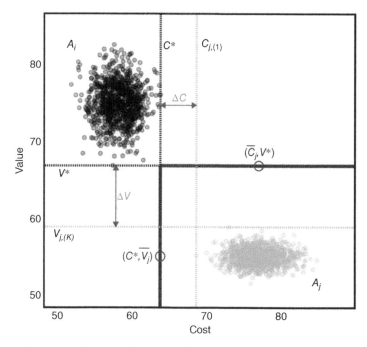

Figure A.3 Realization analysis Level 0 example. Source: Caddell et al. [1]/John Wiley & Sons.

which can be expressed more compactly using its complementary event (i.e., none of the Q future realizations are greater than $V_{j,(K)}$):

$$\eta_q(K, Q) = 1 - \eta_0(K, Q) = 1 - \frac{\binom{K+Q-1}{Q}}{\binom{K+Q}{K}} \qquad (A.2)$$

By symmetry, given K independent and identically distributed realizations of A_j's cost ($C_{j,k}, k = 1, \ldots, K$), the probability that one or more of Q future realizations of A_j's cost ($C_{j,q}, q = 1, \ldots, Q$) is less than its smallest current realization ($C_{j,(1)}$, the first order statistic) is also given by the right-hand side of Equation (A.2).

Armed with Equation (A.2), the probability that additional realizations of A_j's value or cost might nullify A_i's presumed deterministic dominance can be quantified. For example, by generating a single additional sample point for either value or cost (i.e., $Q = 1$), the probability that this realization will be more valuable/less expensive than the most valuable/least expensive of the K current realizations is 0.00099; it is an unlikely event. On the other hand, by treating value and cost independently and doubling the total number of realizations in both dimensions so that $K = 2000$ (i.e., $Q_V = 1000$ and $Q_C = 1000$), this probability jumps to 0.75. In either case, quantifying the probabilities of potentially nullifying A_i's presumed deterministic dominance via additional simulation realizations provides a mechanism to address the cloudplots' "strength of evidence" with a decision maker. In general, the more realizations used in simulation, the stronger the evidence is. In this case, strength is achieved by decreasing the likelihood Q future realizations will breach $V_{j,(K)}$ and $C_{j,(1)}$. If the decision maker is satisfied that $\eta_q(K, Q)$ is sufficiently small, A_j can be safely eliminated. Otherwise, additional analysis is required.

To this end, the above methodology ignores a critical aspect of Figure A.3, namely the distances between V^* and $V_{j,(K)}$ (ΔV), and C^* and $C_{j,(1)}$ (ΔC). Put another way, $\eta_q(K,Q)$ only quantifies the likelihood of being left of and above $C_{j,(1)}$ and $V_{j,(K)}$ respectively; it tells nothing about "how far." Accordingly, if ΔV and ΔC are large, the likelihood of A_i deterministically dominating A_j may be extremely high, immaterial of the value of $\eta_q(K,Q)$.

With this in mind, a recent, multivariate generalization of the classic Chebyshev inequality [3] can be applied, in which:

$$
P\left(\overbrace{(A_{j,K+1} - \mu_j)^{\mathsf{T}} \Sigma_j^{-1} (A_{j,K+1} - \mu_j)}^{D_M^2(A_{j,K+1})} \geq \lambda^2 \right)
$$

$$
\leq \min\left\{ 1, \frac{2(K^2 - 1 + K\lambda^2)}{K^2 \lambda^2} \right\} \tag{A.3}
$$

where $A_{j,K+1}$ is the first future realization of A_j or $[C_{j,K+1}, V_{j,K+1}]$; μ_j and Σ_j are the empirical mean vector and unbiased covariance matrix of the current K realizations of A_j; and λ is a positive real number. In short, when the bivariate distribution of A_j's realizations is unknown, this inequality provides a way to calculate an upper bound for the probability that the squared Mahalanobis distance of $A_{j,K+1}$ (i.e., $D_M^2(A_{j,K+1})$) meets or exceeds a given threshold. Unlike $\eta_q(K,Q)$, this calculation also takes into account any correlation between value and cost.

In Figure A.3, if $A_{j,K+1}$ lies along the highlighted lower right quadrant boundary formed by V^* and C^*, then A_i no longer deterministically dominates A_j. As such, by assuming A_i is fixed and equating λ^2 with the minimum squared Mahalanobis distance along this boundary, the right-hand side of Equation (A.3) provides an upper bound for the probability A_j is no longer deterministically dominated by A_i. Furthermore, if A_j's value and cost are uncorrelated, then the value of λ^2 is given by $\min\{D_M^2([C^*, \overline{V_j}]), D_M^2([\overline{C_j}, V^*])\}$.

For instance, the empirical covariance of V_j and C_j in Figure A.3 is -0.0167, and a subsequent permutation-based hypothesis test with $H_0 : \sigma_{V_j,C_j} = 0$ returns a p-value of 0.83. Assuming that A_j's value and cost are uncorrelated produces:

$$
\min\{D_M^2([C^*, \overline{V_j}]), D_M^2([\overline{C_j}, V^*])\}
$$

$$
= \min\{D_M^2([61.50, 58.01]), D_M^2([74.99, 68.33])\}
$$

$$
= 28.99
$$

Using this result for λ^2 and solving Equation (A.3) gives:

$$
P(D_M^2(A_{j,K+1}) \geq 28.99)
$$

$$
\leq \min\left\{ 1, \frac{2(1000^2 - 1 + 1000 \times 28.99)}{1000^2 \times 28.99} \right\} = 0.0710
$$

These results show that by generating an additional realization of A_j, the probability that A_i will continue to deterministically dominate A_j is at least 0.9290. In light of this information, many, if not most, decision makers would likely feel comfortable eliminating A_j from further consideration. Recalling the cloudplots in Figure A.1, no alternative deterministically dominates any of the others. As such, extensive Level 0 analysis is unnecessary, and all six alternatives are placed in the initial choice set.

A.2 LEVEL 2 ANALYSIS—POST-SELECTION INSIGHTS

During Level 1 analysis for this example discussed in Chapter 10, realizations of each choice set alternative were analyzed against other alternatives using pairwise comparisons. Although the choice set has been winnowed down, the decision maker is still confronted with four viable alternatives in the tradespace. And, although a preferred alternative may be identified, there could still exist some nagging uncertainty in the decision maker's mind as to the selection he or she made versus those foregone. Level 2 analysis is designed to address this issue by comparing all of the possible realizations for the selected alternative against what might have been expected from another choice set member insofar as value and cost returns.

For example, suppose that a decision maker selects alternative A_G (average dominance score [ADS] = 0.295) using Level 0 and 1 analyses, based on a logic that it represents the best value return for cost among the choice set, thereby ruling out A_R for pragmatic cost reasons. In Figure A.4, this self-imposed cost limit is shown as "Budget Limit," noting for clarity that all choice set alternatives are cost feasible and that the budget limit shown is a preference item, not a constraint.

A discussion ensues that solicits the additional amount that the decision maker would be willing to commit to obtaining $E[V_G]$. Denoting this additional amount as Δ, A_B now presents itself as the next best alternative given that the decision maker is willing to commit at least $E[C_G]$ with a buffer of Δ to get $E[V_G]$. Level 2 analysis concerns itself with producing an estimate of the probability that this next closest Pareto efficient alternative (A_B) might outperform alternative A_G at a lower cost. This is an issue of expectation, providing the rationale to select $E_B[C, V]$ as the basis for making similar pairwise comparisons, as done with Level 1 analysis using this near competitor. Moreover, it is motivated by a desire to provide the decision maker with an estimate addressing this dimension of potential regret now that an alternative has been selected.

Level 2 analysis is based on examining the location of all possible realizations for the selected alternative (A_G), as characterized by six zones of consideration with respect to the near competitor (A_B). Being non-selected, A_B exists only in expectation for the decision maker since it was not selected. Level 2 analysis uses the six zones shown centered on $E_B[C, V]$, essentially fixing its tradespace position, and proceeds to count the number of A_G realizations that lie in each zone in the following way.

First, by extending a vector from $E_B[C, V]$ through $E_G[C, V]$, one partitioning of the tradespace necessary to establish the six relevant zones of consideration is created. The slope of this line represents the tradeoff the decision maker is willing to make by selecting A_G over A_B. This notion is the same described for deterministic tradespace analysis in Section 9.5 regarding a "bang for buck" tradeoff ratio.

Next, a second partitioning vector is created by selecting a point along the horizontal extension from $E_G[C, V]$ in the direction of Δ. Finally, horizontal and vertical reference lines are drawn through $E_B[C, V]$ to complete the partitioning. Figure A.4, this self-imposed cost illustrates these zones for the ongoing example, and their interpretations for a realization of alternative G (i.e., $A_{G,k}$) are described below. Notice that each $A_{G,k}$ tradespace location defines the realization of a new trade

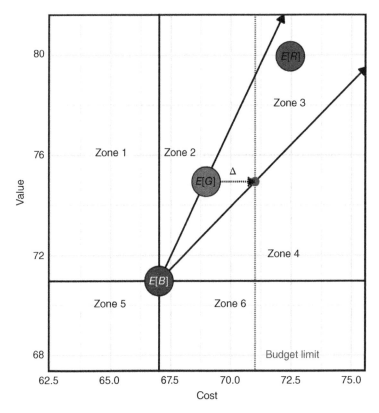

Figure A.4 Zone partitioning in realization space.

occurring between the foregone $E_B[C, V]$, and this potential resulting trade is being compared to the trade the decision maker committed to by selecting $A_{G,k}$ over A_B.

- *Zone 1.* $A_{G,k}$ dominates $E_B[C,V]$; the trade is significantly better than expected (good decision, great outcome)
- *Zone 2.* $A_{G,k}$ is Pareto optimal (+) with respect to $E_B[C,V]$; the trade made is better than expected (good decision, good outcome).
- *Zone 3.* $A_{G,k}$ is Pareto optimal (+) with respect to $E_B[C,V]$; the trade is worse than expected but still acceptable (good decision, good outcome).
- *Zone 4.* $A_{G,k}$ is Pareto optimal (+) with respect to $E_B[C,V]$; the trade is worse than expected and unacceptable (good decision, disappointing outcome).
- *Zone 5.* $A_{G,k}$ is Pareto optimal (−) with respect to $E_B[C,V]$; the trade is worse than expected and unacceptable (good decision, bad outcome).
- *Zone 6.* $A_{G,k}$ is dominated by $E_B[C,V]$; the trade is significantly worse than expected and unacceptable (good decision, disastrous outcome).

Counting trade results for $A_{G,k}$ simulation realizations in Zones 1, 5, and 6 is done in a similar fashion as was done during Level 1; although pairwise slope comparisons are not necessary for Level 2 analysis. However, for Zones 2, 3, and 4 we first identify A_G cloudplot realizations lying

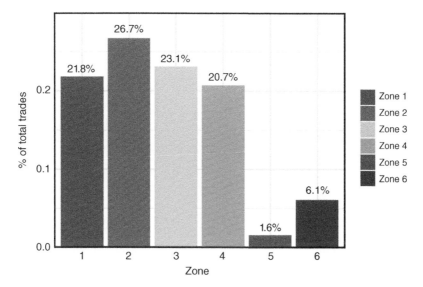

Figure A.5 Trade zones for alternative G.

in the upper right quadrant similar to the comparisons done with Level 1. Then, successive pair-wise comparisons are performed between the slopes of lines extending from $E_B[C, V]$ to each $A_{G,k}$ realization and the slopes of the two partitioning lines shown. For example, if the slope of a line drawn from $E_B[C, V]$ to an alternative G location $A_{G,i}$ is greater than the slope of the partitioning line through the Δ reference point but less than the slope of the decision maker's committed trade between $E_B[C, V]$ and $E_G[C, V]$, then the realization is allocated to the Zone 3 count.

Figure A.5 shows the results of applying Level 2 analysis to the this ongoing example. Based on the zone characterization described, there is a 71.6% likelihood of a good outcome (Zones 1, 2, 3) being realized against the intended trade. There is potential opportunity in these realizations, should they occur. On the other hand, there is a 22.3% chance of being disappointed (Zones 4, 5) by an unacceptable trade realization, and a potentially significant nonzero probability (6.1%) that the intended trade will result in a disastrous outcome (Zone 6). Depending on the decision maker's risk tolerance, these downside realization probabilities could be significant enough to warrant putting mitigation plans in-place after the decision is made to select A_G.

REFERENCES

1. Caddell, J., Dabkowski, M., Driscoll, P., Dubois, P. (2020) 'Improving stochastic analysis for tradeoffs in multi-criteria value models,' *Journal of Multi-Criteria Decision Analysis*, 27(5–6), pp. 304–317.

2. David, H.A., Nagaraja, H.N. (2003) *Order Statistics*. Wiley Series in Probability and Statistics, 3rd ed. Hoboken, NJ: John Wiley & Sons, Inc.

3. Stellato, B., Van Parys, B.P.G., Goulart, P.J. (2017) 'Multivariate Chebyshev inequality with estimated mean and variance,' *The American Statistician*, 71(2), pp. 123–127.

Appendix **B**

Software Fundamentals

B.1 SYSTEMITOOL

SystemTool is a Java-based systemigram drawing and visualization application currently maintained by the Systems Engineering Research Center (SERC), a University Affiliated Research Center of the U.S. Department of Defense. The SERC leverages the research and expertise of senior lead researchers from 22 collaborator universities throughout the United States. The SERC is unprecedented in the depth and breadth of its reach, leadership, and citizenship in systems engineering through its conduct of vitally important research and the education of future systems engineering leaders.

SystemiTool is available free for download at https://sercuarc.org/serc-tools/ in both a Windows and Mac version. SERC also has an online *SystemiTool* application for use. The download consists of a single executable file that will install *SystemiTool* on your computer to default `Program Files` location on the C-drive. As will most stand-alone application installations on Windows 10, we recommend that you disconnect from WiFi to do the installation to avoid accidentally installing the program on your OneDrive.

After completing the installation, launching the application opens the main drawing environment shown in Figure B.1. The drawing, labeling, and colorizing options used to create systemigrams are easily understandable if you have used any digital drawing application feature before. In fact, there really is no Help option despite the menu item at the top.

One unique item with *SystemiTool* that is useful for systemigrams is the "Container tool." It appears as the bottom oval in the left window in Figure B.1. This is the tool used to create a main system that has subsystems that you want to identify within the system boundary, such as was done with the EV systemigram in Figure 3.7. The other oval tool is for creating individual nodes. To use a tool, select and drag it to the drawing pallet. The full range of editing options become available in the right side window as so as you place it on the pallet. Connections between nodes are made by selecting one of the line tools, dragging to the pallet, and dragging the end points

Decision Making in Systems Engineering and Management, Third Edition.
Patrick J. Driscoll, Gregory S. Parnell, and Dale L. Henderson
© 2023 John Wiley & Sons, Inc. Published 2023 by John Wiley & Sons, Inc.

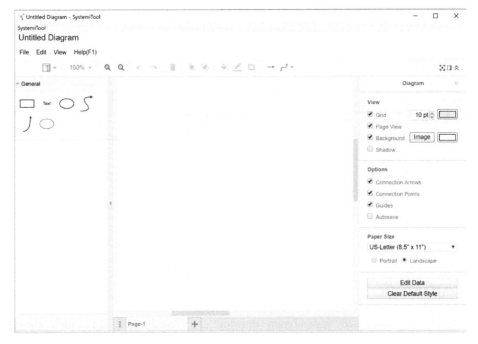

Figure B.1   *SystemiTool* main drawing environment.

of the line to the nodes that you want to connect. Labeling is obvious. Once you are satisfied with your systemigram, save it as a *SystemiTool* file. If you want to use your systemigram in another program, `Export` the image in one of the options available and import it into your other program. Optionally, you could use a snipping tool to capture what you need.

B.2   CAMBRIDGE ADVANCED MODELER (CAM)

Cambridge Advanced Modeler (CAM) is a software platform created by the Engineering Design Centre (EDC) at Cambridge University, England. It is a free application that can be downloaded online at: http://www-edc.eng.cam.ac.uk/cam/. CAM's functionality is organized into toolboxes that provide features for modeling and analyzing dependencies between elements in both products and processes. CAM is implemented in Java for MS Windows. We've been using it in a Windows 10 environment with no issues. EDC says that it may also run on OS X and Linux.

After downloading the application, double-clicking on the installer launch a command window that installs all the necessary files in a default location. Choosing the appropriate Java batch file (*.bat) in the CAM folder (32-bit or 64-bit) opens a command window and launches the workspace environment. Selecting "Create a new workspace" will start a new workspace and begin the dependency structure matrix (DSM) modeling process, as shown in Figure B.2.

Next, select the notebook icon in the lower left of the main window. This launches the workbook options window shown in Figure B.3. Selecting "DSM" will create a workbook for a binary DSM. The option "DSM - 1 text field per dependency" is what was used to create the CAM DSM shown in Figure 3.13 where the type of dependency needed to be labeled. Each of these are suitable for basic system modeling.

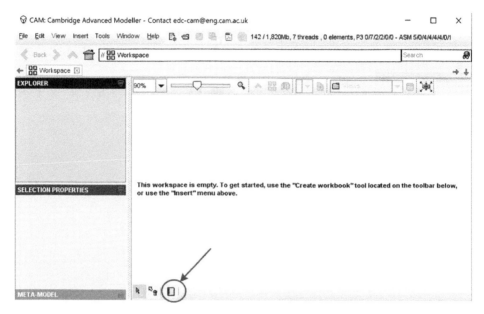

Figure B.2 CAM workspace environment.

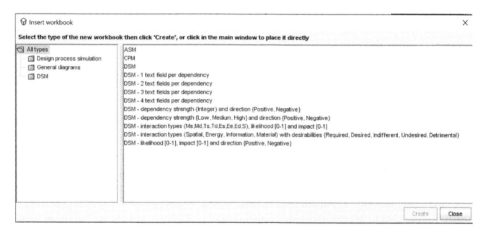

Figure B.3 CAM workbook options.

As more advanced DSMs are desired, the options below these are also available for use. In particular, what gets little attention but seems to surface as a need in system representations is the intensity of dependencies, recognizing that these can matter when deciding to create subsystem modules. CAM's two options for doing this are unique among the current set of available tools.

Double clicking on the new workbook shows a default view of the DSM worksheet, one of several that are available. Double clicking again opens up a new worksheet ready for editing, which is where the DSM is created and select analytics are applied. This is shown in Figure B.4. Highlighted with callout boxes are the two main DSM tools: a system element tool that allows you to create all the row/column elements needed, and a connection tool which is used to click on a particular row *i*

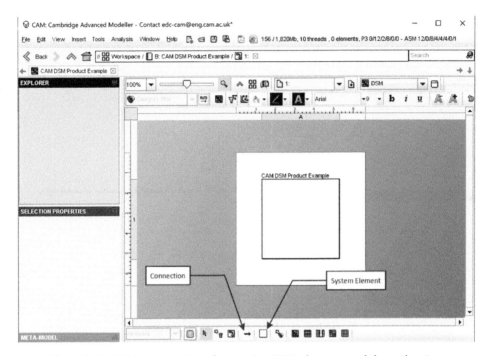

Figure B.4   CAM menu options for creating DSM elements and dependencies.

column *j* location, enter information as it pertains to the type of DSM option selected, and thereby establish a dependency relationship between two system elements. The direction of dependency is from *i* to *j*, meaning that element *j* depends on something that element *i* is providing.

B.3   *MATHEMATICA*

Wolfram Software initially developed *Mathematica* as a computer algebra system (CAS), but over time *Mathematica* has evolved well-beyond this into one of the most powerful computational, visualization, and programming applications available to the science, technology, engineering, and mathematics community. *Mathematica* is commercially available through the Wolfram website: https://www.wolfram.com/mathematica/ at a variety of pricing plans designed to accommodate all types of users.

Once downloaded and installed, *Mathematica*'s functionality is accessed in a workbook environment using a command line interface that is syntax-specific. Commands are entered on an input line (*In[*]:=*) using keystrokes `Enter` for carriage return and `Shift-Enter` for execution by the kernel. Numerical, analytical, and graphical results appear as output (*Out[*]=*) that can be reformatted, copied, and saved to accommodate many options (including imagery used in this book).

The AW101 adjacency matrix in Section 3.5.2 was entered directly by entering `AW101 =`, and using the menu items `Insert -> Table/Matrix -> New`. After specifying the matrix size, a template appears for entering the specific binary DSM entries. `Shift-Enter` stores the adjacency matrix into memory. Optionally, a *CSV file can be imported directly using the `Import["name.ext","CSV"]` format.

The sequence of commands used in the Section 3.5.2 examples are:

- *In[*]:=* `AW101 = *enter matrix as described*` This stores the adjacency matrix as object AW101.
- *Out[*]=* Displays the adjacency matrix.
- *In[*]:=* `AW101g = AdjacencyGraph[AW101]` Converts the matrix to a graphics object and plots the adjacency graph.
- *Out[*]=* Displays the adjacency graph shown in Figure 3.18a.
- *In[*]:=* `FindGraphCommunities[AW101g]`
- *Out[*]=* `{1, 2, 3, 4, 5, 8, 9, 11, 12}, {10, 13, 14, 15, 16, 17, 18, 19}, {6, 7}` These are the three modules identified as communities.
- *In[*]:=* `CommunityModularity[AW101g]` Estimates the percent modularity of the system as an adjacency graph.
- *Out[*]=* `0.0940157`, or 9.5%.
- *In[*]:=* `CommunityGraphPlot[AW101g, FindGraphCommunities[AW101g]]` Plots the communities (modules) identified earlier as a clustered digraph.
- *Out[*]=* Displays the modules shown in Figure 3.18b.

B.4   GEPHI

Gephi is a system visualization and exploration software application that allows the user to interact directly with the visualization. All of the nodes can be dragged to new locations as desired, as was done here so that all of the system element labels could be read. This is one example of the dynamic interaction that *Gephi* affords. Colorization and changes to node and connection size can be used to emphasize subsystems or individual nodes. Two excellent references for *Gephi* are: "Mastering Gephi Network Visualization," by Ken Cherven (PACKT Publishing, 2015), and "Gephi Cookbook," by Devangana Khokhar (PACKT Publishing, 2015).

Once a system is represented as a network graph in *Gephi*, a full suite of network analysis measures are available for use. These appear in the right panel of the workspace. Figure B.5a shows a typical network measure options window that provides a short description of embedded calculations and ability to differentiate between directed and undirected system connections. Figure B.5b shows the result of applying the modularity measure to the AW101 DSM. The *Gephi* modularity measure identifies modules as modularity classes starting at 0. The class size distribution then displays a count of class member subsets: 10 elements in class 0, 6 elements in class 1, and 3 elements in class 2. It uses the same communities calculations as *Mathematica*, so it is not surprising that the results are identical.

Gephi also has a suite of powerful algorithms for dynamically reconfiguring the graph layout depending on characteristics such as strength of connections, node dependencies, and number of in-degree and out-degree connections that system elements (node) have. Figure B.6a shows an automatic reconfiguration using the Fruchterman Reingold algorithm [1] option using the dropdown menu in the left workspace panel. Right-clicking any node of interest in the graph (e.g., one with many or few dependencies) provides an option to highlight it in the Data Table and vice-versa, a very useful feature for structural exploration purposes.

Figure B.6b shows the *Gephi* Data Table with the Tail Rotor system element selected. Doing so automatically highlights this element and the directed connections with its immediate (first order) neighboring elements in the graph layout. Changing the color of the node and its size then highlights

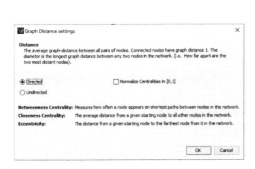

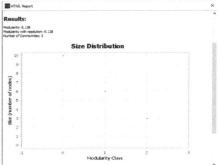

(a) Example Gephi network measure window   (b) Modularity measure applied to AW101 DSM

Figure B.5   Example network measure interface and AW101 modularity results.

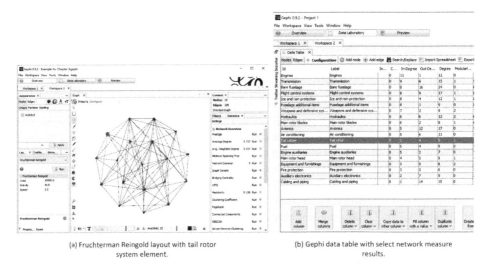

(a) Fruchterman Reingold layout with tail rotor   (b) Gephi data table with select network measure
system element.   results.

Figure B.6   *Gephi* layout reconfiguration, data table, and node highlighting.

this element. The Data Table also contains the numerical results when running network measures. Here, each node's `In-Degree`, `Out-Degree`, `Degree`, and `Modularity Class` identifier is shown.

B.5   VENSIM PLE

Ventana Systems, Inc. has three products useful for systems engineering and systems decision support purposes: Vensim® Professional, Vensim Personal Learning Edition (PLE), and Vensim Model Reader. Vensim® is the full professional version requiring licensing for all uses. Vensim PLE is a version free for educational and research purposes, and the Model Reader is a freely distributable application that can allow clients to open models created in *Vensim Pro* and *Vensim*

PLE but not edit. We used *Vensim PLE* for all the examples in Chapter 3. The *Vensim PLE* free download is available at: https://vensim.com/free-download/. You must provide your name and a valid email address for Ventana to send download instructions to you. You can opt to subscribe or not to their newsletter.

Ventana Systems provides excellent tutorials and user guides on their website: www.vensim .com. If you are not familiar with system dynamics modeling, we highly recommend that you walk through the tutorials to understand how the software operates and how to get at its basic functionality. Most system dynamics modeling with *Vensim PLE* and *Vensim Pro* follows the pattern: create the causal loop diagram to organize your effort, then build the stock and flow diagram that gets executed as a simulation. This application is not as user friendly at the start, but once you discover how to do what you want to accomplish by watching one or two video tutorials, it gets much easier. The logic is consistent throughout the application. As system dynamics models become more complicated, the additional tutorial links available on their website will be needed.

B.6 SIPMATH

SIPmath is one of several software tools developed by Probability Management, a 501(c)(3) nonprofit dedicated to making uncertainty actionable through tools, standards, applications, and training. *SIPmath* functions as an Excel Add-in. The *SIPmath* Modeler Tools leverage the native Excel Data Table function to bring interactive Monte Carlo simulation to all Excel users. The models built with these tools do not require the tools to run in Excel. For more details, see Video Tutorial by Feature at: https://www.probabilitymanagement.org/sipmath-modeler-tools.

For systems decision support in which a majority of stochastic multiple criteria value modelling (MCVM) are built in Excel, *SIPmath* is a great tool because it simply builds on the deterministic tradespace models for cost and value already constructed. Both the ease and power behind *SIPmath* is that the developers leverage the data table functionality of Excel to create Stochastic Information Products (SIP) that can be imbedded in any calculation, logical expression, formula, or macro to model uncertain or probabilistic elements.

A fully functional version of *SIPmath* is available free of charge at the same location. The download is an executable installer that for Windows installs all of its components in the Program Files folder on the C-drive. From experience with Windows 10, we recommend that you disconnect from your WiFi for installation so that it does not default install to the OnDrive location.

After installation is complete. The *SIPmath* Modeler Tools file needs to be installed as an Add-in with Excel. To do this, from the top menu in Excel, select `File` -> `Options` and `Add-ins` from the left window. At the bottom of the window, select `Excel Add-ins` from the drop down menu, select `Go`. Next, you need to locate the *SIPmath* Modeler Tools file on your C-drive. Select `Browse` and navigate to the file. Select the file, then `OK`. The filename should appear in the Add-ins available listing. Select the box next to the file and click `OK`, returning you to the Excel worksheet. At the top of the menu, a new choice called SIPmath Modeler Tools should appear. Selecting this menu item switches to the *SIPmath* main menu shown in Figure B.7.

The basic pattern for using *SIPmath* to model uncertainty in spreadsheet multiple criteria value models (MCVM) is:

1. Initialize the model using the upper left menu icon. Select the number of random samples to be drawn for every uncertainty distribution you intend to use instead of fixed input or parameter values.

Figure B.7   *SIPmath* main menu.

2. Decide what distributions you are going to use to model uncertainty. Create a table to store the distribution's parameters. You will link to these when you Generate Input.

3. Select the desired distribution from the Generate Input menu item. Link the inputs to cell locations on your model. If you want your results to be repeatable (as often is the case), select the HDR button at the bottom and link the `Start Variable ID` to a starting seed value that you have in your table. Typically, easy to remember values in numerical order work fine: 101, 102, and so on. If you want different random samples to be generated every time Excel calculates the worksheet, select `RAND`, which uses the Excel `=Rand()` formula. We recommend that you change the Excel menu item `Formulas` -> `Calculation Options` to `Manual` so that you have control over when this occurs.

4. When you complete a `Generate Input` action, the data is written to an XML file that is not visible, and it has not yet become a SIP. It is, however, able to be used in formulas linking to the specific cell location.

5. To make it visible, select `Define Outputs`, name the random sample output (no space are allowed). Select the location that you want a mini-histogram to appear in a cell that shows you approximately what the distribution you selected looks like. This is called a Sparkline. You typically want this location to take the place of the input or parameter that you are replacing with an uncertainty distribution. Select `Ok`. Two new worksheets get added to your workbook. One called `PMtable` houses each one of your named random sample Outputs in columns. A second worksheet called `SIPmath Chart Data` stores information used to produce charts.

6. One note: you should only turn cell locations into named Output for the ones that are important for analysis purposes. Otherwise, you will over populate the PMtable worksheet with data you don't care about. Eventually this will slow down calculations if you have a lot of them. For MCVMs, we typically test one or two input locations just to make sure everything is working fine. Then, the only locations we name as Output are ones that are involved with stochastic tradespace information such as cloudplots, stochastic dominance checks and so on.

Although most people start out by just replacing input data and other fixed modeling parameters with uncertain distributions and then target final modeling output cells such as Total Value and Total Cost locations to become named Outputs, the real power of using *SIPmath* is that once you replace a number with a distribution, *any cell along involved with that cell location, either directly or indirectly, can be turned into named Output*. So if you are interested in what the distribution of an intermediate calculation looks like, select that cell and name it as Output.

The best reference for all of *SIPmath*'s menu options is online at the website noted. Scrolling down the webpage takes you to a location on the webpage shown in Figure B.8 where individual short tutorials are available for every menu item.

Video Tutorial by Feature

Click on a button below to watch the feature's tutorial.

DETAILED BUTTON
DESCRIPTIONS

MORE TOOLS
VIDEOS

Figure B.8 *SIPmath* main menu: video tutorials.

B.7 MACRO CODE

The following two Visual Basic for Applications (VBA) macro code modules must be installed as an Excel Add-in to use the value table approach described in the book. `ValuePL` was the original macro used for years for MCVM. `ValuePL4` is a revision of the original code to correct for interpolation errors that occasionally happened when *x*-axis scales are arranged in decreasing order. It works for all 2D value function tables.

To install the macros, first make sure the Developer menu item appears in the top menu items for the Excel workbook. If it does not, select `File` -> `Options` -> `Customize Ribbon`, and select `Developer` from the list of Popular Commands in the left window, choose `Add` -> and then OK. The Developer menu item should now appear at the top menu of the workbook.

Next, select `Developer` -> `Visual Basic`. The left upper window shows you several items. Under `VBAProject(<filename>)` you see two subfolders: Microsoft Excel Objects and Modules. If both functions are available, you will see two Module windows in the big grey window showing the code for both. If the big grey window is empty and there is not a Module1 and Module2 appearing under the Modules folder, then two new modules need to be created. and copy paste the following code into each new blank module.

From the menu, select `Insert` -> `Module`, then copy paste the following code for `ValuePL`:

```
Function ValuePL(x, Xi, Vi)
  i = 2
  Do While x > Xi(i)
    i = i + 1
  Loop
  ValuePL = Vi(i - 1) _
```

```
        + (Vi(i) - Vi(i - 1)) * (x - Xi(i - 1)) / (Xi(i) - Xi(i - 1))
End Function


Function ValueE(x, Low, High, Monotonicity, Rho)
    Select Case UCase(Monotonicity)
        Case "INCREASING"
            Difference = x - Low
        Case "DECREASING"
            Difference = High - x
    End Select
    If UCase(Rho) = "INFINITY" Then
        ValueE = Difference / (High - Low)
    Else
        ValueE = (1 - Exp(-Difference / Rho)) / (1 - Exp(-(High - Low) / Rho))
    End If
End Function
```

Next, select `Insert` -> `Module` to create a second VBA module, and copy paste the following code for **Value PL4** :

```
Function ValuePL4(x, Xi, Vi)

Dim NewXi() As Double
Dim NewVi() As Double

NumOfElements = WorksheetFunction.Count(Xi)

ReDim NewXi(NumOfElements) As Double
ReDim NewVi(NumOfElements) As Double

Xi_Array = Range(Xi.Cells(1, 1).Address, Xi.Cells(NumOfElements, 1).Address)

i = 0
Do While i < NumOfElements
    i = i + 1
    NewXi(i) = WorksheetFunction.Small(Xi, i)
    Position = Application.Match(WorksheetFunction.Small(Xi, i), Xi_Array, False)
    NewVi(i) = Vi(Position)
Loop

If x < NewXi(1) Then
   ValuePL4 = NewVi(1)
ElseIf x > NewXi(NumOfElements) Then
   ValuePL4 = NewVi(NumOfElements)
Else
  i = 2
  Do While x > NewXi(i)
    i = i + 1
  Loop
  ValuePL4 = NewVi(i - 1) _
      + (NewVi(i) - NewVi(i - 1)) * (x - NewXi(i - 1)) / (NewXi(i) - NewXi(i - 1))
End If
End Function
```

When complete, close the Visual Basic window. Test that the functions are available for your use by beginning to type the expression `=ValuePL4` into a cell. If both macros appear as a choice from the automatic dropdown selection menu, all is well. If not, go thru the installation sequence again. Once these VBA macros are installed, remember to save the file as an Excel macro-enabled file with the `*.xlsm` filetype. You may need to adjust the macro settings to both enable macros to run and to trust access to the VBA project object model. To do this, select `Developer` -> `Macro Security` and check the radio button and box for the two options. Note that because these are custom functions, Excel does not have help associated with them. So be sure to pay attention as to how to use these.

REFERENCE

1. Fruchterman, T.M.J., Reingold, E.M. (1991) Graph Drawing by Force-directed Placement, *Software – Practice and Experience,* 21(11), pp. 1129–1164.

Index

Decision Making in Systems Engineering and Management, Third Edition.
Patrick J. Driscoll, Gregory S. Parnell, and Dale L. Henderson
© 2023 John Wiley & Sons, Inc. Published 2023 by John Wiley & Sons, Inc.

Printed and bound by CPI Group (UK) Ltd, Croydon, CR0 4YY

27/10/2024

14580677-0004